T0202950

Lecture Notes in Computer Science 11899

More information about this series at http://www.springer.com/series/7409

Antonios Liapis · Georgios N. Yannakakis ·
Manuel Gentile · Manuel Ninaus (Eds.)

Games and Learning Alliance

8th International Conference, GALA 2019
Athens, Greece, November 27–29, 2019
Proceedings

Editors
Antonios Liapis
University of Malta
Msida, Malta

Georgios N. Yannakakis
University of Malta
Msida, Malta

Manuel Gentile
National Research Council of Italy
Palermo, Italy

Manuel Ninaus
Leibniz-Institut für Wissensmedien
Tübingen, Germany

ISSN 0302-9743 ISSN 1611-3349 (electronic)
Lecture Notes in Computer Science
ISBN 978-3-030-34349-1 ISBN 978-3-030-34350-7 (eBook)
https://doi.org/10.1007/978-3-030-34350-7

LNCS Sublibrary: SL3 – Information Systems and Applications, incl. Internet/Web, and HCI

This Springer imprint is published by the registered company Springer Nature Switzerland AG
The registered company address is: Gewerbestrasse 11, 6330 Cham, Switzerland

Preface

The 8th International Conference on Games and Learning Alliance (GALA 2019), organized by the Serious Games Society (SGS) and the University of Malta (UM), was held in the classical yet modern city of Athens, Greece, during November 27–29, 2019.

The GALA series of conferences provide an excellent opportunity to foster the discussion of relevant topics in the growing field of serious games. The conference is a venue for academic researchers, industrial developers, teachers, and corporate decision-makers to meet and exchange experiences and knowledge in this multidisciplinary and challenging area. GALA 2019 received 77 submissions. We were happy that a total of 215 authors contributed their work to GALA 2019, with over 20% based in Greece. While the majority (85%) of authors are based in Europe, North and South America, Oceania, and the Middle East were also represented in the submissions. On average, papers received 2.8 reviews from Program Committee members: 38 of these papers were selected for presentation at the conference and 19 papers for presentation at a poster session of the conference. A total of 18 countries were represented in papers presented at the conference.

The conference featured a location-based game centered around the conference venue, and a competition for the best serious game in terms of impact. It was an honor to have Maria Roussou, from the University of Athens, Greece, and Sander Bakkes from Utrecht University, the Netherlands, as keynote speakers at GALA 2019. The conference featured eight sessions of paper presentations, and topics ranged from serious game design practices, studies on engagement, learning, and usability of serious games, as well as virtual reality, tabletop games, storytelling, creativity, and awareness. Significant to this year, the conference was accompanied by an exhibition of serious games with a focus on impact. The exhibition was hosted at the Technopolis City of Athens, in collaboration with INNOVATHENS powered by Samsung. The exhibition was open to the general public and featured a number of games developed by local industries and institutions as well as European institutions. The exhibition concluded with a panel discussion about the future of serious games and their impact.

As in previous years, selected best papers of the GALA conference will be published in a dedicated special issue of the *International Journal of Serious Games*, the scientific journal managed by the SGS, which is a great reference point for academics and practitioners to publish original research work on serious games and be informed about the latest developments in the field. We thank the authors for submitting many interesting, field-advancing papers, the Program Committee for reviewing these papers, and the SGS and UM for organizing the conference.

November 2019

Antonios Liapis
Georgios N. Yannakakis
Manuel Gentile
Manuel Ninaus

Preface

Organization

General Chair

Antonios Liapis — University of Malta, Malta

Program Chairs

Georgios N. Yannakakis — University of Malta, Malta
Manuel Gentile — CNR–ITD, Palermo, Italy
Manuel Ninaus — Leibniz-Institut für Wissensmedien, Germany

Exhibition Chair

Elina Roinioti — Panteion University, Athens, Greece

Tutorials and Keynotes Chair

Jannicke Baalsrud Hauge — BIBA, Germany, and KTH, Sweden

Awards Chair

Iza Marfisi-Schottman — Le Mans University, France

Publication Chair

Riccardo Berta — University of Genoa, Italy

Communication and Promotion Chair

David Melhart — University of Malta, Malta

Administrative and Financial Chair

Francesco Bellotti — University of Genoa, Italy

Local Arrangements Chair

Iro Voulgari — National and Kapodistrian University of Athens, Greece

Program Committee

Mario Allegra	Italian National Research Council–ITD, Italy
Alessandra Antonaci	Welten Institute–Research Centre for Learning, Teaching and Technology, Open University, The Netherlands
Angeliki Antoniou	University of Peloponnese, Greece
Aida Azadegan	The Open University, UK
Per Backlund	University of Skövde, Sweden
Riccardo Berta	University of Genoa, Italy
Rafael Bidarra	Delft University of Technology, The Netherlands
Lucas Blair	Little Bird Games, USA
Tharrenos Bratitsis	University of Western Macedonia, Greece
Maira B. Carvalho	Tilburg University, The Netherlands
Giuseppe Città	Consiglio Nazionale delle Ricerche–Istituto per le Tecnologie Didattiche di Palermo, Italy
Michael Coovert	University of South Florida, USA
Valentina Dal Grande	Consiglio Nazionale delle Ricerche, Italy
Alessandro De Gloria	University of Genoa, Italy
Teresa de La Hera Conde-Pumpido	Erasmus University Rotterdam, The Netherlands
Kurt Debattista	The University of Warwick, UK
Michael Derntl	University of Tübingen, Germany
Joao Dias	INESC-ID, Portugal
Frank Dignum	Utrecht University, The Netherlands
Jeffrey Earp	ITD-CNR, Italy
Luis Miguel Encarnacao	Innovation by Design International Consulting, USA
Georgios Fesakis	University of Aegean, Greece
Jan Dirk Fijnheer	Utrecht University, The Netherlands
Laura Freina	National Research Council, Italy
Samir Garbaya	ENSAM Art et Metiers ParisTech, France
Dimitris Grammenos	FORTH-ICS, Greece
Dirk Ifenthaler	University of Mannheim, Germany
Carolina A. Islas Sedano	Ubium Oy, Finland
Kostas Karpouzis	National Technical University of Athens, Greece
Vlasios Kasapakis	University of the Aegean, Greece
Michael Kickmeier-Rust	Graz University of Technology, Austria
Ralf Klamma	RWTH Aachen University, Germany
Georgios Kritikos	University of the Aegean, Greece
George Lepouras	University of Peloponnese, Greece
Theo Lim	Heriot-Watt University, UK
Sandy Louchart	Glasgow School of Art, UK
Heide Lukosch	Delft University of Technology, The Netherlands
Ioanna Lykourentzou	Utrecht University, The Netherlands
Katerina Mania	Technical University of Crete, Greece
Samuel Mascarenhas	Universidade de Lisboa, Portugal

Adam Mayes	Uppsala University, Sweden
Michela Mortara	CNR-IMATI Genoa, Italy
Thierry Nabeth	P-Val Conseil, France
Rob Nadolski	Open University of the Netherlands-Welten Institute, The Netherlands
Lucia Pannese	Imaginary, Italy
Davide Parmigiani	University of Genoa, Italy
Sobah Abbas Petersen	Norwegian University of Science and Technology, Norway
Petros Petridis	University of Thessaly, Greece
Johanna Pirker	Graz University of Technology, Austria
Yurgos Politis	University College Dublin, Ireland
Maria Popescu	Carol I National Defence University, Romania
Rui Prada	Universidade de Lisboa, Portugal
Marius Preda	Institut TELECOM, France
Ion Roceanu	National Defence University, Romania
Margarida Romero	Laboratoire d'Innovation et Numérique pour l'Education, Université de Nice Sophia Antipolis, France
Pedro A. Santos	Universidade de Lisboa, Portugal
Avo Schönbohm	Berlin School of Economics and Law, Germany
Yoones A. Sekhavat	Tabriz Islamic Art University, Iran
Christos Sintoris	Human–Computer Interaction Group, University of Patras, Greece
Panote Siriaraya	Delft University of Technology, The Netherlands
Yannis Skarpelos	Panteion University, Athens, Greece
Heinrich Söbke	Bauhaus-Universität Weimar, Germany
Ioana Andreea Stefan	Advanced Technology Systems, Romania
Krassen Stefanov	Sofia University St. Kliment Ohridski, Bulgaria
Matthias Teine	University Paderborn, Germany
Maria Tsourma	Information Technologies Institute, Centre for Research and Technology Hellas (CERTH), Greece
Pauliina Tuomi	Tampere University of Technology, Finland
Erik Van Der Spek	Eindhoven University of Technology, The Netherlands
Herre Van Oostendorp	Utrecht University, The Netherlands
Spyros Vosinakis	University of the Aegean, Greece
Wim Westera	CELSTEC-Centre for Learning Sciences and Technologies, Open University, The Netherlands
Josef Wolfartsberger	University of Applied Sciences Upper Austria, Austria
Stelios Xinogalos	University of Macedonia, Greece
Zerrin Yumak	Utrecht University, The Netherlands

Contents

Posters

Serious Game Design and Pedagogical Foundations

Using Ludo-Narrative Dissonance in *Grand Theft Auto IV* as Pedagogical Tool for Ethical Analysis

Bo Kampmann Walther(✉)

University of Southern Denmark, Odense, Denmark
walther@sdu.dk

Abstract. This paper presents and discusses the findings and results of a series of tests carried out by the author in the Danish educational system among pupils and teachers using the game *Grand Theft Auto IV* (GTA IV) as a case study for investigating the problematic but also fruitful relation between gameplay and fiction, known as ludo-narrative dissonance. In analyzing this dissonance, the paper further discusses the transcendental nature of play (Gadamer), the fact that play seems to play itself, and the delicate way in which the game insists on a meta-ethical theme while at the same time setting up utterly violent game rules and mechanics. As it turns out, this skirmish of fiction versus gameplay is exactly the gravitational point zero of 'ethics' in the stigmatized game of GTA IV and thus a locus for joyful learning.

Keywords: Didactics · Ethics · Ludo-narrative dissonance · Gameplay · Theory

1 Introduction and Didactical Background

During a timespan of roughly six years, from 2010 to 2016, I conducted a series of hands-on tests and workshops in the Danish school system (8th grade and onwards) as well as in high schools with the intention of showing the pedagogical potentials of the new media known as computer games. My encounters with pupils and teachers did not flow through a rigid method design – qualitative questionnaires, quantitative surveys, and the like – but instead consisted of phenomenological observations and stored in the catalogue of my continuous journey to propagate the muscles and fiascos, the good stuff and the bad stuff of games and new media in the age of information technology. In the Danish educational system this is widely known as *'lange viden over disken'*, literally to hand knowledge across the (teacher's) desk. I took a lot of notes in the process, and some of these formed the backdrop of a series of readings and pedagogical tips and tricks in my books *Computerspillets fortællinger* (The stories of computer games 2010), *Computerspil og nye mediefortællinger* (Computer games and new media stories 2012), and *Computerspil: Dannelse, pædagogik og svedige håndflader* (Computer games: Knowledge, pedagogic and sweaty palms 2016).

My aim throughout the educational testing and workshopping was threefold: (A) To make teachers (so) curious about the science of computer games, ludology, to the point where they would feel empowered to integrate the new techniques, tools, and

A. Liapis et al. (Eds.): GALA 2019, LNCS 11899, pp. 3–12, 2019.
https://doi.org/10.1007/978-3-030-34350-7_1

methods into their already established canon and theory books. I know from experience, and so do a lot of professionals in the knowledge business, that solid knowhow combined with just the right amount of *Verfremdung* can kickstart a process of both innovation and creativity. (B) I also wanted, on purpose, to alienate the pupils as regards the analytical levels of playing computer games, and thus to push them from an instrumental practice to a mode of interpretation and critical scrutiny. The goal was to make them see a high ceiling rather than a straightforward route from A to B and which buttons to press. And, finally, (C) I wanted – and still want – to make a point for the use of commercial games in conjunction with edutainment and 'gamified' teachers' material as means for societal, ethical, and socio-semantic discussions in class. What follows are extracts from my notebook on deploying a popular and stigmatized computer game to cultivate a qualified, meta-ethical, and critical discussion.

2 Meta-ethical Dilemmas in *Grand Theft Auto IV*

In *Grand Theft Auto IV* (Rockstar Games 2008) the player is controlling Niko Bellic, a petty criminal immigrant from former Yugoslavia who arrives in the United States seduced by the usual clichés: freedom, happiness, and money. As it turns out, this is somewhat of an illusion. Niko gets trapped in the unforgiving and vicious gangland of Liberty City (a city loosely based on the real New York) with not much else to do than roam around, do the odd theft job, chop cars, and fight. Essentially, the core narrative of GTA IV portrays not only how Niko swerves and frissons his way up to the mafioso summit, it furthermore showcases his futile struggle to escape his destiny. He seems to be irresistibly tied to – and tied up with – his felonious vitae, as it is part and parcel of his interesting and playable ontology. Not to mention Bellic's backstory. At some point it is implied that his father was an abusive alcoholic and that he suffered many traumas as a teenage soldier in the Bosnian War. Niko witnessed and committed numerous atrocities that shaped his cynical approach to life but also a certain degree of repentance, depression, and emotional friability. And on top of that, he is caught in a computer game that you and I are playing for fun.

The rules of GTA IV are quite simple. Niko, aka the player, needs to be good at handling guns and stealing cars. Game rules evolves around the understanding and enactment of a restrained set of potential actions in order to overcome the game's obstacles and to progress in the fictitious space (Salen and Zimmerman 2004), the game world of *Grand Theft Auto*, Liberty City. The problem is that these impending actions (Walther and Larsen 2019), which are the results of rules and how they should be obeyed, not only converge into fluent gameplay but also contain a socio-semantic dimension.

For instance, the game is constructed in such a fashion that the player gets extra points for spending time with a prostitute since this activity boosts the health score. However, one has to pay for the sexual services; but as it happens one can kill or otherwise harm the woman and retrieve the cash. Voila.

Here, the dilemma is obvious. From a game-centric design perspective the prostitute scene is yet another rule (including a matching mechanic) to be followed, a bit like making sure a falling polygon lands properly on the surface, in *Tetris*. Do you need money? No problem; go kill someone! Yet, the rule is problematic viewed from a societal and moral point of view. This is where the game world kicks in: We do not only play by the rules, as noted by Sicart (2009), but are also immersed into the simulation, its world, fiction, and characters. Gameplay and drama, or narrative immersion, are not two opposing things; they weave into one another, enhance and subtract energy from each other. Hence the added fun of playing *Quake* with elaborate textures rather than strict vector graphics, or the thrill of enjoying a game of chess with delicate marble statuettes instead of rude pieces of stick. And hence the joyful experience of being absorbed by Liberty City and its lost souls.

Read this way, GTA IV becomes a game that questions the very existence of the presence of morality. Is this meta-morality somehow implanted in the game world; or does it solely rest in the eye of the beholder? Our anti-hero, Bellic, has arguably huge existential challenges in facing the punitive set of rules in this world (first encountered when we meet his cousin, Roman Bellic, who owns a taxi company, the Express Car Service, which is later burnt down by the Russian Mafia). He wants to be emancipated from his criminal record, hunt down the villains of his unforgettable past. It is safe to say that we understand him; but in realizing the Utopia that he set out for himself he precisely has to gather and master all of the violent and depraved techniques required for the game to be a success. Success for who? The player, of course. As Miguel Sicart writes in *The Ethics of Computer Games*:

> We think, and play, as ethical agents beyond being players, but also as cultural beings. We play as body-subjects. That's why playing *Grand Theft Auto IV* becomes an exploration of meaning and purpose, of values and actions. Previous iterations of the *Grand Theft Auto* series used humor to distance the player, to allow her a moment of reflection to interpret the game as subversive satire. *Grand Theft Auto IV* does not use humor, but tragedy: we empathize with Niko, yet we are forced to drive him to crime. Do we really want to do that? Further, will we also be criminals when we can play in free-form, when we don't have to complete the missions in the game? What does this power say about who we are as ethical beings? (Sicart 2009, p. 105).

The mainstream player would rather have Bellic cling to crime because otherwise the game loses its forthright fascination. Thus, the *narrative* closure and the success of *gameplay* (almost like 'fiction' as opposed to 'reading') point in two drastically different directions. Ultimately, the game is fun because closure and success do not mutually reconcile. The more fun we have, as players, the more unhappy Niko Bellic becomes.

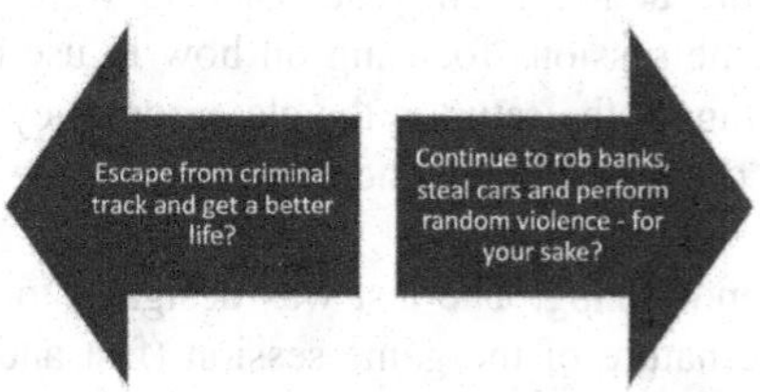

Fig. 1. Confronting Bellic' and the player's dilemma in GTA IV.

The Fig. 1 above depicts the drama of Niko Bellic. This drama is also the conflict that initiates or may initiate the player's moral contemplation in *Grand Theft Auto IV*.

For this to happen, though, we need to pay close attention to the interior of the game, those cracks in which the shrewd, uncertain connection between fiction and play reveal themselves (cf. Frasca 2003). This was the point I tried to put across the teacher's desk by having the students play the game and pondering its ironic setup: that numerous critical and *moralizing* readings of GTA IV tend to be one-dimensional. They miss the meta-moral interior of the game. GTA IV has a ruthless mechanic, a moralistic story, and these two combined is precisely an ethical marker.

3 GTA in the Classroom

I divided the class (a lot of classes) into two groups, determined by two distinctly different game sessions. One game session was dictated solely by the bliss of gameplay, the gaming experience. I then asked the youngsters to note *what* they did, *why* they did it, and how they would *retell* it, as they fought, kicked, smashed into cars, violated pedestrians, etc. Keeping emotional responses off the grid, so to say, was tricky, but eventually they got the hang of it. After a while they simply enjoyed the game and forgot about the agenda of the classroom test and, as a result, forgot to take notes.

The people in the second game session were told to do the exact opposite: take the aspirations and desires of Niko seriously (they took a lot of notes). Then the actual gameplay shifted radically, from a rule- and score based against-the-clock race to a more sophisticated navigation along the alleyways and intersections of the GTA narrative. The first group was playing a kind of urban *Counter-Strike* (get weapon, drive car, cash-in, get out); the second was 'reading' the fictional landscape vis-à-vis a number of background material much more tenderly trying to bridge the socio-cultural landscape of Liberty City with the implicit duty of the protagonist.

Using exploration design inspired by phenomenology I also handed out pre-printed note sheets to the students: 'What action did you just perform?', 'Why did you do that?', and 'How would you retell this action to your classmates?'. The progression of the questions corresponded with a common methodological knowledge, namely that one should begin with factual questions and then proceed with questions of more complex nature. Furthermore, it was part of my hypothesis (which I did not reveal to the students) that the 'retell'-part would cue more into the socio-semantic setup of GTA, in group 2, whereas group 1 would tackle 'retell' as the ability to communicate the very experience of the action itself. The teachers were given a lecture and/or workshop prior to the game sessions focusing on how to use (commercial) computer games as a tool for learning; at the setup in the classroom they usually played the role of observers while many of them, in fact, ended up playing the game as well (aided by the pupils).

However, I was not moralizing. The test was designed to make the students recognize that no matter the nature of the game session (fast and furious as opposed to sweet analysis), the structural result was the same:

Group 1: Gameplay violates/disrupts fiction
Group 2: Fiction violates/disrupts gameplay

Let me elaborate on this point (and this *chiasm*) by first turning the attention to the concept of ludo-narrative dissonance, and second compare it with the peculiar ontology of 'play' put forward by Gadamer, before finally returning once more to my findings of the GTA test and what we may learn from it.

4 Ludo-Narrative Dissonance

The contradictory semantics of the gameplay-fiction scheme above cue right into what has been labelled 'ludo-narrative dissonance'. The term was coined by Clint Hocking (2007) in response to the game *Bioschock* which, Hocking argued, endorses the theme of egocentric behavior through its gameplay and the game's mechanics while at the same time promoting the opposing theme of selflessness through its narrative. As a consequence of this crooked dichotomy of gameplay and fiction the game creates a violation of aesthetic distance that seems to pull the player out of the game. Hocking's point is that there is a recurrent conflict in games between the ludic and the narrative structure, and thus between what the player is allowed to do (i.e. the rules) and why the player is asked to do it, i.e. the (fictional) context of the game. Related to *ludo* we find controls, choices, and consequences while the realm of narrative in games usually contain graphics, dialogue, cutscenes, and, obviously, characters.

Remedy Studios writer Mikko Rautalahti has the following to say about storytelling in video games:

> I think it can be difficult to tell stories in video games. There are all these conventions – you are expected to have a certain amount of combat, a certain minimum number of gameplay hours, etc. These conventions aren't really engineered with storytelling in mind. So, a lot of the time, you end up kind of glossing over some of the details in your head – I mean, if you're playing the lone hero, in terms of the story, does that guy really rack up a four-digit body count? Does he really get repeatedly shot with high-calibre weapons and mysteriously heal himself? And if you really get stuck at a difficult part, does that really mean that the hero also spent an hour just running around in frustration and then quit. Probably not, you know (Rautalahti, in Hernandez 2010).

In response to these practical and far-reaching tasks of joining the rules and narratives of games one may imagine two radically different solutions:

As Brett Makedonski writes, the first option is to create games that are *ever evolving* and wholly responsive to any actions that the player makes. Rather than focusing on telling a particular story, the developers would have to give the player the means to make a story. The second solution is for developers to make games that give the player little to *no control* over any in-game decisions. Doing this will eliminate the possibility of the player diverging from the exact path that the developers intended (Makedonski 2012).

It is easy to see that the first solution is effectively a simulation of life whereas the second solution is a simulation of a fixed sequence of narrative elements, i.e. a linear 'story'. Thus, in trying to solve the puzzle of ludo-narrative dissonance we either get too much (life) or too little (story). From a design-centered perspective ludo-narrative dissonance is widely considered to be something that needs 'fixing', alteration, or, at the very least, a more fine-tuned balance. However, as I shall argue, the very existence of the dissonance between gameplay and fictional complexity, and the ethical challenges it poses, is a good thing in the case of *Grand Theft Auto IV*.

5 Play Plays (Gadamer)

The respondents in group 1 were told to go all in on the violent, non-emphatic gameplay. By doing so they systematically disrupted the agenda of group 2 who, eventually, became more focused on piecing together elements of the game world, the fiction, and the study of its main character into an articulate 'story' based on ethical choices and moral consequences.

The exploits of group 1 was a classroom spectacle in itself, and I witnessed how quickly they got sucked into the game, almost as if the game was playing them, and not the other way around. The second group, having a distinctively different and more eloquent purpose, was constantly attentive to the *test itself*. Perhaps subconsciously they mustered all their interpretation skills to gravitate towards what they thought I, the 'funny teacher' from the 'planet of Ludology', was up to. In short, group 1 simply played a game and had loads of fun. Group 2 tried their very best to humor me. Sure, they were enjoying themselves, yet they were playing a 'serious game'. Actually, the second group was not playing a game at all; they were playing the 'game' that would easily serve as a natural extension of my curricular Q and A.

Gadamer (2006) points out that play is a mode of being that do not simply belong to subjectivity (Larsen and Walther 2019). Being in play is not something we choose by volition. Play takes hold of us and is performed through the players, but it is not something we can control by command. Thus, Gadamer seems to point to a transcendental structure of play as something that can grab us from "outside" beyond our conscious control.

This subsistence of play's transcendental nature, the fact that play plays itself and pushes its own ontology on top of ours, and not the other way around, seemed to resonate strongly with the test pupils in group 1 (although I did not explicitly present Gadamer to them). It also applied, though to a lesser extent, or rather in a negative fashion, to their teachers who were extremely self-conscious and at first a little edgy about the whole setup: 'Are we just going to smash cars and drive them into the harbour? Come on!', as one member of staff replied. It further correlates with Salen and Zimmerman's (2004) view of the dynamics of inside and outside. Here too play happens in an interstitial space, a space which is rooted somehow between the actual, physical place of play and the locus that play itself forcefully but playfully colonizes; spaces that are thus simultaneously present and absent. My test mission was, I found, omnipresent in group 2 as a guiding principle from the 'outside'. Here, play played itself as part of an onsite work assignment. I was the emperor of play dictating both action and teleology, what to do and what to aim for. In group 1 it was opposite: The game itself, GTA IV, was present and kept its presence both instrumentally and transcendentally. Thus, at some point, while taking notes on the behavior of group 1, I recalled Gadamer's view that play almost seems to be an agency of its own exceeding the will of its players.

Gadamer further explains the dynamics of play by incorporating Buytendijk's (1933) description of to-and-fro movement devoid of any goal that would bring an end to the play activity. Not only does play exist in interstitial spaces, it also rests on a particular structure of movement. This dialectic feature makes it possible for play to renew "itself in constant repetition" (Gadamer 2006, p. 104), but the activity is not generated for its own purpose because when we play, we always play some*thing*—and that something is very often a game. In Gadamer's phenomenological depiction of play, it is the game that orders and shapes the movement where play can happen, but it happens as an experience that grabs us from the outside beyond our explicit intentions. The latter is not far from Sicart (2014) when he describes play as appropriative taking over the unfolding activity and the place in which play situationally finds itself as the result of players negotiating rules and setting up communities around play. As Gadamer points out, play carries yet another interesting feature, which is that when in play we cannot say we are in play since it would disturb the experience and bring us "out of play." Self-reflection kills play (aka the destiny of group 2). It is only before and after the play, we are under the control of play.

6 Symbolic Versus Allegorical: Classroom Findings

As a result of the two groups playing and reflecting on GTA IV, I detected the following distinct features:

Group 1: *Unreflected (violent) gameplay -> symbolic game session => naïve interpretation.*

Group 2: *Reflected (ethical) gameplay -> allegorical game session => forced interpretation.*

The test said quite a lot about group dynamics and behavioral sociology among youngsters in the educational system, yet it was important for me not to make the findings nor the results of one of the two sessions stand out as the 'better' or proper way of playing the game. The behavioral aim was *not* for the pupils to conduct some sort of upright, civic performance but to stay true to the test, whatever the ramifications. Both sessions exposed the Pandora's box of ludo-narrative dissonance, and effectively so; the symbolic reading counting all the emotional shouting and passionate, mechanical immersion seemed to renounce the complexity of the fiction altogether, while the forced reading of group 2 who painstakingly took notes and discussed crime and violent forces of our contemporary world along the way missed the efficacy (and fun) of *ludus* and happy-go-lucky play.

A rash conclusion would be, then, that the game of GTA IV suffers from a ludo-narrative disease since the game either becomes (too) naïve or (too) forced. There is a gap between gameplay and story, mechanics and fiction, the argument goes, and this would also purport a critical stance towards the game: It is brutally one-dimensional and should therefore be banned. Or it proves that 'ethics' is really in the eyes of the beholder (in this case the author who carried out the test) and therefore GTA IV transforms into a dismal meta-game with nothing but predictable agendas. Furthermore, the case of reflection among the students, and the lack hereof, was evidenced in the notetaking. As I mentioned earlier, the symbolic game session of group 1 implied a degeneration and disruption of reflexive consideration (and hence of taking notes), while, conversely, the allegorical game session of group 2 clearly pushed them into a very 'wordy' interpretation of the game as well as a continual devotion to the unspoken agenda. The people of group 2 tried their best to relate the authorial outline of the test as such, the sub-text, with the task (the 'text') at hand (Table 1).

Table 1. A table of opposing elements of group sessions 1 and 2.

Group 1	Group 2
Instrumental session Symbolism	Meta-game session Allegorical
Naïve Enjoying a game on its own	Forced Playing a game to do homework
The game plays itself Too much violence	The 'game' of the teacher's implied mission plays itself Too much auto-prophecy (the teacher's agenda) Reading for a sub-text

An interesting aspect about GTA IV from a learning perspective, however, is not the despotic ability to cherry-pick between the persuasive meta-game construction of session 2, to the point where the students lose track of the actual game they are playing, and the blood and gore of session 1 where the game strikes a transcendental, symbolic pose and maybe becomes too much game and too little reflection. Lots of notes versus no notes. Rather, and more significantly, *Grand Theft Auto IV* must be understood, I will argue, as a meta-ethical game because of the *confrontation* of the two modes and ways of playing (or, rather, ways of demanding a certain type of play). The 'ethics' in GTA IV lies in the *dilemma* of either playing symbolically, smacking automobiles and using violence, or playing allegorically, i.e. taking a lot of notes in pursuit of the sub-text that clarifies everything. The million dollar question of ethical game design, as put forward by Sicart (2010), and whether it is possible or in fact preferable, is somewhat beside the point since 'ethics', in this case, emerges not only from a design-centric 'within' but rather as (1) an interesting *result* of the ludo-narrational, dissonant architecture of the game, and (2) as a *confrontational synthesis* of two characteristically different interpretations or actual gameplays.

7 Concluding Remarks

Ludo-narrative dissonance may be a problem in games such as *Bioschock* or *Mass Effect* (Makedonski 2012) but in GTA IV it is rather a solution. One could even say that the upshot of uniting the mutual inadequacies of session 1 and session 2, the fact that one cannot have fun and mature choices at one and the same time, *resonate* in the apparent dissonance of fun versus ethics. Ludo-narration, as it unfolds in GTA IV, is a didactical birthplace, a battle of competences and knowledge, a potential for interesting rattles of ways of playing games and the *modus vivendi* for heated discussions in the classroom, as I soon found out. Why did group 1 stop taking notes as the symbiotic experience took over – 'we began to play with our bodies more than our heads', one sub-group pointed out afterwards – and the game seemed to play itself, as Gadamer writes? And why did group 2 zealously look for inklings within the narration of the game to credit the teacher's intentions? Why did group 2 transform GTA IV into a serious meta-game?

Playing a commercial and already much debated and stigmatized game such as *Grand Theft Auto IV* with a group of 15–19-year old's, and their teachers, exposes not only the need for elevating learning from an instrumental level to a meta-reflexive level. Commercial games can be used to scaffold learning and push the students towards zones of both future insights and past knowledge, i.e. where learning takes off. For me, such 'zones of proximal development' (Vygotsky 1978) were places of both personal and professional recognition: The narrow gap between what a learner can do and conceptualize without help and what he or she can achieve with guidance and encouragement from a skilled partner turned out to be precisely the locus of qualified discussions of ethical and societal matters. Moreover, the inherent reward and feedback structure of games seems to stimulate productive, adaptive, and responsive learning environments. Helped by curious teachers, a specialized toolbox, and thought-provoking dilemmas, games are perfect vehicles for the effective feedback that according to Hattie answers three questions: Where am I going? (feed up). What is next step? (feed forward). Where am I in the learning process? (feed back) (Hattie and Timperly 2007; Hattie 2009). As shown in this paper the students received different answers to different game sessions but still, nevertheless, arrived at the same conclusion because of the confrontational synthesis: That ludo-narrative dissonance is not a design hiccup but a gift of interpretation.

References

Buytendijk, F.J.J.: Wesen und Sinn des Spiels: Das Spielen des Menschen und der Tiere als Er-cheinungsform der Lebenstriebe. Kurt Wolff Verlag/Der Neue Geist, Berlin (1933)

Frasca, G.: Sim Sin City: Some thoughts about grand theft auto 3. Game Stud. 3(2) (2003). http://gamestudies.org/0302/frasca/

Gadamer, H.G.: Truth and Method, Continuum, London (2006)

Hattie, J.A., Timperly, H.: The power of feedback. Rev. Educ. Res. **1**, 81–112 (2007)

Hattie, J.A.: Visible Learning A Synthesis of Over 800 Meta-Analysis Relating to Achievement. Routledge, Oxon (2009)

Hernandez, P.: Alan Wake Writer Blames Ludonarrative Dissonance on Game Expectations. http://nightmaremode.thegamerstrust.com/2010/11/30/alan-wake-writer-blames-ludonarrative-dissonance-on-game-expectations/

Hocking, C.: Ludonarrative dissonance in Bioschock (2007). https://clicknothing.typepad.com/click_nothing/2007/10/ludonarrative-d.html

Larsen, L.J., Walther, B.K.: The ontology of gameplay: toward a new theory. Games Culture Spring, 1–23 (2019)

Makedonski, B.: Ludonarrative dissonance: the roadblock to realism (2012). https://www.destructoid.com/ludonarrative-dissonance-the-roadblock-to-realism-235197.phtml

Salen, K., Zimmerman, E.: Rules of Play—Game Design Fundamentals. MIT Press, Cambridge (2004)

Sicart, M.: The Ethics of Computer Games. MIT Press, Cambridge (2009)

Sicart, M.: Wicked games: on the design of ethical gameplay. In: Proceedings of the 1st DESIRE Network Conference on Creativity and Innovation in Design. ACM Digital Library (2010)

Sicart, M.: Play Matters. MIT Press, Cambridge (2014)

Vygotsky, L.S.: Mind in Society: The Development of Higher Psychological Processes. Harvard University Press, Cambridge (1978)

Walther, B.K.: Computerspillets Fortællinger (The Stories of Computer Games). Gyldendal, Copenhagen (2010)

Walther, B.K.: Computerspil og nye mediefortællinger (Computer Games and New Media Stories). Samfundslitteratur, Copenhagen (2012)

Walther, B.K.: Computerspil: Dannelse, pædagogik og svedige håndflader (Computer Games: Knowledge, Pedagogic and Sweaty Palms). Turbine, Aarhus (2016)

Walther, B.K., Larsen, L.J.: Bicycle kicks and camp sites: towards a phenomenological theory of game feel with special attention towards 'rhythm'. Convergence (2019, in press)

A Participatory Approach to Redesigning Games for Educational Purposes

Stamatia Savvani[1](✉) and Antonios Liapis[2]

[1] University of Essex, Essex, UK
stamatia.savvani@essex.ac.uk
[2] University of Malta, Msida, Malta
antonios.liapis@um.edu.mt

Abstract. Even though games designed for educational purposes can be motivating, they usually shelter dated pedagogies, passive learning procedures, and often overlook learners' creativity. In an effort to reinforce the active participation of learners in games, this paper presents a participatory process in which students and teachers are involved in game design. The proposed process concerns redesigning existing commercial games into educational ones and includes establishing the learning goals, identifying appropriate commercial games, adapting the rules and context, crafting and playtesting the game. Using language learning as one application of this process, the paper presents how three well-known tabletop games were redesigned in a foreign language classroom with elementary and intermediate English language learners. The benefits that underlie the process concern students' active participation, boosting their problem-solving skills, and engaging them in creative learning.

Keywords: Game-based language learning · Student-centered pedagogies · Participatory design · Creativity in education · Tabletop games

1 Introduction

Designing games for educational purposes can be a challenging venture as the golden ratio between fun, learning and pedagogy [2] is difficult to achieve. Focusing solely on game elements or complex rules may detach the game from its learning purpose. On the other hand, scattering game elements in an educational activity just for the sake of it may lead to an unsatisfying game experience.

Students today are digital natives and have been exposed to a plethora of digital games. They are immersed daily in unique digital environments, and have learned to adapt easily to demanding game mechanics. Therefore, educational gamified activities might grasp learners' attention in the beginning, but may prove insufficient in the long run [14]. Students are highly perceptive and recognize the struggle of those educators who try to turn a learning exercise into a game. Unless this is done elegantly, they may quickly lose interest in an educational game. Educational digital games often feel more like gamified quizzes [13]

A. Liapis et al. (Eds.): GALA 2019, LNCS 11899, pp. 13–23, 2019.
https://doi.org/10.1007/978-3-030-34350-7_2

and fail to address higher order thinking skills of learners. Even major digital platforms for language learning such as Duolingo employ behaviorist teaching practices, i.e. translation and repetition, mixing them with advanced gamified rewards [18]. A noteworthy exception is Tinycards by Duolingo, which allows the users to create their own flashcards for teaching or learning purposes, thus soliciting their creative skills [18].

This paper contends that merely *playing* games designed with closed-ended, behaviorist teaching practices does not evoke sufficient creative thinking skills by the students. Instead, *creating* game content that others can enjoy, e.g. in Tinycards, requires the utmost of high order thinking skills [8]. To facilitate creation in the classroom, we propose simple and inexpensive paper-based methods for the participatory design of tabletop games (card games, board games, or puzzles). While teachers take the initial decisions regarding the learning goals and constraints of such a game, learners can be involved throughout the process and especially when crafting the game. Games designed in class may be simple (and even behaviorist in their gameplay), but the act of creating the game engages and empowers students, turning them from *passive players* to *active designers*. The focus and examples in this paper are on game (re)design in a foreign language classroom, which matches the principles of Content and Language Integrated Learning [10]. However, the redesign process of popular tabletop games can be applied to any subject and learning goal.

2 Related Work

According to [6], participatory design (PD) refers to a democratic process of design "actively involving all stakeholders (e.g., employees, partners, customers, citizens, users) in the process to help ensure the result meets their needs and is usable." While PD has its roots in User Experience design, it has been applied to a plethora of settings, including education [15]. Participatory design is not always perfectly democratic as it can involve varying degrees of domain expert (end-user) and design expert participation [15]. For instance, informant PD limits the role of end-users, while facilitated PD gives end-users complete freedom and initiative, leaving a supervisory role to the design experts.

Participatory design is essential to new educational practices, as modern pedagogies and technology-enabled classrooms call for more student-centered approaches [5]. It is expected that the role of teachers will shift significantly as emerging pedagogies such as project-based learning, game-based learning or inquiry-based learning require students to be active participants and take responsibility and initiatives in their learning [1].

Active learning strategies [7] often subvert the traditional roles of teachers and learners. The teachers are not expected to be "sages-on-stage" but rather "guides-on-the-side" [11]. While the teacher embraces a supervisory role, this does not lessen teacher effort. On the contrary, the teacher must prepare well beforehand for active learning experiences to be successful [7]. Depending on the activity, the preparation of the teacher may entail deciding on the learning tasks, students' roles, materials provided, and time allocated. This is also true for the game redesign process described in this paper, especially Stages 1 and 2.

3 The Redesign Process

The redesign process follows a number of successive steps, outlined below. Many of the steps require the presence and active participation of both educators and learners (to different degrees). While the process focuses on use in the English language classroom, the steps are simple to follow and provide a practical guide for adapting games that would be suitable for enhancing the learning experience of different school subjects.

Stage 1: Set the Learning Goals: In this stage the teacher identifies the learning goals and focus of the game to be produced. As in lesson planning, it is of major importance to crystallize the game's objectives and have clear and straightforward outcomes expected by students. Establishing the subject-related content needs of the game is a starting point of the game design process [20]. Useful questions to ask are "What will I teach with this lesson-game?" and "What will my students achieve?" [3] to determine the goal of the game. For instance, if a language teacher decides to co-design with her students a game that would reinforce vocabulary connected to holidays, then that would be the learning goal. The second question should be answered with action verbs that demonstrate student outcome, e.g. spell words related to holiday correctly, identify meaning of words. Deciding on the game's learning outcome helps the teacher search for appropriate games in Stage 2.

Stage 2: Choose a Commercial Game: In this stage, the teacher chooses a popular game that could be adjusted to meet the specific learning goals set. The more experienced the teacher is with different kinds of games and their mechanics, the easier it may be to get inspiration. While there are many tabletop games and genres to choose from, not all are suitable for educational purposes: the four main criteria for choosing an appropriate game are *popularity*, *playtime*, *complexity*, and *theme*. It is advisable to ask students about games they enjoy or are most familiar with, as this would increase their engagement while reducing teacher effort to explain the game. Playtime is especially important, as the games will usually be played within a (small) portion of a teaching hour. Complexity should also be considered; the heavier the game is in terms of rules and/or components, the harder it would be to explain, adapt and redesign. Last, the theme of the game itself should be considered, maturity- and age-wise. The boardgamegeek[1] database can be a helpful source of inspiration during this stage as it offers crucial statistics about commercial games such as intended number and age of players, playing time, complexity (as "weight"), categories and mechanisms. If we look up the *Gaia project* (Feuerland Spiele, 2017) on boardgamegeek[2], for instance, we find that it is a poor choice for a language

[1] https://boardgamegeek.com.

[2] https://boardgamegeek.com/boardgame/220308/gaia-project.

classroom given that its playtime can last up to 150 min and its weight scores 4.28 out of 5. Adapting the rules of such a game in Stage 3 would likely be more difficult than designing one from scratch.

Stage 3: Adapt the Rules: In this stage, rules are removed, added or changed to match the target audience, learning goals, and playtime. This stage can be the most laborious, requiring multiple playtests (Stage 6). This stage involves removing unnecessary subsystems of games, modifying winning conditions, simplifying reward mechanics, and introducing rules specific to the learning goals.

As an example, if the game to be redesigned is Monopoly, one may opt to keep the set collection mechanic but remove the Chance and Community Chest card components or the subsystem of building hotels and houses. Similarly, while in Monopoly the winner is the player who does not go bankrupt, this condition may be modified to shorten playtime and match more pedagogical sensibilities; instead, the game could end when one player occupies all properties of one color (set). Lastly, additions would be made to include learning content, e.g. substituting the sets of street names in Monopoly with verb sets, featuring the present, past and past participle of an English language verb. Similar to Monopoly, the player landing on an unoccupied property must use the verb of the property in a sentence correctly (new mechanic) in order to occupy it.

As with the learning goals, the game mechanics (what a player does in this game) should be defined clearly with action verbs, such as move, collect, describe [19]. As argued above, making a poor choice for a base game in Stage 2 may require more class effort to adapt and remove rules than on learning goals. The audience needs to engage more with the language and content of the lesson than the rules of gaming [9]. After students have designed a number of games with the teacher, they may have their own ideas of what could also work as a rule system. However, game (re)design can be an intensive, time consuming process. Therefore, it is best if the teacher initially preoccupies herself with this stage.

Stage 4: Adapt the Content: In this stage, the class brainstorms the content that could fit into the game, drawing from the goals established in Stage 1. Modifications can be made to the theme of the base game, making it more age- and level-appropriate for learners. The vocabulary on the board and game cards can be adjusted to fit the learning purposes and learners' language level. Language may even be absent from the game components altogether, but it may be elicited during gameplay. The learning content to be included could be established during a pre-game design activity. For instance, the teacher may ask students "Which words from today's lesson did you find most difficult?". Students then share their feedback on the vocabulary taught and create a word list with the teacher, which would then be used as part of the game's word cards. It is important that such interactions take place, as they help learners reflect on their knowledge and address their metalignuistic awareness [12], while also engaging them in the design process.

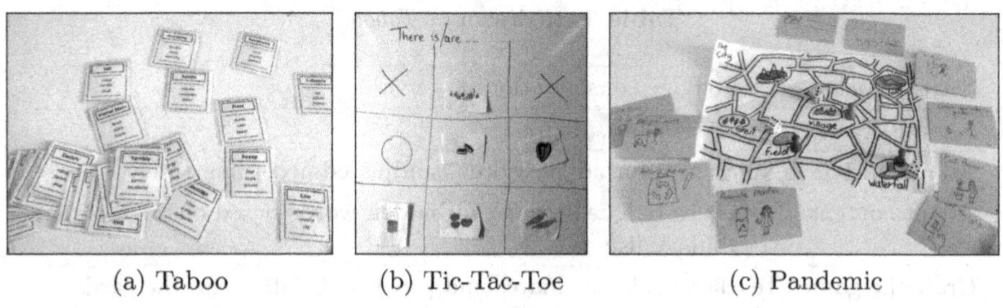

(a) Taboo (b) Tic-Tac-Toe (c) Pandemic

Fig. 1. Tabletop games redesigned for the English language classroom.

Stage 5: Craft the Game: Crafting the game is the implementation stage of the process, requiring the active engagement of both teacher and learners. First, the teacher should make the game rules clear so that learners can craft the game accordingly, and lead a short objective discussion of the game to finalize the game goals and expectations. Crafting the game involves learners creating game components: writing words, drawing a board, cutting cards, and finding appropriate pawns. Having learners lead the crafting process, or even undertake it in full, can increase their personal investment in the game. For instance, being able to personalize their tokens to match their identity can have a strong impact on enjoyment and presence [22]. Ideally, the game parts should include language, topics and content taught previously. With more advanced learners, a manual with the adapted rules could also be crafted in the target language.

Stage 6: Playtest the Game: In a successful game redesign, playing the game in the classroom may mark the end of the activity. Often, however, the first playtest will reveal flaws that require further adjustments. The teacher can discuss the results of the playtest with students. This not only solicits critical thinking about both the rules and the content, but can lead to new redesign iterations (often at Stage 3 or 4) and another playtest.

4 Cases of Redesign for the English Language Classroom

To further demonstrate how the process can be practically implemented in real-world settings, this section describes the redesign process of three commercial games: *Taboo*, Tic-Tac-Toe, and *Pandemic* (see the resulting games in Fig. 1). These games were redesigned during the school year 2018–2019 in a small private school for teaching English as a foreign language (EFL). Elementary and intermediate language learners participated in the design of these games; the students' age ranged from 10–13 years old. Classes consisted of 6 to 10 students, and students' native language was Greek. The first author was the EFL teacher, with four years of prior experience working in the same school. She supervised the redesign process at all times, and had spent adequate time preparing and searching for suitable games that could easily be redesigned within a teaching

Table 1. Redesign of *Taboo*

Set the goals	Vocabulary consolidation
Choose a game	*Taboo* (Hasbro, 1989)
Adapt rules	Number of forbidden words is adjusted according to level
Adapt content	Words to be guessed and forbidden words based on vocabulary list
Craft the game	Teachers' role: evaluates and provides feedback on the cards
	Learners' role: create Taboo cards and add forbidden words

hour (approximately 45 min). The teacher was primarily responsible for Stages 1–3 while learners largely undertook Stages 5 and 6 under the teacher's supervision. The games listed below address mainly vocabulary and grammar skills of learners, but can be easily adjusted to suit learning objectives other than consolidating linguistic content. Choices made in the first 5 stages are also summarized in tables, while results of the playtests are discussed in Sect. 5.

4.1 Taboo for Vocabulary Consolidation

Taboo (Hasbro, 1989) is a well-known party game in which players have to guess a hidden word. The player who knows the word can use any hints to describe the word apart from the forbidden words listed on the word card. *Taboo* can be used in the EFL classroom as a vernacular game [16]. Authentic materials can prepare students for real-life communication scenarios and provide meaningful context to language [21]. However, they are targeted to native speakers and frequently address cultural topics or colloquial language that might be unknown to EFL learners, while they are not carefully graded learning materials. Thus, vernacular games should be adjusted to the language context, e.g. the language level of students, their age, and other factors that may impact understanding [17].

In this case of redesign, students were asked to create "*Taboo*-style" cards for words that they have been taught and then play with them (see Table 1). In this case, the teacher adapted the number of forbidden words per card, reducing them to make the game easier (Stage 3). Students chose the words to be guessed and the forbidden word cards (Stage 4), wrote the first version of the cards on post-it notes (Stage 5) and tested it in class. The teacher evaluated whether their choice of forbidden words is successful and gave ideas on how to improve their word cards. After several playtests (Stage 6) where cards were adjusted and re-created as post-it notes, the teacher used a word processor to create stylized word cards (see Fig. 1a) based on students' post-it notes. The students helped in cutting and laminating the cards in a second iteration of Stage 5.

Redesigning *Taboo* cards provided a two-fold benefit. Students were exposed to the language (e.g. vocabulary lists) they had to learn and created a game that they can play with and understand. Given the popularity of *Taboo*, the teacher's effort in describing the game or assistance in redesigning rules and content was

Table 2. Redesign of Tic-Tac-Toe

Set the goals	Vocabulary and sentence structure practice
Choose a game	Tic-Tac-Toe
Adapt rules	Grid with images instead of blank grid. Use target language to claim and acquire an image on the grid
Include content	Images as prompts to evoke language
Craft the game	Teachers' role: provide ideas for images to be placed on the grid
	Learners' role: choose, draw and color images

minimal. The teacher's role was important for assessing correct use of vocabulary or fair level of challenge between cards. This procedure can take place several times in a school year, e.g. before term exams to revise important vocabulary. By the end of the year, the students can combine all word cards made in different sessions and have a game with key vocabulary learned throughout the year.

4.2 Tic-Tac-Toe for Syntax Practice

Tic-Tac-Toe (or Noughts and Crosses) is a popular, simple pen-and-paper game in which a player claims a place on a three-by-three grid by drawing a circle or a cross; the winner must have three of these in a row. In a digital gamified version of Tic-Tac-Toe designed for EFL purposes by Burlington books, learners have to answer correctly a grammar or vocabulary question (in multiple-choice form) to claim a place on the grid. This behaviorist, filling-in-the-blanks practice does not solicit language productivity as it involves choice among a few options, and generally requires lower order thinking skills. Students are asked to recall their knowledge and identify the correct answers between two options, but they do not produce language. This game feels like a gamified closed-ended quiz [13].

Tic-Tac-Toe was redesigned during the teaching of quantifiers in English to describe food and object quantities (see Table 2). The key vocabulary of the specific class were the quantifiers, i.e. "(a) few", "(a) little", "a lot of", "lots of", "many", "much" and structures such as "There is(n't)/ There are(n't)". After learners were taught these structures, they brainstormed food items with the teacher (Stage 4) and were asked to create an image for each food item (one per student). This resulted in the production of 9 different drawings of food (Stage 5) which were placed on a classic blank Tic-Tac-Toe grid (see Fig. 1b). Students were then invited to play a Tic-Tac-Toe game, adapting the rules (Stage 3) so that students should use the target language to describe the image in order to claim that grid position.

Producing an entire sentence (e.g. "there are a few carrots") is an open-ended task and requires more creativity from the learners compared to the digital Tic-Tac-Toe gamified quiz. From a pedagogical viewpoint, it is more challenging

Table 3. Redesign of *Pandemic*

Set the goals	Practice vocabulary relating to pollution and nature, raise awareness on environmental issues
Choose a game	*Pandemic* (Z-man games, 2008)
Adapt rules	Reduce number of locations, remove infection cards, epidemics, disease cubes, simplify actions to two, new randomization and tracking of locations' threat, new winning condition, no losing condition
Adapt content	Locations, types of pollution (air, water, earth), solution cards based on environmental policies
Craft the game	Teachers' role: elicit environmental solutions from learners, choose number & types of cards, inspect language used
	Learners' role: brainstorm environmental solutions, design the board, craft cards with text and images

to ask a student to produce a correct utterance by themselves than have them choose between options, as is the case with gamified grammar quizzes [13].

4.3 Pandemic for Content and Language Integrated Learning

Pandemic (Z-man games, 2008) is a cooperative board game with a fairly long playtime. The players' (common) objective is to use their characters' powers and special cards to cure diseases in different locations on the world map. Locations keep getting infected with disease cubes and the game is neither easily winnable nor simple to understand. Players have many possible actions to perform such as move, exchange cards, build structures, remove disease cubes etc.

The redesign of *Pandemic* was the most ambitious project, as both the rules and the theme were adapted extensively; it also shows the impact of choosing a more complex game in Stage 2 for redesign (see Table 3). The game was designed around Content and Language Integrated Learning [10] principles, which refers to the teaching of a subject through a foreign language. Thus, the learning goal (Stage 1) was two-fold: (a) expose learners to vocabulary related to nature and pollution, and (b) raise awareness on environmental issues. To shorten and simplify gameplay, the teacher undertook Stage 3 on her own and removed most subsystems of *Pandemic*. Players only take two actions in sequence: move to an adjacent location and use solution cards to alleviate the pollution from their location. Rather than using disease cubes as additional components, each location's pollution was recorded with a die (and initialized with a die roll). The board included rural and urban locations (see Fig. 1c).Students would collect and use solution cards to decrease and finally remove the pollution in each location. Solution cards are eco-friendly actions that learners could take in real life, such as "Pick up litter", "Use the bicycle more than the car", etc.

Students primarily participated in brainstorming locations and solution cards (Stage 4) and in crafting the game (Stage 5). Environment-friendly actions were elicited through discussion and prompts by the teacher, who also chose the theme of each card (e.g. water, air) which determines the location where it can be used (water solution cards can be used at the river and the lake). During this process, students had to discuss and reflect on social issues in the target language, increasing their interest as the actions affect their daily lives. During the crafting process, a student volunteered to draw the board at home while other learners created solution cards on post-it notes (see Fig. 1c). Due to the expansive changes to the base game, it is necessary to perform many playtests in the classroom or by the teacher alone, and the version of the game described can still be improved. In such expansive redesign attempts, the class can participate in multiple redesign iterations and platesting (re-running Stages 3 to 6) and teacher-led reflective discussion at regular intervals throughout the school year.

5 Conclusion

As illustrated by the use cases discussed above, the participatory design followed is friendly to amateurs in game design and even to students. Modifying an existing game is significantly easier than creating one from scratch.

Drawing from the experience of implementing the redesign process in the language classroom, the first author reports high level of engagement from students. While learners treat digital games designed for language learning as break time, they were actively involved during the redesign process of tabletop games. Adapting *Taboo* required effort from the teacher only in Stages 1 and 2; during Stages 4 and 5 the teacher embraced a supervisory role offering feedback on the cards created. While redesigning *Pandemic*, students offered many ideas in Stage 4 and overtook Stage 5 themselves, as they were happy to offer their artistic skills. Adapting Tic-Tac-Toe also required basic artistic input from students in Stages 4 and 5; while this game was by far the easiest to craft (each student created one card), students engaged in intense competition when playing it.

One may argue that some of the adapted games presented do not challenge students' higher order thinking skills, which was the main criticism for current language learning games. The main focus of the adapted *Taboo* and Tic-Tac-Toe is still vocabulary and grammar drilling, albeit with production of original language. However, higher order thinking skills of learners (such as creativity, evaluation, and cooperation) are addressed *during the design process*. Students are actively involved in the game design experience, which strongly resembles a lesson design experience. They are asked to reflect on knowledge they already know (Stage 4) and to assess their learning after playtesting (Stage 6).

The main limitation of this design approach is the amount of time and work invested in and out of class. On the other hand, the redesign process needs only to take place once; the games generated could be showcased to future classes, who could adapt the games already designed by their classmates (focusing on Stages 4 and 5). Another limitation is that the process has been tested in small language classrooms; the same process may be very demanding in larger classrooms (e.g. in a public school). This could be mitigated by breaking the class into groups that would create different variations of the same game. Lastly, a certain amount of game literacy is required from the teacher in order to make the procedures flow. This can be ameliorated by studying and playing commercial games available or by involving students earlier in the process (e.g. Stage 2).

While this paper focused on applying game redesign for EFL, the process can be used for any school subject. Content can be easily adapted, e.g. using learners' drawings of landmarks in a Geography-based Tic-Tac-Toe. Even rules can be adapted to suit the subject, e.g. to show attracting and repulsive forces as pawn movement rules in a Physics-based game redesign. Future work should evaluate the impact of the redesign process on users' engagement, learning effects, and personal impact such as increased environmental awareness [4]. The goal of this paper is not to assess the impact of the redesign process but rather to convince practitioners not to fear involving learners in challenging game design tasks.

References

1. Albion, P.: Project-, problem-, and inquiry-based learning. Big Issues and Critical Questions, Teaching and Digital Technologies (2015)
2. Carrión, M., Santórum, M., Pérez, M., Aguilar, J.: A participatory methodology for the design of serious games in the educational environment. In: Congreso Internacional de Innovacion y Tendencias en Ingenieria (2017)
3. Farrell, T.S.: Lesson planning. In: Methodology in Language Teaching: An Anthology of Current Practice, pp. 30–39 (2002)
4. Gualeni, S., Gomez Maureira, M.: Self-transformative effects of designing videogames and the challenge of capturing them quantitatively: a case study. In: Proceedings of the Foundation of Digital Games (2018)
5. Hannafin, M.J., Hannafin, K.M.: Cognition and student-centered, web-based learning: issues and implications for research and theory. In: Spector, J., Ifenthaler, D., Isaias, P., Kinshuk, S.D. (eds.) Learning and Instruction in the Digital Age, pp. 11–23. Springer, Boston (2010). https://doi.org/10.1007/978-1-4419-1551-1_2
6. Hartson, R., Pyla, P.: Chapter 11 - Background: understand needs. In: The UX Book, 2nd edn. Morgan Kaufmann (2019)
7. Johnson, R.T., Johnson, D.W.: Active learning: cooperation in the classroom. Annu. Rep. Educ. Psychol. Jpn. **47**, 29–30 (2008)
8. Krathwohl, D.R., Anderson, L.W.: A Taxonomy for Learning, Teaching, and Assessing: A Revision of Bloom's Taxonomy of Educational Objectives. Longman (2009)
9. Kultima, A.: Casual game design values. In: Proceedings of the 13th International MindTrek Conference: Everyday Life in the Ubiquitous Era, pp. 58–65. ACM (2009)
10. Marsh, D.: CLIL/EMILE-The European dimension: actions, trends and foresight potential. University of Jyväskylä (2002)
11. Morrison, C.D.: From 'sage on the stage' to 'guide on the side': a good start. Int. J. Sch. Teach. Learn. **8**(1), 4 (2014)
12. Nagy, W.: Metalinguistic awareness and the vocabulary-comprehension connection. In: Vocabulary Acquisition: Implications for Reading Comprehension, pp. 52–77 (2007)

13. Nicholson, S.: Making gameplay matter: designing modern educational tabletop games. Knowl. Quest **40**(1), 60 (2011)
14. Prensky, M.: Digital game-based learning. Comput. Entertain. **1**(1), 21 (2003)
15. Read, J.C., Gregory, P., MacFarlane, S., McManus, B., Gray, P., Patel, R.: An investigation of participatory design with children-informant, balanced and facilitated design. In: Interaction Design and Children, pp. 53–64. Eindhoven (2002)
16. Reinhardt, J.: Gameful Second and Foreign Language Teaching and Learning: Theory, Research, and Practice. Springer, Cham (2018). https://doi.org/10.1007/978-3-030-04729-0
17. Reinhardt, J.: Learnful L2 gaming. Gameful Second and Foreign Language Teaching and Learning. NLLTE, pp. 19–43. Springer, Cham (2019). https://doi.org/10.1007/978-3-030-04729-0_2
18. Savvani, S.: State-of-the-art duolingo features and applications. In: Auer, M.E., Tsiatsos, T. (eds.) ICL 2018. AISC, vol. 917, pp. 139–148. Springer, Cham (2019). https://doi.org/10.1007/978-3-030-11935-5_14
19. Sicart, M.: Defining game mechanics. Game Stud. **8**(2) (2008)
20. Sørensen, B.H.: Educational design for serious games. In: Serious Games in Education, pp. 101–122. Aarhus Universitetsforlag (2011)
21. Tomlinson, B.: Materials development. In: The Encyclopedia of Applied Linguistics (2012)
22. Trepte, S., Reinecke, L.: Avatar creation and video game enjoyment: effects of life-satisfaction, game competitiveness, and identification with the avatar. J. Media Psychol. **22**, 171–184 (2010)

Requirements Analysis of a Serious Game for Deaf Players

Platt-Young Zoë[1(✉)], Shahri Bahareh[2(✉)], Sutherland Dean[3(✉)], and Hoermann Simon[1,2(✉)]

[1] Human Interface Technology Lab, University of Canterbury, Christchurch, New Zealand
zoe@zoeplattyoung.com, simon.hoermann@canterbury.ac.nz
[2] School of Product Design, University of Canterbury, Christchurch, New Zealand
bahareh.shahri@canterbury.ac.nz
[3] School of Psychology, Speech and Hearing, University of Canterbury, Christchurch, New Zealand
dean.sutherland@canterbury.ac.nz

Abstract. Talk Town is a serious digital game to overcome social isolation in Deaf children by combating stigma associated with hearing impairments and providing modelling of social communication skills. This paper presents the research process and outcomes to ensure that Talk Town is engaging and useful for players, educators and parents. It is described and framed using Cooper's Requirements Definition and qualitative methods. The motivation for the game-based intervention is illustrated with findings from a structured literature search and supported with insights gained from qualitative enquiries. Findings and themes from interviews and co-design activities are discussed, personas and artefacts illustrated, and relevant content, game and design recommendations for future work in this area presented.

Keywords: Serious game · Game-based intervention · Deaf and Hard of Hearing (DHH) · Requirements Definition · Design · User experience (UX)

1 Introduction

1.1 Context

Deaf and Hard of Hearing (DHH) children can face significant barriers to social communication despite the advent of sophisticated audiological technologies such as the cochlear implant providing improved access to sound [1–3].

The majority of DHH students are born to hearing parents and educated in mainstream settings where they may be the only DHH student, a situation which can have implications on the development and application of social communication [4]. Contextual barriers can compound the challenges which DHH students face, particularly when encountering stigma. Self-advocacy skills are necessary to recognize the barriers to successful interaction, find possible solutions and employ strategies for their communication needs [5, 6]. Particular challenges exist with pragmatic skills around

A. Liapis et al. (Eds.): GALA 2019, LNCS 11899, pp. 24–31, 2019.
https://doi.org/10.1007/978-3-030-34350-7_3

expressive and receptive language [7, 8], stigma, theory of mind and executive function [2, 9, 10]. In light of these varied challenges, a serious game-based intervention was proposed to promote Deaf players' social communication skills and develop confidence related to a range of everyday social and learning activities, by modelling effective strategies in an engaging format.

2 Literature Review

2.1 Structured Literature Search

A search for relevant past work into digital game-based interventions that targeted social and pragmatic skills for DHH students was conducted, which yielded no comparable precedents to incorporate into the research and requirements definition.

A systematic literature search was therefore conducted to identify game or technology-based interventions that targeted social communication for DHH players, or for children with Autism Spectrum Disorder (ASD), with inclusion and exclusion criteria developed and published on PROSPERO [11]. The search was widened to include ASD related interventions because of the dearth of game intervention research relevant to individuals who were DHH. Though the aetiology is different, some similarities exist in terms of presentation, for example delays in Theory of Mind development compared to hearing peers. Seven databases were systematically searched to identify relevant work, with key search criteria including optimized string variants of theory of mind, self-efficacy, self-advocacy, social skills, social pragmatics, AR, VR, and Game. Once the initial screening was completed, papers identified as relevant were peer-reviewed in teams of two for their accuracy in meeting inclusion criteria. Only a small number were deemed relevant, although of these no single intervention which targeted multiple target areas was identified. This indicated that research, like the one presented in this paper, to inform an intervention in the target areas was well justified.

3 Methods/Framework

3.1 Framework and Approach

Given the multidisciplinary nature of the challenge, an approach that combined Cooper's Requirements Definition [12], Grounded Theory Methods [13, 14] and human-centred Co-Design principles [15] was determined most suitable for the research.

The pre-discovery phase comprised of preliminary observational work in context, interviews with stakeholders and reviewing existing research. Questions to guide the content and structure of workshops and interviews were iterated based on this process.

3.2 Design and Qualitative Methods

Artefacts for co-design workshops and interview scripts for semi-structured interviews [16, 17] were developed following the 'pre-discovery' phase, and both research activities piloted with test participants. Particularly for interviewing Deaf respondents, it was crucial to pilot the interview sessions to ensure communication and the interview environment was as clear as possible.

In the co-design workshops, an adapted focus group format [18] was created that incorporated a segment for group discussion, followed by an active ideation component utilising 10 prompt resources inspired by human-centred design tools developed by IDEO [15]. Participants were encouraged to write their ideas on Post-Its (Fig. 1), allowing the researchers to ask follow-up questions relating to their motivations and thinking behind the contributions, as well as to record ideas for the purpose of later study. Results were collated in summary transcripts from each session and coded, tables produced for all visual data, and full transcripts of interviews were prepared.

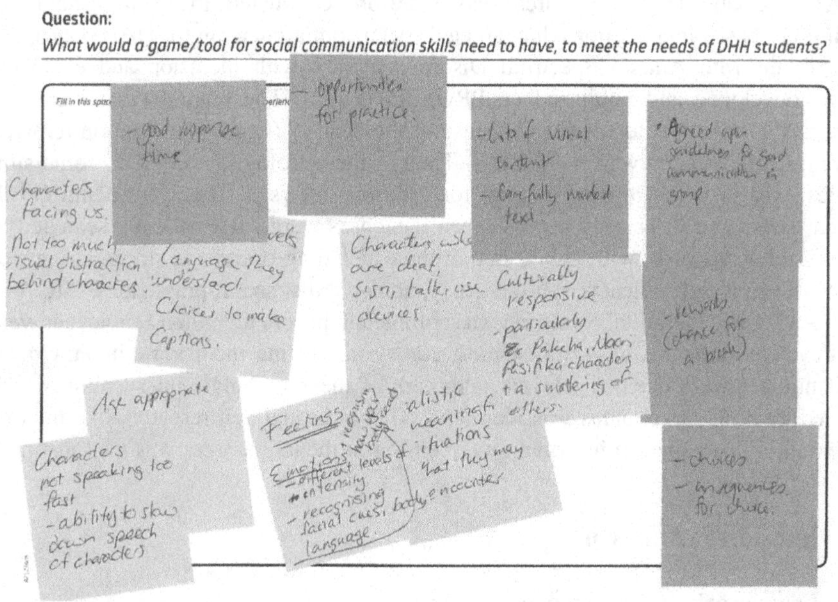

Fig. 1. Co-design resource developed for ideation sessions with Educators and Specialists

3.3 Respondents and Session Structure

Specialists, educators, and parents contributed to the research with their involvement in interviews and focus groups. Overall, 17 respondents participated in the primary research. Three focus groups and 7 interviews with subject matter experts were carried out. Interviews were conducted remotely via video conferencing tools, to allow respondents more flexibility in participation throughout the country. Four Deaf education specialists who were Deaf themselves contributed, adding another layer of experience to the data.

Personas and Scenarios

To guide the design and development efforts, personas and scenarios (Fig. 2) were developed based on the data collected in interviews and co-design workshops [12]. An unintended outcome was learning that education specialists had used cases for the personas, and they described the artefacts as helpful for their practice. Personas and scenarios were designed iteratively in collaboration with a member of the Deaf education community who was a Speech Language Therapist, and whose involvement served as an additional point of triangulation [19].

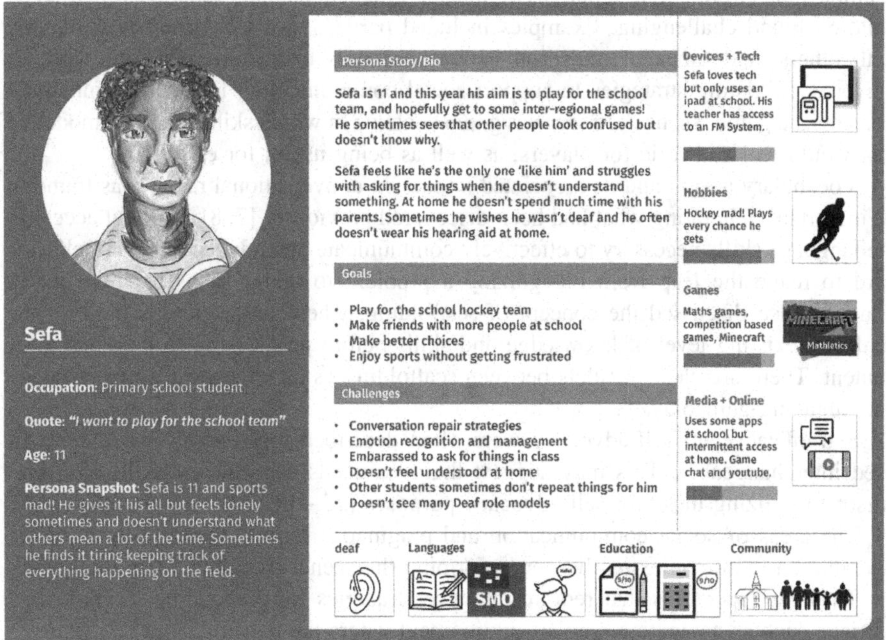

Fig. 2. Sefa, the primary persona, created based on primary and secondary data [20]

3.4 Analysis Framework

Thematic content analysis was used to interpret qualitative data and transform it into insights, findings and themes [20, 21]. Codes were developed following transcription, where ideas discussed by respondents were described by labels that communicated the essence of the phrases being coded. Memoing, member checking, and peer review of a sample of the coded transcripts and negative cases were supporting methods employed to limit impact of bias and arrive at validated themes [22–24].

4 Findings

4.1 Areas of Social and Pragmatic Skills

Social and pragmatic skills encompass themes relating to communication and their deployment in social settings. Many recurring phrases and examples were discussed by parents and educators. The importance of contextual barriers, self-efficacy and advocacy, theory of mind, conversational repair and vocabulary were among the most prominent themes.

"Contextual barriers and scene inspiration" was a combined code used to describe examples that were given about environments, interactions and scenarios which DHH children found challenging. Examples included parties, sports environments, playing with others, and times of transition between schools and from school to work or university. Existing strategies to support social communication formed recommendations for the game 'scenes', to serve as game contexts in which skills could be modelled that would feel authentic for players, as well as being useful for educators.

Vocabulary access and its associated impact on conversational repair was found to be important, reiterating what had been discovered previously [7, 8]. Without access to the language skills necessary to effectively communicate and advocate for oneself, it is hard to make the leap from recognizing a problem to taking steps to solve for it. Teachers also discussed the concept of scaffolding, where knowledge is built on the students' existing level of knowledge and skills before progressing to more complex content. There are clear parallels between scaffolding as an effective learning strategy and engaging gameplay.

Self-efficacy and self-advocacy were often described together by respondents or used interchangeably. This may suggest that one needs self-efficacy skills as a precursor to utilizing these for self-advocacy purposes [25–28].

The areas of social communication and pragmatics formed the core focus of the intervention, with contextual barriers informing the scenarios displayed in the game.

These are scenarios that require effective strategies for responding to contextual barriers, such as navigating a noisy environment where the player character's vision is blocked, reducing their capacity to recognise facial cues of characters in the scene. The player is asked to choose from a range of options how to respond, which promotes both self-efficacy by offering player choice and advocacy by modelling how one may speak up for their needs in a challenging environment.

4.2 Games and Play

Games and play concerned the areas perceived important in a game-based intervention so that it would be engaging for DHH players. Themes included existing games played by students, play-based activities employed by teachers, user experience elements of games, levels and progression, game mechanics and reinforcement. Recommendations included: provision of choice to reinforce the concept that players had influence on outcomes, high visual contrast for legibility, and progression to motivate players and provide a feeling of accomplishment and reinforcement. The context of play was also important – educators described how they would play games with their students, and use these to provoke conversations and additional learning beyond the game. Resource teachers of the Deaf (RTD) may be uniquely placed to augment this learning, as they have more one-to-one contact time directly with the student. RTDs are specialists that have a caseload of DHH children they work closely with, and often develop or configure activities to augment and reinforce learning. For this reason, a secondary persona of an RTD was created to aid the design of the intervention in this area (see Fig. 3).

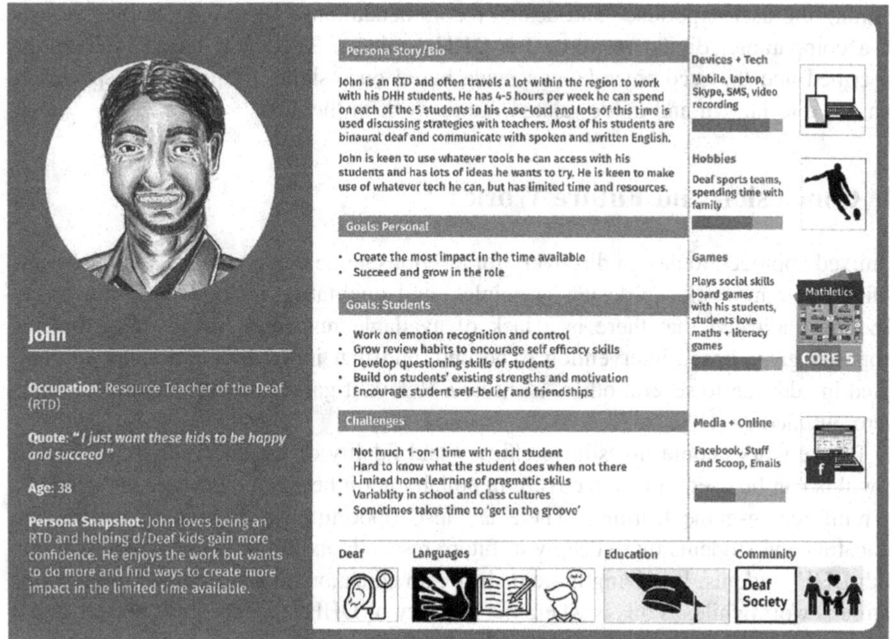

Fig. 3. John, a secondary persona representing a resource Teacher of the Deaf

4.3 Identity, Culture and Relationships

Identity, culture, and relationships related to themes of Deaf identity, relationships with hearing peers, stigma, identity, friendships and culture.

A strong sense of Deaf culture was discussed by respondents as being a protective factor for individuals to counteract stigma relating to hearing loss. Other codes were related to cultural dimensions of deafness, for example, what it means to be "Māori and Deaf" (respondent comment from Focus group 3). A recommendation for the intervention was to promote positive Deaf identity through characters from a range of backgrounds and to depict a range of audiological devices, enabling players to self-select their device and identity.

4.4 Discussion and Recommendations

The areas that emerged from the analysis informed the recommendations for the game-based intervention. The core areas assumed to be important for the intervention were validated, and many others emerged through this research enquiry have been incorporated in the development of the intervention.

A plethora of potential scenes for the game, based on the lived expertise of respondents were suggested, coupled with educational best practices and observations forming the user experience and design recommendations. There is an evidential lack of a comparable, digital resource for DHH students. The game-based intervention described and the recommendations made based on insights from domain specialists can serve to inform and guide related future work in the area.

5 Conclusion and Future Work

A mixed approach to design discovery for a serious game that combines a requirements definition framework, co-design principles, and qualitative methods was illustrated. Findings indicated that there is a lack of available resources in this area, that the proposed game-based intervention is needed, and that initial problem areas are validated in addition to several others identified. Relevant game and user experience areas were outlined.

Future work should investigate efficacy and fidelity of the intervention, as well as how this can be used most effectively in collaboration between educators and students to reinforce in-game learning. There are also opportunities to involve mainstream educators and students more deeply in future research and to play-test the intervention with DHH students. Involving more mainstream educators in research enquiries of this nature is worthwhile, as this is where the majority of DHH students are educated, and it appears promising to examine the challenges within these settings in a more comprehensive manner in the future.

References

1. Church, A., Paatsch, L., Toe, D.: Some trouble with repair: conversations between children with cochlear implants and hearing peers. Discourse Stud. **19**(1), 49–68 (2017)
2. Figueras, B., Edwards, L., Langdon, D.: Executive function and language in deaf children. J. Deaf Stud. Deaf Educ. **13**(3), 362–377 (2008)
3. Hebert, A.M.: An exploratory study of characteristics associated with postsecondary educational attainment in students who are deaf or hard of hearing. Dissertation/Thesis, ProQuest Dissertations Publishing (2012)
4. Kent, B.A.: Identity issues for hard-of-hearing adolescents aged 11, 13, and 15 in mainstream setting. J. Deaf Stud. Deaf Educ. **8**(3), 315–324 (2003)
5. Reed, S., Antia, S.D., Kreimeyer, K.H.: Academic status of deaf and hard-of-hearing students in public schools: student, home, and service facilitators and detractors. J. Deaf Stud. Deaf Educ. **13**(4), 485–502 (2008)
6. Michael, R., Zidan, H.M.: Differences in self-advocacy among hard of hearing and typical hearing students. Res. Dev. Disabil. **72**, 118–127 (2018)

7. Thagard, E.K., Hilsmier, A.S., Easterbrooks, S.R.: Pragmatic language in deaf and hard of hearing students: correlation with success in general education. Am. Ann. Deaf **155**(5), 526–534 (2011)
8. Yoshinaga-Itano, C.: The missing link in language learning of children who are deaf or hard of hearing: pragmatics. Cochlear Implant. Int. 16(suppl.) S53–S54 (2015)
9. Jones, A.C., Gutierrez, R., Ludlow, A.K.: Confronting the language barrier: theory of mind in deaf children. J. Commun. Disord. **56**, 47–58 (2015)
10. Peterson, C.C., Siegal, M.: Representing inner worlds: theory of mind in autistic, deaf, and normal hearing children. Psychol. Sci. **10**(2), 126–129 (1999)
11. Platt-Young, Z., Hoermann, S.: Computer-based interventions for social skills training of deaf and hard of hearing children and youths, and of interventions for ASD children and youths in which the area being studied is related to those also experienced by deaf and hard of hearing students. In: PROSPERO 2018, CRD42018092708 (2018). http://www.crd.york.ac.uk/PROSPERO/display_record.php?ID=CRD42018092708
12. Cooper, A.: About Face: The Essentials of Interaction Design, 4th edn. (no. Book, Whole). Wiley, Indianapolis (2014)
13. Glaser, B.G.: The grounded theory perspective: its origins and growth. Grounded Theory Rev.: Int. J. **15**(1) (2016)
14. Moore, J.: An exploration of the origin of classic grounded theory: Jennifer Moore looks at the origin, development, misinterpretation and misuse of grounded theory. Nurse Res. **17**(1), 8–14 (2009)
15. Ideo (ed.) The Field Guide to Human-Centered Design: Design Kit, 1st. edn, pp. 189. IDEO, San Francisco (2015)
16. Turner, A.M., Reeder, B., Ramey, J.: Scenarios, personas and user stories from design ethnography: evidence-based design representations of communicable disease investigations. J. Biomed. Inform. **46**(4), 575–584 (2013)
17. Daae, J., Boks, C.: A classification of user research methods for design for sustainable behaviour. J. Clean. Prod. **106**, 680–689 (2015)
18. Krueger, R.A., Casey, M.A.: Focus Groups: A Practical Guide for Applied Research, 5th edn, pp. 280. Sage Publications (2014)
19. Morse, J.M.: Critical analysis of strategies for determining rigor in qualitative inquiry. Qual. Health Res. **25**(9), 1212–1222 (2015)
20. Hutchinson, S.A.: Education and grounded theory. J. Thought **21**(3), 50–68 (1986)
21. Guest, G., Bunce, A., Johnson, L.: How many interviews are enough?: An experiment with data saturation and variability. Field Methods **18**(1), 59–82 (2006)
22. Birks, M., Mills, J.: Grounded Theory: A Practical Guide. Sage (2015)
23. Savin-Baden, M., Major, C.H.: Qualitative Research: The Essential Guide to Theory and Practice (no. Book, Whole). Routledge, Abingdon (2012)
24. Aldiabat, K.M., Le Navenec, C.-L.: Data saturation: the mysterious step in grounded theory method. Qual. Rep. **23**(1), 19 (2018)
25. Marschark, M., Walton, D., Crowe, K., Borgna, G., Kronenberger, W.G.: Relations of social maturity, executive function, and self-efficacy among deaf university students. Deaf. Educ. Int. **20**(2), 100–120 (2018)
26. Cassidy, S.: Resilience building in students: the role of academic self-efficacy. Front. Psychol. Orig. Res. **6**, 1781 (2015). (in English)
27. Bandura, A.: Self-efficacy mechanism in human agency. Am. Psychol. **37**(2), 122–147 (1982)
28. Bandura, A.: Social Foundations of Thought and Action: A Social Cognitive Theory, 1st edn, p. 640. Prentice Hall, Englewood Cliffs (1985)
29. Test, D.W., Fowler, C.H., Wood, W.M., Brewer, D.M., Eddy, S.: A conceptual framework of self-advocacy for students with disabilities. Remedial Spec. Educ. **26**(1), 43–54 (2005)

Debriefing and Knowledge Processing an Empirical Study About Game-Based Learning for Computer Education

Maud Plumettaz-Sieber(✉), Catherine Bonnat, and Eric Sanchez

University of Fribourg, CERF, P.-A. de Faucigny 2, 1700 Fribourg, Switzerland
{maud.sieber, catherine.bonnat, eric.sanchez}@unifr.ch

Abstract. This paper deals with debriefing for game-based learning. Using a design-based research methodology, our goal consists of modeling debriefing and helping teachers to implement debriefing into their teaching practices. This model has been tested during experimentations carried out in upper secondary classes (15–17 years old) in Switzerland. Four game-based courses using the game "Programming Game" have been analyzed. In this paper we focus on the debriefing phase. In order to identify how knowledge is processed during the debriefing, we used an annotation software for categorizing interactions between the teacher and the students. Results show that practices differ among teachers regarding debriefing and that the processing of knowledge (named institutionalization) is not fully performed.

Keywords: Debriefing/institutionalization · Computational thinking · Game-based-learning

1 Introduction

Game-based learning (GBL) is not limited to the use of a game. GBL also refers to the use of a learning scenario where debriefing is recognized to be important for the metacognition and the transfer of knowledge [1]. However, debriefing is not often implemented and not often addressed by educational researchers. This paper aims to contribute to fill in this gap. This paper deals with an empirical study about the debriefing after the use of "Programming Game" [2], a game dedicated to computer education. For this study, we adopted a design-based methodology [3] enabling to combine the development and implementation of the learning scenario (including the use of a game) and analysis of data collected during classroom observations. For this study we analyze how debriefing has been implemented based on experiments carried out in 4 upper secondary classes and we proposed a model of debriefing focused on the processing of knowledge called institutionalization.

First, we present computational thinking and institutionalization, the theoretical foundations of our study. Then we present the research questions and the research settings grounded on a design-based methodology. Results are discussed in the last part of this paper and prospects are presented in the conclusion.

A. Liapis et al. (Eds.): GALA 2019, LNCS 11899, pp. 32–41, 2019.
https://doi.org/10.1007/978-3-030-34350-7_4

2 Theoretical Foundations

The learning scenario designed for this study is a game-based learning situation dedicated to computer education. By using "Programming Game", secondary school students face challenges that can be addressed by writing specific algorithms. Therefore, it is expected that they develop computational thinking skills. However, we also consider that the learning scenario should not be limited to the use of the game but should include a debriefing session. In the following we present the theoretical foundation for computational thinking and debriefing.

2.1 Computer Education and Computational Thinking

Computational thinking (CT) is now recognized as an important skill for 21st century citizens [4]. However, no unique definition emerges from the scientific literature. According to Wing [4], computational thinking consists of a set of problem-solving skills which integrate knowledge from computer science. For Csizmadia et al. [5] "It is the process of recognizing aspects of computation in the world that surrounds us and applying the tools and techniques from computing to understand and reason about natural, social and artificial systems and processes" [5, p. 5]. Computational thinking integrates five concepts: logical and algorithmic thinking, decomposition, generalization (pattern recognition), modelling, abstraction and evaluation [4, 5]; and five techniques: reflecting, coding, designing, analyzing and applying [4]. By playing "Programming Game", it is expected that the students learn the following concepts: sequence, variable, function, condition, loop. In this respect "Programming Game" focuses on computational thinking skills that include coding [6]. For this study, students were introduced to computational thinking through algorithms and coding.

2.2 Debriefing vs Institutionalization

Based on the work carried out by Brousseau for the Theory of Didactical Situations [7], a game-based learning situation consists of an action's situation. The player/learner interact with the game which returns feedback. Based on feedback learners can assess his way of acting and thinking. Then, misconceptions are made visible and the player/learner can adapt his strategy and try to find another solution for addressing the challenge. Thus, Brousseau's work is grounded in the constructivist theory developed by Piaget: learning results from an adaptive process. Brousseau also makes a distinction between *connaissances* (contextualized knowledge acquired during the game) and *savoirs* (decontextualized and transferable knowledge). In addition, the knowledge acquired during the game session might be incomplete or incorrect. This is the reason why teachers should take into account the need for the *institutionalization* of knowledge, i.e. to decontextualize knowledge and make it transferable and reusable for other situations. As a result, *institutionalization* is a key step for game-based learning.

We identify differences between debriefing [8] and institutionalization [7] and we consider the transformation of knowledge at the core of game-based learning [9]. On the one hand, debriefing "relates to the learning, the emotional or the behavioral content and, depending on the purpose of the game, the content of debriefing, different scenario might be used by debriefers" [9, p. 244]. On the other hand, institutionalization is "a situation that is unraveled by passing from a knowledge of its role as a means of resolving a situation of action, formulation or proof, to a new role, that of reference for future personal or collective uses" [10, p. 4]. For example, a student who managed to optimize an algorithm with a loop should be able to name a loop, to understand how a loop works and when it is relevant to use it. Previous descriptions of debriefing mainly focus on the cognitive, behavioral and psychological dimensions of the game experience. Meanwhile institutionalization is more focused on the transformation of the knowledge [9].

In a previous work [9], we already advocated for better taking into account the transformation of knowledge and, therefore, for focusing on *institutionalization* as the part of debriefing dedicated to processing knowledge. We have identified five steps. This article is based on a revised version of our model. This new model consists of four dimensions (which refers to the five previous steps):

Dimension 1: **Feelings.** It is a self-reflection about the feelings (fun, stress, happiness, …) that emerged from the experience. The learners express feelings and their willingness to play again.

Dimension 2: (2.a) **Awareness**. This dimension consists of raising awareness and making knowledge visible. Students are invited to express the acquired knowledge and to think about the meaning of the experiment, especially about the learned concepts and acquired skills. (2.b) **Desyncretization.** Students are expected to distinguish and discuss the links between the game and the learned concepts. It is also an opportunity to discuss about mistakes and misconceptions. Solutions for addressing the challenge offered by the game are discussed. Students explain what they did and describe the good and bad strategies. This is a first step for the decontextualization of knowledge and for making visible the learned concepts and acquired skills. Then, knowledge embedded in the game and the game itself become separated (desyncretization).

Dimension 3: **Validation.** This dimension consists of naming, clarifying, legitimizing and validating the concepts embedded in the game. The students are encouraged to explain their solutions. These solutions are rephrased in a scientific way by the teacher. Additional information is provided. The knowledge is legitimized and validated.

Dimension 4: **Generalization.** The students are asked to imagine different situations for which it would make sense to use the new knowledge (concepts and skills).

Through debriefing, we also refer to the Socratic maieutic, also called "Socratic method" [11]. The place of the dialogue between the teacher and the students is important to enable the students to develop their own meaning, but also to identify the gap with previous knowledge. During the institutionalization phase, the teacher is responsible for helping the students to question themselves about their knowledge and, therefore, for making possible the transformation of knowledge.

According to Sensevy [12], for the design of a teaching-learning situation, the teacher is responsible for the roles, the *milieu* and the time. The is expected to take decisions about these 3 dimensions of a learning situation. The roles refer to the teacher and the students' performed tasks. Who is in charge for institutionalizing the knowledge? Who asks questions during the debriefing phase? Who answers the questions? The *milieu* refers to the design of the setting of the debriefing. What kind of objects are used by the teacher? How the situation is setting up? What material is used? The time refers to the time dedicated to the debriefing and the evolution of the knowledge during this phase. In the following, we will refer to this concept and the four dimensions of debriefing to identify the process of debriefing and to modeling it.

3 Research Questions and Objectives

The literature review shows that debriefing is a core element of game-based learning. However, we know little about debriefing and there is a need to clarify how this phase should be implemented. Previous works about debriefing seems to have failed to capture how knowledge is processed during debriefing. In this regard, the Theory of Didactical Situation [7] offers an opportunity to emphasize this dimension. This paper is dedicated to test the model described above. We want to identify, in the practice of four computer science teachers, (Q1) Which knowledge is institutionalized by the teachers? (Q2) Which dimensions of institutionalization are taken into account by the teachers?

4 Research Settings

In the following, we describe the research setting as the co-design of the game and the learning scenario according to a design-based methodology. We also describe the experiments and the data collected.

4.1 Co-design of the Game and the Learning Scenarios

For this research, we adopt a design-based research (DBR) [3] methodology. Since August 2018, an interdisciplinary team composed of five computer science teachers, three computer scientists, two researchers, one graphic designer and one game designer worked together to co-design the "Programming Game" and the learning scenarios. During this phase dedicated to co-design, we defined (1) the expected learning outcomes of the game and targeted concepts (sequences, variable, function, condition, loop), (2) the dashboard enabling for the teacher to assess the students and (3) how to use the game in class (learning scenarios).

For the co-design of learning scenarios, we first decided how the teachers should introduce the game. We decided to hide the learning objectives and to challenge the students: "you have the possibility to move the blond character on the screen of the computer by writing specific instructions. The challenge consists of moving the blond character so that he joins the red character". The teachers also explain the functionalities of the game interface. During the game session, the teachers are not expected to help the students if they encounter difficulties except if there is a risk that they give up. Regarding the phase dedicated to debriefing, we failed to reach a consensus about how to implement it. Despite the arguments derived from the scientific literature on the needs to conduct a debriefing phase to bring out knowledge and contextualize them, teachers were reluctant to script and conduct this phase. So, we let the teachers free to implement this phase.

4.2 Experiments

Experiments took place in four different classes located in Switzerland (canton of Fribourg) with students from 15 to 17 years old (1st and 3rd level) during spring 2019. Beside the teacher, one researcher and one computer scientist were present. They had two separate roles, the computer scientist was responsible for any possible technical incidents, and the researcher was taking notes based on a grid. All experiments took place in a computer room of the school, one computer for each student. Depending on the school, there were about twenty students per class.

The whole learning scenario, including the introduction, the game session and the final conclusion was video-taped. The videos were tagged with ELAN[1], a software which enable for the transcription and the annotations of videos. All teachers and students' interactions were tagged. For this study, we considered only the institutionalization phase. Teacher-student interactions registered during the game sessions were not tagged. Related to our research questions, we designed a methodology dedicated to categorize interactions. Based on a previous project [13], we identified 11 categories described in Table 1, and for some of them we proposed different subcategories. These categories are linked to the debriefing dimensions described previously (Sect. 2.2) and to Sensevy's depiction of a learning situation (role, *milieu*, time). For example, we specified one category (line number 9) in order to describe the nature of the teacher's intervention according to the 4 dimensions of debriefing. We designed another (line number 10) which specify how the concepts are handled (*milieu*). Besides, we defined categories which describe how the teacher scaffold the students' activity (lines number 3, 5, 6) (role). Finally, we considered the course material used by teachers (line 8). To do this, we distinguished between the course material designed before the debriefing (presentation, questionnaire, dashboard) and those designed during the session.

We have created annotations every 15 s, and considered as an event (line number 1) interactions that refer to the same topic.

[1] ELAN is a multimedia file annotation software developed by the technical group of the Max Planck Institute for Psycholinguistics (Nijmegen, Netherlands).

Table 1. Categories and subcategories designed in Elan software

Nb	Categories	Subcategories
1	Event	(number)
2	Teacher's intervention target	Class - student - Unknown
3	Type of intervention	Give instruction - enrich the instruction - ask questions - feedback (correct) - feedback (wrong) - give an information - other - Unknown
4	Student's intervention target	Teacher - teacher and class - Unknown
5	Nature of feedback (if correct)	Rephrases - validate - ask for an opinion - ask to complete - other - Unknown
6	Nature of feedback (if wrong)	Give correct answer - indicates error - explain error - ask to check - ask for an opinion - other - Unknown
7	Teacher's position	Board - desk - beamer - static - movement - next to a student - other - Unknown
8	Course material used	For class produced during course - for class produced before course - individual produced during course - individual produced before course - dashboard - other - Unknown
9	Intervention nature	Usability - emotion - game step - resolution strategies - purpose of activity - concept - competence - other - Unknown
10	Intervention content (*if concept*)	Indicate error - give definition - write answer (game) - mime - explain the use of concept - write answer - other - Unknown
11	Comments	(Notes and verbatim)

Data was stored in a.csv file dedicated to a quantitative analysis. In addition, qualitative analysis was performed with the verbatim (line number 11).

5 Results and Discussion

This section is dedicated to a discussion of the results that emerged from data analysis. We (1) describe how debriefings are performed by the teachers and (2) identify and specify the four dimensions of the theoretical model described above.

Table 2, presents the main characteristics of the debriefings performed by the different teachers.

The duration of the debriefing for these four teachers varies widely, from 2 to 11 min. However, we notice that there is no real discussion between the teacher and his students. Only one or two asked questions for teachers T1, T2 and T3 and none for the teacher 4 which debriefing is longest. All teachers used this time to provide information. We will characterize its nature in the following paragraph.

Table 2. Main debriefing characteristics for the four teachers

Teacher	Duration (mn)	Teacher's interventions	Course material
T1	2'	1': question to student 1': class (give information)	Dashboard displayed on the screen Teacher stands in front of the students, static
T2	6'15	2': question to student 4'15: class (give information)	Questionnaire displayed on the screen Teacher stands in front of the students or the screen
T3	8'15	30": question to student 7'45: class (give information)	Student's screenshots displayed Static in front of the screen and the desk
T4	11'45	11'45: class (give information)	Presentation designed live and projected Static in front of the screen and the desk

Although no consensus was found during the co-design of the debriefing with the four teachers who tested the game, we observe that 4 teachers conducted the debriefing, but only 3 teachers conducted what we consider to be the institutionalization of the knowledge acquired during the game session. Therefore, we assume that the teachers considered this phase important, which is consistent with the Brousseau's theory [3].

Regarding the roles taken by the teacher and the students [12], we observe that the discussion is mainly led by the teachers. They perform face-to-face sessions dedicated to explain the concepts expected to be learnt. One of them use a questionnaire enabling to assess the student's errors based on the registered history of the coding. Observations made during the game period are also used.

In terms of *milieu* [12] these results show a difference related to the course material used by teachers. Indeed, one of them (T4) designed his own material while he was talking, whereas the others (T2 and T3) used a material already designed before the session. We conjecture that this is one of the reasons why they adopt a face-to-face setting.

In terms of time [12], the time invested to debriefing differs between teachers and does not seem to have any link with the time available in the session. Moreover, during the debriefings, we see different practices among teachers for the institutionalization of knowledge. For our analysis, we need to consider an important fact: teachers face constraints so that they organized the activity in different ways. Indeed, T1 spent only 45 min for the whole activity, whereas T2 benefited from 2 different 45-minutes sessions, T3 had spent two 90-minutes sessions and T4 only two 45-minutes sessions. As a result, two of them (T2 and T3) benefited to the time for reflecting about student's achievements and preparing the debriefing session. However, in terms of available time for the three teachers, the time devoted to debriefing was quite short, which should have an impact on their content. The next paragraph presents what they did during this time.

Table 3 shows the speaking time distribution (in percent) according to the four debriefing dimensions described in Sect. 2.2. We also indicate the concepts mentioned by the teacher (dimension 3).

Table 3. Speaking time distribution (in percent) according to the five institutionalization dimensions and concepts mentioned

	Teacher 1	Teacher 2	Teacher 3	Teacher 4
Dimension 1	100	–	–	–
Dimension 2	–		3	44
Dimension 3	–	100 Variable, affectation	97 language, syntax	56 instruction, instruction order, variable, conditions, even number
Dimension 4	–	–	–	–

We observe that, in terms of allocated time, the dimension the most represented is the one relating to making knowledge explicit and visible. Only T1 focuses on dimension 1. He only asks questions about students' feelings and if his students want to play again: "What do you think about it, is it interesting?". However, as we had noticed previously, it should be a consequence of a lack of time and of the implementation of a unique session (2').

Regarding how the other three teachers (who performed dimensions 2 and 3) processed and treated the knowledge involved, we notice:

T2: interactions refer to questions asked in the form. He gives the answers without concretely reporting errors. He doesn't define or explain the concepts related to errors and gives no concrete example: "The two correct answers are as follows", "the answer is 30". This teacher doesn't refer to the activity with the game.

T3: using screenshots from the game, he starts the debriefing by pointing the student's errors made during the game session. These mistakes relate to the language used and the teacher only corrects the language without explaining related concepts. For example: "some of you have written here something like this…you have to use the correct language instruction…you cannot invent it".

T4: after having recalled the main goal of the activity ("the purpose of the game is to learn how to program"), he lists concepts that seemed to have been difficult for the students. For each one, most of the time, after defining the term, he demonstrates how to use it in the game, writing concrete instructions expected from the students. Sometimes he contextualizes the concept using an example from the game. Concepts refer to various learning outcomes (that will be described in the next paragraph). For example: "an instruction sequence is when we put several [instructions] together, enabling a sequence of movements for the character. It will move it forward twice then go to the right, and we will write "move - move"." Besides, to explain one of the main identified mistakes, the teacher mimes the consequence of a wrong instruction "for some of you, I noticed that "turn right" means "go and turn".

The analysis of the knowledge processed by the teachers highlights three types of learning outcomes that, according to our knowledge haven't been described yet in the literature:

- The language: it is about the coding itself, the specific symbolism of this language type. For example (T3) “the “=” symbol is the symbol of the assignment” or “others write “move” without quotation marks”.
- The concept involved: the language translates concepts related to programming. For example (T4) “an instruction is a command given to the computer” or “the variable is called the computer memory”
- The computer operation: all these concepts make it possible to describe how the computer operates. For example (T4) “you have to tell the computer everything he has to do… it will take the value, and the program will perform the instruction…”

Dimension 3 (Validation) is the most represented during the debriefing following a “Programming Game” session. Teachers also performed dimension 2 (Awareness. However, we did not managed to find dimension 4 (Generalization) in the teachers’ practices.

Regarding the type of institutionalized knowledge, we found that T1, only performed dimension 1 so that no knowledge has been institutionalized. T2 referred only to knowledge-concepts did not made connections with the game experience, while T3 has gone back and forth between the game experience and the language used for the coding. T4 adopted another strategy. He made connections between the game experience, the problem-solving strategies within the game, the translation of this problem-solving strategy into computer language (written on the board), and the knowledge-concepts and knowledge-computer operation. In our opinion, the ability to make links between challenges, problem-solving strategies (language) and concepts means computational thinking [4–6] skills. This feature deserves further analysis.

We also emphasize that computer skills and attitudes were not clearly named and defined by teachers during debriefing.

6 Conclusion

Our research purpose was to test a preliminary debriefing model following a learning game session. The main question was based on the idea that learning from a game, implies getting out from the session dedicated to play. We consider that debriefing plays an important role and that the processing of knowledge (institutionalization) is at the core of debriefing.

Based on the analysis of four teachers’ practices, we identified different strategies. Due to their own constraints, they organized debriefing in different ways. However, the main subject of their short debriefing session was dedicated to knowledge. The results of this preliminary study show that practices differ among teachers regarding debriefing. They also show that not all teachers pay specific attention to debriefing and there is a risk that learning fail. Indeed, due to the fact that the need for decontextualizing knowledge, there is a risk that the students do not manage to identify the concepts implemented into the game. More specifically, we found that the teachers pay little attention to the desyncretization of knowledge (dimension 2 of our model) and generalization (dimension 4). These results are an argument for fostering teacher education regarding game-based learning.

Further work will be devoted to a next iteration of the project. For this next step, we plan to design and implement a debriefing session based on the model that we developed. We expect that the teachers will accept to carry out the debriefing accordingly to the four dimensions of our model and that we will have the possibility to assess its relevance.

References

1. Sanchez, E.: Game-based learning. In: Tatnall, A. (ed.) Encyclopedia of Education and Information Technologies, pp. 1–9. Springer, Cham (2019). https://doi.org/10.1007/978-3-319-60013-0
2. AlbaSim: Programming Game. Serious Game (2018). https://www.albasim.ch/fr/nos-serious-games/. Accessed 14 Jan 2019
3. Sanchez, E., Monod-Ansaldi, R., Vincent, C., Safadi-Katouzian, S.: A praxeological perspective for the design and implementation of a digital role-play game. Educ. Inf. Technol. **22**, 2805–2824 (2017)
4. Wing, J.M.: Computational thinking. Commun. ACM **49**(3), 33–35 (2006)
5. Csizmadia, A., et al.: Computational Thinking: A Guide for Teachers, Computing at School. Hodder Education (2015)
6. Krauss, J., Prottsman, K.: Computational Thinking and Coding for Every Student: The Teacher's Getting-Started Guide, Teachers Guide edn. Corwin, Thousand Oaks (2016)
7. Brousseau, G.: Théorie des situations didactiques. La pensée sauvage, Grenoble (1998)
8. Lederman, L.: Intercultural communication, simulation and the cognitive assimilation of experience: an exploration of the post-experience analytic process. Presented to Conference of the Speech Communication Association of Puerto Rico San Juan (1983)
9. Sanchez, E., Plumettaz-Sieber, M.: Teaching and learning with escape games from debriefing to institutionalization of knowledge. In: Games and Learning Alliance, pp. 242–253 (2019)
10. Brousseau, G.: Glossaire de quelques concepts de la théorie des situations didactiques en mathématiques (2010)
11. Parlebas, P.: Un modèle d'entretien hyper-directif: La maïeutique de Socrate. Revue française de pédagogie **51**, 4–19 (1980)
12. Sensevy, G.: Théories de l'action et action du professeur. In: Baudouin, J., Friederich, J. (eds.) Théories de l'action et éducation. De Boeck Supérieur, Bruxelles (2001)
13. Bessot, A., et al.: Décisions didactiques des enseignants de sciences. In: Problèmes du rapport scolaire et social aux mathématiques : identification des causes et propositions de solutions, Lyon (2013)

Designing a 2D Platform Game with Mathematics Curriculum

Varvara Garneli(✉), Christos Sotides, Konstantinos Patiniotis, Ioannis Deliyannis, and Konstantinos Chorianopoulos

Ionian University, Corfu, Greece
{cl3garn, pl2soti, cl5pati, yiannis, choko}@ionio.gr

Abstract. New technologies and media aim at triggering student interest in mathematics and at making learning an entertaining process. However, playful math games need to provide learners with a better experience, which is connected with an engaging gameplay. Popular game mechanics could be used in order to integrate learning in the playing activities. This research employs the Super Mario game format for the design of a playful educational serious game in the context of math education. Mario Maths is addressed to students of 12 and 13 years old and aims to the practice of divisibility criteria. Mario collects numbers instead of coins that must be exactly divided with the number - target, avoiding or eliminating the wrong answers. A wrong choice transports Mario to a subterranean world which informs him for his mistake, but with no influence on the final goal achievement according to a constructive error and trial method. In the end of each track, the player is taking feedback of his effort in a self-assessment process. Mario Maths was developed to be used as a complementary educational tool for students who might be attracted from such forms of media. (https://github.com/ionio-seriousgames/mario-maths).

Keywords: Educational serious games · Math games · Game design

1 Introduction

Math curriculum could be enhanced through various educational media, such as math games for practicing trivial tasks, virtual environments for try-out, simulations for making conjectures, strategic games for manipulating & combining, visualizations of structure(s), or explorations in 2D and 3D geometry [7]. Moreover, real problems could be employed to contextualize math education, such as money calculation or x and y coordinates location on a map. Many math games rely on the puzzle gameplay mechanics, e.g. Tic Tac Toe or they apply a separate set of questions to be answered beyond the gameplay mechanics, e.g. Up, Up, and Away [13]. Another approach uses multiple-choice questions which unhide parts of a hidden picture with math cartoon [2] while Angle Jungle game provides a series of puzzles for practicing angles on ipads [14]. However, different game genres could result in different learning outcomes depending on different gaming experiences [4]. Therefore, playful math games are tightly connected to the applied gameplay. According to Guardiola [11], gameplay could be defined as "all the actions which are performed by the player, influencing the

A. Liapis et al. (Eds.): GALA 2019, LNCS 11899, pp. 42–51, 2019.
https://doi.org/10.1007/978-3-030-34350-7_5

outcome of a game situation in which he is engaged in. Similarly, Fabricatore (2007) defines gameplay as "the set of activities that can be performed by the player during the ludic experience, and by other entities belonging to the virtual world, as a response to the player's actions and/or as autonomous courses of action that contribute to the liveliness of the virtual world". The gameplay influences users' experience through several mechanics which are "atomic rule-based interactive subsystems capable of receiving an input and reacting by producing an output" [8]. From this viewpoint, popular video game formats could be used for the design of playful math games [3]. Although game designers have employed formats of several game genres e.g. the Motion Math which is a Tetris inspired game [18] or the Gem Game which is a side scrolling platform game [10], the integration of leaning in the gameplay mechanics is still a real challenge. Therefore, more research could be conducted on how math curriculum could be effectively integrated in popular game mechanics resulting in playful math games.

Our intention is to be inspired from a popular video game format and to employ its methods for getting players to learn. Super Mario Bros is a popular run and jump platform game, providing an adventure on two-dimensional levels. In particular, the player can move his avatar from left to right avoiding obstacles and interacting with various game objects. Mario can jump, run or shoot fireballs against his enemies being in three different states; small, big, or fire [17]. Various elements of Super Mario Bros gameplay could be employed in order to integrate educational content, such as the divisibility criteria.

The rest of the paper is structured as follows: in the next section Methodology is described, followed by the Discussion and Conclusions section.

2 Methodology

Fabricatore (2007) argues that the gameplay is the most important pillar of the game design activity due to its connection with the player's experience. Our intention is to apply the Super Mario Bros gameplay in the design of Mario Maths, providing players with challenge, mastery and reward to sustain and enhance motivation and entertainment. Mario Maths could be used as a complementary educational tool for practicing the divisibility criteria, a course that is taught in the 6th grade of Greek Elementary School and in the 1st grade of Greek Medium School. The most common method for determining divisibility is to perform the process of division. The divisibility criteria could be alternatively used in order to determine divisibility with not much calculation [21]. Students learn and practice the rules of divisibility in order to advance in more complicated calculations. Therefore, students learn the content and then practice their skills by determining the divisibility of various numbers by 2, 3, 4, 5, 8, 9, 10, 25, and 100 [22]. Drill and practice methods could be used from students in order to acquire such skills through disciplined and repetitious exercise which is the "building blocks" of a more meaningful learning [15]. However, the integration of the curriculum in a popular gameplay could make the learning activity playful while additionally learners are encouraged to construct their knowledge, using various game elements. As a result, the game world becomes an educational environment which supports active and self-regulated learning, according to the constructivist perspective [12]. Game designers and educators worked together, designing a playful math game.

2.1 Designing Mario Maths Based on Familiar Gameplay Mechanics

According to Loguidice and Barton [16], Super Mario Bros provides players with the task to save Princess Toadstool from the evil Bowser, the king of the Koopas. The game has one or two players mode and the playable characters are Mario or Luigi. The player is assigned with the mission to complete each board before the time runs out. If Mario fails, he loses a life and must restart the board. Similarly, we designed Mario Maths as a game aiming at learning the divisibility criteria. The game can be played from one player each time, using one playable character, Mario or Luigi. The player's mission is to find the key and unlock the exit door, at the end of each track by collecting 10 numbers which can be divided exactly with the chosen number (See Fig. 1).

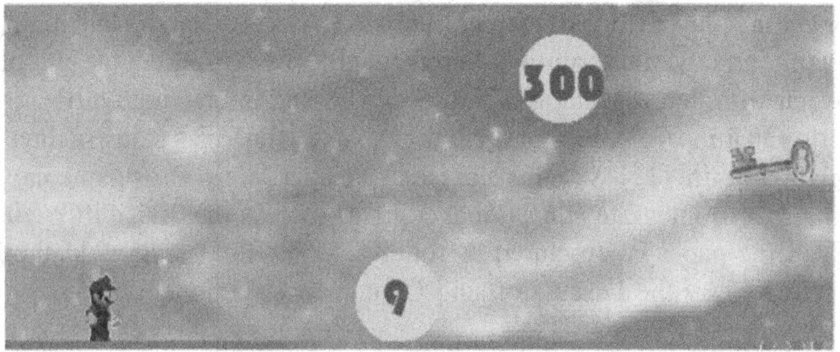

Fig. 1. Mario needs to find the key and unlock the exit door

Mario is free to explore the game-world till no correct numbers are available. The game provides 4 tracks for the numbers 2, 3, 5, and 10. After the end of each track Mario can restart it with the same or another number. During the game, the player collects numbers according to the different each time divisibility criteria in the same way that coins, mushrooms, fire-flowers, and star-men are collected at the Super Mario Bros (See Fig. 2).

Fig. 2. Mario must collect the numbers which can be exactly divided with the number 3

Similarly, to the Super Mario Bros, the enemies to be defeated by the player are Koopas, Mushrooms, and numbers which cannot be divided with the target number (See Table 1).

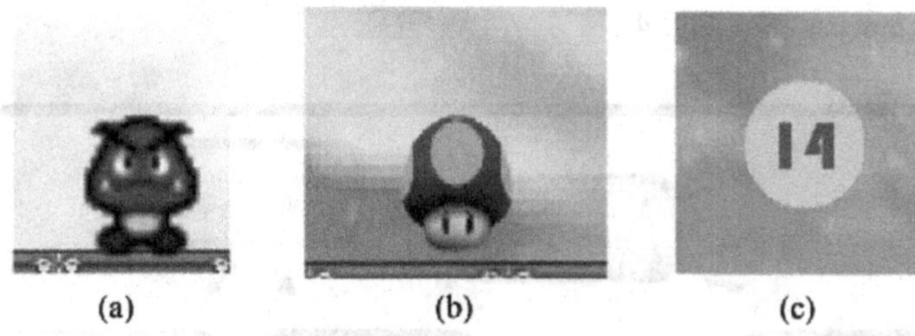

Fig. 3. Game Enemies. a & b: Koopas and Mushrooms are natural enemies used similarly to both games. c: The player needs to collect number - coins which are divided exactly to the number - target. The numbers' shape resembles that of coins in Super Mario. The number is an educational enemy in case that it is not divided exactly with the number - target.

Moreover, Mario attacks the enemies similarly with the classic platform game, jumping on top of them or shooting them with fireballs. Natural enemies, such as Koopas and Mushrooms take him to a previous point of the track depending where he is. Moreover, Mario can jump and destroy blocks, uncovering hidden information. Besides defeating enemies, Mario must navigate his way over and under obstacles. Getting or falling into the sea or into lava will result in losing a life (See Fig. 3).

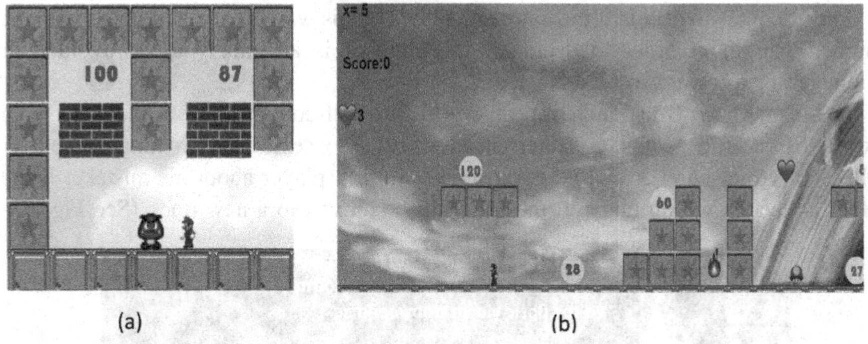

Fig. 4. Mario's navigation in the game-world, collecting numbers, avoiding/eliminating enemies. a. Mario loses a life and goes back when touching enemies from the side. b. Mario loses one life when touching the fire or the mushroom

The feature of teleportation also exists in Mario Maths, allowing the character to instantly travel from one part of the stage to another. Finally, important "statistics" are visible to the player, such as the point score, number of lives as in the classic Super Mario Bros (See Fig. 3).

2.2 Integrating Learning in the Playing Activities

Mario Maths is designed to be used as an educational tool for teaching math curriculum. Therefore, we describe the core learning mechanics using a flowchart according to the Gameplay Methodology [8]. Dark blue shapes are used to represent the In-Game Actions and the light blue shapes the Out-Game ones which are related to the learning process (See Fig. 4).

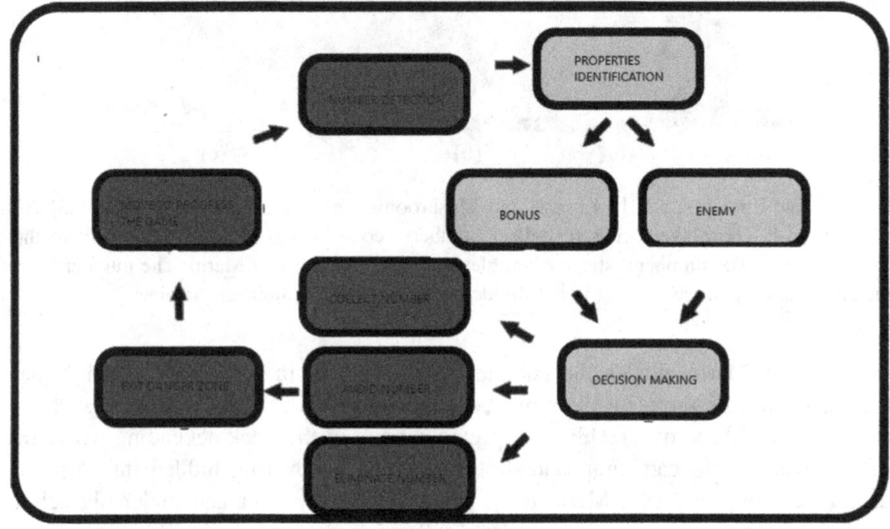

Fig. 5. Learning integrated in the playing gameplay [8] (Color figure online)

Player comes to decide if the number he finds on his way is exactly divided with the number - target in order to decide if this number is an enemy to be avoided or eliminated or a reward to be collected.

In Super Mario Bros, subterranean worlds are self-contained areas that offer coin rewards. In Mario Maths, a subterranean world is accessible each time the player collects a wrong number and its purpose is to inform player about his mistake. If the player collects a wrong number, the user will be moved to a new track (See Fig. 6).

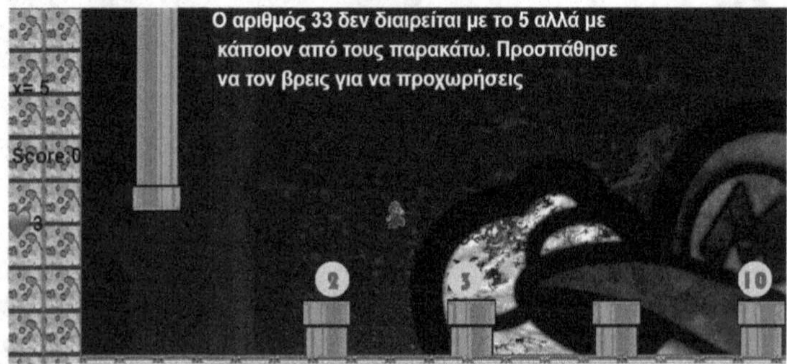

Fig. 6. Educational subterranean world

There, the player will be informed that the number is not divided by the number he chose to play. Within this new track, there will be the remaining three numbers and the user will have to choose the right one. Once he has chosen the correct number, he will be transferred to the spot on the main track and will be able to continue his course. An educational message is displayed informing the user about the rule to learn from his errors (Fig. 6).

Finally, there is an educational rewards system when the player collects the right numbers or eliminates the wrong ones (See Table 1).

Table 1. Rewards system. The player is rewarded when he collects numbers that can be divided with the number - target and when he eliminates numbers that cannot.

	Score	Life	Extra number
Collects 1 correct number	√		
Collects 5 correct numbers		√	
Eliminates 1 wrong number			√
Eliminates 5 wrong numbers		√	

As the player progresses through the game's levels, he encounters a lot of numbers that may or may not divide exactly the number they have chosen to play with. Choosing a correct number will increase the score by a hundred points. At the same time, the player comes one step closer to finding the key. Also, if he finds five correct numbers, then he will earn a life as an educational bonus. If while using the shooting ability, the player eliminates a wrong number, then it will win a life and if it manages to eliminate five, then a more correct number will be displayed at the end of the track.

2.3 Educational Results

Although the Mario Maths goal is to collect 10 correct numbers – coins to find the key, the player is encouraged to explore the world in order to achieve better educational results in the end. When the user touches the key or the door, the track ends and a screen with its educational results is displayed. Through this screen the player is informed of the number of correct and wrong choices, the number of total available options and what his wrong choices were specifically. Therefore, educational results appear to the player regardless of his performance. This is how learning analytics were used and the player can see his overall effort in numbers at the end of each game track as learning analytics involve the collection and analysis of student effort [6]. Students expect that learning analytics could be used to support the learning process, providing self-assessment, delivering recommendations, and producing personalized analyses [19]. On the same screen there is a button that allows the user to start the track from the beginning if he so desires. Finally, the game may also end when the player has no other available lives, where in this case he will be informed of his educational results.

2.4 Introductory Scene

The introductory screen of the game features two buttons, labeled 'Play' and 'Controls'. 'Play' button begins the game, while 'controls' features information about the control of the game. Choosing the 'play' option, will lead to a screen which will inform the player that in order to win the game he/she must select ten numbers that will be divided exactly by the number he has to practice. This will result in finding the hidden key that will "unlock" the door to exit the level. Also, the screen informs the user, that whenever a correct number is chosen, this will be displayed at the top of the screen. The use of the shooting function is also mentioned, to avoid the wrong numbers but also to get rid of other enemies on the screen. The last thing mentioned is the feature of teleportation that exists in game, making it possible for the character to instantly travel from one part of the stage to another. At the end of the instructions the player is prompted to choose between Mario and Luigi to start the game, as well as the number he would like to practice with. The available numbers are 2, 3, 5, 10 and the player's goal is to find the numbers that are exactly divided by the number they choose. A skip intro button is also provided, and if pressed the player is transported directly to the player and number selection screen. In-game, information is displayed on the top of the screen: the number of remaining lives, the score, and the number that the player has chosen to practice with.

2.5 User Interface and Game Controls

As in traditional Mario Games, Mario and Maths features a traditional side-scrolling, 2D view. Score and lives are displayed at the top left of the screen, and Mario (or Luigi) can move left or right, jump, with the use of arrow keys on the keyboard, or fire, using the spacebar.

2.6 Game Aesthetics

The aesthetics of the game are an important part for the game's success in communicating with the players. The backgrounds that appear in the narrative and on the slopes have been chosen to match the character of Super Mario. Also, all the numbers along the track are shown through yellow circular frames so the user can not only see them, but also remind them of the Super Mario coins. Finally, several images have been added to various screens, messages and game elements to make the user's environment more friendly. Music is also added to the game as well as "point sounds" whenever something important is happening. Events that might trigger sound effects are the right or wrong choice of number, contact with an enemy and the use of the elevator and the propeller.

2.7 Development

For the development of Mario and Maths, the Phaser tool was used because it contains important functions for the video game development. Also, the Tiled tool was used for the design of the game track. It has also been chosen the JavaScript and the HTML programming languages for designing a video game which runs on the Internet.

On the contrary with most educational serious games, we do not only provide the game online on the internet for students and teachers to use it, but additionally, we developed Mario Maths as an open source educational serious game, available on the internet for modifications/improvements. This transparency is aiming at supporting innovation, knowledge sharing, and community building [5].

3 Discussion and Conclusions

This study aim is the design and development of a math game to be used complementary as an educational tool for those students who find attractive such type of educational media. The design process was based on the gameplay mechanics of a popular video game in order to provide players with a joyful experience. We were inspired by Super Mario Bros methods for getting players to learn. Designers of good video games employ effective methods for getting people to learn long, complex and difficult games, in a joyful way [9]. We carefully integrated the educational content in the Super Mario Bros mechanics, preserving the entertaining parameter of the game. Super Mario Bros is a video game with a significant educational value; players must learn to jump between platforms, break blocks to get points and power ups or eliminate enemies, such as Bowser, Koopas, and Boos. Moreover, players need to solve problems and puzzles during their navigation in the game world. As a result, Super Mario Bros is considered a fun and engaging game [1]. The use of Super Mario Bros popular elements, such as the characters and the way they move inside the game world, advancing the game and defeating their enemies was aiming at making Mario Maths an appealing game that embeds math curriculum. We integrated content that is addressed to students of 12 and 13 years old, for practicing divisibility criteria. Therefore, Mario collects numbers, instead of coins, which must be exactly divided with the number - target and avoids or eliminates those ones which are not. Following Super Mario Bros format, the player needs to unlock the track's door instead of saving Princess Toadstool, using Mario or Luigi. All the gaming activities of Mario Maths exist in the Super Mario too. The player attacks the enemies, jumping on top of them or shooting them with fireballs or jumps and destroys blocks, uncovering hidden information. Teleportation is a game element that also exists in Mario Maths too and instantly travels the character from one part of the stage to another. "Statistics", such as the point score, number of lives are displayed on the screen in the same way. However, all this gameplay embeds learning activities (See Table 2).

Table 2. Super Mario Bro and Mario Maths gameplay

Super Mario	Mario Math
Entertainment	Entertainment + learning the divisibility criteria
The player needs to save Princess Toadstool from the king of the Koopas	The player's need to find the key and unlock the exit door
One or two players mode/Playable characters: Mario or Luigi	One player mode/Playable characters: Mario or Luigi
Each board must be completed before the time runs out	Each board must be completed according to the educational rules.
If Mario fails, he loses a life and must restart the board	Mario is free to explore the track till no correct numbers are available. After ending a track, Mario can restart the track with the same or another number
The player collects coins, mushrooms, fire-flowers, and star-men	The player collects numbers according to the different each time divisibility criteria
Enemies to be defeated by the player are Koopas, Boos, and Mushrooms	Enemies to be defeated by the player are Koopas, Mushrooms and numbers based on the educational rules
Subterranean worlds are self-contained areas that offer coin rewards	Subterranean world are accessible each time the player makes a mistake in order to learn

Therefore, players construct their knowledge, using the various elements of the game world. Finally, we adopted a constructive trial and error method in order to encourage players in achieving the learning purposes, an element that exist in similar educational games, such as the gem game [10]; when the user makes a wrong choice, he is not punished but he is informed of his error and encouraged to continue trying [3]. Nevertheless, this cannot influence the social meaning of a rewards system as the final statistics allow players to use it for purposes of comparison and social interaction [20].

The current version of the game offers the ability to learn the divisibility criteria with numbers 2, 3, 5 and 10. All the game is progressing to a basic track and the user has the option to choose the number with which he wants to practice before the beginning of the game. However, in the future, more numbers could be added to the game, in order to increase the difficulty. A further meaningful expansion of the game could build on this math curriculum, providing more complex educational activities aiming at extending and enriching student understanding. Finally, we are planning to evaluate Mario Maths, in terms of learning and entertainment in the formal school settings for potential improvements.

References

1. Becker, K.: Battle of the titans: Mario vs. MathBlaster. In: EdMedia + Innovate Learning, pp. 2707–2716. Association for the Advancement of Computing in Education (AACE), June 2007
2. Beremlijski, P., Vondráková, P., Litschmannová, M., Mařík, R.: Math games for one player. In: Proceedings of the 12th International Technology, Education and Development Conferences, pp. 2395–2402 (2018)

3. Chorianopoulos, K., Giannakos, M.N.: Design principles for serious video games in mathematics education: from theory to practice. Int. J. Serious Games **1**(3), 51–59 (2014)
4. Connolly, T.M., Boyle, E.A., MacArthur, E., Hainey, T., Boyle, J.M.: A systematic literature review of empirical evidence on computer games and serious games. Comput. Educ. **59**(2), 661–686 (2012)
5. Dabbish, L., Stuart, C., Tsay, J., Herbsleb, J.: Social coding in GitHub: transparency and collaboration in an open software repository. In: Proceedings of the ACM 2012 Conference on Computer Supported Cooperative Work, pp. 1277–1286. ACM, February 2012
6. Dietz-Uhler, B., Hurn, J.E.: Using learning analytics to predict (and improve) student success: a faculty perspective. J. Interact. Online Learn. **12**(1), 17–26 (2013)
7. Eliëns, A., Ruttkay, Z.: Math games: an alternative (approach) to teaching math. In: GAMEON, pp. 68–74, November 2009
8. Fabricatore, C.: Gameplay and game mechanics. a key to quality in videogames. In: ENLACES (MINEDUC Chile) – OECD Expert Meeting on Videogames and Education, 29–31 October 2007, Santiago de Chile, Chile (2007). http://eprints.hud.ac.uk/id/eprint/20927/1/39414829.pdf. Accessed 15 Oct 2019
9. Gee, J.P.: What video games have to teach us about learning and literacy. Comput. Entertain. (CIE) **1**(1), 20 (2003)
10. Giannakos, M.N., Chorianopoulos, K., Jaccheri, L., Chrisochoides, N.: "This game is girly!" perceived enjoyment and student acceptance of edutainment. In: Göbel, S., Müller, W., Urban, B., Wiemeyer, J. (eds.) E-Learning and Games for Training, Education, Health and Sports, pp. 89–98. Springer, Heidelberg (2012). https://doi.org/10.1007/978-3-642-33466-5_10
11. Guardiola, E.: The gameplay loop: a player activity model for game design and analysis. In: Proceedings of the 13th International Conference on Advances in Computer Entertainment Technology, p. 23. ACM, November 2016
12. Hung, D.: Theories of learning and computer-mediated instructional technologies. Educ. Media Int. **38**(4), 281–287 (2001)
13. Ke, F.: A case study of computer gaming for math: engaged learning from gameplay? Comput. Educ. **51**(4), 1609–1620 (2008)
14. Khan, J., et al.: Angle Jungle: an educational game about angles. In: Extended Abstracts Publication of the Annual Symposium on Computer-Human Interaction in Play, pp. 633–638. ACM, October 2017
15. Lim, C.S., Tang, K.N., Kor, L.K.: Drill and practice in learning (and beyond). In: Seel, N.M. (ed.) Encyclopedia of the Sciences of Learning. Springer, Boston (2012). https://doi.org/10.1007/978-1-4419-1428-6_706
16. Loguidice, B., Barton, M.: Vintage Games: An Insider Look at the History of Grand Theft Auto, Super Mario, and the Most Influential Games of all Time. Focal Press (2012)
17. Ortega, J., Shaker, N., Togelius, J., Yannakakis, G.N.: Imitating human playing styles in super mario bros. Entertain. Comput. **4**(2), 93–104 (2013)
18. Riconscente, M.M.: Results from a controlled study of the iPad fractions game Motion Math. Games Cult. **8**(4), 186–214 (2013)
19. Schumacher, C., Ifenthaler, D.: Features students really expect from learning analytics. Comput. Hum. Behav. **78**, 397–407 (2018)
20. Wang, H., Sun, C.T.: Game reward systems: gaming experiences and social meanings. In: DiGRA Conference, pp. 1–15, September 2011
21. Vorobyov, N.N.: Criteria for Divisibility. University of Chicago Press (1980)
22. http://ebooks.edu.gr/modules/ebook/show.php/DSGYM-A200/293/2065,7177/

Planet Dewey: Designing a Hybrid Game to Boost Students' Information Literacy

Elina Roinioti(✉) and Eleana Pandia

Panteion University for Social and Political Science, Athens, Greece
eleni.roinioti@gmail.com, eleana.pandia@gmail.com

Abstract. This paper presents a case study of the key design choices that were made during the development of «Planet Dewey», a 2D hybrid co-op game for students aged 11–14 years old for strengthen their information literacy skills. The game was tailor made for a Greek charitable foundation library. Using as a starting point the information literacy circle and through puzzle-based missions, scavenger hunt elements and an age-appropriate narrative structure, we aimed to increase intrinsic and extrinsic motivation. Experimental design through controlled frustration was another aspect of our approach.

Keywords: Game design · Information literacy · Library · Hybrid game

1 Introduction

Computer games are an integral part of our social and cultural environment [6]. Serious games in particular are nowadays an established means of imparting knowledge and raising awareness on important issues, while a number of studies have indicated that they are effective learning tools because they increase motivation and boost cognitive engagement during gaming sessions [3, 26]. Playing educational digital games offers players a "mental workout" as it requires a number of cognitive skills. Players have to make a stream of decisions, develop problem-solving strategies in order to complete a series of complex tasks [17]. Garris, Ahlers, and Driskell [13] indicate that educational games engage students in repeated judgment–behavior–feedback loops. Additionally, knowledge or skills learned and practiced through gaming, transfer more easily than when practiced on a single kind of problem [14]. Once mastered, knowledge and skills can be utilized further to provide overlearning [22]. With over-learning, the knowledge and skills become automatized and integrated in memory, so that the player can begin to focus consciously on comprehending and acquiring new skills [4, 9].

Planet Dewey is a 2D hybrid puzzle and narrative-based serious game, combining physical and digital gaming, designed for the purpose of educating schoolchildren on media literacy, the function of the information cycle, and the importance of knowing how to seek, evaluate, cross reference, fact check and use information properly. The game was developed in Unity 3D, using C#, for Windows, Mac and Linux.

A. Liapis et al. (Eds.): GALA 2019, LNCS 11899, pp. 52–61, 2019.
https://doi.org/10.1007/978-3-030-34350-7_6

2 Designing Planer Dewey

2.1 Narrative Design

Games are above all interactive experiences, worlds we tend to inhabit, stories we co-write, places we produce through our actions, our cultural capital, our everyday practices and perceptions. Games are spatial stories [16], through which we transmit values and educational context, enabling players to engage themselves with the story, the heroes and the fictional environment.

In the case of Planet Dewey we drew inspiration from popular young adult literature such as The Hunger Games and The Divergent Trilogy and employed the main characteristics of their plot lines to make Planet Dewey a game about discovering one's individual identity.

The main characters in the books are adolescents struggling for a higher cause which usually refers to personal freedom and the need to question the status quo, taking place in some future dystopia with magical or outer space settings. Following this trend, we decided to create our own imaginative universe, giving the opportunity to our players to lead their own revolution and ask themselves one simple but ethical question: should they defy the social contract and pursue their own individual path to happiness or choose to become integrated in a system that seems oppressive but has proven its value to the common good?

Our game narrative unfolded like this: In a galaxy far away, there is an unusual planet called Dewey where all the inhabitants are books- millions of books from every day and age on any possible topic living in peace and harmony. The cities look like enormous libraries and host books that "know their place", because part of each book's "coming of age" ritual is their classification according to their content aiming for them to find purpose and be active members of the Planet Dewey society. Books that fail to be categorized are forwarded to a shelf until their fate is decided. There are five books players on our story Trickster, Merlina, Mystic Ocean, Reikai and Daotan. While waiting to be classified an Ancient Old One urges them to go on an adventure to discover what they truly want to do, learn about their shared history and then decide if they want to become a part of the Planet Dewey society or not.

The choice of applying non-human avatars, was not of minor importance. On the contrary, it was a conscious design choice to avoid gender identification with human representations that could lead to gender segregation among players and possible reinforcement of stereotypes [18], or even gender dilemmas due to the fact that our players were teenagers. The game was designed for children aged 11–14 years old. This particular developmental stage [8] signifies the onset of puberty. The brain undergoes a burst of electrical and physiological development, simultaneously to the maturation of the frontal lobe, the part of the brain that is mainly responsible for decision making and reasoning [1]. During early adolescence girls and boys become more aware of their gender and start to adjust their behavior and appearance to fit in and comply with what they perceive to be socially acceptable and which often leads to sex segregation regarding peer activities and socializing [20]. Bearing that in mind, we worked towards a more integrative mode of design aiming to facilitate team building and co-operation among mixed gendered groups, in an effort to avoid gender bias or gender-based teams. Gender neutral avatar options, was also a choice it had to be made (Fig. 1).

Fig. 1. Planet Dewey graphic design

Avatars are considered to be digital representations of individuals that appear and/or behave like the users [2]. They are also thought of as the medium of self in the medium, in other words as a virtual self and as tools that can extend the unmediated self into the virtual environment [23]. It seems that avatars can be integrated into the avatar user's conception of the self, in the same way that physical tools can be integrated into the neurological gestalt of the self [24]. And indeed, there is evidence of some sort of merge between the avatar and the self with regard to the player's self- perception and behavior [30]. Even though there are no role-playing elements in the game, personalized avatars served two interrelated purposes: the first is enhancing the narrative structure. For example, Trickster is an index book consisting of a collection of phrases from books that are no longer preserved and therefore cannot be classified due to the fact that it would be impossible for anyone to verify the authenticity of his texts. The second, serves a game design choice, namely, player and avatar matching allowed the recording of player's choice at the end of the game (i.e. Trickster chose to join Planet Dewey's society, Mystic Ocean left the Planet Dewey society).

2.2 Information Literacy Through Game Design Lenses

Our main educational goal was to create a playful environment where the basic principles of information literacy could be applied and at the same time guide students through a creative path of collaborative learning. The term information literacy coined by Paul Zurkowski in 1974 was introduced to highlight the need to understand the value of information, to evaluate, taxonomize it and reuse it in another context. Media and information literacy have become an integral part of European Commissions' policies (2016) as a key area for economic growth and as a framework that empowers people and helps them make critical decisions in an ever-changing, high-demanding digital environment [10]. At the heart of information literacy lies the concept of democracy, citizens' participation in the new digital era and at the end of the day, access to a variety of different public resources.

Information literacy and library instruction is an essential part of academic librarianship [27], but although gaming in public libraries has become popular over the past decade academic libraries have been somehow reluctant to follow suit. However, interest in game- based learning in college and university libraries is high [19]. An early example of a digital game aiming to provide students with an introduction to library research was *The Data Game* in Colorado. It consisted of a set of four tutorials presented in the style of popular quiz shows [29]. A few years later Fletcher Library at Arizona State University created an online information literacy game titled *Quarantined! Axl Wise and the Information Outbreak.* The initial creation was a board game called *Information Pursuit*, designed to evaluate student responses to using games in library instruction, and resulted in the release of *Quarantined!*, a digital adventure game in which players acquired information literacy skills while trying to contain a viral outbreak on campus [12]. Librarians at the University of North Carolina at Greensboro created a web-based board game called *The Information Literacy Game*, designed to meet information literacy learning goals for first-year students.

Gameplay. Planet Dewey is a digital multiplayer game that can be played with 2–5 players. Each player has to first pick the book-avatar of his choice and together as a team and as the narrative commands, to embark on a journey of knowledge. The narrative of the game unfolds as the players solve riddles either by using their knowledge (multiple questions) or following the clues that the game provides and look for answers in the physical environment of the Eugene Library- discovering hidden items carefully positioned as archives, examining library signs placed in specific areas etc. Quite often the game sets challenges like searching for a specific librarian and ask for her help or becoming familiar with older classification systems of information in order to proceed. These challenges can be solved with teamwork through role-sharing. Whenever a solution/clue is found, players have to type their answers and the game will either proceed or in case of incorrect answers, will urge them to continue their efforts. Even though the game can be confined into one session of players and one PC, Planet Dewey can be played as a competitive game using more than one PC and thus more than one team, promoting a competitive game mode. The end goal is to successfully overcome all the obstacles and gather all the information needed in order for each player to make a decision for his own future: joining Planet Dewey and live his life in a specific shelf or decide to look his fate elsewhere and deny everything that he knows so far. By answering this final question, the game counts how many new residents have joined the book society and how many have declined the offer. The game is played with the help of librarians or educators, acquiring the role of game masters-helping when is needed while monitoring the entire game session (Fig. 2).

Fig. 2. Typing the answer of a scavenger hunt riddle

One of the most challenging issues during a serious game design process is to transform the learning objectives to game objectives and thus, game mechanics. In the case of Planet Dewey, we had to transform the information literacy principles to game mechanics of a narrative game. In general, we applied three design strategies: first, we applied traditional scavenger hunt elements of finding, locating and combining information in order to promote information literacy skills related to gathering, locating and use of different sources of information i.e. children had to find a classification book number by decoding a map they had previously found in the library and then return the book to the right shelf. Secondly, to understand the concepts of quality and authenticity of information through mini games and mini challenges like playing with references and detecting the information provided through them or searching in dictionaries for concepts like copyright. Thirdly, we tried to promote a value i.e. recognizing the need for information to solve problems, by exposing the player to a situation where this value was absent, a strategy we called **controlled frustration**.

Controlled Frustration as a Learning Game Mechanic. Frustration is defined as the player's emotional situation when he/she cannot overcome an in-game obstacle or when he/she can't figure out how to complete a challenge [5]. Even though frustration may disrupt the flow of the game [7], it does not always bare negative results for the game experience. In specific, game researchers talk about positive frustration or *in-game frustration* when the player needs to maximize his efforts resulting in high level engagement, in contrast with negative frustration or *at-game frustration* that is due to poor game design and results in players' disassociation with the game [15, 21].

Even though in the serious game research spectrum, frustration is tied to boredom and consequently, to disengagement, in the case of Planet Dewey we experimented with controlled frustration. By designing mini challenges that were never meant to be solved due to the fact that they were based on a common but undetectable mistake or because we had included a substantial omission that wasn't visible in the first place, we managed to evoke learning fruitful dialogues and capture children's interest. The presence of facilitators acting as game masters in order to assure controlled reactions from the children and at the same time, the existence of complementary strategies that will drive game progress despite player's actions and choices, helped us to produce a game experience that was fun and educational at the same time. Due to these circumstances, the moments of frustration were easily deconstructed in their educational elements, avoiding any episode that could harm the fun aspect of the game (Fig. 3).

Fig. 3. Changing the rules of conduct inside a library

Setting of the Game, Extrinsic and Intrinsic Motivation. In order to successfully designing a serious game one also has to take into consideration important parameters like the *setting of the learning* that refers to the *Whens* and *Wheres* of a playful condition and the *learning conditions* that relates with the users' level of knowledge and familiarity with the specific subject [31]. In our case, our game would be placed inside a library and specifically in the Eugenides Foundation Library, in Athens which on a stable basis hosts educational programs for students. The consequences of this fact were: a. The environment of a library posed specific behavioral limitations that needed to be taken into consideration b. The duration of the game had to be limited to the duration of a school visit and c. Children and adolescents that visit the Eugenides Library are more or less familiar with a library environment and the principles of information literacy, thus we needed to design a challenging game. For this reason and to slightly change the common library experience, we added real-life scavenger hunt elements- something which practically meant that the hallways of the library would be filled with children running and laughing. Within a short amount of time the library environment was transformed to a vivid ludic experience, maximizing engagement and interactivity [28], disrupting and at the same time redefining children's relationship not only with books and information, but with the library itself. Changing the rules of conduct in a heterotopian place like libraries, can stimulate creativity and fantasy while at the same time, offered a sense of controlled anarchy that was important for our game narrative.

Extrinsic and intrinsic motivation were paramount for our design. Extrinsic motivation was reinforced through the competition with the other teams, while inter-team collaboration allowed our young players to develop their own team dynamic and to distribute individual roles that would optimize their results [25]. The role of the instructors as game masters was crucial for fostering a healthy competitive attitude, managing time, steering children's thought during the controlled frustration moments and of course, making sure that no unnecessary actions would disrupt the ecosystem of the library.

3 Playtesting

We played Planet Dewey with over 30 children aged 10–15 during a science and technology event organized by the Eugenides Foundation. Our initial concern was to playtest the game mechanics, to identify possible weak points which made it difficult for the players and of course, test the combination of physical and digital challenges. For that reason, members of the game design team were located in specific checkpoints observing and recording players' behavior throughout the entire game.

Testing how control frustration would affect the game flow, was another challenge. According to short interviews that we conducted after each session, the game moments in which we applied controlled frustration were unpleasant at first, but with the help of the instructors the fun factor wasn't altered and the educational goals became clear. For example, through controlled frustration children understood why a specific research question is needed before we initiate an inquiry. This principle has manifested itself in-game by prompting players to embark on a journey of knowledge, but without providing a specific starting point or in practice, with no indication of the kind of question the player had to type in order to continue the game.

Turning the library into an active playground that could be rediscovered through location-based elements, was as expected, something the children truly enjoyed while at the same time, most of the children admitted that through Planet Dewey, they became more familiar with the function of the contemporary library especially with regard to the dissemination and preservation of knowledge.

How the game influenced the library's ecosystem and more generally, how a game could affect the surrounding environment, was also of great importance. Even though the librarians were very eager to help children find their way during scavenger hunting, as expected, visitors seemed rather annoyed. A solution to this problem was the use of Planet Dewey during specific occasions and library events.

4 Discussion

Designing a game for information literacy for students was a challenging task due to specific factors, like the age group we were addressing, the setting of the game and the specific learning goals we had to reach. Planet Dewey is a game that combines an exciting narrative with allegories that pose questions concerning issues of identity and the role of information in contemporary civic issues and different game modes during which the players had to collaborate in order to find the hidden clues, split into two different teams and accomplish different but complementary tasks and simultaneously, make decisions as individual persons. The term of controlled frustration was chosen as an experimental game design element that could cause temporary confusion in order to attract high level engagement from the young players. Possible relation between in game frustration, flow and their effect on learning process with respect to the ethics in education, is important to be subjected to further in-depth research.

Our experience with Planet Dewey has taught us that working with children means that we have to think and work more as game designers and maybe less as educators, produce games that can in a way compete with other recreational means that are already in children's daily routine. Experiment with different game modes and blend different game mechanics may offer a solution on to how to capture children's interest, especially when the game is played in a public space where there are many external factors that can affect the end experience. Schoolchildren and especially adolescents are a highly demanding audience: they know their way around technology and specifically video games, they lose their interest relatively quickly and last but not least, they have been growing up inside a continuous training and learning environment. Thinking out of the box, offering creative game-based learning solutions and even more exciting serious games, seems like a one-way path for educators.

Acknowledgements. Planet Dewey was a project designed in 2016 by GameLab Panteion team, a research PhD group based in Panteion University lead by Professor Yannis Skarpelos with the collaboration of a Greek game development studio called Gameness Monster. We would also like to thank the entire personnel of the Euginides Foundation Library and specifically Hara Brindesi director and scientific collaborator of the project. Planet Dewey wouldn't be possible without the valuable help of Anna Kartasi, Myrto David (game graphics) and Yiouli Yannakariou.

References

1. Arain, M., et al.: Maturation of the adolescent brain. Neuropsychiatric Dis. Treat. **9**, 449–461 (2013)
2. Bailenson, J.N., Blascovich, J.: Avatars. In: Bainbridge, W.S. (ed.) Berkshire Encyclopedia of Human-Computer Interaction, pp. 64–68. Berkshire Publishing Group, Great Barrington (2004)
3. Baker, R.S.J.D., D'Mello, S.K., Rodrigo, M.M.T., Graesser, A.C.: Better to be frustrated than bored: the incidence, persistence, and impact of learners' cognitive affective states during interactions with three different computer-based learning environments. Int. J. Hum. Comput. Stud. **68**, 223–241 (2010)
4. Broussard, M.J.S.: Secret agents in the library: integrating virtual and physical games in a small academic library. Coll. Undergrad. Libr. **17**(1), 20–30 (2010)
5. Canossa, A., Drachen, A., Sørensen, J.R.M.: Arrrgghh!!!: blending quantitative and qualitative methods to detect player frustration. In: Proceedings of the 6th International Conference on Foundations of Digital Games, pp. 61–68. ACM, June 2011

6. Crawford, G., Gosling, V.K., Light, B. (eds.): Online Gaming in Context: The Social and Cultural Significance of Online Games. Routledge, Abingdon (2011)
7. Csikszentmihalyi, M.: Flow: The Psychology of Optimal Experience. Harper Perennial, New York (1990)
8. Curtis, A.C.: Defining adolescence. J. Adolesc. Fam. Health **7**(2), 2 (2015). https://scholar.utc.edu/cgi/viewcontent.cgi?article=1035&context=jafh. Accessed 24 June 2019
9. Eichenbaum, A., Bavelier, D., Green, C.S.: Videogames: play that can do serious good. Am. J. Play **7**(1), 50–72 (2014)
10. European Commission: The European Digital Competence Framework for Citizens (2016)
11. Froschauer, J., Seidel, I., Gartner, M., Berger, H., Merkl, D.: Design and evaluation of a serious game for immersive cultural training. In: The Proceedings of the 16th International Conference in Virtual Systems and Multimedia, Seoul, Korea, 20–23 October 2010 (2010)
12. Gallegos, B., Allgood, T.: The Fletcher Library game project. In: Harris, A., Rice, S.E. (eds.) Gaming in Academic Libraries: Collections, Marketing and Information Literacy. Association of College and Research Libraries, Chicago (2008)
13. Garris, R., Ahlers, R., Driskell, J.: Games, motivation and learning: a research and practice model. Simul. Gaming **33**(4), 441–467 (2002)
14. Giannakos, M.N.: Enjoy and learn with educational games: examining factors affecting learning performance. Comput. Educ. **68**, 429–439 (2013)
15. Gilleade, K.M., Dix, A.: Using frustration in the design of adaptive videogames. In: Proceedings of ACE 2004, pp. 228–232. ACM Press (2004)
16. Jenkins, H.: Game design as narrative. Computer **44**, 53 (2004)
17. Johnson, S.: Everything Bad is Good for You: How Today's Popular Culture is Actually Making Us Smarter. Allen Lane, London (2005)
18. Lim, C., Harrell, F.: Developing computational models of players' identities and values from videogame avatars. In: Proceedings of the 10th International Conference on the Foundations of Digital Games, Pacific Grove, 22–25 June 2015 (2015)
19. McDevitt, T.R. (ed.): Let the Games Begin! Engaging Students with Interactive Information Literacy Instruction. Neal-Schuman Publishers, New York (2011)
20. Mehta, C.M., Strough, J.: Sex segregation in friendships and normative contexts across the lifespan. Dev. Rev. **29**, 201–220 (2009). https://doi.org/10.1016/j.dr.2009.06.001
21. Miller, M., Mandryk, R.: Differentiating in-game frustration from at-game frustration using touch pressure. In: ACM Interact Surfaces Spaces – ISS 2016, Niagara Falls, pp. 225–234 (2016). https://doi.org/10.1145/2992154.2992185
22. Paraskeva, F., Mysirlaki, S., Papagianni, A.: Multiplayer online games as educational tools: facing new challenges in learning. Comput. Educ. **54**(2), 498–505 (2010)
23. Ratan, R.A.: Self-presence, explicated: body, emotion, and identity extension into the virtual self. In: Luppicini, R. (ed.) Handbook of Research on Technoself, pp. 322–336. IGI Global, New York (2012)
24. Ratan, R.A., Dawson, M.: When Mii is me: a psychophysiological examination of avatar self-relevance. Commun. Res. **43**(8), 1–30 (2015)
25. Roinioti, E., Pandia, E., Skarpelos, Y.: Sociability by design in an alternate reality game: the case of the trail. In: Antero, G., Niemeyer, G. (eds.) Alternate Reality Games and the Cusp of Digital Gameplay. Bloomsbury Publishing (2017)
26. Sitzmann, T.: A meta-analytic examination of the instructional effectiveness of computer-based simulation games. Pers. Psychol. **64**, 489–528 (2011)
27. Smale, M.A.: Learning through quests and contests: games in information literacy instruction. J. Libr. Innov. **2**(2), 36–55 (2011)
28. Swiatek, C., Gorsse, M.: Playing games at the library: seriously? LIBER Q. **26**(2), 83–101 (2015)

29. Thistlethwaite, P.: The Data Game: Colorado State University's animated library research tutorial. Colorado Libr. **27**(3), 12–15 (2001)
30. Yee, N., Bailenson, J.N., Ducheneaut, N.: The proteus effect: implications of trans-formed digital self-representation on online and offline behavior. Commun. Res. **36**, 285–312 (2009)
31. Weitze, C.L.: Developing goals and objectives for gameplay and learning. In: Schrier, K. (ed.) Learning, Education and Games, Volume One: Curricular and Design Considerations. ETC Press (2014)

Designing Serious Games for People with Special Needs: Implications from a Survey

Stelios Xinogalos(✉) and Stavros Tsikinas

Department of Applied Informatics,
University of Macedonia, Thessaloniki, Greece
{stelios, s.tsikinas}@uom.edu.gr

Abstract. Serious Games (SGs) are games that have a serious purpose besides the entertainment of the player. SGs are used in various sectors with quite promising results. One field that SGs are used is education, since SGs are considered to offer promising technology enhanced learning opportunities. This paper focuses on SGs that aim to deal with the limitations that people with Intellectual Disabilities (ID) and Autism Spectrum Disorder (ASD) have in acquiring conceptual, social, practical and cognitive skills. In particular, we present the results of a questionnaire designed to investigate the perceptions of special education professionals and teachers regarding the use of SGs in the education of people with ID and ASD. Specifically, we investigate the usefulness and the effectiveness of SGs as teaching/learning tools, the ease of use by people with ID and ASD, and the ideal age group for SGs targeted to various skills. Ninety-three special education professionals and teachers participated in the study. The participants evaluated positively SGs for all the examined skills in terms of their usefulness, usability and effectiveness. Moreover, we recorded some interesting implications that can assist the design of SGs for people with ID and ASD, as well as open issues for further research.

Keywords: Serious Games · Serious games design · Intellectual Disabilities · Autism Spectrum Disorder · Participatory design

1 Introduction

Serious Games (SGs) are games that use entertainment to enhance training, education, health, public policy [1] and generally games that assist in achieving a "serious" purpose. In order for a SG to be effective it is not enough just to resemble a game [2]. A number of factors and interrelations between them must be met and the use of a specialized SG design framework is considered necessary. Some widely known SG design frameworks are the *Conceptual Framework for SGs* [3], the *Serious Educational Game (SEG) Design Framework* [4], the *Four Dimensional Framework* [5], the *Educational Games (EG) Design Framework* [6], and the *Design, Play, experience Framework* [7].

SGs have been successfully included in special education and more specifically in the learning process of people with Intellectual Disabilities (ID) and people with Autism Spectrum Disorder (ASD). People with ID have limitations in conceptual,

A. Liapis et al. (Eds.): GALA 2019, LNCS 11899, pp. 62–72, 2019.
https://doi.org/10.1007/978-3-030-34350-7_7

social and practical skills, but also in intellectual functioning skills [8]. People with ASD have limitations mainly in social and emotional skills and show repetitive behaviors [9]. Therefore, the learning process of people with ID and people with ASD is challenging and the educational methods need to be carefully chosen.

In SGs targeted to people with ID and people with ASD, *participatory design* is considered necessary [10, 11]. This means that special education teachers and professionals, parents and people with ID and ASD must participate in the design process. Having this fact in mind, we prepared a specialized questionnaire for investigating the perceptions of special education professionals and teachers regarding the following issues: (1) the *usefulness* of SGs as teaching tools for a variety of skills that people with ID and ASD have limitations; (2) the *effectiveness* of SGs in improving each one of the examined skills; (3) the *ease of use* of SGs targeted to each one of the defined skills by people with ID or ASD; (4) the most appropriate *age group* that SGs should be used for each skill.

We considered that this information would help researchers and game designers that focus on SGs for people with ID and ASD to make design and utilization decisions that are more informed. Ninety-three participants filled the questionnaire and the results were analyzed using descriptive statistics.

The rest of the paper is organized as follows. In Sect. 2, the methodology of the study is presented. In Sect. 3 the results are analyzed, while in Sect. 4 the findings of the survey are discussed. Finally, in Sect. 5, we present the conclusions and open issues for future research.

2 Methodology

As already mentioned, this study aims to investigate the perceptions of special education professionals and teachers on various aspects of utilizing SGs for improving skills that people with ID and ASD have limitations in. In order to achieve this, an online questionnaire was prepared using Google forms. The questionnaire included a definition of SGs, the aim of the study and closed type questions. The aim of the study was to investigate the participants' perceptions on the usage of technology in general and SGs in particular in the education of people with ID and ASD. We must note that we did not ask the participants to evaluate specific SGs for the investigated skills, but rather to share their perceptions based on their own experiences on utilizing SGs. Since we were not able to find an established questionnaire sharing the same aims, we developed it from scratch taking into account relevant literature. The questionnaire was validated by two experts, namely one Professor from the field of Special Education and one from the field of Computer Science and Educational Technology.

The questions that refer to the usage of technology in general are analyzed in [12] and will be briefly summarized in the next section. In this study, we focus on the following questions:

Question 1.1 (Q1.1): Do you believe that SGs can be *useful* in teaching each one of the defined skills to people with ID?

Question 1.2 (Q1.2): Do you believe that SGs can be *useful* in teaching each one of the defined skills to people with ASD?
Question 2.1 (Q2.1): Do you believe that SGs can be *easily used* by people with ID for each one of the defined skills?
Question 2.2 (Q2.2): Do you believe that SGs can be *easily used* by people with ASD for each one of the defined skills?
Question 3.1 (Q3.1): Do you believe that SGs can be *effective* for people with ID for each one of the defined skills?
Question 3.2 (Q3.2): Do you believe that SGs can be *effective* for people with ASD for each one of the defined skills?
Question 4.1 (Q4.1): In which *age group* of people with ID do you believe that SGs can be more effective for each one of the defined skills?
Question 4.2 (Q4.2): In which *age group* of people with ASD do you believe that SGs can be more effective for each one of the defined skills?

For each one of the aforementioned research questions we investigated skills falling into the following categories [8]: *Conceptual skills* - Letters, Money, Numbers, Language; *Social skills* - Emotions, Social Interaction; *Practical skills* - Safety, Diet, Hygiene, Travel, Transportation, Work-related; *Cognitive skills* - Perception, Rules.

All the questions were closed-type and the first three used a five point Likert scale: 1 = Not at all; 2 = A little; 3 = More or less; 4 = Very; 5 = Extremely. The age groups of the fourth question were: up to 4 years old; 5–13; 14–24; 25–35; more than 36 years old.

An email containing the aim of the study and a link for the questionnaire was sent to the principals of all the special education primary and secondary schools and institutions in Greece with the request to distribute it to special education professionals and teachers working in these schools/institutions. Ninety-three (93) people anonymously filled in the questionnaire in a voluntary basis. The participants comprised of 64 females and 29 males working in Preschool/Elementary Education (50.5%), Secondary Education (11.8%), Vocational Training (32.3%), and Extracurricular Organizations (5.4%). The vast majority (90%) of the participants was special education teachers and the rest of them special education professionals. The participants had on average 9.8 years of experience in special education.

The participants' replies were analyzed using SPSS. The mean value and standard deviation, as well as frequencies and percentages for each possible response in each question were calculated.

3 Results

An initial analysis of some general questions included in the questionnaire [12] showed that special education teachers and professionals consider the role of technology in the learning process as much or very much important both for people with ID (94.6%) and ASD (88.2%). However, people with ASD are considered to be more familiar with technology than people with ID (ASD: 57%, ID: 28%).

Special education professionals and teachers utilize both educational software and SGs in the learning process, with a clear preference in educational software. One out of five participants stated that uses much or very much SGs and twice as many educational software in the educational process, while one fourth of them use SGs and educational software averagely [12].

In this paper, we focus on investigating for what skills the participants find SGs more useful and effective as teaching tools, as well as the underlying ease of use of the corresponding games for people with ID and ASD. Moreover, we investigate in what skills the SGs should aim at based on the age group of the learners. In Table 1 we present the mean value and standard deviation for questions Q1, Q2 and Q3 and in the following subsections we briefly summarize the results for all four questions.

Table 1. Mean value and standard deviation for usefulness, usability and effectiveness

	Usefulness		Usability		Effectiveness	
	ID Q1.1	ASD Q1.2	ID Q2.1	ASD Q2.2	ID Q3.1	ASD Q3.1
	Mean (St. Dev)	Mean (St. Dev)	Mean (St. Dev)	Mean (St. Dev)	Mean (St. Dev)	Mean (St. Dev)
Letters	4.29 (.802)	4.05 (.925)	3.98 (.780)	4.08 (.797)	4.18 (.779)	4.09 (.775)
Money	4.22 (.832)	3.97 (.914)	3.90 (.835)	3.92 (.824)	4.12 (.778)	4.05 (.826)
Perception	4.19 (.800)	4.02 (.909)	3.85 (.779)	3.83 (.842)	3.96 (.871)	3.88 (.806)
Numbers	4.16 (.825)	4.04 (.932)	3.96 (.793)	3.98 (.766)	4.03 (.814)	4.06 (.805)
Safety	3.86 (1.028)	3.82 (.988)	3.58 (.993)	3.59 (.888)	3.69 (1.063)	3.66 (.915)
Language	4.09 (.905)	3.97 (.890)	3.88 (.907)	3.88 (.845)	4.00 (.834)	4.00 (.766)
Diet	3.85 (1.021)	3.87 (1.013)	3.74 (.943)	3.67 (1.004)	3.83 (.928)	3.62 (.896)
Emotions	3.84 (1.046)	3.73 (1.105)	3.47 (1.038)	3.55 (1.068)	3.65 (1.049)	3.62 (.955)
Rules	4.03 (.914)	4.02 (.884)	3.71 (.939)	3.80 (.904)	3.85 (.943)	3.81 (.850)
Social Interaction	3.57 (1.21)	3.65 (1.185)	3.42 (1.056)	3.51 (1.090)	3.56 (1.005)	3.54 (1.099)
Travel, Transportation	3.46 (1.128)	3.53 (1.049)	3.37 (.998)	3.41 (.992)	3.52 (.940)	3.44 (1.026)
Hygiene	3.86 (.996)	3.82 (1.073)	3.72 (.948)	3.69 (.967)	3.68 (.991)	3.76 (.949)
Work-related	3.80 (.920)	3.49 (1.138)	3.61 (.944)	3.46 (1.038)	3.62 (.955)	3.47 (1.079)

3.1 Usefulness of SGs as Didactical Tools

The results of the survey regarding the usefulness of SGs as tools for teaching various skills to people with ID (Q1.1) and ASD (Q1.2) were rather positive. The majority of the participants considered SGs as very or extremely useful as didactical tools for all the defined skills both for people with ID and ASD. The only exception was the practical skill of *travel and transportation* for people with ID where 48.4% of the participants considered SGs as very or extremely useful tools for teaching the specific skill, while 36.6% of the participants were neutral. A possible reason is that the specific skill refers more to independent living and it is not as common as the rest ones.

SGs are considered as *very or extremely useful* as didactical tools both for people with ID and ASD by at least 3 out of 4 participants for the following skills: *letters* (ID: 87.1%; ASD: 82.8%), *numbers* (ID: 81.7%; ASD: 77.4%), *language* (ID: 78.5%; ASD: 75.2%), *money* (ID: 87.1%; ASD: 77.4%), *perception* (ID: 84.9%; ASD: 81.7%) and *rules* (ID & ASD: 78.5%).

3.2 Usability of SGs as Learning Tools

The results of the survey regarding the *ease of use* of SGs by people with ID (Q2.1) and ASD (Q2.2) as learning tools for acquiring the defined skills were analogous to the results regarding their usefulness. The majority of the participants considered that people with ID and ASD are able to use easily SGs that are targeted to the defined skills with a few exceptions. Specifically, the participants considered less usable SGs that refer to *travel and transportation* (very or extremely usable - ID: 44.1%; ASD: 49.4%), *emotions* (ID: 48.4% very or extremely usable), and *social interaction* (ID: 46.2% very or extremely usable).

The participants consider that people with ID and ASD will find *very or extremely easy to use* SGs that refer to the following skills: *letters* (ID: 75.3%; ASD: 80.7%), *numbers* (ID: 73.1%; ASD: 76.3%), *language* (ID: 74.2%; ASD: 71%), and *money* (ID: 70.9%; ASD: 76.4%).

3.3 Effectiveness of SGs

The results of the survey regarding the *effectiveness* of SGs targeted to the defined skills for people with ID (Q3.1) and ASD (Q3.2) are quite positive as well. The majority of the participants consider SGs as *very or extremely effective* for all the defined skills and both groups. The only exception is the skill of *travel and transportation* for people with ID that was considered very or extremely *effective*, as well as *useful* as a didactical tool by nearly half (48.4%) of the participants.

Three out of four, or even more, participants consider as *very or extremely effective* SGs that are targeted to the following skills: *letters* (ID: 86.1%; ASD: 82.8%), *numbers* (ID: 80.7%; ASD: 79.6%), *language* (ID: 79.6%; ASD: 77.4%), *money* (ID: 83.9%; ASD: 80.6%), *perception* (ID & ASD: 76.4%) and *rules* (ID: 73.2%; ASD: 74.2%). SGs that refer to the specific skills are also considered to be useful didactical tools (see Sect. 3.1), which is an indication that the results of the survey are consistent.

3.4 Effectiveness of SGs in Relation to Age Group and Skills

When designing a SG it is of vital importance to take into account the target group of the game. Several characteristics of the *learner* must be examined, such as [5]: age, gender, culture, preferences and skills. So, in the survey the participants were asked to define the *age group* that a SG for each one of the defined skills would be more effective. Five age groups were defined as shown in Figs. 1 and 2 where the results of Q4.1 and Q4.2 are presented.

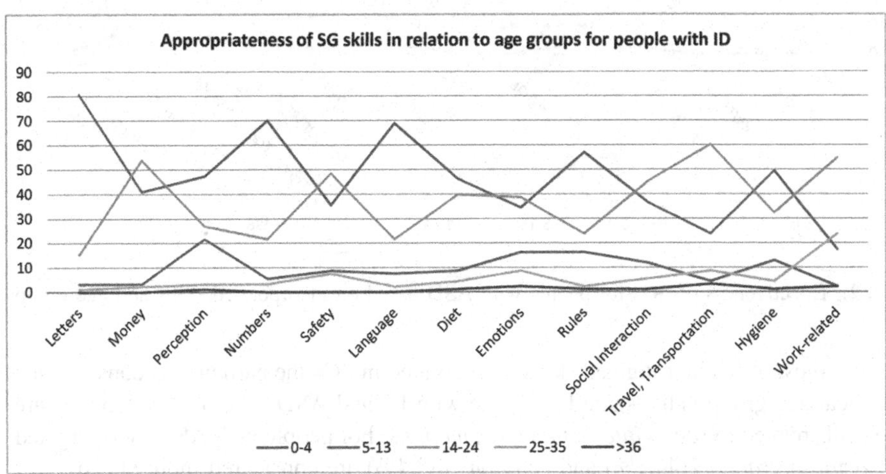

Fig. 1. Effectiveness of SGs for people with ID based on incorporated skills and age group

Based on the results we can draw the following conclusions:

SGs are generally considered *more effective* for the age groups of *5–13* and *14–24* years old.

SGs for *preschool ages* (0–4 years old) targeted to *perception* are considered by one out of five participants effective both for children with ID and ASD.

SGs for the age group of *5–13 years* old are more effective for the skills of *letters* (ID: 80.6%; ASD: 82.8%), *numbers* (ID: 69.9%; ASD: 71%), *language* (ID: 68.8%; ASD: 67.7%), *hygiene* (ID: 49.5%; ASD: 55.9%), *rules* (ID: 57%; ASD: 53.8%), *perception* (ID: 47.3%; ASD: 57%), and *diet* (ID: 46.2%; ASD: 49.5%).

SGs for the age group of *14–24 years* old are more effective for the skills of *travel and transportation* (ID: 60.2%; ASD: 52.7%), *work-related* skills (ID: 54.8%; ASD: 49.5%), *money* (ID: 53.8%; ASD: 55.9%), and *safety* (ID: 48.4%; ASD: 41.9).

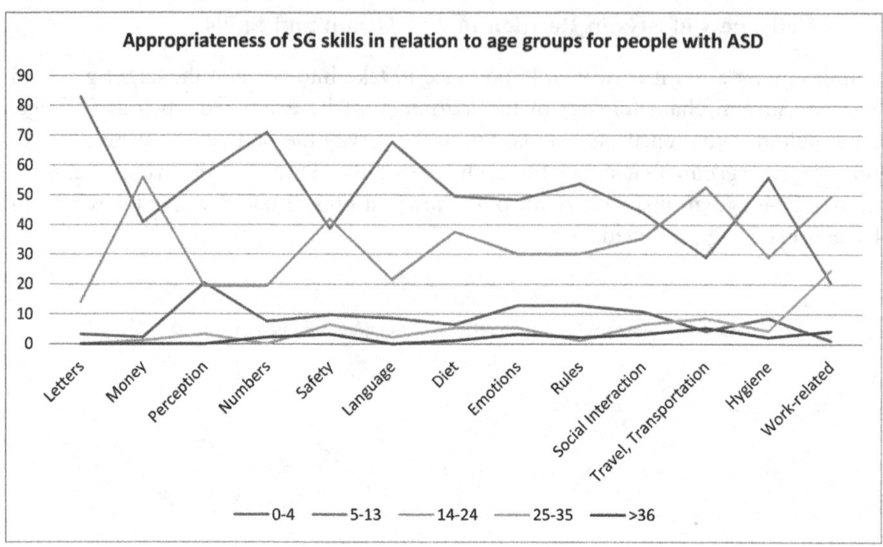

Fig. 2. Effectiveness of SGs for people with ASD based on incorporated skills and age group

For most of the investigated skills incorporated in SGs the participants consider that the ideal age group is the same for people with ID and ASD. The only exceptions are the skills related to *social interaction* and *emotions*. For people with ASD, SGs targeted to *social interaction* (44.1%) and *emotions* (48.4%) are considered more effective for the age group of 5–13 years old, followed by the age group of 14–24 years old (social interaction: 35.5%; emotions: 30.1%). This is logical, since people with ASD have severe limitations in skills related to social interaction and emotions and they have to work on it as long as they start school life and interact with people besides their family. On the contrast, for people with ID, SGs targeted to *social interaction* (45.2%) and *emotions* (38.7%) are considered more effective for the age group of 14–24 years old, followed by the age group of 5–13 years old (social interaction: 36.6%; emotions: 34.4%). This might be attributed to the fact that people with ID are getting prepared for independent living at the age of 14–24 and they have to interact constantly and effectively with people they do not know for daily living activities.

4 Discussion

A large number of SGs has been developed the last years that aim to improve various skills that people with ID/ASD and their teachers strive to improve [13]. However, professionals/teachers in special education do not utilize SGs extensively in the learning process [12] and this is quite unexpected, since the research so far has shown that SGs have a positive impact on improving various skills of people with ID/ASD [13].

Regarding the results of the survey, it is interesting that although the vast majority of the participants consider SGs as *useful* and *effective* learning tools and *easy to use* for all the defined skills both for people with ID (Fig. 3) and ASD (Fig. 4), their penetration in the teaching/learning process is considerably lower. Specifically, as recorded in the preliminary analysis of the survey [12] half the participants stated that rarely utilize SGs in the teaching/learning process, while the use of educational software is more widespread. The reasons for the limited utilization of SGs were not investigated in this study, but this is certainly an interesting issue that should be further studied. The limited number of freely available SGs that support the mother language of the target group is the most obvious reason, but surely other reasons exist as well.

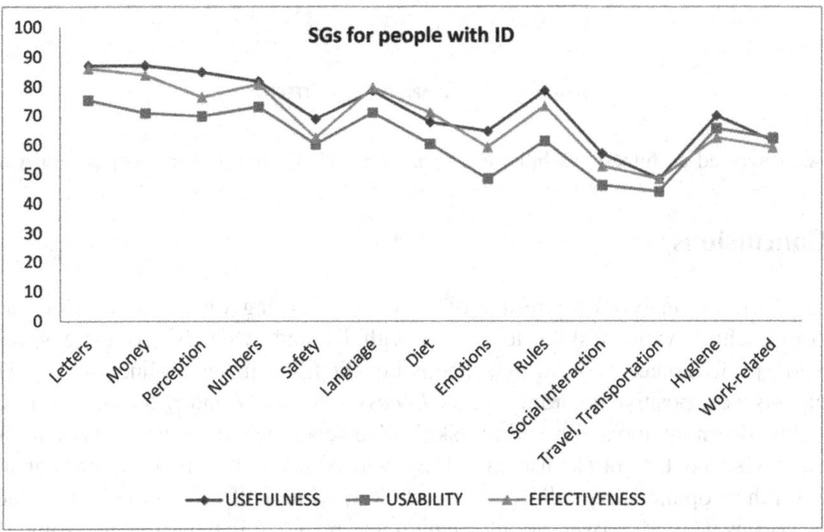

Fig. 3. Perceived usefulness, usability & effectiveness of SGs per skill for people with ID

Regarding the most appropriate *age group* that each skill would be more effectively approached using SGs, it turned out that the results are analogous for people with ID and ASD. The only exceptions are the skills related to social interaction and emotions that should be better approached in younger students with ASD.

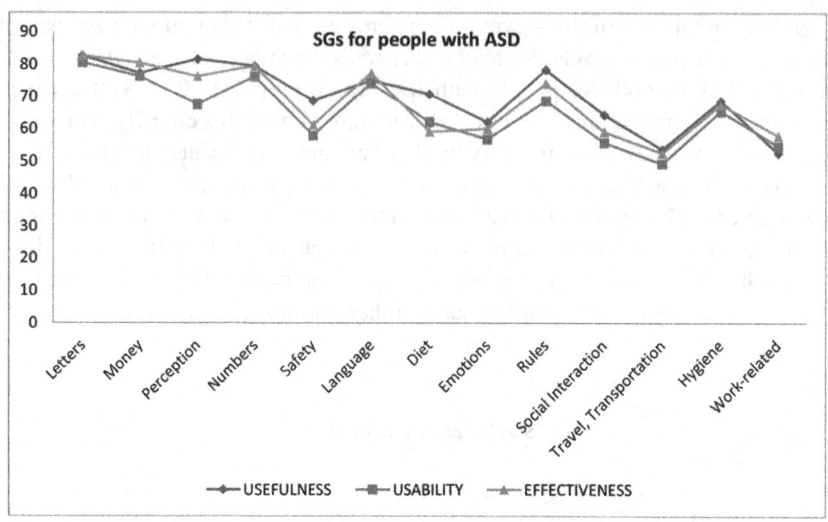

Fig. 4. Perceived usefulness, usability & effectiveness of SGs per skill for people with ASD

5 Conclusions

In this paper, we analyzed the results of a survey regarding various aspects of using SGs for teaching various skills to people with ID and ASD. Ninety-three special education professionals and teachers anonymously filled in an on-line survey. The participants were positive regarding the *usefulness*, *ease of use* and *effectiveness* of SGs as teaching/learning tools for various skills. However, we must note that half the participants stated that rarely use SGs [12], which means that half the participants reflect on their opinions regarding the use of SGs, while half of them reflect on their experiences as well. Moreover, no information was recorded in this study regarding the SGs that the participants have used, which definitely would lead to stronger conclusions. Besides these limitations, the study has helped us draw some interesting results regarding the perceptions of special education teachers/professionals on the use of SGs for various skills, implications for designing SGs and open research questions on the field.

The *implications* for designing SGs for people with ID and ASD that were drawn from the survey are the following: (1) SGs aiming at *letters*, *numbers*, *language*, *hygiene*, *rules*, *perception*, and *diet* should better be targeted to young students (ages 5–13) both for ID and ASD; (2) SGs aiming at *travel and transportation*, *work-related* skills, *money*, and *safety* should better be targeted to older students and young adults (ages 14–24) both for ID and ASD; (3) SGs aiming at *social interaction* and *emotions* should better be targeted to young students (5–13) with ASD and older students/young adults (ages 14–24) with ID; (4) Incorporating *role-playing* is important for the effectiveness of a SG for people with ID and ASD [12].

Regarding the limited utilization of SGs in special education in comparison to the high percentage of special education professionals and teachers that consider SGs to be useful, usable and effective more research is needed. It is interesting to study what are the reasons for the limited utilization of SGs in special education, as well as to replicate this study taking into account its limitations in order to generalize the results. Two reasons that we believe that affect the decision to utilize or not SGs and could be investigated are the following: the degree that a SG comes with *clear and concise utilization guidelines* for teachers regarding its effective usage by students with ID and ASD in and out of school; the existence of *monitoring mechanisms* for students' achievements in the game.

Finally, the results of this study could assist special education teachers and professionals in selecting appropriate SGs for their students based on their age, as well as game designers in making more informed decisions when designing SGs for specific target groups based on their age and special needs.

Acknowledgments. This research is funded by the University of Macedonia Research Committee as part of the "Principal Research 2019" funding program.

References

1. Zyda, M.: From visual simulation to virtual reality to games. IEEE Comput. **38**(9), 25–32 (2005)
2. Van Eck, R.: Digital game-based learning: it's not just the digital natives who are restless. EDUCAUSE Rev. **41**(2), 16–30 (2006)
3. Yusoff, A., Crowder, R., Gilbert, L., Wills, G.: A conceptual framework for serious games. In: 9th IEEE International Conference on Advanced Learning Technologies, ICALT, pp. 21–23. IEEE (2009)
4. Annetta, L.A.: The "I's" have it: a framework for serious educational game design. Rev. Gen. Psychol. **14**(2), 105–112 (2010)
5. De Freitas, S., Jarvis, S.: A framework for developing serious games to meet learner needs. In: Interservice/Industry Training, Simulation and Education Conference, Florida (2006)
6. Ibrahim, R., Jaafar, A.: Educational games (EG) design framework: combination of game design, pedagogy and content modeling. In: International Conference on Electrical Engineering and Informatics, vol. 1, pp. 293–298. IEEE (2009)
7. Salen, K., Zimmerman, E.: Rules of Play: Game Design Fundamentals. The MIT Press, Cambridge (2004)
8. Schalock, R.L., et al.: Intellectual Disability: Diagnosis, Classification, and Systems of Supports, 11th edn. American Association on Intellectual and Developmental Disabilities, Washington, DC (2010)
9. Iovannone, R., Dunlap, G., Huber, H., Kincaid, D.: Effective educational practices for students with autism spectrum disorders. Focus Autism Dev. Disabil. **18**(3), 150–165 (2003)
10. Tsikinas, S., Xinogalos, S.: Designing effective serious games for people with intellectual disabilities. In: Proceedings of IEEE Global Engineering Education (EDUCON), Santa Cruz de Tenerife, 17–20 April 2018, pp. 1902–1909 (2018)
11. Tsikinas, S., Xinogalos, S.: Design guidelines for serious games targeted to people with autism. In: Uskov, V., Howlett, R., Jain, L. (eds.) Smart Education and e-Learning 2019. SIST, vol. 144, pp. 489–499. Springer, Singapore (2019). https://doi.org/10.1007/978-981-13-8260-4_43

12. Tsikinas, S., Xinogalos, S., Satratzemi, M., Kartasidou, L.: Using serious games for promoting blended learning for people with intellectual disabilities and autism: literature vs reality. In: Auer, M., Tsiatsos, T. (eds.) IMCL 2017. AISC, vol. 725, pp. 563–574. Springer, Cham (2018). https://doi.org/10.1007/978-3-319-75175-7_55
13. Tsikinas, S., Xinogalos, S.: Studying the effects of computer serious games on people with intellectual disabilities or autism spectrum disorder: a systematic literature review. J. Comput. Assist. Learn. **35**(1), 61–73 (2019)

From Skeptics to Advanced Adopters: Investigating Digital Game Adoption Practices, Challenges and Needs of Teachers in Swedish Schools

Melinda Mathe(✉), Harko Verhagen, and Mats Wiklund

Stockholm University, Stockholm, Sweden
melinda@dsv.su.se

Abstract. To effectively support digital game adoption in education, stakeholders need to understand teachers' current game-based teaching practices, challenges, and needs. This study investigates digital game use of teachers at compulsory and upper secondary school levels in Sweden. Data were collected from 181 respondents during spring 2019 through an online survey. Cluster analysis and descriptive statistics are used to establish the characteristics of game-using teachers and explore their teaching practices, challenges, and professional development needs. Based on their disposition, three subsets of game-using teachers are identified. Findings indicate that a more positive disposition is related to increased pedagogical integration, a greater variety of game use, higher and more varied educational outcomes, as well as interest in professional development. Perceptions of inhibiting factors of games-based teaching tend to shift with teachers' level of game-based teaching competency. Results highlight teachers' need for good quality games with curricular relevance as well as relevant professional development options. Moreover, the potential of games to facilitate a collaborative form of learning and skill development may not have been yet fully realized in Swedish schools. Future research should have a twofold focus; the development of adequate game resources that can support collaborative forms of learning and higher-level skills development, as well as competency development solutions for teachers relevant to their needs.

Keywords: Digital games-based teaching · Educational games · Games-based learning

1 Introduction

The interest in research regarding the use of digital games in education has been significant in the past decades. Digital games can be valuable learning environments [1, 2] increase student motivation and engagement, improving cognitive learning outcomes about processes, understanding causes and effects, programming, and developing collaborative skills [2, 3]. Nevertheless, solid empirical evidence for games as effective learning tools is sparse and mixed [1, 4]. Research in the field focuses predominantly on controlled experiments [5] often assuming that effectiveness can be

A. Liapis et al. (Eds.): GALA 2019, LNCS 11899, pp. 73–82, 2019.
https://doi.org/10.1007/978-3-030-34350-7_8

attributed solely to the game effect [6]. Recent studies point out the critical role of the teachers [3, 7] as they have the most significant impact on student achievement [8]. Nonetheless, teachers have been underrepresented in game-based learning literature and teachers practice-based use of games is still somewhat unexplored [6, 7]. Thus, this study addresses the research gap and investigates teachers' practices, challenges, and needs regarding digital games-based teaching (DGBT) in Swedish schools.

The study uses a broad interpretation of digital games that includes any form of games played on any kind of digital device. Digital games specifically designed for educational use are often short, easy-to-use games that fit a class period and can be used to practice specific learning objectives [9]. However, they may not provide any significant educational value nor meet learner expectations [10]. The challenge of more complex educational games relates to the integration of learning content with game mechanics and addressing curricular requirements [6]. Entertainment games can provide interactive and immersive experiences but they require more extensive expertise and gaming literacy from teachers as well as technological resources [6, 11]. Another approach is building and modifying digital games that situate teachers and learners as co-designers of digital games [2]. Gamification motivates learners through rewards, leaderboards or playful narrative, however may not enhance learning and students may not appreciate these tools beyond their novelty [6].

Navigating a variety of game designs and adopting require coordination of various knowledge domains [12] which can be daunting for teachers. Previous research points out obstacles [10, 11] including costs, technical issues, the lack of access to good quality games, and time for preparation. Teachers may not know how to integrate games into their teaching [16] and few games come with teacher support [11, 13–15]. Thus, to realize the potentials of digital games in education, educational stakeholders need to understand teachers' characteristics, current DGBT practices, and challenges.

In Swedish schools, digital skills are promoted by the Swedish national curriculum [16]. Digital games are an integral part of life for most Swedish youth outside the classroom, but their role in schools is yet little understood.

Thus, the aim of this study is to explore how teachers use digital games in the context of contemporary Swedish education at compulsory and upper secondary levels. We seek to establish the characteristics of game-using teachers and explore how teachers' disposition towards DGBT relate to their teaching practices and challenges. More specifically, the research questions are the following:

- How can game-using teachers be characterized based on their disposition towards Digital Games-based Teaching?
- How does their disposition relate to their digital games-based teaching practices, challenges, and professional development needs?

2 Theoretical Underpinning

Educational tools cannot be understood by studying either the learning tool or the educational context in isolation from one another [17]. Activity Theory (AT) is a widely used theoretical and analytical approach in education [18]. Its core idea is the notion that people develop and use tools to achieve their objectives [18, 19]. The model was developed by Lev Vygotsky and then further developed by Leont'ev who introduced the concept of activity, object, and division of labor. Later, Engeström introduced the ideas of community, rules, and outcomes. Based on this model, Activity Theory constitutes Subjects, Object, Tools, Community, Rules, Division of Labor and Outcomes [18]. In this study, the elements of AT are reflected in the following ways: Subjects represent the teachers who are involved in DGBT activities. They use Tools (digital games) to carry out their teaching activities. Object represents their objectives for engaging in DGBT (e.g. knowledge and skills development.) which are then transformed through teaching-learning activities into Outcomes (e.g. knowledge and skills outcomes). Rules refer to regulations, cultural norms (e.g. curriculum, school regulations). Community represents both the physical and conceptual environment in which DGBT is carried out (e.g. students, teachers, school management, parents). The Division of Labor component reflects roles and responsibilities of teachers (e.g. preparation, classroom roles, professional development responsibilities). The framework considers teachers as an individual as well as a member of a larger community and provides a way to understand the perspectives of teachers in Swedish schools.

3 Methodology

Data was collected through an online survey during spring 2019 in Sweden. Prior to the survey, a pre-study was conducted [20]. The survey was designed based on the pre-study findings, a relevant previous survey studies on DGBT [10] and AT. Altogether 37 scaled, multiple and single choice, and open-ended questions were included in the survey and pre-tested by teachers. The survey was distributed via teacher social media forums and sent to 1200 schools across Sweden randomly selected from the central database of the National Agency for Education. Data was collected using Survey and Report tool of Stockholm University and exported into SPSS. The total number of respondents to the survey was 181. Challenges of the online survey were related to the risk of non-responses and accessing relevant participants.

Out of the 181 respondents, 123 teachers indicated experience with digital games in an educational context at some point of time and were selected for analysis in this study. Non-game user teachers will be discussed in a separate study. Around 40% of the game using teachers are 40–49 years old, 69% of them are female and have typically over ten years of teaching experience.

While there are different types of classification techniques, a widely applied tool in the field of education is k-means clustering [21]. This study draws on the study by Takeuchi and Vaala [10] who applied k-means analysis to investigate DGBT practices of 694 K-8 teachers. K-means clustering requires the selection of variables and cluster numbers prior to the analysis. In this study, the selection of the variables is based on the research questions and tie into the Subject dimension of AT. Current research on game-based pedagogy competency shows that for effective implementation of digital games, personal interest and playful stance are important together with the knowledge of games-based learning processes and practical technological skills [6]. The selected disposition variables are understood as teachers' self-reported interest in digital games for entertainment and educational purposes as well as their self-reported level of pedagogical, technological, and digital game competence to plan, implement and evaluate DGBT activities. These include (1) personal interest in playing games for entertainment purposes as found in [20], (2) interest in applying games in teaching as found in [20], and (3) comfort levels of applying games in education [10]. The variables were assessed on a 5-point Likert scale measuring interest and comfort levels.

After the standardization of the variables, a k-means cluster analysis was run to determine group classification. Cluster values from two to four were assessed and compared. Visualization and cross-tabulation were used to assess the different cluster solutions and to understand how the algorithm perceived the similarities and differences of the clusters [21]. Reliability of the clustering and the consistency of characteristics in each cluster was assessed by measuring dispersion expressed as standard deviation and range. This was helpful to assess how much variation exists on each variable in each cluster, as clusters may include teachers with a high level of variability. Due to the high dispersion, the two-cluster solution was unhelpful to answer the research questions. The four-group solution included a cluster with few members (N = 6) and did not meaningfully contribute to the research question. Considering the SPSS iteration statistics, significance statistics for each variable's contribution to the clustering, number of cases in the clusters, and dispersion, the three-group solution was determined to be optimal. While k-means analysis was used by Takeuchi and Vaala [10], other clustering techniques can be helpful to investigate whether clusters are consistent.

To investigate cluster validity, a two-step cluster analysis was conducted both with automatic analysis and a specified number of three. The automatic analysis returned a two-cluster solution. Both the automatic analysis and the manual three-cluster grouping had silhouette coefficient of 0.5 suggesting a fair separation distance between the clusters in both cases. Comparing the three-cluster results from the two methods showed minor differences on the individual level (9.7% of the cases reassigned) while the main cluster characteristics remained consequent across both methods. Thus, the three-cluster was deemed most informative for our sample.

The additional features of clusters are described below using descriptive statistics. Similar to the study by Takeuchi and Vaala [10] the additional features were not used to form the clusters. Here, they investigate other dimensions of AT, such as Tools (digital games), Object (pedagogical objectives, teaching, and assessment practices), Outcomes (perceived efficacy of the activities). Challenges are explored in relation to Tools, Community (students, teachers, school management, and parents), Rules (curriculum), and Division of Labor (preparation and professional development). Perceived efficacy was assessed on a 5-point Likert scale while other the features were assessed using multiple-choice questions.

4 Findings

Cluster 1 (C1) is the smallest cluster (N = 16, 13%). Teachers here are mostly uninterested in playing entertainment games (75%), uninterested in applying games in education (100%), and feel uncomfortable about using them in their teaching (87%). Cluster 2 (C2) members form the second largest group in the survey (N = 36, 30%).

They are also typically uninterested in playing games for their own entertainment (94%), but they are interested (89%) in applying games for teaching. They also feel comfortable or very comfortable about using games in their teaching (81%). Cluster 3 (C3) is the largest cluster (N = 71, 57%). We find that 97% expresses interest or strong interest in playing entertainment games, and applying games in education (100%) while 92% of them feel comfortable about using digital games in their teaching.

4.1 Types of Digital Games Used

C1 teachers (56%) mostly apply gamification tools (e.g. Kahoot, Mentometer) and to lesser extent educational games (25%). C2 teachers report a wider repertoire and use gamification tools (67%) and educational games (72%) the most extensively (e.g. Elevspel, Rixdax). They use game creation tools (e.g. Scratch) most frequently among the clusters (27%). Difference between C2 and C3 can be observed in terms of entertainment game use (e.g. Gone Home, Battlefield 1, Pokemon Go) and entertainment games modified for educational use (e.g. Minecraft) as C3 teachers tend to use these entertainment games more frequently (21%) than C2 (2.8%). C3 group similar to the other clusters report the use of gamification tools (75%) and educational games (72%) most frequently. Few C2 (8%) and C3 (7%) teachers report the use of games designed by teachers such as self-made Jeopardy game and music game developed by teachers.

4.2 Teaching and Assessment Practices

C1 teachers' primary aim with using games is to motivate their students and practice already taught knowledge (50%). C2 and C3 teachers move beyond motivation and practice. C2 (50%) and C3 (62%) teacher use games to increase interaction. 12% of C1, 42% of C2, and 58% C3 teachers use games to teach new knowledge and skills, and 48% of C3 use them to conduct formative evaluation.

The majority of the C1 (81%), C2 (94%), and C3 teachers (75%) use games for a shorter time, as a part of a lesson. Only a few C3 teachers (7%) indicate that they have gameplay over one full lesson or several lessons but none of C1 or C2 teachers. Across the clusters, C1 (25%), C2 (64%), and C3 (47%) teachers have their students play individually, around 10% of all teachers across the cluster design activities around smaller groups, and 5% or less with another classmate.

When it comes to assessment, more than half of the C1 teachers tend not to assess game-based learning activities (56%). This is characteristic of C2 teachers (50%) as well, however, they use whole-class discussions (33%), game points (25%), in-built assessments (31%), and their own assessments (28%) more frequently than C1 teachers. In contrast, C3 teachers are more likely to assess game-based learning activities (69%). They have whole-class discussions (47%), use the game points (34%), and create their own assessments (41%) more frequently than C2 teachers.

4.3 Perceived Efficacy of Digital Games

Teachers across the clusters perceive that digital games are most effective in increasing student motivation and engagement. C1 teachers perceive games the least effective among the cluster, while C3 teachers report the highest benefits. Games are perceived to be the least effective in teaching communicative, meta-cognitive, and analytical skills. This opinion is characteristic of all clusters but to a varying extent (Fig. 1).

4.4 Challenges of Games-Based Teaching

C1 teachers report uncertainty about finding good quality games (43%), unfamiliarity with digital game-related technology (38%), and the lack of belief in digital games as a teaching-learning tool (38%). This group encompasses most teachers who are concerned about health implications of games on students (19%) and are the least sure

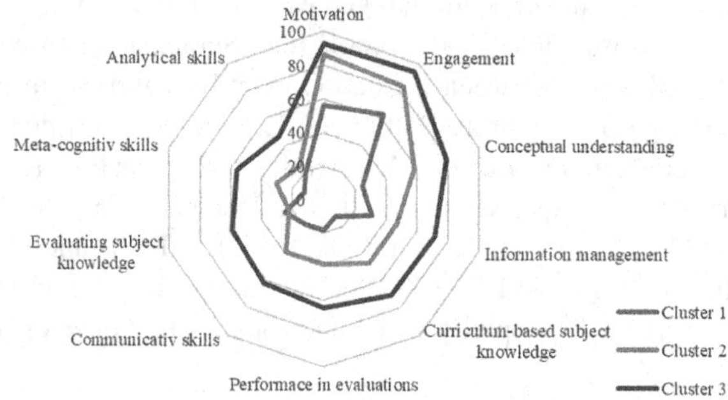

Fig. 1. Perceived efficacy of digital-games based teaching (% of teachers)

among the clusters regarding the integration of games in their teaching (19%). For C2 teachers, the lack of preparation time (50%), game costs (47%), and locating good quality resources (47%) that match the curriculum (42%) are the biggest obstacles. C3 teachers indicate that game costs (45%) and the difficulty of finding curriculum-related games (42%) are the most pressing hurdles. Finding good quality resources is an important challenge for them as well, but somewhat less so than for any other cluster (31%). This group is the least concerned about the lack of time to prepare (21%) and the most familiar with game-related technologies (93%).

4.5 Digital Game-Related Professional Development

Currently, somewhat more than half the teachers in all cluster learn about games from their colleagues. C2 (47%) and C3 (46%) teachers utilize online discussion forums to a much greater extent than C1 teachers (12%). Less than 10% of the teachers across the clusters go to gamer forums, and only C3 teachers (7%) visit online gamer groups. Currently, none of the C1 teachers and few C2 teachers learn from web-based video resources (6%) and online courses (3%). Some C3 teachers use video resources (12%) but very few learn from online courses (3%) about DGBT. However, 97% of C2, 99% of C3, and 56% of C1 teachers indicated interest in future professional development options. The most preferred options across all the clusters are workshops in the respective schools of teachers. C2 teachers (72%) are the most interested in learning through discussions with their colleagues, while C3 teachers are the most interested to learn from online video resources (17%), online courses (51%), and participate in game-specific teacher groups and discussion forums (38%) in the future.

5 Discussion

Using cluster analysis, three subsets of teachers could be identified:

- Teachers with a generally negative disposition towards DGBT indicate little interest in gameplay or educational use of games and feel generally uncomfortable about applying games.
- Teachers with a mixed disposition are interested in the educational potentials of games without being interested in playing games. They feel mostly confident in their own skills to apply digital games.
- Teachers with a generally positive disposition are typically interested in playing games, see the educational potential of games, and are confident in their own skills to apply games.

Investigation of additional cluster characteristics shows that a more positive disposition generally relates to increased pedagogical integration, a greater variety of game use, higher and more varied educational outcomes, and interest in professional development. Inspired by their cluster characteristics, in this study we call teachers with a generally negative disposition the Skeptics, mixed disposition teachers the Curious Adopters, and teachers with strongly positive disposition the Advanced Adopters. Skeptics, Curious Adapters, and Advanced Adopters are concerned about a somewhat different set of inhibiting factors regarding DGBT adoption.

Skeptics have used digital games at some point in time but generally do not believe in games-based teaching. They are the least apt to use games for teaching and are unsure where to find good quality games. They mostly use gamification tools and perceive these effective in motivating and engaging students but do not see them useful to teach new knowledge, skills, or to increase interaction. They typically do not assess the learning outcomes of these activities. Inhibiting factors for Skeptics are their lack of belief in the educational potentials of games, inability to find good quality games, and unfamiliarity with digital game technology. Many of these teachers do not engage in any form of game-related professional development while 60% of them are interested in school workshops and discussions with their colleagues in the future.

The C2 cluster of teachers can be called Curious Adopters due to their increased interest in educational application and comfort levels of using games. They use a wider repertoire of games including educational games, gamification, and game creation tools. Their purpose of game use is also primarily to motivate and engage their students, however, they also set pedagogical objectives for increased interaction, teaching new knowledge and skills, or conduct formative evaluation. Typically, they do not assess the learning around games-based activities, but when they do, they tend to prefer discussions with the whole class. They perceive games more effective than the Skeptics and report higher outcomes in conceptual understanding, information management, subject knowledge, and communicative skills. Curious Adopters are intent to develop their DGBT practices through discussions with their colleagues and workshops in their school contexts. The biggest hurdle is their lack of time to prepare and find good quality resources that match the curriculum.

Advanced Adopters have high levels of interest and comfort in the educational application of games. They are most likely to apply entertainment games in their teaching. This confirms previous research that teachers with more DGBT experience will on average consider digital games as more suited to fit the curriculum than teachers with less experience [22]. Advanced Adopters tend to assess game-based learning activities and report the highest levels of education outcomes. They see the lack of time to prepare as less of a challenge possibly due to that fact that they are also the aptest users of game-related technologies. Their foremost concerns are the game costs and finding good quality resources that match the curriculum. Around one-quarter of the Advanced Adopters report having a lack of technological resources. They are strongly interested in developing their game-based teaching practices and would primarily prefer to participate in workshops at their schools and learn through discussions with their colleagues. They are somewhat apter in using web-based resources and game-specific groups for professional development than the other clusters. Due to their game-aptness, these teachers might be more aware of relevant online resources such as video tutorials and online communities [6].

While most teachers in this study are interested in the educational use of digital games, some teachers are skeptical. During the DGBT adoption process, teachers can come to rejection if they perceive it as less adequate than their previous practice [22]. The findings press the need for a critical position towards DGBT with a focus on the particular circumstances under which games can increase the quality and effectiveness of teaching [12]. Moreover, DGBT requires pedagogical, technological, collaborative, and creative teacher competency development [6]. Teachers need adequate content [23], showcases of good practice [12, 24, 25], support from their local school contexts, and access to technical support and game-related resources [24].

In summary, this study has identified three types of game-using teachers based on their DGBT disposition. Results indicate that the more positive teachers' disposition is, the more likely they are to integrate games, apply a greater variety of games, report higher and more varied educational outcomes, and show interest in professional development. Contrast exists in current professional development practices and needs and indicates that the majority of game-using teachers are interested in developing their competency, but lack the supporting tools, programs, and opportunities to do so.

Teachers at different stages of a DGBT competency are concerned about a somewhat different set of inhibiting factors. This indicates that DGBT competency development is a dynamic process where different challenges arise with the increase of competency. Moreover, results show that game-based learning activities are generally individual activities and a short part of a lesson. Social settings around gameplay and longer game-based learning activities are not typical. Games are perceived the least effective in supporting communicative, meta-cognitive, and analytical skills. Thus, the potential of games to facilitate a collaborative form of learning and skill development may not have been yet fully explored in Swedish schools.

Future research should focus on the development of adequate game resources that can support collaborative forms of learning and higher-level skills development, as well as competency development solutions for teachers relevant to their needs.

References

1. Connolly, T.C., Boyle, E.A., Hainey, T., McArthur, E., Boyle, J.M.: A systematic literature review of empirical evidence on computer games and serious games. Comput. Edu. **59**(2), 661–686 (2012). https://doi.org/10.1016/j.compedu.2012.03.004
2. Kafai, Y.B., Burke, Q.: Constructionist gaming: understanding the benefits of making games for learning. Edu. Psychol. **50**(4), 313–334 (2016)
3. Huizenga, J.C., Ten Dam, G.T.M., Voogt, J.M., Admiraal, W.F.: Teacher perceptions of the value of game-based learning in secondary education. Comput. Edu. **110**, 105–115 (2017). https://doi.org/10.1016/j.compedu.2017.03.008
4. Hainey, T., Connolly, T.M., Boyle, E.A., Wilson, A., Razak, A.: A systematic literature review of games-based learning empirical evidence in primary education. Comput. Edu. **102**, 202–223 (2016). https://doi.org/10.1016/j.compedu.2016.09.001
5. Boyle, E.A., et al.: An update to the systematic literature review of empirical evidence of the impacts and outcomes of computer games and serious games. Comput. Edu. **94**, 178–192 (2016). https://doi.org/10.1016/j.compedu.2015.11.003
6. Nousiainen, T., Kangas, M., Rikala, J., Vesisenaho, M.: Teacher competencies in game-based pedagogy. Teach. Teach. Edu. **74**, 85–97 (2018). https://doi.org/10.1016/j.tate.2018.04.012
7. Kangas, M., Koskinen, A., Krokfors, L.: A qualitative literature review of educational games in the classroom: the teacher's pedagogical activities. Teach. Teach. **23**(4), 451–470 (2017)
8. Hattie, J.: Teachers make a difference: what is the research evidence? New Zealand Council of Educational Research, Wellington, pp. 3–26 (2002)
9. Clark, D.B., Tanner-Smith, E., Hostetler, A., Fradkin, A., Polikov, V.: Substantial integration of typical educational games into extended curricula. J. Learn. Sci. **27**(2), 265–318 (2018). https://doi.org/10.1080/10508406.2017.1333431
10. Takeuchi, L.M., Vaala, S.: Level up learning: a national survey on teaching with digital games. The Joan Ganz Cooney Center, New York (2014)
11. Marklund, B.: Unpacking Digital Game-Based Learning: The Complexities of Developing and Using Educational Games. University of Skövde, Skövde (2015)
12. Bourgonjon, J., Grove, F.D., Smet, C.D., Looy, J.V., Soetaert, R., Valcke, M.: Acceptance of game-based learning by secondary school teachers. Comput. Edu. **67**, 21–35 (2013). https://doi.org/10.1016/j.compedu.2013.02.010
13. Hamari, J., Nousiainen, T.: Why do teachers use game-based learning technologies? The role of individual and institutional ICT readiness. In: Proceedings of the 48th Hawaii International Conference on System Sciences, pp. 682–691. IEEE Computer Society, Hawaii (2015)
14. Becker, K.: Choosing and Using Digital Games in the Classroom: A Practical Guide. AGL. Springer, Cham (2017). https://doi.org/10.1007/978-3-319-12223-6
15. Hanghøj, T.: Game-based teaching: practices, roles and pedagogies. In: New Pedagogical Approaches in Game Enhanced Learning: Curriculum Integration, pp. 81–101. I. Global (2013). https://doi.org/10.4018/978-1-4666-3950-8.ch005
16. Utbildningsdepartementet: Nationell digitaliseringsstrategi för skolväsendet. Utbildningsdepartementet, Stockholm (2017)

17. Mwanza-Simwami, D.: Activity theory and educational technology design. In: Handbook of Design in Educational Technology, pp. 176–189. Routledge, New York (2013)
18. Gedera, D.S., Williams, J.P.: Activity Theory in Education. Sense Publishers, Rottardam (2016)
19. Kaptelinin, V., Nardi, B.N.: Acting with Technology: Activity Theory and Interaction Design, pp. 29–73. MIT Press, London (2006)
20. Mathe, M., Verhagen, H., Wiklund, M.: Digital games in education: exploring teachers' practices and challenges from play to co-design. In: Proceedings of the 12th European Conference on Games Based Learning, pp. 388–395 (2018)
21. Bahr, P.R., Bielby, R., House, E.: The use of cluster analysis in typological research on community college students. New Dir. Inst. Res. **2011**(S1), 67–81 (2011)
22. Emin-Martinez, V., Ney, M.: Supporting teachers in the process of adoption of game based learning pedagogy. In: ECGBL 2013-European Conference on Games Based Learning, pp. 156–162, ACPI, Porto (2013)
23. Grove, F.D., Bourgonjon, J., Looy, J.V.: Digital games in the classroom? A contextual approach to teachers' adoption intention of digital games in formal education. Comput. Hum. Behav. **28**(6), 2023–2033 (2012). https://doi.org/10.1016/j.chb.2012.05.021
24. Ketelhut, D.J., Schifter, C.C.: Teachers and game-based learning: Improving understanding of how to increase efficacy of adoption. Comput. Edu. **56**(2), 539–546 (2011). https://doi.org/10.1016/j.compedu.2010.10.002
25. Sardone, N.B.: Attitudes toward game adoption: preservice teachers consider game-based teaching and learning. Int. J Game-Based Learn. **8**(3), 1–14 (2018). https://doi.org/10.4018/IJGBL.2018070101

Reinforcing the Attitude-Behavior Relationship in Persuasive Game Design

Four Design Recommendations for Persuasive Games for Societal Interventions

Annebeth Erdbrink([✉]), Rens Kortmann, and Alexander Verbraeck

Delft University of Technology, Jaffalaan 5, 2628 BX Delft, The Netherlands
a.e.erdbrink@tudelft.nl

Abstract. Persuasive games for societal interventions aim to shape, reinforce or change players' attitudes and behavior to help solving complex societal issues. In earlier work, we explored how persuasive game mechanics may contribute to the formation of attitudes in persuasive games. As a follow-up, this paper presents four design recommendations that could increase the chance that these attitudes will actually lead to the desired behavior shown by players after the game: viz., these attitudes require the right conditions to become a predictor of the desired, post-game behavior.

In order to arrive at these recommendations we looked at relevant work from the field of social psychology. Next we linked our insights to the context of persuasive game design. This yielded four conceptual design recommendations for maximizing the likelihood for an attitude influenced by a persuasive game to result in the desired behavior in the real world;

1. aligning the degree of specification of a game's message and the desired behavior
2. emphasizing the function of the attitude to be influenced
3. enabling players to reflect on their internal states
4. emphasizing personal relevance of an attitude to a behavioral choice

So far, these recommendations are still theoretical in nature. We therefore discuss how future work should empirically examine these, including their implications for the effective use of persuasive game mechanics.

Keywords: Persuasive games · Societal interventions · Persuasive game design · Attitude-behavior relationship

1 Introduction

Policymakers at all different levels are concerned with grand societal challenges such as public health, food safety, climate change, clean energy and smart transport [1]. In order to tackle these challenges public administration has three different types of strategies at its disposal: regulatory (rights and prohibitions), financial (taxes, levies, subsidies) and communicative (information and public campaigns) [2]. A notable

A. Liapis et al. (Eds.): GALA 2019, LNCS 11899, pp. 83–91, 2019.
https://doi.org/10.1007/978-3-030-34350-7_9

application within this communicative strategy is the use of games to increase awareness amongst involved stakeholders concerning certain challenges in complex systems [3]. These games can effectively contribute to the process of social problem solving because they can produce interactive learning environments [4].

An increased interest exists in games that aim for more than just informing about complex societal issues; they aim to influence the attitude or behavior of its players concerning these matters [5]. From changing the attitude towards homeless people [6] to improve home energy behavior [7]. These games are generally referred to as 'persuasive games', since they are explicitly designed with the goal to shape, reinforce or change players' attitudes and behavior that exists beyond the gaming session [8].

In the pursuit of secure, inclusive, and reflective societies, it seems only logical that persuasive games often aim to reach a broad variety of citizens. In that way persuasive games can support civic engagement, which is considered "instrumental to democracy" [9]. However, unfortunately their accurate design still involves many ambiguities [10, 11].

According to Bogost [12] games can persuade due to the rhetoric that is embedded in a game's system and rules. Further analyzing the dynamics of persuasive game design beyond this proceduralist view, De la Hera [8] presented a more holistic view of persuasive elements. In her conceptual model several persuasive "dimensions" are described through which games can channel persuasion; such as through sounds, text, narrative and emotions.

Although this research is very valuable for game analysis, from a more practical point of view there are still a lot of unanswered questions concerning the effective design for persuasion through games [11]. Next to the fact that some useful methods are proposed for the overall design process [10, 13], there is still notably little practical knowledge on how to effectively implement persuasive game mechanics in the design [13]. Since game mechanics can be considered the key drivers of a game's success [14], new knowledge on persuasive game mechanics will benefit the discipline by reducing the risk of their ineffective or even counterproductive implementation [15]. As there is still limited empirical evidence available to prove the overall effectiveness of persuasive games, this focus of research seems to be even more relevant [16].

Previously we already explored how persuasive game mechanics can either enhance or reduce the motivation and/or ability of the player to comprehensively evaluate the persuasive message of the game [17], based on the Elaboration Likelihood Model [18]. Expanding these insights concerning persuasive game design and attitude formation, this paper subsequently focuses on design recommendations concerning the right conditions under which attitudes become predictors of the desired behavior after the game.

Because one cannot assume that a persuasive game that effectively generates a desired attitude formation automatically leads to the subsequent desired (long-term) behavior. The influence of attitudes on behavior is in fact by no means simple and direct [19]. According to the well-known Theory of Planned Behavior [20] for example attitudes can help predict someone's intention to behave in a certain way, which in turn is related to performing that behavior. Besides the relationship between attitudes and behavior is unfortunately by no means always demonstrable [21].

This paper therefore focuses on the formulation of design recommendations that could increase the attitude-behavior relationship of persuasive games for societal interventions. Through a literature study in the field of social psychology (with attitude/behavioral change as a key research area), several possible predictors of the attitude-behavior relationship were identified. Next we linked these psychological insights to the context of persuasive game design in order to provide four conceptual design recommendations for maximizing the likelihood for a (new) attitude to result in the (long-term) desired behavior in the real world. Finally conclusions, as well as limitations and suggestions for future research are discussed.

2 Four Design Recommendations to Reinforce the Attitude-Behavior Relationship

To a large extent persuasive games can be considered as part of Persuasive Technology, a class of technologies "*intentionally designed to change a person's attitude and/or behavior*" [22]. Remarkably this 'and/or' part is rather undefined and unsubtle. It therefore seems that the substantial attitude-behavior relationship that is inherent to long-term persuasion seems ignored in Persuasive Technology [11]. Within persuasive game design it is also often not specifically described and explained if the design of a persuasive game aims to influence a certain attitude, certain behavior or even both and why this is the case. This seems a rather unfortunate situation, because this indiscriminate vision could influence the design choices and thus eventually lead to potentially disappointing results concerning the often intended long-term outcomes of the game session(s).

In response to this issue we claim that the design of persuasive games should in principle focus on shaping, reinforcing or changing the attitude of the players concerning the persuasive message of the game. In persuasion theory and research persuasion is in fact conceived as fundamentally involving attitude change [19]. So even if the ultimate goal of a persuasive game is specific long-term behavioral change to occur after the gaming session, one cannot ignore the formation of the subsequent attitude that goes with that desired behavior. Additionally from a more practical perspective Jacobs [23] even argues that persuasive games should specifically focus on attitude formation because they are "*inherently incapable of physically forcing players to perform behaviors, not during play sessions and afterwards*".

With our legitimate focus on attitude formation, we conducted a literature review in the field of social psychology as a theoretical basis for our design recommendations. Before these recommendations are described in the following paragraphs of this section we firstly specify how we conducted this literature study in the next paragraph.

2.1 Review Methodology

In order to formulate design recommendations that could increase the attitude-behavior relationship of persuasive games for societal interventions, we conducted a literature review in the field of social psychology (with attitude/behavioral change as a key research area) to extract several possible predictors of the attitude-behavior relationship.

Search Strategies. Two different search strategies were used: a conventional database search and backwards snowballing. For the database search we compiled relevant search terms regarding the right conditions under which attitudes become possible predictors of the desired behavior after the game. These search terms were based on personal knowledge. For the second search strategy we searched for relevant references and citations in other papers.

Databases and Keywords. For the review the databases of Delft University of Technology and Scopus were used. The following keywords and combinations were used for the database search: ("attitude-behavior" AND "relationship")/("attitude-behavior" AND "consistency")/("attitude" AND "predictor" AND "behavior").

Selection Criteria. Literature was selected based on the following criteria: 1. it described social psychological studies/theories 2. it contained empirical findings concerning the conditions under which attitudes could become predictors of behavior 3. findings seemed to be applicable in a persuasive game design context 4. it was published post-1970. 5. it was written in English.

As expected, our initial search with the above described keywords and combinations provided thousands of articles. However, based on selection criteria 2 and 3, we concluded that the majority of these articles were not relevant for the specific focus of this paper and were thus excluded from this literature study. Within the remaining selection of literature lots of overlap was found; the same principles and researchers were repeatedly referred to. This convinced us that there is a fairly small group of possible predictors of the attitude-behavior relationship, but each with a strong argumentation. Based on the selection criteria we eventually selected only 7 relevant papers and 3 books for the theoretical foundation on the basis of which the aimed recommendations could be drawn up. This review finally resulted in the following four conceptual design recommendations based on the psychological insights we collected, as described in the next paragraphs of this section.

2.2 Aligned Degree of Specification of Game's Message and Desired Behavior

The first insight concerns the correspondence between attitudinal and behavioral measures. This might sound like an open door, but it is often easily overlooked in the design of persuasive games. Whether one finds consistency between an attitudinal measure and a behavioral measure depends in part on the nature of the measures involved [19]. According to the *correspondence principle* [24] close attitude-behavior correlations can only be expected if both measures agree in their degree of specification. In other words, specific attitudes predict equally specific behaviors.

When applied in the context of persuasive game design, this principle shows that the level of the persuasive message of the game (that should influence the attitude) should be presented at the same specific level as the intended behavior to occur after the game. An example: when one designs a persuasive game that aims to positively influence the attitude of players concerning the sustainable consumption of energy, one has to be very clear about what specific behavior concerning this consumption is desired and the specific attitude and thus message that goes with it. The goal of the game for example could be to persuade people to wash their clothes less often than they are used to. In that case, simply positively influencing the general attitude of sustainable energy use with a corresponding general persuasive message in the game would probably not achieve the desired result according to this principle. Simply because the degree of specification of the game's message is not aligned with the desired behavior. In this case, the recommendation would then be to adjust the game's message from a general one about sustainable energy use into one that specifically says that one should wash their clothes less often than they are used to.

2.3 Emphasizing the Function of the Attitude to Be Influenced

In order to effectively change a particular attitude is it useful to know which specific function it serves. Two main attitude functions that can be seen as the essence of different theoretical approaches are: 1. serving knowledge organization and guiding approach and avoidance (utititarian) 2. serving higher psychological needs (value expressive, social adjustive) [21].

Attitudes and behavior are more closely related if those aspects of the attitude that are highly accessible at the time of attitude measurement are also accessible at the time the behavior is performed, also known as *functional matching hypothesis* [25]. This implies that attitudes will more strongly predict behavioral intention if the emphasized attitude function matches the function that is normally associated with the attitude object. If we apply these insights in the context of persuasive game design, this could imply that the relevant function of the attitude must be made salient in the game. This is only possible if you actually know what that function is (through for example target group research). In some cases this is easier than in others. Besides an attitude can have several functions at the same time and the functions can also differ per individual [21].

But if we look again at the example of the persuasive game concerning the sustainable consumption of energy this could mean that emphasizing the knowledge function of the attitude towards sustainable energy consumption would not increase the likelihood of the desired sustainable behavior as much as making the value-expressive function of that attitude salient in the game (through the persuasive message of the game). If, of course, indeed the great value that someone attaches to a sustainable world is more salient than new knowledge about sustainable energy consumption at the moment the sustainable behavior should be performed.

2.4 Enabling Players to Reflect on Their Internal States

There are several personality traits that have been linked to individual differences in attitude-behavior consistency. In our earlier work [17] we already mentioned the role of the trait *need for cognition* in attitude formation and change. People high in need for cognition are believed to form stronger attitudes that are highly resistant to change and predictive to behavior because they tend to think more deeply about things and therefore put more effort in processing a persuasive message [26]. We concluded however that within the context of persuasive game design no design mechanic could indirectly enhance the motivation of the player to elaborate on the persuasive message of the game by influencing the *need for cognition,* being a personal trait. But interestingly the effects of two specific traits; *self-monitoring* and *self-awareness,* can function as an implication for effective persuasive game design. They are both namely considered to affect the relative importance of attitudes in guiding behavior. People low in self-monitoring, whose social behavior is generally more reflective of their internal states [19, 27], show higher attitude-behavior correlations than people in high self-monitoring. The latter are more guided by situational demands and the expectation of others. For people high in self-awareness a closer attitude-behavior relation is found as well [28]. They also tend to focus more on their internal states, including their attitudes. Therefore their attitudes are more likely to be accessed and used for decisions concerning the related behavior.

In terms of persuasive game design this could mean that the relation between the aimed attitude formation by the game and the desired resulting behavior after the gaming session would be stronger in case the game enables the players to reflect on their internal states, including their attitudes. In the context of the prior example of the persuasive game that aims to positively influence the sustainable consumption of energy that would imply that the game should enable players to think about their current energy consumption and to what extent it is sustainable (like "*What types energy am I using?*/"*For what purposes and how often?*"/"*To what extent are my choices sustainable?*" etc.) and make them reflect on their current attitude towards this topic (like: "*How important is sustainable consumption of energy for me?*"/"*What do I think about my current consumption of energy?*" etc.).

2.5 Emphasizing the Personal Relevance of an Attitude to a Behavioral Choice

Whether one will act consistently with their attitudes depends in part on whether those attitudes are perceived as relevant to their behavioral choices [19]. So one last factor influencing the attitude-behavior relationship that will be described is the perceived relevance of the attitude to the action.

According to the Elaboration Likelihood Model [18] high motivation and ability support the formation of attitudes through effortful processing of all potentially relevant detail information, whereas either low motivation or low ability leads to lower effort in processing the persuasive message and thus evaluations based on simple rules. Earlier we concluded that persuasive games should focus on the first so called 'central route' to attitude formation because attitude change is considered to be the most resistant and enduring via this route [17]. These different routes however have also been linked to different degrees of attitude-behavior consistency [21]. Attitudes that are formed via the central route are considered more predictive of behavior than those via the so called peripheral route [18].

Specifically the role of personal relevance plays an important role here. Attitudes of people who process a persuasive message under conditions of high personal relevance are considered more predictive of behavior than those of people who process under conditions of low relevance [29]. In general, "*it may be only when individuals explicitly define their attitudes as relevant and appropriate guides to action that they can be expected to turn their general attitudinal orientations for guidance in making their behavioral choices"* [30].

So for a persuasive game it seems important to make the player aware of the personal relevance of the concerned attitude to the desired action. This implies that a persuasive game should emphasize the personal relevance of the (possibly already existing) attitude to a behavioral choice. Like with the earlier example of the persuasive game about sustainable energy consumption, this implies that the game should emphasize the personal relevance of the player concerning sustainable energy consumption. If this is not emphasized in the game, it could be possible that although the player might belief sustainable energy is important for society, he/she will still not personally make sustainable choices concerning energy use since the personal relevance it not made salient.

3 Conclusion, Discussion and Future Work

In this paper we aimed to formulate conceptual design recommendations that could increase the attitude-behavior relationship of persuasive games for societal interventions. Through a literature study in the field of social psychology, several possible predictors of the attitude-behavior relationship were identified and then linked to the context of persuasive game design. In this way, the following design recommendations for maximizing the likelihood for an attitude influenced by a persuasive game to result in the (long-term) desired post-game behavior were presented:

1. aligning the degree of specification of a game's message and the desired behavior
2. emphasizing the function of the attitude to be influenced
3. enabling players to reflect on their internal states
4. emphasizing the personal relevance of an attitude to a behavioral choice

These design recommendations can contribute to the overall effectiveness of a persuasive game because through their application they enable the right conditions for the attitude to be influenced by the game to become a predictor of the desired, post-game behavior. So far persuasive game design is often based on insights from Persuasive Technology [22], where the substantial attitude-behavior relationship that is inherent to long term persuasion seems to be ignored. With this paper we aim to contribute to a broader, nuanced view on the effective design of persuasive games for societal interventions.

It should be highlighted however that in this paper we specifically focused on improving the persuasive effects of a persuasive game through reinforcing the attitude-behavior relationship and left out the engaging aspects that might also contribute to the overall persuasive power of the game.

We also realize that the attitude-behavior relationship is very complex and therefore very difficult to control. In this paper we only looked at increasing the chance that attitudes influenced by a persuasive game could lead to the desired behavior after the game. But we must emphasize that not only attitudes can be predictors of the desired behavior, other factors play a role in this process as well; like norms and expectations of the social environment, the extent to which people think they can carry out the desired behavior and affective determinants of the behavior [19]. This means that a persuasive game for a societal intervention can never guarantee to result in the desired societal change alone, but should be deployed as part of a larger intervention next to other strategies to tackle grand societal challenges.

Although this paper provides interesting insights from social psychology to the field of persuasive game design, we must also stress that so far this work is limited through its theoretical nature. Future work should therefore consist of empirical studies where the proposed conceptual design recommendations are applied in different persuasive games for societal interventions, with pre- and post-attitude measurements and post-game long-term behavior measurement. Automatically within these future studies it could be investigated what these design recommendations imply for the effective implementation of popular persuasive mechanics such as *simulation*, *comparison*, *suggestion* or *customization* [31]. For example *comparison* could potentially be used to emphasize a possible social adjustive function of an attitude and *customization* for emphasizing the personal relevance of an attitude to a behavioral choice. Results from this empirical research should ultimately contribute to the overall effectiveness of persuasive games for societal interventions, so these games can become impactful tools to reach a broad variety of citizens and enable civic engagement.

References

1. Kuhlmann, S., Rip, A.: Next-generation innovation policy and grand challenges. Sci. Public Policy **45**(4), 448–454 (2018)
2. McCormich, J.: Carrots, Sticks and Sermons - Policy Instruments and Their Evaluation. Transaction Publishers, New York (1998)
3. Lukosch, H.K., Bekebrede, G., Kurapati, S., Lukosch, S.G.: A scientific foundation of simulation games for the analysis and design of complex systems. Simul. Gaming **49**(3), 1–36 (2018)
4. Klabbers, J.H.G.: On the architecture of game science. Simul. Gaming **49**, 207–245 (2018)
5. Antle, A.N., Tanenbaum, J., Macaranas, A., Robinson, J.: Games for change: looking at models of persuasion through the lens of design. In: Nijholt, A. (ed.) Playful User Interfaces. GMSE, pp. 163–184. Springer, Singapore (2014). https://doi.org/10.1007/978-981-4560-96-2_8
6. Ruggiero, D.: The effect of a persuasive game on attitude towards the homeless. Unpublished thesis, Purdue University (2013)
7. Reeves, B., Cummings, J.J., Scarborough, J.K., Flora, J., Anderson, D.: Leveraging the engagement of games to change energy behavior. In: International Conference on Collaboration Technologies and Systems (CTS) (2012)
8. De la Hera Conde-Pumpido, T.: Conceptual model for the study of persuasive games. DiGRA 2013 - DeFragging Game Studies (2013)
9. Checkoway, B., Aldana, A.: Four forms of youth civic engagement for diverse democracy. Child. Youth Serv. Rev. **35**(11), 1894–1899 (2013)
10. Visch, V., Vegt, N., Anderiesen, H., van der Kooij, K.: Persuasive game design: a model and its definitions. In: CHI 2013. ACM, Paris (2013)

11. Kors, M.J.L., van der Spek, E.D., Schouten, B.A.M.: A foundation for the persuasive gameplay experience. In: Proceedings of the 10th Annual Foundations of Digital Games Conference Foundations of Digital Games. Foundations of Digital Games (2015)
12. Bogost, I.: Persuasive Games: The Expressive Power of Videogames. MIT Press, Cambridge (2010)
13. Siriaraya, P., Visch, V., Vermeeren, A., Bas, M.: A cookbook method for persuasive game design. Int. J. Serious Games **5**, 37–71 (2018)
14. Schrier, K.: Designing games for moral learning and knowledge building. Games Cult. 1–38 (2017)
15. Kaptein, M., De Ruyter, B., Markopoulos, P., Aarts, E.: Adaptive persuasive systems. ACM Trans. Interact. Intell. Syst. **2**(2), 1–25 (2012)
16. Soekarjo, M., van Oostendorp, H.: Measuring effectiveness of persuasive games using an informative control condition. Int. J. Serious Game **2**(2), 37–55 (2017)
17. Erdbrink, A., Kortmann, R., Verbraeck, A.: The context dependency of four persuasive game design principles. In: Hamada, R., et al. (eds.) Neo-Simulation and Gaming Toward Active Learning. Translational Systems Sciences, vol. 18, pp. 453–463. Springer, Singapore (2019). https://doi.org/10.1007/978-981-13-8039-6_43
18. Petty, R.J., Cacioppo, J.T.: The elaboration likelihood model of persuasion. Ad. Exp. Soc. Psychol. **19**, 123–205 (1986)
19. O'Keefe, D.J.: Persuasion: Theory and Research. SAGA Publications, USA (2002)
20. Ajzen, I.: The theory of planned behavior. Organ. Behav. Hum. Decis. Process. **50**, 179–211 (1991)
21. Bohner, G., Wänke, M.: Attitudes and Attitude Change. Psychology Press, Cornwall (2002)
22. Fogg, B.J.: Persuasive technologies. Commun. ACM **42**(5), 27–29 (1999)
23. Jacobs, R.S.: Play to win over: effects of persuasive games. Erasmus University Rotterdam, The Netherlands (2017)
24. Ajzen, I., Fishbein, M.: Attitude-behavior relations: a theoretical analysis and review of empirical research. Psychol. Bull. **84**, 888–918 (1977)
25. Shavitt, S., Fazio, R.H.: Effects of attribute salience on the consistency between attitudes and behavior predictions. Pers. Soc. Psychol. Bull. **17**, 507–516 (1991)
26. Cacioppo, J.T., Petty, R.E., Feinstein, J.A., Jarvis, W.B.G.: Dispositional differences in cognitive motivation: the life and times of individuals varying in need for cognition. Psychol. Bull. **119**, 197–253 (1996)
27. Snyder, M.: Self-monitoring of expressive behavior. J. Pers. Soc. Psychol. **30**, 526–537 (1974)
28. Gibbons, F.X.: Sexual standards and reactions to pornography: enhancing behavioral consistency through self-focused attention. J. Pers. Soc. Psychol. **36**, 976–987 (1978)
29. Leippe, M.R., Elkin, R.A.: When motives clash: issue involvement and response involvement as determinants of persuasion. J. Pers. Soc. Psychol. **52**, 269–278 (1987)
30. Snyder, M.: When believing means doing: creating links between attitudes and behavior. In: Consistency in Social Behavior: The Ontario Symposium, vol. 2, Lawrence Erlbaum, Hillsdale (1982)
31. Orji, R., Vassileva, J., Mandryk, R.L.: Modeling the efficacy of persuasive strategies for different gamer types in serious games for health. User Model. User-Adapt. Interact. **24**, 453–498 (2014)

Incorporating Theories of Metacognitive Learning in the Design of a Serious Game on Emotion Regulation

Styliani Chytiroglou[1(✉)], Isabella Pollak[2], and Helen Pain[1]

[1] University of Edinburgh, Edinburgh, UK
stella7hitiroglou@yahoo.com
[2] University of Birmingham, Birmingham B15 2TU, UK

Abstract. The ability to regulate one's emotions is inextricably linked to positive life outcomes. Emotion regulation, however, is a skill that ranges between individuals and often does not reach appropriate patterns of development all the way into adulthood. Current research in the field suggests that the ability is trainable. This research aimed at identifying the design requirements for the development of a digital touchscreen game with the long-term goal of enhancing children's awareness regarding their emotion regulation (ER). A review of the literature suggested that in order to achieve the aforementioned goal, such a game needed to take the form of a story-creation activity and elicit (self-) reflection regarding ER strategy use. Based on theoretical considerations, it was proposed that a metacognitive approach, facilitated by questions, would succeed in promoting the above aims. The present paper, aims to present the implementation of this approach into a story-creation game and, in particular, describe the process of incorporating metacognitive theories of learning into the design choices.

Keywords: Emotion regulation · Metacognitive learning · Educational games

1 Introduction

Emotion regulation (ER) refers to all behaviours related to the increase, maintenance and decrease of negative and positive emotions (Gross 1998). Difficulties with emotion regulation have not only been linked to unfavourable long-term outcomes (Nelis et al. 2011), but have been shown to impact a person's life from the early years (Rubin et al. 1995; Rydell et al. 2003). ER abilities vary depending on early experiences, as well as intrapersonal factors (Denham 2007; Thompson 1991). Given that initial situational ER strategy preferences are likely to manifest over time and develop into trait-like ER behaviours (Cole et al. 1994). The creation of a serious game for young children that allows for the exploration of different ER strategies and prompts conversation around their outcomes arises as particularly useful. Though there are a number of games for young children that touch upon the topic of emotional learning (e.g. Sesame Street, Daniel Tiger's Neighbourhood), these are rarely constructed on a theoretical base. Accounting for the literature on emotion regulation the present research aimed to design a game which facilitates exploration of ER strategies and discussion of ER

A. Liapis et al. (Eds.): GALA 2019, LNCS 11899, pp. 92–102, 2019.
https://doi.org/10.1007/978-3-030-34350-7_10

strategy use and related outcomes. Importantly, the game aims to elicit metacognitive reflection related to ER strategies.

Recent educational theories support that a promising area of instruction is metacognitive learning (Larkin 2009). Metacognition is the conscious self-awareness of one's own knowledge of task, topic and thinking and the conscious self-management of the related cognitive processes (Jacobs and Paris 1987). Extensive evidence indicates that metacognition plays an important role in learning (Wang et al. 1990; Veenman and Spaans 2005, Michalsky et al. 2009). Metacognitively aware learners perform better in tasks compared to their peers (Garner and Alexander 1989; Pressley and Ghatala 1990). It promotes understanding and problem solving skills and it has been linked with enhanced planning and monitoring abilities, thus promoting durable and transferable learning (Alexander and Judy 1988; Garner and Alexander 1989; Schoenfeld 1992; White 1992). Indeed, interventions targeting metacognitive knowledge of strategy use were found to be most effective in terms of enhancing student's academic performance (de Boer et al. 2018).

The present paper aims to describe the formation of the design requirements for the aforementioned game. Specifically, design elements that elicit discussion of emotion regulation strategies, and particularly the process of incorporating theories of metacognition in the creation of the game.

2 Target Users

The development of metacognition does not occur automatically in all children (de Jager et al. 2005). Children's awareness of cognitive functions lies at one end of a developmental progression that materializes in complex meta-knowing abilities often unmastered by many adults (de Jager et al. 2005; Kuhn 2000). Although the age at which metacognitive knowledge and skills emerge remains unclear, findings show that instances of metacognition are present in very young children. Research has linked the early emergence of various executive functions, such as inhibition, control and attention with self-regulatory abilities in children up to 6 years old (Rothbart et al. 2006). Therefore, a form of metacognition emerges early in life. However, in a major review of the field, Veenman et al. (2006) reported that much of the literature still suggests that metacognitive skills emerge between 8–11 years of age. In adherence to this the design of the present game identified a particular user demographic as optimal for metacognitive training, with the game addressing users between the ages of 8–11.

3 Incorporating Metacognitive Theory into Game Design

3.1 Incorporating Metacognitive Guidance: The Game Structure

The phase the metacognitive guidance is provided in is important for cognitive learning (Michalsky et al. 2009). Most authors agree that during any experience or task there are three opportunities for metacognitive guidance; before, during and after the experience. For Michalsky et al. (2009) these opportunities are beMeta (occurring prior to the experience), duMeta (occurring at the moment) and afMeta (occurring after the experience).

Thus, the game comprises of three parts, each designed to be played with the accompaniment of an adult. The three parts correspond to an Introduction, Main Body, and Reflection, and are to be completed consecutively. Following the literature the game provided three opportunities for metacognitive guidance; prior, during and after task. This was reflected in the creation of three distinct sections, each allowing for metacognitive guidance at a different point in time. The Introduction allowed for reflection before the story-creation task and included questions like *"How do humans experience emotions differently in different contexts?"* and *"What are good and bad ways to control your emotions?"* The Main Part included reflective questions which facilitated reflection after each story (e.g. How does the character feel? Why do they feel like that? What should they do next? How will their reaction make others feel?), while the Reflection promoted own strategy use reflection upon completion of all storylines. On reflecting on the users ER knowledge of context for example, the question of *"Do you handle your emotions differently in different environments?"* was posed.

3.2 Incorporating Direct Instruction: The Intro and the Reflection

The impact of direct instruction on cognitive outcomes has been widely demonstrated (Kruit et al. 2018; Muijs and Reynolds 2001; Pressley and McCormick 1995). Particularly for metacognitive learning, Veenman (1992) suggests that a model of direct instruction that encompasses the training of metacognition can be efficiently used in modern educational practice. In the context of ER interventions, Weytens et al. (2014), found that presenting and explaining the task to learners increases positive effects. According to de Young and Monroe (1996), learning is very selective and strongly biased towards certain informational characteristics. Direct experience is thought to contain many of these characteristics, with studies indicating that attitudes and knowledge developed through direct experience are better predictors of future behaviour (de Young and Monroe 1996). An effective substitute for direct experience in educational contexts has been suggested to be the use of stories, with research indicating that can facilitate exploration and internalization of new knowledge (Bahman and Maffini 2008; Jonassen and Hernandez-Seranno 2002; Monroe and Kaplan 1988; Monroe and de Young 1994; Wells 1986). At the same time, inquiry-based approaches have been shown to be well suited for use in narrative learning paradigms (McQuiggan et al. 2008).

Fig. 1. Opening scene

Fig. 2. Introduction

Fig. 3. Mike's interactive list

In order to account for the benefits of explicit instruction, the game starts by giving an introduction of the story and presenting all relevant components of ER (Fig. 2). The opening screen depicts the character "Mike", set on a yellow background, with a prompt button 'Play with Mike' inviting the user to play (Fig. 1). Once clicked, the user is taken to the first scene of the introduction, where an audio-visual narration sets the context of Mike the alien, who has come to earth to learn how humans control their emotions, so that he can teach his friends (Fig. 2). Users are invited to help Mike read his list: an interactive image providing information regarding ER (Fig. 3). Through clicking on the items on the list, the users were given basic information about the impact of different environments on ER, interpersonal differences in ER, different ER strategies and the process of ER. Once all items of the list are read, users can proceed to the main body of the tool comprising of a story-creation activity. To ensure users are aware of these aspects of ER while navigating through the stories, interactive questions are guiding the user's thought process when making decisions regarding the storyline. Once all stories are completed, the adult directs the attention to the Reflection (Fig. 5). This comprises of a collection of open-ended questions posed by Mike, with the user required to reflect on these and discuss them with the adult. The discussion is facilitated by interactive on-screen questions that provide audio cues relating to each question. Each guiding question relates to a different aspect of ER and is posed in a new pop-up screen. Explicit references to all ER components were presented as discussion with adults or peers has been identified as crucial for children's emotional socialization (Denham 2007; Holodynski and Friedlmeier 2006). To proceed to the next question, the user clicks on a button labelled 'GO'. Ensuring discussion is not hindered, the button appears after a 20 s delay.

3.3 Incorporating Metacognitive Questions: The Story Creation Game

The Inquiry Process

Metacognitive learning is thought to be elicited through processes of inquiry, with evidence showing that such approaches promote learning in various academic domains by supporting self-reflection (Mevarech and Susak 1993; Schoenfeld 1987). Questions activate metacognitive processes, resulting in more effective learning (Mevarech and Kramarski 1997). Moreover, discussions with adults and peers provide opportunities for the collaborative construction of metacognition (Garrison and Akyol 2015; Lewis 2017). An example of an inquiry-based approach, targeting metacognitive mathematical reasoning, is the IMPROVE method (Mevarech and Kramarski 1997). The method proposes the use of a series of self-addressed metacognitive questions regarding comprehension of the phenomenon, construction of links between previous and new knowledge, appropriate strategy use and reflection on the solution process.

As such, the present game assumed the format of a story-creation game in which the users themselves shaped the storyline. Intricate narratives with complex, interesting characters the user can identify with and remember, were created to prompt engagement with the topic. The Main Menu allows the users to choose the character they want to play with (Fig. 4). Once selected, users build a story with this character by choosing between different response options. These options are presented as possible responses to questions posed by Mike, which help guide the development of the story. This way, the game adopted an inquiry approach and a set of questions was incorporated to guide the story-creation activity and the final reflection. Each story incorporates different ER strategies and depending on the response chosen, a different narrative is created. Maladaptive strategies, such as acting out or ruination lead to unfavourable outcomes, while choosing adaptive strategies, such as attention reorientation or capitalizing (adapted from strategies identified by Nelis et al. 2011) lead the players to a happy ending. Upon completion of each story, the accompanying adult facilitates conversation around the strategies used in the story. To promote a higher control over the learning process and effective learning outcomes, the questions incorporated in the game aimed to guide learners to formulate and answer questions that elicit elaborate explanations of their concept of ER (e.g. How does the character feel? Why do they feel like that?), create between-topic comparisons (What should the character do next?) and justify strategy use (How do they feel in the end?).

Fig. 4. Main menu

Fig. 5. Reflection level

Metacognitive Skills and Metacognitive Knowledge

Metacognition can be differentiated into the components of metacognitive knowledge and metacognitive skills (Flavel 1976; Lucangeli et al. 1995; Whitebread et al. 2009). Metacognitive knowledge is the awareness and understanding of one's cognitive processes and products (Flavell 1976). Metacognitive skills conversely, can be seen as the voluntary control people have over their own cognitive processes (Brown 1987). In educational contexts, metacognitive knowledge refers to the knowledge learners have about their own cognition, cognitive functioning and that of others' (de Jager et al. 2005). For the purposes of the present research metacognitive reflection is defined as what Thompson (1999) referred to as meta-emotive understanding. That is, knowledge of the relationship between an antecedent situation and the emotion reaction, knowledge of the consequences of an emotional response and knowledge of the strategies of self-regulation. Incorporating what more recent researchers have referred to as interpersonal metacognition, the third component is expanded to further include knowledge of strategies others use to regulate their emotions, (Liskala et al. 2004; Vaurus et al. 2003; Whitebread et al. 2009).

Following the literature, two levels of stories were created to address both metacognitive knowledge and metacognitive regulation within the game. The first level addressed metacognitive knowledge and included questions that elicited reflection on the components of the situation and raised awareness of the relation between strategies and outcomes. For example, a first level story that addresses the emotion of anger is that of Lewis and the canceled weekend trip. Within the story, the users are presented with the situation of Lewis, whose "*family had planned a trip to the Fun Park over the weekend. Lewis loves the Fun Park because there are a lot of slides and carousels. He is very excited. But oh dear! His mum, Mrs. Smith, forgets to buy the tickets in time and they are all sold out!*" As part of the story creation activity, the level included questions and the answers that affected the storyline. These questions addressed knowledge of persons (*How does Lewis Feel?*), tasks (*Why does Lewis feel angry?*) and strategies (*What should Lewis do? How does Lewis feel in the end?*). Depending on the users' answer choices, a different storyline is created.

Addressing Metacognitive Regulation of ER strategy use Level 2 in turn, included questions that make the user reflect on ER strategy use by addressing how strategies are chosen, how this makes them and other people feel and how this leads to positive/negative outcomes. In this level the emotional and practical goals are introduced by the narrator (*Lewis is very angry but he doesn't want to fight with his mum*) and the user has to reflect on the proper ER strategy to use in the story (*What do you think Lewis should do?*). Finally, the Main Part, as well as the Introduction and Reflection, included explicit references on the role of people, environments, process of ER and strategies.

4 Game Evaluation and Results

Following the development of the high fidelity prototype a series of evaluation workshops was conducted with experts and children of the target age in order to assess the final design and provide feedback on the tool's suitability for the target population.

4.1 Expert Evaluation

Three experts participated in the evaluation of this research. They came from both a Psychology and Education background. The workshops lasted approximately one hour and took the form of an interview which aimed to aim to:

- To evaluate the theoretical soundness of the game.
- To evaluate the instructional soundness of the game.
- To evaluate the appropriateness of various features of the game (e.g. narratives, agent) for the target users.
- To identify design problems and get suggestions for improvements.

The experts reaffirmed the appropriateness of the game design for the target ages, particularly the use of stories to promote emotional engagement and facilitate recall of the target skill. They also agreed that most aspects of the theory were implemented in the tool design, as for example with the three part structure. Similarly the incorporated questions were seen as facilitating metacognitive thinking and self-reflection. Although the game was designed for individual use, the experts underlined its appropriateness for educational settings and its usefulness for current classroom demands. At the same time, slight changes in the complexity of the storylines and characters were suggested as better to promote all emotion regulation aspects. For this purpose, the experts suggested the creation of three distinct levels, each of which corresponded to regulation in the self, ER behavior impact on others and reflection on how to respond to other people's emotions.

4.2 Children Evaluation

Following the expert evaluations, a series of individual workshops was conducted with children of the target age. Given the time limitations of this research, these sessions aimed only to provide a proof of concept and not a detailed measurement of the tool effects. The evaluations included a total of 6 participants, who ranged between the ages of 9 and 11.

Each session lasted approximately one hour. Each child evaluated the prototype individually. During the first part of the sessions the researchers described briefly the aims and content of the tool and obtained the participant's consent. For the main part of the session, the child went through the different stories and explored the various outcomes. The participant was guided through the tool by one of the researchers who followed an adult guidance script developed for the purposes of the evaluation sessions. A set of criteria was formed, based on the initial literature review, to assess the extent to which the different components of the tool successfully met the research goals set.

The findings showed that the game facilitated exploration of ER strategies. The stories engaged the children and evoked their curiosity with the participants making spontaneous comments about the stories (e.g. "Wow", "Penguins!"). One in particular commented extensively on the story content, drawing comparisons with real life. With the exception of one, all children expressed the desire to go back and explore the outcomes of the different options. Most participants mainly wanted to explore adaptive options (e.g. "I will actually go for a different option to see if this would lead to a happy ending."). However, one child, though initially choosing an adaptive option during the free exploration level, asked to go back and explore what happens when one chooses the maladaptive option (e.g. "I want to see what happens if you click the wrong one."). At the same time, participants were attentive to the story contexts. Two participants drew comparisons across storylines and between storylines and pictures, while four of the participants read the options aloud. P6 interacted verbally with the tool (e.g. "Yes, I'm sure!"), while P2 and P4 were eager to see how the story unfolds and get new options. The participants did not refer back to the stories during the discussion part of the tool, with the exception of P3, who used one of the storylines as an example to explain his emotional reactions.

Similarly, the narratives and questions included in the game were found to facilitate discussion. The narrative elements evoked discussion with all participants - apart from one- spontaneously commenting on the proposed strategies. In the case where only maladaptive options were provided, comments included "I wouldn't do any of those" (P3) and "Oh no! They are both sad options!" (P6). In the case of adaptive storylines, discussion was again facilitated, with one of the participants comparing the proposed strategies and relating them to possible outcomes prior to making a choice. No spontaneous comments were made regarding the characters' behaviours in relation to the storylines. At the same time, none of the participating children spontaneously referred to personal experiences.

The questions posed on the storylines by either the system or the guiding researcher, engaged participants in conversation. P2 and P4 talked about the proposed strategies after being prompted in the context of questions posed by the researcher (i.e. "Do you think it was a good idea to think about the things that could go wrong?" "Do you think Lucy's first reaction to yell at Daniel in the Zoo was good?"). Questions initiated by the system also resulted in discussion. P6 for example, was prompted to identify the maladaptive options and explaining why they are dysfunctional. With the exception of P1, the use of questions also prompted participant comments on the ER behaviours of the characters. P3 for example, engaged in detailed discussion concerning strategy preferences by each character and the reasons that could result in this. When posed with the explicit question of talking about their personal experiences, only P1 and P4 referred to own experiences.

Metacognitive reflection was found to be facilitated by the questions used in the tool. Particularly concerning knowledge of persons, all participants exhibited metacognitive knowledge of self-used regulatory strategies. Half of the participants exhibited metacognitive understanding of ER strategy use by others, while metacognitive understanding of universals of ER strategy use were present in all participants with the exception of P1 and P5. P3 for example, initiated a detailed conversation on how different people show different strategy preferences, while P4 and P6 reflected on their strengths.

Knowledge of tasks was also facilitated, with participant statements demonstrating long-term memory knowledge in relation to elements of ER within the story. Two participants stated that they use different strategies in different environments. P3 extensively referred to situational factors, describing how the difficulty of ER processes changes with varying emotional causes and circumstances.

Finally, all participants except P1 exhibited an understanding of the strategies used when aiming to achieve a particular emotional goal. Particularly the example strategies and question within the Reflection prompted metacognitive reflection around ER strategies. All participants differentiated between adaptive and maladaptive strategies. P2 and P4 specifically commented on their own usage patterns, while P2, P3 and P4 linked strategies to likely emotional consequences for the characters.

5 Discussion

The present research followed an interdisciplinary approach accounting for theories from the fields of psychology and education. Importantly the design of the tool, with its three-part structure, different levels and particular features, was informed by theory and was developed, so as to mirror the ER components and patterns of metacognitive development identified in the literature. More particularly, following recent findings the design of the game incorporated theories of metacognitive learning. The use of a metacognitive approach not only adheres to modern educational research findings, but ensures that the target skill is transferable outside of the tool context in real life social situations that call for ER.

A series of evaluation workshops conducted with children of the target user age gave promising results, with the design of the game eliciting metacognitive reflection. The workshops revealed that the form of the game was indeed well accepted by the children, engaging them in the story-creation activity and prompting discussion around emotion regulation. The collected verbalizations indicated that questions posed throughout both the Main Part, and during the Reflection, evoked metacognitive answers. As metacognitive theory identifies interpersonal metacognition (Whitebread et al. 2009), the game, particularly the Reflection, aimed to direct attention on the participants' own behaviours. The children used the game as a basis for expressing their beliefs, often comparing the story content to their own behaviour. Although not all participants showed the same level of reflection, their verbalizations revealed that the tool prompted metacognitive reflection for all components of ER. The difference between participants is expected, given the developmental span of metacognition is broad (Veenman et al. 2006).

As shown in the evaluation workshops, the chosen game design supported the users' reflection processes by creating a coherent context in which users could build their beliefs. At the same time however, certain limitations arise. Although the evaluation sessions provide evidence confirming the initial hypotheses, these can only be seen as proof of concept. The small participant sample and subjective nature of the measurement used cannot affirm the findings. As such, further work and a more systematic evaluation of the game are needed for concrete conclusions to be reached.

References

Alexander, P.A., Judy, J.E.: The interaction of domain-specific and strategic knowledge in academic performance. Rev. Educ. Res. **58**(4), 375–404 (1988)

Bahman, S., Maffini, H.: Developing Children's Emotional Intelligence. Bloomsbury Publishing (2008)

Brown, A.L.: Metacognition, executive control, self-regulation and other more mysterious mechanisms. In: Weinert, F.E., Kluwe, R.H. (eds.) Metacognition, Motivation and Understanding, pp. 65–116. Erlbaum, Hillsdale, NJ (1987)

Cole, P.M., Michel, M.K., Teti, L.O.D.: The development of emotion regulation and dysregulation: a clinical perspective. Monogr. Soc. Res. Child Dev. **59**(2-3), 73–102 (1994)

de Boer, H., Donker, A.S., Kostons, D.D., van der Werf, G.P.: Long-term effects of metacognitive strategy instruction on student academic performance: a meta-analysis. Educ. Res. Rev. **24**, 98–115 (2018)

de Jager, B., Jansen, M., Reezigt, G.: The development of metacognition in primary school learning environments. School Effect. School Improve. **16**(2), 179–196 (2005)

Denham, S.A.: Dealing with feelings: how children negotiate the worlds of emotions and social relationships. Cogn. Brain Behav. **11**(1), 1–48 (2007)

Flavell, J.H.: Metacognitive aspects of problem solving. In: Resnick, L.R. (ed.) The Nature of Intelligence, pp. 231–235. Erlbaum, Hillsdale (1976)

Garner, R., Alexander, P.A.: Metacognition: answered and unanswered questions. Educ. Psychol. **24**(2), 143–158 (1989)

Garrison, D.R., Akyol, Z.: Toward the development of a metacognition construct for communities of inquiry. Internet High. Educ. **24**, 66–71 (2015)

Gross, J.J.: The emerging field of emotion regulation: an integrative review. Rev. Gener. Psychol. **2**, 271–299 (1998)

Holodynski, M., Friedlmeier, W.: Development of Emotions and Emotion Regulation. Springer, New York (2006)

Jacobs, J.E., Paris, S.G.: Children's metacognition about reading: issues in definition, measurement, and instruction. Educ. Psychol. **22**(3–4), 255–278 (1987)

Jonassen, D.H., Hernandez-Serrano, J.: Case-based reasoning and instructional design: using stories to support problem solving. Educ. Tech. Res. Dev. **50**(2), 65–77 (2002)

Kruit, P.M., Oostdam, R.J., Van den Berg, E., Schuitema, J.A.: Effects of explicit instruction on the acquisition of students' science inquiry skills in grades 5 and 6 of primary education. Int. J. Sci. Educ. **40**(4), 421–441 (2018)

Kuhn, D.: Metacognitive development. Curr. Dir. Psychol. Sci. **9**(5), 178–181 (2000)

Larkin, S.: Metacognition in Young Children. Routledge (2009)

Lewis, H.: Supporting the development of young children's metacognition through the use of video-stimulated reflective dialogue. Early Child Dev. Care, 1–17 (2017)

Liskala, T., Vauras, M., Lehtinen, E.: Socially-shared metacognition in peer learning? Hellenic J. Psychol. **1**(2), 147–178 (2004)

Lucangeli, D., Galderisi, D., Cornoldi, C.: Specific and general transfer effects following metamemory training. Learn. Disabil. Res. Pract. **10**(1), 11–21 (1995)

McQuiggan, S.W., Rowe, J.P., Lee, S., Lester, J.C.: Story-based learning: the impact of narrative on learning experiences and outcomes. In: Woolf, B.P., Aïmeur, E., Nkambou, R., Lajoie, S. (eds.) ITS 2008. LNCS, vol. 5091, pp. 530–539. Springer, Heidelberg (2008). https://doi.org/10.1007/978-3-540-69132-7_56

Mevarech, Z.R., Kramarski, B.: IMPROVE: a multidimensional method for teaching mathematics in heterogeneous classrooms. Am. Educ. Res. J. **34**(2), 365–394 (1997)

Mevarech, Z.R., Susak, Z.: Effects of learning with cooperative-mastery method on elementary students. J. Educ. Res. **86**(4), 197–205 (1993)

Michalsky, T., Mevarech, Z.R., Haibi, L.: Elementary school children reading scientific texts: effects of metacognitive instruction. J. Educ. Res. **102**(5), 363–376 (2009)

Monroe, M.C., DeYoung, R.: The role of interest in environmental information: a new agenda. Child. Environ., 243–250 (1994)

Monroe, M.C., Kaplan, S.: When words speak louder than actions: environmental problem solving in the classroom. J. Environ. Educ. **19**(3), 38–41 (1988)

Muijs, D., Reynolds, D.: Being or doing: the role of teacher behaviors and beliefs in school and teacher effectiveness in mathematics, a SEM analysis. In: Annual Meeting of the American Educational Research Association, Seattle, WA (2001)

Nelis, D., Quoidbach, J., Hansenne, M., Mikolajczak, M.: Measuring individual differences in emotion regulation: the emotion regulation profile-revised (ERP-R). Psychol. Belgica **51**(1), 49–91 (2011)

Pressley, M., Ghatala, E.S.: Self-regulated learning: monitoring learning from text. Educ. Psychol. **25**(1), 19–33 (1990)

Pressley, M., McCormick, C.: Cognition, Teaching, and Assessment. HarperCollins College Publishers, New York (1995)

Rothbart, M.K., Posner, M.I., Kieras, J.: Temperament, attention and the development of selfregulation. In: McCartney, K., Phillips, D. (eds.) Blackwell Handbook of Early Childhood Development. Blackwell, Oxford (2006)

Rubin, K.H., Coplan, R.J., Fox, N.A., Calkins, S.D.: Emotionality, emotion regulation and preschoolers' social adaptation. Dev. Psychopathol. **7**, 49–62 (1995)

Rydell, A.M., Berlin, L., Bohlin, G.: Emotionality, emotion regulation, and adaptation among 5- to 8-year-old children. Emotion **3**(1), 30 (2003)

Schoenfeld, A.H.: What's all the fuss about metacognition. Cogn. Sci. Math. Educ. **189**, 215 (1987)

Schoenfeld, A.H.: Learning to think mathematically: problem solving, metacognition, and sense making in mathematics. In: Handbook of Research on Mathematics Teaching and Learning, pp. 334–370 (1992)

Thompson, R.A.: Emotional Regulation and Emotional Development. Educ. Psychol. Rev. **3**(4), 269–307 (1991)

Thompson, R.A.: Early attachment and later development. In: Cassidy, J., Shaver, P.R. (eds.) Handbook of Attachment: Theory, Research, and Clinical Applications, pp. 265–286. The Guilford Press, New York (1999)

Vauras, M., Liskala, T., Kajamies, A., Kinnunen, R., Lehtinen, E.: Shared regulation and motivation of collaborating peers: a case analysis. Psychol.: Int. J. Psychol. Orient **46**, 19–37 (2003)

Veenman, M.V.J., Spaans, M.A.: Relation between intellectual and metacognitive skills: age and task differences. Learn. Individ. Diff. **15**, 159–176 (2005)

Veenman, M.V.J., Van Hout-Wolters, B.H.A.M., Afflerbach, P.: Metacognition and learning: conceptual and methodological considerations. Metacogn. Learn. **1**, 3–14 (2006)

Veenman, S.A.M.: Effectieve instructie volgens het directe instructiemodel [Effective instruction based on the direct instruction model]. Pedagogische Stud. **69**(4), 242–269 (1992)

Wang, M.C., Haertel, G.D., Walberg, H.J.: What influences learning? A content analysis of review literature. J. Educ. Res. **84**, 30–43 (1990)

Wells, G.: The Meaning Makers: Children Learning Language and Using Language to Learn. Heinemann Educational Books, Inc., London (1986)

Weytens, F., Luminet, O., Verhofstadt, L.L., Mikolajczak, M.: An integrative theory-driven positive emotion regulation intervention. PLoS One **9**(4), e95677 (2014). 59

White, R.T.: Implications of recent research on learning for curriculum and assessment. J. Curric. Stud. **24**(2), 153–164 (1992)

Whitebread, D., et al.: The development of two observational tools for assessing metacognition and self-regulated learning in young children. Metacogn. Learn. **4**(1), 63–85 (2009)

Young, R.D., Monroe, M.C.: Some fundamentals of engaging stories. Environ. Educ. Res. **2**(2), 171–187 (1996)

Teaching Educational Game Design: Expanding the Game Design Mindset with Instructional Aspects

Kristian Kiili[1,2](✉) and Pauliina Tuomi[1,2]

[1] Faculty of Education and Culture, Tampere University, Tampere, Finland
{kristian.kiili,pauliina.tuomi}@tuni.fi

[2] Information Technology and Communication, Tampere University, Pori, Finland

Abstract. It is argued that we are witnessing a paradigmatic shift toward constructionist gaming in which students design games instead of just consuming them. However, only a limited number of studies have explored teaching of educational Game Design (GD). This paper reports a case study in which learning by designing games strategy was used to teach different viewpoints of educational GD. In order to support design activities, we proposed a CIMDELA (Content, Instruction, Mechanics, Dynamics, Engagement, Learning Analytics) framework that aims to align game design and instructional design aspects. Thirty under-graduate students participated in the gamified workshop and designed math games in teams. The activities were divided into eight rounds consisting of design decisions and game testing. The workshop activities were observed and the designed games saved. Most of the students were engaged in the design activities and particularly the approach that allowed students to test the evolving game after each round, motivated students. Observations revealed that some of the students had isolated design mindset in the beginning and they had problems to consider design decisions from game design and instructional perspectives, but team-based design activities often led to fruitful debate with co-designers and helped some students to expand their mindsets.

Keywords: Game-based learning · Game design · Educational game · Design mindset

1 Introduction

During the past decade the use of game-based learning solutions have increased. Nevertheless, it seems that the quality of game-based learning solutions varies a lot and the field is lacking of generally acknowledged theoretical frameworks for developing engaging and effective game-based learning solutions. Since digital games as a learning approach was proposed, game designers have faced challenges to integrate instructional and game design aspects [e.g. 1–3]. For example, Quinn [2] has stated that educational games have to be well-designed to incorporate engagement that integrates with educational effectiveness. In fact, Habgood and Ainsworth [3] have proven that deep integration of game's core mechanics and its learning content is crucial for creating

A. Liapis et al. (Eds.): GALA 2019, LNCS 11899, pp. 103–113, 2019.
https://doi.org/10.1007/978-3-030-34350-7_11

intrinsically motivating and effective game-based learning solutions. However, the integration of content knowledge and game mechanics is not enough, but also the domain specific instructional knowledge should be considered when designing the core mechanics and dynamics of an educational game. Unfortunately, previous research has shown that systematic investigation of learning integration in games is lacking [4] and for example in the context of game-based rational number learning the intrinsic integration has been rare [5]. Thus, in order to teach educational GD for undergraduate students we designed a workshop that aimed to explore students' game design preferences as well as to support the development of integrated educational GD mindset. With integrated mindset we refer to such educational GD practices in which instructional knowledge, content knowledge, game design knowledge as well as target group characteristics are considered in the game design decisions. In this paper we propose a framework for educational GD and game research that is built upon the idea of integrated educational GD mindset. The proposed framework helps to design learning activities in the educational GD subject and it was applied in the design of the game design workshop that was build upon an existing number line math game engine. Moreover, one aim of the workshop was to evaluate the feasibility of the idea to develop a game design workshop authoring tool around an existing game.

1.1 Related Work

According to Koivisto and Hamari [6] game-like characteristics of our world are increasing and gamification of activities, systems, and services has become more common. With gamification authors [6, pp. 191] refer to "designing information systems to afford similar experiences and motivations as games do, and consequently, attempting to affect user behavior". Although most of the students have used gamified products and played digital games, only few are able to design and create games. According to Resnick et al. [7] digital fluency requires more than just interacting with media, it requires ability to collaboratively design, create, and invent with media. In this paper we report results of a study in which an emerging pedagogical strategy, learning by designing games was used to teach educational GD in a gamified workshop. The pedagogical idea behind learning by designing games approach relies on the assumption that game design activities help students to reformulate their understanding of the subject matter and express their personal ideas about both the subject and the designed game [8]. In line with this, Games's [9] study in which game creation activities were investigated in an online Gamestar Mechanic environment (www.gamestarmechanic.com) showed that students can learn to analyze designs articulated by others as well as to articulate their own designs, which facilitates a deeper understanding of the expressive possibilities of games as a medium.

Kafai and Burke [10] have argued that we are currently witnessing a paradigmatic shift toward constructionist gaming in which students design games for learning instead of just consuming games created by professionals. They note that the popularity of Minecraft is the clearest indicator that constructionist gaming approach has arrived. According to recent literature reviews [10, 11], learning by designing/making games approach has been used to teach several subjects such as programming, computational concepts/strategies/thinking, mathematics, arts, and language & writing skills, but the studies in which the educational GD is a main learning objective are rare.

Nevertheless, a model of creative and playful learning [12], Smiley Model [13], and MDA (Mechanics, Dynamics, and Aesthetics) framework [14] can be applied in structuring learning by designing games activities. The creative and playful learning model distinguishes (1) orientation to tools, methods and the topic of learning, (2) game design and creation, (3) game play, and (4) elaboration, reflection and evaluation learning phases. The Smiley Model is a detailed framework for designing engaging learning experiences in games and it has been found to be useful in scaffolding the learning game design process [13]. On the other hand, the MDA framework proposes more general, formal approach, for game design and game research. MDA aims to bridge the gap between game design, game criticism, and technical game research. However, as the MDA is a general game framework we propose an extended CIMDELA (Content, Instruction, Mechanics, Dynamics, Engagement, Learning Analytics) framework to better fit to the educational game context (Fig. 1).

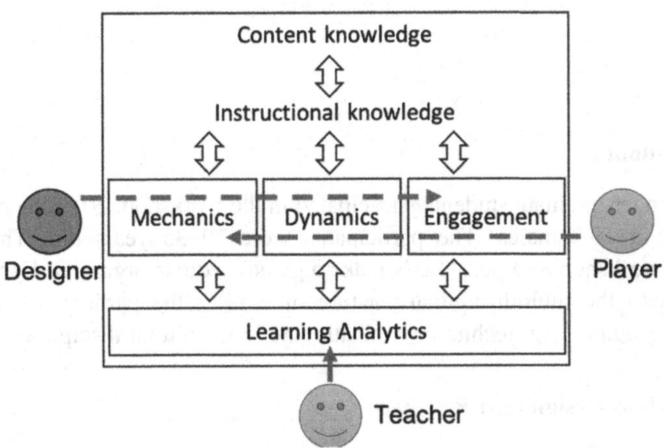

Fig. 1. CIMDELA framework for educational game design and game research

In the proposed framework the aesthetics component is replaced with engagement component while it conceptualizes the meaning and consequences of aesthetics better in the educational game context. The mechanics generates dynamic system behavior, which aims to create certain experiences in players. The engagement component describes the desirable cognitive, behavioral, and emotional responses that interacting with the educational game system evokes in the player. The framework encourages to consider not only the designer's perspective, but also player's and teacher's perspectives that in contrast to feature-driven design facilitates experience-driven and learning-driven design. The most important extension to the original MDA framework is addition of instructional knowledge, content knowledge, and Learning analytics components. With these components the CIMDELA framework aims to facilitate intrinsic integration of learning domain specific content knowledge, instructional knowledge, and learning analytics with mechanics, dynamics, and engagement components.

1.2 The Present Study

The educational GD workshop was held as a part of HYPE, which is a three-year long project funded by European Social Fund (ESF). The aim of HYPE is to develop new educational practices in the field of serious games in close collaboration with working-life partners and educational organizations. The project generates new patterns and models for cross-sectoral collaboration between various educational levels, industries, and organizations relying strongly on digital learning solutions. In this paper, we report a study in which we explored the usefulness of learning by designing games approach in teaching different viewpoints of educational GD. Furthermore, the aim was to evaluate students' tendencies to consider both game design and instructional design aspects when making game design decisions as well as to evaluate the feasibility of the idea to develop a game design workshop authoring tool around the game used in the workshop.

2 Methods

2.1 Participants

Overall, 30 under-graduate students participated in the workshop. 20 of the participants were male and 10 females. The participants were 19–35 years old. The students attended the workshop as a part "Let's make a game" -course organized by the HYPE-project. Due to the multidisciplinary nature of HYPE, the participants came from various backgrounds (e.g. technology, health-care, and cultural disciplines).

2.2 Workshop Design and Progress

The three-hour workshop consisted of three main phases. First, a short lecture about serious games and design of digital game-based learning solutions were given. The themes of the lecture were derived from the proposed CIMDELA framework and Smiley Model [13]. The aim of the lecture was to orient students to the game-based learning topic and to the tools used in the workshop. The lecture provided several design principles that students could apply in the second phase that consisted of game design and game play activities. Finally, in the third phase, debriefing was carried out and teams' game design decisions were evaluated and elaborated.

The phases 2 and 3 formed a gamified part of the workshop. Several gamification elements such as points, leaderboard, tasks, teams, competition, narrative, and game rounds were used. Narrative elements were utilized to provide a context for the game design activities. The participants were divided into five design teams that worked in the same publishing company. The company had just started a new project in which they were developing a math game about fraction numbers for primary schools (10–12 years old pupils) and the task of the teams was to design a game demo for the next board meeting of the company. The teams competed between each other as only the best demo was promised to present in the forthcoming board meeting.

The teams did not have to start designing from the scratch, but the marketing department of the publishing company had already benchmarked the fraction games available in the market. Based on the benchmarking activities a prototype of the number line estimation game engine was already developed and several possible game mechanics were identified. Figure 2 shows the appearance of the game in the beginning of the workshop. The task of the teams was to decide what kind of game mechanics, aesthetics, and features were included in their final game demo and balance the dynamics. In practice the design activities were divided into eight game rounds that each included 1–3 design decisions to make. The rounds included decisions that were related to feedback and scaffolding mechanics, activable special skills, task types, scoring rules, obstacles, character movement, game balancing, and adaptation rules. Most of the decision tasks were designed in a way that the available options were conflicting with each other with respect to different design mindsets, entertainment mindset versus instructional mindset. For example, some mechanics would be nice additions to entertainment games enhancing emotional engagement, but in educational games these features could increase unnecessarily extraneous cognitive load and possibly even disturb learning or features could make the interpretation of learning analytics harder. The aim of such kind of conflicts was to trigger reflection between possible design choices and design perspectives and that way expand the design mindset of the participants.

Fig. 2. The appearance of the number line-based math game in the beginning of the workshop

In practice the participants did not have to do any programming or graphical design, but only design decisions. In each round, the participants got design documents in which the possible design options were described (see Fig. 3 for an example of one design option). One round could include 1–3 design tasks. At the end of each round the teams provided their design decisions to the two game masters that implemented the decisions to the game through a game configuration file (implementation took couple minutes/team). After the implementation process the teams could play their game and experience the implemented features in action. During the game designing phase, the teams did not get any external feedback about their decisions, but from time to time they were reminded to pay attention also on instructional aspects and target group characteristics. Thus, the playing/testing experience was the only feedback channel during the design phase. Finally, in the debriefing phase all the decisions were elaborated and the achieved points from each decision was revealed. During the debriefing session a leaderboard was visible and players could see how their final rank was determined.

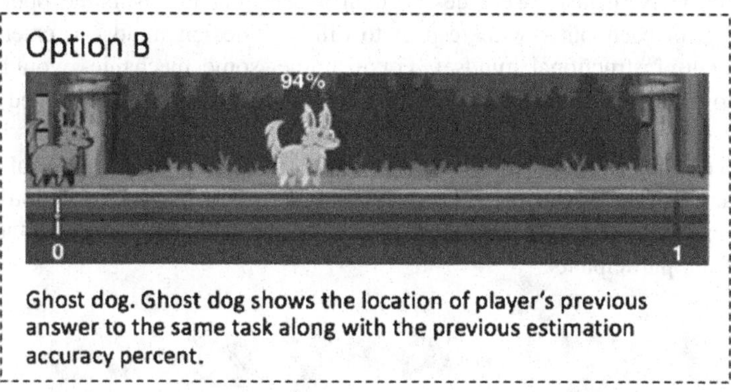

Fig. 3. An example of a design option of the scaffolding round

2.3 Research Materials

The research material consists of observational data and participants game design decisions. In respect to ethical manner, the participants were aware of being observed [15]. As suggested in Merriam [16], the observation focused on physical environment, participants, activities, and interaction/communication and the observation themes were derived from the purpose of the study [16] focusing on decision making, game testing, game design justifications, and collaboration. The observation took place in the classroom and it followed the method of observing ongoing behavior within small groups. The observation was conducted by three researchers. One operated as a main observer and did not partake in any workshop activities. The observation sheet for the main observer was half-structured and it focused on the actual atmosphere, faced challenges, co-design activities, and concrete statements done by the workshop participants. Two other researchers (game masters of the workshop) observed the groups and their decision making in unstructured manner and discussed with participants during the workshop. The whole duration of the workshop (approx. 3 h) was observed.

3 Results

3.1 General Experiences About the Game Design Workshop

The learning by designing educational games concept functioned well and the participants seemed to like the designing activities. Most of the participants were fully concentrated on the topic, but a small number of students seemed to occasionally do some external activities while the rest of the team considered the design options. However, in most cases all the members of the teams took part in the final decisions of the design rounds. In general, the collaborative design approach worked well while participants had to justify their opinions and negotiate the final design decisions. Collaborative aspect clearly made the participants to consider design options from different perspectives. It was evident that 4/5 groups had a more or less clear leader, who strongly influenced on team's decision-making process for example by making suggestions or making the team to vote on the options. One leader clearly indicated that he is a leader by stating that "I'm the leader, but I'm trying to be democratic so I'll ask your opinions".

Participants thought that 2-hour design session was appropriate. During the design phase the majority of the participants eagerly waited for the next round to start. In general, the round-based structure worked well and sequenced the activities into meaningful learning chunks. In fact, the most useful element of the design phase seemed to be the fast-based design-playing cycles. All the teams were eagerly waiting to see how their design choices changed the game as the statements of one team indicate "Yes, we will soon see what was the effect!… If that is critical adjustment for game play, I'm amazed". The playing of the game after each round made participants to think and reflect on the design choices they had made as the following statements indicate: "So why it is now giving this?… Really? Oh, ok, it goes like THAT… Annoying, we didn't think about that… Hey, this feedback was great. It really helps to teach what fraction is". Usually there was one person in the group that played the game while others watched. Such approach facilitated discussions while the teams tested the game. On the other hand, the playing experience also helped participants to consider the options of the following design rounds in a meaningful context. There was also some frustration caused by the lack of competence during the workshop, both on the substance (fractions) and game design aspects as the following comments illustrate: "Argh, I don't know how to count these!… Nooooo, help!… This is hard, even for a person as smart as I am."

Based on the observational data, the competitive element did not play a significant role until the very end when the results were announced. This might be due to the fact that the competition was not emphasized in the beginning, but it was only a part of the background story of the workshop. Furthermore, the competition did not involve any external rewards or prizes and thus the extrinsic motivation was low. In fact, some of the participants even forgot that the competitive element was involved. For example, one participant was frustrated when he remembered the competition and realized that no prizes existed as the following statement shows "Yeah right, so you actually won just a good mood." In spite of a lack of external rewards most of the players were very excited and the round by round evolving game seemed to provide an intrinsically motivating learning context. A real time scoring approach could have increased motivation and meaning of the competitive element. However, in several rounds there were overlapping learning themes and real time scoring would have undermined the instructional value of certain design rounds.

3.2 Students' Game Designs and Design Trends

As a part of the debriefing phase the game designs of the teams were scored. The mean (sd) score was 100.67 (3.11). The best team scored 106 points from 120 maximum points. Overall, all the teams make quite good design choices and considered design decisions from several perspectives. However, in the individual level we identified students that had problems to take both instructional and game design aspects into account, but the team-based approach expanded their design mindset. The deeper analyses of teams' design choices revealed several design trends.

The participants acknowledged the preconditions given in the beginning of the workshop and paid a lot of attention to target group characteristics. For example, one participant tried to figure out what is the best approach for kids and made a design suggestion of a new task type: "Text-based? I don't think that would be the best fit for the children? Perhaps a visual approach?" Another participant reminded the rest of the team to remember the target group by saying that "We should carefully consider the target group and keep in mind what is the competence of a 3rd grader". It became also evident that the participants were aware that math is not the most liked school subject and thus they did not want to design games that rely too much on mathematics that sometimes undermined the instructional value. For example, none of the teams did not include any mathematical obstacles in their game, but preferred non-mathematical obstacles that did not provide any instructional value. This was surprising while in many cases the teams tended to consider choices mostly from instructional point of view. Nevertheless, in several occasions the teams were able to consider the meaning of design choices from both learning and gameplay perspectives as the following argument shows "The last option would be the most accurate - most useful for learning, but the first one would be the funniest choice". The teams clearly became aware of the fact that even if a chosen feature would be great for the gameplay experience, it might not enhance the actual learning and might even disturb learning. In this sense, some of the teams paid attention also to emotional aspects. For example, one of the teams discussed the meaning of a time limit and an obstacle type for playing experience: "If we add the time limit, it might cause more stress - which might hinder the actual learning… I would prefer choosing the ball, it causes no further stress and one would probably then learn more".

As the teams wanted to create very positive learning experiences to the players, they preferred to use rewards and bonuses instead of such assessment mechanics that would more clearly reveal mathematical competences (learning analytics). In fact, students rarely thought the game from teacher's perspective. The participants did not realize that the lack of competence metrics complicates the integration of game playing activities to classroom practices while teachers may face challenges to interpret reward-based in-game metrics. In fact, it became evident that the teams considered only the needs of the players that have difficulties in math. For example, all teams preferred adaptive scaffolding features over adaptive difficulty adjustment that would have taken also the needs of the high achieving players into account. Nevertheless, the design choices and discussions indicated that the participants understood the instructional power of scaffolding mechanics and elaborated feedback in contrast to simple corrective feedback.

If participants did not understand the mathematical meaning of a game mechanic they tended to justify their design decision with fun factors. For example, one team did not understand how the jumping movement might support understanding of unit fractions and they chose it, because they thought that it might be fun for the gameplay. We also noticed that sometimes teams decided to add a certain mechanic to their game, because they liked it so much and wanted to experience that mechanic in action. Thus, it would be reasonable to provide possibilities for participants to try all mechanics before making design decisions instead of just providing an example figures and descriptions of the mechanics as it was done in this study. All in all, the debriefing session was very useful, because the mechanics and design options were considered from different perspectives and participants could reflect on their own choices in the new light.

4 Discussion and Conclusions

This study contributes to the discussion of development of methods to teach design of game-based learning solutions. We explored the usefulness of learning by designing games approach to teach different viewpoints of educational GD to novice designers. We extended the MDA game framework [14] to CIMDELA framework (Content knowledge, Instructional knowledge, Mechanics, Dynamics, Engagement, Learning Analytics) and used the proposed framework to create such design tasks that require alignment of the game design and instructional design aspects. We observed students co-design activities and analyzed their game designs as a part of three-hour workshop that consisted of a short lecture, gamified design activities, and a debriefing session.

In general, the results showed that students were motivated and excited about the game design tasks that is consistent with results of Weitze [13]. However, although the design activities were gamified, the results indicated that the gamification was too loose and thus the gamified parts did not have large effect on students' engagement and motivation. Gamification should be better integrated to core learning activities and students should be constantly aware of gamification elements and state of the system. On the other hand, the round-based structure worked well and sequenced the activities into meaningful learning chunks. The approach in which the students could test how their design decisions changed the gameplay motivated students a lot and the testing sessions facilitated deep discussions about the game designs. However, although the round-based structure worked well, the debriefing session in which the design options were finally elaborated at the end of the workshop were very important for learning and supported the development of the integrated design mindset.

Overall, the analyses of the observation notes indicated that learning by designing game-based learning solutions can be successfully utilized with novice game designers taken that the design activities do not require mastery of game programming. Our results provided evidence that some students had isolated design mindset and they had problems to consider design decision from multiple perspectives. There were students that tended to consider design choices either only from fun or instructional perspectives, but the team-based design activities helped them to expand their design mindset and consider decisions from multiple perspectives. The team-based design activities facilitated learning as students had to articulate and justify their design suggestions often leading to fruitful debate with co-designers. In our opinion the tasks in which design decisions can be justified from several perspectives (e.g. from entertainment or instructional design points of views) worked best as the participants had to consider the meaning of possible options more exhaustively. Although we did not measure learning outcomes, we believe that participants benefited from the design activities and their educational GD mindset expanded. To conclude, based on our experience the proposed CIMDELA framework can be a useful tool for designing learning activities about educational GD. However, we suggest to utilize also other frameworks such as Smiley Model [13] to form more detailed grounding of the design activities. In future, we aim to develop a game design workshop authoring tool around our math game engine to facilitate the organization of similar game design workshops.

References

1. Kiili, K.: Digital game-based learning: towards an experiential gaming model. Internet High. Educ. **8**(1), 13–24 (2005)
2. Quinn, C.: Engaging Learning: Designing E-Learning Simulation Games. Pfeiffer, San Francisco (2005)
3. Habgood, M.J., Ainsworth, S.E.: Motivating children to learn effectively: exploring the value of intrinsic integration in educational games. J. Learn. Sci. **20**(2), 169–206 (2011)
4. Ke, F.: Designing and integrating purposeful learning in game play: a systematic review. Educ. Technol. Res. Develop. **64**(2), 219–244 (2016)
5. Kiili, K., Koskinen, A., Ninaus, M.: Intrinsic integration in rational number games – a systematic literature review. In: CEUR Proceedings, pp. 36–46 (2019). http://ceur-ws.org/Vol-2359/
6. Koivisto, J., Hamari, J.: The rise of motivational information systems: a review of gamification research. Int. J. Inf. Manag. **45**, 191–210 (2019)
7. Resnick, M., et al.: Scratch: programming for all. Commun. ACM **52**(11), 60–67 (2009)
8. Kafai, Y.B.: Playing and making games for learning: instructionist and constructionist perspectives for game studies. Games Cult. **1**(1), 36–40 (2006)
9. Games, I.A.: Gamestar mechanic: learning a designer mindset through communicational competence with the language of games. Learn. Media Technol. **35**, 31–52 (2010)
10. Kafai, Y.B., Burke, Q.: Constructionist gaming: understanding the benefits of making games for learning. Educ. Psychol. **50**(4), 313–334 (2015)
11. Caponetto, I., Earp, J., Ott, M.: Gamification and education: a literature review. In: 8th European Conference on Games Based Learning, pp. 50–57, ECGBL, Germany (2014)
12. Kangas, M.: Creative and playful learning: Learning through game co-creation and games in playful learning environment. Thinking Skills Creativity **5**(1), 1–15 (2010)
13. Weitze, C.L.: Designing for learning and play: the smiley model as a framework. Interact. Design Archit. **29**(1), 52–75 (2016)

14. Hunicke, R., LeBlanc, M., Zubek, R.: MDA: a formal approach to game design and game research. In: Proceedings of the AAAI Workshop on Challenges in Game AI, vol. 4, no. 1 (2014)
15. Kawulich, B.: Participant observation as a data collection method. In: Forum Qualitative Sozialforschung/ Forum: Qualitative Social Research, [S.l.], vol. 6, no. 2 (2005)
16. Merriam, S.B.: Qualitative Research and Case Study Applications in Education. Jossey-Bass Publishers, San Francisco (1998)

AI and Technology for SG

A Pilot Study on the Feasibility of Dynamic Difficulty Adjustment in Game-Based Learning Using Heart-Rate

Manuel Ninaus[1,2](✉), Katerina Tsarava[1,2], and Korbinian Moeller[1,2,3]

[1] Leibniz-Institut für Wissensmedien, Tübingen, Germany
{m.ninaus,k.tsarava,k.moeller}@iwm-tuebingen.de
[2] LEAD Graduate School and Research Network, Eberhard-Karls University, Tübingen, Germany
[3] Department of Psychology, Eberhard-Karls University, Tübingen, Germany

Abstract. Personalization and adaption have become crucial in game-based learning to optimize user experience and performance. Recent advances in sensor technology allow for acquiring physiological data of players which, in turn, allows for acquiring more fine-grained information on internal changes of the player than conventional user interaction data. Therefore, the current pilot study assessed the feasibility of dynamic difficulty adjustment (DDA) in a digital game-based emergency personnel training using heart rate data. In particular, the game became harder/easier when learners heart rate fell below/exceeded predefined thresholds based on leaners individual baseline heart rate. For the adaptive version of the game, we observed that heart rate changes indeed triggered the game to become easier/more difficult. This also altered completion rates as compared to a non-adaptive version of the same game. Moreover, players reported the adaptive version to be more challenging, fascinating, and harder than the non-adaptive one. At the same time players felt that the difficulty in the adaptive version was just right, while the non-adaptive one was rated to be harder than just right. In sum, DDA using heart rate seems feasible. However, future studies need to determine effects on performance and user experience of such adjustments in more detail and different contexts.

Keywords: Personalization · Adaptation · Game-based learning · Serious games · Biofeedback · Physiological data · Heart rate

1 Introduction

One crucial aspect of learning or interacting with digital games is the possibility to acquire a large amount of data and game metrics (e.g. [1]). These data have the potential to provide deeper insights into the learning process beyond simple aggregated scores or grades after finishing playing (for an overview see [2]). Therefore, adaptivity and personalization of digital game-based learning environments have become one of the most interesting topics to promote performance, user experience, as well as

A. Liapis et al. (Eds.): GALA 2019, LNCS 11899, pp. 117–128, 2019.
https://doi.org/10.1007/978-3-030-34350-7_12

motivation [3]. However, most games still rely on simple pre- or post-test measures for assessing learner skills [4].

In recent years, physiological sensors became easier to use and more affordable allowing to track learning processes in different learning scenarios and situations (for a review see [5]). One major advantage of utilizing physiological data is that they can be acquired continuously throughout the learning experience and provide fine-grained information on internal changes of the learner (cf. [2]). Physiological data, such as heart rate (HR; e.g. [6]), galvanic skin response (e.g. [7]), or brain activity (e.g. [8]), have been successfully used to identify a range of different cognitive, motivational, and emotional states relevant for learning [2, 9]. However, most of the studies rely on classifying these states post-hoc rather than in real-time. Importantly though, the latter is required for optimal personalization or adaption, respectively.

Dynamic difficulty adjustment (DDA) reflects an automatic way of adapting, for instance, game difficulty to performance levels of a given player in real-time. Usually, predefined parameter thresholds are used to decide when the difficulty of the game should be increased or decreased [3]. DDA is probably best known from entertainment games, in particular racing games. For instance, so-called rubber banding artificially boosts, for instance, the speed of the players racing car allowing him/her to catch up with cars ahead [10]. However, in game-based learning DDA is still scarce (e.g. [11]). In an optimal scenario, the game-based learning environment would, for instance, detect when a learner is overstrained or gets bored. Accordingly, the game would react in real-time by decreasing or increasing its difficulty. Detecting such learning relevant states, however, is no trivial endeavor, which might explain the lack of empirical studies. Physiological data might therefore be helpful as they allow to identify even small changes in inner states of the user [2].

Optimizing performance by dynamic adaptations in game-based learning requires careful balancing (cf. [12]). In this context, the Yerkes-Dodson Law [13] offers a theoretical framework for implementing adaptive components within a game. It postulates an inverted U-shaped relationship between performance and arousal. Hence, a moderate level of arousal and/or stimulation facilitates best performance in new or complex tasks and is similar to flow [14]. In contrast, performance decreases when arousal becomes too high (e.g. learner is stressed) or too low (e.g. learner is bored). Previous studies demonstrated that arousal can be detected in games by physiological data such as heart rate (e.g. [15, 16]) because heart rate increases with arousal. Hence, heart rate data might be feasible to realize DDA in game-based learning.

In the current pilot study, we aimed at adjusting the difficulty of a game-based learning environment in real-time by utilizing heart rate data. In particular, we implemented DDA in the game-based emergency personnel training *Emergency* (https://www.serious-games-solutions.de/einsatzkraeftetraining/), which simulates critical scenarios such as traffic accidents or structural fires. Accordingly, players have to learn to coordinate and manage these scenarios by patching up wounded persons, preventing houses and vehicles from catching fire, and by evacuating persons. Generally, the game was developed as game-based staff training for emergency personnel, such as firefighters, police, as well as rescue services.

The difficulty of the game-based learning environment is assumed to be mainly driven by the number of tasks or events that need to be addressed simultaneously.

Therefore, the game might create rather stressful and high arousing situations, offering a good opportunity to evaluate dynamic difficulty adjustment. For a pre-pilot experiment, we developed three different scenarios (i.e., *Traffic Accident, Building Fire, and Train Crash*) with three levels of difficulty each (easy – middle – hard). The scenarios and levels of difficulty were designed in such a way that more difficult scenarios and levels required the player to manage more tasks simultaneously. The main objective of our pre-pilot experiment was to determine whether this mechanic made the game indeed more difficult. Accordingly, easier scenarios and levels of difficulty should be solved more often than more difficult ones. In the actual pilot study, we used the information gained from the pre-pilot and implemented DDA utilizing heart rate data to assess players' level of arousal. Consequently, the game should become more/less difficult when players' arousal was lower/higher than baseline heart rate to keep the players as long as possible within the game-loop and thereby affecting not only completion rates but also players' subjective experiences.

2 Pre-pilot Study

2.1 Aim

Aim of the pre-pilot experiment was to evaluate whether the implemented mechanisms to vary difficulty of the simulation work successfully in that the level of difficulty increases across the 3 game scenarios, and across 3 levels of each scenario.

2.2 Methods

Participants. In the experiment, 7 (3 male) undergraduate and postgraduate students participated voluntarily and provided informed consent prior to the experiment. Their average age was 27.9 years (*SD* = 6.79).

Dependent Variable. We were interested in in-game performance, this means whether participants completed a scenario successfully or not (coded 1 vs. 0, respectively) as well as in what time they completed the scenarios, in case they were successful. This information was derived from time stamped events in the log files for each scenario.

Procedure. Participants were invited to play the 3 game scenarios (see Fig. 1) in the following order: i. *Traffic Accident*, ii. *Buildings Fire,* and iii. *Train Crash*. For each game scenario participants had to play 3 different levels, starting with level 1 (easy), continuing with level 2 (medium), and finishing with level 3 (hard). Each game scenario and level had specific requirements for finishing it correctly and time limits: *Traffic Accident* had a limit of 5 min, *Buildings Fire* had 7.5 min and *Train Crash* 10 min. Before starting playing the actual games, participants went through an on-screen interactive tutorial for 2 min.

Game Description. *Emergency* scenarios simulate emergency situations and require players to coordinate emergency personnel efficiently, in order to handle life-threatening events and secure victims' lives. Emergency units involved in all game

Fig. 1. Screen shots from the 3 scenarios of the game, namely the *Traffic Accident* (left), the *Buildings Fire* (middle), and the *Train Crash* (right) to illustrate gameplay.

scenarios are fire fighters, paramedics, and ambulances. In each scenario, there is a predefined number of events occurring during the gameplay. During the *Traffic Accident,* emergency personnel has to evacuate injured individuals from vehicles involved in the accident (done by fire fighters), initially treat the injured passengers on site (paramedics) and then transfer them safely to hospital (ambulances). During the *Buildings Fire,* emergency personnel has to evacuate the burning buildings, extinguish existing fires, prevent further fire from spreading (by fire fighters), provide first aid (paramedics) and transfer injured people to hospital (ambulances). In the *Train Crash* scenario emergency personnel has to combine tasks from the two aforementioned scenarios, by evacuating injured individuals from all vehicles involved in the accident and extinguishing fires and preventing new vehicle to catch fire (fire fighters), then treating injured people on site (paramedics), and transfer them to the hospital (ambulances). In all three game scenarios, both emergency personnel as well as civilian bystanders can get hurt during gameplay. When wounded persons are not treated by paramedics quickly enough, they may succumb to their wounds. In that case, ambulance personnel nevertheless has to collect the bodies and transfer them to a hospital.

2.3 Outcomes

Analyzing in-game performance (see Table 1), we observed that our difficulty manipulation within and across scenarios seemed to be working. On the scenario level, successful completions decreased from the *Traffic Accident* scenario over the *Building Fire* to the *Train Crash* (i.e., 95% vs. 66% vs. 53%, respectively, see Table 1). This strengthened our assumption that the *Traffic Accident* scenario is in general easier to complete successfully than the *Building Fire* scenario, which is again easier to complete compared to the most advanced *Train Crash* scenario. Levels within each scenario, also showed increasing difficulty, especially in the *Building Fire* scenario and the *Train Crash* scenario. In the *Buildings Fire* there were more successful completions for the easy (86%) than for the medium (71%) and than for the hard level (43%). In the Train Crash we observed a very similar pattern of successful completions for the easy (100%), medium (43%), and hard level (14%, see Table 1). This overall pattern of results with increasing difficulty across and within scenarios was further substantiated considering the time spent at each game scenario and respective level. Looking at the time spent with each scenario despite completing successfully or not provides more fine-grained information. Again, we observed that as the game scenarios and levels progress from easier to more difficult across and within scenarios as the time needed to complete the respective scenarios increased accordingly. On average participants completed the *Traffic Accident* scenarios 52 s (*SD* = 34 s), the *Building Fire* scenarios 1 min and 39 s (*SD* = 1 min and 32 s), and the *Train Crash* scenarios 1 min and 16 s (*SD* = 1 min and 21 s) before the respective time limits. The same pattern of increasing average game completion time was also observed for the three levels of difficulty within each scenario, especially in the *Building Fire* and the *Train Crash* scenario. In the *Traffic Accident*, average time left until the time limit was reached was similar across the easy, medium, and hard level with 53 s, 55 s, and 50 s, respectively, probably indicating a learning effect on game handling. In the *Building Fire* scenarios the easy, medium, and hard level were finished on average 3 min and 1 s, 1 min and 30 s, and 26 s before the time limit, respectively. In the *Train Crash*, we observed the same pattern of game completion with on average 2 min and 55 s, 40 s and 11 s to the time limit for the easy, medium, and hard level, respectively. Taken together, results of the pre-pilot study demonstrated that the mechanic of adding tasks/events that need to be addressed simultaneously works well for adjusting the difficulty of the game and thus can be used for DDA in the pilot study.

Table 1. Pattern of successfully and not successfully completed levels of the simulation scenarios per participant (P1 to P7). Dark green = more than 1 min left upon completion; light green = less than 1 min left; red = scenario not completed. Remaining time in mm:ss format.

	Traffic Accident			Buildings Fire			Train Crash		
	Easy	Medium	Hard	Easy	Medium	Hard	Easy	Medium	Hard
P1	00:22	01:01	00:33	03:30	02:06	00:00	03:28	01:30	00:00
P2	00:41	00:58	00:45	04:06	01:45	00:19	03:01	00:00	00:00
P3	02:05	01:35	01:14	04:15	02:06	01:54	03:37	01:59	01:19
P4	00:35	00:58	01:43	00:00	03:06	00:00	02:34	01:14	00:00
P5	00:36	00:39	00:36	02:36	00:00	00:46	02:20	00:00	00:00
P6	00:01	00:00	00:12	02:42	00:00	00:00	02:28	00:00	00:00
P7	01:48	01:11	00:44	03:55	01:30	00:00	02:59	00:00	00:00

3 Pilot Study

3.1 Aim

Aim of the pilot study was to initially explore game experience of players during the non-adaptive and the adaptive version of the *Emergency* simulation in 3 scenarios of increasing difficulty. Additionally, feasibility of adaptations based on real-time heart rate data was evaluated.

3.2 Methods

Participants. Fifteen participants voluntarily completed the experiment. All provided signed consent prior to the study. For technical reasons data of 3 participants was partially or completely lost. For that reason, we only included data of 12 participants (5 males) in the following analyses. Their average age was 28.83 years (SD = 5.25).

Dependent Variables. Identical to the pre-pilot study, data on whether participants completed a scenario successfully or not (coded 1 vs. 0, respectively) as well as the time need to complete the scenarios were derived from time stamped events in the log files. From the log files, we also collected data related to the adaptations triggered during gameplay, this means, how often an adaptation of the game was triggered and whether this adaptation made the game easier or harder for the respective participant.

Furthermore, we used the German Flow-Short-Scale (FKS; [17]), a self-assessment instrument with 13 items and two subscales (namely *Fluency of performance* and *Absorption by activity)* which measure the flow during gameplay, using a Likert scale (from 1 = *completely disagree* to 7 = *completely agree*). The FKS questionnaire includes 3 additional questions to be answered on a 9-point Likert scale. The questions are Q1. *Compared to all the other activities I do, the current one is…* (1 = easy to 9 = difficult), Q2. *I think my abilities in this field are…* (1 = low to 9 = high), and Q3. *For me personally the current challenges are…* (1 = too low to 5 = just right and to 9 = too high). The questionnaire was administered twice, once after participants completed the non-adaptive and once after the adaptive version of the simulation.

At the end of the session, participants also had to answer an additional 8-item questionnaire asking them to directly compare the two played versions of Emergency (Questions: *Which version was better/easier/more pleasant to play/more stressful/more exciting/more challenging/more fascinating/more interesting*). By the time of answering the questionnaire, participants were not aware about whether they played the adaptive/non-adaptive version first.

Procedure. Participants again had to play 3 scenarios (see Fig. 2) of the simulation in its highest difficulty in the following order: i. *Traffic Accident* (level 3 - hard), ii. *Buildings Fire* (level 3 - hard), and iii. *Gas Station Fire* (level 3 – hard). They played this sequence of scenarios twice, once the initial non-adaptive version of the scenarios (see Sect. 2.2, *Games Description*) and once an adaptive version (see *Adaptive Games Description* below). Order of playing adaptive/non-adaptive versions was counterbalanced across participants (i.e. half of participants started with the adaptive version). Before starting to play the actual scenarios, participants completed an on-screen interactive tutorial for 2 min and then had a baseline measurement for 3 min, so that the system got calibrated on each participant's baseline heart rate. Each game scenario had a specific time limit, but finishing requirements differed between the two versions. For the non-adaptive version, finishing requirements were pre-defined, whereas for the adaptive version, finishing requirements were adapted dynamically based on the biofeedback of the players. The overall time limit of the *Traffic Accident* was 5 min, of the *Buildings Fire* 7.5 min and of the newly developed scenario *Gas Station Fire* 10 min.

Adaptive Game Description. The initial version of the *Traffic Accident* and *Buildings Fire* scenarios that were used in this experiment are already described for the pre-pilot experiment above. In the *Gas Station Fire* scenario, which was developed to create an even harder scenario, emergency personnel has to evacuate injured individuals from

Fig. 2. Screenshots illustrating the three scenarios *Traffic Accident* (left), the *Buildings Fire* (middle), and the *Gas Station Fire* (right).

burning vehicles as well as extinguish the intensive fire and prevent fire expansion (done by fire fighters), initially treat the injured passengers on site (paramedics) and then transfer them to hospital (ambulances).

The adaptive mode of those games does not affect the sort of events happening during the gameplay, but the frequency of their occurring and their difficulty. For example, if in a specific scenario there were 4 pre-specified fire events in total, but the participant's heart rate value fell at least 5 bpm below baseline (as acquired during the baseline measurement) for at least 10 s, then the scenario was adapted to the detected low arousal of the player by triggering the appearance of additional bystanders that got hurt, which could happen multiple times in each scenario. The 5 bpm threshold was defined based on previous pilot tests with the same game. On the opposite, if participants' heart rate increased at least 5 bpm over the respective baseline for at least 10 s, then the scenario was adapted to the detected high arousal and stress of the player by triggering a helpful action, like the appearance of a verticopter that assists transportation of an injured person to hospital, which could also happen multiple times in each scenario.

3.3 Outcomes

Analyzing the in-game performance based on the successful or not completion of each game, we observed decreased successful game completions across the game scenarios in both the adaptive and the non-adaptive versions (see Table 2). In the non-adaptive setting, successful completions decreased especially from the *Traffic Accident* scenario (60%) to the *Building Fire* (12%) and *Gas Station Fire* scenario (24%). In the adaptive setting successful completions were lower and again decreased from the *Traffic Accident,* over the *Building Fire* to the *Gas Station Fire* scenario (i.e., 30% vs. 12% vs. 0%). The results in both settings confirmed our assumption that the *Traffic Accident* scenario should be in general easier to complete than the *Building Fire* scenario. The newly developed *Gas Station Fire* scenario was of comparable difficulty as the latter. The results of the adaptive setting strengthened the assumption that the adaptive features of the game are sensible and do not make it too easy or difficult in comparison to the performance in the non-adaptive setting.

This overall pattern of results with increasing difficulty across scenarios in both versions and particularly so in the adaptive one, was further substantiated considering the time spent at each game scenario and respective level (see Table 2). We observed that as the game scenarios progress from easier to more difficult time left until reaching

Table 2. Pattern of successfully and not successfully completed levels of the simulation scenarios per participant (P1 to P12). Dark green = more than 1 min left upon completion; light green = less than 1 min left; red = scenario not completed. Remaining time in mm:ss format.

	Non-Adaptive Versions			Adaptive Versions		
	Traffic Accident (hard)	Buildings Fire (hard)	Gas Station (hard)	Traffic Accident (hard)	Buildings Fire (hard)	Gas Station (hard)
P1	00:49	00:00	00:00	00:00	00:00	00:00
P2	00:00	00:00	00:00	00:00	00:00	00:00
P3	00:00	00:00	00:00	00:00	00:00	00:00
P4	00:00	00:00	00:00	00:11	00:00	00:00
P5	00:04	00:00	00:00	00:00	00:00	00:00
P6	00:00	00:00	00:00	00:00	00:24	00:00
P7	00:50	02:41	01:55	00:58	00:00	00:00
P8	00:26	00:00	00:00	00:16	00:00	00:00
P9	00:00	00:00	00:00	00:00	00:00	00:00
P10	00:00	00:00	00:00	00:00	00:00	00:00
P11	01:02	00:00	00:00	00:00	00:00	00:00
P12	01:30	00:00	00:42	00:48	00:00	00:00

the time limit decreased. In the non-adaptive setting, on average participants completed the game 23 s (*SD* = 31 s) before the time limit on average for the *Traffic accident* and 13 s before the time limit for both the *Building Fire* (*SD* = 46 s) and for the *Gas Station Fire* (*SD* = 34 s). The same pattern was even more nuanced for the adaptive version. Participants finished the *Traffic Accident* – on average – 11 s (*SD* = 20 s), the *Building Fire* 2 s before the time limit was reached (*SD* = 6 s), and the *Gas Station Fire* scenario was not completed in time at all (*SD* = 0 s). Comparing results between the non-adaptive and the adaptive version, we observed that adaptations made players playing longer towards the time limit to complete the scenarios.

Importantly, the in-game data for the adaptive triggers that were activated during the gameplay indicated that in total a mean of 3.5 (*SD* = 2.47) helpful and a mean of 6.5 (*SD* = 2.02) demanding triggers occurred during the adaptive versions' gameplay reflecting that the game was indeed adapted due to changes in participants' heart rate.

As regards experienced flow during gameplay as assessed by the FKS there were no significant differences between the adaptive and non-adaptive version of the game in *Fluency of performance* and *Absorption by activity* as indicated by *t*-tests (both $p > .12$).

We also ran paired-samples *t*-tests to compare the ratings for the non-adaptive and adaptive version on the three 3 additional questions of the FKS. For the present context, the third one (*For me personally the current challenges are*... 1 = too low to 9 = too high) was the most important one. There was no significant difference between participants' ratings for the non-adaptive ($m = 5.75$, $SD = .97$) and adaptive condition ($m = 5.17$, $SD = 1.19$), $t_{(11)} = 1.629$, $p = .408$. However, testing mean ratings against the middle of the scale (5 = difficulty just right) indicated that the players rated challenges significantly higher than the middle of the scale for the non-adaptive $t_{(11)} = 2.691$, $p = .021$ but not the adaptive version $t_{(11)} = .484$, $p = .638$. For Q1 and Q2, there were no significant differences between the non-adaptive and adaptive version (both $p > .40$).

Finally, the results of the comparison between the non-adaptive and adaptive version by the non-parametric Wilcoxon test (to account for the small sample size; see Table 3) showed that the adaptive version of the game was perceived significantly more challenging and fascinating than the non-adaptive one. The non-adaptive one, however, was rated as significantly easier.

Table 3. Responses to the 8 questions regarding players' preference between the adaptive and non-adaptive version of the games. Significant differences are in bold.

Which version of the game was...	Non-adaptive version	Adaptive version	*V*	*p*-values
...better?	5	7	45.5	.59
...easier?	**11**	**1**	**6.5**	**<.01**
...more pleasant to play?	8	4	26	.27
...more stressful?	3	9	58.5	.09
...more exciting?	3	9	58.5	.09
...more challenging?	**2**	**10**	**65**	**<.05**
...more fascinating?	**2**	**10**	**65**	**<.05**
...more interesting?	4	8	52	.27

4 General Discussion

The present pilot study aimed at investigating the feasibility of DDA in a digital game-based emergency personnel training based on changes in players' heart rate. In a pre-pilot experiment, we determined that the implemented mechanisms to vary difficulty of the game worked. That is, the number of events that need to be managed simultaneously influenced completion rates of players across and within the 3 game scenarios. In the actual pilot study, an adaptive and a non-adaptive version of the game were compared. Results indicated that the DDA based on players' heart rate altered completion rates and subjective user experience. Importantly, feasibility of DDA in a game-based learning or training scenario using heart rate was demonstrated on three outcome levels:

(i) *Completion rates*: Generally, descriptive completion rates as well as time left were lower in the adaptive version as compared to the non-adaptive one. As desired, the DDA kept the players as long as possible within the game-loop to train such stressful situations when coordinating emergency personnel. Hence, heart rate seems to be a reasonable metric for players arousal and stress, which is in line with previous research [15, 16, 18].

(ii) *User experience*: Participants, who were unaware of the true nature of the pilot study, experienced the adaptive version of the game more challenging and fascinating. On the other hand, the non-adaptive game was rated easier. No differences were found in the perceived flow of the players, which might be attributable to the limited sample size. More importantly though, difficulty of the non-adaptive version was rated to be significantly higher than "just right", while this was not the case for the adaptive version of the game. This is in line with our argument that the implemented DDA worked as expected by making the game neither too easy nor too difficult.

(iii) *Adaptive triggers*: DDA worked in both ways. That is, not only did the game become more difficult due to demanding triggers, but also helpful triggers were activated making the game easier for the players. In this context, it would be interesting to investigate whether and in which way user experience is affected by the number of helpful or demanding triggers within a game. This would not only further substantiate the feasibility of DDA using heart rate but also its validity. However, with the limited sample size of the current pilot study we refrained from reporting these exploratory analyses in the results section. Nevertheless, our current data tend to support the validity of the approach by observing (marginally) significant correlations between the number of helpful triggers that occurred and the perception of the non-adaptive version as easier (r = .57, p = .051) as well as between the number of demanding triggers and the perception of the adaptive version as more stressful (r = .55, p = .066) and challenging (r = .81, p = .001). However, these results need to be treated with great caution. Future studies with larger sample sizes and more dedicated study designs need to investigate this in more detail.

Future studies might also investigate how DDA is realized within a game and whether current results can be generalized to different contexts (e.g. math learning games). In the current study, adjustments made were explicit to the player by prompts indicating that the game became easier or more difficult (e.g., an additional bystander was hurt). In contrast, one could realize such DDA hidden from the players or/and investigate players reaction to adjustments. This is the case, for instance, in many racing car games when employing rubber banding (cf. [10]). Accordingly, dynamic difficulty occurs in the background rather than explicitly notifying the player. This might influence players' experience because such adjustments explicitly evaluate players' skills.

Taken together, current results suggest that heart rate is a feasible means to dynamically adjust the difficulty of gameplay in real-time. The adaptive version of the game exposed players longer to the game and thus the training situation. Accordingly, it was rated more challenging but also fascinating. These results offer first evidence for a better understanding of how adaptive mechanisms based on real-time physiological data might be implemented to optimize game-based learning.

References

1. Kiili, K., Moeller, K., Ninaus, M.: Evaluating the effectiveness of a game-based rational number training - in-game metrics as learning indicators. Comput. Educ. **120**, 13–28 (2018). https://doi.org/10.1016/j.compedu.2018.01.012
2. Nebel, S., Ninaus, M.: New perspectives on game-based assessment with process data and physiological signals. In: Ifenthaler, D., Kim, Y. (eds.) Game-Based Assessment Revisited. Springer (in Press)
3. Streicher, A., Smeddinck, J.D.: Personalized and adaptive serious games. In: Dörner, R., Göbel, S., Kickmeier-Rust, M., Masuch, M., Zweig, K. (eds.) Entertainment Computing and Serious Games. LNCS, vol. 9970, pp. 332–377. Springer, Cham (2016). https://doi.org/10.1007/978-3-319-46152-6_14
4. Smith, S.P., Blackmore, K., Nesbitt, K.: A meta-analysis of data collection in serious games research. In: Loh, C.S., Sheng, Y., Ifenthaler, D. (eds.) Serious Games Analytics. AGL, pp. 31–55. Springer, Cham (2015). https://doi.org/10.1007/978-3-319-05834-4_2
5. Schneider, J., Börner, D., van Rosmalen, P., Specht, M.: Augmenting the Senses: a review on sensor-based learning support. Sensors **15**, 4097–4133 (2015). https://doi.org/10.3390/s150204097
6. Xiao, X., Wang, J.: Context and cognitive state triggered interventions for mobile MOOC learning. In: Proceedings of the 18th ACM International Conference on Multimodal Interaction - ICMI 2016, pp. 378–385. ACM Press, New York (2016). https://doi.org/10.1145/2993148.2993177
7. Nourbakhsh, N., Chen, F., Wang, Y., Calvo, R.A.: Detecting users' cognitive load by galvanic skin response with affective interference. ACM Trans. Interact. Intell. Syst. **7**, 1–20 (2017). https://doi.org/10.1145/2960413
8. Witte, M., Ninaus, M., Kober, S.E., Neuper, C., Wood, G.: Neuronal correlates of cognitive control during gaming revealed by near-infrared spectroscopy. PLoS ONE **10**, e0134816 (2015). https://doi.org/10.1371/journal.pone.0134816
9. Ninaus, M., et al.: Neurophysiological methods for monitoring brain activity in serious games and virtual environments: a review. Int. J. Technol. Enhanc. Learn. **6**, 78 (2014). https://doi.org/10.1504/IJTEL.2014.060022
10. Pagulayan, R.J., Keeker, K., Wixon, D., Romero, R.L., Fuller, T.: User-centered design in games. In: Sears, A., Jacko, J., (eds.) Handbook for Human-Computer Interaction in Interactive Systems, pp. 1–28. CRC Press (2001)
11. Klinkenberg, S., Straatemeier, M., van der Maas, H.L.J.: Computer adaptive practice of maths ability using a new item response model for on the fly ability and difficulty estimation. Comput. Educ. **57**, 1813–1824 (2011). https://doi.org/10.1016/j.compedu.2011.02.003
12. Greipl, S., Moeller, K., Ninaus, M.: Potential and limits of game-based learning. Int. J. Technol. Enhanc. Learn. (in Press)
13. Yerkes, R.M., Dodson, J.D.: The relation of strength of stimulus to rapidity of habit-formation. J. Comp. Neurol. Psychol. **18**, 459–482 (1908). https://doi.org/10.1002/cne.920180503
14. Csikszentmihalyi, M.: Flow: the psychology of optimal experience. Harper & Row (1990)
15. Mandryk, R.L., Atkins, M.S.: A fuzzy physiological approach for continuously modeling emotion during interaction with play technologies. Int. J. Hum Comput Stud. **65**, 329–347 (2007). https://doi.org/10.1016/j.ijhcs.2006.11.011

16. Drachen, A., Nacke, L.E., Yannakakis, G., Pedersen, A.L.: Correlation between heart rate, electrodermal activity and player experience in first-person shooter games. In: Proceedings of the 5th ACM SIGGRAPH Symposium on Video Games - Sandbox 2010, pp. 49–54. ACM Press, New York, (2010). https://doi.org/10.1145/1836135.1836143
17. Rheinberg, F., Vollmeyer, R., Engeser, S.: Die Erfassung des Flow-Erlebens [measuring flow-experience]. In: Diagnostik von Motivation und Selbstkonzept, pp. 261–279. Hogrefe, Göttingen (2003)
18. Jerritta, S., Murugappan, M., Nagarajan, R., Wan, K.: Physiological signals based human emotion Recognition: a review. In: 2011 IEEE 7th International Colloquium on Signal Processing and its Applications, pp. 410–415. IEEE (2011). https://doi.org/10.1109/CSPA.2011.5759912

Modelling the Quality of Visual Creations in Iconoscope

Antonios Liapis(✉), Daniele Gravina, Emil Kastbjerg, and Georgios N. Yannakakis

Institute of Digital Games, University of Malta, Msida, Malta
{antonios.liapis,daniele.gravina,georgios.n.yannakakis}@um.edu.mt, kastbjerg@gmail.com

Abstract. This paper presents the current state of the online game Iconoscope and analyzes the data collected from almost 45 months of continuous operation. Iconoscope is a freeform creation game which aims to foster the creativity of its users through diagrammatic lateral thinking, as users are required to depict abstract concepts as icons which may be misinterpreted by other users as different abstract concepts. From users' responses collected from an online gallery of all icons drawn with Iconoscope, we collect a corpus of over 500 icons which contain annotations of visual appeal. Several machine learning algorithms are tested for their ability to predict the appeal of an icon from its visual appearance and other properties. Findings show the impact of the representation on the model's accuracy and highlight how such a predictive model of quality can be applied to evaluate new icons (human-authored or generated).

Keywords: Online game · Human creativity · Crowdsourcing · Deep learning · Mixed-initiative design · Computational creators

1 Introduction

While creativity has been a source of awe since the ancient years, as an activity of the gods in us [15], modern-day scholars of creativity have established that creative skills can be taught [4]. Indeed, creativity is increasingly being considered as an explicit educational objective within formal education [2,17]. From *LEGO* to *Minecraft* (Mojang, 2011), games have been fostering the creativity of their players in a multitude of ways (construction, exploration, storytelling). Focusing on the theoretical framework of *creative emotional reasoning* [18], re-framing (i.e. changing a routine for performing tasks or a pattern of associations between facts, emotions or actions) can be accomplished through an external stimulus that causes disruption. Re-framing leads to semantic, visual, and emotional *lateral thinking* [4], which respectively target a shift in conceptual structures, visual associations, and one's perception of the effect that a creative solution will have on others' emotional states. A game that is designed explicitly around these concepts would be more targeted in the type of creative processes it elicits. When

A. Liapis et al. (Eds.): GALA 2019, LNCS 11899, pp. 129–138, 2019.
https://doi.org/10.1007/978-3-030-34350-7_13

the game is used in the classroom and with teachers' intervention, it can be a powerful tool in *teaching for creativity* [7]. When the game is played in the wild, however, it would be valuable if the system could predict the visual impact of certain creative outcomes to help provide more targeted stimuli for disruption.

This paper revisits the Iconoscope project which was designed and developed in 2015 [11] and expanded with a web interface in 2017 [10]. Conceived initially as part of the FP7 ICT project *C2Learn* (project No: 318480), the game was intended as one of several classroom activities for young learners, with the teacher acting as facilitator and moderator. In this first version of Iconoscope, players would share a mobile device to draw an icon so that their group members could not always guess which concept it represents. Towards the end of *C2Learn*, and in order to maintain a persistent platform for playing Iconoscope in the classroom or in the wild, the game was redesigned to be played individually on a website in which all user creations would be publicly displayed. The game was further expanded for the purposes of the Erasmus+ project *eCrisis* (Europe in Crisis) with adjustments to the drawing interface and the way concepts were presented. To further enhance its usefulness in the classroom, a Do-It-Yourself (DIY) version of Iconoscope was developed to allow teachers to customize the list of concepts. When played in a classroom, DIY Iconoscope allows educators to discuss and play with specific topics of *eCrisis* such as social inclusion and integration. However, this paper will not focus on DIY Iconsocope but instead will analyze the users' data from the 45 months that Iconoscope has been online.

Given the long-term use of Iconoscope within the classroom (as part of the *C2Learn* and *eCrisis* projects) and in the wild (as the game is available to all on a public website), a large dataset of icons has been collected. Users have also engaged with the public gallery of the Iconoscope website, rating how appealing they find each icon and guessing which concept it represents. Given the recent advances of machine learning, this rich dataset of diagrams and user feedback could be used to train computational models of users' visual styles. This paper takes the first step in this computational modelling task by building predictive models of the crowdsourced visual quality of icons, reaching accuracies as high as 80% when combining image data with metadata on the icon's colors and shapes.

2 Machine Learning for Visuals

Machine learning grants the ability to automatically detect patterns in raw data, such as images, text, or audio. While conventional machine learning methods were held back by the requirement that raw data should be transformed into a suitable representation via a handcrafted feature construction process [1], *deep learning* [5] can circumvent this by automatically learning these representations from raw data through a nonlinear composition of simple data transformations.

Convolutional neural networks (CNNs) [9] are deep learning models applied to 2-dimensional inputs such as images or time-series data. CNNs employ a sequence of two-dimensional trainable filters (convolutions), nonlinear activation functions and pooling operations on the raw input, resulting in a hierarchy of increasingly complex features. By design, CNNs are able to encode the spatial information of their inputs. Since their success in the 2012 ImageNet competition [8], CNNs have become the dominant approach for almost all visual detection and recognition tasks [13,16,20].

Deep learning has also been applied in multimodal learning tasks [22] which involve learning joint representation across multiple and (usually) heterogeneous information sources. Several studies have shown that combining multiple sources of information results in overall better performance, especially when the data size is limited or different tasks need to be learned simultaneously [14]. Literature in multimodal learning distinguishes between early and late fusion: early fusion aggregates information of different modalities via simple element-wise averaging, product and/or concatenation [14], while in late fusion high-level representations for each modality are computed separately and then fused via simple averaging or by stacking another learning model [19]. There is no consensus on which approach is better, and usually it depends on the task at hand.

This paper explores how to model the human perception of visual quality based on users' ratings. We test how different deep learning architectures, inputs and late fusion of different modalities (icons' images and metadata) affect the accuracy of a simple classification task (high rated vs. low rated icons).

3 The Game

Iconoscope is a creation game focusing on the visual depiction of semantic concepts in a creative fashion [12]. Creativity is fostered due to the constrained medium (as players must compose an icon from a small set of primitive shapes and colors) and due to the demand for ambiguity (as players must create icons that will be hard to guess). The game was initially designed for co-located play by a group of learners [11], but has been redesigned as an online game (*web*Iconoscope) which allows players to anonymously submit icons to a public database where all users can browse and provide feedback asynchronously [10].

Game Loop and Drawing Interface: In the online version of Iconoscope, players first select their language of choice (English, Greek and German translations of the game are available) and follow a tutorial. Players are then shown a list of different *concept triplets*, each in a different post-it note. Players select one of the three concepts in a concept triplet, and enter the drawing interface with the triplet and the chosen concept highlighted (top-left corner of Fig. 1a). In the drawing interface, players can add or remove shapes (among the available types on the bottom-left corner of Fig. 1a), change their color through the palette in the top-right corner of Fig. 1a, and move, rotate or resize them by dragging their relevant anchor points. At the same time, computational assistants can provide alternative icons to the user if the latter taps on one of their portraits (top of Fig. 1a). Assistants use computational intelligence methods to change the shapes and colors of the user's icon, and the user can choose to replace their creation with a computer-generated one or ignore it. Each of the four assistants has a different process for generating icons; more details can be found in [10]. When

(a) The Iconoscope drawing interface

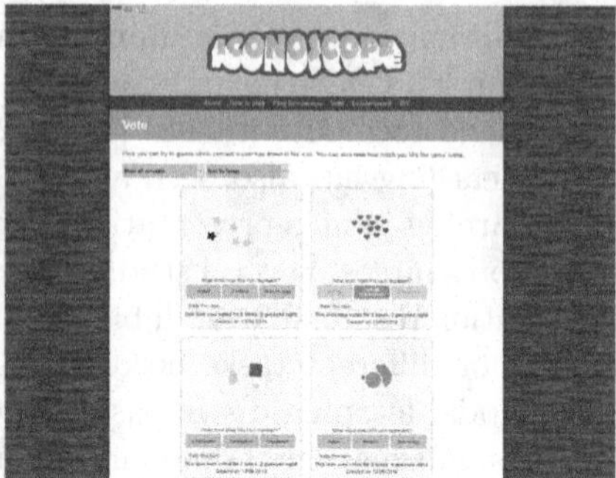

(b) The Iconoscope voting interface

Fig. 1. Interaction methods with the Iconoscope game and website

the player is happy with their icon, or after a maximum of 5 minutes, the icon is sent to the database where everyone can see it and provide feedback (see below).

Concept Triplets: Creativity in Iconoscope lies in the interpretation of a semantic concept through an abstract visual icon that can mislead others to pick different candidate concepts. This is achieved through *concept triplets*, i.e. groupings of three semantically linked concepts, each consisting of one or more words. The three concepts can be linked by lexical similarity (e.g. "Lead, Govern, Dominate"), common social issues (e.g. "Sexual orientation, Gender, Human rights") or overarching theme (e.g. online identities in "Avatar, Communication, Expression").

Public User Feedback Interface: All icons are stored in a database and shown on the Iconoscope website[1]. As with the entire website, the "voting" page (see Fig. 1b) is accessible to any visitor, who can offer feedback anonymously on any of the icons in the database. Under each icon, the three concepts of the triplet selected by the icon's author are shown. The user can attempt to guess which of these three concepts is depicted, and can also see how many other users have guessed correctly. Once the user chooses one of these three buttons, they receive feedback on whether they were right or wrong and can not guess again for this icon. The website allows each IP to make one guess per icon. Additionally, users can "rate" how much they like each icon, on a scale between 1 and 5 stars. Similar to guessing the concept, one rating per icon is allowed from each IP.

Since icons created via Iconoscope are intended to be ambiguous and difficult to guess correctly, the website includes a leaderboard which shows the top 10 icons with the highest ambiguity score. This ambiguity score is calculated based on a balance between correct and incorrect guesses of users, while also rewarding icons which have received more guesses in total; see [10] for more details.

[1] http://iconoscope.institutedigitalgames.com/vote.php.

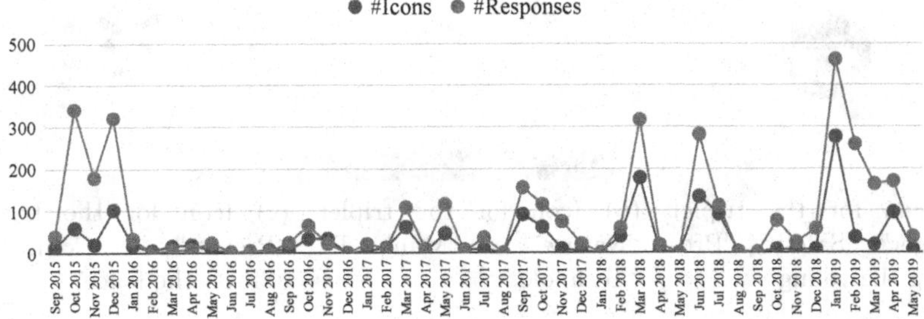

Fig. 2. Monthly interactions with the drawing interface and the voting interface.

4 Data Collection

The online version of Iconoscope was launched in September of 2015. This Section analyzes the data collected from Iconoscope since its launch until 23 May 2019, which is 45 months (almost 4 years) of continuous operation.

Icons Created and User Feedback: After curation by educators and administrators for offensive content and cleanup of corrupt data, a total of 1555 icons were collected during the 45 months examined. These icons received 3774 user responses through the website's gallery: these responses include guesses, ratings, or both. Figure 2 shows the distribution of these interactions over time.

Favored Concepts: In terms of the concept triplets and the selected concepts among them, it is not surprising that some of the concepts were favored more than others for creating icons. The most popular triplet was "Nature, Mankind, Technology" (164 icons), likely because all three concepts seem intuitively straightforward to draw. In contrast, the least popular triplets are "Proactive, Reactive, Inactive" (24 icons) and "Tolerance, Acceptance, Solidarity" (30 icons) which consist of much more abstract concepts. As expected, the most commonly depicted concept was "Nature" (in 102 icons) followed by "Push" (76 icons), "Play" (70 icons), and "Team" (65 icons).

Icon Properties: The icons collected during the 45 months of Iconoscope contained a total of 7912 shapes. While this amounts to 6.1 shapes per icon, icons most often had one shape (14%), two shapes (11%), three shapes (12%) or four shapes (10%). However, 27 icons included 20 or more shapes and the highest number of shapes in one icon was 119. In terms of types of shapes favored, circles were most common (22% of all shapes) followed by elongated rounded rectangles (17%) and squares (14%). From observations of created icons, rounded rectangles were often used as lines (as Iconoscope does not include lines).

In terms of the icons' colors, it is not surprising that 30% of icons only had one color (as 14% of icons had one shape in any case). Most other icons had either two colors (23% of all icons), three colors (18%) or four colors (12%), although there were also several icons with 10 or 11 colors (9 icons and 4 icons, respectively). While all possible colors in icons are 11, only 10 are options on the

(a) Icon for the triplet "Danger", "Safety", "Protecting the young"

(b) Icon for the triplet "Nature", "Mankind", "Technology"

(c) Icon for the triplet "Protest", "Conform", "Sit on the fence"

Fig. 3. Some of the icons rated with the maximum score (5); these icons had the highest number of ratings. In total, 142 icons received an average rating of 5.

interface (eight hues, black, and white). New shapes start as gray, but players do not have an option to recolor shapes to gray. Gray shapes were surprisingly common (32% of all shapes); it is obvious that users often chose not to recolor their shapes. Other popular colors were red (14% of all shapes) and yellow (10%).

Playtime: In terms of the time users spent drawing each icon (i.e. *playtime*), the average playtime was 133 seconds. Users seem able to finish icons fairly quickly (28% of icons were created in under one minute). This is not surprising, considering that many icons had one or two shapes. Indeed, there is a strong positive correlation between the number of shapes and playtime (Pearson correlation coefficient $\rho = 0.47$). On the other hand, 12% of icons were submitted automatically by the system when the time ran out (5 min); this indicates that some users could not identify how to submit icons manually in the interface.

Use of Assistants: It is worthwhile to investigate how users interacted with the four included computational assistants who serve as aides to players' creativity. In total, users selected assistants to receive their suggestions 2575 times; out of those, users applied the suggestions to replace their own icon 499 times. The assumption is therefore that only in 19% of instances were the computational assistants' creations considered helpful—or, to be precise, better than the user's own sketch. A confounding factor, however, is the fact that assistants animated and showed a dialog balloon at random intervals, which may have urged users to select them even when they did not want to change their design.

Public Feedback: As noted above, a total of 3774 responses were collected from the public gallery of the Iconoscope website. Out of those, 835 responses included a rating of the icon in terms of appeal. Such ratings were only offered on 521 of the 1555 icons; it can be assumed that only some of the icons captured the attention of the audience enough to receive ratings (even if that rating was bad). Figure 3 shows a sample of the highest rated icons for different concept triplets. Moreover, 3710 out of 3774 responses included attempts at guessing the depicted concept. Most icons were annotated in this fashion, as 1370 of the 1555 icons (88%) received at least one attempt at guessing the concept. Most icons received one or two guesses, with only 34 icons receiving more than 10 guesses.

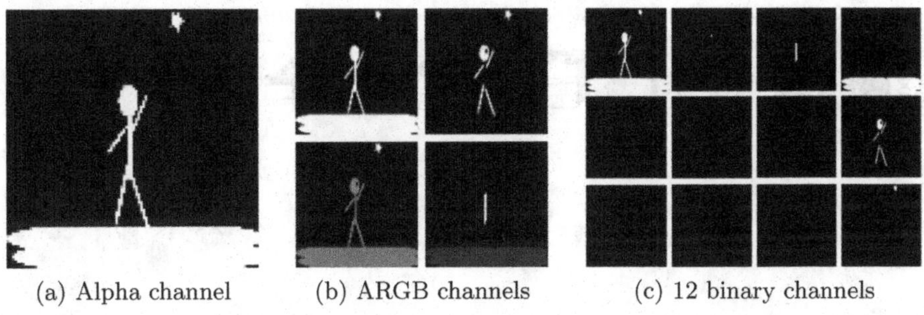

(a) Alpha channel (b) ARGB channels (c) 12 binary channels

Fig. 4. Example pre-processing of the image inputs for the image of Fig. 3b.

5 Modelling Visual Quality

As noted in Sect. 1, the corpus of icons and user feedback can be used to train computational models via machine learning. As a first exploration in this vein, this paper focuses on training models that can predict an icon's visual appeal, using the crowd's ratings of appeal as the ground truth. The application of such a model could be to predict the visual quality of icons that have not received ratings (less than a third of icons have received any rating on appeal). More ambitiously, such a model could be used by the computational assistants which attempt to generate alternatives to the user's icon; instead of or in tandem with the assistants' current objectives, assistants can attempt to improve the predicted visual quality of their generated icons. The next sections discuss how the data is prepared and the results of different machine learning experiments.

Preprocessing: For the task of predicting the rating of icons, the dataset consists of the 521 icons that received at least one rating from users, coupled with the average value of users' ratings for each icon. In order to simplify the task of predicting visual quality, we treat it as a *binary classification* task between "high" and "low" rated icons. To assess where the split between high and low rated icons should be, the average μ of all icons' ratings is calculated ($\mu = 3.15$). In order to avoid ambiguous annotations, the icons with an average rating within 5% of μ, i.e. $[2.99, 3.31]$ are ignored; 84 icons in total are ignored in this fashion. Icons with an average rating below 2.99 are treated as low rated, and icons with average rating over 3.31 are treated as high rated. This split yields 247 high and 190 low rated icons. To validate our machine learning findings, we apply 10-fold cross-validation and apply oversampling to the least common class in the training and the test set individually; this results in 445 training samples and 51 testing samples on average. The baseline accuracy (random choice) is 50%.

This paper explores several ways of processing the icon to be used as input for the machine learning task. The 2D image of the icon is the most straightforward input. Each image is cropped to the icon's bounding box (removing unnecessary empty space) and scaled to 100 by 100 pixels. After this, the scaled-down image is treated here in four different ways (see Fig. 4): as a binary *alpha* channel (transparent versus non-transparent), as RGB channels, as ARGB channels (including

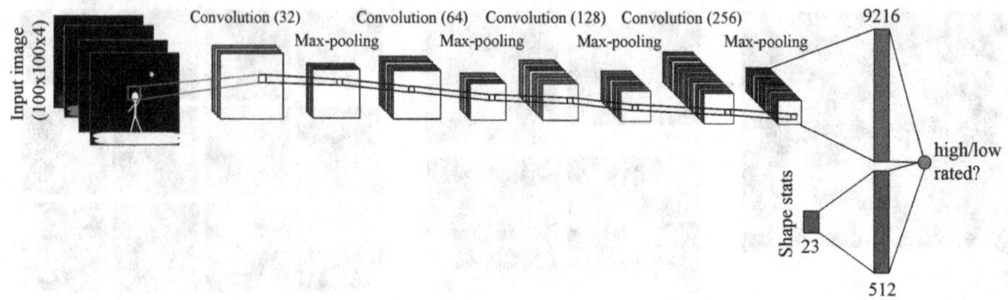

Fig. 5. Late fusion architecture for image channels (here: ARGB) and shape stats.

transparency information) and using a custom 12-binary channel format based on the 11 possible shapes' colors in Iconoscope and the alpha binary channel. In addition to the image, we test the *shape statistics (stats)* of the icon as another modality of input. The shape stats make up a vector of 23 real numbers listing the number of primitives for each possible shape (10), the total number of different shapes (1), the number of primitives for each possible color (11), and the total number of different colors (1).

Results: A number of machine learning structures and input modalities were tested: Table 1 shows the results of these experiments. All networks end in one output node which predicts high (1) or low (0) rated icons. When using shape stats as the only output, an artificial neural network (ANN) is used with a single fully-connected hidden layer of 512 nodes. When using only image inputs, the output of the convolutional network is flattened into a vector and connected to the single output. When combining images with shape stats, the flattened vector from the CNN is concatenated with the 512 nodes which process the shape stats (late multimodal fusion, see Fig. 5). Based on extensive parameter tuning, the CNN we use has four layers of convolution (of size 5×5 with zero padding), with 32, 64, 128 and 256 filters, each followed by a max-pooling layer; this results in a flat vector of 9216 features. Finally, we tested a pre-trained VGG19 [20] which is a very deep architecture trained on the vast ImageNet image corpus; the VGG19 produces a flat vector of 4608 features which is concatenated with the 512 nodes from shape stats or fed directly (image-only) to the output. The VGG19 model accepts RGB images only, and training is only applied to the final layer's weights. All nodes use an ELU activation function [3] and the output of each hidden layer is normalized via batch normalization [6]. All models were trained for 20 epochs, while to avoid overfitting we save the best model obtained during the training process based on validation accuracy. Since the training data is sparse, we use dropout after each hidden layer [21] and reported results in each case are the best across three different dropout values tested (0.1, 0.3, 0.5).

Based on Table 1, we notice that including shape stats generally increased performance. The exception is VGG19, which had comparable accuracy with or without shapes (best performing fold is with images alone: 77%); since VGG19 is trained on millions of real-world images, it is not surprising that it is strong

Table 1. Test accuracies (%) for different networks and inputs, averaged from 10-fold cross-validation. Standard deviation across folds is shown in parentheses.

Input	Image	Image & shape stats
Shapes only (NN)	68.54 (6.26)	
Alpha (CNN)	64.27 (5.31)	69.40 (5.94)
RGB (CNN)	64.71 (5.55)	67.53 (6.29)
ARGB (CNN)	64.18 (5.04)	67.88 (5.97)
12 channels (CNN)	64.45 (4.79)	68.95 (5.36)
RGB (VGG19)	68.12 (5.35)	68.33 (6.21)

in visual pattern detection. Surprisingly, using shapes alone as input achieves comparable accuracies to CNN models (best fold: 81%). Overall, all CNNs were well performing when combining image data with shape stats as input, with the alpha channel component achieving the highest accuracy on average (69%) while the ARGB component reached the highest accuracy at the best fold (83%).

6 Conclusion

Results of Sect. 5 show that average accuracy when predicting visual quality is not very high, but metadata regarding shapes' types and colors can help in that regard. Current models of visual quality (e.g. the best fold) can be used to rank all icons in the corpus, even if these have not received any ratings from users, or even to predict visual quality for new icons as they are created. Predicted visual quality can also be used as a constraint for the computational creators' search processes, ensuring that their suggestions are at least predicted to be high rated. Future work should explore other deep learning models using the icons (and shape stats) as input to predict metrics such as the ambiguity score (based on users' guesses), playtime, or—more ambitiously—the concept being depicted.

References

1. Ballard, D.H., Hinton, G.E., Sejnowski, T.J.: Parallel visual computation. Nature **306**(5938), 21 (1983)
2. Cachia, R., et al.: Creativity in schools in Europe: a survey of teachers (2009). http://ipts.jrc.ec.europa.eu/publications/pub.cfm?id=2940. Accessed Nov 2016
3. Clevert, D.A., Unterthiner, T., Hochreiter, S.: Fast and accurate deep network learning by exponential linear units (ELUs). arXiv preprint arXiv:1511.07289 (2015)
4. De Bono, E.: Lateral Thinking: Creativity Step by Step. Harper Collins (2010)
5. Goodfellow, I., Bengio, Y., Courville, A.: Deep Learning. MIT press (2016)
6. Ioffe, S., Szegedy, C.: Batch normalization: accelerating deep network training by reducing internal covariate shift. arXiv preprint arXiv:1502.03167 (2015)

7. Jeffrey, B., Craft, A.: Teaching creatively and teaching for creativity: distinctions and relationships. Educ. Stud. **30**(1), 77–87 (2004)
8. Krizhevsky, A., Sutskever, I., Hinton, G.E.: ImageNet classification with deep convolutional neural networks. In: Advances in Neural Information Processing Systems (2012)
9. LeCun, Y., Bengio, Y., et al.: Convolutional networks for images, speech, and time series. Handb. Brain Theory Neural Netw. **3361**(10), 1995 (1995)
10. Correia, J., Ciesielski, V., Liapis, A. (eds.): EvoMUSART 2017. LNCS, vol. 10198. Springer, Cham (2017). https://doi.org/10.1007/978-3-319-55750-2
11. Liapis, A., Hoover, A.K., Yannakakis, G.N., Alexopoulos, C., Dimaraki, E.V.: Motivating visual interpretations in iconoscope: designing a game for fostering creativity. In: Proceedings of the Conference on the Foundations of Digital Games (2015)
12. Liapis, A., Yannakakis, G.N., Alexopoulos, C., Lopes, P.: Can computers foster human users' creativity? theory and praxis of mixed-initiative co-creativity. Digit. Cult. Educ. (DCE) **8**(2), 136–152 (2016)
13. Makantasis, K., Doulamis, A., Doulamis, N., Psychas, K.: Deep learning based human behavior recognition in industrial workflows. In: Proceedings of International Conference on Image Processing, pp. 1609–1613. IEEE (2016)
14. Park, E., Han, X., Berg, T.L., Berg, A.C.: Combining multiple sources of knowledge in deep CNNS for action recognition. In: Proceedings of the Winter Conference on Applications of Computer Vision (WACV), pp. 1–8. IEEE (2016)
15. Plato, C.D.: The Collected Dialogues. Princeton University Press (1961)
16. Redmon, J., Divvala, S., Girshick, R., Farhadi, A.: You only look once: unified, real-time object detection. In: Procedings of the IEEE Conference on Computer Vision and Pattern Recognition, pp. 779–788 (2016)
17. Sawyer, K.: Educating for innovation. Thinking Skills Creativity **1**, 41–48 (2006)
18. Scaltsas, T., Alexopoulos, C.: Creating creativity through emotive thinking. In: Proceedings of the World Congress of Philosophy (2013)
19. Simonyan, K., Zisserman, A.: Two-stream convolutional networks for action recognition in videos. In: Advances in Neural Information Processing Systems (2014)
20. Simonyan, K., Zisserman, A.: Very deep convolutional networks for large-scale image recognition. arXiv preprint arXiv:1409.1556 (2014)
21. Srivastava, N., Hinton, G., Krizhevsky, A., Sutskever, I., Salakhutdinov, R.: Dropout: a simple way to prevent neural networks from overfitting. J. Mach. Learn. Res. **15**(1), 1929–1958 (2014)
22. Srivastava, N., Salakhutdinov, R.R.: Multimodal learning with deep boltzmann machines. In: Advances in Neural Information Processing Systems (2012)

Andromeda: A Personalised Crisis Management Training Toolkit

Paris Mavromoustakos Blom[1](✉), Sander Bakkes[2], and Pieter Spronck[1]

[1] Department of Cognitive Science and Artificial Intelligence, Tilburg University, Tilburg, The Netherlands
{p.mavromoustakosblom,p.spronck}@uvt.nl

[2] Center for Game Research, Utrecht University, Utrecht, The Netherlands
s.c.j.bakkes@uu.nl

Abstract. Over the last decades, technological advancements have enabled the gamification of many of modern society's processes. Crisis management training has benefited from the introduction of human-machine interfaces (HMIs) and wearable monitoring sensors. Crisis responders are nowadays able to attend training sessions through computer-simulated crisis scenarios while simultaneously receiving real-time feedback on their operational and cognitive performance. Such training sessions would require a considerable amount of resources if they were to be recreated in the real world. We introduce Andromeda, a toolkit designed to allow remote-access, real-time crisis management training personalisation through an applied game. Andromeda consists of a browser-based dashboard which enables real-time monitoring and adaptation of crisis management scenarios, and a remote server which securely stores, analyses and serves training data. In this paper, we discuss Andromeda's design concepts and propose future studies using this toolkit. Our main focal points are player stress response modelling and automated crisis management training adaptation.

Keywords: Crisis management · Game-based training · Serious games · Personalised games · Real-time adaptation · Player monitoring

1 Introduction

Traditional crisis management training is a paper-based, collaborative dynamic exercise [1]. In simple words, during training, a team of crisis responders are alerted and introduced to a simulated crisis scenario which they have to "solve" rapidly through efficient teamwork. Such training sessions are held frequently so that crisis responders are aware of all the possible threats and maintain a high level of preparedness [2].

However, certain weaknesses in the crisis training scheme have been identified [3]. First of all, often at times training sessions fail to induce high amounts of stress onto the trainees, as expected to happen in a real-life crisis situation. Ideally, crisis management training involves several highly stressful components (e.g.

A. Liapis et al. (Eds.): GALA 2019, LNCS 11899, pp. 139–147, 2019.
https://doi.org/10.1007/978-3-030-34350-7_14

information under/overload, time pressure, peer/media/public pressure etc.). Even though such components are often included in the training scenarios, training sessions are focused towards trainee decision making, meaning that the effect of such stressors is given little attention. Moreover, mainly due to the training scheme's collaborative nature, trainees receive limited individual-level feedback on their performance. Trainee assessment is mostly done at team-level, which means that trainee performance is not measured individually, but with respect to the contribution to the overall team's performance.

This study aims to address the above two points; in order to shift the focus of crisis management training towards the individual trainee, we provide a personalised crisis management training environment through adjustable in-game components and just-in-time, individual-level feedback. Secondly, to study the effects of stress-inducing mechanisms during training sessions, we monitor individual trainee operational performance and stress responses through a real-time monitoring dashboard and wearable physiological sensors.

Our study is based on the dynamic game engine of the Mayor's game [4]. The Mayor's game engine enables the creation of crisis management training scenarios which can be adapted in real-time through adjustable in-game components. Over the last four years, the Mayor's Game has been widely used by crisis management experts in the Netherlands [5]. In the game, players act as the mayor of a fictional town undergoing a crisis. The crisis needs to be solved by answering a series of dilemmas for which, additional information is provided by non-player characters (NPCs) representing various institutions, such as the town's police or fire department. A screenshot of the Mayor's Game is shown in Fig. 1. Our study is aimed towards the training of the administrative crisis management team (off-site) and not the operational crisis management team (on-site), given that the Mayor's Game has been implemented to be played by administrative staff [4]. An example scenario of the Mayor's Game can be found in [6].

2 Related Work

Games have been used as a medium for crisis management training for decades. After World War II, military games were developed at Harvard University and Massachusetts Institute of technology to study the military and political dimensions of crisis management [2]. In more recent years, especially after '9–11', nation-wide crisis management simulations have been run in order to prepare both governmental and local safety agencies for terrorist threats [7]. As a natural consequence, researchers have been investigating ways in which crisis management exercises could be conducted through computer simulations. For an extensive review of crisis management training through serious games, we refer readers to Di Loreto et al. [8].

Walker et al. [9] discuss the usability and efficiency of virtual crisis management systems (CMSs). They describe crises as unique multi-variable entities, defined by location, affected population and relevant support organisations. These variables are continuously changing over time and are difficult to predict

Fig. 1. A screenshot of the Mayor's Game. The main game screen consists of five advisors (top half) which the player can consult in order to answer a series of dilemmas presented to them within a crisis scenario (bottom half).

in advance. Moreover, Walker et al. define four categories which can be fulfilled through crisis management games: *teaching, operations, training* and *experimentation.* Our study revolves around the latter two, *training* and *experimentation*; through Andromeda we aim to improve the performance of crisis mangement trainees by analysing their decision making processes under stressful conditions.

A notable example of a dynamic crisis management training application is Pandora [1]. Pandora provides a training environment for crisis responders, through monitoring of the emotional and behavioural state of the trainees [10]. The developers of Pandora define key "affective factors" which are used to model trainees' emotional state, namely *personality traits, leadership style, background experience, self-efficacy, stress* and *anxiety.* Similar to our study, Pandora recognises trainee stress level as an essential factor based on which, several in-game variables are adjusted in order to provide personalised crisis management training experiences. However, unlike Pandora, Andromeda enables fully remote crisis management training sessions, even when the trainer and/or trainee are not located in their typical working environment.

Physiological sensors have been employed in game-related studies in order to investigate various aspects of player behavior, such as flow state [11], stress management [12] and learning [6,13]. Particularly, Steinrucke et al. [6] use Shimmer3 GSR+ [14] wearable physiological sensors to assess the effect of stress on analytical skill performance during crisis management scenarios in the Mayor's Game. They show that stress induced through time pressure has an effect on players' analytical skills, while they attempt to unobtrusively measure players' experienced stress levels through physiological sensor signals.

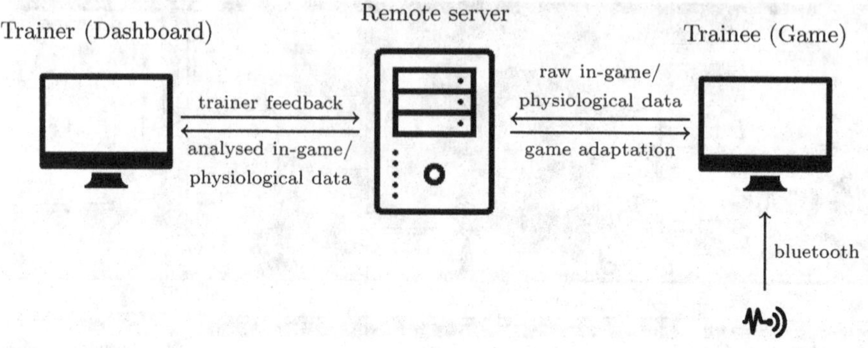

Fig. 2. Andromeda's architecture design. Two remotely located computers run the monitoring dashboard and Mayor's game respectively, while they both independently connect to the remote server. The physiological sensors are connected to the computer running the Mayor's game via bluetooth.

3 Approach

We have implemented Andromeda, a personalised crisis management training toolkit, based on crisis scenarios built for the Mayor's game. Andromeda includes a web-based monitoring and adaptation dashboard, and a remote data server. We have designed Andromeda aiming towards fully remote crisis management training using a centralised architecture, where the remote server undertakes the task of receiving, securely storing, analysing and serving in-game, physiological sensor and game adaptation data. The Mayor's game and trainer dashboard can be run on separate remote locations, connected to the server through persistent two-way connections. The physiological sensors are attached to the trainee and communicate to the remote server through the trainee's computer via a bluetooth connection. A graphical explanation of Andromeda's architecture is illustrated in Fig. 2. Below, we present a detailed description of each of Andromeda's main features.

3.1 Trainee Monitoring and Training Personalisation Dashboard

The trainee monitoring and training personalisation dashboard allows trainers to observe and dynamically adjust crisis management training sessions to the individual trainee, and is illustrated in Fig. 3.

The dashboard is web-based and runs on any modern web browser. Looking at Fig. 3, we identify four main features:

Training Session Controls. In order to allow fully remote monitoring of each training session, we provide a number of basic controls. In the dashboard's top bar (colored area), trainers can select the current user (trainee) from a dropdown

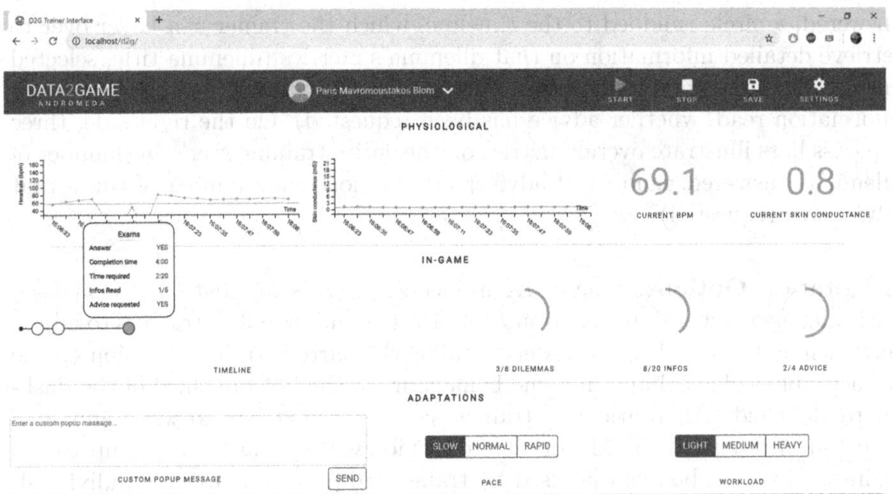

Fig. 3. Andromeda's trainer dashboard, during a crisis management training session. The participant's physiological responses are illustrated in the top third of the dashboard, followed by in-game monitoring (middle third) and adaptations (bottom third). (Color figure online)

menu. Using the four buttons on the right side, trainers can either (1) start training session monitoring, (2) stop/pause training session monitoring, (3) save the current training session to the remote server and (4) change the dashboard's settings (change the data request interval and line chart range).

Physiological Data Visualisation. We aim to manipulate trainee stress levels, in order to achieve a realistic crisis management training environment. To that end, we offer trainers the possibility of monitoring trainee physiological measurements, including heartrate and skin conductance. In the top third of the dashboard (labelled "Physiological"), two line charts are used to visualise the trainee's physiological measurements (heart rate and skin conductance). For these two signals, baseline measurements are extracted before the start of the training sessions, and are illustrated by a horizontal grey line in each respective line chart. Moreover, the current heart rate and skin conductance are illustrated through a large colored text on the right side. We expect the provision of information on trainee physiological measurements to guide trainers towards more effective training scenario adaptations.

In-Game Action Tracking. Apart from monitoring trainee physiological measurements, we provide information on the trainee's in-game actions. Since trainers can monitor training sessions remotely, it is important for them to have an overview of the current crisis management training scenario. In the middle third of the dashboard (labelled "In-game"), we have implemented a timeline (left side) which visualises the trainee's in-game actions. For each dilemma that is answered, a circle is added to the timeline, which the trainer can hover over to retrieve detailed information on that dilemma's metrics (dilemma title, selected answer, dilemma completion time, time required to answer, number of advisor information read, whether advice has been requested). On the right side, three progress bars illustrate overall metrics on the entire training scenario (number of dilemmas answered, number of advisor information read, number of times that advice was requested).

Adaptation Options. One of Andromeda's goals is to create a personalised crisis management training environment. To that end, we allow trainers to adjust certain in-game variables, in order to tailor the current training session to the trainee's physiological and in-game behaviour. In the bottom third of the dashboard (labelled "Adaptations"), trainers can use a text box to write and send a custom message to the Mayor's Game which will appear as a pop-up to the trainee. This text box can be used by trainers to provide real-time, individual-level feedback to the trainees. On the middle and right side, trainers can adapt the scenario pace (speed in which advisor information is presentented to the player) and the scenario workload (amount of advisor information presented to the player).

3.2 Remote Server

The second essential part of Andromeda is the remote server. It is built to receive, analyse, securely store, and serve all the data relevant to the training scenario. This includes physiological sensor data, player in-game actions and trainer dashboard interactions.

Specifically, as illustrated in Fig. 2, the trainer dashboard can either communicate to the remote server to receive training session data or dynamically adapt the training scenario. The trainee's computer can either send in-game and physiological data to the remote server, or receive in-game adaptations (generated by the trainer). The raw physiological signals received from the sensors, will be filtered and analysed by the remote server before being sent to the trainee dashboard.

It is important to note that every data block sent or received by the remote server is labelled with a timestamp, to allow synchronisation of data between the three data channels (Mayor's game, trainer dashboard and physiological sensors). This way, the completed training scenarios can be re-run and the generated data can be analysed in scientific studies.

3.3 Physiological Sensors

We employ physiological sensors to monitor trainee physiological stress responses. Our goal is to provide trainers with realistic, personalised crisis management training scenarios based on stress level manipulation. We expect training scenario adaptations generated by the trainee to have an impact on trainee stress levels.

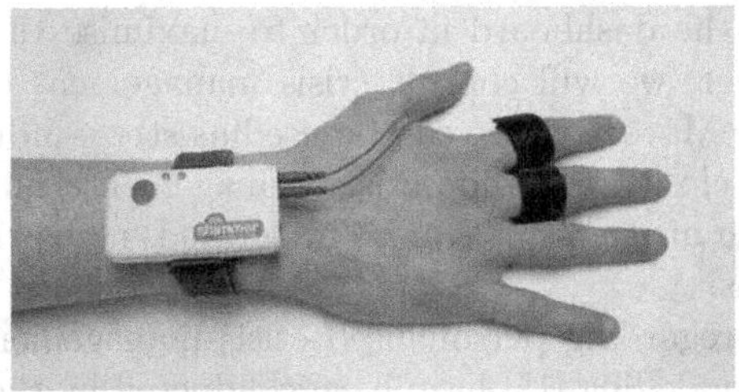

Fig. 4. The Shimmer3 GSR+ wearable sensor, with skin conductance electrodes attached to the index and middle finger.

We have selected to use the Shimmer3 GSR+ wearable sensors (Fig. 4), which are capable of measuring heart rate through photoplethysmography (PPG) and skin conductance (SC) through electrodes strapped to the trainee's fingers. Apart from PPG and SC, the Shimmer3 GSR+ sensors are equipped with a gyroscope, a 3-axis accelerometer, a thermometer and an atmospheric pressure meter. Connection to a computer is made possible through a built-in bluetooth transmitter.

4 Limitations and Future Work

We identify two main limitations regarding Andromeda's practical application. Firstly, this study mostly discusses crisis management training through decision making games such as the Mayor's Game. We consider the Mayor's Game a low-fidelity game, since it's text-based design cannot yield a highly realistic simulation of a real-life crisis. For that reason, we identify Andromeda as a tool which does not aim at replacing the current crisis management training scheme, but become a supplement of it. However, both Andromeda's dashboard and remote server are designed with generalisability in mind; with relatively little effort, they can be adapted to any type of game.

Secondly, remote crisis management training may prove to be a challenging task. Crisis management trainers and/or trainees may lack basic computational training skills, resulting in incorrect use of the dashboard and/or game engine, or misplacement of the physiological sensors. This can result in sub-optimal training conditions, so researchers are should ensure that the crisis management staff is provided with proper tutoring regarding dashboard, game and physiological sensor usage. Furthermore, various visualisation methods will be tested to ensure that crisis management trainers thoroughly understand the physiological sensors' output signals.

We plan on employing Andromeda in scientific studies and experiments. Our main focus is player multi-modal stress response modelling and automated dynamic scenario adaptation. To that end, we aim to collaborate with crisis management experts from the safety association Twente (Veiligheidsregio Twente) in the Netherlands. Our planning includes interview sessions with professional crisis management trainers, to discuss which data visualisations should be added to or removed from the dashboard in order to maximise the efficacy of training sessions. Moreover, we will consult crisis management experts to identify which features of the Mayor's game can be used as stress-inducing mechanisms, in order to create a close to real-life crisis management training environment. Once indicated, those mechanisms can be integrated in the trainer's dashboard as adaptation options.

Previous studies regarding personalised crisis management training [3] and multi-modal player modelling [15] have been conducted by the authors. A study on multi-modal stress response modelling using a static (non-adaptive) version of the Mayor's game is currently being conducted. If accurate models of trainee stress responses are implemented, they may be employed by Andromeda in order to automate the personalisation of training sessions. Within the scope of the Data2Game project, parallel studies such as [16] focus on creating generating textual game assets for serious games in the crisis response field.

Acknowledgment. This study is conducted within the Data2Game project, partially funded by the Netherlands Organisation for Scientific Research (NWO).

References

1. Bacon, L., MacKinnon, L., Cesta, A., Cortellessa, G.: Developing a smart environment for crisis management training. J. Ambient Intell. Hum. Comput. **4**(5), 581–590 (2013)
2. Kleiboer, M.: Simulation methodology for crisis management support. J. Cont. Crisis Manag. **5**(4), 198–206 (1997)
3. Mavromoustakos-Blom, P., Bakkes, S., Spronck, P.: Personalized crisis management training on a tablet. In: Proceedings of the 13th International Conference on the Foundations of Digital Games, p. 33. ACM (2018)
4. van de Ven, J.G.M., Stubbé, H., Hrehovcsik, M.: Gaming for policy makers: it's serious!. In: De Gloria, A. (ed.) GALA 2013. LNCS, vol. 8605, pp. 376–382. Springer, Cham (2014). https://doi.org/10.1007/978-3-319-12157-4_32
5. de Heer, J., Porskamp, P.: Predictive analytics for leadership assessment. In: Kantola, J.I., Nazir, S., Barath, T. (eds.) AHFE 2018. AISC, vol. 783, pp. 516–523. Springer, Cham (2019). https://doi.org/10.1007/978-3-319-94709-9_51
6. Steinrücke, J., Veldkamp, B., de Jong, T.: Determining the effect of stress on analytical skills performance in digital decision games towards an unobtrusive measure of experienced stress in gameplay scenarios. Comput. Hum. Behav. (2019)
7. Helsloot, I.: Bordering on reality: findings on the bonfire crisis management simulation. J. Cont. Crisis Manag. **13**(4), 159–169 (2005)
8. Di Loreto, I., Mora, S., Divitini, M.: Collaborative serious games for crisis management: an overview. In: IEEE 21st International Workshop on Enabling Technologies: Infrastructure for Collaborative Enterprises (WETICE) 2012, pp. 352–357. IEEE (2012)
9. Walker, W.E., Giddings, J., Armstrong, S.: Training and learning for crisis management using a virtual simulation/gaming environment. Cogn. Technol. Work **13**(3), 163–173 (2011)
10. Bacon, L., Windall, G., MacKinnon, L.: The development of a rich multimedia training environment for crisis management: using emotional affect to enhance learning (2011)

11. Berta, R., Bellotti, F., De Gloria, A., Pranantha, D., Schatten, C.: Electroencephalogram and physiological signal analysis for assessing flow in games. IEEE Trans. Comput. Intell. AI Games **5**(2), 164–175 (2013)
12. Al Osman, H., Dong, H., El Saddik, A.: Ubiquitous biofeedback serious game for stress management. IEEE Access **4**, 1274–1286 (2016)
13. Cowley, B., Charles, D., Black, M., Hickey, R.: Toward an understanding of flow in video games. Comput. Entertainment (CIE) **6**(2), 20 (2008)
14. Burns, A., et al.: Shimmer ^{TM}–a wireless sensor platform for noninvasive biomedical research. IEEE Sens. J. **10**(9), 1527–1534 (2010)
15. Mavromoustakos Blom, P., Bakkes, S., Spronck, P.: Modeling behavioral competencies in crisis management scenarios. In: International Meeting of the Psychonomics Society 2018, 10 May 2018–12 May 2018 (2018)
16. van Stegeren, J., Theune, M.: Towards generating textual game assets from real-world data. In: Proceedings of the 13th International Conference on the Foundations of Digital Games, ser. FDG 2018, pp. 43:1–43:4. ACM, New York (2018). https://doi.org/10.1145/3235765.3235809

Towards an Operational Definition of Procedural Rhetoric

Michal Švarný(✉) and Vít Šisler

Institute of Information Science and Librarianship, Faculty of Arts, Charles University, 158 00 Prague, Czech Republic
michal.svarny@ff.cuni.cz

Abstract. Identifying the features that contribute to a game's effectiveness as a learning tool is a key task in game-based learning research. Proponents of procedural rhetoric claim that representation through rule-based systems is crucial for the effectiveness of serious games. Yet, this claim has never been thoroughly tested in empirical research. One possible way of testing the effects of procedural rhetoric is by way of value-added research. This approach has been successfully applied in studies on multimedia learning materials as well as serious games. Nevertheless, in the case of procedural rhetoric, the value-added research approach poses considerable challenges. These challenges arise from the complex relationship between procedural representation and other game elements and modes of communication. The aim of this paper is to overcome these challenges through the operationalization of procedural rhetoric. We propose an analysis procedure based on multi-modal analysis methods combined with existing game analysis frameworks. We illustrate this procedure using an example analysis of the game *We Become What We Behold* (2016). The proposed procedure enables both a formal comparison and analysis of the examined game modifications, something which is indispensable when designing experiments that adopt the value-added research approach.

Keywords: Procedural rhetoric · Operational definition · Value-added research method · Multi-modal analysis

1 Introduction

Shaping the attitudes of students is one of the key challenges of environmental and civic education. Some authors consider video games uniquely suited for this purpose due to their characteristic features [1]. Bogost, for example, while proposing the concept of procedural rhetoric, argues that the procedural nature of games is what makes game-based learning effective [2]. If this is the case, it would be beneficial to provide designers of learning materials with evidence-based guidelines on the use of procedural rhetoric. This would require extensive empirical research on the effects of different design choices pertaining to procedural rhetoric, something which has not yet been done.

One possible way of testing the effects of procedural rhetoric is through value-added research. This approach has been successfully used to provide backing for

A. Liapis et al. (Eds.): GALA 2019, LNCS 11899, pp. 148–157, 2019.
https://doi.org/10.1007/978-3-030-34350-7_15

evidence-based design guidelines [3, 4]. Though promising, the value-added approach does present considerable challenges when studying procedural rhetoric. These arise from the complex relationship between procedural representation and other game elements and modes of communication. The aim of this paper is to overcome these challenges through the operationalization of procedural rhetoric, thereby providing methodological support for experimental research on the application of procedural rhetoric in serious games.

2 Theoretical Background

2.1 Procedural Rhetoric

Bogost defines procedural rhetoric as "the art of persuasion through rule-based representations and interactions rather than the spoken word, writing, images, or moving pictures" [2]. However, key components of the definition remain somewhat vague. Bogost relies on a negative delineation and preexisting understanding of the notions of rules and interactivity. For an operationalized definition of procedural rhetoric, more detailed conceptual definitions of the key underlying concepts are necessary. We have chosen to build the proposed operationalization around the notion of game mechanics as the core of interactivity and adopt Sicart's definition of game mechanics as: "methods invoked by agents, designed for interaction with the game state" [5]. We also adopt Sicart's understanding of rules as "general or particular properties of the game system and its agents [...] evaluated by a game loop" that provide the possibility space for interactions and transitions between game states [5].

Bogost's concept of procedural rhetoric and his notion of persuasive games [2] has sparked debates regarding the role of procedural representation in the meaning-making process of gameplay [6–9]. It is not our intention to enter this debate arguing for a new interpretation of the meaning-making process. However, for a valid operational definition to be attained, all aspects which contribute to persuasive communication through games must be considered in order to control extraneous variables.

2.2 Challenges in Experimental Research on Procedural Rhetoric

Value-added research requires a well-controlled experiment where the experimental and control versions of the game differ only in the feature being studied [4], in our case, procedural rhetoric. Different versions of the experimental game have to be identical with respect to the sound effects, music, visual and textual elements. It is thus necessary to be able to analyze procedural changes and their effects on other modes, as it is only through non-procedural elements that players engage with procedural rhetoric [8]. Critiques of the proceduralist paradigm offer useful insights into the complex relationships and unclear boundaries between procedural rhetoric and other game elements.

Möring [8], for example, notes that analyses of procedural rhetoric often describe games in a "very general way", without referring to any specific game states. He concludes, in accordance with Sicart's objections [9], that from a proceduralist standpoint, games are seen primarily as texts. The importance of actual gameplay, along with the player's interpretation, is thus downplayed. However, since the aim of value-added research is to provide design guidelines, it is advantageous to focus on the designer's perspective.

2.3 Proposed Theoretical Approach

Generally speaking, the operationalization of procedural rhetoric requires identifying different game elements and their relationship to one another, so that any modification of the game is formally comparable to the original version. As a result, this ensures control over the variables in the game's design and enables falsification by other researchers. We have adopted a model proposed by de la Hera [6] to form the foundation of our analysis, taking into account a wide range of layers of persuasive communication in a structured manner (see Table 1).

Table 1. Overview of de la Hera's Conceptual Model for the study of persuasive games [6].

Level of persuasion	Dimensions of persuasion	Example variables
1st level The signs	Linguistic	Names, Instructional texts, Dialogues
	Visual	Interface, Character design
	Sonic	Sound effects, Ambient sound beds
	Haptic	Input, Haptic feedback
2nd level The system	Procedural	Model rules, Goal rules, Meta-rules
	Narrative	Story, Characters, Space, Time
	Cinematic	Framing, Camera, Editing
3rd level The context	Sensorial	Sensorial experiences
	Affective	Basic emotions, Complex emotions
	Tactical	Convergent and divergent thinking
	Social	Reputation, Relationships

Although this model provides a useful analytical framework, it does not elaborate on the relationships between different game elements across different levels and dimensions of persuasion. Another limitation of the model is that it does not provide sufficiently detailed definitions of the identified dimensions, primarily in the case of procedurality, which could facilitate a formal analysis without having to borrow from other models or methods. Semiotics can be applied here to provide the methods necessary for overcoming these limitations.

De la Hera uses the term semiotics to refer to the first level of persuasion [6]. Similarly, Möring describes semiotics as comprising "different modalities, such as visual, textual, auditory and tactile" [8]. We use the term semiotics in a more general sense, referring to the theoretical and methodological approach which also examines other modes of communication outside of the sign level. Brejcha [10], for instance, proposes a semiotic analysis of human-computer interaction. He uses "interaction sentences" to analyze user interaction tasks, similarly to how Sicart [5] describes game mechanics. We propose the use of multi-modal (discourse) analysis [11] for our purposes.

3 Operationalization of Procedural Rhetoric

As an operationalization of procedural rhetoric, we propose an analytical procedure that draws on multi-modal analysis methods [11] and de la Hera's model [6], consisting of the following three steps:

1. General analysis of the overall structure of the game, identifying core mechanics and rules.
2. Detailed multi-modal analysis of the game mechanics selected for modification.
3. Paradigmatic analysis of the selected mechanics or rules, exploring the possible modifications and their expected effects on the game.

In this section, we detail the proposed procedure, showcase it using an existing game, and address possible challenges.

3.1 Example Analysis

We chose to showcase the procedure using the game *We Become What We Behold* (WBWWB) [12]. It is a browser game where the player assumes the role of a news reporter. In the game, cartoon people called "peeps" [12], that have either square or round heads, wander around and interact with each other (see Fig. 1). The player controls the viewfinder, hovering over the characters, and chooses what to report on by taking pictures. WBWWB is a suitable example, as it is relatively simple and short, yet it adopts a wide range of persuasive communication. Also, Case (the creator of the game) acknowledges [13] Bogost's concept [2] as a source of influence, meaning that the use of procedural rhetoric is expected here.

Fig. 1. WBWWB: A screenshot from the beginning of the game [12].

Step 1: General Analysis. A detailed multi-modal analysis of an entire game, even a game as WBWWB, would be unnecessarily complex for our purposes. Instead, we first analyze the overall game structure, identifying the core game mechanics and rules. The nature of the general structural components may vary depending on the game, i.e. different game stages or parallel modes of gameplay. A game's structure might be evident at face value, for example, if game progression is segmented into levels. If the structure of the game is not as well defined, variations in the game mechanics can be used for distinction. We use a modified version of the Gameplay Loop Model [14] to represent the game's overall structure (see Fig. 2), as it serves as a flexible tool for representing player actions at different levels of granularity.

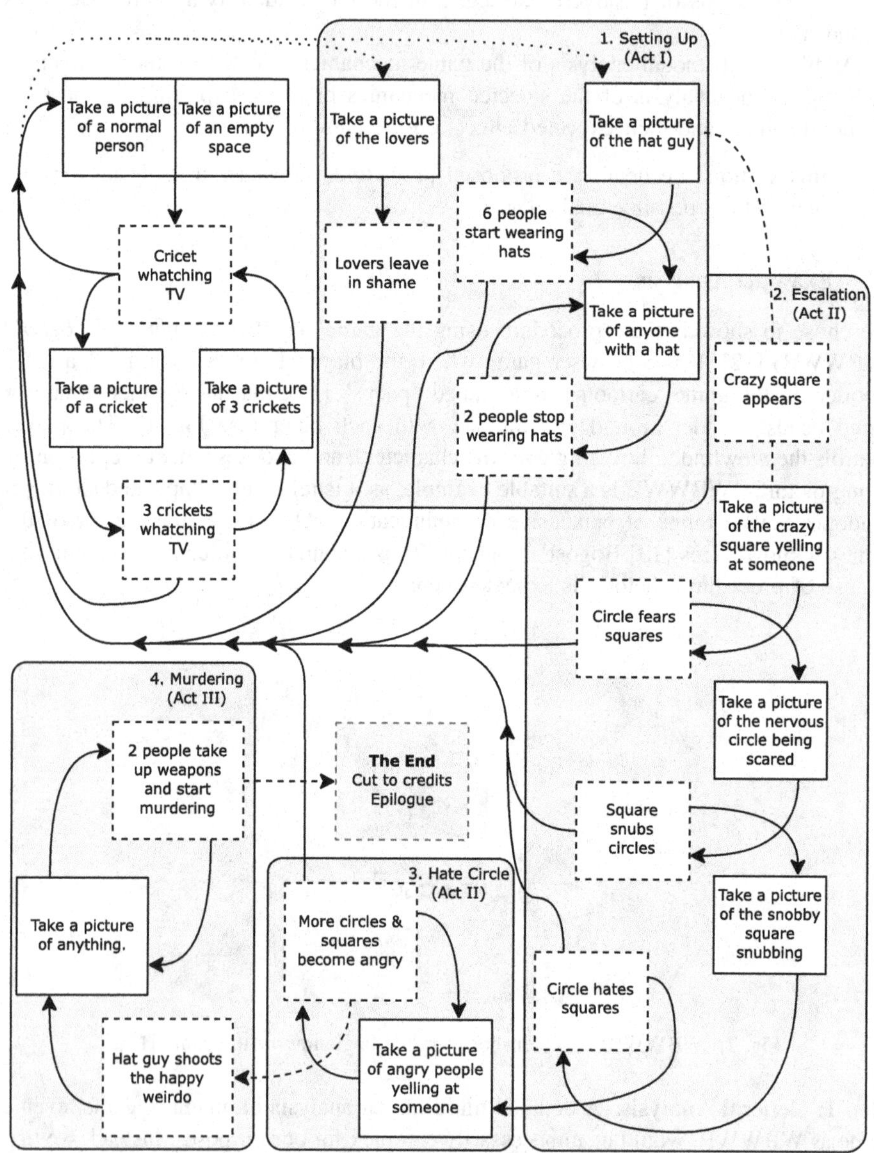

Fig. 2. Overview of WBWWB. Solid lines indicate player actions. Dashed nodes represent game states, dashed lines represent conditional relationships. Dotted arrows are actions available only in Act I. The crazed square's conversion from Act II was omitted for simplification.

In WBWWB, no explicit transitions separate any stages of the game during gameplay. Case [15] divides the game into three acts (indicated also in Fig. 2). Based on changes in the game mechanics, four distinct stages and an epilogue can be distinguished:

1. The beginning of the game allows the player to learn the core game mechanics: The player takes pictures by pointing and clicking (see Fig. 1). Taking pictures of different situations has different consequences on the game state.
2. Shortly after the first consequential picture is taken (a picture of the "hat guy" [15]),[1] a new character appears on the screen: a "crazed square" [12] that yells at the people it meets. Reports of these incidents cause emotions to escalate: ranging from a nervous circle, to a snobby square, to an angry circle.
3. This leads to a vicious circle of hate, until "everyone hates everyone" [12]. Meanwhile, the "crazed square" is converted into a happy "weirdo" [15].
4. At this point, the "hat guy" shoots the happy "weirdo". People start to panic. Any reports of the situation make people lose their minds, get weapons and start murdering. After some more reports are made, the camera starts zooming out and then cuts to the end credits. In an epilogue scene, the lovers and a cricket commemorate the deceased quietly.

In Fig. 2, we focused on the game mechanics. The rules were indicated only as relational connections between nodes. In a more detailed analysis, the rules could be described using labels at each connection. Note that we included the objects of player actions in the nodes representing the game mechanics (see Fig. 2). Sicart [5] only uses simple verbs to describe the game mechanics. In the case of WBWWB, following Sicart's approach would lead us to the conclusion that there is only one mechanic present, that is "to photograph". However, as taking pictures of different scenes has different effects on the game state, each combination can be considered a separate mechanic.

Step 2: Multi-modal Analysis. Based on the general analysis, we can decide which game mechanics or rules should be selected for modification. The multi-modal analysis follows the structure of de la Hera's model [6], however in a multi-modal analysis, elements of different levels and dimensions of persuasion are mapped on a timeline and thus their relationships are more apparent. For our purposes, we have chosen the mechanic: *angry circle (AC) yelling at others* (a non-player invoked interaction, in short *yelling*), and the *player taking a picture* of the said interaction (see Fig. 3).

The Signs. At this level, *yelling* is represented primarily through a sequence of *AC*'s facial expressions (see Fig. 3). The red lines coming from *AC*'s mouth emphasize the accompanying sound effect. The representation of anger is further reinforced by the red color of *AC*'s body. The unfortunate square's only reaction during the whole sequence is a blank, perplexed stare.

[1] Reference to the GitHub repository is made when the quoted label is used in the comments in the game's code and is not present in the game itself.

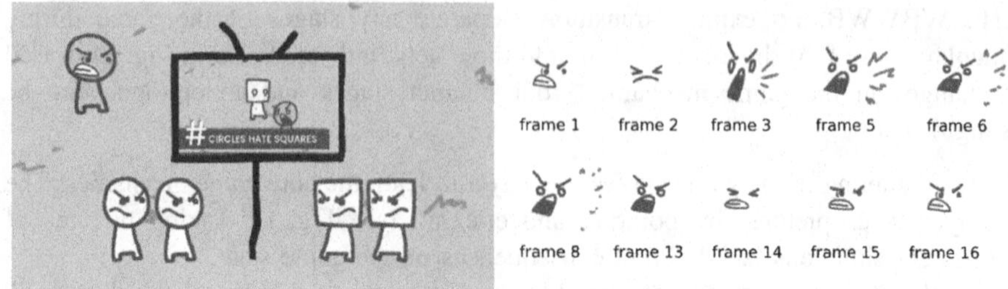

Fig. 3. Left: *Yelling* makes the headlines (screenshot available on the game's website [12]). Right: The sequence of facial expressions of *AC yelling* [15].

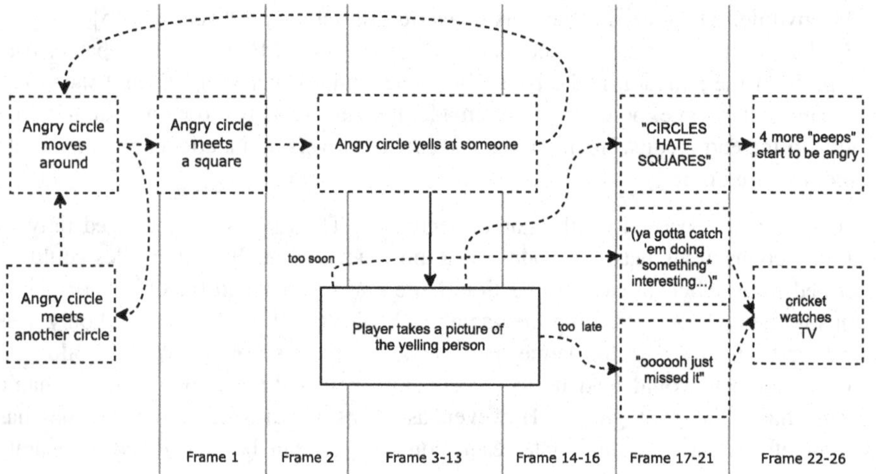

Fig. 4. Procedural and linguistic dimensions of the *yelling* mechanic in WBWWB [12]. The indicated frames correspond to the frames from Fig. 3. Dashed lines indicate non-player actions. Solid lines indicate player actions. In frames 17 to 21, the nodes contain the resulting news headlines.

When the player takes a picture, the camera flashes, and a camera shutter sound effect is played. If the picture is taken during frames 3 to 13, the story makes the headlines (see Fig. 4). Consequently, news of the incident angers other "peeps". In addition to changes in facial expressions, the transformation is marked with a "squeak!" sound. When the picture is taken too early or too late, the sound of a cricket is played instead of the news jingle. Although the cricket does really appear afterward, watching TV, the sound mainly serves as an indication that the report was boring. A caption tells the player what went wrong (see Fig. 4).

The System. The second level consists of narrative, procedural and cinematic dimensions. In the multi-modal analysis of the procedural dimension, we use the Gameplay Loop Model [14] for a more detailed schematization of the chosen mechanic (see Fig. 4). The distinction between the procedural and narrative dimensions poses a significant challenge at this level. In her conception of the narrative dimension, De la Hera [6] includes both the scripted narrative and the "alterbiography", i.e. narrative generated during gameplay. Based on this understanding, any sequence of in-game events is then part of the narrative dimension and thus any distinction between both dimensions in an experimental setting would be impossible, as any meaningful change in the procedural dimension inevitably leads to a change in the alterbiography. In order to distinguish game modifications in these dimensions, we argue that events generated during gameplay should be considered as part of the procedural dimension, as indexical representations of the game's rules and mechanics.

In terms of the cinematic dimension, during most of the game, a stationary bird's-eye extreme long shot shows "peeps" moving around (the same way as in Fig. 1). Every time the player takes a picture, the camera zooms in for a close-up of the photographed scene. An overlay headline appears and the camera zooms out for a long shot of the TV set (see Fig. 3), including "peeps" (or crickets) watching and reacting to the news. Finally, the camera zooms out to the initial set-up.

The Context. An analysis of the third level of persuasion can be fruitful when conducted on the game as a whole. This would therefore be an advisable step to take for a more thorough analysis, though it is beyond the scope of this paper.

Step 3: Paradigmatic Analysis. This is a crucial step in the proposed analytical procedure's use in research design. Chandler describes paradigmatic analysis as follows: "[it] involves comparing and contrasting each of the signs present in the text with absent signs which in similar circumstances might have been chosen and considering the significance of the choices made" [16]. In order to determine the procedural rhetoric variables, the possible modifications of the game mechanics and rules must be considered, which "may involve any of four basic transformations: addition, deletion, substitution, and transposition" [16]. These commutations are then compared based on how they impact the other dimensions of the game, selecting those with a negligible or controllable impact.

Let us consider the addition of a 50% chance that when an angry "peep" yells at someone, the victim becomes nervous – just like the circle in stage 2 (see Fig. 2).

Influence on Other Dimensions. At the sign level, no new sign elements have to be added. The new mechanic consists of existing facial expressions and sound effects, potentially differing in the arrangement of facial expressions only. "Peeps" react to *yelling* with a blank perplexed stare (see Fig. 3). The circle that becomes nervous from watching TV in the original version initially had a neutral facial expression. The proposed mechanic would generate a slightly different sequence of facial expressions, though in our opinion, such a difference could be considered negligible. Alternatively, the proposed modification could be changed so that *yelling* affects witnesses instead of victims. Nearby "peeps" have a neutral facial expression and thus the resulting sequence would be identical.

At the system level, the influence of the proposed modifications on the cinematic and narrative dimensions must be examined. The sequence associated with the player's news reports is completely omitted here. Yet, this isn't the only transformation which occurs in the background, outside the interest of TV news. The conversion of the "crazed square" into a happy "weirdo" is brought about in the same manner. No new element is thus introduced in the cinematic dimension.

In terms of the distinction between the narrative and procedural dimensions, the proposed modification adds events which are the product of non-player actions. Unlike the conversion of the "crazed square", these events are not scripted. Whether or not a victim (or alternatively a witness) becomes nervous is determined by the rules, meaning that this could happen at a different rate and at different times, depending on the game session. These events can thus be considered as part of the procedural dimension.

4 Discussion

When adopting a value-added research approach, it is crucial to be able to distinguish the features of the game being studied in order to minimize extraneous variables [3]. This proves to be a difficult task in the case of procedural rhetoric, as a game's procedural dimension is only experienced through other game elements. Moreover, the existing conceptual definitions of procedural rhetoric are not sufficient for experimental research design.

We propose to overcome these challenges by using an analytical procedure based on semiotic methods [10, 11, 16]. We used de la Hera's model of persuasive communication [6] as our conceptual framework. Within the structure of this model, we adopted Sicart's definition of game mechanics and rules [5] as a key criterion for identifying and distinguishing procedural game elements. The proposed procedure consists of three steps: (1) a general analysis of the game structure and game mechanics, (2) a multi-modal analysis, and (3) a paradigmatic analysis. We showcased the proposed procedure on an example analysis, which we also used to address some more specific issues. Most notably, we argued that events generated during gameplay should be considered as part of the procedural dimension.

One of the main limitations of the proposed approach is that a thorough multi-modal analysis can quickly become unfeasible due to the nearly infinite level of possible granularity and exponential complexity in the case of more complicated games. It is necessary to carefully consider which game mechanics and potential modifications should be analyzed and to what level of detail, in order to maintain a feasible level of complexity. In this respect, the Gameplay Loop Model [14] proves to be a helpful tool, as it can be applied to various levels of granularity.

Although multi-modal analysis has already been employed in game studies, its application as an analytical tool in the context of value-added research presents a new approach. The proposed procedure allows for different game elements, along with their relationship to one another, to be identified and classified in great detail. Any modification can be precisely documented to control the variables in the design of the game being studied, allowing other researchers to reconstruct the analysis for a possible critique. These are essential attributes of any research design, especially when based on the value-added research approach. The proposed procedure could prove beneficial for digital game-based learning research in general. In the case of procedural rhetoric, this approach provides a level of detail and comprehensiveness which, while necessary due to the complex relationship between procedural rhetoric and other game elements, was not available before. This facilitates a new perspective for exploring how serious games affect players, while also serving as a potential gateway towards evidence-based design guidelines for the application of procedural rhetoric.

Acknowledgments. This study was supported by the European Regional Development Fund Project, "Creativity and Adaptability as Conditions for the Success of Europe in an Interrelated World" (No. CZ.02.1.01/0.0/0.0/16_019/0000734) and the Charles University Programs Progress Q15 and PRIMUS/HUM/03.

References

1. Gee, J.P.: What Video Games Have to Teach Us About Learning and Literacy. Palgrave Macmillan, New York (2004)
2. Bogost, I.: Persuasive Games: The Expressive Power of Videogames. MIT Press, Cambridge (2007)
3. Mayer, R.E., Lieberman, D.A.: Conducting scientific research on learning and health behavior change with computer-based health games. Educ. Technol. **51**, 3–14 (2011)
4. Brom, C., Šisler, V., Slussareff, M., Selmbacherová, T., Hlávka, Z.: You like it, you learn it: affectivity and learning in competitive social role play gaming. Int. J. Comput.-Support. Collab. Learn. **11**, 313–348 (2016)
5. Sicart, M.: Defining game mechanics. Game Stud. **8** (2008). http://gamestudies.org/0802/articles/sicart. Accessed 16 Mar 2019
6. de la Hera Conde-Pumpido, T.: Persuasive structures in advergames. conveying advertising messages through digital games (2014)
7. Brathwaite, B., Sharp, J.: The mechanic is the message: a post mortem in progress. In: Ethics and Game Design: Teaching Values Through Play, pp. 311–329, IGI Global (2010)
8. Möring, S.M.: Games and metaphor – a critical analysis of the metaphor discourse in game studies (2013)
9. Sicart, M.: Against procedurality. Game Stud. **11**(3) (2011). http://gamestudies.org/1103/articles/sicart_ap. Accessed 28 Apr 2019
10. Brejcha, J.: Cross-Cultural Human-Computer Interaction and User Experience Design: A Semiotic Perspective. CRC Press (2015). https://doi.org/10.1201/b18059
11. O'Halloran, K.L.: Multimodal discourse analysis. In: Continuum Companion to Discourse Analysis, pp. 120–137. Continuum, New York (2011)
12. Case, N.: We Become What We Behold by Nicky Case (2016). https://ncase.itch.io/wbwwb. Accessed 01 July 2019
13. Case, N., Hart, V.: Parable of the polygons: a playable post on the shape of society (2014)
14. Guardiola, E.: The gameplay loop: a player activity model for game design and analysis. In: Proceedings of the 13th International Conference on Advances in Computer Entertainment Technology - ACE2016, pp. 1–7. ACM Press, Osaka (2016)
15. Case, N.: We Become What We Behold – a minigame about the news! (2019). https://github.com/ncase/wbwwb. Accessed 01 July 2019
16. Chandler, D.: Semiotics: The Basics. Routledge, New York (2017)

Study on Enhancing Learnability of a Serious Game by Implementing a Pedagogical Agent

Daniel Atorf(✉), Ehm Kannegieser, and Wolfgang Roller

Fraunhofer IOSB, Fraunhoferstr. 1, 76131 Karlsruhe, Germany
{daniel.atorf, ehm.kannegieser, wolfgang.roller}@iosb.fraunhofer.de

Abstract. This paper elaborates on a study on the implementation of a pedagogical agent. The agent is meant to improve and enhance the learnability of the serious game Lost Earth 2307. The game is analyzed in order to find the aspects that need to be improved (i.e. problems players might have with learning how to use and handle the game). Based on these findings the implementation of the pedagogical agent and the methods used are presented and elaborated. Furthermore, the question whether a pedagogical agent can improve the learnability of game mechanics in serious games compared to the "Standard form contract"-style tutorials used in Lost Earth 2307, is discussed. A study about the evaluation of the implemented pedagogical agent, its research question and the metrics used, is presented. The paper depicts the setup of the user study using SUS and NASA TLX questionnaires and report in detail about the results and discusses the outcomes.

Keywords: Game design · Pedagogical agent · Digital game-based learning · Usability · Immersion · Study

1 Introduction

The serious game Lost Earth 2307 is about learning how to analyze aerial and satellite images and how to formally describe the identified objects using specific terms and answering to specific tasks. This training domain is rather complex to teach, therefore individual training courses last several months and trainers have a high interest in keeping the students motivated over a long time. The game addresses this need by following the ideas of Digital Game Based learning [1] and Immersive Didactics [2]. It is integrated into the course as an optional element in the informal learning phase where students have to intensify their knowledge through exercises.

The game was evaluated during the iterative development. The evaluation focused on the learning outcome, on game functionality and user experience. However, the evaluation was only preliminary but showed important indicators on these aspects [3]. Further evaluation was proposed with focus on a formal evaluation of engagement including larger test groups.

Feedback mechanisms and the learning outcome did not seem to be an issue in the preliminary evaluation. Concerning immersion and usability, in addition to the known

A. Liapis et al. (Eds.): GALA 2019, LNCS 11899, pp. 158–168, 2019.
https://doi.org/10.1007/978-3-030-34350-7_16

indicators of the preliminary study, further small evaluations on site revealed aspects where the game should be improved.

Tests showed that once the students were familiar with the game mechanics, the core game loop and processes, they had no problem to immerse into the game. However, getting to know how the game works was an issue with some students. Learning how to play a game is the very first step to succeed in it and achieve the learning objectives in a serious game. Usability issues greatly interferes with immersion [4], thus preventing acceptance and good learning outcomes.

With learnability as one of the five key attributes of usability [5], this paper focuses on the hypothesis if the learnability of a serious game can be improved by implementing a pedagogical agent. It addresses the question if a pedagogical agent can improve the learnability of game mechanics in serious games compared to the "Standard form contract"-style tutorials used in Lost Earth 2307. In addition, the paper presents a study to evaluate the implementation and discusses the results and implications on future developments of serious games.

2 Analysis of the Game

To find interesting spots where the learnability of the game can be improved, the status quo of Lost Earth had to be analyzed. This was done by an expert evaluation, as described by Benyon [6]. The current UI was analyzed for commonly acknowledged criteria and principles, namely the ten heuristics for User Interface Design by Nielsen [5]. In addition, Gee's 13 principles were applied [7] in order to extend the model for evaluating serious games.

The analysis revealed several points where the game can be improved. One of the biggest issues were visibility of the current system status and interaction possibilities for the user in general. As an example, the user gets a list of names and rooms where he should go next, but at this point in the game he does not know about the goals and there is no visual hint where to go next. The important design principles neglected here are: error prevention, information 'on demand' and 'just in time'.

Another big issue was the consistent supply of information outside its context and use, as illustrated in Fig. 1. Important information on how to play the game and achieve its goals are combined in one long "wall-of-text"-dialog webbed into a human dialog that makes it longer and more distracting. This can reduce player engagement and leads to players missing important information to succeed in the game. The main neglected design principles here are recognition rather than recall and information 'on demand' and 'just in time'.

To increase the usability and learnability of Lost Earth 2307 significantly, it should be improved in those two fields. Other issues were minor and are not described further.

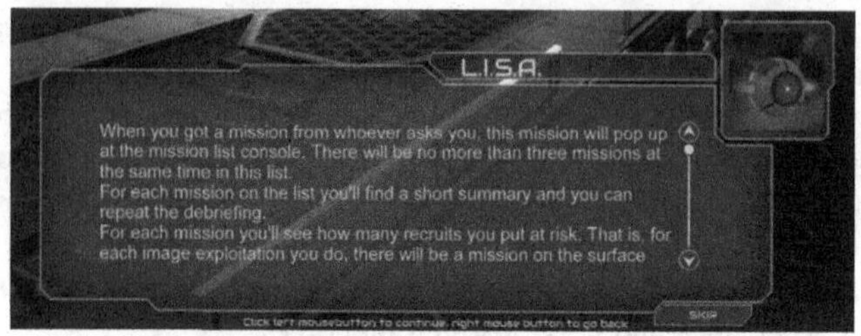

Fig. 1. Example for information outside of context and use

3 Method and Implementation

3.1 Method for Improving the Learnability

Video games often use tutorials to achieve the learnability of the game. Tutorials in video games are sections, sequences, levels, or even simple explanatory texts popping up during gameplay. Their main goal is to teach the player necessary skills, rules and mechanics he needs to succeed in the game. A prominent characteristic of a good tutorial is that it does not feel like one. This can be seen as deep engagement into the matter, which results in higher efficiency [7, 8]. It requires the right level of guidance for the player and involves that he is not overwhelmed by complexity, or bored by simplicity of the tutorial [8]. A solution to this problem are Gee's Fish Tanks [7]: Focusing on the mechanism, strategy or skill to be taught at a specific point in play and stripping it from all unnecessary information.

One method to create engaging tutorials are pedagogical agents. These are autonomous characters that cohabit learning environments with students to create rich, face-to-face learning interactions. [9] In other words, they can be learning companions, tutors, assistants, role-players and much more to the player.

Schroeder et al. conducted a broad meta-analysis on pedagogical agents where they collected different theories and principles that could help in designing pedagogical agents [10]. A suitable approach is the Cognitive Apprenticeship model by Collins et al. [11]. It gives seven characteristics for tutor behavior that lead to positive learning effects: Modeling, Coaching, Scaffolding, Articulation, Reflection, Exploration and Fading (see Table 1).

Table 1. The seven characteristics for tutor behavior by Collins [11]

Modeling is the process of demonstrating a skill or task to be learned, and externalizing usually internal processes for the student to understand better
Coaching. Observing the student while he is carrying out a task and providing feedback, reminders, hints, scaffolding and modeling when needed
Scaffolding is the art of building sound towers from knowledge, using already acquired skills to build it

(*continued*)

Table 1. (*continued*)

Articulation. Letting the student articulate or formulate their knowledge can refine their understanding of concepts and deepen their engagement
Reflection compares student and expert performance to find weaknesses and parts to improve on. Every time getting a bit closer to the preferred expert execution
Exploration means giving the student tools to explore on his own and pushing him into situations where he needs to find solutions for new problems by himself
Fading. The more a student learns and the further he increases his expertise, the more the tutor will get obsolete and not needed anymore. Students need to become independent in their doing and therefore, tutors should intervene less the further the student develops. This goes up to a point where the tutor has completely vanished and the student progresses on his own

3.2 Implementation

Lost Earth 2307 already uses the character LISA as a tutor in its original version. For implementing, the pedagogical agent LISA was improved to support the player in the beginning of Lost Earth 2307, teaching him the needed mechanics to progress further.

The new implementation of LISA followed the model of Collins Cognitive Apprenticeship [11] as described in chapter 3.1 and delivered several characteristics.

The first implemented characteristic was Fading. LISA reduces intervention, the further the player progresses in the game. This is modeled through the number of hints that are presented by LISA in each mission. A mission is a coherent task and after a successful completion new missions are unlocked. The amount of hints by LISA is reduced for each mission the player progresses. Only if new knowledge is taught more hints are added. This also leads to providing more reduced and context-sensitive help instead of providing large amounts of general guidance at the beginning.

Modeling was implemented in form of LISA highlighting next steps. This can be understood as LISA pointing and thereby demonstrating steps to the player. The agents helping behavior is divided into two categories: On-Demand, and Pro-Active.

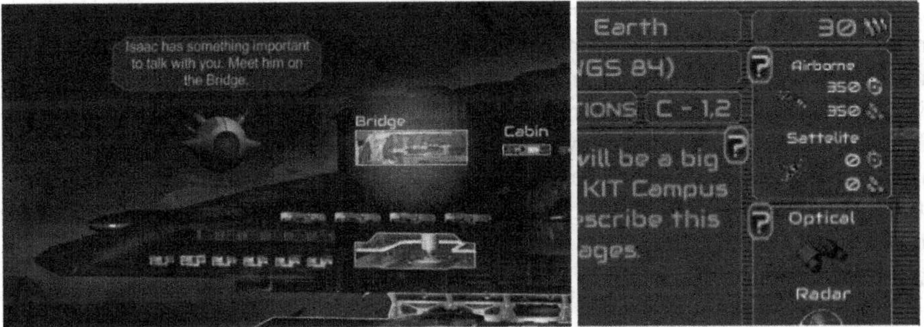

Fig. 2. Example for pro-active hint as a modeless LISA dialog with additional highlighting (left) and example for tooltips in complex menu (right)

On-Demand means that the player himself demands help from the pedagogical agent. On-Demand was implemented in two patterns. The first one is when a player clicks on LISA. Then a speech bubble pops up with a hint for the next step to do. The second one addresses complex menus. Tooltips reveal additional information to specific sections of the menu (see Fig. 2 right).

In the pro-active category, the pedagogical agent LISA "acts on her own" and tells the player about important steps in the current context. This context sensitive, pro-active behavior implements the Coaching characteristic. LISA acts when a player has to do something for the first time. The dialogs presenting hints are divided into modal dialogs and modeless dialogs. The modal dialog blocks all other workflows in the game in order to highlight important information that is obligatory to progress further in the game. Blocking interruptions need to be used carefully because chances are high to annoy the user instead of helping him [12], when used too often. Therefore, wherever possible modeless dialogs are used (see example in Fig. 2 left).

LISA also acts when no interaction from the player is recognized for some time. In this case LISA assumes the player is missing some information to progress further, or does not remember the next step.

The characteristics Scaffolding and Reflection were already implemented in the original version. Scaffolding is covered by the missions' design to build up on each other, and Reflection is given by providing expert solutions in the debriefing phase of each mission.

Having players articulate their knowledge is unusual when learning to play a game. Therefore, the characteristic of Articulation was not implemented.

4 Study

4.1 Research Question and Metrics

As described in the introduction the main question was, if a pedagogical agent can improve the learnability of a serious game. So the main hypothesis is: *Do pedagogical agents used in serious games affect its learnability, compared to "standard form contract"-tutorials.* (H1).

Learnability cannot be measured directly. For the study, it was inferred through the metrics shown in Table 2 and limited to the core game loop (see Fig. 3 left). These metrics had to be analyzed over time, in this case throughout multiple trials (see trials in Fig. 4). This analysis can be represented by learning curves suggested by Albert and Tullis [13] (see Fig. 3 right). Low and flat learning curves are preferred, provided the metrics define lower values as better. When analyzing this curve it is important, how steep the initial drop-off is and how fast the curve converges. The fewer trials it takes for the curve to converge and the flatter the initial drop-off, the easier it is to learn how to use the system [13].

In addition to learnability, the usability was measured because of a tight connection between these two [14]. Usability can give clues about difficult or unclear parts of a task. In general if a task or UI is more pleasant to use it is also easier to learn, regarding to Nielsen's Heuristics [6]. Furthermore, cognitive load is also directly connected to

Table 2. Metrics for learnability of Lost Earth

Metric	Description
1. Mission success	A mission is considered as either a success or a failure. If the mission score (see metric 3) is below 50%, the mission is a failure. The mission also failes if the time limit in this study was reached (30 min per mission). The mission success rate yields over multiple trials
2. Mission Time	Time on task. The time needed from the moment a mission was started until the start of the debriefing phase
2.1 Time to Mission	Time from starting the game until starting the first mission. This metric takes into account, the time needed to read the intro talk (control group only)
2.2 Time to Image Exploitation	Time from starting the game until start of the image exploitation phase
2.3 Image Exploitation Time	Time spent for image exploitation
3. Mission Score	This is the score calculated by the game for each mission. The score reaches from 0–100%, whereas <50% is considered a mission failure. Effects in mission score will be interpreted as a difference in the ability to teach what to do during the image exploitation phase. Missions that fail due to score are still used in the evaluation for time on task

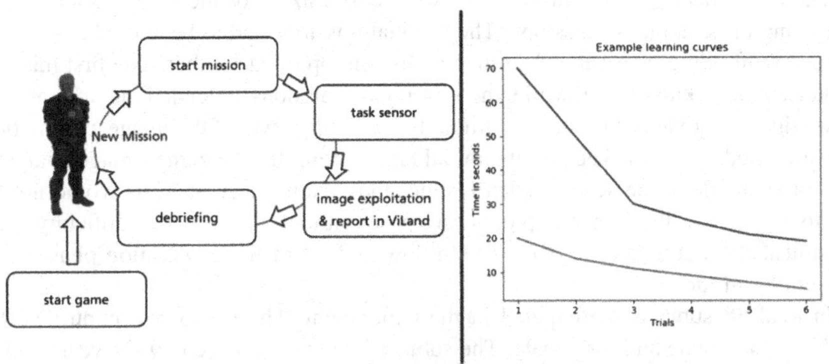

Fig. 3. Left: Core game loop for image exploitation missions Right: example for learning curves according to Albert & Tullis [13]

usability and learnability. If the cognitive load is too low, users are less engaged. When the cognitive load is too high users feel overwhelmed.

4.2 Setup

The study was set up as A/B Testing [13], comparing subjects using the pedagogical agent, to subjects playing the original Lost Earth 2307 implementation. Each session was conducted as a 'Think Aloud Session' [3], where the subjects are asked to verbally illustrate what happens inside their heads.

Three types of questionnaires were applied for the study. For measuring the usability in both groups, the SUS (System Usability Scale) questionnaire was used [15]. The NASA Raw TLX (Task Load Index) questionnaire was presented after each trial to assess the cognitive load of the subject while playing [16]. Finally, an open questionnaire was utilized in order to give subjects the possibility to return feedback or other comments.

The procedure for each experiment in both groups followed seven steps (see Fig. 4). The first step was a short briefing on the game and starting it. The briefing was followed by the first trial where the subject played the first mission in Lost Earth 2307. After this step the subject was asked to fill in the SUS and NASA TLX questionnaire. Then the second trial with mission two and the third trial with mission three followed consecutively. After that the open questionnaire was handed out to gather general feedback. The last step was a debriefing about the test setting and the purpose of the study.

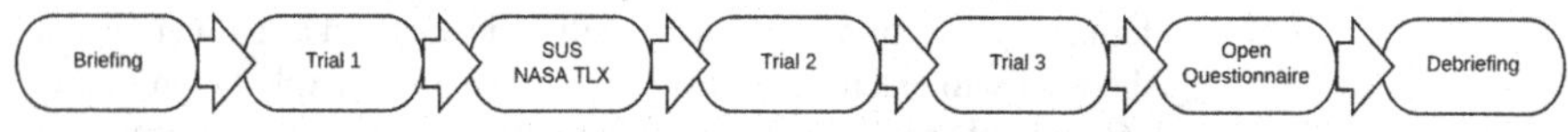

Fig. 4. Procedure of the user study

The three missions used in the trials were customized for the study. Both groups were using these adjusted missions. The original missions had to be altered in order to improve scaffolding (see Table 1), thus to build on top of each other. The first mission introduced new knowledge while the other two missions extended on top of this knowledge and advanced on it. In addition, the difficulty level of the image exploitation was simplified. This was because the initial target group for the game (image analysts) was not available in the scale needed for the study. Non image analysts would not be able to succeed in the image exploitation phase without adjusting the difficulty. The adjustment did not affect the overall workflow and UI of the exploration phase, thus does not harm the study.

In total 38 subjects participated in the experiment. The group was controlled by gender, 50% female and 50% male. The subjects' age was between 19–32 years and at an average of 24 years. None of the subjects had military experience beforehand, and 39% had experience with strategic video games.

To keep the amount of work for the experimenter manageable, sessions were restricted to 1.5 h. The limited session time also helped to avoid overfatigue of subjects and to control for negative effects on the subjects capability in perceiving and remembering the information presented to them during trials.

All information given by the experimenter was formulated in a script, to avoid subjects bias, by missing information or given too much compared to others.

4.3 Results

The data was analyzed using independent T-Test, which results in two values: F and p. A p-value below 0.05 is commonly interpreted as showing some effect between two variables. F-values show the significance of an effect if there is one. Commonly a value above 0.05 is chosen as threshold for showing a significant effect.

For the metric 'mission success' the data showed no significant effect (F = 1.765; p = .476) between the two test groups. There is also no significant effect over multiple trials (F = 351; p = .516).

'Mission Score' also showed no significant difference (F = 2.509; p = .417) between groups. These findings are also true over multiple trials (F = .006; p = .488).

However, evaluating 'Mission Time' showed significant effect (F = .054; p = .000). Furthermore, all other times measured in the first trial showed similar significances. Plots of the raw data can be seen in Fig. 5. Nevertheless, the amount of data gathered for an analysis of learnability (Mission Time over trials) is too small for a statistically authoritative statement. Reason behind this is the low number of subjects which reached the last level of the game (eight in total).

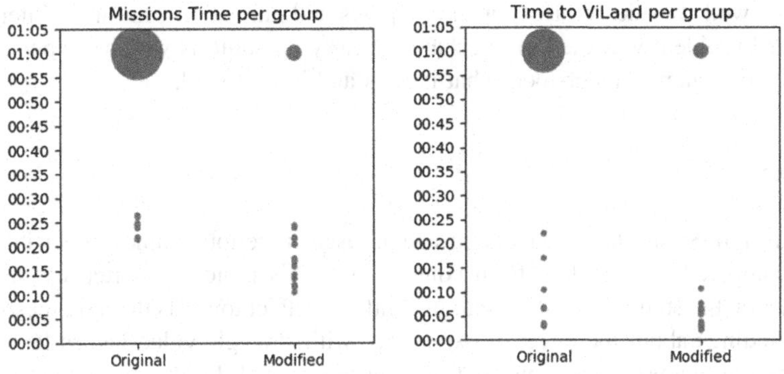

Fig. 5. Results metric "Mission Time' and submetrics

Due to the overall low success rate, analysis for effects between subjects that have experience with strategic video games and those that have no experience seemed to be of interest. T-Test showed the significance distribution of the different metrics is inverse compared to the results shown above. The metrics for time showed no effect. On the other hand, 'Mission Score' and 'Mission Success' showed significant differences between these groups. This leads to the assumption that literacy in strategic games affects the learnability of the game significantly, compared to illiterate control group.

Regarding the usability the group using the pedagogical agent showed better results in SUS (see Fig. 6). The difference between these groups is significant (F = .377; p = .008). The NASA TLX results on the other hand showed no effect (see Fig. 6) But significantly less subjects felt lost when guided by LISA compared to the control group

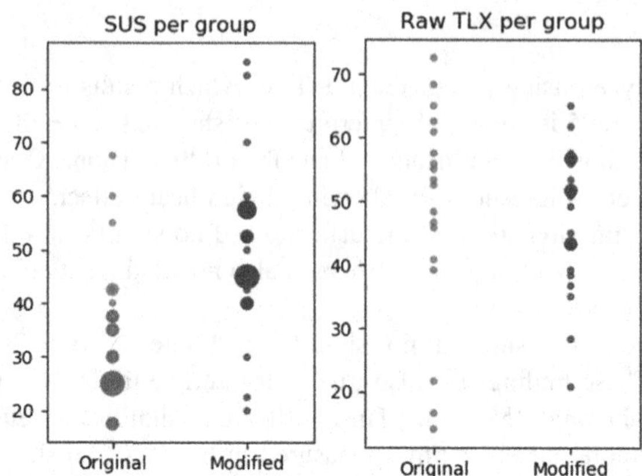

Fig. 6. Results for SUS and NASA Raw TLX

(F = 89.526; p = .010). Also the modified LISA scored significantly lower (F = 1.406; p = .017) on a five point annoyance scale.

The qualitative results from the open questionnaire showed some interesting insights as well. Besides praises for the graphics and animations, the most interesting unexpected problem was the turn mechanic. Nearly no subjects without experience in strategic video games understood what it does and how it works.

5 Discussion

The main hypothesis that pedagogical agents used in serious games affect its learnability, compared to "standard form contract"-tutorials is not supported by the data. Nevertheless, the study showed a small insignificant effect towards the hypothesis. This and the findings about the effect of experience with strategic video games let assume that literacy in games plays a bigger role than anticipated. Furthermore, the insignificant effect on learnability is supported by the results of SUS. LISA as pedagogical agent improves perceived usability significantly, compared to the control group.

As stated before, the subjects were not part of the initial target group. Therefore, a study conducted with image analysts might result in different outcomes. Still, as the general usability score is relatively low in all groups an improvement on usability will improve the learnability independent of the target group.

It is noteworthy that evaluation between genders showed big significant effects in most metrics. Nevertheless when sorting out subjects that had experience with strategic video games these effects disappeared. Only one female subject had previous experience with such video games where on the other side 75% of male subjects had previous experience. This leads to the assumption that the big effect between genders is caused by experience.

The experiments were held in a laboratory setting. Therefore, the ability to generalize results of this study is limited, as this could also have had an influence on the general engagement and thus on SUS and TLX.

6 Conclusion

The paper presented a process on how the learnability of a serious game could be improved and how the implementation was evaluated by a study. At first, the status quo of the game was analyzed. Based on the findings a pedagogical agent was implemented to address the problems. A user study evaluated the effect on learnability. No significant effect on learnability could be found, but a strong effect between subjects with and without experience in strategic video games was observed. In addition, the low score in general usability could be the cause of the agent's limited effect.

Taking into account, that experience in strategic video games seems to be of great importance, the further evaluation of this effect is subject of future work. Although the participants were not part of the initial target group, the low SUS and TLX rating lead to a general improvement of the usability of the game and after that further studies need to be conducted to give clear answers on the learnability effect of pedagogical agents.

Compared to the pure "text-wall" tutorial used in the original version of the game, using a pedagogical agent was an improvement in usability, although the game still suffers from further usability issues. Therefore, in general one can assume that using a pedagogical agent for improving the learnability of a serious game is suggested, in particular if the creators experience the users having problems learning the game.

References

1. Prensky, M.: Digital Game-Based Learning. Paragon House, St. Paul (2007)
2. Bopp, M.: Immersive Didaktik und Framingprozesse in Computerspielen. In: Neitzel, B., Nohr, R.F. (eds.) *Das Spiel mit dem Medium. Partizipation-Immersion-Interaktion. Zur Teilhabe an den Medien von Kunst bis Computerspiel,* pp. 170–186. Schüren, Marburg (2006)
3. Atorf, D., Kannegieser, E., Roller, W.: Balancing realism and engagement for a serious game in the domain of remote sensing. In: Gentile, M., Allegra, M., Söbke, H. (eds.) GALA 2018. LNCS, vol. 11385, pp. 146–156. Springer, Cham (2019). https://doi.org/10.1007/978-3-030-11548-7_14
4. Cheng, M.-T., She, H.-C., Annetta, L.A.: Game immersion experience: its hierarchical structure and impact on game-based science learning. J. Comput. Assist. Learn. **31**(3), 232–253 (2015)
5. Nielsen, J.: Usability Engineering. Academic Press, London (1993)
6. Benyon, D.: Designing Interactive Systems: A Comprehensive Guide to HCI and Interaction Design. Pearson, UK (2019)
7. Gee, J.P.: Learning by design: good video games as learning machines. E-Learn. Digit. Media **2**(1), 5–16 (2005)
8. Hedges, N.: Gamasutra: hedges's blog - video game tutorials: how do they teach? (2017). https://www.gamasutra.com/blogs/NathanHedges/20171013/307378/Video{-}Game{-}Tutorials{-}How{-}Do{-}They{-}Teach.php. Accessed 07 June 2019
9. Johnson, W.L., Lester, J.C.: Face-to-face interaction with pedagogical agents, twenty years later. Int. J. Artif. Intell. Educ. **26**(1), 25–36 (2016)
10. Schroeder, N.L., Adesope, O.O., Gilbert, R.B.: How effective are pedagogical agents for learning? A meta-analytic review. J. Educ. Comput. Res. **49**(1), 1–39 (2013)

11. Collins, A., Brown, J.S., Holum, A.: Cognitive apprenticeship: making thinking visible. Am. Educ. **6**(11), 38–46 (1991)
12. Raskin, J.: The Humane Interface. Addison Wesley, New York (2000)
13. Albert, W., Tullis, T.: Measuring the User Experience: Collecting, Analyzing, and Presenting Usability Metrics. Morgan Kaufmann, Waltham (2013)
14. Nielsen, J., Mack, R.L., Bergendorff, K.H., Grischkowsky, N.L.: Integrated software usage in the professional work environment: evidence from questionnaires and interviews. In: Proceedings of the SIGCHI Conference on Human Factors in Computing Systems CHI 1986, vol. 17, no. 4, pp. 162–167. ACM (1986)
15. Brooke, J.: SUS - a quick and dirty usability scale. Usability Eval. Ind. **189**(194), 189–194 (1996)
16. Cao, A., Chintamani, K.K., Pandya, A.K., Ellis, R.D.: NASA TLX: software for assessing subjective mental workload. Behav. Res. Methods **41**(1), 113–117 (2009)

Scaffolding Open Text Input in a Scripted Communication Skills Learning Environment

Raja Lala[1](✉), Johan Jeuring[1,2], and Marcell van Geest[1]

[1] Computer Science Department, Utrecht University, Utrecht, The Netherlands
r.lala@uu.nl

[2] Faculty of Management, Science and Technology, Open University Netherlands, Heerlen, The Netherlands

Abstract. Serious games, as well as entertainment games, often employ a scripted dialogue for player interaction with a virtual character. In our serious game Communicate, a domain expert develops a structured, scripted scenario as a sequence of potential interactions in an authoring tool. Communicate is widely used and several domain experts have already developed over a thousand scenarios. In the original version of Communicate, a student 'navigates' a dialogue with a virtual character by clicking one of the multiple statement options at a step of a scenario. Open text response often requires more complex thinking from a student. In this paper we explore ways to handle open text input from a student at a step of a scenario. Our goal is to match open text to scripted statements using a Natural Language Processing (NLP) method and explore mechanisms to handle matched and unmatched input.

1 Introduction

Communication skills are best learned through practice, in role play or with a simulated patient [2]. In Communicate [6], a serious game for training communication skills, a student practices a communication skills dialogue with a virtual character, see Fig. 1. Communicate is used in multiple domains to practice diverse communication skills and protocols, including assertiveness training, breaking bad news, visit to a pharmacy and collaboration.

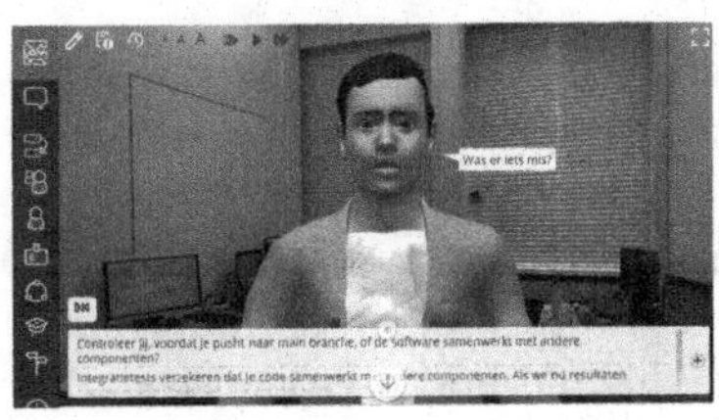

Fig. 1. Communicate game

Authoring content in an Intelligent tutoring system often requires significant effort [1], and authoring tool usability is often at the expense of expressiveness [13]. Communicate provides an authoring tool that combines expressive dialogue constructs with ease of use [7] and runs in a web browser. We release a dialogue scenario editor authoring tool as open-source as part of an EU project RAGE (Realising an Applied

A. Liapis et al. (Eds.): GALA 2019, LNCS 11899, pp. 169–179, 2019.
https://doi.org/10.1007/978-3-030-34350-7_17

Gaming Ecosystem), see gamecomponents.eu. A communication skills teacher, usually a non-programmer, authors a scenario. A scenario is a sequence of interleaved subjects, where each subject is a directed acyclic graph consisting of a sequence of statements alternating between a virtual character and a player. A learning goal is typically encoded as a parameter in a scenario. An author assigns values to this parameter, typically an integer, per player statement option. An author also assigns an emotion to a player statement.

Communicate [6] presents statement options to a player at a step of a communication scenario, see Fig. 1. Choosing a player statement elicits the emotion assigned to the statement from a virtual character. At the end of a simulation, a player gets a score depending on her statement choices during the simulation. Martinez et al. [11] review cumulative research on the cognitive demand of multiple choice versus constructed response test item formats. Test item formats pose trade offs in cognitive demand, psychometric characteristics, and costs of administration/scoring. Multiple choice items often elicit low level cognitive processing from a student but are deterministic and easy to score. Open text response often requires complex thinking, but is more difficult to score. Students consider multiple choice fair, but they pay more attention to content when preparing for an open response test.

Our goal is to enhance Communicate by offering a student the possibility to enter open text at a step of a scenario. Adding an input box for a player to enter open text to our simulation is trivial, the challenge is to process this open text. To process open text, we use Natural Language Processing (NLP) techniques. In a previous experiment we gathered student open text input for a scenario and created a golden dataset on which we ran a range of open source NLP methods [9]. NLP methods that use local information (e.g. string kernels) give better matching results than NLP methods that use a generic corpora (e.g. semantic matching using latent semantic analysis, or paraphrasing). Even with a sizeable dataset, the results of NLP methods are not entirely accurate: NLP methods often require very large datasets to train a model [15]. It is unlikely we will obtain large datasets for all scenarios in Communicate: since authors can easily create and/or modify a scenario, we have over a thousand (variants of) scenarios about different communication protocols in different contexts. Our main contribution in this paper is to introduce open text input without significant additional effort from an author and/or extensive data gathering for a scenario, which is infeasible given the number of scenarios, and to explore mechanisms to handle matched and unmatched input. There is a wider implication for entertainment and learning games using scripted dialogues.

Realdon et al. [14] suggests a scaffolding structure in a learning environment to give a student an opportunity to learn. Given the limitations mentioned in the previous paragraph, our approach is to use an NLP method to match a student open text input and use scaffolding to handle matched and unmatched input. This NLP method takes a scripted scenario as input to build a scenario specific corpus [8]. For matching an open input text, this method uses the scenario specific corpus and returns a match score per scripted statement at a step of the simulation. We established a threshold score for the NLP method [9] and if all match-scores are below this threshold, we consider an open text input as unmatched. If at least one match-score is above the threshold, we consider an open text input as matched. Fowler and Barker [3] find that highlighting improves retention of material and to handle matched input, we highlight the best matching statement. To handle unmatched input, we look at Intelligent Tutoring Systems (ITS). Van Lehn [16] studies common behaviour of ITSs and recommends giving a hint for a next step when a student needs a hint. He recommends sequencing hints, starting with encouraging a student to think herself, and after that giving more detail about a next step. Our research questions (RQs) are: Can we handle matched input by highlighting a statement and unmatched input by providing a sequence of hints? We introduce variations in blended teaching sessions to answer our research questions.

This paper is organised as follows. Section 2 discusses related work. Section 3 describes our method to answer the research questions. Section 4 discusses results and Sect. 5 presents conclusions and future work.

2 Related Work

This section gives related work on introducing natural language input in a learning environment or serious game. We look at different approaches to introduce open text input.

Autotutor [4] is a well known tutoring environment using natural language technologies. In AutoTutor, a student answers a question by means of a paragraph (approximately seven sentences) of text. Autotutor provides feedback on this text, and engages in a turn taking dialogue until a student arrives at a number of correct sentences. To handle open text, AutoTutor uses NLP methods like latent semantic analysis and speech act classifiers; techniques that focus on the general meaning of the input and functional purpose of an expression but also require a large dataset. It is unclear how AutoTutor processes unmatched input that does not fit any classifier in the script. The time and cost of authoring a script is considerable and requires extensive collaboration between computer scientists, cognitive psychologists and content experts.

Lessard [10] investigates the design of a natural language game conversation (built in ChatScript) based on experience from three digital games primarily involving a dialogue between a player and a virtual character. An NLP interaction provides creative conversational play, role playing, content contribution and non-linear conversations in these games. The drawbacks mentioned are: a player expectation that the system understands and responds like a person, leaky fictional coherence, unrestricted input, i.e. a player can say anything and a virtual character cannot have a response for everything and 'amnesia' specific to a chatbot that cannot 'remember' previous utterances.

Higashinaka et al. [5] conduct an experiment to collect question answer pairs from users to create a chatbot character with consistent personality. The authors use a text engine to index the collected question answer pairs. They develop a chatbot that takes an open text input as a query to retrieve the most relevant question and responds with the pair answer. They use different retrieval methods and perform a 'subjective' evaluation to rate an answer in terms of naturalness and consistency. Higashinaka et al. find that the chatbot character has a consistent personality but the text retrieval methods are not entirely accurate. (In)accuracy of an NLP method is related to our work; we use scaffolding to handle an open text input.

Min et al. [12] present a multimodal framework that predicts breakdowns in a student conversation with a pedagogical agent. The authors characterise a dialogue breakdown as a situation in which an agent misinterprets a student utterance and responds incorrectly. The framework incorporates natural language, eye gaze, student gender, and task state. Min et al. investigate this framework in a study of 92 middle school students in a game based learning environment. They find that incorporating eye gaze achieves high predictive accuracy for dialogue breakdown. We give a sequence of hints to a player when an open text input cannot be matched to a scripted statement.

In summary, there is a diversity of methods to introduce open text input in serious games and learning environments. Methods range from collecting and classifying input, semantic matching, chatbots, and agent technology. In our approach we use a scripted scenario as the basis, which ensures consistency, fictional coherence and control in utterances. We use an NLP method that takes a scripted scenario as input to build a scenario specific corpus [8]. We match an open text input using this corpus and use scaffolding to handle matched and unmatched input.

3 Method

To answer our research question, we introduce variations in our teaching intervention. At our University, final year computer science students learn to work together in a software project team. During the project we provide a communication skills blended learning session per team consisting of 10 to 12 students each. In this session, students play a scenario about collaboration. A student needs to converse with a team mate (virtual character) who has not followed quality procedures (integration tests). In a session, an instructor introduces Communicate, students play the scenario, the instructor explains the communication protocol that forms the basis of the scenario, and there is a plenary discussion. To enable open text, we provide a text box at each step of a scenario, see Fig. 2.

We added hints to the Collaboration scenario that we use in the sessions. For example, we added the hint *'Try to give feedback about working together: his code does not work with other components, so you know that he has not performed integration tests'* to the subject *'Express'*, and we added the hint *'verbalise behaviour'* to the player statement, *'You pushed code that does not work with other components'*.

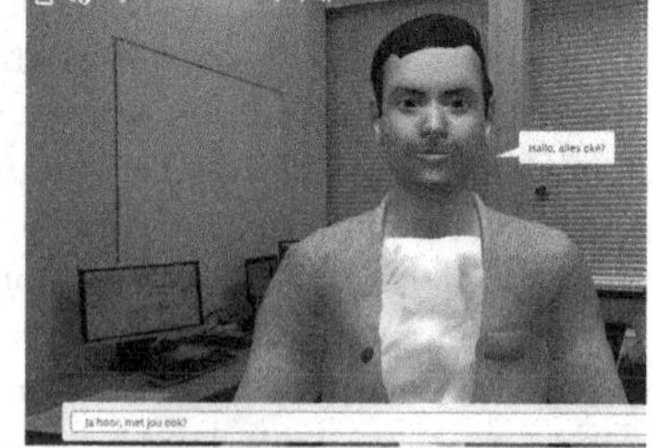

Fig. 2. Open text input box

Our research method is to vary the aspect under consideration. For highlighting our treatment is to let a student match her open text input to a statement option with and without highlighting in separate rounds of sessions respectively. For hints, the treatment is to divide the students randomly into an experimental and control group, where within the same session, a student from the experimental group gets a sequence of hints and the control group get no hints. The design of the sessions in the semester of fall-winter 2018 is shown schematically in Fig. 3.

Round1: student inputs open-text, method matches.

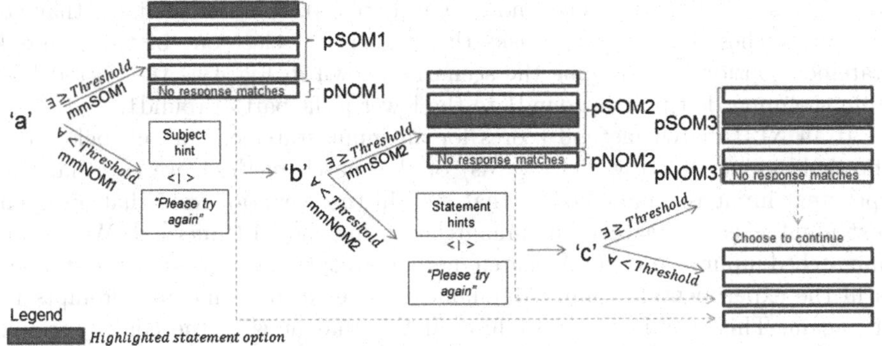

<|> *Student in evaluation group gets a hint versus in control group,"please try again"*

Round2: LearnEnv plays student playthrough from round1

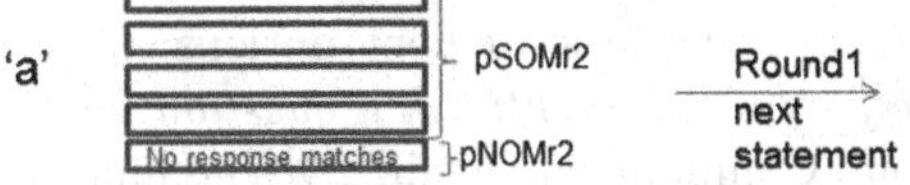

Fig. 3. Setup within sessions of fall-winter 2018

A student fills in an open input text (see Fig. 2, for example 'Ja hoor, met jou ook?') and the NLP match method takes this open input text 'a' and returns a match score per scripted statement option at a step of the scenario. In a previous experiment [9], we empirically determined a baseline threshold value for a match. If at least one statement option has a match score above the threshold value of the match method, we call that an mmSOM (match method some option matches). If a match method detects at least one mmSOM (∃ arrow upwards), Communicate displays all scripted statement options and highlights the best mmSOM match, see Fig. 4, in this example 'Jazeker, met jou ook?'.

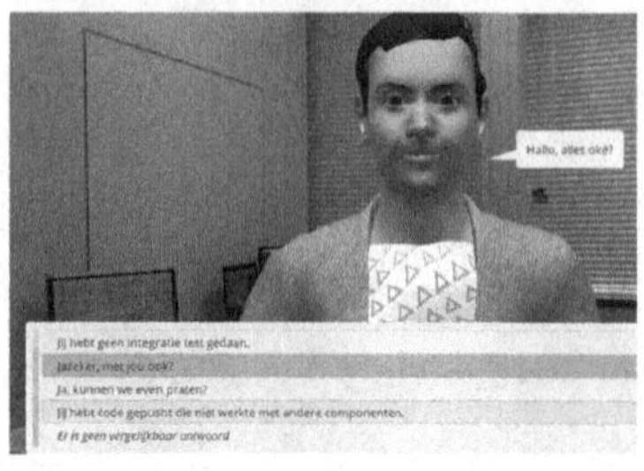

Fig. 4. Highlighted best match

Communicate asks a student to match the closest option to her open input text 'a' from the displayed statement options. If a student selects one of the statement options, we log for statistical comparison (see Sect. 4) as 'pSOM1' (player some option matches). We also log whether a student selects the highlighted option or another option. A student also gets an option to choose 'No response matches' (*Er is geen vergelijkbaar antwoord*). If a student chooses this option, we log this as 'pNOM1' (player no option matches). If a student finds that no option matches, Communicate asks the student to select one of the scripted statement options to continue the scenario, shown in Fig. 4 as the dotted line from the upper left part in round1 to the lower right part of round1.

If all NLP match method scores for an input statement 'a' are below the threshold value (∀ arrow downwards) of the match method, we say that the open text input is unmatched at that step in the scenario. Note that an open text input is either matched or unmatched using the NLP method. We log an unmatched input as mmNOM (match method no option matches). If the student is in the experimental group, Communicate gives a first hint and prompts to try again. This hint is a subject hint. If the student is in the control group, Communicate gives no hint and prompts a student to try again. A student enters a new response 'b', which is matched to obtain an mmSOM or mmNOM. In case the match method finds an mmSOM, we process it in the same way as described in the paragraph above. In case a match method detects an mmNOM again, Communicate displays the hints for all the statement options at that step, e.g: *Try to: verbalise behaviour; refer to agreement; ask a question* for the experimental group. For the control group Communicate again gives no hint and prompts a student to try again. A student enters a new response 'c', which again is matched to obtain an mmSOM or mmNOM. In case of an mmSOM, we again process as described above. In case of an mmNOM, Communicate asks a student to select one of the scripted statement options to continue the scenario.

For the treatment with no highlighting, we conduct a 2nd round of sessions with the students, three weeks after the 1st round. For all students who agreed in their user profile to store their open text input, Communicate presents a student her first playthrough from the 1st round. At each step of the playthrough, the first open text a student entered (the string 'a') in the 1st round is displayed, and Communicate displays all the statement options available at that step of the scenario and the special option *No response matches.* No statements are highlighted unlike in round1. There are a total of 210 open text input statements that students match. Communicate asks a student to match her input (string 'a') to an option, and we log if a student matches to a scripted option or if she chooses *No response matches.* Communicate displays the match the student made in the first round and continues with the next entered input from her playthrough from the 1st round until the end of the playthrough. Other students, who did not agree to store their open text input, played the scenario in multiple choice format.

4 Results and Discussion

In the fall-winter semester 2018, there were a total of 52 students in five project teams, who played the same scenario in a modified version of Communicate where they typed in open text responses. Our research question is whether we can handle matched and unmatched open text input using highlighting and hints respectively. In the majority of open text input in round1 (389 statements out of 503 statements, 77.34%), the match method matched with at least one of the scripted statements. For the remaining statements (114 of 503 statements, 22.66%) for which no match was found: Communicate showed a hint to students in the experimental group for approximately half the unmatched cases (56 statements, 11.13%) versus no hint in the control group (58 statements, 11.53%).

RQ: Can we handle matched input by highlighting a statement?

We compare the match choice from a student in the first round (best matched statement highlighted) versus the second round (no statement highlighted). In the first round, for an mmSOM, a player gets to match her open text input to one of the scripted statements while the best match is highlighted, see Fig. 4. She can choose either the highlighted statement, another statement, or *No response matches.* We analyse the different combination cases that occur. We discuss how a simulation without a highlighting scaffolding (referred as automatic match) would look like. We also gather insight into NLP matching versus student matching. All percentages in this subsection are from a total of 210 open text input statements that students match in round2, see Sect. 3. The comparison between round1 (highlighting) versus round2 (no highlighting) is summarised in Table 1.

Table 1. Highlighting comparison table

	%
Highlighting effect cases	09.05%
True Positive (TP)	17.14%
True Negative (TN)	07.14%
False Negative (FN)	16.19%
False Positive (FP)	01.90%
NLP match differs from student match	20.48%
Student chooses inconsistently	28.10%

Does highlighting increase the chance of matching? We argue that highlighting had an effect when a student matches the highlighted statement in round1 and to a different statement; or to *No response matches* in round2. This occurs in 16 (7.62%) and 3 (1.43%) statements respectively, total 9.05% of the statements (210) matched in the 2nd round, shown in the first row of Table 1.

When a player matches her open input with the match method highlighted statement choice in round1 and chooses the same statement (unhighlighted) in round2, we call this a true positive (TP), 36 statements (17.14%) are TPs, shown in the second row of Table 1. When a player chooses *No response matches* in round2 and the match method also detects no match (mmNOM) in round1, we call this true negative (TN), 15 statements (7.14%) are TN, shown in the third row of Table 1. A TN open text input might be a signal of a missing scripted player statement option at a step of a scenario. In an automatic match, Communicate response would be accurate in these (TP and TN) cases. When a student matches her input to a statement in round2 but the match method detects no match in round1, we call this a false negative (FN, 34 statements, 16.19%). In an automatic match, Communicate would incorrectly provide a hint for an FN. When a student chooses *No response matches* in both rounds but the match method finds at least one match value above the threshold, we call this a false positive (FP, only in 4 statements, 1.90%). For an FP in an automatic match, a virtual character would provide a response, but Communicate should have given a hint.

When the NLP match method matches differently than a student statement match in both rounds (43 statements out of 210, 20.48%), in an automatic match a virtual character would provide a different response than possibly intended by the scenario author. E.g. a student entered, 'De code die je gisteren hebt gepushed conflicteert' for which the NLP method has the best match score to 'Ik wil het even met jou hebben over je werk van gisteren' whereas the student matches to 'Je code werkte niet samen met het geheel'. In this example, the NLP choice is not incorrect, however these statements are opportunities to examine if we can improve the NLP match method further.

There are cases when a student chooses inconsistently: when a student matches to an unhighlighted statement in round1 but chooses a different statement in round2 (43 statements out of 210, 20.48%), coincidentally the same amount but other statements than the statements that the NLP method matches differently than a student. We examined these statements: sometimes an input was a mix of two scripted statements or perhaps the statement options seemed similar to a student. Another inconsistency is when a student chooses *No response matches* in one of the rounds and an unhighlighted option in the other round (16 statements, 7.62%). In automatic processing these cases (total 28.10%, shown in the last row of Table 1), either a virtual character's response or a hint would be somewhat correct.

To answer our research question: using highlighting for matched open text input is not effective. The total of absolute errors in matching: false negative and false positive (18.09%) is limited and we argue on the basis of our results that for a matched open input, Communicate should not use highlighting, and automatically continue with the simulation.

RQ: Can we handle unmatched input by providing a sequence of hints? We evaluate if giving a hint in the experimental group leads more often to a matched input than in the control group.

Table 2. Hint evaluation table

	Control group	Hint group
Initial unmatched statements (mmNOM)	58	56
Observed matches after subject hint	24	28
Expected matches after subject hint	26.4561	25.5439
Unmatched statements after subject hint	34	28
Observed matches after statement hints	16	9
Expected matches after statement hints	13.7097	11.2903

We perform a chi-distribution test, which compares the observed cases versus expected values, see Table 2. The experimental (hint) group matches slightly better than expected after a subject hint and slightly worse than expected after a statement hint. The control group matches the other way around, slightly worse than expected after the first prompt to try again and slightly better than expected after the second prompt to try again. The differences are not significant (p-value 0.2521), and the reasons could be multifold. We paid attention while scripting the hints that a hint would not result in a match by copy-pasting. Perhaps a student tried the same words as in a hint and it could be that a student is perhaps frustrated by having to type something again. The match method is also not entirely accurate, perhaps a hint is similar to a student input which was incorrectly unmatched. To answer our research question, giving a hint for unmatched open text input has no significant impact in our experiment. We recommend to not give hints, but instead to display the available statement options immediately to allow a player to continue a simulation.

5 Conclusions and Future Work

In this paper we take steps to enhance our learning environment from a multiple choice player input to open text player input. Enabling player open text input in our learning environment leads to more student interaction. Scaffolding, highlighting matched open text input and giving hints for unmatched input, has only a limited effect in Communicate. This result can perhaps be generalised for serious games that use a dialogue graph, want to incorporate open text input and have no extensive dataset. Our experiment results in a dataset of open text matched to a statement annotated by a student herself. The total of absolute matching errors by our NLP method on this dataset is small. The dataset provides a good distribution of student open text with corresponding matching and can be used by other NLP methods to improve match accuracy.

For future work, we recommend and plan to have guided sessions with minimal scaffolding, where in case of matched input a simulation continues as if a virtual character has understood the input (i.e. no extra highlight step to confirm a match) and in case of unmatched input, we present the available statement options to a player to select and continue a dialogue. This setup will involve no extra effort for a scenario author.

Acknowledgments. This activity has partially received funding from the European Institute of Innovation and Technology (EIT). This body of the European Union receives support from the European Union's Horizon 2020 research and innovation programme. The authors acknowledge Gemma Corbalan and Matthieu Brinkhuis for their help in the statistical analysis.

References

1. Aleven, V., Sewall, J., McLaren, B.M., Koedinger, K.R.: Rapid authoring of intelligent tutors for real-world and experimental use. In: Sixth IEEE International Conference on Advanced Learning Technologies (ICALT 2006), pp. 847–851. IEEE (2006)
2. Berkhof, M., van Rijssen, H.J., Schellart, A.J.M., Anema, J.R., van der Beek, A.J.: Effective training strategies for teaching communication skills to physicians: an overview of systematic reviews. Patient Educ. Couns. **84**(2), 152–162 (2011)
3. Fowler, R.L., Barker, A.S.: Effectiveness of highlighting for retention of text material. J. Appl. Psychol. **59**(3), 358 (1974)
4. Graesser, A.C., et al.: AutoTutor: a tutor with dialogue in natural language. Behav. Res. Methods Instrum. Comput. **36**(2), 180–192 (2004)
5. Higashinaka, R., Mizukami, M., Kawabata, H., Yamaguchi, E., Adachi, N., Tomita, J.: Role play-based question-answering by real users for building chatbots with consistent personalities. In: Proceedings of the 19th Annual SIGdial Meeting on Discourse and Dialogue, pp. 264–272 (2018)
6. Jeuring, J., et al.: Communicate!—a serious game for communication skills—. In: Conole, G., Klobučar, T., Rensing, C., Konert, J., Lavoué, É. (eds.) EC-TEL 2015. LNCS, vol. 9307, pp. 513–517. Springer, Cham (2015). https://doi.org/10.1007/978-3-319-24258-3_49
7. Lala, R., Jeuring, J., van Dortmont, J., van Geest, M.: Scenarios in virtual learning environments for one-to-one communication skills training. Int. J. Educ. Technol. High. Educ. **14**(1), 17 (2017)
8. Lala, R., et al.: Processing open text input in a scripted communication scenario. In: SEMDIAL 2018: The 22nd Workshop on the Semantics and Pragmatics of Dialogue, pp. 211–214 (2018)
9. Lala, R.: Enhancing free-text interactions in a communication skills learning environment. In: Proceedings of the 13th International Conference on Computer Supported Collaborative Learning, pp. 363–364 (June 2019)
10. Lessard, J.: Designing natural-language game conversations. Proc. DiGRA-FDG (2016)
11. Martinez, M.E.: Cognition and the question of test item format. Educ. Psychol. **34**(4), 207–218 (1999)
12. Min, W., et al.: Predicting dialogue breakdown in conversational pedagogical agents with multimodal LSTMs. In: Isotani, S., Millán, E., Ogan, A., Hastings, P., McLaren, B., Luckin, R. (eds.) AIED 2019. LNCS (LNAI), vol. 11626, pp. 195–200. Springer, Cham (2019). https://doi.org/10.1007/978-3-030-23207-8_37
13. Murray, T.: An overview of intelligent tutoring system authoring tools: updated analysis of the state of the art. In: Authoring Tools for Advanced Technology Learning Environments, pp. 491–544. Springer (2003). https://doi.org/10.1007/978-94-017-0819-7_17

14. Realdon, O., Zurloni, V., Confalonieri, L., Mortillaro, M., Mantovani, F.: Learning Communication Skills Through Computer-Based Interactive Simulations. From Communication to Presence: Cognition, Emotions and Culture Towards the Ultimate Communicative Experience, pp. 281–303. IOS Press, Amsterdam (2006)
15. Ruseti, S., Lala, R., Gutu-Robu, G., Dascalu, M., Jeuring, J., van Geest, M.: Semantic matching of open texts to pre-scripted answers in dialogue-based learning. In: Isotani, S., Millán, E., Ogan, A., Hastings, P., McLaren, B., Luckin, R. (eds.) AIED 2019. LNCS (LNAI), vol. 11626, pp. 242–246. Springer, Cham (2019). https://doi.org/10.1007/978-3-030-23207-8_45
16. Vanlehn, K.: The behavior of tutoring systems. Int. J. Artif. Intell. Educ. **16**(3), 227–265 (2006)

Loud and Clear: The VR Game Without Visuals

Berend Baas, Dennis van Peer, Jan Gerling, Matthias Tavasszy, Nathan Buskulic, Nestor Z. Salamon, J. Timothy Balint, and Rafael Bidarra(✉)

Faculty of Electrical Engineering, Mathematics and Computer Science, Delft University of Technology, Delft, The Netherlands
R.Bidarra@tudelft.nl

Abstract. While visual impairment is relatively common, most sighted people have no idea of what it is like to live without one of the most heavily utilised senses. We developed the game *Loud and Clear* in order to have them experience the difficulties of being visually impaired, as well as to put in evidence the abilities blind people have developed, which sighted people mostly lack. In this game without visuals, the player has to rely solely on audio to complete objectives within the game. The game consists of a number of puzzle rooms the player has to solve. These puzzles illustrate the challenges of being blind in a playful setting, and challenge the player to use different auditory skills that are key to achieving objectives without vision, such as sound localisation, sound recognition and spatial orientation. The game uses audio spatialisation techniques to give the player a realistic and immersive auditive experience. Preliminary tests of this game show that players acknowledge the initial high difficulty of 'living' as a blind person, to which eventually they were able to somehow adapt. In addition, players reported feeling both immersed and educated by the experience.

Keywords: Virtual reality · Audio game · Blindness awareness

1 Introduction

According to the World Health Organisation, in 2017 there were roughly 39 million fully blind people worldwide. Additionally, there are another 217 million people that the WHO labels as moderate to severely visually impaired [4]. However, even with this massive number of cases, many people do not understand the experience of having to live without sight. Sighted people rarely experience either the challenges of (completely) lacking sight or the abilities that blind people develop to cope with those challenges. In order to give them this opportunity, learn from it, and help raise awareness about blindness generally, the game Loud and Clear was developed. This is a Virtual Reality (VR) game without visuals in which the player has to rely on audio cues in order to navigate and recognise

A. Liapis et al. (Eds.): GALA 2019, LNCS 11899, pp. 180–190, 2019.
https://doi.org/10.1007/978-3-030-34350-7_18

the surroundings and clear objectives in the game. Taking the form of an escape-room-like puzzle game, the player is locked in a dungeon consisting of various chambers, each containing a puzzle. The player has a certain amount of time to solve these puzzles in order to progress to the next chamber and eventually escape. The puzzles challenge the player and aim to provide experience of, and insight into, what it means to be blind. Different from real escape rooms, we do not enforce a target finishing time. The player is allowed to freely explore the scenarios, and feedback is provided to help progression as time passes. The game runs on a mobile phone attached to a head mounted device, paired with headphones and a joystick. No specialised hardware is required, making it portable and accessible to a broad audience.

2 Related Work

Creating awareness about the problems faced by visually impaired people is a first step to inclusion, and sight simulators explore that by providing experiences on partial or total sight loss. Applications attempting to provide blind people with the ability to play games are widespread, either by porting games directly targeted at visually impaired people, or by adapting existing games to be playable without a display. Many solutions rely on audio feedback. Audio is both an expressive narrative medium to convey detailed information to the player, and simple and inexpensive due to the general accessibility of audio devices.

Another source of feedback for blind people comes from haptics. While this is a promising area of research to assist the blind in navigating virtual environments [6,20], it poses various constraints (e.g. on resolution, mobility and portability), which might be considered distracting to the player. For that reason, we focus on audio games.

Sight Loss Simulators. Sight Loss Simulators are a category of applications that aim to simulate a variety of visual conditions that impair vision, usually by applying image filters to the graphics of the application that try to mimic the experience of someone with one of these conditions. The *See Now* Sight Loss Simulator simulates the experience of an impaired view to its users with the goal of improving eye care [17]. The effects of cataracts, glaucoma, and retinopathy with adjustable severity are shown to the users by applying a visual filter to a Google Street View impression of their choice. The game can be played on smartphones using any capable browser. Due to the sparse design of the simulator the experience of blindness is not as immersive or intense compared to a virtual reality solution and therefore is not illustrative of people with complete loss of vision. A similar approach was also tested using different simulation glasses [7]. Simulations to create awareness are, however, not always straightforward. Silverman [18] stated that simulating blindness by trying to achieve everyday tasks (for a limited amount of time) only serves to further distance the person trying to understand visually impaired people. All that is simulated is the moment of initial shock and confusion following the loss of vision. Playing a game meant for blind people could distract the player from the initial shock, as described by Silverman, and allow the player to experience one aspect of a visually impaired person's life through the immersion of that game. Games like *Finger Dance* [10] can achieve this goal, as it was designed to be enjoyable by both visually impaired and visually capable people alike.

Audio Games. Audio games in this context are digital games focusing on audio rather than on visual representations. These games use audio cues to make up for the lack of visuals. For example, the game *Blindfold Flappy* [14] mimics the game *Flappy Bird* [12], where the player has to steer a bird in-between gaps of varying height to avoid crashing. In *Blindfold Flappy*, the sound is adjusted so that in the left audio channel a continuous tone of varying pitches represents the vertical height of the bird while the pitch in the right channel represents the height of the gap, which should be matched in order for the player to progress. An application to indicate trajectory and movements was also evaluated as a pictionary-like game converting drawings into sound [15]. Other games are especially designed to help blind people develop new skills, such as *BraillePlay* [11] helping blind children learn braille or navigate through an environment. Echo-House [2] explores how sound waves and their echo reverberations can be used to navigate in an virtual environment. Wu et al. [21] developed a game to train people on using such audio cues to echo-locate. Similarly, *The Legend of Iris* [1] aims at training the navigation skills of blind children relying just on audio. In these games the player must navigate towards sound sources and avoid obstacles and dangerous moving objects by localising the sounds they produce. The key element of *The Legend of Iris* is the use of binaural audio in order to allow the player to localise items in 3D space.

Binaural Audio. Binaural audio is the term for audio which is received with two ears; with the perceived difference in volume and timing of the received sound for both ears, the brain is able to estimate the location of the sound's origin. To blind people this property is exceptionally useful, since they often use audio in order to get a mental model of their orientation and surroundings. The first implementations of binaural audio are from 1881, when Clément Ader displayed dual audio channel headphones that allowed people to listen to a concert over phone lines [9]. After this binaural audio has appeared in music records [13] and television shows [3]. Due to its often expensive setup, it did not gain much popularity during these time over these mediums.

Our work incorporates notions from previous work, but its original focus lies on the exposure of sighted people to a "blind-like" exclusively-auditive experience, rather than on game interaction for visually impaired. *Loud and Clear* relies on binaural audio perception to help players grasp the kind of skills that visually impaired people develop to overcome challenges in their environment. Our target group is focused on people that are of good hearing (as this is a requirement for the game to communicate to the player effectively). The controls are kept as simple as possible, but as buttons are used for moving around, some comfort with using abstract movement controls on a controller is also expected.

3 Game Design

The design of *Loud and Clear* materialises the long-established conclusions of experiential learning [8] in a VR setting. The game design is guided by two main principles, building the experience that is intended to be conveyed to the player. The first is to make the player feel challenged, yet accomplished. This is intended to convey the capabilities of blind people. The second is to not overwhelm the player, as a cognitive overload could have a negative experience, and potentially cause the player to feel inept. These principles are reflected in multiple facets of the game design discussed below. In case of conflicting principles, they were solved by carefully balancing challenge and avoiding extra cognitive load.

The game is designed to be fully wearable; it runs on an Android device mounted on a headset. The device does not render any visuals but is used for head tracking to facilitate both audio localisation and the movement direction. The player can interact with the virtual world using two one-handed controllers.

3.1 Audio Design

The game utilises audio spatialisation to virtually place objects in the room, where the audio adapts to the direction that the player is looking to. Since this is the main form of communication with the player, the selection and design of audio sources and sounds has a large impact on the experience. Therefore, we categorised sound according to characteristics and requirements as follows:

- **Static sounds** exist to illustrate the environment and are repetitive in nature. Since these sounds are a constant presence, particular care must be taken that these sounds are not too distracting or irritating for the player.
- **Dynamic sounds** signify some change in the level, whether by direct or indirect player interaction. These sounds can sometimes be unexpected, hence being able to cause surprise without startling.
- **Feedback sounds** provide direct feedback to player interaction. These are sounds that result from actions, such as footsteps from the player walking around in the level, or sounds to indicate use of an item or pressing a button.
- **Voice acting** is used to provide narrative to the player, which can help illustrate a surprising or unlikely scene. It can also be used in combination with audio spatialisation. It is important that the voice acting is not patronising to the player, as this would work against the intended goal of illustrating the capacities of blind people.

In general, sounds should be reasonably pleasant so that players do not feel uncomfortable taking any new actions and can advance without sensorial/emotional hindrance, thus feeling autonomous while unsighted. Sounds must also be balanced out in such a way that the players do not become frustrated or experience cognitive overload for extended periods of time. Since identification can be quite difficult, chosen sounds should also minimise the risk of confusing multiple objects. Furthermore, it is important that sounds do not become irritating. For example, for a repetitive sound like a static background hum, we slightly modulate it over time without affecting the perception, as to not become annoying or unrealistically monotonous.

3.2 Game Mechanics

Being deprived of vision and having to rely only on audio can be demanding for a sighted person. To avoid this, the game mechanics was designed to be simple and intuitive. Requiring only simple interactions with the environment, even people unfamiliar with interactive experiences should be able to play the game.

- Players can move forward and backward in the direction they are facing by pressing a button on the controller. While traditionally a thumb stick or d-pad is used for movement, we chose to allocate forward and backward movement to two buttons to avoid the misconception that moving to the sides is an option. The player's rotation is controlled by their head orientation.
- To interact with objects in the environment (e.g., a button or a door), the player presses a button on the controller. The interaction can either be the character taking and item to keep it in the hand or simply performing an action with an environment item.
- In order to perform certain interactions, players are able to hold items, one in each hand. If players forget what their hands are holding, they can shake the controller and the held item will make an identifying sound.
- All items in the game will make sounds in order to be easily perceptible by the player. However some of them will only do so after interacting with the environment (e.g. a bell rings after pushing a button).
- From time to time, a talking companion may guide the player toward some important items that otherwise could be missed.

3.3 Gameplay

The story in the game is purposefully kept simple: the player is a skeleton locked up in a dungeon by a necromancer. This character is a guiding presence for the player rather than an antagonist. This idea was inspired by puzzle games such as Valve's Portal series [5].

The player has to escape by solving puzzles of increasing difficulty in order to progress through the chambers. Initially, the character is awoken by a knocking sound on his coffin. The player starts by interacting with the coffin door, thus opening it. The necromancer communicates with the player, explaining that he can only escape by solving the puzzle rooms. The first puzzles are rather simple, exploring the basics of the sight-less game mechanics and the basic game concepts, such as basic movement, interaction, and sound localisation. The levels will get increasingly challenging, exposing new mechanics to the player while providing less feedback, following the *scaffolding* principle [16]. During the puzzles, the necromancer guides the player, explaining chamber settings and providing hints if the player is not able to solve the puzzle after a certain amount of time. When the player clears all the chambers, the game is over.

4 Level Design

In order to challenge the players and allow them to experience the capabilities of their auditory senses, the puzzle design is geared to utilise different auditory aspects. Additionally, the player is required to combine the skills learnt in previous puzzles with more general logical thinking elements. This provides immersion and conveys a feeling of aptitude to players when they succeed.

4.1 The Tutorial Level

The initial level presents to the player the environment, story and the game mechanics. The first steps in the environment do not require visual cues, so the level is designed to ease the player's transition out of a sighted environment and provide a gentle introduction to the controls.

At first, the player cannot move and is required to leave their coffin by interacting with it. This teaches the first game mechanic the player should learn: how to interact in a simple way with the environment. After having interacted with the coffin, the player is asked to go to a corner of the room to get his missing arm. At this moment of the game, the only sound that can be heard is the sound of the pile of bones where the player should go. Now, the player has to familiarise with the sound localisation mechanic within the game. The clear and singular sound in the room is here to show that in this new environment, the only way of getting information is to listen carefully. The player then has to reach the destination and so start to use the moving mechanic of the game. The last remaining task is to locate a button by its buzzing sound, walk to it and interact with it to open the door to the next level.

4.2 Put Out the Fire

The goal of this puzzle is to help assess the comprehension of the main game mechanics previously learnt, namely, interaction and audio localisation, while introducing the puzzle element of the game.

The room consists of 3 elements: a fire in the middle of the room, water dripping from a pipe in a corner, and a bucket in another corner. Narration informs the player that the final goal is to put out the fire. In order to do that, the player first needs to fill up the bucket and then pour the water on the fire. The player is able to hear the three sound sources at the same time, and the goal is to understand the logical connection between them: first interact with the bucket before moving towards the water source. While re-enforcing the sound-only environment, this level also conveys to the player logical challenges that require deductive reasoning.

4.3 Follow the Path

The goal of the third level is to test the ability of localising an object using the sound and traverse to it upon a specific path. The player has to follow a path through the room to be able to activate the end button in order to go to the next room. If the player goes off the path, he falls through the floor and is placed back to the last successful turn he performed.

At the beginning of the path, a mouse is waiting, and flees whenever the player approaches the next turn. At the next turn it stays there, squeaking, to indicate the next turn to be followed by the player. A second mechanic has been added to this room to facilitate the player orientation: if the player starts to go too far off the path, the sounds of his footsteps change from a safe wooden floor to a dangerous cracking floor that feels about to break at any time. By combining the sound of the mouse and the changes in the footsteps the player should be able to follow the right path and reach the final button. This aims at showing that, even without vision, it is possible to navigate in a complex environment by making use of all the available information.

5 Implementation

In order to provide an immersive experience, the game needs to provide a seamless integration between software and hardware. As we do not rely on haptic feedback, the hardware is used solely for input control.

Software. The game is implemented using the Unity game engine and Google VR Cardboard library. With the cellphone attached to the Cardboard, the head movement is tracked by merging the data from the Inertial Measurement Unit of the phone and extrapolating the actual movement from this measurement. The Unity Game Engine has built-in audio SDKs supporting audio spatialisation. Unity implements a binaural head-related transfer function (HRTF) in such a way the player can experience sound directionality through filtering the head and micro-delays between the ears. Furthermore, Unity allows to set custom roll-off curves for the volume of the audio sources, such as linear or logarithmic [19]. Audio samples and model were mostly developed in house, with addition of a few pre-recorded audio samples from standard packages.

Hardware. The hardware on which the game is played is fully wearable, using a mobile phone, stereo headphones, a virtual reality headset (e.g., Google Cardboard, solely for mounting and blocking sight), and the Nintendo Switch Joy Cons. The game is run on a mobile phone running android API Level 19 and Bluetooth 4.1 (or higher). The player has to wear a VR headset in which the mobile device is inserted; the mobile device takes care of both running the game and tracking the rotation of the head while the headset blocks all external light. The headphones can be plugged in directly into the mobile device. The Joy Cons are connected to the mobile device using a Bluetooth connection. The hardware setup is shown in Fig. 1.

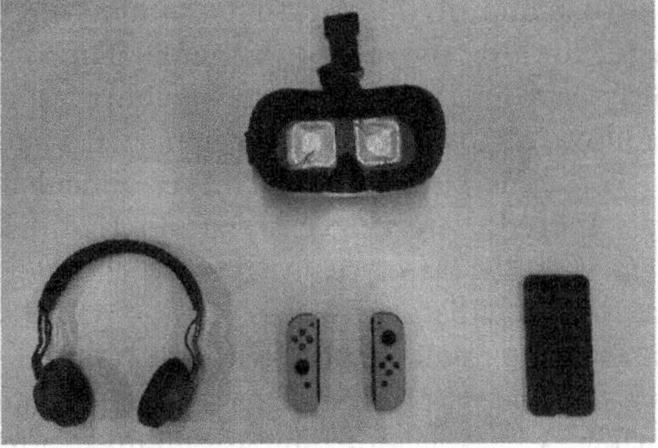

Fig. 1. The setup used to play Loud and Clear

6 Evaluation

The game was evaluated using player feedback, in the form of a questionnaire. This questionnaire had a pre- and post-gameplay component, in order to estimate whether the player's perspective on the experience of the visually impaired had changed. Alongside the survey, the behaviour of players was observed during gameplay and we asked informal questions about the different sounds. These observations and feedbacks were used to improve the game development stage.

We recruited 26 participants (age range 18–25, 8 female, 18 male) randomly divided in 3 groups. We did not repeat participants in order to guarantee the absence of any previous experience with the game. The 3 testing sessions were separated by one week, with one group per session. All players played the first two levels, and when there was time left in the session they also played the third level. Prior to playing, the setup and the controls were quickly introduced. Each player filled out the pre- and post-questionnaire, asking for their views on the difficulty of having to live without sight, along with a small evaluation about the game itself and the direct effects on the player.

6.1 Results and Discussion

Between playtest sessions the game was improved such as to tackle the fundamental difficulties we recorded through our observations and/or feedback of the players. Elements like confusing level design, sounds that are not clearly identifiable and unhelpful or incomplete narrative are examples of points being improved between sessions. Additionally, the playtests showed that not all sounds are equally easy to identify by players. As a result, we identified and replaced problematic sounds, as well as avoided sound sources occluding each other, making it difficult for players to locate and separate audio sources.

Player skills varied greatly during the playtest sessions, with some people having a lot of initial difficulty in locating objects in the tutorial level, while other people finished the game almost as fast as the developers. In either case, everyone improved in locating a sound source during a play session, being clearly faster towards the end of the game. The identification of objects by sounds was fairly easy for the players, and definitely not a major challenge to overcome. In addition, almost every player managed to get through the end of the game.

For many players, it was rather difficult to estimate how far a sounding item was. Indeed, detecting extreme relative distances is quite easy, e.g., when an item is really far or really close to the player; but distinguishing between two intermediate distances turns out to be rather difficult. In the absence of reliable hardware to mimic haptic feedback, collision sounds provided a surprisingly effective solution. Each object has a specific sound triggered when the player collides with it. A bucket, for example, will make a metal clanking sound, indicating that you are bumping into it.

From the pre-questionnaire, our participants thought that locating objects solely by sound and doing daily tasks would be very difficult. After playing the game, they had a different view about this difficulty, finding it easier than expected (Fig. 2). The game received many positive reactions, as participants enjoyed playing the game, declaring that they had learnt from the experience of navigating in an environment based only on audio.

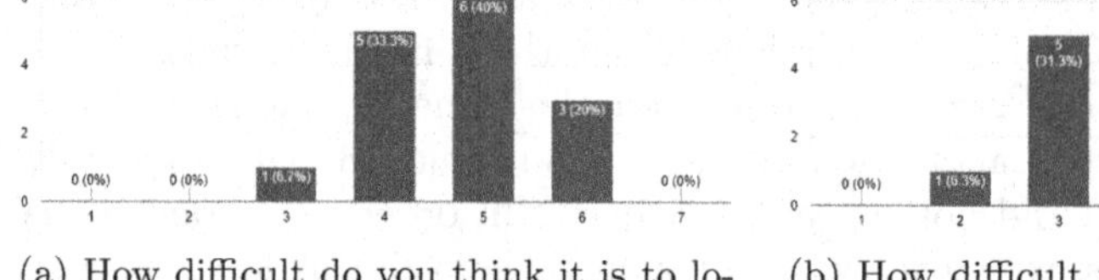

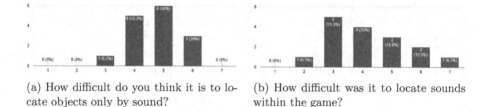

(a) How difficult do you think it is to locate objects only by sound?

(b) How difficult was it to locate sounds within the game?

Fig. 2. Sound localisation perception (a) before and (b) after playing the game.

On average, the playtime of one play-through varied between 10 and 25 min, revealing that getting familiar with this new environment without visuals greatly varied from player to player. According to feedback from the players, the puzzles were neither too challenging nor too hard. While some players took longer than others, they found the puzzles neither too easy nor too difficult or frustrating to solve. Solving the puzzles gave a rewarding feeling for the players. Many players stated having fun while playing the game, as well as becoming aware of what it means not being able to use your vision.

We also confirmed that reducing the available senses increases the cognitive load. Indeed, players had to focus way more than usual to do tasks that would be considered trivial with vision. Starting the game with easy challenges was, therefore, a good strategy to avoid cognitive overload in later puzzles.

7 Conclusion

The game *Loud and Clear* was developed to give sighted people a sense of the experience of being blind. By facing the difficulties of solving puzzles without using their vision, players gain a new perspective on the challenges of visually impaired people, as well as on valuing their abilities.

The playtesting process revealed hard to anticipate issues, and yielded various important improvements, including: (i) the feedback when players get close to an object, as it is often unclear when is it possible to interact with an object; and (ii) a collision sound for each object, helping players in their object interaction, to overcome the total lack of haptic feedback (on which visually impaired persons heavily rely, in their lives). As a result, players quickly became immersed in the game after getting used to the environment and game mechanics.

Our initial evaluation confirmed that *Loud and Clear* contributes towards improving awareness of the challenges of "being blind", as well as the appreciation for the unique skills developed by visually impaired people. We are currently considering how the game could be broadly disseminated, particularly through schools, which will permit a more thorough evaluation. In addition, we are also discussing deploying the game in a special museum in The Netherlands, specifically dedicated to the experience of visually impaired people.

Acknowledgements. The authors would like to thank Bas Dado and Olivier Hokke for their inspiration and support during the project.

References

1. Allain, K., et al.: An audio game for training navigation skills of blind children. In: Proceedings of SIVE (IEEE VR). IEEE (2015)
2. Andrade, R., Baker, S., Waycott, J., Vetere, F.: Echo-house: Exploring a virtual environment by using echolocation. In: Proceedings of the 30th Australian Conference on Computer-Human Interaction, OzCHI 2018 (2018)
3. BBC: Binaural sound: immersive spatial audio for headphones (2012). https://bbc.in/2UqNYor
4. Bourne, F.: Magnitude, temporal trends, and projections of the global prevalence of blindness and distance and near vision impairment: a systematic review and meta-analysis (2017)
5. Corporation, V.: Portal 2 (2011). http://www.thinkwithportals.com
6. Evett, L., Brown, D., Battersby, S., Ridley, A., Smith, P.: Accessible virtual environments for people who are blind-creating an intelligent virtual cane using the Nintendo Wii controller. In: International Conference on Virtual Rehabilitation (ICVDRAT) (2008)
7. Goodman-Deane, J., Waller, S., Collins, A.C., Clarkson, P.J.: Simulating vision loss. In: Contemporary Ergonomics and Human Factors, vol. 347 (2013)
8. Kolb, D.: Experiential Learning: Experience as the Source of Learning and Development. Prentice Hall, Upper Saddle River (1984)
9. Lange, A.: Victor hugo, premier temoin du theatrophon. histoire de la télévision (2002)

10. Miller, D., Parecki, A., Douglas, S.A.: Finger dance: a sound game for blind people. In: ACM SIGACCESS, pp. 253–254. ACM (2007)
11. Milne, L.R., Bennett, C.L., Ladner, R.E., Azenkot, S.: BraillePlay: educational smartphone games for blind children. In: ACM SIGACCESS, pp. 137–144 (2014)
12. Nguyen, D.: Flappy bird (2014). https://bit.ly/2N9uXDV
13. Nusser, D.: Billboard: arista has 1st stereo/binaural disk (1978)
14. ObjectiveEd: Blindfold games: education and entertainment for the visually impaired community (2019). https://blindfoldgames.org
15. Salamon, N.Z., Jacques, J.C., Musse, S.R.: Seeing the movement through sound: giving trajectory information to visually impaired people. In: Brazilian Symposium on Computer Games and Digital Entertainment (SBGAMES). IEEE (2014)
16. Schiller, N.: A portal to student learning: what instruction librarians can learn from video game design. Ref. Serv. Rev. **36**(4), 351–365 (2008)
17. SeeNow, T.F.H.F.: See now (2019). https://seenow.org/
18. Silverman, A.M.: The perils of playing blind: problems with blindness simulation and a better way to teach about blindness (2015)
19. Technologies, U.: Audio spatializer sdk (2018). https://bit.ly/2P0OHH1
20. Todd, C.A., Naylor, K.: A haptic-audio simulator indoor navigation: to assist visually impaired environment exploration. Int. J. Inf. Educ. Technol. **6**(3), 178–186 (2016)
21. Wu, W., et al.: EchoExplorer: A Game App for Understanding Echolocation and Learning to Navigate Using Echo Cues. Georgia Institute of Technology, Atlanta (2017)

Infusing Multimodal Tools and Digital Storytelling in Developing Vocabulary and Intercultural Communicative Awareness of Young EFL Learners

Eleni Korosidou and Tharrenos Bratitsis(✉)

University of Western Macedonia, 3rd Km National Road Florinas-Nikis, 53100 Florina, Greece
koro_elen@hotmail.com, bratitsis@uowm.gr

Abstract. This paper outlines the process of introducing a pilot EFL (English as a Foreign Language) project to 16, 5th graders in a Greek primary school. A multimodal learning environment was created so that learners could engage in a digital storytelling process. Both qualitative and quantitative data were collected (pre/post test, teacher/researcher's journal, semi-structured interviews with students). The effectiveness and applicability of the intervention on learners' vocabulary and intercultural understanding were examined. The results indicated the positive effects of the project on learners' communicative competence. Among the learning gains were the acquisition of topic-related vocabulary, the development of collaborative skills, as well as gains regarding intercultural understanding and digital literacy. Additionally, both teacher and learners' assumptions lead to the conclusion of an exciting learning experience, indicating that language learning was a motivating and intriguing process.

Keywords: Digital storytelling · Foreign language learning · Intercultural awareness

1 Introduction

Phenomena like globalization, transcontinental migration or the refugee crisis are inevitably relevant nowadays, with implications to the educational system and the syllabi adopted. The promotion of multicultural understanding and citizenship awareness is vital, with the issues of equality, identity, culture and diversity being critical for the development of learners' intercultural awareness. As stated in the literature, relating one's culture with the majority and drawing on one's own cultural asset can provide a solid ground for promoting efficient intercultural communication [1].

In addition, as young people increasingly tend to use emerging technologies, educators and educational researchers heavily work on integrating technology to instruction. Mayer [2] refers to the multimedia principle and the ways it can be more effective for learners to learn, when presented with words and pictures rather than words alone. Technological resources offer opportunities for creating audiovisual and interactive language learning environments, making learning concepts more appealing

A. Liapis et al. (Eds.): GALA 2019, LNCS 11899, pp. 191–200, 2019.
https://doi.org/10.1007/978-3-030-34350-7_19

and exciting than traditional instructional tools or more conventional media do [3, 4]. Multimodal tools used in language learning can stimulate students' attention and enhance their motivation [5], while technology based instruction methods apply to young learners by facilitating the successful accomplishment of tasks [6]. In this framework, multimodality calls for a much broader view of literacy.

Digital Storytelling (DS) can be applied as an educational tool embracing a multimodal learning approach. Technological devices allow computer users to develop their own interesting stories and become "creative storytellers" [7, 8]. DS is defined as *the contemporary expression of the ancient art of narration* [9] and refers to *the art of telling stories with multimedia objects including images, audio, and video* [10]. It constitutes a creative process used to capture personal stories in a 3–5 min digital clip [11, 12]. Working on a DS project can foster the development of language learners' multimodal design skills, as they learn to simultaneously brainstorm and design purposively, using different modes to create meaning [13, 14]. It seems that DS can be a powerful tool for language learning, as the use of video and multimedia helps students retain new information and aids the comprehension of difficult material [15]. In addition, DS is enhancing motivation and vocabulary understanding in the context of language learning [15, 16]. Lately it has been utilized as a teaching approach in many disciplinary areas and levels of education [17–20].

In the light of the aforementioned, this study aimed at gaining insight on the potential of a multimodal DS project for developing learners' vocabulary skills, as well as their intercultural understanding. The study focused on the "intercultural dimension", as illustrated by Byram, Gribkova, and Starkey [21]. In more detail, researchers focused on intercultural awareness in the sense of referring to the ability to engage with complexity and multiple identities and achieve communication on the basis of respect for individuals and one's rights during social interaction.

2 Pilot Design and Procedure

2.1 Purpose of the Study

The present pilot project was introduced with the dual aim of examining whether multimodal tools and DS may prove effective regarding: (a) the development of young learners' FL vocabulary and communication skills, and (b) the acquisition of knowledge and skills to view the world from others' perspectives.

More specifically, the following research questions were posed:

- can DS be a useful tool for enhancing foreign language vocabulary learning?
- how are communication skills built when multimodal tools and DS are applied in teaching?
- can young learners' intercultural awareness and their understanding be enhanced when they create their own stories about refugees?

2.2 The Adopted Syllabus

A mini syllabus was designed after considering the learners' perceived needs [22]. A questionnaire was distributed before the intervention, regarding topics of social interest that learners would like to explore by participating in a class project. One of the researchers was also the class teacher; therefore she had identified learners' needs regarding the FL and was able to facilitate them during the learning process. The experimental syllabus was developed on the basis of CLIL criteria for providing successful teaching and learning, as suggested by Coyle's 4Cs-Framework, where content, communication, cognition and culture were inextricably linked [23]. The designed mini - syllabus consisted of three broad thematic areas, with each one consisting of a number of activities. The learners accomplished the activities in pairs or groups of four. Lesson planning was not restrictive or teacher directed but it was a rather ongoing process conducted in cooperation with the learners. The thematic areas were:

1. Human and children's rights and needs, war and refugees' rights, cultural differences, aspects of culture and history of refugees
2. Issues of solidarity, support and integration, developing a positive attitude towards refugees, services provided to refugees in the host countries
3. The refugee crisis through our eyes, combating prejudice and stereotypes, developing cross cultural understanding, developing critical thinking.

2.3 Pilot Setting and Sample

The intervention was piloted on a small scale, in one 5th grade classroom in a semi urban area in southern Greece. Sixteen Greek-speaking students (mean age = 10.75 years-old) of Greek origin participated in the study, 8 boys and 8 girls. They were taught English as a FL as a compulsory subject from the 3rd grade onwards and their language level was identified as A1+ according to the CEFR (Common European Framework for Languages). They participated in a project titled *"Not so far away"* for approximately two months. A total of sixteen 45-minute teaching sessions took place. All students were present during all of the sessions, participating in the learning process and performing the proposed tasks in groups.

2.4 Study Procedure

Aim of the Pilot Project

In the present study authentic multimodal material and applications (storyboardthat.-com, Microsoft movie maker, Mindmup 2) were used for educational purposes, after having considered that the current technological advances seem to offer a great number of interesting alternatives to the teaching process [24]. In more detail, learners could engage in critical discussions in the target-language and DS activities on refugee-related issues. They had opportunities to work in the school lab, use online sources to conduct research, critically process and synthesize information from various sources (blogs, sites, wikis), write scripts, as well as create and present digital stories. A pc or a laptop was available for every pair/group of students. Multimodal texts and videos were used during classes to enhance language learning, collaboration and interaction, while learners were actively involved in decision making processes.

Classroom Activities

Learners were encouraged to undertake a research project related to the topics of refugees/migration, nationality, culture and citizenship and create their digital stories, as mentioned in the above thematic areas, utilizing corresponding applications and tools. The stages described were followed upon the completion of the project procedure.

Stage 1. Speculating on the topic: towards an understanding of the refugees' situation

Within 4 teaching sessions, plenary and group discussions were facilitated concerning refugees and the reasons why they are forced to flee their home and seek for asylum in Greece or other European countries. Learners were encouraged to use Mindmup 2 (https://app.mindmup.com/) in order to identify concepts related to the topic and reflect upon their ideas and understanding of it. Using concept mapping and searching through online sources provided by the teacher they had ample opportunities to process information in both the foreign language and their mother tongue. After having negotiated and taken part in meaning making processes and mediation tasks [25, 26], they collected relevant data, created their maps and shared them with the other groups in class. They presented their ideas in the target language and exchanged views and experiences.

Stage 2. Conducting research in a process of empathizing with refugees

At this stage the groups gathered information from a variety of sources and critically processed it for five teaching sessions. They worked cooperatively in order to organize, categorize and synthesize information gathered from multimodal texts, such as online magazines and encyclopedias. They were asked to watch videos related to issues of forced displacement of population, read contemporary authentic stories that refugee children told or watch authentic videos containing interviews conducted with them. Young learners were encouraged to take notes, summarize and synthesize key information from multimodal texts, paying attention to visual and audio elements. They were asked to engage in meaning making processes. The teacher regularly checked their progress, providing feedback when needed.

Stage 3. Contributing to digital storytelling and sharing stories

First, the concept of DS was introduced. Learners were shown a number of digital stories and were encouraged to identify the modes employed, their communicative strengths and the ways a story can be made powerful and affective for the viewer. Following that introductory phase, they were asked to use StoryboardThat (https://www.storyboardthat.com/) to design storyboards. They choose the layouts, the images for their digital stories and customized story-scenes and characters using both authentic material and their imagination. They drew on information and experiences gathered during Stage 2 to create fictional digital stories. Their stories were based on the authentic ones but they added their views and ideas and a desired ending. During this stage young learners engaged in collaborative writing processes in order to express themselves creatively, to communicate and add personal meaning to their stories [27]. This stage lasted for seven teaching sessions, while at its completion the learning products were storyboards, short clips, narrations and dialogues made by young learners with the movie maker for kids application (https://www.microsoft.com/el-gr/p/movie-maker-for kids).

3 Evaluation of Pilot Implementation

3.1 Assessing Learning Outcomes

Both qualitative and quantitative data were gathered to assess the effect of the intervention on learners' language skills and vocabulary development, as well as the enhancement of their intercultural awareness. The instruments used, following a data triangulation approach [28], were: (a) a pre-and a post-test, (b) a teacher/researcher's journal, and (c) semi-structured interviews.

Pre/post Testing
All participants were assessed on their vocabulary knowledge a week before and a week after the intervention. A pre/post test was distributed, consisting of 25 words. It contained various parts of speech (15 nouns, 7 adjectives and 3 verbs), as presented in Table 1. Learners were asked to provide the meaning of the words in their mother tongue.

Table 1. Pre/post test vocabulary questions

Item	Question	Item	Question
1	Homeless	14	Comfortable
2	Hopeless	15	Country
3	Fighting	16	Shelter
4	Destroy	17	Support
5	Refugee	18	Fear
6	Care	19	Violence
7	Volunteer	20	Secure
8	Illness	21	Scared
9	Safety	22	Nightmare
10	Explosion	23	Starve
11	Scream	24	Thirsty
12	Education	25	Danger
13	Desperate		

Researcher's Journal
A teacher/researcher journal was kept once a week in order to record and reflect on the impact and the applicability of the intervention. It was based on the reflective questions proposed by Richards and Lockhart [29] and the observations of Burns [30] and Wallace [31] as far as journal keeping is concerned.

Semi-structured Interviews

Semi-structured interviews were used for recording learners' interest and their degree of satisfaction with the project, the difficulties they encountered and their perceptions of DS, some of the questions being *(What) did you enjoy (about) this project? What do you think about making your own stories on a pc? What did you learn that was new? Were there any difficulties?.*

4 Results

4.1 Quantitative Data

As the results of the conducted paired sample t-test show (Tables 2 and 3) there was a significant increase in the number of words young learners could recall after the intervention. Therefore, it seems that the provided educational environment could provoke significant learning outcomes, regarding vocabulary acquisition.

Table 2. Pre/post test results

	N	Mean	Std. deviation	Std. error mean
Pre	25	6,56	4,19	0,84
Post	25	11,52	3,73	0,75

Table 3. Pre/post test results (Levene's test for Equality of Variances)

	F	Sig.	t	df	Sig. (2-tailed)	Mean difference	Std. error diff.	95% confidence interval of the difference	
								Lower	Upper
Equal variances assumed	0.096	0.758	−4.41755	48	0.000	−4,96	1.122794	−7.21753	−2.70247
Equal variances not assumed			−4.41755	47.36	0.000	−4,96	1.122794	−7.2183	−2.70168

4.2 Qualitative Data

Journals have been proved to be valuable tools for reflecting on and improving the teaching/learning process [32]. Since they are easy to use and allow great flexibility documenting classroom events and teaching situations [33], journal entries were kept and offered insights into learners' attitudes towards the intervention, post-completion. The qualitative analysis of 8 journals led to the formation of three typologies, and several categories under each one (Table 4). It revealed that employing multimodal material and having learners participate in DS activities promoted the development of their communication skills in the target language, led to their active participation during the learning process and a positive attitude towards FL learning. Moreover, it seems that young learners' multicultural understanding was enhanced.

The qualitative analysis of the interview transcripts revealed that learners enjoyed learning by being involved in DS activities, using technological material and devices. They concluded that they found the video making process *"challenging"*, while being able to compose one's own story was *"both creative and intriguing"*. They underlined that DS applications enabled them to create their own heroes and empathize with them. They especially liked having been involved in collaborative writing, as they were *"able to express their ideas more easily"*. Concerning encountered difficulties, they claimed that *"some vocabulary items related to the topics of refugee crisis, the war and aspects of citizenship were particularly difficult"*. However, they underlined that they usually inferred meaning by *"paying attention to audio or visual elements in multimodal texts"* or paralinguistic features of language when watching videos. They also observed that they had opportunities to *"learn in an alternative, though interesting way"*. They stated that they learned content specific language and gained knowledge about human rights and other cultures, underlining that *"I learned a lot about their culture"* and *"it is now clear to me how they feel when they come in Greece…they have needs, they have rights…"*. They claimed that they *"felt aware of their own ignorance"* on refugee issues, while trying to view and interpret the world from other culture's point.

Table 4. Researcher's journal qualitative analysis

Typology	Categories
A. Teaching process	Developing multiliteracies skills Developing cross cultural skills Developing language skills Multimodal learning environment Research activities Presentations Collaborative writing Whole class discussions Decision making activities
B. Learners' attitudes	Taking initiatives Conducting research Engaging in digital storytelling Learning the target language in a pleasurable way
C. Communication and interaction	L2 use L1 use Code switching between L1 and L2 Negotiating meaning Inferring meaning Multiliteracies meaning making

5 Conclusions

This study aimed at exploring the educational opportunities offered by multimodal tools and DS as a multimodal pedagogy applied in the context of an EFL learning environment in a state primary school in Greece. The analysis demonstrated that learners' experiences were efficient and exciting, as well as effective concerning vocabulary and language learning. Young learners had various opportunities to practice their communication skills and gain vocabulary knowledge *receptively* (in listening or reading) and *productively* (in speaking or writing) [34]. This observation is of particular importance, as it seems that acquiring vocabulary is crucial for the cultivation of communication skills in the target language [35].

The participants managed to seek out relationships between their everyday reality and aspects related to their culture and that of refugee children, gaining culture specific knowledge and respect. Outcomes related to the enhancement of their intercultural understanding were attained through engaging in DS, as the qualitative data analysis illustrated. The activities preceding the DS process enabled young learners to empathize with refugees, exposing them to issues related to multicultural citizenship and raising their awareness of different cultures and human rights. The creation of digital stories allowed for the adoption of a more "personal" view, dispelling prejudice and encouraging them to move beyond their comfort zone. Digital narratives actually helped learners to accept cultural diversity, and become more interculturally competent during social interactions by *"bridging the gap"* between school and community [36, 37].

The conclusions of this study are in line with previous research showing that when learning occurs in virtual environments, as when technology is properly integrated in the teaching process, learners' interest is enhanced [38]. Stimuli provided in a multimodal environment facilitate the enhancement of student motivation and better understanding of the language [39]. Learners' exposure to multimodal material such as texts, images and videos creates a learning environment that significantly influences vocabulary learning [40]. At the same time, the use of digital media allows for collaboration and positively affects dialogue, exchange of ideas and negotiation among students [41].

Although the experience of conducting research on the effectiveness of a multimodal pedagogy at primary FL learning settings indicates positive suggestions for future research, there are limitations to be considered. The study sample was rather small, therefore the applicability of the project in other contexts should be carefully considered.

References

1. Ho, S.T.K.: Addressing culture in EFL classrooms: the challenge of shifting from a traditional to an intercultural stance. Electron. J. Foreign Lang. Teach. **6**(1), 63–76 (2010)
2. Mayer, R.E.: The Cambridge Handbook of Multimedia Learning. Cambridge University Press, New York (2014)
3. Linebarger, D.L., Piotrowski, J.T., Lapierre, M.: The relationship between media use and the language and literacy skills of young children: results from a national parent survey. Paper presented at the NAEYC Annual Conference (2009)
4. Adams, M.J.: Technology for Developing Children's Language and Literacy: Bringing Speech Recognition to the Classroom. The Joan Ganz Cooney Center at Sesame Workshop, NY (2011)

5. Pokrivčáková, S.: CLIL in Foreign Language Education: E-Textbook for Foreign Language Teachers. Constantine the Philosopher University, Nitra (2015)
6. Riconscente, M.M.: Using latent profile analysis to evaluate the 4-phase model of interest development. In: Ainley, M. (ed.) The Next Decade of Interest Research-Processes and Measures, Biannual International Conference on Motivation, Porto (2010)
7. Robin, B.R.: The power of digital storytelling to support teaching and learning. Digit. Educ. Rev. **30**, 17–29 (2016)
8. Robin, B.R.: Digital storytelling: a powerful technology tool for the 21st century classroom. Theory Pract. **47**(3), 220–228 (2008)
9. Digital Storytelling Association: Digital storytelling. http://electronicportfolios.com/digistory/. Accessed 11 Apr 2019
10. Rossiter, M., Garcia, P.A.: Digital storytelling: a new player on the narrative field. New Dir. Adult Contin. Educ. **126**, 37–48 (2010)
11. Lambert, J.: Digital Storytelling: Capturing Lives, Creating Community, 4th edn. Routledge, New York (2013)
12. De Vecchi, N., Kenny, A., Dickson-Swift, V., Kidd, S.: How digital storytelling is used in mental health: a scoping review. Int. J. Mental Health Nurs. **25**(3), 183–193 (2016)
13. Vinogradova, P., Linville, H.A., Bickel, B.: "Listen to my story and you will know me": digital stories as student-centered collaborative projects. TESOL J. **2**(2), 173–202 (2011)
14. Nelson, M.A., Hull, G.A.: Self-presentation through multimedia: a Bakhtinian perspective on digital storytelling. In: Lundby, K. (ed.) Digital Storytelling, Mediatized Stories: Self-Representations in New Media, pp. 123–141. Peter Lang, NY (2008)
15. Verdugo, D.R., Belmonte, I.A.: Using digital stories to improve listening comprehension with Spanish young learners of English. Lang. Learn. Technol. **11**(1), 87–101 (2007)
16. Ohler, J.B.: Digital Storytelling in the Classroom: New Media Pathways to Literacy, Learning and Creativity. Corwin, Thousand Oaks (2013)
17. Bratitsis, T., Kotopoulos, T., Mandila, K.: Kindergarten children as story makers: the effect of the digital medium. In: Xhafa, F., Barolli, L., Köppen, M. (eds.) Proceedings of the IEEE 3rd International Conference on Intelligent Networking and Collaborative Systems - INCoS 2011, pp. 84–91. Fukuoka, 30 November–2 December (2011)
18. Bratitsis, T.: Experiences from digital storytelling training seminars for educators. In: The case of Greece, 9th Panhellenic Conference "ICTs in Education", October 3–5 2014. University of Crete, Rethymno (2014)
19. Melliou, K., Moutafidou, A., Bratitsis, T.: Children's rights: using digital storytelling and visible thinking approaches to create a narrative video in early childhood classroom. Int. J. Electron. Gov. **7**(4), 333–348 (2015)
20. Bratitsis, T., Ziannas, P.: From early childhood to special education: interactive digital storytelling as a coaching approach for fostering social empathy. Procedia Comput. Sci. **67**, 231–240 (2015)
21. Byram, M., Gribkova, B., Starkey, H.: Developing the intercultural dimension in language teaching: a practical introduction for teachers. Language Policy Division, Directorate of School, Out-of-School and Higher Education, Council of Europe (2002). http://discovery.ucl.ac.uk/1562524/1/Starkey_InterculturalDimensionByram.pdf
22. Moon, J.A.: Reflection in Learning & Professional Development: Theory and Practice. Kogan Page, London (2000)
23. Coyle, D., Hood, P., Marsh, D.: CLIL: Content and Language Integrated Learning. Cambridge University Press, Cambridge (2010)

24. Parhizkar, B., Gebril, Z.M., Obeidy, W.K., Ngan, M.N.A., Chowdhury, S.A., Lashkari, A. H.: Android mobile augmented reality application based on different learning theories for primary school children. In: International Conference on Multimedia Computing and Systems (ICMCS), pp. 404–408 (2012)
25. Stathopoulou, M.: Cross-Language Mediation in Foreign Language Teaching and Testing. Multilingual Matters, Bristol (2015)
26. Council of Europe.: Common European Framework of Reference for Languages: Learning, teaching, assessment. Cambridge: Cambridge University Press (2001)
27. Button, K., Johnson, M.J., Furgerson, P.: Interactive writing in a primary classroom. Read. Teach. **49**(6), 446–455 (1996)
28. Kember, D.: To control or not to control: the question of whether experimental designs are appropriate for evaluating teaching innovations in higher education. Assess. Eval. High. Educ. **28**(1), 89–101 (2003)
29. Richards, J.C., Lockhart, C.: Reflective Teaching in Second Language Classrooms. Cambridge University Press, Cambridge (1994)
30. Burns, A.: Collaborative Action Research for English Language Teachers. Cambridge University Press, Cambridge (1999)
31. Wallace, M.J.: Action Research for Language Teachers. Cambridge University Press, Cambridge (1998)
32. Griva, E., Kofou, I.: Alternative assessment in Language learning: Challenges and Practices, vol. I. D Kyriakidis, Thessaloniki (2018)
33. Mackey, A., Gass, A.: Second Language Research Methodology and Design. Lawrence Erlbaum Associate, London (2005)
34. Nation, I.S.P.: Learning Vocabulary in Another Language. Cambridge University Press, Cambridge (2001)
35. Zarei, A.A., Mahmoodzadeh, P.: The Effect of multimedia glosses on L2 reading comprehension and vocabulary production. J. Engl. Lang. Lit. **1**(1), 1–7 (2014)
36. Frazel, M.: Digital Storytelling: Guide for Educators. International Society for Technology in Education, Washington (2010)
37. Miller, C.H.: Digital Storytelling: A Creator's Guide to Interactive Entertainment. Taylor & Francis, UK (2013)
38. Peterson, M.: Learner participation patterns and strategy use in second life: an exploratory case study. ReCALL **22**(3), 273–292 (2010)
39. Wang, A.I., Lieberoth, A.: The effect of points and audio on concentration, engagement, enjoyment, learning, motivation, and classroom dynamics using Kahoot. In: European Conference on Games Based Learning, pp. 737–748. Academic Conferences International Limited (2016)
40. Bakhsh, S.A.: Using games as a tool in teaching vocabulary to young learners. Engl. Lang. Teach. **9**(7), 120–128 (2016)
41. Vivitsou, M.: Digital storytelling in teaching and research. In: Tatnall, A., Multisilta, J. (eds.) Encyclopedia of Education and Information Technologies. Springer (2018). https://doi.org/10.1186/s40561-014-0006-3

Lessons Learned from the Development of a Mobile Learning Game Authoring Tool

Pierre-Yves Gicquel(✉), Iza Marfisi-Schottman, and Sébastien George

Le Mans Université, EA 4023, LIUM, 72085 Le Mans, France
{pierre-yves.gicquel,iza.marfisi, sebastien.george}@univ-lemans.fr

Abstract. Students and schools are increasingly equipped with smartphones and tablets. These mobile devices can enhance teaching in many ways. Mobile Learning Games (MLGs) for example, have shown great potential for increasing student's motivation and improving the quality of situated learning. For the past few years, the research community has been working on authoring tools that allow teachers to create and distribute their own MLGs. The development of these authoring tools is challenging and time consuming and even more so if the objective is for these tools to actually be used in classrooms. The Design-Based Research (DBR) paradigm was precisely developed to address these central issues of Technology Enhanced Learning. It involves co-designing and testing with end-users from the beginning of the project. Although DBR increases the acceptance of new educational tools, it also adds several challenges, including the complexity of involving teachers and students in real-world situations and creating several versions of the tools that will be improved iteratively. In this paper, we aim at providing design principles and practical guidance on the way to develop such authoring tools, based on our experience. We conclude on lessons learned from this project and discuss some systematic issues we faced.

Keywords: Game-based learning · Authoring tool · Mobile Learning · Situated learning · Design-Based Research

1 Designing Mobile Learning Game Authoring Tools

Authoring tools for Mobile Learning Games (MLGs) provide teachers with a simple way of designing and using applications that fit their specific needs. Teachers especially like using MLGs for educational outing and field trips. Indeed, MLGs combine all the ingredients necessary to attract students' attention and engage them in learning activities [1–3]: game mechanics such as competition, rewards and exploration, situated learning in real contexts and the physical effort necessary to go to the right place. Several MLG authoring tools have recently been proposed [4, 5]. The conception, development and administration of such authoring tools are arguably challenging and time-consuming tasks for researchers.

The first challenge is related to the complex nature of MLGs itself. Despite an active research community, no MLG model has reached a consensus and the know-

A. Liapis et al. (Eds.): GALA 2019, LNCS 11899, pp. 201–210, 2019.
https://doi.org/10.1007/978-3-030-34350-7_20

how required to select the best game mechanics to create pedagogically effective MLGs remains difficult to pinpoint. In addition, the main objective of authoring tools is to fit the needs of a large number of users. The MLG model used by the authoring tool therefore needs to be as generic as possible while still providing enough structure and guidance to help teachers.

Moreover, designing authoring tools that actually meet the needs of real teachers is very challenging. Many researchers such as Virvou and Eythimios [6] were confronted to the difficulty of adapting the user interface to the needs of teachers because they waited for the end of the project to involve end-user. The use of Design-Based Research (DBR) seems like a good alternative to maximize the acceptability of authoring tools in class [7, 8]. This movement started in the 1990s and was developed to address several central issues of Technology Enhanced Learning (TEL) such as the need to find solutions with the end-users (teachers and students) and the need to study learning phenomena in the real world rather than in a laboratory.

Although DBR is a powerful paradigm for addressing these needs, it also brings major technical challenges for the development of TEL tools. First of all, DBR implies the co-design of tools with the end-users in an iterative way. Researchers therefore need to develop not one, but several prototypes, in close collaboration with the end-users. In the case of MLG authoring tools, this means that the authoring tool and the underlying MLG model will be modified, several times, until they meet the teachers' needs. DBR also emphasizes the fact that the tools should be tested in real-world learning environments. The MLGs, designed by teachers with the authoring tool, therefore need to support many simultaneous connections during field trips. Finally, DBR strongly depends on the help of teachers. If they want to benefit from their full collaboration, researchers must provide robust tools that teachers will be able to use, long after the research project is over.

As we have shown, the design of MLG authoring tools with DBR raises many technical challenges. Yet, to our knowledge, very few researchers have provided theoretical or practical guidelines for the development of such tools. In this paper, we propose design principles and an example of software architecture, based on our experience developing a MLG authoring tool, named MOGGLE, with DBR.

In the second section of this paper, we will detail the constraints related to developing authoring tools and supporting DBR. In the third section, we propose several design principles that are adapted to these constraints and illustrate them with the architecture we set up for MOGGLE. Section four provides elements of validation of our proposition through the numerous iterations and modifications that MOGGLE was put through before reaching a final version. Finally, in section five, we conclude on lessons learned from the development of MOGGLE, and discuss systematic issues we faced at different stages of the project.

2 Challenges Brought by Design Based Research

Design-Based Research is "a systematic but flexible methodology aimed to improve educational practices through iterative analysis, design, development, and implementation, based on collaboration among researchers and practitioners in real-world settings, and leading to contextually-sensitive design principles and theories" [12]. The use of DBR is paramount for designing tools that meet the needs of teachers and that will actually be used in class. However, DBR also comes with a set of constraints that complicates the development of these tools. In this section we identify the constraints that DBR sets on the development of MLG authoring tools.

2.1 User-Centered Design

DBR gives a central position to the end-users. The design of MLG authoring tools should therefore be carried out with teachers, who will use the authoring tool to create MLGs, and students, who will play these MLGs. Usability and utility are therefore a central concern. In terms of usability, the authoring tool should be **simple enough for teachers to create MLGs rapidly**. In order to feel at ease with these tools and confident enough to use them in class, teachers also need to be able to control what the final MLG will look like for the students. This is especially true when designing MLGs, that are new to them. This implies developing a **preview or testing system** that can immediately show what the final MLG will look like. In addition, like any educational material, MLGs need to be adjusted before reaching the satisfactory final version. The authoring tool therefore needs to offer **the means to modify MLGs** to facilitate incremental design. Finally, authoring tools need to offer maximum utility to teachers. In other terms, they should allow them to create MLGs that are adapted to their educational field trips. Such educational outings are used in many domains such as geology, botany, history, archaeology but also arts and sports. For many of these domains, it is important for the MLGs to offer specific activities such as plant and rock identification or augmented reality. The authoring tool therefore needs to **offer the possibility of adding new types of domain specific activities**.

2.2 Iterative Design

DBR supports the idea that the theoretical learning model and the learning tools are gradually improved through iterative co-design and testing with end-users. In the context of MLG authoring tools, two models are at stake: the MLG model and the authoring tool model. Indeed, there are many different ways of designing an authoring tool based on the same MLG model. Given the fact that DBR encourages multiple iterations to reach a satisfying version of these models and the limited resources available for research projects, the **initial models need to be highly modular and expandable** in order to build on them and not start from scratch each time.

2.3 Tests in Real-World Situations

Finally, the last important constraint that is brought by DBR, is the fact that learning tools need to be tested in real-world situations. This means that the MLGs designed by the teachers, with the authoring tools, need to be **robust** enough to withstand field trips with 30 or more students, who will probably not use the MLGs as they were initially intended to be. Furthermore, the genericity of MLG authoring tools needs to be tested with teachers in several different domains. Given the complex organization of field trips, it is not rare for several tests to overlap. It should therefore be possible **to set up independent instances of MLG authoring tools** for each user group.

In the next section, we propose several design principles that support these three major constraints and illustrate them with the software architecture uses for MOGGLE.

3 Design Principles to Support Design-Based Research

MOGGLE (MObile, Geolocated Games for Learning) is composed of two applications: **MOGGLE-Editor** (referred to as Editor) that allows teachers to create their MLGs and **MOGGLE-Player** (referred to as Player), which allows students to play these MLGs (Fig. 1). The instances of MLGs are stocked in a shared database.

Fig. 1. MOGGLE MLG authoring tool

The first key decision, taken at the beginning of the project, was to use **only web technologies** to develop the Editor and the Player. There are several reasons for this choice. First of all, web applications can be accessed from all types of devices and operating systems (PC, Mac, Android, IOS, Windows tablets…). This is very advantageous, given the fact that the types of devices available in schools are very heterogeneous. Secondly, web applications do not require complex installation. Users simply need to have access to the Internet and connect themselves via their usual web browser. This definitely facilitates the use of tools for teachers and students in a learning context. One might think that the need to have a connection can be a constraint but some web technologies allow connection breaks by using a cache system (local storage) while allowing data to be transferred when the connection is restored. Furthermore, from an ergonomic point of view, responsive web apps are getting closer and closer to native applications. Finally, web applications can be updated very easily without requiring any actions from the end-users. Knowing that DBR implies many iterations and updates, this seemed like an important advantage. The choice of web technologies was justified for MOGGLE but seems well adapted for the development of any TEL tool, especially if they are designed with the DBR paradigm. We therefore propose **to only rely on Web technologies as our first design principle**.

Below, we will propose seven other design principles to support the constraints detailed in the last section. Note that we will not detail the basic design principles derived from software engineering such as system versioning, server security or programming design patterns.

3.1 User-Centered Design

Interactive Preview of Elements Being Designed

As mentioned in the previous section, it is important for teachers to able to preview what their MLG will look like on students' smartphones and test its interactions. Ideally, this preview should be available while they are designing the elements, so that they can adjust them directly in order to obtain the desired interface. We therefore advocate the integration of an **interactive preview of the MLG elements** into the MLG authoring tool.

This design principle was used for MOGGLE. As shown in the Fig. 2, teachers can test the player interface (on the top right) while they are designing the MLG activities. To offer this interactive preview, we used the same web component for the Player and the Editor's preview system. The interactive preview is updated, in real time, when the teachers fill in the form on the left. This was done with two-way data binding. In *HTML/JavaScript*, data binding refers to the binding of a variable declared in the main script directly to an HTML tag's attribute (i.e. the attribute "value" of an input tag *<input value = {{boundVariable}}>*). When the attribute is modified, the value of the variable is also modified. By using the same variable in another tag's attribute element, real time synchronization between functionally independent components can be achieved.

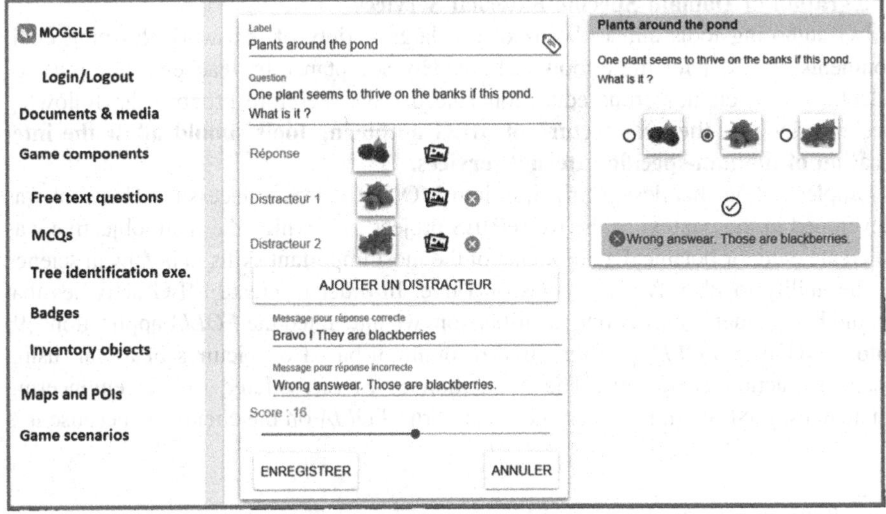

Fig. 2. MOGGLE-Editor interface for creating an MCQ with the interactive preview

Incremental Design

As for any type of educational content, teachers will need to adjust their MLG's scenario several times, until they reach the desired product. For instance, after testing the MLG, the teacher might want to change an image or add educational feedback. It is therefore important, in terms of user experience, to support incremental design by **providing functionalities to incrementally edit and test MLGs.**

This design principle was implemented in MOGGLE using the dual server architecture presented in Fig. 3. Each instance of MOGGLE is composed of two separate virtual machines: the Editor server and the Player server. The Editor and the Player both share the same MLG model and communicate through a unique MLG database. When an element is created or updates in the Editor, it is immediately updated in the database which is used by the Player. Teachers can therefore immediately test the new versions of their MLGs, while editing them.

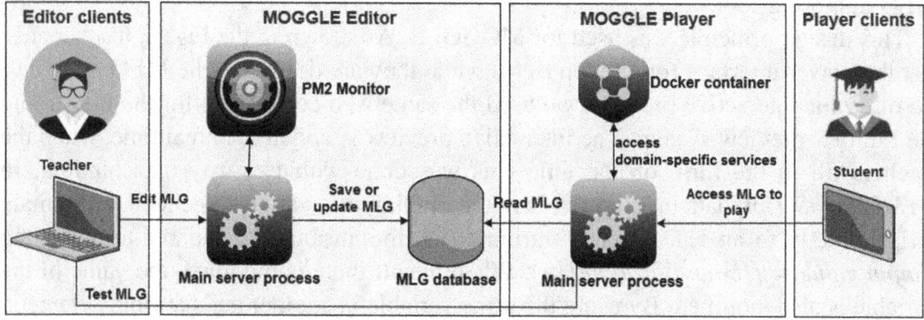

Fig. 3. MOOGLE architecture

Integration of Domain-Specific External Services

MLG authoring tools aim to be used in a large variety of real-world learning environments. In order for these tools to be widely acceptance by teachers, they must be adaptable to their numerous educational needs. We therefore propose the following design principle: **the architecture of MLG authoring tools should allow the integration of domain-specific external services.**

Implementing this design principle into MOGGLE was a necessity. This tool was developed in the context of the ReVeRIES project[1], for which the main objective was to create outdoor botanical games. One of the most important skills in botanical science is the ability to identify the species of a tree. In order to create MLG activities that would help students master tree identification, we integrated the *FOLIA* application[2] [9] into MOGGLE. *FOLIA* performs tree recognition based on pictures of a leaf, using shape extraction algorithms. The integration of *FOLIA* offered several engineering challenges. First of all, it was not possible to run *FOLIA* on the client side because it is

1 http://reveries-project.fr/.

2 https://apps.apple.com/fr/app/folia/.

a binary executable file. It also requires multiple dependencies that need to be compiled manually. In order to avoid unnecessary dependencies and a tedious compilation process for each new deployment, we chose to encapsulate *FOLIA* in a *Docker* container accessible as a web service (Fig. 3). *Docker* containers are similar to virtual machines, they encapsulate an operating system and applications and can be run on a host system with precise resources allocation (CPU, RAM, disk space). This method can easily be applied to other existing services such as speech recognition or Augmented Reality to create domain specific MLG activities without compromising the security, robustness and genericity of the authoring tool.

3.2 Iterative Design for Mobile Learning Game Authoring Tools

Extensible Data Model and Document-Based Data Persistence
DBR encourages iterative co-design. As shown in Sect. 2, it is therefore crucial for the MLG model to be designed with future extensions in mind. Such extensions inevitably require the flexibility of the data persistence mechanism. Relational databases are not well adapted for handling structural modifications. Indeed, their schemas are fixed at the beginning and are very time consuming to modify. NoSQL databases, on the other hand, do not store the data in fixed schemas. Instead of using tables, they store the data in *documents*. A *document* is an association of key-values, similar to *JSON*, with loose constraints on the existence of keys and on the type of the values. Thus in a NoSQL database, it is possible to add new kinds of *documents* without impacting what previously exists. As a design principle we therefore propose that MLG authoring tools should use **extendable MLG models and a document-based data persistence system.**

In the case of MOGGLE, we used a highly modular and adaptable MLG model, described in previous work [10], and the document-oriented database *MongoDB* that offers a high-level performance on a large number of documents.

Modular Interfaces
As seen previously, iterative co-design will refine the MLG model but also the Editor's and Player's user interfaces. The interfaces should therefore offer **maximum modularity by minimizing functional dependencies** between its different parts.

This design principle was implemented in MOGGLE by using web components to represent each level of granularity of a MLG. At the lowest level, MLGs are composed of elementary resources (images and videos) that can be combined into multimedia documents. These resources and documents can then be used to create situated activities such as multiple-choice questions, free text questions or tree identification exercises. These activities can then be associated to a point of interest, at a specific location, in order to create MLG units. Finally, these units are organized to form a MLG. Each level being independent, it is easy to modify the design process of a MLG according to the user needs. Technically, this design process is supported by the use of *web-components* that allow the definition of *custom elements* which are usable directly as HTML tags (e.g. *<div/>*, *<span/>*). We defined tags for each level of granularity above, the high-level tags (e.g. *<mlg-unit/>*) being structured with generic fillers, to avoid functional dependencies with lower level tags.

3.3 Tests in Real-World Situations

Server Fallback Mechanism
A very important constraint brought by DBR is the necessity to provide teachers with a consistent access to the application. When performing daily changes on a code, even proper testing cannot guarantee against a failure of the server. Such failures could have serious consequences on the collaboration with end-user: if teachers lose access to the MLGs they spent hours designing, they will likely be reluctant to use the system again. As a design principle we therefore propose to **set up a fallback mechanism in case of server crash**.

In MOGGLE, we use a *PM2 Monitor* (Fig. 3) as process manager and fallback mechanism in case of server failure. *PM2* monitors the state and the resources used by a process in real time. Additionally, *PM2* can detect when a process is in failure state and perform a proper restart of this process.

Separate Group-Based Web Portals
Teachers put a significant amount of effort into understanding how to design MLGs. It is therefore important not to change the version of the tools they use during this process. The use of distinct group-based web portals allows to perform incremental changes on the MLG authoring tool without disturbing the end-users. Each web portal is accessible through a unique URL which is provided to a group of users (usually teachers from the same school). This way, two groups are able to work at the same time on two distinct versions of the authoring tool. We therefore advocate the use of **separate web portals for each users' group.**

This design principle was implemented in MOGGLE through the use of virtual machines. Each new machine, associated with a unique subdomain of our main domain reveries-project.fr (e.g. moggle1.reveries-project.fr).

4 Iterative Experimental Validation of MOGGLE

In this section we provide elements of experimental validation of MOGGLE regarding the DBR constraints we identified.

The first constraint was the User-Centered Design. We integrated a preview system for the MLG elements in the Editor and propose an incremental MLG design process, meaning that teachers can easily test the MLG being designed and modify them until they reach satisfaction. We gathered elements of validation for these principles through a qualitative evaluation of MOGGLE involving five teachers from various domains: history, geography, mathematics and foreign language. They were asked to design a MLG adapted to their teaching domain after a short introduction to MOGGLE. They all managed to create a MLG adapted to their specialty in less than an hour, with minimal assistance from the experimenter. The iterative MLG design process we proposed, proved to be useful since the teachers directly tested their games and updated them. The integration of domain specific tools was evoked by the history teacher. She questioned the possibility to integrate Augmented Reality layer of visualization to provide reconstitution of ancient buildings.

The second constraint is to use an iterative design in MLG authoring tool. We proposed a modular design pattern for the client side in order to simplify modifications resulting of these iterative circles. This modular design pattern based on web component was proven useful for integrating new features. The integration of *Youtube* videos was added after using MOGGLE with a natural park manager and the scoring mechanism was changed after another iteration. Other features, such as the integration of sound files in multimedia documents, were removed because they were never used. The modular design pattern, and the generic data structure we proposed, allowed us to add and remove these features with only minor changes.

The third constraint was to be able to test MOGGLE in real-world learning environments. We proposed the use of group-based web portal for that feature. These portals were deployed for each user group which facilitated the test of MOGGLE with several groups at the same time. We are currently in the process of deploying portals for two new groups of teachers. The ability to deploy up-to-date web portals on demands proved to be very useful to offer a private space to end-users but also for testing purposes.

5 Lessons Learned and Perspectives

In this article, we identify the three main constraints related to the design of Mobile Learning Game (MLG) authoring tools with Design-Based Research (DBR) and propose design principles. These design principles result from our experience in developing MOGGLE, a MLG authoring tool, designed in collaboration with several groups of teachers and that went through many iterative cycle of refinement.

The **first design principle we propose is to rely only on web technologies**. This design principle, justified in detail Sect. 3. From this quite generic principle we derive seven design principles (Table 1). We illustrate technological implementation of each principle in terms of software architecture.

Table 1. Design principles for the development of Mobile Learning Game authoring tools

DBR Constraints	Proposed design principles	MOGGLE software architecture
User-centered design	Interactive preview of elements being designed	Web components & data binding
	Incremental MLG design	Shared database
	Integration of domain specific external services	Web services & Docker
Iterative design	Extensible data model & document-based database	Extensible MLG model & MongoDB
	Modular design patterns on the client side	Web components
Test in real-world situations	Server Fallback Mechanism	PM2
	Separate Group-Based Web Portals	Separate virtual machines for each user group

However, we faced some systematic issues, related to the incredibly fast evolution of web technologies between the project beginning and today [11]. At the beginning of the project, in early 2016, we choose *Polymer 1.0* that was recently released by Google and was very promising for the use of web-components. *Polymer 2.0* was released in the beginning of 2017 with no backward compatibility and *Polymer 3.0* was released in 2018 equally without backward compatibility. Due to limitations in human resources we had to keep using *Polymer 1.0* even though it is now deprecated.

A related systematic issue is the unpredictability frameworks trends. *VueJS* and *ReactJS* (which are also component-oriented framework) now largely surpass *Polymer*, although initially these two frameworks were not as promising. The question of framework evolution and deprecation creates many concerns in the web developer community while few publications focus on this question. This question raises important practical challenges in TEL and would deserve further investigations.

References

1. Marfisi-Schottman, I., George, S.: Supporting teachers to design and use mobile collaborative learning games. In: Proceedings of the International Conference on Mobile Learning, Madrid, Spain, pp. 3–10 (2014)
2. Bianchi-Berthouze, N.: Understanding the role of body movement in player engagement. Hum. Comput. Interact. **28**(1), 40–75 (2013)
3. Bellotti, F., Kapralos, B., Lee, K., Moreno-Ger, P., Berta, R.: Assessment in and of serious games: an overview. Adv. Hum.-Comput. Interact. **2013**, 1:1 (2013)
4. Karoui, A., Marfisi-Schottman, I., George, S.: Mobile learning game authoring tools: assessment, synthesis and proposals. In: Bottino, R., Jeuring, J., Veltkamp, R.C. (eds.) GALA 2016. LNCS, vol. 10056, pp. 281–291. Springer, Cham (2016). https://doi.org/10.1007/978-3-319-50182-6_25
5. Karoui, A., Marfisi-Schottman, I., George, S.: JEM iNVENTOR: a mobile learning game authoring tool based on a nested design approach. In: Mobile Learning European Conference, Larnaca, Cyprus, pp. 1–4 (2017)
6. Virvou, M., Eythimios, A.: Mobile educational features in authoring tools for personalised tutoring. Comput. Educ. **44**(1), 53–68 (2005)
7. Collins, A., Joseph, D., Bielaczyc, K.: Design research: theoretical and methodological issues. J. Learn. Sci. **13**(1), 15–42 (2004)
8. Sanchez, E., Monod-Ansaldi, R., Vincent, C., Safadi-Katouzian, S.: A praxeological perspective for the design and implementation of a digital role-play game. Educ. Inf. Technol. **22**(6), 2805–2824 (2017)
9. Bertrand, S., Cerutti, G., Tougne, L.: Bark recognition to improve leaf-based classification in didactic tree species identification. In: International Conference on Computer Vision Theory and Applications, VISAPP, Porto, Portugal, pp. 435–442 (2017)
10. Marfisi-Schottman, I., Gicquel, P.-Y., Karoui, A., George, S.: From idea to reality: extensive and executable modeling language for mobile learning games. In: Verbert, K., Sharples, M., Klobučar, T. (eds.) EC-TEL 2016. LNCS, vol. 9891, pp. 428–433. Springer, Cham (2016). https://doi.org/10.1007/978-3-319-45153-4_38
11. Pano, A., Graziotin, D., Abrahamsson, P.: Rationale leading to the adoption of a JavaScript framework. arXiv preprint. arXiv:1605.04303 (2016)
12. Wang, F., Hannafin, M.J.: Design-based research and technology-enhanced learning environments. Educ. Technol. Res. Dev. **53**(4), 5–23 (2005)

Bolstering Stealth Assessment in Serious Games

Konstantinos Georgiadis[1](✉), Tjitske Faber[2], and Wim Westera[1]

[1] Open University of the Netherlands, 6419AT Heerlen, The Netherlands
{konstantinos.georgiadis,wim.westera}@ou.nl
[2] Erasmus University of the Netherlands, 3015GD Rotterdam, The Netherlands
t.faber@erasmusmc.nl

Abstract. Stealth assessment is an unobtrusive assessment methodology in serious games that use digital player traces to make inferences of players' expertise level over competencies. Although various proofs of stealth assessment's validity have been reported, its application is a complex, laborious, and time-consuming process. To bolster the applicability of stealth assessment in serious games; a generic stealth assessment tool (GSAT) has been proposed, which uses machine learning techniques to reason over competence constructs, player log data and assess player performance. Current study provides empirical validation of GSAT by applying it to a real-world game, the *abcdeSIM* game, which was designed to train medical care workers to act effectively medical emergency situations. GSAT demonstrated, while relying on a Gaussian Naive Bayes Network, to be highly robust and reliable, achieving a three-level assessment accuracy of 96%, as compared with a reference score model defined by experts. By this result, this study contributes to the alleviation of stealth assessment's applicability issues and hence promotes its wider uptake by the serious game community.

Keywords: Stealth assessment · Generic tool · Statistical model · Machine learning · Stepwise regression · Serious games · ABCDE-method

1 Introduction

As opposed to traditional classroom teaching, the use of serious games yields a bulk of digital traces of learner actions, which open up new opportunities for the in-depth assessment of learners: so-called stealth assessments (SA), unobtrusively based on the learner's behavioural traces in the game, without the need for explicit test items.

SA is grounded in a principled methodology [1], combining a design framework for modeling the assessment process and advanced data science technologies. Evidence-Centered Design (ECD) [2] has served as the design framework that provides a generic layout for developing competency, task, and evidence (i.e. data) constructs. Most notably, these constructs lead to the development of statistical models–describing the relationships between competencies, tasks and evidence, which can be used to meaningfully represent gameplay data within machine learning (ML) algorithms to produce

A. Liapis et al. (Eds.): GALA 2019, LNCS 11899, pp. 211–220, 2019.
https://doi.org/10.1007/978-3-030-34350-7_21

valid inferences (i.e. classifications). Several empirical studies [3–5] have provided a proofs of concept for SA.

Notwithstanding the proofs that SA can indeed provide valid and reliable assessments, its practical application turns out to be complex, laborious, and time-consuming. Applying SA in serious games requires substantial expertise in different domains including assessment, data science, statistics, game development, machine learning, etc. Until recently, no tools existed to automate the data processing (ML) part of SA in a generic way, thus forcing anyone who wants to apply SA to manually develop it from scratch in a hardcoded manner. This not only turns applying SA into a time-consuming process, but it also reduces its transferability to other serious games, increases development costs, and makes it prone to mistakes. Overall, these practicable barriers turn an otherwise exquisite assessment methodology into an unattractive assessment alternative for a wide spectrum of the serious game community.

In a recent study, a generic tool for applying SA has been proposed [6, 7], which tackles these issues and allows its broader application in serious games. The Generic Stealth Assessment Tool (GSAT) is a full-functional stand-alone software application that (a) handles numerical datasets from any serious game, (b) automatically runs ML processes, and (c) allows the easy arrangement of diverse ECD models. GSAT has been successfully tested for its robustness against several conditions with simulation datasets of different sizes and normality significance levels, with different ML algorithms, and different ECD models [8]. Current study goes beyond simulation data: it examines the robustness and reliability of GSAT with real-world data collected from the serious game *abcdeSIM*. This game supports healthcare practitioners and students at the acquisition of emergency medical care skills. The players are trained in properly applying an emergency treatment method called the *ABCDE*-method. A detailed rating system developed by experts was implemented within the game to evaluate the players' performances by registering points to them after every correct or false action. Using these expert scores a benchmark for assessment allowed to study and compare the quality and validity of the SA approach that was established using GSAT.

The structure of this paper is as follows. Background information about SA is provided in Sect. 2. Information on GSAT is presented in Sect. 3. Background information on the *ABCDE*-method can be found in Sect. 4. Details regarding the game and the collected data are presented in Sect. 5. The methodology that was used for the purposes of the study is described in Sect. 6. Section 7 presents the results of this study, while a discussion over the results and our final conclusions are in Sect. 8.

2 Stealth Assessment Background

As mentioned above, SA is essentially the combination of a principled conceptual framework for designing data-driven assessments in serious games. It relies on the ECD framework along with ML algorithms.

2.1 Evidence-Centered Design

The ECD [2] is a framework for designing assessments in serious games on the basis of several generic conceptual models. ECD describes the assessment design as part of three such models. These are: (a) the competency model, which describes the assessed competency and its underlying facets (i.e. sub-skills), (b) the task model, which describes the in-game tasks that can elicit data relative to the assessed competency constructs, and (c) the evidence model, which describes the relationships of the elicited data (i.e. game variables/observables) to both the tasks in the game and the competency constructs. In particular, the relationship between game data and competency constructs, which commonly referred to as the statistical model, is crucial for applying SA. GSAT was designed to solely focus on the assessment aspects of ECD (such as the statistical and competency models).

2.2 Machine Learning

ML being a subset of artificial intelligence technology is considered to be on the verge of data science due to its capability for providing probabilistic solutions to non-binary and non-deterministic problems. Generally speaking, a wide array of ML algorithms exists that are usually categorized as supervised, unsupervised, or semi-supervised learning algorithms. Supervised ML algorithms produce inferences by using as reference point a set of labeled training data (e.g. a pre-annotated dataset with classifications by experts). Unsupervised ML algorithms can provide classifications by applying clustering techniques on unlabeled datasets. Semi-supervised ML algorithms fall in-between the previous two categories were both labeled and unlabeled data is used to provide classifications. The ML algorithms belonging to these categories can be further distinguished according to the different types of data (e.g. numerical, categorical, ordinal, etc.) that they can process.

As mentioned previously, serious games offer the opportunity to capture vast amounts of data far beyond a teacher's grasp within a traditional classroom. After structuring this data into meaningful statistical models (e.g. through ECD) allows for the use of ML algorithms to assess (i.e. classify) the learners' performances. So far, various ML algorithms (such as Bayesian Networks, Support Vector Machines, Decision Trees, and Deep Learning) have been used for SA [9, 10]. Nevertheless, Bayesian Networks have been the first and foremost used algorithm in existing SA studies [3–5] probably due to its generative nature. In this study, Gaussian Naive Bayes Network (GNBN) was opted as we deal with numerical data in a supervised manner. Also, GNBN has turned out to be the highest performing algorithm in our simulation studies with GSAT [8].

3 GSAT

SA is essentially a generic methodology as its two components (i.e. ECD and ML) are generic in nature by default. However, so far SA has only been applied in a hardcoded manner, that is, directly implemented within a game's source code and thus specifically destined for assessing a certain competency within the context of a specific game.

GSAT offers a generic tool to define and operate SA across diversity of competencies and game contexts. GSAT is currently a stand-alone software solution that offers fully automated processing of numerical datasets with ML, and that exclusively deals with the diagnostic aspects of SA. It allows for declaring the competency model and once it is fed with player log data it uses ML classifiers to deliver the player-related performance assessments. The tool is a client-side console application developed in the C# programming language using the.NET framework. A more detailed description of GSAT including its technical architecture, workflow design, external libraries, etc. can be found in previous studies [6, 7].

4 The ABCDE-Method

The *ABCDE-method* is an emergency medical care protocol used by healthcare providers all over the world for assessing and treating acutely ill patients. This method relies on the principle of "treat first what kills first". This means that the healthcare practitioner needs to follow a systematic approach when dealing with acutely ill patients. This approach is divided into five phases, using a simple mnemonic: Airway, Breathing, Circulation, Disability, and Exposure/Environment (ABCDE). See Table 1 for a brief description of each phase.

Table 1. Descriptions of the five phases of the ABCDE-method (not exhaustive).

Phases	Description
Airway	Check for abnormalities indicating airway obstruction by addressing the patient, listening for abnormal breathing and inspecting the oral cavity for blood, vomit, swelling. In case of obstruction, manual airway manoeuvers or airway devices should be used. If the airway is blocked, specialist help should be called
Breathing	Check for pulmonary disorders (e.g. pneumonia, asthma, etc.). If the ventilation and oxygenation of the patient is inadequate, the practitioner must put the patient in a sitting position, administer oxygen and treat the underlying cause. Consider manual or mechanical ventilation in severe cases
Circulation	Check for loss of circulating volume, decreased cardiac contractility, and loss of vascular pressure. In case of disorders, establish intravenous access, and, depending on the underlying issue, administer fluids or vasoactive medication. Specific cases require consultancy from specialists
Disability	Evaluate patient's neurological status by examining his/her consciousness, meninges, pupillary response to light, and glucose levels. Look for signs of intracranial hemorrhage, intoxication, hypoglycemia, or electrolyte disorders. Treat the underlying disorder, with specialist help if needed. Protect the airway: obstruction may occur when consciousness deteriorates
Exposure/Environment	Look for skin and other physical abnormalities (e.g. injury signs). Treat disorders that require immediate attention, consult appropriate specialists, and cover the patient to avoid hypothermia

5 The Game: abcdeSIM

The *ABCDE-method* is generally taught to healthcare practitioners in face-to-face courses across several contexts (e.g. trauma, medicine, obstetric, and pediatric courses). Although such courses are generally effective, still there is room for improvement since the costs are high [11] and the opportunities for distributed practice are limited [12]. It has been suggested to use a serious game for addressing these issues, which would also allow to teach complex cognitive skills in an engaging, flexible and patient-safe way [13].

Therefore, a serious game called *abcdeSIM* was developed in close collaboration between medical practitioners, game designers, and educationalists from the Erasmus University Medical Center, Rotterdam and VirtualMedSchool, Rotterdam. The aim of the game is to prepare residents in emergency medicine care by applying the *ABCDE-method*. The *abcdeSIM* game has already been used in research [14] and training. Now, the game is used for testing and validating the SA produced by GSAT.

5.1 Gameplay

In the *abcdeSIM* game, the player takes on the role of a physician who is presented with an acutely ill patient in a virtual emergency department. The virtual nurse provides a brief handover containing information on patient's condition. All tools and information available in a real-life emergency department are available to the player. Among other things, the player can perform physical examinations, talk to the patient, administer medication, order diagnostic tests, and ask for help from a specialist. In fifteen minutes, the player must complete a full examination of the patient and initiate necessary treatments.

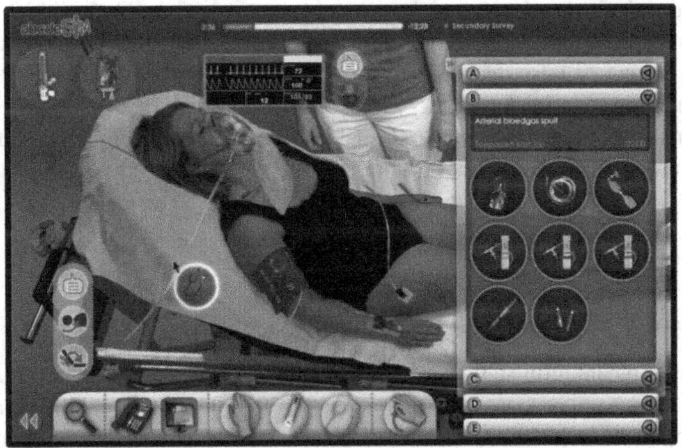

Fig. 1. A snapshot from the *abcdeSIM* gameplay.

Vital parameters and the condition of the patient are generated by a complex physiological model that is influenced by the player's actions. This results in a realistic feel of the scenario (Fig. 1). Afterwards, the player can choose to proceed on a "secondary survey". At this point, corrective feedback, a game score based on an expert rating system, and a narrative on how the patient fared after their care are provided. Several patient cases are available with different medical conditions and levels of sickness.

For the purpose of this study, a game scenario concerning a patient suffering from subarachnoid hemorrhage was used. The patient presents with an obstructed airway, necessitating the use of the *ABCDE-method* to improve her condition swiftly. Before playing this scenario, players are advised to first follow a gameplay tutorial, complete a practice scenario without any illness, and apply their skills in an emergency scenario. This ensures their familiarity with the game interface.

5.2 Game Logs

For this study, we looked at log files of first attempts at completing the scenario containing anonymized raw data collected during gameplay from 267 players. Each log file was parsed using a specialized JavaScript parser, which allowed extracting and categorizing logged events based on actor (player or patient), action type (examination, exploration, intervention, history, diagnostics, help-seeking from specialist, reflection), and the concurrent *ABCDE-method* phase if applicable. From this parsed log we calculated the total number of actions for the player and patient and the total number of actions per action type. In addition, aggregated game variables were devised for each action type, that is, ratio of the number of times each action type was performed to the total number of player's actions. Finally, to quantify adherence to the *ABCDE-method*, we calculated systematicity scores for each session using a Hidden Markov Model as described by Lee and colleagues [15].

The rating system (developed by content experts) embedded within *abcdeSIM* allowed for logging final game scores for each player. The game score depends on the number of correct or false decisions made according to the *ABCDE-method*. Harmful interventions (e.g. administering the wrong medication) subtract points, while helpful interventions add points to the players' final game score. Completing a case faster than fifteen minutes rewards additional points.

6 Methodology

6.1 Statistical Model

For deriving a meaningful statistical model from the logged data it is important to first describe a competency construct that specifies the underlying abilities needed to properly apply the *ABCDE-method*. During each of the *ABCDE-method's* phases the players have to perform a series of actions that require medical and game procedural abilities. The medical part covers three theoretical aspects of the medical care process: (a) ability to properly diagnose the medical problem, (b) ability to apply according treatments, and (c) ability to systematically follow the ABCDE-method and reflect on the outcomes of each phase. The game procedural part relates to the practical aspects of performing the correct actions (e.g. navigating the game environment, selecting tools, applying the tools to the correct areas).

To investigate and establish the statistical relationships between the game variables and the competency construct a linear stepwise regression analysis on the data was applied. Beforehand, certain regression assumptions were first examined, such as the linearity the relationship of the game variables (independent variables) and the final game scores from the expert rating system (dependent variable), as well as the collinearity between the game variables. In this way, we minimized the set of game variables that should be included into the regression analysis and thus maintain only the most influential ones. Finally, five game variables made it into the regression analysis: (1) relative examination ratio: no. of examinations to no. of player actions, (2) relative reflection ratio: no. of reflections to no. of player actions, (3) relative diagnostics ratio: no. of diagnostics to no. of player actions, (4) systematicity, and (5) inversed relative exploration ratio: inversed no. of exploration to no. of player actions. The model turns out to explain 53% of the variance (*Adjusted* R^2= 0.53) of the dependent variable and shows an acceptable level of internal consistency (Cronbach's α = 0.602). Figure 2 provides a view of the statistical model.

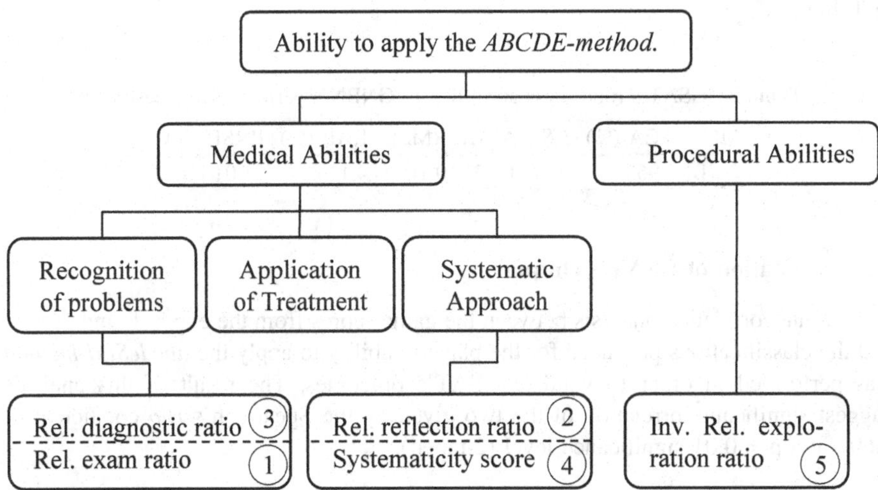

Fig. 2. A view of the statistical model for the players' ability to apply the *ABCDE-method.*

6.2 GSAT's Configuration and ML Performance Measures

In order to classify the ability of the players in applying the ABCDE-method we imported the statistical model to GSAT along with the respective data. Since the data originally was not labelled (by experts or otherwise), a clustering approach described in [8] was first applied to label the data. Then, a GNBN algorithm was used to produce inferences with regard to three classes (Low, Medium, and High performance).

A percentage split rule was used to train (65% of the samples used) and test (remaining 35% of the samples used) the classifier. In accordance with to [16] several performance measures were used to evaluate the performance of the GNBN classifier including the classification accuracy (CA), the kappa statistic (KS), the mean absolute error (MAE), the root mean squared error (RMSE), the relative absolute error (RAE), and the root relative squared error (RRSE), respectively.

6.3 Validation Process

To validate the outcomes of GSAT we examined the Spearman's *rho* correlation coefficients of the classifications produced by GSAT and the game scores from the expert rating system. To this end, the game scores were first clustered using a k-means clustering approach (3 clusters) in order to have both variables aligned in an ordinal form.

7 Results

7.1 GSAT's Performance

The various performance measures (cf. Sect. 6.2) for the GNBN classifier are presented in Table 2.

Table 2. GSAT's robustness according to GNBN's performance measures.

ML	CA (%)	KS	MAE	RMSE	RAE (%)	RRSE (%)
GNBN	96.8	0.94	0.03	0.18	4.11	21.01

7.2 Validation of GSAT's Outputs

A bivariate correlation analysis between the game scores from the expert rating system and the classifications produced for the players' ability to apply the *abcdeSIM-method* was performed in order to validate GSAT's outcomes. The result of this analysis suggest significant correlation of the two given by the Spearman's *rho* coefficient of 0.607 at a p = 0.01 significance level (2-tailed).

8 Discussion and Conclusions

In this study on the *abcdeSIM* game we managed to derive a statistical model effectively describing meaningful relationships between the collected log data and the abilities that are needed to apply this *ABCDE* protocol in the abcdeSIM game environment. The statistical model displayed internal consistency at an acceptable level (Cronbach's $\alpha = 0.602$). Entering this model into GSAT allowed for making inferences regarding the players' performances. The classifications produced by GSAT are highly correlated (Spearman's *rho* = 0.607 at a 0.01 significance level) with the expert scores.

Concerning GSAT's performance it was found that when applying a GNBN algorithm on the declared statistical model its classification accuracy (being the most important performance measure) is beyond 96%. This means that the classifier was able to accurately assess most of the tested cases.

A substantial limitation of the study is the limited size of the dataset. As a consequently, the statistical power and accordingly the number of behavioral predictors (cf. Sect. 6.1) are constrained. Notably, in this setting no relevant game variable could be identified that would cover applying proper treatments. One explanation is that a portion of data (e.g. certain mouse clicks relating to dosage or response to double-check procedure) that could potentially relate to this facet was not logged in the first place. Another explanation could be that after correctly diagnosing the patient condition, players naturally follow the indicated treatment procedures so a strong covariance with examination actions exists. Another explanation could be that the game mechanics do not allow for capturing enough data relating to the treatment, which is quite likely because the treatment procedures within the game are collected in the game log as whether or not they are initiated, without operational details. Hence, one might conclude that the game does not particularly teach the detailed execution of treatment procedures. Overall, *abcdeSIM* offered an excellent opportunity to detail the practical application of the SA method with GSAT, demonstrating the potential of automation tools that can lift the barriers of SA and allow its wider application in the domain of serious games.

Acknowledgements. We wish to thank IJsfontein, serious game company in Amsterdam, for making the game and extensive logging utility available and Virtual Medschool for providing (anonymised) game log data. We also acknowledge Jeroen Donkers of the School of Health Professions Education, Maastricht University, the Netherlands, for assisting at calculating systematicity scores and data processing. Finally, we thank Tin de Zeeuw, Lent, The Netherlands, for his assistance in processing the raw game log data.

References

1. Shute, V.J.: Stealth assessment in computer-based games to support learning. Comput. Games Instr. **55**(2), 503–524 (2011)
2. Mislevy, R.J.: Evidence-centered design for simulation-based assessment. CRESST Report 800. National Center for Research on Evaluation, Standards, and Student Testing (CRESST) (2011)
3. Shute, V.J., Ventura, M., Kim, Y.J.: Assessment and learning of qualitative physics in Newton's playground. J. Educ. Res. **106**(6), 423–430 (2013)
4. Ventura, M., Shute, V., Small, M.: Assessing persistence in educational games. Des. Recomm. Adapt. Intell. Tutoring Syst. Learn. Model. **2**, 93–101 (2014)
5. Shute, V.J., Wang, L., Greiff, S., Zhao, W., Moore, G.: Measuring problem solving skills via stealth assessment in an engaging video game. Comput. Hum. Behav. **63**, 106–117 (2016)
6. Georgiadis, K., Van Lankveld, G., Bahreini, K., Westera, W..: Accommodating stealth assessment in serious games: towards developing a generic tool. In: 2018 10th International Conference on Virtual Worlds and Games for Serious Applications (VS-Games), pp. 1–4. IEEE (2018)

7. Georgiadis, K., Van Lankveld, G., Bahreini, K., Westera, W..: Learning analytics should analyse the learning: proposing a generic stealth assessment tool. In: Accepted at the IEEE Conference on Games (CoG) (2019)
8. Georgiadis, K., Van Lankveld, G., Bahreini, K., Westera, W..: On the robustness of steath assessment. In: Submitted to IEEE Transactions on Games (2019)
9. Sabourin, J.L.: Stealth assessment of self-regulated learning in game-based learning environments (2013)
10. Min, W., et al.: DeepStealth: leveraging deep learning models for stealth assessment in game-based learning environments. In: Conati, C., Heffernan, N., Mitrovic, A., Verdejo, M. Felisa (eds.) AIED 2015. LNCS (LNAI), vol. 9112, pp. 277–286. Springer, Cham (2015). https://doi.org/10.1007/978-3-319-19773-9_28
11. Perkins, G.D., et al.: Improving the efficiency of advanced life support training: a randomized, controlled trial. Ann. Intern. Med. **157**(1), 19–28 (2012)
12. Cook, D.A., et al.: Comparative effectiveness of instructional design features in simulation-based education: systematic review and meta-analysis. Med. Teach. **35**, e867–e898 (2012)
13. Kalkman, C.J.: Serious play in the virtual world: can we use games to train young doctors? J. Grad. Med. Educ. **4**(1), 11–13 (2012)
14. Dankbaar, M.E., et al.: Preparing residents effectively in emergency skills training with a serious game. Simul. Healthc. **12**(1), 9 (2017)
15. Lee, J.Y., Donkers, J., Jarodzka, H., van Merriënboer, J.J.G.: How prior knowledge affects problem-solving performance in a medical simulation game: Using game-logs and eye-tracking. Comput. Hum. Behav. **99**, 268–277 (2019)
16. Domingos, P.M.: A few useful things to know about machine learning. Commun. ACM **55** (10), 78–87 (2012)

Cyber Chronix, Participatory Research Approach to Develop and Evaluate a Storytelling Game on Personal Data Protection Rights and Privacy Risks

Rosanna Di Gioia(✉), Stéphane Chaudron, Monica Gemo, and Ignacio Sanchez

European Commission, Joint Research Centre, 21027 Ispra, Varese, Italy
Rosanna.Di-Gioia@ec.europa.eu

Abstract. This paper describes the participatory approach chosen to develop and evaluate a new serious game called Cyber Chronix developed in the format of a digital comic strip with storytelling branches. The aim of the story entitled "Finding Data" is to raise awareness about the privacy risks and the data protection rights in the new European Union (EU) General Data Protection Regulation (GDPR), whilst delivering a pleasant and enjoyable experience. In the evaluation phase, students acted as assessors with the assignment of looking at the key factors contributing to engage in reading, to enhance curiosity and to raise awareness of EU GDPR concepts. Here we report on how students perceived the different dimensions of the story and how the game can help to disseminate knowledge of EU GDPR rights and raise awareness of privacy risks.

Keywords: Storytelling · Branching game · Personal data protection rights · Privacy risks · Digital competences · Engagement

1 Introduction

Storytelling [1] is a winning formula for engagement [2] as narrative can help human beings in making sense of the world around them. Everyone has listened to fairy tales told either by grandparents or parents and, if we simply look back to history, we immediately realise the impact that stories have had on shaping our lives. We initiated this development from the assumption that learning through serious games provides situated learning and has educational values that are based on intrinsic motivation [3] and learning concepts advocated by constructivist psycho-cognitive theories [4]. Storytelling is the approach that we chose to design a new game, Cyber Chronix (Fig. 1), created to raise awareness on privacy risks and data protection rights stated in the new EU General Data Protection Regulation (GDPR) [5]. Its main goal being to empower data subjects, namely citizens, to better control their personal data and to mitigate privacy risks. Reading and understanding a regulation is not an easy task, especially at a young age.

A. Liapis et al. (Eds.): GALA 2019, LNCS 11899, pp. 221–230, 2019.
https://doi.org/10.1007/978-3-030-34350-7_22

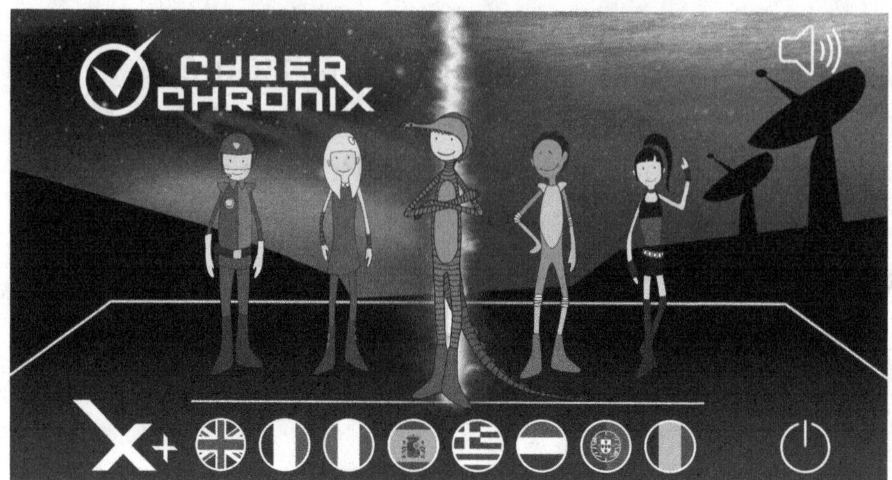

Fig. 1. Cyber Chronix graphical presentation.

To ensure the success of the EU GDPR, it is important that citizens are aware of their data protection rights and understand how to exercise them to control their data and mitigate privacy and security risks. In Cyber Chronix, players are taken to a futuristic planet several light years from Earth. The player's aim is to help the main character to make it to a party, while he encounters several data protection-related obstacles along the way. As the player progresses through the game, she/he has to make choices that will affect the storyline and eventual outcome. Several storylines are possible depending on the branches that the player's choice has developed. The game is also designed to introduce young people to EU GDPR concepts with an informal educational approach. Concepts such as the "Right to be forgotten", "Personal Data Breach", "Data Portability", can be unusual terms for those new to this language. In Cyber Chronix, some of these terms are firstly introduced in an informal way during the dialogues and interactions among characters. Additionally, quiz questions called XRay add gaming elements and appear unexpectedly (Fig. 2) to challenge the player during the game session. Moreover, a dedicated educational part called XRay+ (Fig. 3) is always available for the player who wishes to know more. Behind the choice of the XRay term, there is the idea that Cyber Chronix XRay can provide a "picture of knowledge" as it happens with the medical x-ray imaging.

2 Theoretical Framework

Cyber Chronix edutainment contributes to the debate on how digital technology can support the enhancement of digital competences among youngsters. Cyber Chronix was conceived under a theoretical framework that takes grounds on digital competences framework (DigComp) [6–8], storytelling [1] and notions of

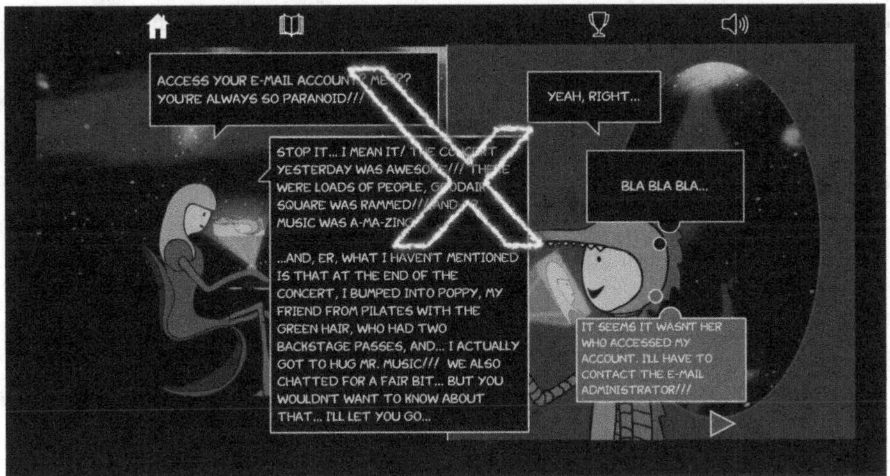

Fig. 2. Example of XRay appearing during game play.

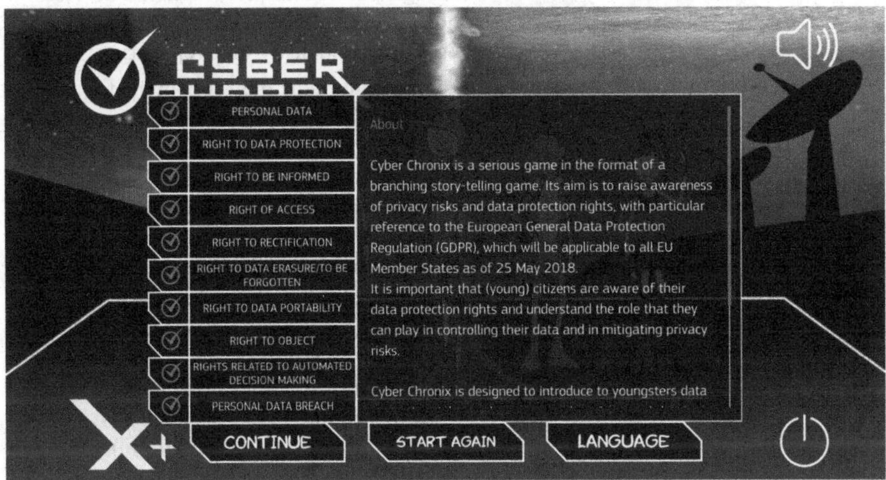

Fig. 3. Summary of XRay + educational sheets.

engagement in reading [2] with the aim to get concepts treated in the EU GDPR through to youngsters. The EU GDPR [5] from 25th May 2018 has replaced current data protection laws in the European Union. The EU General Data Protection Regulation is an essential step to strengthen citizens' fundamental rights for the protection and management of data in the digital age. To give some examples, individuals have significantly strengthened rights to obtain details about how their data is processed by an organisation or business (Right of Access); to obtain their data from an organisation and to have that data transmitted to another organisation (Right of Data Portability); to have incorrect or incomplete data corrected (Rights to Rectification); to obtain by the data controller report of any breaches of personal data (Personal Data Breach) to the National Data Protection Authority.

Table 1. DigComp areas.

Area	Description
1. Information and data literacy	To articulate information needs, to locate and retrieve digital data, information and content. To judge the relevance of the source and its content. To store, manage, and organise digital data, information and content
2. Communication and collaboration	To interact, communicate and collaborate through digital technologies while being aware of cultural and generational diversity. To participate in society through public and private digital services and participatory citizenship. To manage one's digital identity and reputation
3. Digital content creation	To create and edit digital content to improve and integrate information and content into an existing body of knowledge while understanding how copyright and licences are to be applied. To know how to give understandable instructions for a computer system
4. Safety	To protect devices, content, personal data and privacy in digital environments. To protect physical and psychological health, and to be aware of digital technologies for social well-being and social inclusion. To be aware of the environmental impact of digital technologies and their use
5. Problem Solving	To identify needs and problems, and to resolve conceptual problems and problem situations in digital environments. To use digital tools to innovate processes and products. To keep up-to-date with the digital evolution

Digital competences are fundamental to boost effective privacy safeguards strategies that also rely on the skills and attitudes of the people concerned. As defined in the EC Recommendation on Key Competences the notion of competence involves the confident and critical use of Information and Communication Technology (ICT) (i.e. the knowledge, skills and attitudes) for employment, learning, self-development and participation in society. In this work we refer to the Digital Competence framework (DigComp) [6–8] (Table 1) and more specifically, we focused on area one (1) "Information and data literacy", area two (2) "Communication and collaboration", with particular emphasis on the digital identity and reputation management, and area four (4) "Safety" for the protection of devices, content, personal data and privacy in digital environments. It is important to note that data literacy, including the understanding, articulation and usage of personal data have been included in the DigComp framework (Area 1- DigComp 2.0).

3 Cyber Chronix Development

Cyber Chronix development is the result of a process that can be summarized in the following steps: (1) Idea and proposal; (2) First dialogue writing; (3) Storyboard development; (4) Images and Sound creation; (5) Educational content creation and validation; (6) Assessment by users; (7) Feedback gathering and reflection; (8) Adjustment and re-testing; (9) First publication:

1. In the preliminary phase, the research team agreed on the project concept and main ideas. The theoretical framework was defined and the branching storytelling game format was chosen. The story tale was developed from scratch using basic tools such as Power Point and Word. Story scenes with branches and dialogues are now available in Dutch, English, French, Italian, Greek, Portuguese, Romanian and Spanish, and they are the result of the imagination of the authors and consultants helping with the development.
2. Text and dialogues were first tested internally among researchers.
3. This first test led us to develop a storyboard.
4. In this phase, in addition to the text, illustrations were added to the serious game (Figs. 1, 2 and 3). At first, the main character Iggy was designed. The development of other characters (Fig. 4) was carefully thought so that they could support the narrative understanding and recall familiar real roles

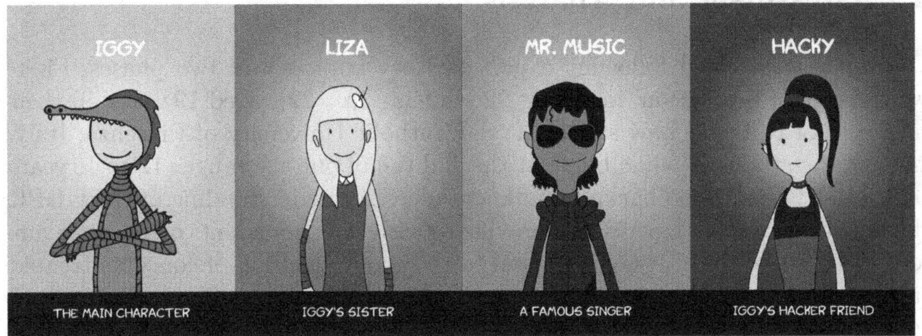

Fig. 4. Some of the Cyber Chronix characters.

for the reader (e.g. sister, policeman, hacker, famous singer, events organiser, friends). Sounds were chosen to give to the branching game a "light" suspense and some hypnotic atmosphere, avoiding either a too intense or noisy effect. The aim of this is to accompany the game in the reading and at the same time to distinguish musically different characters' personalities and game situations.

5. The educational section was developed with experts in privacy and data protection matters and digital education guided by the DigComp Area 1, 2 and 4 (Table 1). The game presents 10 questions with a situation, conceived to recreate a possible real case, where a citizen could imagine and use critical thinking to exercise rights, control data and mitigate risks. In addition, there are dedicated sheets for each presented concept for in-depth information.
6. Cyber Chronix assessment was carried out with a participatory research approach with young citizens. More details are described under section "Result and discussion".
7. Feedback and suggestions were considered and analysed.
8. A new version of the tool was developed taking into consideration the results of the feedback and suggestions.
9. Cyber Chronix was published on 25th May 2018, the day on which the EU GDPR became applicable in all EU Member States. Cyber Chronix can be a versatile tool both for individual use and also to create an informal educational session within a community. An example is the live competition which was organised by JRC researchers to celebrate the EU GDPR day on 25th May 2018. On this occasion, ten Italian schools represented by the so-called "quartets" formed by a girl, a boy, a teacher and a parent attending the event, where the winner's team finished the challenge of recognising and describing the 10 EU GDPR concepts within the game. Such methodology can help to fill in generational gaps towards digital technology use and enhance discussion among actors (children and adults) on subjects related to the themes treated within the game (privacy, personal data protection, online safety, fair communication, etc.) [9–11].

4 Assessment and Analysis

Our game was tested following a participatory approach in two phases. First, we ran a pilot evaluation, involving 22 students ($n = 22$), aged 19 years, in their first year of ICT and Law studies at the Catholic University of Piacenza, Italy. Indeed, the students, while being at the end tail of our age range (12 to 19 years old), already had some background knowledge and understanding of the GDPR document, which was essential to provide us with their comments on how the various elements of the story contributed to the comprehension of concepts treated in the educational XRay and XRay+ sheets, to the quality of the reading and finally to the gamification experience [12]. The results of this first pilot evaluation were promising. Generated comments were taken into account and lead us to review the game and propose a second wave of testing ($n = 39$) with students aged 12 to 15 in schools of Friuli Venezia Giulia Region (Italy) in the frame of the Memorandum of Understanding signed with the Joint Research Centre. To gather and analyse data from the items and related dimensions listed in Table 2, we referred to the work developed by Rubegni and Landoni [2] concerning the evaluation of engagement in reading (narrative presence, continuous desire to read and/or explore new branches, etc.) and previously presented by Zagalo et al. [1]. Finally, the understanding of the concepts presented in questions 8 to 17 were evaluated against the DigComp framework (Table 1).

Table 2. Questionnaire items and related theoretical dimensions

Item	Description
1. Introduction	Curiosity
2. Theme	Narrative presence
3. Engagement and general comment	Emotional engagement and enjoyment
4. Characters	Character Identification
5. Context/Environment	Additional transportation and story-worl
6. Story elements	Adherence to the story structure
7. Narrative and style	Narrative presence and comprehension
8–17 Concepts	Education and awareness raising on EU GDPR

While the first questionnaire was administered to a small sample of 22 students, as described above. The results of this first evaluation were the following, described following the structure of Table 2. Most of the sample considered the introduction as original and interesting, meaningful and clear (item 1). The Narrative was understood very positively by the sample (item 2) as was the Emotional Engagement (item 3). The Characters were considered in a positive way by almost the totality of the sample (item 4); Context with visual and descriptive elements were clear for the majority of the sample (item 5–6); Comprehension and narrative also received positive comments (item 7). The educational part presents a mixed evaluation (item 8–17). Students remembered the concepts presented, however some concept explanations remained not completely clear (i.e. Biometric data, Data Protection Authority). Overall, the evaluations remained positive. Nevertheless, as a general comment it was suggested we try a younger age target. These comments led us to reflect on the importance of different game elements and to propose a new assessment with a different age group. In this second wave of assessment, the beta-version of the game was tested with two different schools, we administered a questionnaire to children aged between 12–15. We present here the results of the second assessment considering that multiple answer solution to questions was chosen. From the first assessment, it appeared that an introduction was needed to better explain to end-users several game elements. Namely context, branching-game mechanism, characters, key-educational tools as XRay and XRay + (Plus) with prizes. Most of the students considered the introduction (item 1) as clear, meaningful, original and interesting.

Results show that more than two-thirds of students understood the proposed theme (item 2). From the theoretical point of view, this question would elicit information about Narrative Presence and the sense of realism children will get when reading. Emotional engagement received positive comments (item 3) (Fig. 5). According to our assessors, characters (item 4) were well developed and described and maintained their own identity throughout the story. Context-Environment (item 5) was also appreciated by the majority of the students. Visual and descriptive details in the text were considered important links to the treated theme. Story elements (i.e. main characters, antagonist, helper, etc.) (item 6) were recognised as partially present and interrelated. The narrative style and comprehension (item 7) was satisfying. Most of the concepts presented (items 8 to 17) were recognized and more than the half were considered as new learning with clear explanations. The evaluation was grounded within the DigComp theoretical framework (Table 1).

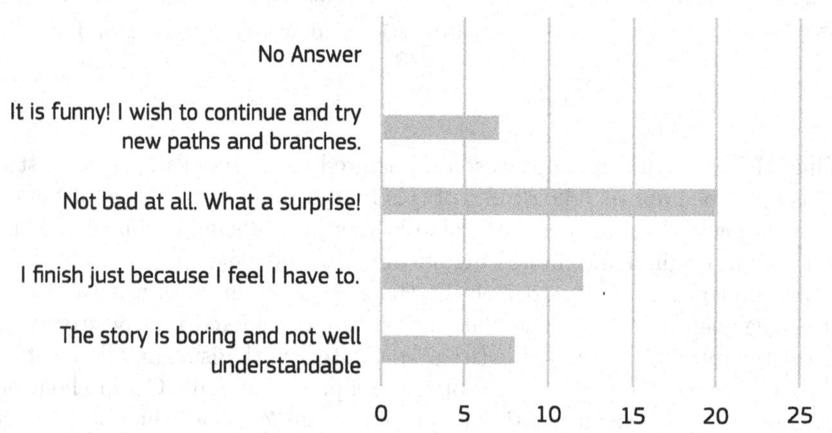

Fig. 5. Emotional engagement and enjoyment - 2nd wave of testing

5 Results and Discussion

Developing a product that could satisfy both enjoyment and educational needs is a challenging task and the EU GDPR jargon added a layer of complexity to the entire process. We overcame this difficulty thanks to the participatory approach and the close collaboration between researchers and experts on Privacy, Data Protection and Digital Education. This allowed for the "translation" difficult concepts into more understandable terms, whilst maintaining the essence of the legal aims. While there are several online and offline guides to better understand the EU GDPR, we aimed at delivering a tool, for a participatory, jargon-free, informal, co-constructive and meaningful learning model. As anticipated, informal educational sessions were arranged and others are foreseen. Future works with broader samples and in countries other than Italy would be beneficial to better understand the validity of the tool at cross-national level. An added value would be a comparative analysis on the different artefacts proposed, namely digital (App and Web versions) and paper-based one. Future planning envisages the development of new tales under a more economic and sustainable format. From our previous work with the Happy Onlife [13] toolkit, it emerged that the versatility of the toolkit in its paper and digital versions is an added value to the learning and citizen engagement process. To meet paper-oriented gamer's needs, a comic strip version is under development. Cyber Chronix digital game is now available in Dutch, English, French, Italian, Greek, Portuguese, Romanian and Spanish. In collaboration with stakeholders, we are planning new informal educational sessions with the tool as it would be beneficial to re-test it with a broader sample to investigate cross-national findings.

Acknowledgments. This research project benefited from the support of members belonging to the International Working Group on Privacy and Digital Education and Constructing an Alliance for Value-driven Cybersecurity (CANVAS) EU-funded project. Cyber Chronix is the result of a multidisciplinary work carried out by JRC researchers, IT developer architect William Peruggini, graphical designer Massimiliano Gusmini and illustrator Giuliana Gusmini. Thanks to Laurent Beslay for guidance and support in Privacy and Data Protection matters and to Henrik Junklewitz for his enthusiastic help in the storytelling reviewing. We are grateful to Monica Landoni, University of Italian Switzerland and Elisa Rubegni, University of Applied Sciences and Arts of Southern Switzerland (SUPSI), whose work and suggestions inspired the evaluation methodology. The assessment was arranged in collaboration with Professor Mariachiara Tallacchini of Catholic University, Piacenza (Italy) and Friuli Venezia Giulia Region (Italy) in the frame of the Memorandum of Understanding signed with Joint Research Centre. Many thanks to Katheryn Hands for proofreading.

References

1. Zagalo, N., Louchart, S., Soto-Sanfiel, M.T.: Users and evaluation of interactive storytelling. In: Aylett, R., Lim, M.Y., Louchart, S., Petta, P., Riedl, M. (eds.) ICIDS 2010. LNCS, vol. 6432, pp. 287–288. Springer, Heidelberg (2010). https://doi.org/10.1007/978-3-642-16638-9_44
2. Rubegni, E., Landoni, M.: Evaluating engagement in reading: comparing children and adult assessors. In: Proceeding of the 2014 conference on Interaction Design and Children, Manchester (2016)
3. Sailer, M., Hense, J., Mandl, H., Klevers, M.: Psychological perspectives on motivation through gamification. Interact. Des. Archit. J. **19**, 28–37 (2013)
4. Novak, J.: Meaningful learning: the essential factor for conceptual change in limited or inappropriate propositional hierarchies leading to empowerment of learners. Sci. Educ. **86**(4), 548–571 (2002). https://doi.org/10.1002/sce.10032

5. European Parliament and Council: General Data Protection Regulation (EU) 2016/679. Official Journal of the European Union, Luxembourg (2016)
6. Carretero, S., Vuorikari, R., Punie, Y.: DigComp 2.1: the digital competence framework for citizens with eight proficiency levels and examples of use. Publications Office of the European Union, Luxemburg EUR 28558 EN (2017). https://doi.org/10.2760/38842
7. Ferrari, A., Punie, Y., Brečko, N.: DIGComp: a framework for developping and understanding digital competences in Europe. Joint Research Centre - European Commission, EUR 26035 EN, Seville (2013). https://doi.org/10.2788/52966
8. Vuorikari, R., Punie, Y., Carretero Gomez S., Van den Brande, G.: DigComp 2.0: the digital competence framework for citizens. update phase 1: the conceptual reference model. Publication Office of the European Union, EUR 27948 EN, Luxembourg (2016). https://doi.org/10.2791/11517
9. European Commission Science Hub page, Understanding GDPR: new game from the JRC. https://ec.europa.eu/jrc/en/news/understanding-gdpr-new-game-jrc. Accessed 05 Sept 2019
10. European Commission Science Hub page, Cyber Chronix, a game to understand data protection rights and raise awareness on privacy risks. https://ec.europa.eu/jrc/en/research-topic/security-privacy-and-data-protection/cyber-chronix. Accessed 05 Sept 2019
11. Better Internet for kids web page, Cyber Chronix, a new game from the JRC to better understand the GDPR. https://www.betterinternetforkids.eu/web/portal/practice/awareness/detail?articleId=3187316. Accessed 05 Sept 2019
12. Kapp, K.M.: The Gamification of Learning and Instructions: Game-based Methods and Strategies for Training and Education. Wiley, San Francisco (2012)
13. Di Gioia, R., Gemo, M., Chaudron, S.: Empowering children and adults for a safe and responsible use of ICT, EUR 27702. Publications Office, Luxembourg (2016). https://doi.org/10.2788/942647

Some Notes on the Possibile Role of Cognitive Architectures in Serious Games

Manuel Gentile[1,2(✉)], Giuseppe Città[1], Antonio Lieto[2,3], and Mario Allegra[1]

[1] Institute for Educational Technology, National Research Council of Italy, Palermo, Italy
{manuel.gentile,giuseppe.citta,mario.allegra}@itd.cnr.it

[2] Dipartimento di Informatica, Università di Torino, Turin, Italy
manuel.gentile@edu.unito.it, antonio.lieto@unito.it

[3] ICAR, National Research Council of Italy, Palermo, Italy
http://www.pa.itd.cnr.it/, https://www.antoniolieto.net

Abstract. This paper provides a preliminary analysis of the possible role of cognitive architectures in the field of Serious Games. The seminal works that explore the use of Cognitive Architecture in games will be analyzed in the light of an emerging perspective of the games AI research area. Finally, an initial proposal of application of Cognitive Architecture for the design and implementation of non-player characters will be presented.

Keywords: Serious games · Cognitive Architecture · Cognitive Science · Artificial Intelligence

1 Introduction

Serious games are tools designed with a purpose other than pure entertainment, such as educational games [19]. According to Dorner et al. [14] serious games can be described as digital games developed not with the only intention to entertain but to achieve at least a goal named "characterizing goal". Usually such a goal is to enhance learning or to foster the development of skills and abilities through the use of a highly motivating teaching technology. Moreover, on the basis of their natural engagement and learning features, serious games allow:

- to extend the learning time, taking advantage of non-school times as a reinforcement mechanism;
- to develop skills and abilities in domains where it is difficult to have training opportunity through a realistic simulation of complex scenarios;
- to train soft skills such as problem-solving and decision-making [20], social and communication skills [7], etc.

In the literature, an interesting research area focuses on the use of serious games in Educational Sciences [9] but, despite the growing interest in the sector, some

A. Liapis et al. (Eds.): GALA 2019, LNCS 11899, pp. 231–241, 2019.
https://doi.org/10.1007/978-3-030-34350-7_23

scholars [16,23,46] highlight and suggest that Serious Game (SG) sector can benefit from a constructive dialogue with another field of knowledge, Cognitive Science (CS), that could and should provide an essential theoretical reference for dealing with some crucial issues such as modeling the player's behaviour and evaluate his/her interaction. Specifically, CS would be able to provide SG research with results and research methodologies on cognitive principles and models for explaining the cognitive processes that underlie learning through SG [23]. This kind of research would help researchers in the design and the evaluation process of an SG giving valuable indications on how cognitive skills, and in particular, according to Anderson [5], declarative and procedural knowledge are acquired in the game phases.

On the other hand, analyzing this relationship from the inverse point of view, SGs could provide CS with an appropriate experimental environment able to overcome the limitations of some cognitive experiments. In CS, experimental designs are generally carried out in aseptic environments (e.g., the laboratories) very distant from everyday reality to isolate all the factors that could influence the studies. Unfortunately, this approach leads to results often refuted when tested and analyzed in "real" contexts. SGs can represent a good compromise between structured experimental settings and less structured experimental settings closer to daily reality. In fact, SGs are generally designed to be realistic, and research confirms that SGs can "immerse" the player in a cognitive flow that leads him to experience the situation as if it were real. In addition, the handcrafted nature of SGs gives the researchers the possibility to manipulate the game to stimulate/test and verify certain cognitive processes. The analysis of the user's interactions collected during the gameplay would allow researchers to verify the validity of the theorized models, thus representing a promising research paradigm for the cognitive sciences of the computational approach.

In this paper, by focusing on a specific Computational branch of Cognitive Science, we deepen the specific aspect related to Cognitive Architectures (CA) and their possible role in the SGs domain.

In the next section, starting from the analysis of the literature in the intersection between games and AI, we present the proposal of organization of the new *games AI* field by Yannakakis and Togelius [49]. After a brief introduction of the cognitive architecture concept, we will analyze the contributions that apply cognitive architectures in the field of games and more specifically, where present, in the field of serious games according to the proposed perspective. Finally, we will sketch a preliminary analysis on the limits and possible solutions that derive from the use of cognitive architectures in the realization of non-player characters.

2 Artificial Intelligence and Games

Since its foundation, Artificial Intelligence (AI) has considered games one of the main fields of study and experimentation. From the analysis of classic board games such as chess, backgammon and more recently Go [44] the interest of AI researchers has been growing during the time. Also thanks to the development of the digital games market a new field of research called games Artificial Intelligence (games AI) [49] has emerged.

Workshops such as the first and second International Workshop on Agents for Games and Simulations [12,13] and conferences such as the AAAI Artificial Intelligence and Interactive Digital Entertainment (AIIDE) [37,43] and IEEE Computational Intelligence and Games (CIG) [1,2] played an essential role for the consolidation of the *games AI* research area.

A fundamental step in this process took place in May 2012 when, during the Dagstuhl seminar [35], about 40 world-leading experts convened to discuss future research directions and key research challenges for artificial and computational intelligence in games. While the studies on board games were almost exclusively aimed at creating virtual "players" able to compete with human opponents, according to the experts the new *games AI* field was supposed to include a broader range of research objectives. The experts identified ten different research themes (i.e. Non-player character (NPC) behavioral learning, Search and planning, Player modelling, Games as AI benchmarks, Procedural content generation, Computational narrative, Believable agents, AI-assisted game design, General game AI, AI in commercial games).

After this first attempt to give shape to this new sector, over time other works [13,48] have contributed to the definition of the field of research. Among others, the recent book "Artificial Intelligence and Games" [49] presents a systematic review of this field, coming to identify three main areas of research:

- playing game;
- generating content;
- player modeling.

The *playing game* area collects large portion of the research done to the date in games AI, which concerns two main themes: (1) the development of intelligent systems capable of playing independently with performance behaviours comparable to those of a human player; (2) the research on systems able to control the so-called non-player characters (NPCs) present in the game, in order to endow them with human-like behaviors and thus make them credible and engaging for human players. The *generating content* area refers to methods for generating game content (e. g. levels, maps, game rules, textures, stories, objects, missions, music, weapons, vehicles, characters), autonomously or with a limited human contribution. Content generation has seen an explosive growth of interest in the gaming industry. Examples of games incorporating automatically generated content already exist since the early 1980s, such as Rogue [8] and Elite [17]; however, in the second half of the last decade interest in academic research has increased significantly. Finally, the *player modeling* area collects all those researches that aim at the detection, prediction, and expression of the human characteristics of the player using cognitive, emotional and behavioral models during the game. Player modeling mainly studies the use of AI methods for the construction of players' computational models, i.e., representations capable of capturing the underlying functions between the player's characteristics and his/her interaction with the game.

The modeling of the player's behavior and experience has a primary value in the application of games AI because it has a direct influence also in the other two areas. Just think for example of the problem of the game adaptivity according to the player's profile that leads to the need of automatic content generation [38,41].

According to this perspective, we will investigate the contributions that apply cognitive architectures in the field of games and serious games.

3 Toward the Use of Cognitive Architectures in Serious Games

3.1 A Brief Overview About Cognitive Architectures

Cognitive architectures have been historically introduced in the fields of AI and Computational Cognitive Science (i) to capture, at the computational level, the invariant mechanisms of human cognition, including those underlying the functions of control, learning, memory, adaptivity, perception and action [40] (ii) to reach human level intelligence in a non narrow setting, by means of the realization of artificial artifacts built upon them and (iii) to form the basis for the development of artificial cognitive capabilities through ontogeny over extended periods of time (this goal is one of the main target of the so called emergent perspective) [47]).

During the last decades many cognitive architectures have been realized, - such as SOAR [27], ACT-R [4] etc. - and have been widely tested in several cognitive tasks involving learning, reasoning, selective attention, recognition etc. The modern instantion of the most mature cognitive architectures is, tipically, a hybrid computational model describing, as accurately as possible, the basic infrastructure of an intelligent agent. Current cognitive architectures, in fact, usually combine low-level neural components for the modeling of perceptual aspects and high-level logical and symbolic components for automatic reasoning and planning activities [31]. Over the last 30 years, these systems have had an extensive application in the various sectors: from robotics to tutoring systems [34]. The use of cognitive architectures, in fact, allows the construction of artificial agents able to use decisional and behavioral heuristics of cognitive inspiration, thus proposing specific models for the creation and the analysis of the mechanisms of such agents [32]. Kotseruba and Tsotsos provide an updated and broad overview of the last 40 years of research in cognitive architectures [25]. In this review, the authors analyze a set of 84 architectures, 49 of which are still actively developed.

3.2 Cognitive Architecture in Games AI

Literature reports a few examples of the application of cognitive architectures in games and obviously an even smaller number in the specific field of SG. In this section, we analyze these works according to the organization of the *games AI* area described in the previous section, emphasizing the possible role of cognitive architectures in games.

In the *playing game* area, the aim is to automatically control the player character or the non-player character of the game. Controlling the player character allow experts in AI to focus on optimizing the play-performance and/or testing the advancements algorithms and techniques for general cognitive processes such as perception, planning, decision-making and so on. From the point of view of game designer, the availability of intelligent agent able to human-like play game is an opportunity to test and evaluate of the game design.

About the design of non-player character, Ramirez [10] have pointed out that the enormous progress in game technologies to improve the physical realism of environments and characters does not correspond to an adequate level of "cognitive" realism of the characters.

In this area falls the work of Laird, the creator with Newell and Rosenbloom of the cognitive architecture SOAR [28,29]. He was one of the first researchers exploring the use of cognitive architectures in games [26]. In fact, with his research group, Laird has been investigating the use of games as an experimental environment in which testing the CAs features to control either the player character or the non-player character of the game [26,30]. As an example, Magerko et al. [36] applied the Soar architecture to design and develop complex AI characters in their games *Haunt 2*.

According to Streicher [45] CAs can play a primary role in *player modeling* area. It is a matter of fact that, one of the successful application of cognitive architecture is the creation of intelligent tutoring systems [34]. One demonstration is the application of ACT-R for the creation of an intelligent tutoring system widely used in the educational context of the United States [6,42]. In the same area, Ghosh and Verbrugge [21] offer an example of an application of the PRIM cognitive architecture.

In this context, the use of CAs may also provide the basis for overcoming the lack of adequate tools able to overcome traditional evaluation methodologies (e.g., questionnaires, self-evaluation tests), that, being external tools, do not allow to exploit the potential offered by SGs. The growing interest in learning analytics is leading the trend towards the realization of embedded objective measures able to evaluate the progress of students in real time; measures defined starting from the considerable amount of data generated by the "high frequency" interactions of the player with the SG.

However, despite the potential offered by these tools, the analysis of the literature shows that the learning analytics methods rarely refer to cognitive models. Liu et al. [33] conducted a systematic review to understand what are the evidence there are in using analytics in SG to support teaching and learning. Recently, Alonso-Fernández et al. [3], presented a review of their experiences in Game Learning Analytics for serious games.

The cognitive-grounded analysis of the user's interactions collected during the gameplay would represent a promising research paradigm both for the cognitive sciences of the computational approach as well as for serious games scientists.

Moreover, starting from a cognitive model of the player, it will be possible to improve also the research in personalization and adaptivity of the "game content" to the specific needs of the player.

According to this analysis, it emerges that cognitive architectures can naturally play a primary role in all three areas.

3.3 A Proposal of Application NPC

Despite the interest of academics and researchers, several factors have limited the applicability of cognitive architectures for these purposes. In this section, we propose a possible line of exploration to overcome the limits of applicability of CA in games, and in particular with reference to the creation of NPCs.

As stated by Dignum [13], among the main reasons that limit its applicability, there is undoubtedly a purely technical and technological reason. At present, cognitive architectures are difficult to integrate into the platforms currently used for the creation of games (e.g., Unity and Unreal). As the game engine, also the CAs demand a considerable computational capacity to satisfy the needs of responsiveness required by many types of game.

In order to overcome these problems, several solutions have been proposed based on the creation of communication middleware able to connect a proxy version of the agent that lives inside the game with a remote and complex one, based on cognitive architectures [18,26,30,39]. These solutions have been designed to theoretically interact with any cognitive architecture unless of the creation of a specific integration module.

Even though the quality of the proposed solutions, the effort required in terms of design and development and some technical limitations, such as the inability to take advantage of algorithms already integrated in game development environments, have limited the applicability of such solutions.

The proposed approach is based on the assumption that it is possible to create a mapping between "complex" agents and "simplified" agents to overcome all the computational limitations raised above. The goal is to allow designers, to model agents according well-grounded cognitive model, and allow the developers to implement simplified agents directly integrated into the gaming platforms (e.g., Unity and Unreal), but able to "simulate" complex behaviors.

Evidences from CS suggest that the simplification could be achieved at the cognitive level, modelling cognitive processes on the base of heuristics able to preserve the input-output functions of cognitive architectures through an efficient development of the dynamics of information processing provided by them. In other words: the computational model instantiated with a cognitive architecture can be compliant with the architectural constraints of the system but, at the same time, can implement more flexible heuristics enabling the creation of a computational model that is easier to integrate with other technological environments.

Heuristics (or judgements heuristics) are, according to the positive definition from Gigerenzer [22], shortcuts of thought that take a minimum amount of time, knowledge and calculation (computation) to process adaptive choices in concrete environments. This kind of shortcuts guides, on the basis of empirical rules (emerging from previous experience and knowledge), our daily actions that must be carried out immediately or in a short time and relying on limited knowledge. Kahneman [24] defines them in terms of paths of reasoning or mental events that occur automatically, have to do with both some innate skills (e.g. recognizing objects, orienting attention, perceiving the world) and learned skills (e.g. reading and/or understanding the shades of a situation) and take the form of automatic activities of different types (e.g. reading the words on a billboard, understanding simple sentences, noticing that an object is further away than another, driving a car etc.). Cognitive heuristics can be described as fast, automatic and implicit paths of reasoning that reduces the load on working memory. They characterize precisely the steps of collection and processing of information that are involved in certain decision-making processes and therefore it is possible to instantiate them in computational terms [22]. This approach is part of the research on dual systems, that suggests a path to consolidate process of type 2 cognitive processes in automatic processes typical of the type 1 system [15].

4 Conclusion

In this paper, we have proposed some preliminary insights about the possible role of cognitive architectures in the context of Serious Games. To instantiate these insights, new tools and frameworks for the aforementioned gaming platforms need to be created in order to improve game design according to more realistic modeling of human cognition. This is true both about the creation of intelligent NPCs as well as for the modeling of the player and the subsequent real-time adaptation of the game itself. As a mid-term goal, we aim at verifying to what extent cognitive architectures can be integrated into game technologies as they are, or instead they need to be specifically adapted/extended for the implementation of NPC in games. The research could highlight the need to use technologies such as deep learning and probabilistic models to reproduce the behavior of intelligent agents realized through cognitive architectures. As an additional goal of this investigation, we aim at providing useful guidelines about how to make cognitive architectures a ready-to-use tool (1) for the design and implementation of games especially in relation to the creation of so-called non-player characters and (2) for player modelling, as a fundamental step in the generation of adaptive content that can keep the player in a state of flow [11].

References

1. In: IEEE Conference on Computational Intelligence and Games, CIG 2017, New York, NY, USA, 22–25 August 2017. IEEE (2017). http://ieeexplore.ieee.org/xpl/mostRecentIssue.jsp?punumber=8067294
2. In: IEEE Conference on Computational Intelligence and Games, CIG 2018, Maastricht, The Netherlands, 14–17 August 2018. IEEE (2018). http://ieeexplore.ieee.org/xpl/mostRecentIssue.jsp?punumber=8473398

3. Alonso-Fernández, C., Cano, A.R., Calvo-Morata, A., Freire, M., Martínez-Ortiz, I., Fernández-Manjón, B.: Lessons learned applying learning analytics to assess serious games. Comput. Hum. Behav. **99**, 301–309 (2019). https://doi.org/10.1016/j.chb.2019.05.036. http://www.sciencedirect.com/science/article/pii/S0747563219302171
4. Anderson, J.R., Bothell, D., Byrne, M.D., Douglass, S., Lebiere, C., Qin, Y.: An integrated theory of the mind. Psychol. Rev. **111**(4), 1036 (2004)
5. Anderson, J.R., Corbett, A.T., Koedinger, K.R., Pelletier, R.: Cognitive tutors: lessons learned. J. Learn. Sci. **4**(2), 167–207 (1995). https://doi.org/10.1207/s15327809jls0402_2
6. Anderson, J.R., Gluck, K.: What role do cognitive architectures play in intelligent tutoring systems. Cognition & Instruction: Twenty-five Years of Progress, 227–262 (2001)
7. Augello, A., Gentile, M., Dignum, F.: Social agents for learning in virtual environments. In: Bottino, R., Jeuring, J., Veltkamp, R.C. (eds.) GALA 2016. LNCS, vol. 10056, pp. 133–143. Springer, Cham (2016). https://doi.org/10.1007/978-3-319-50182-6_12
8. Cerny, V., Dechterenko, F.: Rogue-like games as a playground for artificial intelligence – evolutionary approach. In: Chorianopoulos, K., Divitini, M., Hauge, J.B., Jaccheri, L., Malaka, R. (eds.) ICEC 2015. LNCS, vol. 9353, pp. 261–271. Springer, Cham (2015). https://doi.org/10.1007/978-3-319-24589-8_20
9. Cheng, M.T., Chen, J.H., Chu, S.J., Chen, S.Y.: The use of serious games in science education: a review of selected empirical research from 2002 to 2013. J. Comput. Educ. **2**(3), 353–375 (2015). https://doi.org/10.1007/s40692-015-0039-9
10. Conde Ramírez, J.C., Sánchez López, A., Sánchez Flores, A.: An architecture for cognitive modeling to support real-time adaptation and motivational responses in video games. In: Castro, F., Gelbukh, A., González, M. (eds.) MICAI 2013. LNCS (LNAI), vol. 8265, pp. 144–156. Springer, Heidelberg (2013). https://doi.org/10.1007/978-3-642-45114-0_12
11. Csikszentmihalyi, M.: Toward a psychology of optimal experience. Flow and the Foundations of Positive Psychology, pp. 209–226. Springer, Dordrecht (2014). https://doi.org/10.1007/978-94-017-9088-8_14
12. In: Dignum, F. (ed.) Agents for Games and Simulations II - Trends in Techniques, Concepts and Design [AGS 2010, The Second International Workshop on Agents for Games and Simulations, Toronto, Canada, 10 May 2010, Lecture Notes in Computer Science, vol. 6525. Springer (2011). https://doi.org/10.1007/978-3-642-18181-8
13. Dignum, F., Bradshaw, J., Silverman, B., van Doesburg, W. (eds.): AGS 2009. LNCS (LNAI), vol. 5920. Springer, Heidelberg (2009). https://doi.org/10.1007/978-3-642-11198-3
14. Dörner, R., Göbel, S., Effelsberg, W., Wiemeyer, J. (eds.): Serious Games Foundations, Concepts and Practice. Springer, Cham (2016). https://doi.org/10.1007/978-3-319-40612-1
15. Evans, J.S.B., Stanovich, K.E.: Dual-process theories of higher cognition: advancing the debate. Perspect. Psychol. Sci. **8**(3), 223–241 (2013)
16. Frutos-Pascual, M., Zapirain, B.G.: Review of the use of AI techniques in serious games: decision making and machine learning. IEEE Trans. Comput. Intell. AI Games **9**(2), 133–152 (2017). https://doi.org/10.1109/TCIAIG.2015.2512592
17. Gazzard, A.: The platform and the player: exploring the (hi) stories of elite. Game Stud. **13**(2) (2013)

18. Gemrot, J., et al.: Pogamut 3 can assist developers in building AI (not only) for their videogame agents. In: Dignum, F., Bradshaw, J., Silverman, B., van Doesburg, W. (eds.) AGS 2009. LNCS (LNAI), vol. 5920, pp. 1–15. Springer, Heidelberg (2009). https://doi.org/10.1007/978-3-642-11198-3_1
19. Gentile, M., Allegra, M., Söbke, H. (eds.): GALA 2018. LNCS, vol. 11385. Springer, Cham (2019). https://doi.org/10.1007/978-3-030-11548-7
20. Gentile, M., et al.: The effect of disposition to critical thinking on playing serious games. In: Gentile, M., Allegra, M., Söbke, H. (eds.) GALA 2018. LNCS, vol. 11385, pp. 3–15. Springer, Cham (2019). https://doi.org/10.1007/978-3-030-11548-7_1
21. Ghosh, S., Verbrugge, R.: Studying strategies and types of players: experiments, logics and cognitive models. Synthese **195**(10), 4265–4307 (2018). https://doi.org/10.1007/s11229-017-1338-7
22. Gigerenzer, G., Todd, P., Group, A.: Simple Heuristics that Make Us Smart. Evolution and Cognition. Oxford University Press, Oxford (2000). https://books.google.it/books?id=4ObhBwAAQBAJ
23. Greitzer, F.L., Kuchar, O.A., Huston, K.: Cognitive science implications for enhancing training effectiveness in a serious gaming context. J. Educ. Resour. Comput. **7**(3), 2 (2007). https://doi.org/10.1145/1281320.1281322
24. Kahneman, D.: Thinking, Fast and Slow. Penguin Books Limited, Westminster (2011). https://books.google.it/books?id=oV1tXT3HigoC
25. Kotseruba, I., Tsotsos, J.K.: 40 years of cognitive architectures: core cognitive abilities and practical applications. Artif. Intell. Rev. (2018). https://doi.org/10.1007/s10462-018-9646-y
26. Laird, J.E.: Using a computer game to develop advanced AI. Computer **34**(7), 70–75 (2001). https://doi.org/10.1109/2.933506
27. Laird, J.: The Soar Cognitive Architecture. MIT Press, Cambridge (2012)
28. Laird, J.E.: Extending the soar cognitive architecture. In: Artificial General Intelligence 2008, Proceedings of the First AGI Conference, AGI 2008, University of Memphis, Memphis, TN, USA, 1–3 March 2008, pp. 224–235 (2008) http://www.booksonline.iospress.nl/Content/View.aspx?piid=8310
29. Laird, J.E., Newell, A., Rosenbloom, P.S.: SOAR: an architecture for general intelligence. Artif. Intell. **33**(1), 1–64 (1987). https://doi.org/10.1016/0004-3702(87)90050-6
30. van Lent, M., et al.: Intelligent agents in computer games. In: Proceedings of the Sixteenth National Conference on Artificial Intelligence and Eleventh Conference on Innovative Applications of Artificial Intelligence, Orlando, Florida, USA, 18–22 July 1999, pp. 929–930 (1999). http://www.aaai.org/Library/AAAI/1999/aaai99-143.php
31. Lieto, A., Lebiere, C., Oltramari, A.: The knowledge level in cognitive architectures: current limitations and possible developments. Cogn. Syst. Res. **48**, 39–55 (2018)
32. Lieto, A., Bhatt, M., Oltramari, A., Vernon, D.: The role of cognitive architectures in general artificial intelligence. Cogn. Syst. Res. **48**, 1–3 (2018). https://doi.org/10.1016/j.cogsys.2017.08.003. http://www.sciencedirect.com/science/article/pii/S138904171730222X. cognitive Architectures for Artificial Minds
33. Liu, M., Kang, J., Liu, S., Zou, W., Hodson, J.: Learning analytics as an assessment tool in serious games: a review of literature. In: Ma, M., Oikonomou, A. (eds.) Serious Games and Edutainment Applications, vol. 2, pp. 537–563. Springer, Cham (2017). https://doi.org/10.1007/978-3-319-51645-5_24

34. Lopes, R., Bidarra, R.: Adaptivity challenges in games and simulations: a survey. IEEE Trans. Comput. Intell. AI Games **3**(2), 85–99 (2011). https://doi.org/10.1109/TCIAIG.2011.2152841
35. Lucas, S.M., Mateas, M., Preuss, M., Spronck, P., Togelius, J.: Artificial and computational intelligence in games (dagstuhl seminar 12191). In: Dagstuhl Reports, vol. 2, no. 5, pp. 43–70 (2012). https://doi.org/10.4230/DagRep.2.5.43
36. Magerko, B., Laird, J.E., Assanie, M., Kerfoot, A., Stokes, D.: AI characters and directors for interactive computer games. In: Proceedings of the Nineteenth National Conference on Artificial Intelligence, Sixteenth Conference on Innovative Applications of Artificial Intelligence, San Jose, California, USA, 25–29 July 2004, pp. 877–883 (2004)
37. Magerko, B., Rowe, J.P. (eds.): Proceedings of the Thirteenth AAAI Conference on Artificial Intelligence and Interactive Digital Entertainment (AIIDE-17), Snowbird, Little Cottonwood Canyon, Utah, USA, 5–9 October 2017. AAAI Press (2017). http://www.aaai.org/Library/AIIDE/aiide17contents.php
38. Mehm, F., Radke, S., Göbel, S.: 80days: adaptive digital storytelling for digital educational games. In: Proceedings of the 2nd International Workshop on Story-Telling and Educational Games, in conjunction with the 8th International Conference on Web-based Learning, STEG@ICWL 2009, RWTH Aachen University, Aachen, Germany, 21 August 2009 (2009). http://ceur-ws.org/Vol-498/steg09_submission_9.pdf
39. van Oijen, J.: Cognitive agents in virtual worlds : a middleware design approach. Ph.D. thesis, Utrecht University, Netherlands (2014). http://dspace.library.uu.nl:8080/handle/1874/300548
40. Oltramari, A., Lebiere, C.: Pursuing artificial general intelligence by leveraging the knowledge capabilities of ACT-R. In: Bach, J., Goertzel, B., Iklé, M. (eds.) AGI 2012. LNCS (LNAI), vol. 7716, pp. 199–208. Springer, Heidelberg (2012). https://doi.org/10.1007/978-3-642-35506-6_21
41. Peirce, N., Conlan, O., Wade, V.: Adaptive educational games: providing non-invasive personalised learning experiences. In: The 2nd IEEE International Conference on Digital Game and Intelligent Toy Enhanced Learning, DIGITEL 2008, Banff, Canada,, 17–19 November 2008, pp. 28–35 (2008). https://doi.org/10.1109/DIGITEL.2008.30
42. Ritter, S., Anderson, J.R., Koedinger, K.R., Corbett, A.: Cognitive tutor: applied research in mathematics education. Psychon. Bull. Rev. **14**(2), 249–255 (2007)
43. Rowe, J.P., Smith, G. (eds.): Proceedings of the Fourteenth AAAI Conference on Artificial Intelligence and Interactive Digital Entertainment, AIIDE 2018, Edmonton, Alberta, Canada, 13–17 November 2018. AAAI Press (2018). http://www.aaai.org/Library/AIIDE/aiide18contents.php
44. Schaeffer, J., van den Herik, H.: Games, computers, and artificial intelligence. Artificial Intelligence **134**(1), 1–7 (2002). https://doi.org/10.1016/S0004-3702(01)00165-5. http://www.sciencedirect.com/sciGhoshence/article/pii/S0004370201001655
45. Streicher, A., Smeddinck, J.D.: Personalized and adaptive serious games. In: Entertainment Computing and Serious Games - International GI-Dagstuhl Seminar 15283, Dagstuhl Castle, Germany, 5–10 July 2015, Revised Selected Papers, pp. 332–377 (2015). https://doi.org/10.1007/978-3-319-46152-6_14
46. Vermillion, S.D., Malak, R.J., Smallman, R., Becker, B., Sferra, M., Fields, S.: An investigation on using serious gaming to study human decision-making in engineering contexts. Des. Sci. **3**, e15 (2017). https://doi.org/10.1017/dsj.2017.14

47. Vernon, D.: Artificial Cognitive Systems: A primer. MIT Press, Cambridge (2014)
48. Yannakakis, G.N., Togelius, J.: A panorama of artificial and computational intelligence in games. IEEE Trans. Comput. Intell. AI Games **7**(4), 317–335 (2015). https://doi.org/10.1109/TCIAIG.2014.2339221
49. Yannakakis, G.N., Togelius, J.: Artificial Intelligence and Games, 1st edn. Springer, Heidelberg (2018). https://doi.org/10.1007/978-3-319-63519-4

Gamification

Towards a Reality-Enhanced Serious Game to Promote Eco-Driving in the Wild

Rana Massoud[1,2(✉)], Francesco Bellotti[1(✉)], Stefan Poslad[2(✉)], Riccardo Berta[1(✉)], and Alessandro De Gloria[1(✉)]

[1] Elios Lab, University of Genoa, Genoa, Italy
{rana.massoud, franz, berta}@elios.unige.it, alessandro.degloria@unige.it

[2] IoT2US Lab, Queen Mary University of London, London, UK
{r.massoud, stefan.poslad}@qmul.ac.uk

Abstract. Reality-enhanced serious games (RESGs) incorporate data from the real world to enact training in the wild. This – with the proper cautions due to safety - can be done also for daily activities, such as driving. We have developed two modules that may be integrated as field user performance evaluators in third-party RESGs, aimed at improving driver's fuel efficiency. They exploit vehicular signals (throttle position, engine revolutions per minute and car speed), which are easily accessible through the common On-Board Diagnostics-II (OBD-II) interface. The first module detects inefficient and risky driving manoeuvres while driving, in order to suggest improvement actions based upon fuzzy rules, derived from analyzing naturalistic driving data. The second module provides an eco-driving categorization for a drive via two indicators, fuel efficiency and throttle position values. The estimation of fuel efficiency for the whole trip relies on the mentioned signals, plus the OBD-II calculated engine load. Data from 'enviroCar' project's, a naturalistic driving archive, was used in a simulation. The results are promising in terms of accuracy and encourage further steps towards more effective modules to support a better driving performance, for RESGs.

Keywords: Eco-driving · Gamification · Serious game (SG) · Reality-enhanced serious game (RESG) · Driving pattern · Fuel consumption (FC) · Fuel efficiency

1 Introduction

In addition to smarter vehicles and roads, improving driver behavior still has a significant potential to increase road safety, fuel efficiency and reduce emissions [1, 2]. It has been estimated that vehicle drivers can save up to 25% of fuel by adopting efficient driving patterns [3], with variations depending on the type of a vehicle [4].

Studies have demonstrated that eco-driving (economic or ecologic driving) advice supports fuel-saving [5]. This can decrease fuel consumption (FC) from 5 to 25% [3]. Thus, there is a need to continuously motivate the drivers towards eco-driving. However, advice might also be misinterpreted, which may lead to a worse performance [4]. Hence there is a need to provide drivers with proper and understandable advice.

A. Liapis et al. (Eds.): GALA 2019, LNCS 11899, pp. 245–255, 2019.
https://doi.org/10.1007/978-3-030-34350-7_24

Encouraging eco-driving could be promoted using serious games (SGs) and gamification, which applies game-style mechanics and experience designs in non-game contexts and activities [7–9]. These techniques have been trialled in the automotive and transportation sector because of their motivating and inspiring potential [10, 11]. Given the frequently critical operation context, user experience must be carefully designed [12]. Furthermore, users' privacy should be taken into account [13, 14].

A SG can improve the user experience by combining training and entertainment. In the emerging genre of reality-enhanced serious games (RESGs), in-game progress is due not only to the digital gaming ability of the player, but also it depends on sensing a user's performance in the actual target field [1, 11, 15]. This is an evolution of pervasive gaming [16], where the game's fictive world blends with the physical world connecting a digital game environment with reality, and allows opening and exploiting a direct, possibly real-time (RT), link between a game and a training objective. Therefore, field users' performance becomes a key factor [11] and should be easily understandable to supply effective coaching feedback to players.

This paper contributes to the field by proposing two driving profiling algorithms (for RT feedback and for trip-level categorization), usable as pluggable modules in RESGs towards reducing FC. Given the effectiveness of monitoring a driver's behavior [17], the outcome of the former module can be used to provide direct feedback via voice prompts and/or other means suited to the driving environment. Both algorithms analyse the changes of throttle position (TPS), revolutions per minute (RPM) and car speed. Those vehicular signals are easily understandable to any driver. They are accessible through the On-Board Diagnostics-II (OBD-II) interface [18]. We also considered the OBD-II calculated engine load in the FC estimation for the second algorithm.

Significant changes in TPS, RPM and speed are detected as FC-relevant events, e.g., signaling overtaking. We developed our algorithms exploiting open data extracted from the enviroCar project that collects naturalistic drive trips [19].

Following the introduction in the first section, Sect. 2 reviews the literature; Sect. 3 presents the methodology and data; Sect. 4 describes the two proposed modules for (i) RT driving feedback and (ii) trip-level eco-drive categorization; Sect. 5 presents the analysis, assessment and a simulated case study; Conclusions and future work are given in Sect. 6.

2 Related Work

Several studies have shown the benefits of providing eco-driving advice in reducing FC and emissions using different approaches. [20] proposed a control strategy to drive efficiently using fuzzy logic (FL) by determining the adequate speed and gear. [21] presented a driver evaluation system for assessing driver's skills, based upon the achieved fuel efficiency and acceleration using in-mobile sensors and car's OBD-II system. [22] developed a smartphone fuzzy application to reduce energy consumption via providing hints to drivers using statistical analysis of speed, acceleration and FC.

Driving- and travel-related SGs can have a range of objectives such as encouraging the use of different transport mode and route choices [23]. Studies have also used gamification's motivation towards more fuel-efficient driving (e.g., [24]) and safer driver behavior (e.g., [25]). Some of those motivations were achieved by combining gamification with social networks. [26] developed an incentive system for comparing individual driver's FC average with the average FC of all drivers in a group that is formed with similar vehicles, routes, and time of day. [27] presented a social awareness system to promote eco-driving and safe-driving by implementing some social experiments on a website through communication technology that gathers information about driving patterns using GPS and motions sensors. [4] implemented a driving game to encourage drivers to save fuel, comparing the vehicle telemetry with other users with similar characteristics. Drivers can share their scores with others, e.g., via social networks. Their experiments (on three routes by 36 drivers) showed that gamification tools and eco-driving assistants, help drivers to not lose interest in fuel saving.

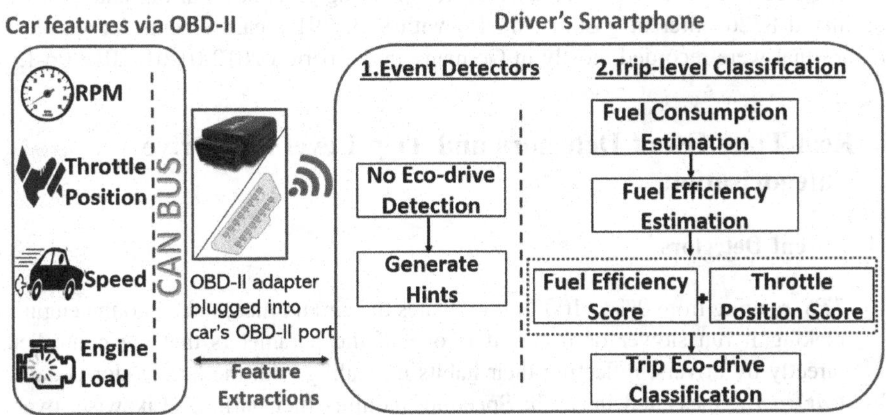

Fig. 1. Methodology – in-car features' extraction via OBD-II system used as inputs for the two modules (running in drivers' smartphones): (i) RT driving feedback when inefficient manoeuvres are detected and (ii) eco-drive classification after a drive

3 Experimental Environment

3.1 Methodology

Figure 1 depicts the followed methodology. The inputs are periodically captured from the vehicle OBD-II interface, through an OBD-II adapter and delivered to a driver's smartphone via a Bluetooth connection. A careless (aggressive) driving style results in more FC than a normal one. Our system thus detects in RT aggressive/inefficient driving manoeuvres by analyzing the three signals (TPS, car speed and RPM) and triggers warnings on what actions the driver could do to better control the fuel economy. Beside RT event's detection, we also estimate instant FC for fuel efficiency's calculation after a trip, which might be used as a part of self/peer competitions (e.g., [10]). FC is not directly accessible through the OBD-II interface, as the 'Engine fuel

Rate' is not supported by all cars (not mandatory in the OBD-II standard protocol) [19]. Thus, it has to be estimated from the available OBD-II signals and information.

3.2 Experimental Data

We analysed the requested OBD-II enviroCar data – a community-based open data collection platform for gathering pseudonymized naturalistic driving car sensor data (cars are just identified by ID numbers for the privacy of drivers) [19]. Data was sampled at regular time intervals (every 5 s, for most of the tracks we used), together with GPS information for spatial-temporal analysis. Derived parameters, such as FC and Carbon dioxide (CO_2) emissions, are computed post-hoc and added to the server.

To build our dataset, we developed a software system that requests the data through a JSON (JavaScript Object Notation) interface, using the enviroCar REST APIs. Data is then stored in a local relational database for querying purposes. For our analysis, we considered 8726 different gasoline tracks, with 983, 291 measurements for gasoline engines that were recorded mostly in Germany in the period 2012-01-01–2016-06-15.

4 Real-Time Event Detectors and Trip-Level Eco-Drive Categorisation

4.1 Event Detectors

(a) *TPS*, ranging from 0% to 100%: It regulates the air and fuel intake into the engine, making it run slower or faster. It is one of the parameters that are controlled directly by drivers, reflecting their habits in dealing with the accelerator pedal.

(b) *Car speed,* measured in km/h: Speeding requires fuel burning. Likewise, overspeed is a crucial metric to characterize driver safety compliance. Overspeeding events are triggered if the car's speed is greater than the legal speed limit, which is obtained through a web service access, based on OpenStreetMap (OSM) [28]. Table 1 presents the driving classification with this indicator.

(c) *RPM* expressed as the number of revolutions per minute: The higher the RPM, the more the fuel is consumed [1, 29]. Optimal RPM value differs between cars (e.g., engine characteristic) and depends on road type (e.g., uphill or downhill).

(d) *Engine Load (calculated),* ranging from 0% to 100%: It measures how much air and fuel are sucking into the engine. The more the engine is loaded (close to 100%), the more the fuel is burned. We categorised this feature into three classes low-loaded 'LL', typical 'T' and Loaded 'L', when its ranges in 0–39, 40–59 and 60–100 respectively.

In [1], we modelled FC resorting to FL, exploiting TPS, speed and RPM signals. Table 2 presents the driving feedback, extracted from our deduced fuzzy rules for the case FC is high 'H' or very high 'VH' [1].

Table 1. Driving profiling with overspeeding (CS: current speed, MS: OSM maximum speed).

Speed (km/h)	Class	Recommendation
CS < MS–5%	M	–
MS–5% $\leq$ CS $\leq$ MS + 5%	M	Be careful, reaching the legal speed limit
CS > MS	A	Overspeeding, slow down for safety and fuel saving

Table 2. Extracted fuzzy rules and proposed feedback in case FC is High or Very High (L: Low, M: Medium; H: High, VH: Very High).

	FL rules
1	if RPM is L & TPS is H & Speed is H then FC is VH
2	if RPM is L & TPS is H & Speed is VH then FC is H
3	if RPM is H & TPS is M & Speed is M then FC is H
4	if RPM is H & TPS is M & Speed is (H or VH) then FC is H
5	if RPM is H & TPS is H then FC is H
6	if RPM is VH & TPS is M then FC is H
7	if RPM is VH & TPS is H then FC is VH
Corresponding driving feedback	
F1	Whether upshift the gear or slow down
F2	Whether upshift the gear or slow down
F3	Downshift the gear
F4	High RPM caused by high speeds, downshift the gear to drive at a lower speed
F5	High RPM caused by high speeds, downshift the gear to drive at a lower speed
F6	Downshift the gear
F7	High RPM caused by high speeds, downshift the gear to drive at a lower speed

4.2 Trip-Level Eco-Driving Categorization

We implemented an eco-driving categorisation for a trip as a trade-off between the two indicators, fuel efficiency (75%) and TPS (25%). TPS is introduced to balance the impact of driving patterns and other factors on fuel economy (e.g., weather conditions) [2]. This could be a powerful indicator of fuel efficiency and driving style simultaneously. The trip is classified as (1) Saver 'S' for a score is in 60–100; (2) Typical 'T' if the score is in 40–59; (3) Careless 'C' for a score is in 0–39.

(a) *Quantitative FC estimation:* In [2], we proposed a FC predictor for gaming via three vehicular signals TPS, RPM and car speed, using Random Forests (RF). FC is impacted by other factors in addition to driving styles [29]. Consequently, we involved the calculated 'engine load' sensed from OBD-II, as a further FC predictor. In the analysed data, we consider the computed FC (l/h) by enviroCar following the formula given in [30], focusing on gasoline engines, as their FC estimation provides the best accuracy [19]. For implementing the RF model, we used the 'RandomForestRegressor' of the 'Sklearn.ensemble' python library [31], dividing our dataset in 80% learning and 20% testing. We have adjusted its two most important settings, (1) the number of trees in the forest 'n_estimators' and (2) the number of features considered for splitting at each leaf node 'max_features'. In addition to 'max_depth', which is the max number of levels in each decision tree.

(b) *Eco-driving categorization:* Fuel efficiency relates distance travelled by a vehicle and the amount of fuel consumed. For estimating the fuel efficiency score, we followed the proposed approach in [21] (Fig. 2). It compares the fuel efficiency achieved by a driver with the current maximum recorded fuel efficiency value by any previous driver, who is driving a similar car model. The TPS score is an average of the instantaneous values obtained as 100-TPS. The higher the TPS score, the better the driver's estimated performance.

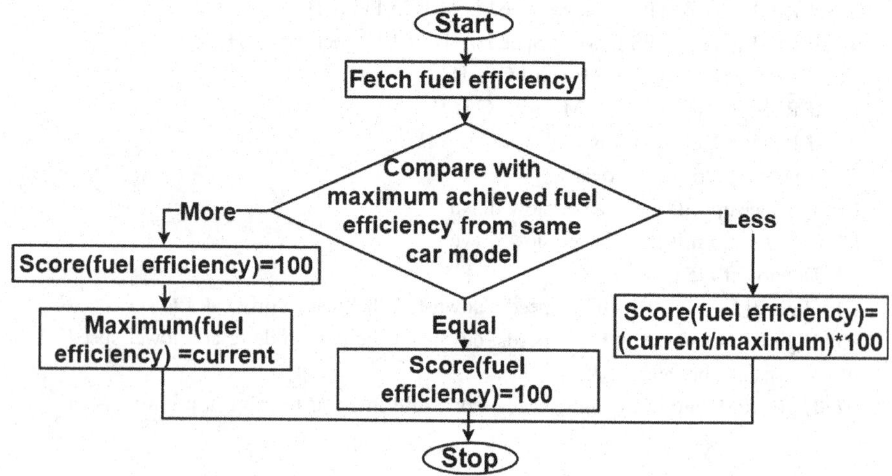

Fig. 2. Fuel efficiency score algorithm [21].

5 Results Case Study and Discussion

For our analysis, we selected from the enviroCar database, a 71 km and 50 min track, with 575 measurements, recorded in Germany in 2016, with a Volkswagen Polo 9 N 2009, gasoline engine. Figure 3 shows the analysis done for the considered indicators. The trips were mostly driven on a highway. The last picture at the bottom of Fig. 3, visualizes the time evolution of FC predicted by the RF model versus the actual enviroCar estimated one for the studied track. We considered 800 trees, 100 levels and square root of the number of features to split at each leaf node, as found in [2]. Involving engine load, increases the performance of the model, giving a lower Mean-squared-error (0.82 vs 1.5) and a slightly higher squared correlation coefficient (0.94 vs 0.896) than without it. Figure 4 shows the fit of the RF model.

Speeding requires a high RPM, leading to a drop in fuel efficiency. On the motorway (the speed is higher than 60 km/h), the values of RPM are higher compared to urban roads at the start and the end of the trip, where the OSM speed limit is about 70 and 30 km/h respectively. In those cases, the values of engine load are higher, since the engine has to work harder for moving the car at high speeds, which implies more FC. Further, the FC fluctuates more than RPM on motorways. This is caused by engine load variations which is clear from the engine load timeline. This might be due to car configuration changes (e.g., caused by the use of heated seats and demister blowers in cold weather as the trip was recorded at the beginning of February) or changes in the use of car accessories such as playing the entertainment system more loudly. This is the reason for involving the engine load in the FC estimation.

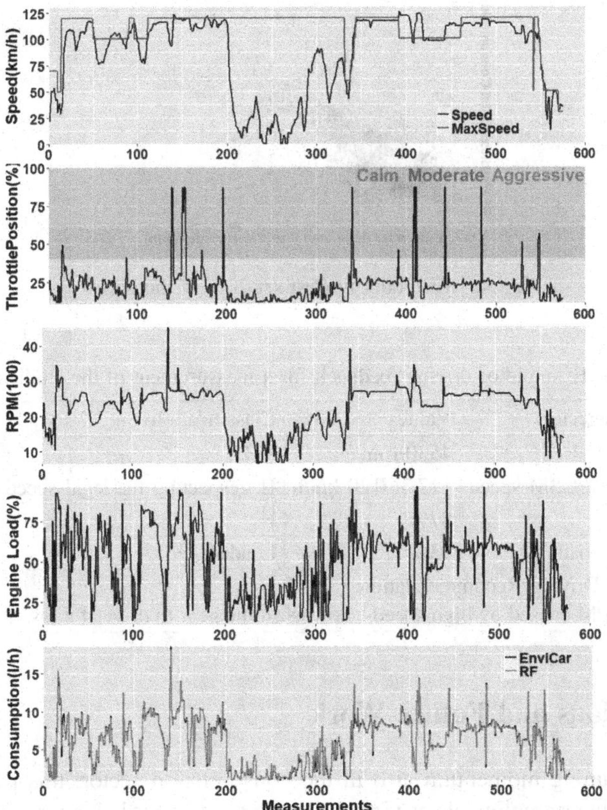

Fig. 3. Car data behavior along with the trace: speed, TPS, RPM, engine load and FC (RF prediction vs enviroCar estimation).

Higher values of TPS are translated into higher FC values, regardless of other factors. Also, when a driver releases the accelerator pedal, the FC decreases. This validates involving TPS in the eco-driving profiling, since it affects strongly the fuel economy and it is directly controllable by a driver. Table 3 shows an example of an instant driving recommendation.

The achieved fuel efficiency for the studied trip is 0.021 km/l/h, while the maximum efficiency achieved by 111 tracks for the same car type, in the same region is 0.037 km/l/h. Hence, the score of fuel efficiency is 56.25 over 100 (normal trip). The score for the TPS is 77 over 100 (calm, saver trip). The eco-driving score for the trip is 61.44 over 100, which again indicates a saver behavior.

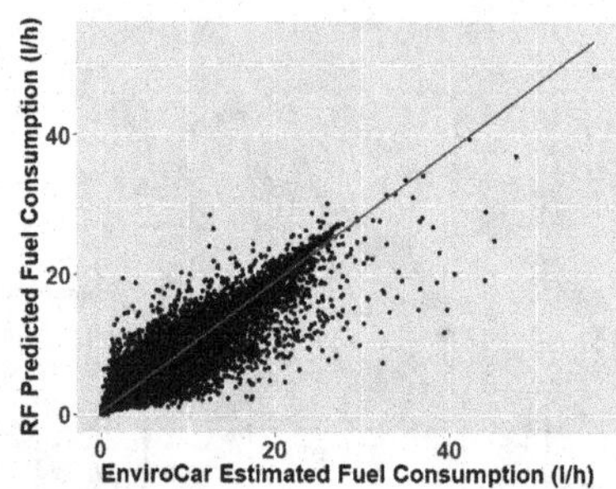

Fig. 4. RF model fit (test set 20% of the data).

Table 3. Example of driving feedback for a measurement of the studied track.

Event detectors	Values	Classifications
RPM	4530 rpm	VH
Car speed/OSM speed	117.36/120 km/h	H, respecting the legal speed limit
TPS	87%	H
Engine Load	93%	Loaded
****** Driving Recommendation ******		
High RPM caused by high speeds, downshift the gear to drive at a lower speed		

6 Conclusions and Future Work

As SGs are gaining momentum also in the transportation sector, this paper has proposed two modules employable as virtual sensors for driver's behavior assessment. The first algorithm detects no eco-driving events and provides instant related recommendations for keeping the driver aware of fuel economy. Source signals are accessed from the OBD-II standard interface for estimating a driver's style and fuel economy. These are numerical values and verbal messages, that can be easily encapsulated into a variety of game mechanics inside a RESG (e.g., as points, energy, bonuses/maluses) [32].

The second algorithm processes data sampled from a whole trip to classify it with respect to three classes, 'Saver', 'Typical' and 'Careless'. The algorithm exploits two indicators: (i) the achieved fuel efficiency (the most important metric in eco-driving) and (ii) the throttle position, which is a good indicator for the driving style, also considering the influences on FC by other factors (e.g., environmental). As above, the provided quantitative score for each drive can be exploited through proper game mechanics. Those games' motivation elements are expected to encourage continuous improvement towards more fuel-efficient and safer driver behavior.

Our future work will focus on improving validation. Drivers will be evaluated under different driving conditions in order to tune feedback provision to improve fuel economy. We believe that this work opens significant perspectives, as similar algorithms may be designed and integrated into SGs (e.g., as software services [33]) in order to improve the field performance in various types of activities.

Acknowledgements. This research was partially funded as part of a Joint Doctorate Interactive and Cognitive Environments (JD-ICE) between the University of Genova, Elios Lab, in agreement with Queen Mary University of London. We also acknowledge technical support given by the enviroCar open Citizen Science Platform (in from 52 North).

References

1. Massoud, R., Poslad, S., Bellotti, F., Berta, R., Mehran, K., De Gloria, A.: A fuzzy logic module to estimate a driver's fuel consumption for reality-enhanced serious games. Int. J. Serious Games **5**(4), 45–62 (2018)
2. Massoud, R., Bellotti, F., Poslad, S., Berta, R., De Gloria, A.: Exploring fuzzy logic and random forest for car drivers' fuel consumption estimation in IoT-enabled serious games. In: IEEE International Symposium on Autonomous Decentralized Systems (ISADS) (2019)
3. Van Mierlo, J., Maggetto, G., Van de Burgwal, E., Gense, R.: Driving style and traffic measures-influence on vehicle emissions and fuel consumption. Proc. Inst. Mech. Eng. D J. Automob. Eng. **218**, 43–50 (2004)
4. Magana, V.C., Munoz-Organero, M.: GAFU: using a gamification tool to save fuel. IEEE Intell. Transp. Syst. Mag. **7**(2), 58–70 (2015)
5. Zhao, X., Wu, Y., Rong, J., Zhang, Y.: Development of a driving simulator based eco-driving support system. Transp. Res. Part C Emerg. Technol. **58**, 631–641 (2015)
6. Tulusan, J., Soi, L., Paefgen, J., Brogle, M., Staake, T.: Eco-efficient feedback technologies: Which eco-feedback types prefer drivers most? In: 2011 IEEE International Symposium on a World of Wireless, Mobile and Multimedia Networks, pp. 1–8. IEEE (2011)
7. Deterding, S., Sicart, M., Nacke, L., O'Hara, K., Dixon, D.: Gamification. using game-design elements in non-gaming contexts. In: CHI 2011 Extended Abstracts on Human Factors in Computing Systems, 2425–2428. ACM (2011)
8. Bellotti, F., Berta, R., De Gloria, A.: Designing effective serious games: opportunities and challenges for research. Int. J. Emerg. Technol. Learn. (iJET) **5**(2010) (2010)
9. Ritterfeld, U., Cody, M., Vorderer, P.: Serious Games: Mechanisms and Effects. Routledge, Abingdon (2009)
10. Bellotti, F., et al.: TEAM applications for collaborative road mobility. IEEE Trans. Ind. Inf. **15**(2), 1105–1119 (2018)

11. Drakoulis, R., Bellotti, F., Bakas, I., Berta, R., Paranthaman, P.K., et al.: A gamified flexible transportation service for on-demand public transport. IEEE Trans. Intell. Transp. Syst. **19** (3), 921–933 (2018)
12. Diewald, S., Möller, A., Roalter, L., Stockinger, T., Kranz, M.: Gameful design in the automotive domain: review, outlook and challenges. In: Proceedings of the 5th International Conference on Automotive User Interfaces and Interactive Vehicular Applications, 262–265. ACM (2013)
13. Poslad, S., Hamdi, M., Abie, H.: Adaptive security and privacy management for the internet of things (ASPI). In: Proceedings of the ACM conference on Pervasive and Ubiquitous Computing Adjunct Publication, pp. 373–378 (2013)
14. Djordjevic, I., Dimitrakos, T.: Towards dynamic security perimeters for virtual collaborative networks. In: Jensen, C., Poslad, S., Dimitrakos, T. (eds.) iTrust 2004. LNCS, vol. 2995, pp. 191–205. Springer, Heidelberg (2004). https://doi.org/10.1007/978-3-540-24747-0_15
15. Fijnheer, J.D., van Oostendorp, H.: Steps to design a household energy game. In: de De Gloria, A., Veltkamp, R. (eds.) GALA 2015. LNCS, vol. 9599, pp. 12–22. Springer, Cham (2016). https://doi.org/10.1007/978-3-319-40216-1_2
16. Bellotti, F., Berta, R., Ferretti, E., DeGloria, A., Margarone, M.: VeGame: exploring art and history in venice. IEEE Comput. Spec. Issue Handheld Comput. **36**(9), 48–55 (2003)
17. Johnson, D.A., Trivedi, M.M.: Driving style recognition using a smartphone as a sensor platform. In: 14th International IEEE Conference on Intelligent Transportation Systems (ITSC), pp. 1609–1615 (2011)
18. Godavarty, S., Broyles, S., Parten, M.: Interfacing to the on-board diagnostic system. In: 52nd IEEE Vehicular Technology Conference (IEEE-VTS), vol. 4 (2000)
19. Bröring, A., Remke, A., Stasch, C., Autermann, C., Rieke, M., Möllers, J.: Envirocar: a citizen science platform for analyzing and mapping crowd-sourced car sensor data. Trans. GIS **19**(3), 362–376 (2015)
20. Saboohi, Y., Farzaneh, H.: Model for developing an eco-driving strategy of a passenger vehicle based on the least fuel consumption. Appl. Energy **86**(10), 1925–1932 (2009)
21. Khedkar, S., Oswal, A., Setty, M., Ravi, S.: Driver evaluation system using mobile phone and OBD-II system. Int. J. Comput. Sci. Inf. Technol. **6**(3), 2738–2745 (2015)
22. Araújo, R., Igreja, A., De Castro, R., Araujo, R.E.: Driving coach: a smartphone application to evaluate driving efficient patterns. In: Intelligent Vehicles Symposium. IEEE, pp. 1005–1010 (2012)
23. Mei, H., Poslad, S., Du, S.: A game-theory based incentive framework for an intelligent traffic system as part of a smart city initiative. Sensors **17**(12), 2874 (2017)
24. Poslad, S., Ma, A., Wang, Z., Mei, H.: Using a smart city IoT to incentivise and target shifts in mobility behaviour – is it a piece of pie? Sensors **15**(6), 13069–13096 (2015)
25. Law, F.L., Kasirun, Z.M., Wang, Z., Mei, H.: Gamification towards sustainable mobile application. In: Malaysian Conference in Software Engineering, pp. 349–353. IEEE (2011)
26. Liimatainen, H.: Utilization of fuel consumption data in an ecodriving incentive system for heavy-duty vehicle drivers. IEEE Trans. Intell. Transp. Syst. **12**(4), 1087–1095 (2011)
27. Ando, R., Nishihori, Y., Ochi, D.: Development of a system to promote eco-driving and safe-driving. In: Balandin, S., Dunaytsev, R., Koucheryavy, Y. (eds.) NEW2AN/ruSMART -2010. LNCS, vol. 6294, pp. 207–218. Springer, Heidelberg (2010). https://doi.org/10.1007/978-3-642-14891-0_19
28. OpenStreetMap. http://www.openstreetmap.org. Accessed 26 June 2019
29. Massoud, R., Bellotti, F., Poslad, S., Berta, R., De Gloria, A.: Eco-driving profiling and behavioral shifts using IoT Vehicular sensors combined with serious games eco-driving profiling and behavioral shifts using IoT vehicular sensors combined with serious games. In: IEEE Conference On Games (COG) (2019)

30. Faiz, A., Weaver, C.S., Walsh, M.P.: Air pollution from motor vehicles: standards and technologies for controlling emissions. The World Bank (1996)
31. 'RandomForestRegressor' package. http://scikit-learn.org/stable/modules/generated/sklearn.ensemble.RandomForestRegressor.html. Accessed 26 June 2019
32. Carvalho, M.B., et al.: An activity theory-based model for serious games analysis and conceptual design. Comput. Educ. **87**, 166–181 (2015)
33. Carvalho, M.B.: A case study on service-oriented architecture for serious games. Entertain. Comput. **6**, 1–10 (2015)

Gamifire - A Scalable, Platform-Independent Infrastructure for Meaningful Gamification of MOOCs

Roland Klemke[1,2](✉), Alessandra Antonaci[1], and Bibeg Limbu[1]

[1] Welten Institute, Open University of the Netherlands, Heerlen, The Netherlands
roland.klemke@ou.nl

[2] Cologne Game Lab, TH Köln, Köln, Germany

Abstract. Gamification aims at addressing inherent problems of massive open online courses (MOOC): high dropouts, lack of engagement, isolation, lack of individualization. However, each MOOC platform offers different features and technical interfaces. Also, each platform collects different sets of data about user interaction, learning progress, or completion and success rates. This is an obstacle to the theoretically sound application of gamification in a vendor independent way and to the evaluation of the impact of gamification. We define our understanding of meaningful gamification, introduce requirements for platform-independent gamification, present the resulting Gamifire infrastructure, and describe application cases. We also point out planned development activities.

Keywords: Gamifire · Gamification · Architecture · Scalability · MOOC · Platform independence · Infrastructure

1 Introduction and Related Work

MOOCs, announced to improve worldwide education [16], come with downsides like high-drop out rates [4] and low learner engagement [7]. Gamification was introduced to improve situations of motivational gaps: applying game elements to boring activities adds the fun [6]. Relying on mostly extrinsic motivational factors (such as points, badges, and leaderboards), gamification does not yet exploit the potential of motivation and passion for learning [10].

However, *meaningful gamification*, i.e. gamification that is thoughtfully integrated with the learning process, using a composition of game elements [5] supporting the desired effects according to selected theories, can be beneficial to learners [15]. Designing meaningful gamification is complex and implementing it into MOOC platforms is another obstacle: platforms differ in technology, functionality and extensibility [20].

We studied this situation and developed the GaDeP framework for the design of gamification [1,2], which we will briefly describe below. In this article, we highlight the technical side by introducing backgrounds and related works, describing our design and development approach, listing requirements, resulting in a

A. Liapis et al. (Eds.): GALA 2019, LNCS 11899, pp. 256–265, 2019.
https://doi.org/10.1007/978-3-030-34350-7_25

description of the system architecture and implementation. We describe planned fields of application and conclude on insights gathered.

A categorization of gamification requirements is reported in [13]. We derive different requirements, as their approach focuses on business applications rather than open distance education. A corresponding gamification architecture [12] provides basic elements for a gamification platform, likewise focused on business platforms, lacking the openness required for platform-independence. A gamification framework for K-6 education collects elements for educational purposes and derives motivational goals [19], without reporting technical aspects. Another gamification platform focuses on software development processes [11], where specific software development tasks and process elements are gamified. Building on the mentioned approaches, we add a sound methodology, platform independence, scalability, and a focus on online learning.

2 Research Design, and Development Approach

Applying gamification to MOOCs is complex and comprises a number of decisions to be taken from interdisciplinary perspectives, such as: game design, psychology, learning science, technology-enhanced learning, human-computer interaction, and software engineering [17]. Many gamification attempts fail due to the lack of a clear design methodology [18]. Therefore, we investigate the following research questions: (RQ1) Can we develop a platform-independent, scalable platform to support the meaningful gamification of MOOC? (RQ2) Can we resolve the conflict between platform-independence and the required platform integration for meaningful gamification? (RQ3) Can Gamifire support different MOOCs and their educational contexts? To answer RQ1-RQ3 and to base Gamifire on solid grounds, our approach comprises three main perspectives:

1. A *design perspective*, combining game design with problem-based selection of theories into an evaluation-based continuous improvement cycle.
2. A *user-experience and usability perspective*, taking the interplay of learning environment and gamification into account.
3. A *software-engineering perspective*, transforming outcomes of the other perspectives into implementable requirements and architectural specifications.

Gamification design frameworks have been discussed in [18]. In [1,2] we outline the six steps of our gamification design process (GaDeP) in detail, covering the first two perspectives: (1) *application scenario analysis* to understand characteristics of the application context, (2) *problem definition* to analyse specific problems to be addressed by gamification, (3) *theoretical framework* to understand the background of how to address the problem, (4) *game element selection* to find appropriate game elements matching the theoretic framework, (5) *design and implementation* to realise the selected game elements, and (6) *evaluation* to measure the resulting effects and continuously improve the approach. This article takes the software-engineering perspective, covering steps (4–6) of GaDeP.

3 Requirements

The requirements for Gamifire are based on the application field and the gamification framework GaDeP (see Table 1). Our *Field of application* is online learning in MOOCs. This defines (non-functional) attributes of the user environment and technical constraints. The *gamification methodology* defines functional aspects. It requires game elements and user processes to be interwoven. This impacts the selection of game elements and the way the MOOC platform and the gamification platform are integrated. Based on game elements selected in [2] we reflect this from a software engineering standpoint.

Table 1. Non-functional Requirements related to the Field of Application (Nx) and Functional Requirements related to the Gamification Methodology (Fx)

No.	Requirement description
	Non-functional requirements related to the field of application (Nx)
N1	*Scalability.* MOOCs are designed for high numbers of learners. The gamification platform has to serve this amount of learners without significant run-time impact. This comprises scalability in terms of computing power, data storage, and network traffic
N2	*Platform independence.* As different MOOC platforms exist, a gamification engine should cover many of these. At the same time, the integration of gamification into the target platform needs to be seamless in order to deliver a continuous learner experience
N3	*Content integration.* Many game elements only make sense in connection to the content. The gamification engine needs to allow for these connections by tracking learner progress and learner interaction
N4	The *User experience* of learners interacting with the MOOC platform should be enhanced by the gamification engine
N5	*Extensibility.* The platform should be easily extensible to additional use cases. This covers adding new game elements, adapting existing game elements, or adding other functionality
N6	*Stability.* The platform should provide a stable and reliable service with minimal human intervention
N7	*Security.* The platform needs to store user related data in a secure way
N8	*GDPR.* The data storage needs to be GDPR compliant
N9	*Multi-user support.* Online learning may lead to a feeling of isolation, even if numerous learners share the same platform. Thus, the platform needs to support collaborative or competitive multi-user game elements
N10	*Web front-end.* MOOC platforms are commonly accessed via web-browsers. The gamification platform needs to offer web front-ends
N11	*User Group Size.* The gamification platform and the choice of game elements should not restrict the number of MOOC users
N12	*Seamless integration.* The user interface (UI) of the gamification platform needs to integrate with the MOOC platform to appear as part of the MOOC UI without the user having to navigate between the systems

(*continued*)

Table 1. (*continued*)

No.	Requirements description
N13	*Responsive UI.* The design, layout, and interaction mechanisms used should adapt to various end-user devices. The UI elements added to the MOOC should support all platforms the MOOC platform supports
Functional Requirements related to the Gamification Methodology (Fx)	
F1	*Data collection.* GaDeP requires an evaluation step to be performed. To measure effects in different experimental settings requires to collect data about learner interaction in a flexible but structured way
F2	*User management integration.* MOOC users register with the MOOC platform. The gamification platform needs to gather user information to avoid double registrations to provide the personalized service to the user (e.g. displaying individual information in the HUD to the MOOC user)
F3	*Choice of game elements.* The platform shall support a variety of combinable game elements to provide meaningful, gameful interaction. In the context of MOOC, these should according to GaDeP comprise at least the ones listed in F4-F12
F4	*Communication.* The platform needs to support synchronous and asynchronous forms of communication
F5	*Stimulated planning* helps users to plan activities and to follow that plan. It thus requires functionality for planning, plan-based feedback and communication
F6	*Clans* (or Guilds, Teams) organize users into groups, which can receive group-related assignments for collaborative or competitive work. This requires support for the grouping phase and group-based concepts of content visibility and access
F7	*Collaboration and Cooperation.* Group members should be able to work together on some tasks
F8	For *Group competition*, groups need some form of group-privacy to hide working progress from other groups
F9	*Individual and group challenges* are assignments to be solved according to constraints (e.g. time limits, number of attempts, competition/collaboration modes). Challenges shall motivate users and are (usually) not part of the formal learning success calculation but count for users' engagement and may contribute to perceived social presence and sense of community
F10	A *Narrative* presents learning content with a story line, that connects learning episodes and contextualizes learning content with this story. The gamification platform should allow to include narrative elements
F11	In games *Head-up displays (HUDs)* show contextual information to the player. The gamification platform should include HUDs for relevant information in a non-intrusive way, to support the learning process and not interfering with it
F12	*Avatars.* Users should be able to personalize their appearance in the game, by using an avatar representation

4 Gamifire

This section describes the design decisions leading to the architecture and implementation of Gamifire based on the requirements. It also reports on trade-offs and limitations.

To have many of the listed requirements covered on platform-level, Gamifire is implemented on top of the Google App Engine (GAE) cloud platform using a three-tier architecture, with database back-end (cloud data-store), application server, and front-end user-interface (UI) widgets. Choosing GAE enables us to meet the following requirements immediately:

- *Scalability (N1)* and *Stability (N6)* are core principles of GAE.
- *Extensibility (N5)* Gamifire is distributed as an open source solution[1].
- *Security (N7)* and *GDPR compliance (N8)* are inherent aspects of GAE.
- Support for *web front-ends (N10)* is supported within GAE.
- GAE's native session management delivers *multi-user support (N9)*.
- For *Data collection (F1)* Gamifire stores interaction information in the back-end data-store and supports treatment/control groups.

Covering (F1), the back-end stores log information about user interactions, time-stamps, and progress related data. The application server handles user related sessions, tracks user interactions, manages logging operations and generates feedback and UI-related content.

With platform-independence (N2) in mind, Gamifire uses user interface widgets to integrate into the MOOC platform through front-end integration. No back-end integration has to be performed (integrating data models, server interaction, session management or other back-end services). However, each game element/widget can store widget specific data. From the MOOC platform, Gamifire gathers the user, who is currently logged in and synchronizes Gamifire's user data with the MOOC at hand. In combination with the multi-user support and the scalability, this allows to support the same *user group size (N11)* as the MOOC platform itself.

To generate the UI in line with the front-end integration approach, Gamifire comprises a library of game element widgets, which provide the individualized views with respect to the user status. These widgets are embedded into the MOOC platform by adding them to the web-based front-end of the MOOC platform as HTML components. Through JavaScript introspection, they gather user information from the MOOC platform to synchronize user sessions and data between MOOC and Gamifire. Figure 1 shows the Gamifire component architecture and its integration into a MOOC platform. Figure 2 shows selected UI components displaying different game elements and components.

Content integration (N3) is in conflict with platform-independence. In section *Trade-offs and limitations* we discuss this situation. To keep the *user experience (N4)* close to the MOOC environment, we use style-sheets in Gamifire's front-end to adapt look and feel to the MOOC environment. This also supports the creation of responsive *UI components (N13)*. In combination with the front-end integration, this also supports seamless integration into the MOOC platform *(N12)*, where an important aspect of the front-end integration is the recognition of the user logged into the MOOC platform, which supports *user management integration (F2)*.

[1] A public distribution of Gamifire is currently under preparation.

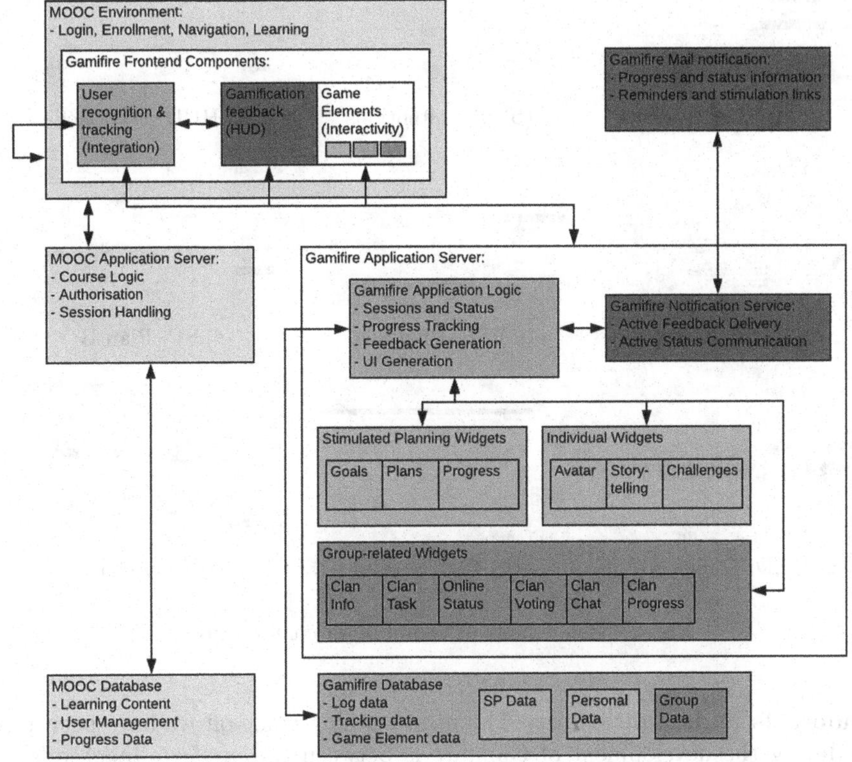

Fig. 1. Architecture of the Gamifire platform

Gamifire supports a number of game elements, as represented by the game element front-end components and the game element widget library: stimulated planning widgets, individual game element widgets, and group-related widgets. With this collection of game elements, requirements *F4-F12* are covered: *stimulated planning* is directly supported with a set of specific widgets and front-end components *(F5)*, the set of group-related widgets and components support *communication channels (F4)*, *clans (F6)*, *collaboration* via clan tasks and clan voting *(F7)*, *competition* via online status and clan progress *(F8)*, *individual and group challenges (F9)* are supported via challenges (individual) as well as clan tasks (group). *Narrative* is supported with specific information components as individual game element *(F10)*. The *HUD (F11)* combines the Gamifire application logic with the gamification feedback front-end. The user avatar component implements the game element *avatars (F12)*. The avatar is used to personalize the feedback component and online status, clan voting, clan chat, clan tasks and clan progress. With this coverage of game elements in Gamifire, also requirement *F3 (choice of game elements)* is covered. However, we do not claim completeness: additional game elements are planned to be added to Gamifire for a broader support of application cases and gamification scenarios.

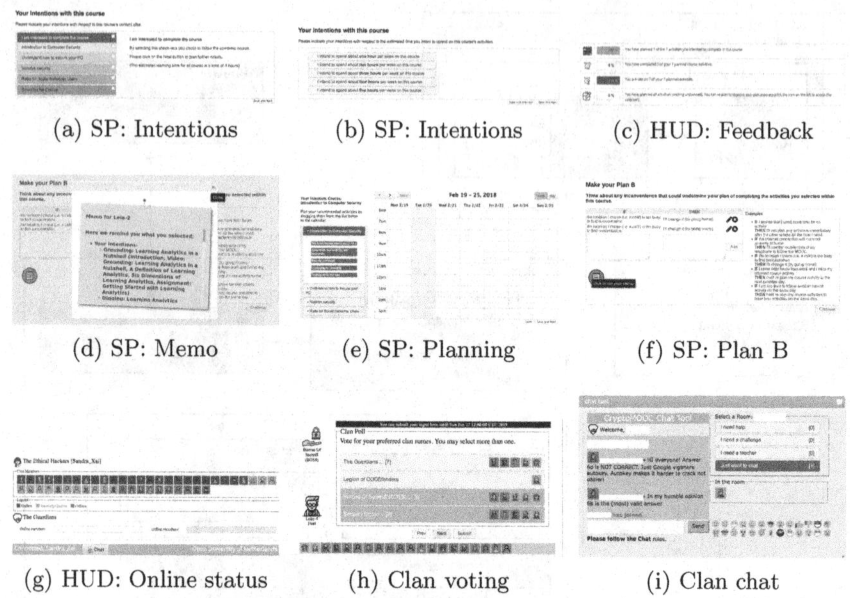

(a) SP: Intentions (b) SP: Intentions (c) HUD: Feedback

(d) SP: Memo (e) SP: Planning (f) SP: Plan B

(g) HUD: Online status (h) Clan voting (i) Clan chat

Fig. 2. Screen-shots of Gamifire UI components.

Trade-Offs and Limitations. The most striking trade-off we have been facing during the development of Gamifire is between the *platform-independence (N1)* and the concept of meaningful gamification *(F3-F12)* combined with the functional-requirement for seamless integration *(N12)*: while the former requires us to rely on shallow integration of Gamifire and the MOOC environment by means of front-end integration, the latter requires some understanding of the learning content and the corresponding learner progress within Gamifire. We addressed this trade-off with the following concept: when preparing a gamified MOOC, Gamifire is configured with a mirrored content structure (only the outline, not the contents itself), assigning content ids to recognizable page URIs. Through the tracking feature of the front-end integration, Gamifire can thus keep track of learner interactions within the MOOC and calculate interaction rates, learning progress, completion rates, etc. on its own data without having to query the MOOC platform's back-end. While this solution allows to keep the technical integration independent, it requires some extra effort to mirror the content structure into Gamifire. Especially, when a MOOC undergoes many changes, this may represent a bottleneck and a source of possible mistakes.

While this article mainly focuses on technical aspects, conflicts may also arise in the combination of game elements: narrative e.g. is in conflict with stimulated planning. A narrative connects learning contents into episodes of a story, stimulated planning allows users to plan individual learning activities, which requires a degree of independence. Gamifire does not automatically detect such conflicts and it is in the responsibility of the design team to make sure that the game elements used are not in conflict with each other.

The shallow integration according to the required platform-independence leads to another conflict in relation to narratives: narratives can be seen as part of the MOOC content but also expected to be part of the gamification design. For now, Gamifire does not resolve this conflict with a technical solution but leaves it to the course and gamification design team to resolve, where to apply which elements of a narrative: at this point learning design and gamification design need to be performed as a team-work.

5 Application Cases and Results

Even though the architecture and implementation of Gamifire meet the requirements set out in Sect. 3, a proof of the applicability of the solution can only be achieved by applying it to a variety of cases. Gamifire has been applied to three different application cases, where different game elements have been selected and implemented due to a different focus of the application case:

(1) In a MOOC on information security, we explored the impact of planning behaviour on goal achievement by implementing the game element "stimulated planning" according to the implementation intention theory [8]. Participants had to state their goals, plan their activities (including a coping plan for inconveniences), received plan related feedback, and were stimulated to re-plan, when the plan was not met. We applied the first version of Gamifire to Moodle first and to Open EdX later. This platform switch confirmed the platform-independence of Gamifire, by restricting the number of modifications necessary mainly to the front-end integration scripts. This version of Gamifire also underwent a usability study [1], which informed the further development of Gamifire.

(2) A MOOC on cryptography aimed at fostering engagement through perceived social presence and the development of a sense of community [9]. We implemented several game elements (clans, avatars, group activities, communication channels, online status) according to concepts described in [14]. Group awareness and team interactions were at the focus of this version, requiring fast updates and exchange of status information, activities, and communication, to allow Gamifire to keep group members informed about other group members' activities and states in close to real-time. This focus required us to balance server communication load, caching mechanisms, and load balancing mechanisms to allow fast communication without increasing server load too much [3].

(3) A MOOC on trusted learning analytics has been chosen for an updated version of the stimulated planning game element, which included an improved user interface, enhanced browser compliance, and updated feedback mechanisms.

To test Gamifire as data collection tool, we applied it to a MOOC on marine pollution without implementing specific game elements and collected student interactivity data for an A-B-Test designed within the features of the MOOC. The data collected here currently being analyzed.

6 Conclusions and Future Work

With the implementation of Gamifire, we were able to show that it is possible to deliver a "scalable, platform-independent, cloud-based Infrastructure for meaningful gamification of MOOC". We were able to meet the requirements collected for such a platform and to apply and test Gamifire in several application cases.

However, as we have seen from our application cases, the implementation and application of Gamifire faces a number of trade-offs, which show, that some conceptual issues have to be addressed in future work: (1) The solution found addressing the trade-off between platform-independence and meaningful gamification as highlighted in Sect. 4 requires to be re-thought, in order to get rid of erroneous extra work. (2) The conflicts found between some of the game elements requires us to offer more guidance to designers of MOOCs and gamification in order to share a more clear understanding of which game elements combine well for which gamification goals. To achieve this, more research on the effects of specific game element configurations needs to be performed.

Gamification remains a process requiring well-defined procedures and concepts. We hope, that Gamifire based on the methodology presented contributes to a better understanding and application of meaningful gamification in online learning.

Acknowledgements. We thank teachers and participants for their support. Studies reported are approved by the university's ethical committee (cETO).

References

1. Antonaci, A., Klemke, R., Dirkx, K., Specht, M.: May the plan be with you! a usability study of the stimulated planning game element embedded in a MOOC platform. Int. J. Serious Games **6**(1), 49–70 (2019)
2. Antonaci, A., Klemke, R., Kreijns, K., Specht, M.: Get gamification of MOOC right! how to embed the individual and social aspects of MOOCs in gamification design. Int. J. Serious Games **5**(3), 61–78 (2018)
3. Antonaci, A., Klemke, R., Lataster, J., Kreijns, K., Specht, M.: Gamification of MOOCs adopting social presence and sense of community to increase user's engagement: an experimental study. In: Scheffel, M., Broisin, J., Pammer-Schindler, V., Ioannou, A., Schneider, J. (eds.) EC-TEL 2019. LNCS, vol. 11722, pp. 172–186. Springer, Cham (2019). https://doi.org/10.1007/978-3-030-29736-7_13
4. Atiaja, L., Proenza, R.: The MOOCs: origin, characterization, principal problems and challenges in higher education. J. e-Learn. Knowl. Soc. **12**(1) (2016)
5. Björk, S., Holopainen, J.: Patterns in Game Design (Game Development Series), vol. 54, 1st edn. Charles River Media, Needham (2004)

6. Deterding, S.: Gamification: designing for motivation. Interactions **19**(4), 14–17 (2012)
7. Dillon, J., et al.: Student emotion, co-occurrence, and dropout in a MOOC context. Educational Data Mining (2016)
8. Gollwitzer, P.M., Sheeran, P.: Implementation intentions and goal achievement: a meta-analysis of effects and processes. Adv. Exp. Soc. Psychol. **38**, 69–119 (2006). https://doi.org/10.1016/S0065-2601(06)38002-1
9. Gunawardena, C.N., Zittle, F.J.: Social presence as a predictor of satisfaction within a computer-mediated conferencing environment. Am. J. Dist. Educ. **11**(3), 8–26 (1997). https://doi.org/10.1080/08923649709526970
10. Hamari, J., Koivisto, J., Sarsa, H.: Does gamification work?-a literature review of empirical studies on gamification. HICSS **14**, 3025–3034 (2014)
11. Herranz, E., Colomo-Palacios, R., de Amescua Seco, A.: Gamiware: a gamification platform for software process improvement. Systems, Software and Services Process Improvement. CCIS, vol. 543, pp. 127–139. Springer, Cham (2015). https://doi.org/10.1007/978-3-319-24647-5_11
12. Herzig, P., Ameling, M., Schill, A.: A Generic Platform for Enterprise Gamification. In: Joint Working Conference on Software Architecture and 6th European Conference on Software Architecture (2012). https://doi.org/10.1109/WICSA-ECSA.212.33
13. Herzig, P., Ameling, M., Wolf, B., Schill, A.: Implementing gamification: requirements and gamification platforms. In: Reiners, T., Wood, L.C. (eds.) Gamification in Education and Business, pp. 431–450. Springer, Cham (2015). https://doi.org/10.1007/978-3-319-10208-5_22
14. Luo, N., Zhang, M., Qi, D.: Effects of different interactions on students' sense of community in e-learning environment. Comput. Educ. **115**, 153–160 (2017). https://doi.org/10.1016/j.compedu.2017.08.006
15. de Marcos, L., Garcia-Lopez, E., Garcia-Cabot, A.: On the effectiveness of game-like and social approaches in learning: comparing educational gaming, gamification & social networking. Comput. Educ. **95**, 99–113 (2016)
16. McAuley, A., Stewart, B., Siemens, G., Cormier, D.: The MOOC model for digital practice (2010)
17. Meschede, C., Knautz, K.: Gamification and interdisciplinarity: challenges in the modern knowledge society. Int. J. Inf. Commun. Technol. Hum. Dev. **9**(3), 1–13 (2017)
18. Mora, A., Riera, D., Gonzalez, C., Arnedo-Moreno, J.: A literature review of gamification design frameworks. In: VS-Games 2015–7th International Conference on Games and Virtual Worlds for Serious Applications. IEEE (2015)
19. Simões, J., Redondo, R., Vilas, A.: A social gamification framework for a K-6 learning platform. Comput. Hum. Behav. **29**(2), 345–353 (2013)
20. Taneja, S., Goel, A.: MOOC providers and their strategies. Int. J. Comput. Sci. Mob. Comput. **3**(5), 222–228 (2014)

A Data-Driven Approach to Analyze User Behavior on a Personalized Gamification Platform

Balázs Barna and Szabina Fodor(✉)

Corvinus University of Budapest, Budapest, Hungary
contact@balazsbarna.hu, szabina.fodor@uni-corvinus.hu

Abstract. This paper presents a study on data retrieved from a gamified teambuilding application (named Battlejungle [1]), which promotes employees' joint sport activities. The aim of this work is to identify and evaluate behavior and usage patterns, and user engagement indicators based on interaction data gained from the application. In order to determine behavioral patterns, users have been tested for system use, for participation at events and competitions, and for having tendency in social interactions. Our results reveal that we were able to distinguish engaged and non-engaged users. The *Non-Engaged* users were characterized as a group who were initially eager to use the application; however, this enthusiasm disappeared quickly. The study classified three typologies of engaged users. The *Achievers* who are motivated by the reward of achieving long-term goals, the *Socializers* who enjoy interacting with others and *Seekers* who enjoy exploring things and discovering new situations.

Keywords: Personalized gamification · Motivational information system · User behavior pattern

1 Introduction

Motivation is one of the most important factors affecting human behavior and performance. Individual and group motivation levels have a great impact on all aspects of achievement. One of the key indicators to measure the level of interest is user engagement [2, 3]. The term 'engagement' has a variety of meanings. In this work we consider user engagement as the willingness to have emotions, affect directed towards the mediated activity in order to achieve a specific goal. Several studies underline the importance of the users' engagement in different fields such as education [4], health-related activities [5–7] and Web applications [8]. While motivation refers to goals and values in a given area, engagement refers to behavioral displays of effort, time, and persistence in attaining desired outcomes [9, 10]. Engagement is also a critical issue in interactive mediated activities, defined as human activities supported by digital interactive technologies such as computer applications, mobile platforms, Internet, or virtual reality systems.

Engagement can be defined qualitatively. From this perspective, it is characterized as a state of involvement with the technology. Yardley et al. [11] make a distinction of

A. Liapis et al. (Eds.): GALA 2019, LNCS 11899, pp. 266–275, 2019.
https://doi.org/10.1007/978-3-030-34350-7_26

engagement at the micro and macro levels. The micro level reflects the moment-to-moment interactions that occur as a user engages with features of the technology, while the macro-level engagement refers to how the user engages with the overall behavior change goal. The aim of our research is to propose an approach to identifying users' macro-engagement and qualifying their engagement behavior from the history of users' actions collected in real time from their interactions with a gamified application. We used data gathered among the users of Battlejungle (https://battlejungle.com/), an exercise encouragement application that combines three motivational technologies as gamification, quantified-self and social networking. Since users are different, therefore a variety of classes of motivational design may have a differential fit for them. Being able to distinguish a given user's typology, motivational design could be better tailored [7, 12].

2 Related Work

Over the last decades, many studies related to behavior theory and user engagement were conducted in social psychology, behavioral economics and marketing [13]. Several works focused on how to use technology to motivate healthier lifestyle [14–16]. However, some studies pointed to the limitations of the one-size-fits-all approach especially when the change is aimed at health behavior [17]. The realization of this fact led to a growing interest in finding ways of tailoring interventions to various users. Kaptein et al. revealed that the users' personality is an important determinant of motivation [18] and Halko and Kientz showed the relationship between the users' personality and the success of different motivational strategies [19]. Approaches to measure user engagement can be divided into three main groups: self-reported engagement, cognitive engagement, and online behavior metrics. In this paper, we explore user engagement from a quantitative perspective, such as number of logins and likes per day, or time spent on using our interactive system: an application to foster joint sporting activities. We use this personalized gamification platform as a case study for developing quantitative typologies of user engagement.

2.1 User Typology

Several personality models have been published during the recent years, such as the Myers-Briggs Type Indicator (MBTI) [20], the Five Factor Model (FFM) [21], the Bartle four gamer types [22] or the BrainHex model of seven gamer types [23]. In this study we used the BrainHex model as it is empirically based so it can be validated. The BrainHex model identifies the following seven types of players:

- *Achievers* are motivated by the reward of achieving long-term goals.
- *Conquerors* are challenge-oriented.
- *Daredevils* are excited by taking risks.
- *Masterminds* enjoy solving puzzles, devising strategies.
- *Seekers* enjoy exploring things and discovering new situations.
- *Socializers* enjoy interacting with others.

- *Survivors* love the experience associated with frightening situations.

The BrainHex model admits that users cannot be categorized into one gamer type exclusively; we can only recognize users' primary gamer type and further types.

3 Method

We used the Battlejungle [1] social platform that gives support with organizing and encouraging (mostly) sport related events among employees within organizations. Several gamification elements help to enhance the motivation and team building such as points, performance- and activity-based badges, leader boards, recognitions and awards. The Battlejungle has a strong social dimension as it promotes sharing game events on social networks and it also promotes social interactions. Quantified-self features include activity tracking of exercise and performance indicators.

3.1 Research Model

We propose an approach of identifying engaged behaviors from the users' interactions. This study sets the following research questions:

Q1: *Can engaged behaviors be distinguished from non-engaged behaviors based on the collected data?*
Q2: *Can we identify the type of players and motivations based on the collected data?*

Users have been characterized by 9 use-based attributes (see in Table 1) collected from the teambuilding application between 1 July 2016 and 31 May 2019.

Table 1. List of use-based attributes

Usage	Period (A1)	Time period between the date of registration and the date of last login in days; number of usage days
	Logins (A2)	Number of logins
Badge & social	level (A3)	The reached level
	badges (A4)	Number of collected badges
	likes (A5)	Number of positive reactions ('like') given to posts
	posts (A6)	Number of written posts
	comments (A7)	Number of written comments
Activities	induvidual_race (A8)	Number of individual race*
	team_race (A9)	Number of team race**

*a competition in which individuals separately (e.g. running race)
**a competition in which two teams play with each other (e.g. football)

We also used feedback answers given through service interface to map the motivations of the users. The questions can be divided into four topics:

- Changes in workplace atmosphere
- Quality and quantity of relations between organization members
- Frequency of doing sports
- Motivation-related opinions.

In this study, we used just the responses of motivation-related questions (see in Table 2). For each question, 5 answers are available, one of which can be selected by the user, and giving the answer is always optional. A feedback is done by answering one question, which is selected from a predetermined question bank depending on what activity has just been done by the user, what side of the system is being used and what kind of similar questions have been answered recently.

Table 2. Motivation-related feedback questions

Abbreviation	Question
Player-level	Do you check yours and/or others' player-level?
Bandages	Do you like the Badges?
Points	Does the Karma[a] motivate you to participate in activities and challenges?
Leaderboard	How often do you check the main Leaderboard page (which lists all members)?
Others' profile	How often do you check others' profile page?

[a]Point is named Karma in the used gamified platform.

3.2 Participants

Participants[1] (N = 1012) ranged in age from 18 to 54, though 62.5% were 25–34 years old, and the second largest group were between the ages of 35 and 44 (20.2%). There were approximately the same number of males (51.6%) as females (48.4%). In terms of country-by-country classification, Hungary ranks first (42%), followed by German users (27%), and the third largest group is from the UK (15%).

4 Results

Our main question was whether users can be distinguished as engaged and non-engaged users on a behavioral basis. Users were divided into the following three groups:

1. **'new users':** they registered less than 100 days earlier.
2. **'engaged users':** they registered at least 100 days ago and they returned at least two times ('login') to the application.

[1] Only those visitors who reached the internal surface (which needs registration) of the service at least once and signed up for at least one competition, were counted.

3. **'non-engaged users'**: they registered at least 100 days ago and they did not return more than once after the registration.

As a result of separation, 3.2% of the users (N = 32) were categorized as 'new user', 81.7% (N = 827) as 'engaged user' and 15.1% (N = 153) as 'non-engaged user'. Data show that new users have the highest daily activity (see Fig. 1 panel A). On average they post and give likes the most, and for one day, they participate in most competitions. The lowest performance in group competitions is surprising at first sight, but if we think over, organizing a group competition is relatively time consuming and short (on average 32 days) is not enough to organize many major sport events. Comparing the engaged and non-engaged group we can see an engaged person is more active (see Fig. 1 panel B).

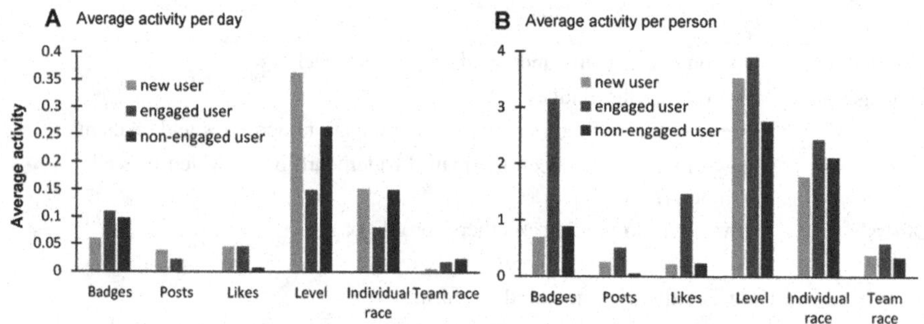

Fig. 1. Average activities per group

We statistically tested our three groups and the distributions of the aforementioned populations – according to attributes described in Sect. 3.1 – were compared with the Kolmogorov-Smirnov test. Based on the results, there were significant distribution differences in cases of the nine attributes. As for answering **Q1**, there is a difference between the general activities of the three populations.

4.1 Identifying Behavior Types

Agglomerative Hierarchical Clustering (AHC) was done by using Pearson Correlation Coefficient to identify the behavior types within engaged users using the nine collected attributes (see Table 3). The dendrogram divided these users into three major clusters. The first cluster (*class-1*) encompasses 651 individuals, the second cluster (*class-2*) has

Table 3. Summary statistics of the use-based attributes for engaged user

	A1	A2	A3	A4	A5	A6	A7	A8	A9
Min.	1	2	1	0	0	0	0	0	0
Max.	935	741	14	128	137	29	113	35	5
Mean	148.1	19.1	3.9	3.1	1.5	0.5	5.3	2.4	0.6
Std. dev.	180.2	44.6	2.0	6.2	6.8	2.1	11.7	3.2	0.9

124 and the third cluster (*class-3*) has 52 individuals. The variance decomposition for the optimal classification values are 16.6% for within class variation while 83.4% for the between-class differences and the cophenetic correlation is 0.772.

If we depict engaged users by class (see in Fig. 2, panel A), we can immediately notice that *class-1* users logged in, took part in individual and group competitions the most and reached the highest level time proportionally. If we take into account their responses to feedback questions (see in Fig. 3), it appears that those in this group are most interested in others' profile. So, taken together these users are stimulated by interaction with others, that is, they are the *Socializer* type based on the BrainHex model. It is worth noting that 64% of engaged users are in this cluster.

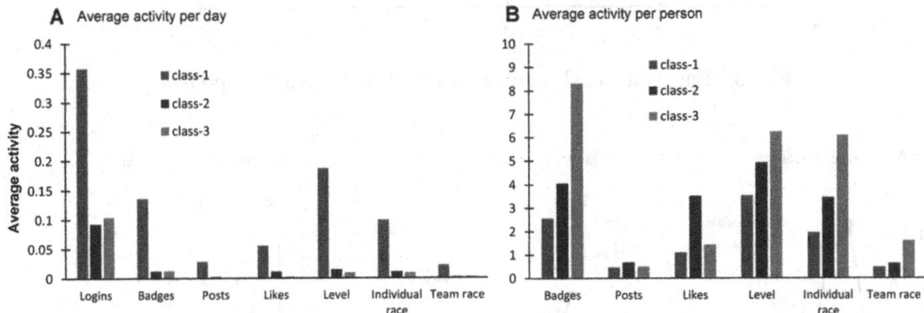

Fig. 2. Engaged users' average activities per classes

In Fig. 2, panel B, when we see personalized data, we see that the *class-3* members have collected most of the badges, most of them have participated in most tournaments, while the least social activity (like, post) is given.

If we look at Fig. 3, which reveals users' motivation, we can see that users from *class-3* are very motivated by points, badges, but they are less interested in others' performance. In the BrainHex list we could identify them as *Achivers* who are motivated by the reward of achieving long-term goals. They are the smallest cluster of engaged users (5% of all engaged users). It is worth noting that users of *class-3* t are the longest time to use the application on average (data not shown).

The characterization of the *class-2* user group is somewhat challenging, as they are socially active, they give likes and comments and they post. They are also moderately motivated by points, badges and leaderboards. However, their striking feature is that *class-2* users participate in individual races rather than in group competitions (see in Fig. 2). Furthermore, members of *class-2* reported in their feedback responses that they are doing more sports since the application was in use.

Overall, they are the '*Seekers*' in BrainHex model who enjoy exploring things and discovering new situations.

While exploring motivations, we examined how the activities related to social activity change in time for each group (Fig. 4). The figure shows that, although members of the *class-1* group are the most active in time, it is noticeable that the

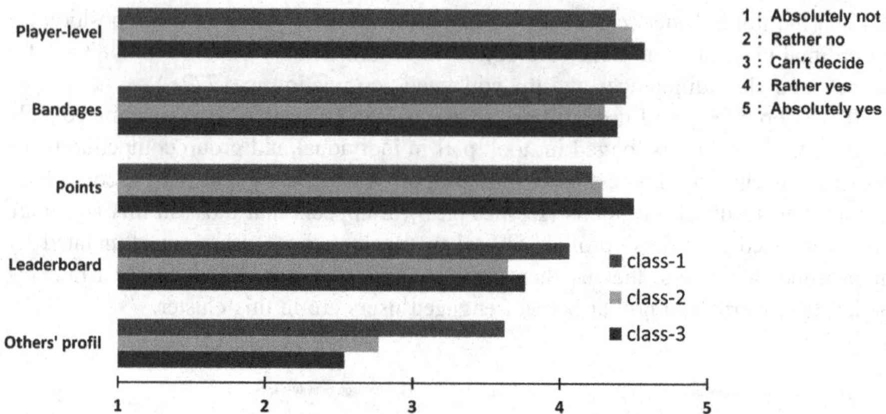

Fig. 3. Engaged users' motivation based on feedback responses

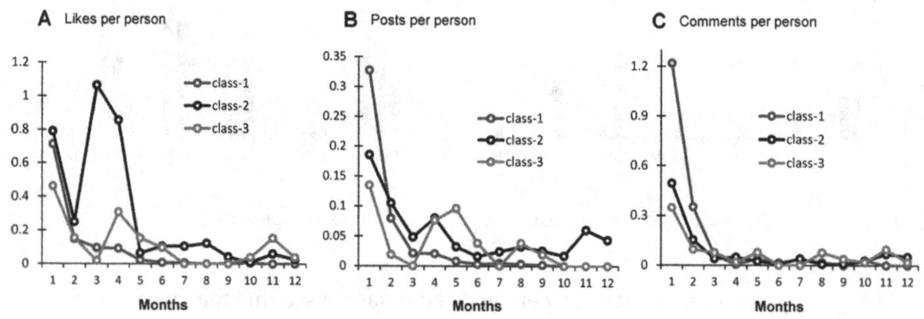

Fig. 4. Social related activity per class

vanishing of the enthusiasm is the highest as well in that group. After the enthusiasm of the first months, the number of posts and likes is significantly reduced.

Adding together, **Q2** question could be answered as we could dependably identify users with different motivations based on the data collected.

4.2 Further Factors Affecting Engagement

During the investigation of engagement the text-mining of content of comments clearly showed that the level of engagement is influenced by organizational culture e.g. whether the organization is allowed to play tournaments during working hours or there are one or two people within the organization who also act as organizers. We have studied the proportion of committed participants depending on the number of participants in the organization (see in Fig. 5).

The figure shows that engagement rate below 50% couldn't be found ('new' users are not included); this high level of engagement is understandable as only registered users were counted in the study, which already shows interest. Based on the data, it can

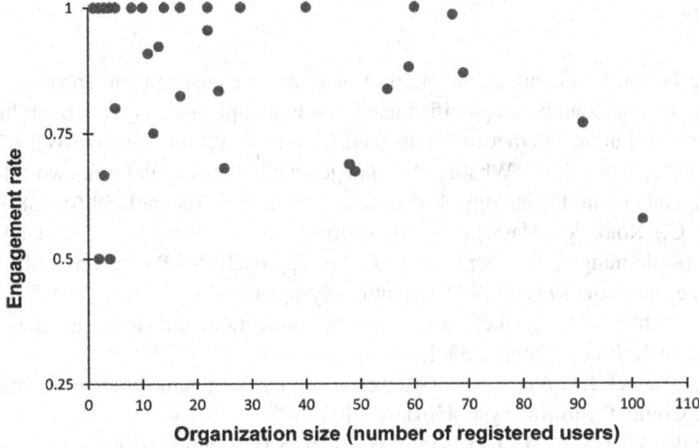

Fig. 5. Engagement rate depending on the size of the organization

be said that the number of registered users within the organization varies within a relatively large range (1–102) and higher levels of engagement can be observed in the case of lower organization 'size'. The latter confirms that the level of engagement is also influenced by an 'organizer' or 'personal' factor.

4.3 Limitations and Future Research

Our study is limited by the fact that the feedback responses gathered by the application are, obviously, self-reported. Use of self-reported data is likely to affect the results as the users responding are most probably actively engaged with the service, and eager to participate in activities related to it.

5 Conclusion

In conclusion, it has been found that behavior patterns among users (who use the examined service, at least in a minimal way) can be distinguished significantly by their usage time. After separation, we could identify different behaviors' pattern for engaged and non-engaged users. Users who are already engaged can be well distinguished by their behavioral patterns, and these clusters can help to identify the *Socializers*, *Achievers* and *Seekers*. The study was also able to reveal additional influencing factors beyond personal behavior pattern.

In further development of the service, it is suggested to motivate those who do not use any social function because their general participation is expected to be low. While the rate of participation among users who have tendency to take part in team competitions may be satisfactory, it is suggested to set up personally achievable challenges for those who like to act individually because these challenges can be motivational for them.

References

1. Barna, B., Fodor, S.: Gamification's impact on employee engagement: enhancing employee well-being with a cloud based gamified team-building application. In: 2018 6th International Conference on Future Internet of Things and Cloud Workshops (FiCloudW). IEEE (2018)
2. O'Brien, H.L., Toms, E.G.: What is user engagement? A conceptual framework for defining user engagement with technology. J. Am. Soc. Inform. Sci. Technol. **59**(6), 938–955 (2008)
3. Law, E.L.C., Roto, V., Hassenzahl, M., Vermeeren, A.P. and Kort, J.:. Understanding, scoping and defining user experience: a survey approach. In: Proceedings of the SIGCHI Conference on Human Factors in Computing Systems. ACM (2009)
4. Garris, R., Ahlers, R., Driskell, J.E.: Games, motivation, and learning: a research and practice model. Simul. Gaming **33**(4), 441–467 (2002)
5. Huang, Z., Cappel, J.J.: Assessment of a web-based learning game in an information systems course. J. Comput. Inform. Syst. **45**(4), 42–49 (2005)
6. Kankanhalli, A., Taher, M., Cavusoglu, H., Kim, S.H.: Gamification: a new paradigm for online user engagement. In: International Conference on Information Systems, ICIS (2012)
7. Silverman, R.E.: Latest game theory: mixing work and play. Wall Street J. (2011)
8. Attfield, S., Kazai, G., Lalmas, M., Piwowarski, B.: Towards a science of user engagement (position paper). In: WSDM Workshop on User Modelling for Web Applications (2011)
9. Guthrie, J.T., Wigfield, A., You, W.: Instructional contexts for engagement and achievement in reading. In: Christenson, S., Reschly, A., Wylie, C. (eds.) Handbook of Research on Student Engagement, pp. 601–634. Springer, Boston (2012). https://doi.org/10.1007/978-1-4614-2018-7_29
10. Klauda, S.L., Guthrie, J.T.: Comparing relations of motivation, engagement, and achievement among struggling and advanced adolescent readers. Read. Writ. **28**(2), 239–269 (2015)
11. Yardley, L., et al.: Understanding and promoting effective engagement with digital behavior change interventions. Am. J. Prev. Med. **51**(5), 833–842 (2016)
12. Hamari, J., Hassan, L., Dias, A.: Gamification, quantified-self or social networking? Matching users' goals with motivational technology. User Model. User-Adap. Inter. **28**(1), 35–74 (2018)
13. den Akker, H., Jones, V.M., Hermens, H.J.: Tailoring real-time physical activity coaching systems: a literature survey and model. User Model. User-Adapt. Interact. **24**(5), 351–392 (2014)
14. Grimes, A., Kantroo, V., Grinter, R.E.: Let's play!: mobile health games for adults. In: Proceedings of the 12th ACM International Conference on Ubiquitous Computing. ACM (2010)
15. Orji, R., Vassileva, J., Mandryk, R.L.: LunchTime: a slow-casual game for long-term dietary behavior change. Pers. Ubiquit. Comput. **17**(6), 1211–1221 (2013)
16. Berkovsky, S., Freyne, J., Coombe, M., Bhandari, D.: Recommender algorithms in activity motivating games. In: Proceedings of the Fourth ACM Conference on Recommender Systems. ACM (2010)
17. Berkovsky, S., Freyne, J., Coombe, M., Bhandari, D.: Adaptive persuasive systems: a study of tailored persuasive text messages to reduce snacking. ACM Trans. Interact. Intell. Syst. (TiiS) **2**(2), 10 (2012)
18. Kaptein, M., Lacroix, J., Saini, P.: Individual differences in persuadability in the health promotion domain. In: Ploug, T., Hasle, P., O-K, H. (eds.) PERSUASIVE 2010. LNCS, vol. 6137, pp. 94–105. Springer, Heidelberg (2010). https://doi.org/10.1007/978-3-642-13226-1_11

19. Halko, S., Kientz, J.A.: Personality and persuasive technology: an exploratory study on health-promoting mobile applications. In: Ploug, T., Hasle, P., O-K, H. (eds.) PERSUASIVE 2010. LNCS, vol. 6137, pp. 150–161. Springer, Heidelberg (2010). https://doi.org/10.1007/978-3-642-13226-1_16
20. Myers, I.B., McCaulley, M.H., Most, R.: Manual: A Guide to the Development and Use of the Myers-Briggs Type Indicator. Consulting Psychologists Press, Palo Alto (1985)
21. Goldberg, L.R.: The structure of phenotypic personality traits. Am. Psychol. **48**(1), 26 (1993)
22. Bartle, R.: Hearts, clubs, diamonds, spades: players who suit MUDs. J. MUD Res. **1**(1), 19 (1996)
23. Nacke, L.E., Bateman, C., Mandryk, R.L.: BrainHex: preliminary results from a neurobiological gamer typology survey. In: Anacleto, J.C., Fels, S., Graham, N., Kapralos, B., Saif El-Nasr, M., Stanley, K. (eds.) ICEC 2011. LNCS, vol. 6972, pp. 288–293. Springer, Heidelberg (2011). https://doi.org/10.1007/978-3-642-24500-8_31

Tower of Questions (TOQ): A Serious Game for Peer Learning

Nafisul Kiron(✉), Ifeoma Adaji(✉), Jeff Long, and Julita Vassileva

University of Saskatchewan, Saskatoon, SK, Canada
{ni.kiron, ifeoma.adaji, jeff.long, julita.vassileva}@usask.ca

Abstract. Research has shown that educational games are effective in motivating and engaging students to learn. To contribute to ongoing research in the area of educational games, we developed and evaluated a peer-quizzing game, Tower of Questions (TOQ). In TOQ, students are anonymous and can create towers virtually by asking questions and can conquer towers by answering questions. Students receive incentives for asking and correctly answering questions. To evaluate the game, 37 first-year university students played the game regularly as part of an introductory programming course during an entire academic term. We compared the engagement of the students considering their gender, preferred mode of studying (cooperative and individualistic), and their final course grade.

Keywords: Gamification · Serious game · Peer learning · Game-based testing · Peer-quizzing · Incentives · Engagement

1 Introduction

Several studies in the use of educational games to facilitate learning suggest that educational games are effective in motivating students to learn [1, 3, 4, 18]. Motivation is important because students learn better when motivated [2]. Educational games have been found to be effective as means for engaging students in self-directed learning [17]. Furthermore, educational games have been found by learners to be useful [3], easy to use [11], and provide students with various learning opportunities [6]. Research on educational games suggests that they significantly improve students' performance [5, 10, 11].

Game designers often use mechanics from existing games in developing educational games. For example, "Mario Teaches Typing" is developed to teach players educational skills like mathematics, reading or typing by solving puzzles [13]. Tower Defense (TD) is a sub-genre of strategy games that is often used in the design of educational games. Lin et al. [14] used TD mechanics in the development of chemical bond concept learning game for high school students. Thorton and Guillermo [19] similarly used the TD mechanics to develop a game that teaches end users to choose strong passwords. Furthermore, Hernàndez-Sabaté et al. [9] used TD dynamics to develop a game to teach mathematics to students. Despite the use of TD mechanics in these studies, the games that were developed did not promote peer learning. Peer

A. Liapis et al. (Eds.): GALA 2019, LNCS 11899, pp. 276–286, 2019.
https://doi.org/10.1007/978-3-030-34350-7_27

learning online has been shown to facilitate student learning experiences, while minimizing the isolation students face while learning online [16]. To bridge this gap, we developed Tower of Questions (TOQ), a peer learning online game based on TD game mechanics. In this paper, we present the initial results regarding the student engagement in peer learning from a field study involving 37 students who played the game regularly as part of an introductory programming course during a 4-month long academic term at our university.

2 Literature Review

The use of games to enhance the experience of learners is an active research area. Chow et al. [5] studied the use of an educational game to improve undergraduate students' understanding and retention in an introductory statistics course. They compared the understanding and learned retention of students who played the game to those who did not. According to the authors, the learned retention rate for students who played the game was 95% compared to 59% for those who did not play the game. The game developed by the authors based on the popular TV show "Deal or No Deal[1]" and thus it differs from our proposed game, TOQ. The game was synchronous (all players had to be online at the same time) and not anonymous.

Papastergiou [15] investigated the learning effectiveness and motivational appeal of a computer game in teaching computer science concepts to students. The author developed a single player game that taught computer science concepts to students. The results suggested that the use of the computer game was more effective in promoting the students' knowledge of the concepts being taught compared to a non-gaming approach. Similarly, the use of the game was more motivational to the students compared to a non-gaming approach. Unlike the game described in this study, TOQ is a multi-player game that promotes peer learning among students.

In their study of a game to teach requirements collections and analysis in software engineering, Hainey et al. [8] developed and evaluated a role play game and compared the performance of the game's players to that of students that were taught using the traditional approach. Their results suggest that game-based learning was well suited to higher education learners and provided them with a supplementary learning experience. TOQ differs from the game developed by the authors because TOQ is not a role-play game. Everyone in TOQ can build or conquer towers which represents asking and answering questions respectively.

3 TOQ Game Design

The TOQ is a web-based gamified quizzing application using some game mechanics from Tower Defense (TD) games, which is a subgenre of strategy games [1]. Some of the TD features used in our game are points in the form of gems, territory, building and

---

1 https://www.nbc.com/deal-or-no-deal.

attacking towers and a section containing fallen towers. The students should learn about a subject domain be able to earn points and while they play the game. Our goal is to provide students with the opportunity to learn by forming questions about the learning content, answering questions of other students, and to earn points and status in the game. It is important to ensure anonymity, to prevent shy students from embarrassment and fear of asking too simple questions, and also to prevent gaming by collusion among by pairs or groups of students aiming to maximize their points.

When a player logs in for the first time, they are presented with the game's dashboard showing the option to ask new questions and information about the current status of the game: the gems remaining in the bank, the gems they have earned, questions they have asked (their own towers). Initially, the game starts with 5000 gems in the bank. The bank is a virtual place in the game where all the un-earned gems are stored. Each time a player asks a question in the game, a virtual tower is created, and 10 gems are awarded to that player from the bank. As long as there are sufficient gems left in the bank, players can ask questions and build new towers.

The Player who create a question is called *Lord of the tower* or simply *Lord*. For each successful attack on other Lords' towers, the attacker receives 6 out of the 10 gems awarded to the Lord for creating the tower. The game has a finite number of gems in the bank to keep the in-game economy alive and prevent players from asking trivial questions. However, this amount can be increased by the instructor/moderator.

There are three types of questions in the game: Multiple choice questions (MCQ), true/false, and short answer. When asking a question, the Lord needs to provide the question, an answer, the answer options (for MCQ and true/false type questions) and the territory to which the tower will belong to. Territories are the chapters from the course syllabus. The new tower is placed in the "Open towers" section and is available for attacks for one week. If the tower is not conquered in one week, the Lord of the tower keeps all of the ten gems, and the tower is marked as *safe*. The safe tower is then made open to the public for viewing. Each player can attempt to attack a tower only once. If a player fails to answer the question correctly, the tower for that question is closed to that player but remains open to other players.

For short answer type questions, after receiving an answer, the tower is placed on hold (cannot be attacked) until the Lord of the tower reviews the answer. After reviewing and marking the answer as correct, the tower is placed in the "Conquered towers" section, and both the Lord's and attacker's answers are made public. The "Conquered towers" section is an important section in the game. This section is designed to help players study questions and answers already solved in the game. The secondary purpose of this section is to build a question and answer bank for the instructors, to use as they see fit. For example, high-quality questions can be used in tests or quizzes. Figure 1 shows a snapshot of the "Conquered towers" section of the game.

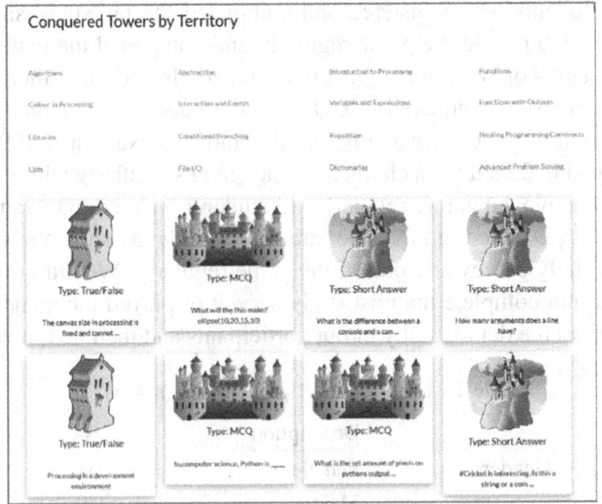

Fig. 1. A screenshot of the Conquered towers section

Players can punish Lords for posting inappropriate questions by using the flagging feature in both the "Open towers" and the "Conquered towers" section. The game has five types of flags: "Duplicate," "Off-topic," "Poor Question," "Poor answer," and "Objection!". The "Poor Question" and "Poor Answer" flags are used to flag rudimentary questions, and answers in the game and are only present in the "Conquered towers" section. "Duplicate" and "Off-topic" are self-explanatory. "Objection!" is a special type of flag and is only available for short answer type questions. This flag allows players to object to answers that are similar to their own but have been chosen as the correct answer by the Lord of the tower whereas their answer was marked wrong. Towers that receive a considerable number of flags of similar types are sealed with a label mentioning the type of violation and the gems for that tower are returned back to the bank.

4 Field Study

In the following section, we describe the results of a field-study using TOQ.

4.1 Recruitment of Participants

We recruited 106 first-year students from the University of Saskatchewan to play the game for one school term as part of their Introduction to Computer Science course. The students were required to complete a pre-study survey before playing the game and a post-study survey at the end of the term. The intent of the pre-study survey was to learn about the students' gender, preferred study hours, familiarity with TD games, and preference to work alone or in a group. The post-study survey aimed to gather information about their experience of playing the game. Each student was assigned a pseudo name so they could remain anonymous.

Of the 106 students who registered and completed the pre-study survey, only 37 students (M:18, F:19) played the game regularly and completed the exit survey. These students created a total of 186 towers (MCQ: 57, True/False: 67, and Short-Answer: 62), of which 171 towers were conquered (MCQ: 51, True/False: 65, and Short-Answer: 55). Of the 186 questions, 77 were created before the midterm exam, and 109 were created before the final exam. 23 students claimed to play games regularly while 14 did not. Of the 23 students who played games regularly, 12 students claimed to be familiar with TD games. The results presented in this paper are based on the 37 students who completed the pre and post study survey and played the game regularly. We did not include those students who did not complete the post study survey or played the game occasionally. Table 1 summarizes the demography of our participants and their activities in the game.

Table 1. Description of participants (n = 37)

	Description	%
Gender	Female	51
	Male	49
Study preference	Prefer studying alone	57
	Prefer group study	43
Towers created	Multiple choice questions	31
	True/False	36
	Short Answer	33
Towers conquered	Multiple choice questions	30
	True/False	38
	Short Answer	32

4.2 Measures for Student Engagement

One of the aims of this study was to measure students' engagement with TOQ. Engagement describes how active the students are in the system. We hypothesize that the active students were able to learn more from their peers compared to the inactive ones. We measure engagement using several metrics described below.

Points Earned

In TOQ, participants earn points by creating towers (asking questions) and conquering towers created by others (answering questions created by others). The more towers created or conquered, the more points the participant earns. Thus, someone who has earned several points has used the system on several occasions and is thus, more engaged than others.

Number of Towers Created

Towers are created by asking questions in the game. A student who has created many questions is considered more active than a student who has not.

Number of Towers Conquered

Towers are conquered by correctly answering the questions of others in the game. A student who has correctly answered more questions is considered more active than a student who has not.

Number of Conquered Towers Visited

The aim TOQ is to encourage students to learn from their peers. Apart from asking and answering questions, viewing already answered questions (conquered towers) is another way that students can learn from their peers. A student that frequently visits correctly answered questions is considered more active in the game than students who do not.

4.3 Methodology

To determine the engagement of students in the game, we computed the average of each of the metrics defined above. Research has shown that males and females are engaged differently in playing games [20]. Thus, we compared the differences in the average measures of engagement of our participants based on their gender.

Research suggests that people learn in different ways [12]. Some learn by cooperating with other learners in a group, while others learn by being competitive with group members. Others learn by working alone or being individualistic [12]. The preferred modes of learning are important in serious game development because they can be used to personalize influence strategies to individuals or groups of similar individuals. For example, students who prefer working in groups could be given group tasks with similar others instead of individual tasks. To determine the differences in preferred learning modes, we computed the average metrics for students based on their study preference: studying alone or in groups. We excluded competitive learning because of the controversy that surrounds it [7].

To determine if on average, the students' engagement levels differed based on their final grades, we computed the average of these metrics based on the final overall grade of the students.

5 Results

In the following section, we present the results of the analysis we carried out on the engagement metrics: points earned, number of towers created, number of towers conquered, and number of conquered towers visited based on the gender of our participants, their learning mode preference and their final course grade.

5.1 Gender

As shown in Fig. 2 and Table 2, the male students, on average, earned more points, created more towers (asked more questions), and conquered more towers (answered more questions) compared to the female students. The female students, on the other hand, visited more conquered towers (answered questions) compared to the male students. This suggests that male students contributed more to the bank of questions and answers. This is similar to research [20] that suggests that males are more active game players than females.

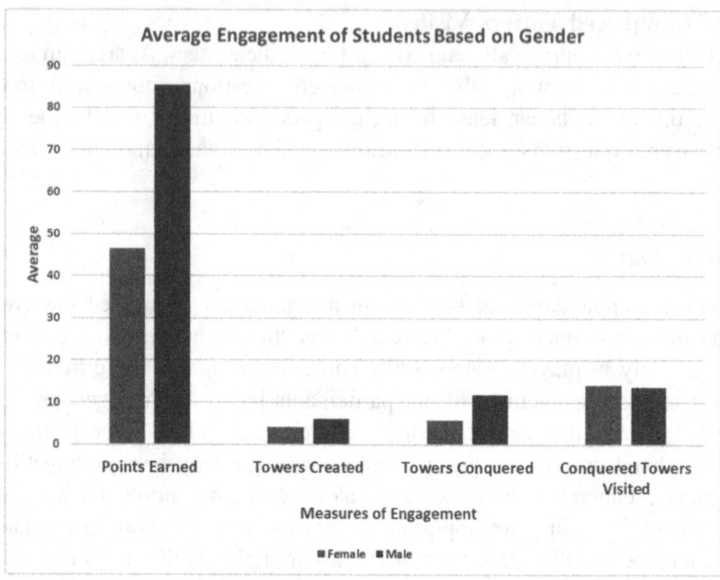

Fig. 2. Average engagement of students based on gender. (n = 37)

Despite earning more points and being more engaged, the male students' average final grade for the course (as shown in Table 2) was less than the average final grade of the female students.

Table 2. Average engagement and overall course grade based on gender. (n = 37)

Gender	Average				
	Points earned	Towers created	Towers conquered	Conquered towers visited	Overall course grade
Female	46.53	4.05	5.79	14.21	79.52
Male	85.44	6.06	11.78	13.72	75.97

5.2 Study Mode Preference

To determine the students' study mode preference, we included a question in the pre-game survey that asked participants to choose which best describes their study preference: studying alone or in a group.

Our results as shown in Fig. 3 and Table 3 suggest that the students who prefer group study earned more points in the game and created more questions compared to students who prefer studying alone. On the other hand, students that prefer studying alone conquered more towers (answered more questions) and visited more conquered towers (correctly answered questions).

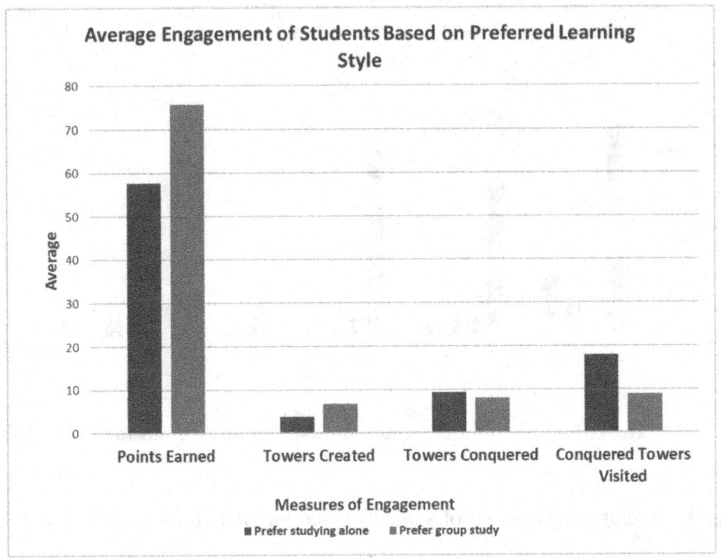

Fig. 3. Average engagement of students based on study preference. (n = 37)

As shown in Table 3, on average, the students that prefer studying alone had a higher average overall course grade compared to the students that prefer studying in groups. In the future, we will carry out more statistical analysis to determine if there is a significant difference in the averages of the two groups.

Table 3. Average engagement and overall course grade based on learning preference. (n = 37)

Study preference	Average				
	Points earned	Towers created	Towers conquered	Conquered towers visited	Overall course grade
Alone study	57.62	3.71	9.24	17.90	81.42
Group study	75.75	6.75	8.0	8.81	73.04

5.3 Overall Course Grade

To determine if the level of engagement of students have any impact on their learning outcome, we compared the engagement metrics for the students based on their overall course grade. We split students into five groups based on their grade: 90% and above, between 80 and 89.99%, between 70 and 79.99%, between 60 and 69.99% and 59.99% and below. Figure 4 shows the average engagement metrics of the students in each of these groups.

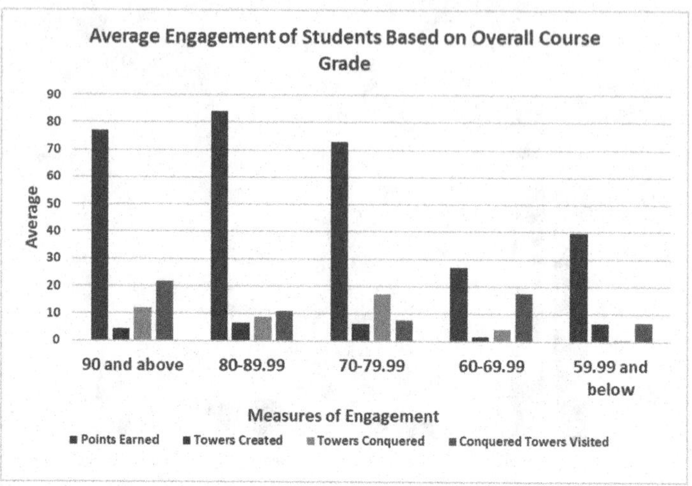

Fig. 4. Average engagement of students based on final course grade. (n = 37)

Our result shown in Fig. 4 and Table 4 suggests that the highest average points earned in the game were from students who scored between 80 and 89.99%, followed by those who scored 90% and above and those who scored in the 70% range. However, the students who visited the highest number of conquered towers (correctly answered questions) on average scored 90% and above overall in the course, followed by those in the 60% range. In addition, the students who conquered the least number of towers (answered the least number of questions), on average, scored the least overall grade of 59.99% and below. While these results suggest interesting findings, we need to establish the significance of the differences in the results between the various groups through deeper analysis and future studies.

Table 4. Average engagement and overall course grade based on learning preference. (n = 37)

Grade	Average			
	Points earned	Towers created	Towers conquered	Conquered towers visited
90 and above	77.11	4.44	12.00	21.67
80–89.99	83.85	6.46	8.69	11.00
70–79.99	73	6.25	17.25	7.5
60–69.99	26.86	1.57	4.29	17.43
59.99 and below	39.5	6.5	0.5	6.75

6 Conclusion and Future Work

Research has shown that educational games are effective in influencing learning in students. To contribute to ongoing research in this area, we developed and evaluated a new game, Tower of Questions, which uses some of the game mechanics from Tower

Defense games. Because engagement has been shown to influence learning, we measured students' engagement in the game based on their gender, their preferred mode of study and their final course grade. We analyzed the data of 37 students who played the game for one term. Our results suggest that the average points, towers created, and towers conquered for the male students were more than those of the female students. However, the average conquered towers visited by the female students and the average final grade for the female students were more than those of the male students. In addition, while the students who preferred group study earned the highest average points, the students who preferred studying alone, on average, visited more conquered towers and their final grade in the course was higher. Furthermore, the students who scored between 80 and 89.99 had the highest average number of points, while students who scored 59.99 and below visited the least number of conquered towers.

In the future, we plan to carry out further statistical analysis to determine the significance of the averages we reported here. In addition, we plan to explore if visiting the conquered towers (correctly answered questions) significantly influences the students' final course performance.

References

1. Azriel, J.A., et al.: Answers, questions, and deceptions: what is the role of games in business education? J. Educ. Bus. **81**(1), 9–13 (2005). https://doi.org/10.3200/JOEB.81.1.9-14
2. Bergin, S., Reilly, R.: The influence of motivation and comfort-level on learning to program. In: 17th Workshop on Psychology of Programming - PPIG (2005), pp. 293–304 (2005)
3. Bourgonjon, J., et al.: Students' perceptions about the use of video games in the classroom. Comput. Educ. **54**(4), 1145–1156 (2010)
4. Burguillo, J.C.: Using game theory and competition-based learning to stimulate student motivation and performance. Comput. Educ. **55**(2), 566–575 (2010)
5. Chow, A.F., et al.: Deal or no deal: using games to improve student learning, retention and decision-making. Int. J. Math. Educ. Sci. Technol. **42**(2), 259–264 (2011). https://doi.org/10.1080/0020739X.2010.519796
6. Crocco, F., et al.: A proof-of-concept study of game-based learning in higher education. Simul. Gaming. **47**(4), 403–422 (2016). https://doi.org/10.1177/1046878116632484
7. Ediger, M.: Cooperative learning versus competition: which is better? J. Instr. Psychol. **23** (3), 204 (1996)
8. Hainey, T., et al.: Evaluation of a game to teach requirements collection and analysis in software engineering at tertiary education level. Comput. Educ. **56**(1), 21–35 (2011). https://doi.org/10.1016/J.COMPEDU.2010.09.008
9. Hernández-Sabaté, A., et al.: Mathematics learning opportunities when playing a tower defense game. Int. J. Serious Games **2**(4), 57–71 (2015)
10. Hwang, G.-J., et al.: A contextual game-based learning approach to improving students' inquiry-based learning performance in social studies courses. Comput. Educ. **81**, 13–25 (2015). https://doi.org/10.1016/J.COMPEDU.2014.09.006
11. Hwang, G.-J., et al.: A knowledge engineering approach to developing educational computer games for improving students' differentiating knowledge. Br. J. Educ. Technol. **44**(2), 183–196 (2013). https://doi.org/10.1111/j.1467-8535.2012.01285.x
12. Johnson, D.W., Johnson, R.T.: Learning together and alone: overview and meta-analysis. Asia Pac. J. Educ. **22**(1), 95–105 (2002). https://doi.org/10.1080/0218879020220110

13. Ju, E., Wagner, C.: Personal computer adventure games: their structure, principles, and applicability for training. ACM SIGMIS Database. **28**(2), 78–92 (1997). https://doi.org/10.1145/264701.264707
14. Lin, Y.-C., et al.: Valence bond;-integrating scientific visualization mechanism in a tower defense game for chemical bond concept learning in high school. In: 2015 IIAI 4th International Congress on Advanced Applied Informatics, pp. 725–726, July 2015
15. Papastergiou, M.: Digital game-based learning in high school computer science education: impact on educational effectiveness and student motivation. Comput. Educ. **52**(1), 1–12 (2009)
16. Raymond, A., et al.: Peer learning a pedagogical approach to enhance online learning: a qualitative exploration. Nurse Educ. Today. **44**, 165–169 (2016). https://doi.org/10.1016/J.NEDT.2016.05.016
17. Salen, K., et al.: Rules of Play: Game Design Fundamentals. MIT Press, Cambridge (2004)
18. Sung, H.-Y., Hwang, G.-J.: A collaborative game-based learning approach to improving students' learning performance in science courses. Comput. Educ. **63**(2013), 43–51 (2013)
19. Thornton, D., Journal, G.F.: Gamification of information systems and security training: issues and case studies. Inform. Secur. Educ. J. **1**(1), 16–24 (2014)
20. Williams, D., et al.: Who plays, how much, and why? Debunking the stereotypical gamer profile. J. Comput.-Mediat. Commun. **13**(4), 993–1018 (2008)

Albiziapp: A Gamified Tool Dedicated to Tree Mapping

Pierre-Yves Gicquel, Ludovic Hamon(✉), Florian Plaut, and Sébastien George

LIUM - EA 4023, Le Mans University, 72085 Le Mans, Cedex 9, France
{pierre-yves.gicquel,ludovic.hamon,florian.plaut.etu, sebastien.george}@univ-lemans.fr

Abstract. Identification and mapping of trees through a Geo Collaborative Inventory (GCI) platform is an important task for research in botany, citizen sciences and education. The quantity and veracity of the recorded data rely mainly on the motivation and engagement of each participant. However, for a non-botanist, tree mapping can be perceived as an unstructured and tedious task that requires advanced skills. In addition, existing GCI applications deliver poor or nonexistent feedbacks regarding identification and mapping skills as well as progression in these skills. Structuring GCI sessions and enhancing them with game mechanics and clear objectives may have a positive effect on the inventory quality. Inventory situations being highly context dependant, a descriptive model of the GCI task is required to create adapted activity scenarios usable in various situations. This paper presents Albiziapp: a web collaborative and mobile tool, based on OpenSteetMap, that operationalizes any gamified scenario, consistent with a descriptive model built from a structural analysis of the GCI task.

Keywords: Tree mapping & learning · Collaborative inventory · Gamification

1 Introduction

Geo-locating trees and learning to identify them is especially interesting for domains such as botany, citizen sciences and education [6,13,14]. One can use a mobile device with a Geo-Collaborative Inventory (GCI) application to create Point Of Interests (POI) representing trees together with information (*e.g.* name, genus, species, size). Getting relevant and regular Volunteered Geographic Information (VGI) relies mainly on the motivation, engagement and skills of participants. However, despite the existence of numerous web or native GCI applications, such as OpenStreetMap (OSM)[1] or Spotteron[2], most of them suffer from several issues linked to: (a) a non-adapted interaction paradigm to record new trees in a short time (b), the absence of structures leading the users in the task

[1] https://www.openstreetmap.org.
[2] https://www.spotteron.net/.

A. Liapis et al. (Eds.): GALA 2019, LNCS 11899, pp. 287–297, 2019.
https://doi.org/10.1007/978-3-030-34350-7_28

and (c) appropriate mechanisms enhancing their motivation, engagement and identification skills [11].

In the gamification domain, this can be counterbalanced by structuring the inventory process through an adapted scenario. This scenario must define: (i) clear objectives, (ii) possible user actions (iii), immediate and appropriate feedbacks for these actions and (iv), clear progress indicators in terms of tree recognition and mapping skills [5]. The learning and inventory situations being various (*e.g.* residential areas, natural parks dedicated to some species), a descriptive model is required from which an adapted inventory and a gamified scenario can be formalized and tested.

This paper presents Albiziapp[3], a web application dedicated to the operationalization of gamified scenarios for the collaborative inventory of trees at a large scale. The main contribution of this work lies in the design of a descriptive model formalizing gamified scenarios for collaborative inventories. This model aims to tackle the following challenge: to allow everyone to write a gamified scenario that is operationalized by Albiziapp. The player will follow a set of activities made of clear objectives (*e.g.* add, identify, check a number of trees), actions (*e.g.* give the genus/species, confirm/disconfirm data, take a photo) and, instant or short-delayed rewards related to game mechanics (*e.g.* scores, timer, trophies, status).

In the next section, the GCI related work is studied from the tree inventory perspective. Section 3 proposes the descriptive model for the formalization of a structured and gamified scenario. The Abliziapp architecture and main functionalities are described in Sect. 4. A discussion around the model and the current architecture is made in Sect. 5.

2 Related Work

For mapping and sharing geo-located objects, OSM is one of the most popular and efficient web services from which, several web or native mobile applications were built, such as: Osmand, OSMContributor, StreetComplete, GoMaps, Vespuchi, MapContrib[4].

Most of these applications relies on the visualization, creation and edition of POIs. In the context of tree mapping, the users can choose and fill a form dedicated to trees or create their own fields for the species, the genus, the common name, etc., of a tree. Searching the appropriate tree form and/or creating the missing required fields for each POI is time consuming for one only interested in plants and trees inventories. With MapContrib, a layer specializing the inventory for a specific category of POI can be created. Once a layer is activated, each new POI will automatically display the appropriate form made of the same set of fields to fill. Nevertheless, it is not possible to edit OSM POIs, while the reading and editing of the user's POIs can only be done after an expert validation.

---

[3] https://pre-prod.albiziapp.reveries-project.fr/.

[4] https://www.mapcontrib.xyz.

More ergonomic applications for gathering knowledge about trees and plants can be found in the crowdsourcing domain. Nguyen *et al.* reviewed the systems dedicated to botanical data collection and their automatic identification tools [11]. Various efficient applications are associated with a botanical database for automatic or semi-automatic plant identification such as Pl@ntNet [11], CLOVER [10], Flower Checker[5], MyGarden Answers[6], Garden Compass[7], Garden Tag[8]. Yet, one well-known issue of crowdsourcing pointed by Misra *et al.* is "Recruiting and retaining the participant" [11].

Two other well-known issues in GCI can be noted: (a) the uneven geographic distribution of new POIs and (b), the uneven ratio between POIs creation and edition [2]. To counterbalance these issues, Antoniou *et al.* built a simulation of a gamified version of OSM with virtual players following the principles of geogames [2]. Geogames are games where the navigation task in the real world is at the core of the game scenario [7]. Despite their interesting "theoretical" results in terms of motivation and engagement, they did not simulate the user's interests for the POI categories. In addition, to our knowledge, few works addressed the recurrent problems of GCI through geogames and none were specialized in trees. Dhuny *et al.* built a web mobile system, based on an HTML5 framework, to geo-tag various fruit trees, medicinal herbs and share their location in a public database [4]. This initiative aimed to encourage planting for feeding purposes. Each POI could contain usual data about the plant with fructification and flowering information. A badge mechanism was implemented, despite its unclear aspect in terms of feedback and customizable features. Finally, the proposed authoring aspect was also fuzzy and seems to rely only on the framework itself.

The presented work is conducted as part of the ReVeRies project[9] and is supported by the French National Agency for Research (ANR). This work contributes to a research axe led by the following hypothesis: a gamified activity of geo-collaborative inventory of trees can enhance: (a) data quantity and veracity and (b), motivation and engagement of the participants. However, given the diversity of inventory situations, GCI scenarios and their game mechanics must be adaptable. This adaptation process implies to: (i) analyze and structure this activity in terms of relevant action units (ii), develop a model describing gamified scenarios. The next section presents an analysis of the tree-based GCI activity, followed by a proposition of such a descriptive model.

3 Toward a Descriptive Model of Gamified Scenario

3.1 Requirements for a GCI Activity

The minimal set of information expected by botanists for tree identification seems to be the GPS coordinates, the species and a picture [11]. For a GCI,

[5] http://www.flowerchecker.com/.
[6] http://www.gardenanswers.com/.
[7] https://www.gardencompass.com/.
[8] https://gardentags.com/.
[9] http://reveries-project.fr.

each of these pieces of information being a valid contribution, a POI with at least one of those fields is acceptable. The enhancement of the record veracity and completeness by the community is a relevant problematic for citizen sciences [2]. As a consequence, the possibility for everyone to make new records and/or edit them must be taken into account. However, records verification is a tedious task that is mostly done by experts. Tools for the automatic identification of plants from leaves can also be used with VGI systems such as Pl@ntNet [11] or, in the ReVeRies project, FOLIA [3]. Therefore, actions that "encourage" the data verification (*e.g.* the use of FOLIA, consulting the record history to edit it, records confirmation/disapproval, etc.), must be available and promoted. Finally, to motivate and engage the users, their progress in terms of tree identification and inventory skills must be characterized through appropriate feedbacks. Depending on the inventory and learning situation, several contextual reward mechanisms can be applied based on all or a part of the completion of the scenario and/or the user's actions.

3.2 Descriptive Model of a Scenario for GCI

Figure 1 proposes a descriptive model for GCI scenarios. A record is a set of data containing, at least, the GPS coordinates of the tree. The genus, species, common name and photos, can be added. To create scenarios, we modeled the concept of "mission" as a set of "activities" (Fig. 1, black part, *cf.* "ActivityList" class). An activity (*cf.* "Activity" class) is a task to perform that can have three "Types" (in bracket): (a) make X new records [INVENTORY] (b) check and/or edit X records of another participant [VERIFY] and (c) identify X trees [IDENTIFY].

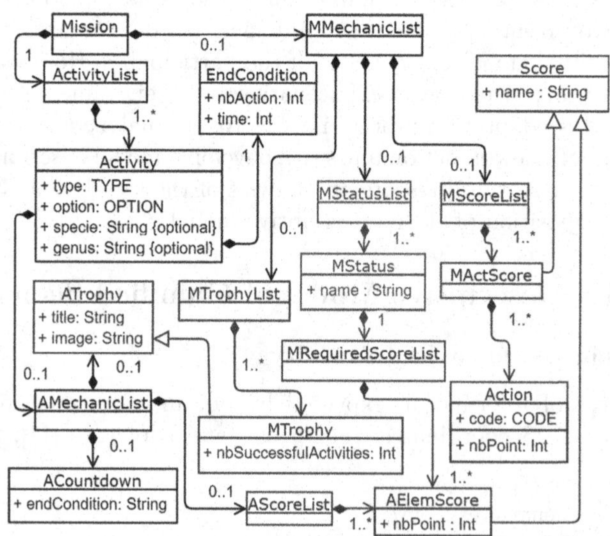

Fig. 1. UML diagram of the descriptive model (Color figure online)

This last activity aims to test the identification skills of the user (*cf.* Sect. 5 for more details). An expert geo-tags some trees in the field beforehand. Then, the user has to go to the tree location and fill its data that will be compared with those of the expert. Points are given to the user for each correct answer (*cf.* Sect. 3.3). Each of those types or goals can be refined with an "Option" (*cf.* "Activity" class), asking to perform the activity: (i) on a specified species or genus [SPECIES/GENUS] (ii), with different species or genus [DIFFERENT SPECIES/GENUS] and (iii), freely regarding the tree nature [NONE]. If the "Option" value is either [SPECIES] (or [GENUS]), the "specie" (or "genus") member must be added to the "Activity" object and its value specified. Besides, an activity requires an end condition (*cf.* "EndCondition" class) that can be the number X of records ("nbAction" field), a limited time (*cf.* Sect. 3.3) or both.

3.3 Descriptive Model of Game Mechanics

According to Zichermann *et al.* and Haaranen *et al.* cited by [4], reward mechanisms are simple, understandable and powerful mechanics to motivate and engage the user . A scenario can be enhanced with two kinds of game mechanics: (i) those associated at the mission level (*cf.* "MMechanicList" class) depending only on the user's actions and (ii) those associated at the activity level (*cf.* "AMechanicList" class) depending on the current activity.

Mission mechanics are made of trophies, scores and status (Fig. 4, right). First of all, the user can receive trophies (*i.e.* a name and an image, *cf.* "MTrophy" class) for successfully completing a specified number of activities.

A set of scores can also be defined (*cf.* "MScoreList" class). Being composed of a name (*cf.* "Score" class) and points, each score rewards the user each time a specific action is performed (*cf.* "MActScore" classe). Referring by a "code", an action can be ("code" value in bracket): create a POI [GPS], fill/edit the genus/species/common name field [complete/edit GENUS/SPECIES/COMMON], take a picture [photograph], confirm the record data [validate], doubt the tree existence [question] or use FOLIA [useFOLIA]. Each coded action can be performed at any time and contribute to the GCI regardless the activity type. However, only the appropriate actions can move the activity forward.

A status consists in one "name" or title (*cf.* "MStatusList" and "MStatus" classes) given to the user once a threshold is reached. This threshold is defined by a set of values of one or several previously defined scores (*cf.* "MRequiredScores" classes). Once a new status is obtained, it replaces the previous obtained one (*cf.* Fig. 3, right).

Activity mechanics are made of: a countdown to limit the activity in time (*cf.* "ACountdown" class), trophies and scores for successfully completing the targeted activity (*cf.* "ATrophy" and "AElemScore" class).

Note that the "code" vocabulary contains also the keywords [identifiedGENUS], [identifiedSPECIES] and [identifiedCOMMON] to set up a score, giving points for a correct answer on the genus, the species and/or the common name during an [INVENTORY] activity (*cf.* Sect. 3.2). Finally, all the game mechanics are optional as a GCI scenario can also be defined without them.

3.4 A JSON Example

The descriptive model allows formalizing a gamified scenario according to a JSON structure. Figure 2 shows an example of such a structure compatible with Albiziapp. The left and middle-up sides show the mission activities. The first activity aims to find and map 5 new trees of the "Acer" genus. The second one aims to identify 3 trees mapped by an expert (*cf.* Sect. 3.3) and give 20 "knowledgePoints" once this activity is done, whereas the last one aims to map as many trees as possible in less than 15 min. The middle-down and right sides represent the mission mechanics. A score named "explorationPoints" give 2 points for each "photograph". The trophy "3 activites done" is given to the user once 3 activities are completed. The user will receive the status "Traveler" after reaching 64 "explorationPoints".

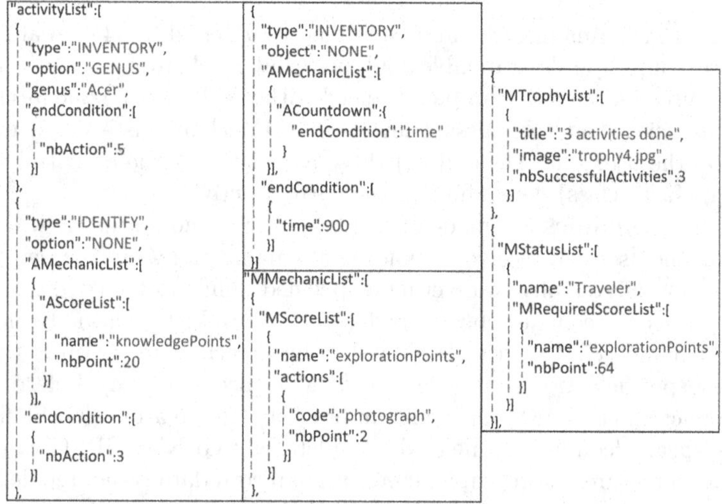

Fig. 2. A JSON mission example: three activities with a score and a countdown mechanic (left and middle-up) and 3 mission mechanics (middle-down and right).

The next section details the key features of Albiziapp, its architectural and design principles for the implementation of these features.

4 Albiziapp Architecture and Main Functionalities

4.1 A Full-Web, Mobile, Real-Time Collaborative Application

Figure 3 (left) gives a high-level representation of the server architecture and the data flow. Albiziapp (See footnote 3) is a full-web application, using only standardized web technologies without relying on a specific platform. It has been designed to be used at a large scale. Any mobile or desktop device with a web-browser can run Albiziapp. Nonetheless, performances and user experience of a web application are known to not be as good as native ones [1]. We detail in this section, how we mitigate these issues.

Figure 3 (left) gives a high-level representation of the server architecture and the data flow. There are, at least two main keys and user-related features directing the back-end architecture (server): (i) recording new trees in a persistent database and (ii), visualizing and editing other participants' records and her/his own in real time.

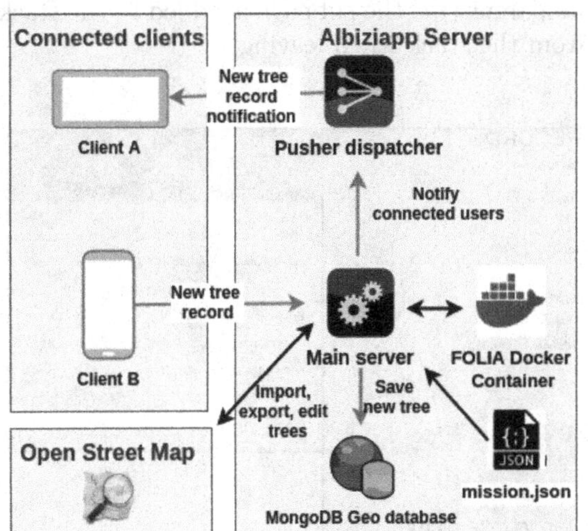

Fig. 3. High level server architecture (left), Albiziapp map page (right) (Color figure online)

The first feature entails constraints on the database schema. For a record, there are innumerable types of information that could be relevant when one inventories trees[10], for instance: phenological information (*e.g.* date of flowering), health information (*e.g.* parasite, disease). Various use-cases are likely to arise. Therefore, the database must be able to handle: (a) modifications in the data structure and (b), the coexistence of different structures. Consequently, the NoSQL paradigm was chosen with a document-oriented NoSQL database [9]: MongoDB[11].

The second feature entails real-time communication between connected users. When a user adds a tree, the tree must show up on other participants' map. Such real-time communication is efficiently performed with *websockets* for broadcasting [12]: a client notifies the server that he added a tree, the server then broad-

[10] https://wiki.openstreetmap.org/wiki/Tag:natural%3Dtree.

[11] https://www.mongodb.com/.

casts the message to all other clients. Therefore, *websockets* were used to communicate.

4.2 Interacting with Albiziapp: The Client Side

The web application was designed to be similar to a native application, reusing well-known good practices in terms of interaction[12]. The main interactions are navigation through the different pages and creation/editing/deleting tree records. The navigation follows two usual patterns in mobile applications: (a) the main pages are always accessible through a tab bar and (b) a subpage follows the stack pattern by overlaying its parent (*i.e.* the subpage is added to the stack for access, the page is removed from the stack when leaving).

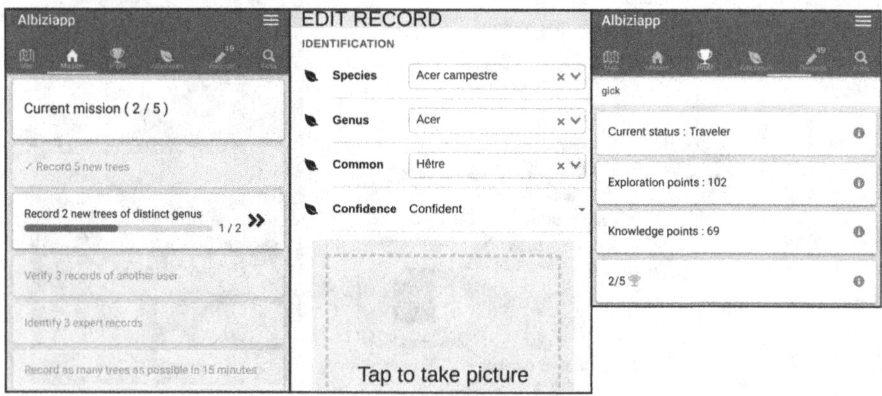

Fig. 4. The mission page (left), the record page (middle) and the profile page (right). (Color figure online)

The JSON scenario can be loaded thanks to an option in the main menu protected by an administrator password. Then the mission page is presented with the set of successive activities that must be completed (Fig. 4, left). The user can also give up an activity to go to the next one. Interactions involving tree records are initiated from the map page (Fig. 3, right). The user can touch the map (*i.e.* create a new POI) or a circle (*i.e.* edit an existing POI) and fill its data through a dedicated form (Fig. 4, middle). A color code allows distinguishing the user's records (*i.e.* red) from those of other participants (*i.e.* green). The users can interact with the POI data with its dedicated page (Fig. 4, middle) *i.e.*: perform actions listed in Sect. 3.3 and export their records to OSM. The user is informed of all rewards, in real-time thanks to a toast mechanism (Fig. 3, right). All the rewards are gathered in the user profile page, accessible *via* the main

[12] https://www.nngroup.com/articles/ten-usability-heuristics/, *cf.* "consistency and standard" included in "Follow platform conventions".

menu (Fig. 4, right): each mechanic has its own bar that can be touched to see its functioning and history.

The next section discusses the advantages and drawbacks of the current version of Albiziapp and our scenario model with an highlighting on the human learning aspect.

5 Discussion and Conclusion

The Albiziapp architecture and descriptive model allow anyone creating a structured scenario, with highly customizable game mechanics for tree-based GCI. The system limitations lies in the JSON format requiring the understanding of its syntax. A more accessible HCI must be developed by, for example, the association of visual components for activities, actions and game mechanics [8]. Nonetheless, the choice of this format was related to a generator, under development, that can create JSON scenarios depending on the inventory, game and learning objectives. In addition, adding a new type of game mechanics is still a challenge with the current architecture.

Making relevant feedbacks regarding the user's progress in terms of tree identification skills is still an issue. We provide the [IDENTIFY] activity to set up some identification exercises (*cf.* Sect. 3.2). Nevertheless, an expert is not necessarily available and this activity does not make a contribution to the inventory. Another strategy is to give to the user some points if another participant checks/edits her/his records and give similar information for the genus, the species or the common name. This has been implemented in our model *i.e.* in the JSON file, a score can be specified and linked to the respective action code: [sameGENUSPropagation], [sameSPECIESPropagation], [sameCOMMONPropagation] (*cf.* Sect. 3.3). Obviously, this second option does not guarantee the veracity of the record data. However, it can be relevant in terms of "instant" feedback giving an insight of the user's identification skills. Nevertheless, the propagation formula could be enhanced as it does not take into account and detect, for example, the access to the record history by the participant making the verification.

This paper presents Albiziapp, a web application for the Geo-Collaborative Inventory (GCI) of trees. Keeping participants engaged in a GCI task is crucial to enhance the number of records, their completeness, their geo-distribution and veracity. Toward the variety of inventory situations, the questionable or nonexistent feedbacks provided by the applications of the literature and the absence of scenarios guiding the user, a descriptive model of gamified scenarios was proposed. This model was built thanks to a simple structural analysis of the GCI task according to: (i) its goals and requirements and (ii) the macro-elementary user's actions. Each scenario, conformed to our model, can be formalized thanks to a JSON file that is operationalized by Albiziapp. To enhance the motivation and engagement of the participant, our descriptive model can specify four types of fully customizable reward-type mechanics at the activity level and/or the action level. In addition to the future work suggested in the previous section, a comparative study (GCI VS gamified GCI) will be conducted to analyse the influence of the gamification elements on: (a) the quantity and veracity of the recorded data during the inventory task and (b) the user's motivation, engagement and identification skills.

Acknowledgment. This work is supported by the French National Agency for Research with the reference ANR-15-CE38-0004-01 (ReVeRIES project).

References

1. Ahmad, A., Li, K., Feng, C., Asim, S.M., Yousif, A., Ge, S.: An empirical study of investigating mobile applications development challenges. IEEE Access **6**, 17711–17728 (2018)
2. Antoniou, V., Schlieder, C.: Addressing uneven participation patterns in VGI through gamification mechanisms. In: Ahlqvist, O., Schlieder, C. (eds.) Geogames and Geoplay. Advances in Geographic Information Science, pp. 91–110. Springer, Cham (2018). https://doi.org/10.1007/978-3-319-22774-0_5
3. Cerutti, G., Tougne, L., Mille, J., Vacavant, A., Coquin, D.: Understanding leaves in natural images - a model-based approach for tree species identification. Comput. Vis. Image Underst. **117**(10), 1482–1501 (2013)
4. Dhuny, R., Sajeevan, G., Pardeshi, S.: An open framework to geotag and locate plants around the world. In: International Conference on Smart Technologies and Management for Computing, Communication, Controls, Energy and Materials (ICSTM), pp. 153–158 (2015)
5. Filsecker, M., Hickey, D.T.: A multilevel analysis of the effects of external rewards on elementary students' motivation, engagement and learning in an educational game. Comput. Educ. **75**, 136–148 (2014)
6. Frisch, J.K., Unwin, M.M., Saunders, G.W.: Name that plant! Overcoming plant blindness and developing a sense of place using science and environmental education. In: Bodzin, A., Shiner Klein, B., Weaver, S. (eds.) The Inclusion of Environmental Education in Science Teacher Education, pp. 143–157. Springer, Dordrecht (2010). https://doi.org/10.1007/978-90-481-9222-9_10
7. Ahlqvist, O., Schlieder, C.: Geogames and Geoplay, Game-Based Approaches to the Analysis of Geo-Information. Springer, Heidelberg (2018). https://doi.org/10.1007/978-3-319-22774-0
8. Gicquel, P.-Y., George, S., Laforcade, P., Marfisi-Schottman, I.: Design of a component-based mobile learning game authoring tool. In: Dias, J., Santos, P.A., Veltkamp, R.C. (eds.) GALA 2017. LNCS, vol. 10653, pp. 208–217. Springer, Cham (2017). https://doi.org/10.1007/978-3-319-71940-5_19
9. Han, J., Haihong, E., Le, G.I., Du, J.: Survey on NoSQL database. In: 6th IEEE International Conference on Pervasive Computing and Applications, pp. 363–366 (2011)
10. Nam, Y., Hwang, E., Kim, D.: CLOVER: a mobile content-based leaf image retrieval system. In: Fox, E.A., Neuhold, E.J., Premsmit, P., Wuwongse, V. (eds.) ICADL 2005. LNCS, vol. 3815, pp. 139–148. Springer, Heidelberg (2005). https://doi.org/10.1007/11599517_16
11. Nguyen, T.T.N., Le, T.L., Vu, H., Hoang, V.S., Tran, T.H.: Crowdsourcing for botanical data collection towards to automatic plant identification: a review. Comput. Electron. Agric. **155**, 412–425 (2018)

12. Pimentel, V., Nickerson, B.G.: Communicating and displaying real-time data with websocket. IEEE Internet Comput. **16**(4), 45–53 (2012)
13. Roman, L.A., McPherson, E.G., Scharenbroch, B.C., Bartens, J.: Identifying common practices and challenges for local urban tree monitoring programs across the United States. Arboric. Urban Forest. **39**(6), 292–299 (2013)
14. Skjoth, C.A., et al.: An inventory of tree species in European essential data input for air pollution modelling. Large Scale Comput. Environ. Model. **217**(3), 292–304 (2008)

Applications and Case Studies

Lifelong Learning with a Digital Math Game: Performance and Basic Experience Differences Across Age

Simon Greipl[1(✉)], Korbinian Moeller[1,2,4], Kristian Kiili[3], and Manuel Ninaus[1,4]

[1] Leibniz-Institut für Wissensmedien, Tübingen, Germany
{s.greipl,k.moeller,m.ninaus}@iwm-tuebingen.de
[2] Department of Psychology, Eberhard-Karls University, Tübingen, Germany
[3] TUT Game Lab, Tampere University of Technology, Pori, Finland
kristian.kiili@tut.fi
[4] LEAD Graduate School and Research Network, University of Tübingen, Tübingen, Germany

Abstract. Gaming is acknowledged as a natural way of learning and established as a mainstream activity. Nevertheless, gaming performance and subjective game experience were hardly examined across adult age groups for which the game was not intended to. In contrast to serious games as specific tools against a natural, age-related decline in cognitive performance, we evaluated performance and subjective experiences of the established math learning game *Semideus* across three age groups from 19 to 79. Observed decline in performance in terms of processing speed were not exclusively predicted by age, but also by gaming frequency. Strongest age-related drops of processing speed were found for the middle-aged group aged 35 to 59 years. On the other hand, more knowledge-dependent performance measures like the amount of correctly solved problems remained comparably stable. According to subjective ratings, the middle-aged group experienced the game as less fluent and automatic compared to the younger and older groups. Additionally, the elderly group of participants reported fewer negative attitudes towards technology than both younger groups. We conclude that, albeit performance differences with respect to processing speed, subjective gaming experience stayed on an overall high positive level. This further encourages the use of games for learning across age.

Keywords: Game-based learning · Life-long learning · Reliability · Applicability · Number-line estimation · User-experience · Elderly

1 Introduction

While gaming is largely established as a mainstream activity among teenagers and (young) adults alike [e.g. 1], there is also a substantial share of gamers aged 50 and above. The ESA reports that with 21% of gamers beyond the age 50 this age group shows the second highest percentage together with the age group of individuals 18 years and younger [2]. In the vein of Huizinga's 'Homo Ludens' [3], there seems to be

A. Liapis et al. (Eds.): GALA 2019, LNCS 11899, pp. 301–311, 2019.
https://doi.org/10.1007/978-3-030-34350-7_29

no decline in the engagement in playful activities with age. This leads to the intriguing question why the attempt to exploit, for instance, the motivational potential of games for learning still focuses primarily on younger populations [e.g. 4]. Educational studies widely acknowledge that play is a natural way for children to learn [5]. Yet, there seems to be a traditional dichotomy between learning and playing [6]. Moreover, the gradual detachment of learning and playing with higher levels of the educational system [7] seems paradoxical [8]. In the current study, we try to apply a math game on fraction knowledge, usually played by primary and/or secondary school students, to age groups from 19 to 79 in order to explore differences of game-related performance as well as subjective experiences with respect to the game-based learning environment.

(Serious) Games and Their Applications for the Adult and Elderly Population. Serious games for rehabilitation purposes are becoming increasingly popular [9] and can be distinguished in three types: physical, cognitive, and social as reported in the review of Ngyuen and colleagues [10]. While games aiming at physical and cognitive effects make up most of the studied effects, about 75% of studies also found a positive impact on well-being in the elderly [10]. However, there are restrictions in the interpretation of these results. Most of the reviewed games were utilized to compensate impairments and disabilities on the physical or cognitive level (e.g., memory, attention, problem solving, etc.), acquired through diseases or injury, and to overcome repetitive characteristics of therapy and training processes [11]. Besides actual clinical conditions, there is a natural association between aging and a decline in cognition and perception as well as an increase in physical impairments which should be considered in the design of games [e.g. 12, 13]. So far, most articles examined the impact of digital games on well-being, brain plasticity or decreasing cognitive abilities in (children and) seniors. However, healthy adult populations were found to benefit from game-based trainings as tools to enhance cognitive and emotional skills as well [14]. Importantly, a recent book takes a perspective on senior gamers and games for the elderly in general and goes beyond aspects of compensation of age-related or incidence-related declines. It explicitly avoids the view of reducing "…older players to a stereotype or design for them without talking and testing game designs with them." [15] but includes knowledge and experience of older generations by establishing a framework for game-based lifelong learning [6] or intergenerational game-design workshops [16] to promote, for instance, intergenerational learning and exchange.

Gaming Through the Lifespan. The *gerontoludic manifesto* [17] suggests (amongst others) that gaming research and design should focus on heterogeneity but not on stereotyping, because older gamers vary considerably in terms of preferences, experiences or health status. Not only for the adult, but also for the (healthy) elderly population, this raises the question whether commonly used games in the context of learning or even entertainment maintain their applicability with respect to their main qualities, they are usually evaluated on. While mobile applications were already successful in, for instance, assessing cognitive functions across the lifespan [e.g. 18], to our knowledge only one study examined the same gaming environment on heterogeneous age samples. The authors assessed motor development with a Kinect sensor across the lifespan embedded in a serious game for rehabilitation [19]. The study replicated that cognitive performance across the lifespan first increases and then decreases again – a quadratic trend known from neuropsychological evidence on maturation [20] and aging [21] suggesting a climax of cognitive performance in terms of processing speed in the mid 30's.

To advance and extend this knowledge to the cognitive domain in terms of acceptance and applicability of serious games, we used a tablet-based math game that is usually played by and designed for high school aged children. According to previous research, the "acceptance of serious games is independent of gender, technical expertise, gaming habits, and only weakly influenced by age. Determinants of acceptance are perceived fun and the feeling that the users can make playing the game a habit" [22]. This means that subjective experiences should have a high impact on the acceptance of serious games. In contrast, performance in the game should mostly be influenced by age and previous gaming experience [22]. For the current purpose, we followed a similar distinction, separately evaluating the game with respect to the domains *Cognition* and (subjective) *Player Experiences/Attitudes.*

Cognition. The present game aims at assessing and training fraction understanding. Generally, deficits in numerical competencies can have critical drawbacks on an individual as well as societal level [23]. The game comprises two tasks, of which the first one, *number-line estimation*, requires the player to navigate an avatar along a horizontal number-line to accurately indicate the correct location of a target fraction (e.g. where goes 4/7 on a number line from 0–1?). This type of task is commonly used for training number magnitude understanding [e.g. 24] and performance in this task is associated with mathematical achievement [25]. In the second task, *magnitude comparison*, the magnitudes of two fractions need to be compared. Both tasks can be evaluated in terms of speed (how much time to solve a comparison/number-line estimation) and error rate (how many correct items per session). The number-line estimation task also captured accuracy (how close was the indicated solution to the correct location).

Age related cognitive declines are most significantly found in components of fluid cognition [26] such as processing speed [27], whereas the crystallized part of cognition, this means knowledge and experience, is comparably stable, rarely starting to decline until the age of 65 [26]. While in-game performance measure such as speed can clearly be attributed to the former part of cognition, error rate/accuracy should be more (fraction) knowledge-dependent and therefore part of the latter domain. We generally expected an overall age-related decline in performance. However, this should be true for measures associated with speed, but not necessarily for others (e.g. accuracy). We further hypothesise that in-game performance metrics might be influenced by participants' prior tablet use and their gaming frequency.

Player Experiences/Attitudes. Additionally, we were interested in whether and how players across different age groups might perceive and experience the game differently. Therefore, we assessed participants' experienced flow, a widely used measure in game-based learning [28]. We further captured other aspects of user experience such as attractiveness, pragmatic quality (e.g. handling) and hedonic quality (e.g. novelty) of the game, that are often investigated when evaluating software [29, see e.g. 30]. Finally, we also try to shed light on the question whether there is an age-related change in general affinity and attitude towards technology [31, 32], which in the context of serious games, has not been evaluated so far.

2 Methods

The game took about 10–15 min, involved both number line estimations and magnitude comparisons, and was completed by 3 different age groups (see Sect. 2.1 below). For both tasks we compared performance across 3 age groups. Data presented in this paper is preliminary and part of a larger ongoing project including other measures such as basic intelligence scales and assessments of basic math competencies, which are not relevant for the current study.

2.1 Participants

78 adults from three age groups participated in the current study: (i) 33 participants below 35 years of age ($M = 25.15$ years; $SD = 3.76$ years; 25 females), (ii) 21 participants between 35 to 59 years of age ($M = 46.05$ years; $SD = 6.83$ years; 25 females) and (iii) 24 participants aged 60 years and above ($M = 66.04$ years; $SD = 4.35$ years; 11 females). Participants were recruited via online and newspaper advertisements. The study was approved by the local ethics committee.

2.2 Measurements

The first and main part of the current study was the assessment with the learning game *Semideus*. As mentioned above, the game consisted of two tasks, *number-line estimation* and *magnitude comparison*. In the former, participants are asked to indicate the spatial position of a target number/fraction (e.g. 5/8) along a number-line with fixed ends (e.g. 0 and 1; see Fig. 1). This task is complemented by the comparison task, in which participants had to put two fractions, represented by two piled blocks that displayed two different fractions, in ascending order with regard to the numerical magnitudes depicted on them (e.g., which is larger 4/7 or 1/2). The game was played on an Apple iPad. The main mechanics of the game required controlling the avatar walking along the number-line by tilting the Tablet. All other operations such as confirming to be on the right position on the number line are realized via button presses on top-left or top-right positions on the touchscreen. The game-session involved an onboarding phase and the actual assessment phase. The former was assisted by the experimenter and aimed at familiarizing players with controls and game mechanics. Hence, whole numbers instead of fractions were used in this phase. The latter was played without assistance and only these data were analysed in the current study (for further details see also [33], Fig. 1 and https://youtu.be/rhl88VvGCvI). Therefore, assessments regarding the *Cognition* domain took place in-game. The time to solve each item (speed), the number of correct items (error rate), and for number line estimation the accuracy of correct estimations were used (note that an estimation was considered correct when not more than 8% off the correct location).

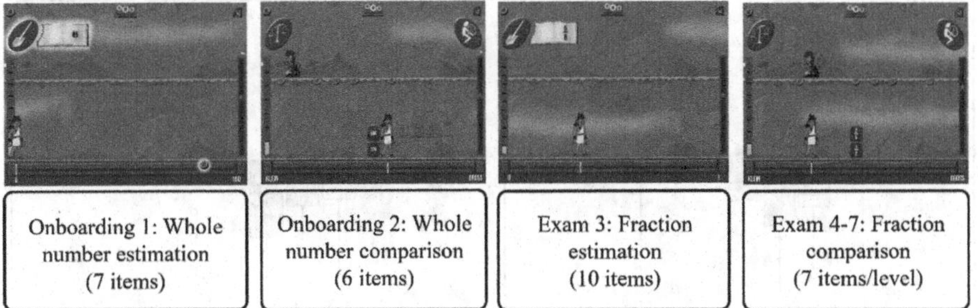

Fig. 1. Screenshots of "Semideus" showing the level structure.

The second part of the current study comprised questionnaires regarding the (subjective) *experiences* domain. To measure subjective experiences with the game and attitudes towards technology we employed the Flow-Scale (FKS [34], subscales: automaticity, absorption), the User Experience Questionnaire (UEQ [29], subscales: attractiveness, pragmatic quality, hedonic quality), and a questionnaire regarding general affinity for technology (Fragebogen zur Technikaffinität (TA-EG) [35], negative/positive attitude toward technology).

Finally, gaming frequency (never = 5 to daily = 1, scale was recoded for analysis) and tablet use (never = 1 to daily = 7) was assessed on a Likert scale.

2.3 Procedure

Before playing the game on the tablet participants received written instruction on the handling and the tasks within the game. Next, participants started the onboarding phase which included 7 number-line estimation tasks and 6 magnitude comparison tasks, both with whole numbers instead of fractions to lower the initial hurdle. This phase contained one level with 10 estimation items and three comparison levels with 7 items each. Game-play was immediately followed by the utilized questionnaires.

3 Results

Cognition. We analyzed group differences using regression models, comparing each age group against its younger one using gaming frequency and tablet use as additional predictors. Performance variables were divided into speed, error, and accuracy measures for both tasks with accuracy only evaluated for number line estimation. Hence, we analyzed a total of five models. The only significant model in our analysis was the one on speed in the comparison task. It explained 27.4% of variance [$adj.\ R^2 = .274$, $F(4,73) = 8.272$, $p < .001$][1]. Group 2 (35–59 years) showed a significant increase in time needed to solve the comparison task ($\beta = 0.256$, $p < .05$) in comparison to group

[1] Results did not change substantially when age was used as continuous variable: [$adj.\ R^2 = .309$, $F(3,73) = 12.36$, $p < .001$]

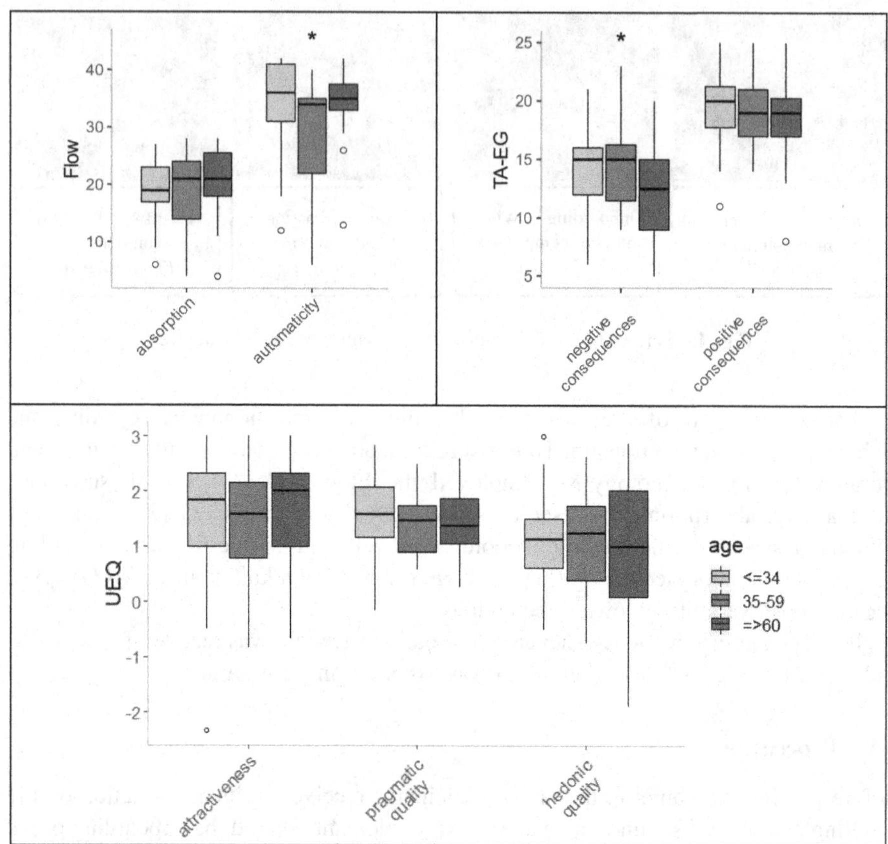

Fig. 2. Top left: Flow scale. Top-right: Affinity for technology scales. Bottom: User Experience Questionnaire – UEQ. The bold horizontal line represents the median and the lower and upper hinges correspond to the first and third quartiles. Upper and lower whiskers extend from the hinge no further than 1.5 * inter-quartile range. Asteriscs indicate significant comparisons.

1 (19–34 years), but this was not present for group 3 (60 years and above) when compared to group 2 ($\beta = 0.181$, $p = .13$). Additionally, higher gaming frequency significantly predicted higher speed in the comparison task ($\beta = -0.266$, $p < .05$). Tablet use did not account for unique parts of the variance ($\beta = -0.097$, $p < .05$). The model on number of errors for magnitude comparison was not significant [*adj.* $R^2 = .049$, $F(4,73) = 1.998$, $p = .104$].

No significant models were identified for speed [*adj.* $R^2 = .053$, $F(4,73) = 2.076$, $p < .1$][2], number of errors [*adj.* $R^2 < .01$, $F(4,73) = 0.607$, $p = .65$], and accuracy for number line estimation tasks [*adj.* $R^2 < .01$, $F(4,73) = 1.04$, $p = .39$].

[2] Results did not change substantially when age was used as continuous variable: [*adj.* $R^2 = .016$, $F(3,73) = 1.41$, $p = .246$]

Player Experiences/Attitudes. We used separate multivariate analyses of variance (MANOVAs) for each questionnaire to examine differences between age groups. For the flow-scale, the analysis revealed marginally significant group differences [F (4,148) = 2.0695, p = .088, η^2 = .053; see Fig. 2]. Univariate post-hoc t-tests showed that group 2 (M = 29.380) felt the game experience to be more fluent or automatic, respectively (p < .05). No differences were found for absorption.

Affinity for technology scales showed a significant effect for age groups [(F (4,146) = 2.070, p = .019, η^2 = .077; see Fig. 2]. Univariate post-hoc t-tests indicated that means for both group 1 (M = 14.515) and group 2 (M = 14.650) were significantly higher than for group 3 (M = 12.126, both p < .05). That is, groups 1 and 2 anticipated more negative consequences for society from technology use than the elderly group.

Finally, no significant group effect was revealed with respect to the user experience questionnaire [F(12,140) = 1.2141, p = .279, η^2 = .094; see Fig. 2].

4 Discussion and Conclusion

In the current study, we focussed on two domains of game-based learning across age, *cognitive* factors such as performance and subjective *experiences* as a user/player. By addressing these aspects across age, we gained new insights into the applicability and usability of an existing, evaluated, and well documented game-based learning environment for age groups other than it was originally intended and designed for.

With respect to the cognitive domain, we hardly found age-related changes of performance. Findings related to speed were largely congruent with evidence on general cognitive ageing in terms of an age-related decline in speeded performance [27]. However, strong speed-related effects of age were only present in the comparison task. Moreover, gaming frequency was another significant predictor of speed differences alongside age. That is, young players between 19 and 34 years of age responded to faster than participants aged 35–59. Interestingly, a similar effect was not found for number-line estimation. However, our predictors or model, respectively, did not explain number line estimation data significantly so that it is likely that there is/are an unknown factor/s influencing speed in number-line estimation. For the comparison task, we may assume that, on the one hand, processing speed reflects overall age-related performance decline, but, on the other hand, handling differences between tasks might have affected results as well. These might arose because the comparison task required players to perform a more complex combination of tilting and pressing two additional buttons on the tablet to successfully solve an item as compared to the number line estimation task. In magnitude comparison trials players had to pick up the stones/fractions (button press) and place them (tilting) according to their numerical magnitude. This might have placed additional obstacles for older participants than the number line estimation task, where only tilting (i.e., navigating the avatar to the correct location) and one button press (i.e., confirming the location) was required. However, this alternative interpretation was not substantiated by our results as player's tablet use did not significantly predict speed in magnitude comparison (or number line estimation). Moreover, pragmatic quality (i.e. handling) of the game was rated similar across age groups.

Our analysis showed that the most significant performance drop as regards speed occurred in the group aged between 35 to 59 and not within the age group above 60 years. Finally, we were not able to explain any differences in error rates or accuracy across age. This might be due to the fact that the ability to just correctly or accurately solve the tasks of the game is primarily knowledge-based and part of the crystallized part of cognition, which is rather stable across age [26].

Differences in (subjective) experiences across age groups were found for flow experience and affinity for technology. Participants aged between 35 and 59 experienced gaming as a less automatized process (e.g. "having more trouble to concentrate") compared to both other age groups. Furthermore, together with the youngest group of participants they seemed to anticipate more negative influences of technology use/digitalization on society than the group aged 60 and above. Seemingly consistent with above reported results on performance, a more negative attitude towards technology and less experience of automaticity during gameplay may accompany the performance decline in the middle-aged group. Most prominently, we did not find differences across age in terms of perceived quality of the game or its attractiveness to the individual participant.

Accordingly, we found no signs of a decline of the perceived entertaining nature of the game nor its pragmatic quality (including its controllability and handling). Generally, players across all age groups rated the game equally positive.

From a game-design perspective, we may conclude that games using, for instance, scaffolded feedback and high scores that depend on player's in-game performance should adapt these features to age appropriate norms. Particularly with respect to speed related feedback elements, there might be the chance that, for example, inappropriate or even continuously lowered rewards because of lower speeded play might lead to undesirable effects like demotivation and frustration of elderly player.

Future studies should continue to investigate factors influencing age-related performance differences in digital games. Our analyses revealed that age, gaming frequency, and tablet use do not cover the entire variance at least in the non-speed-related performance measures of our study. First, educational and professional background may be potentially relevant variables contributing to differences not only within but also across age groups. Second, education/profession and gaming experience should be assessed and examined in more detail. For instance, gaming experience may qualitatively vary over the lifespan, for instance, different game genres played or devices used by different age groups [e.g. 2, 18]. Literature, for instance, suggests that video game experience is differentially associated with cognitive markers like memory and attention in older adults compared to the younger population [18]. Additionally, more attention should be drawn on the details of the relationship between experiential and performance dimension in game-based learning environments across age.

In conclusion, we did only find age-related declines in in-game performance measures reflecting processing speed. However, the observed relationship was never exclusively due to age but also influenced by gaming frequency. A significant drop in speed seemed to take place within the age range of 35 to 59 rather in the range above 60. Although designed for a different target group (i.e., elementary and secondary school students), we did not find conclusive evidence that individuals of different higher ages perceived or experienced the game differently in general. Only the middle-aged group experienced playing the game as a less "fluid" or automatic process, whereas elderly participants and younger adults rated the game comparably positive. In sum, alongside literature-consistent performance differences, experiences with the math-game originally designed for a younger target group did not seem not to vary significantly across the ages from 19 to 79.

References

1. Lenhart, A., Kahne, J., Middaugh, E., Macgill, A.R., Evans, C., Vitak, J.: Teens' gaming experiences are diverse and include significant social interaction and civic engagement. Pew Internet & American Life Project (2008)
2. ESA: Entertainment Software Association (2019). https://www.theesa.com/wp-content/uploads/2019/05/ESA_Essential_facts_2019_final.pdf
3. Huizinga, J., Flitner, A.: Homo Ludens: vom Ursprung der Kultur im Spiel. Rowohlt Taschenbuch Verlag, Hamburg (2017)
4. Hainey, T., Connolly, T.M., Boyle, E.A., Wilson, A., Razak, A.: A systematic literature review of games-based learning empirical evidence in primary education. Comput. Educ. **102**, 202–223 (2016). https://doi.org/10.1016/j.compedu.2016.09.001
5. Edwards, C.P.: Three approaches from Europe: Waldorf, Montessori, and Reggio Emilia. Early Child. Res. Pract. **4**, n1 (2002)
6. Romero, M., Ouellet, H., Sawchuk, K.: Expanding the game design play and experience framework for game-based lifelong learning (gd-lll-pe). In: Romero, M., Sawchuk, K., Blat, J., Sayago, S., Ouellet, H. (eds.) Game-Based Learning Across the Lifespan. AGL, pp. 1–11. Springer, Cham (2017). https://doi.org/10.1007/978-3-319-41797-4_1
7. Ritterfeld, U., Cody, M.J., Vorderer, P. (eds.): Serious Games: Mechanisms and Effects. Routledge, New York (2009)
8. Greipl, S., Moeller, K., Ninaus, M.: Potential and limits of game-based learning. Int. J. Technol. Enhanced Learn. (in press)
9. Bonnechère, B., Jansen, B., Omelina, L., Van Sint Jan, S.: The use of commercial video games in rehabilitation: a systematic review. Int. J. Rehabil. Res. **39**, 277–290 (2016). https://doi.org/10.1097/MRR.0000000000000190
10. Nguyen, H., et al.: Impact of Serious Games on Health and Well-being of Elderly: A Systematic Review, vol. 10
11. Rego, P., Moreira, P.M., Reis, L.P.: Serious games for rehabilitation: a survey and a classification towards a taxonomy. In: 5th Iberian Conference on Information Systems and Technologies, pp. 1–6 (2010)
12. Fisk, A.D., Czaja, S.J., Rogers, W.A., Charness, N., Czaja, S.J., Sharit, J.: Designing for Older Adults: Principles and Creative Human Factors Approaches, 2nd edn. CRC Press (2018). https://doi.org/10.1201/9781420080681
13. Farage, M.A., Miller, K.W., Ajayi, F., Hutchins, D.: Design principles to accommodate older adults. Glob. J. Health Sci. **4** (2012). https://doi.org/10.5539/gjhs.v4n2p2
14. Pallavicini, F., Ferrari, A., Mantovani, F.: Video games for well-being: a systematic review on the application of computer games for cognitive and emotional training in the adult population. Front. Psychol. **9** (2018). https://doi.org/10.3389/fpsyg.2018.02127

15. Romero, M., Sawchuk, K., Blat, J., Sayago, S., Ouellet, H. (eds.): Game-Based Learning Across the Lifespan: Cross-Generational and Age-Oriented Topics. Springer, Cham (2017). https://doi.org/10.1007/978-3-319-41797-4
16. De Schutter, B., Roberts, A.R., Franks, K.: Miami six-o: lessons learned from an intergenerational game design workshop. In: Romero, M., Sawchuk, K., Blat, J., Sayago, S., Ouellet, H. (eds.) Game-Based Learning Across the Lifespan. AGL, pp. 13–27. Springer, Cham (2017). https://doi.org/10.1007/978-3-319-41797-4_2
17. De Schutter, B., Vanden Abeele, V.: Towards a gerontoludic manifesto. Anthropol. Aging **36**, 112–120 (2015). https://doi.org/10.5195/aa.2015.104
18. Lee, H., et al.: Examining cognitive function across the lifespan using a mobile application. Comput. Hum. Behav. **28**, 1934–1946 (2012). https://doi.org/10.1016/j.chb.2012.05.013
19. Bonnechère, B., Sholukha, V., Omelina, L., Van Vooren, M., Jansen, B., Van Sint Jan, S.: Suitability of functional evaluation embedded in serious game rehabilitation exercises to assess motor development across lifespan. Gait Posture **57**, 35–39 (2017). https://doi.org/10.1016/j.gaitpost.2017.05.025
20. Teulier, C., Lee, D.K., Ulrich, B.D.: Early gait development in human infants: plasticity and clinical applications: early gait development. Dev. Psychobiol. **57**, 447–458 (2015). https://doi.org/10.1002/dev.21291
21. Trewartha, K.M., Garcia, A., Wolpert, D.M., Flanagan, J.R.: Fast but fleeting: adaptive motor learning processes associated with aging and cognitive decline. J. Neurosci. **34**, 13411–13421 (2014). https://doi.org/10.1523/JNEUROSCI.1489-14.2014
22. Wittland, J., Brauner, P., Ziefle, M.: Serious games for cognitive training in ambient assisted living environments – a technology acceptance perspective. In: Abascal, J., Barbosa, S., Fetter, M., Gross, T., Palanque, P., Winckler, M. (eds.) INTERACT 2015. LNCS, vol. 9296, pp. 453–471. Springer, Cham (2015). https://doi.org/10.1007/978-3-319-22701-6_34
23. Beddington, J., Cooper, C.L.: The mental wealth of nations. Nature **455**, 3 (2008)
24. Siegler, R.S., Opfer, J.E.: The development of numerical estimation: evidence for multiple representations of numerical quantity. Psychol. Sci. **14**, 237–243 (2003). https://doi.org/10.1111/1467-9280.02438
25. Geary, D.C., Hoard, M.K., Nugent, L., Byrd-Craven, J.: Development of number line representations in children with mathematical learning disability. Dev. Neuropsychol. **33**, 277–299 (2008). https://doi.org/10.1080/87565640801982361
26. Cavanaugh, J.C., Blanchard-Fields, F.: Adult Development and Aging. Wadsworth/Thomson Learning, Belmont (2006)
27. Salthouse, T.A.: The Processing-Speed Theory of Adult Age Differences in Cognition, vol. 26
28. Perttula, A., Kiili, K., Lindstedt, A., Tuomi, P.: Flow experience in game based learning – a systematic literature review. Int. J. Serious Games **4** (2017). https://doi.org/10.17083/ijsg.v4i1.151
29. Laugwitz, B., Schrepp, M., Held, T.: Konstruktion eines Fragebogens zur Messung der User Experience von Softwareprodukten. In: Heinecke, A.M., Paul, H. (eds.) Mensch und Computer 2006: Mensch und Computer im Strukturwandel, pp. 125–134. Oldenbourg Verlag, München (2006)
30. Giannopoulos, I., Kiefer, P., Raubal, M.: GazeNav: gaze-based pedestrian navigation. In: Proceedings of the 17th International Conference on Human-Computer Interaction with Mobile Devices and Services - MobileHCI 2015, pp. 337–346. ACM Press, Copenhagen (2015). https://doi.org/10.1145/2785830.2785873
31. Czaja, S.J., Sharit, J.: Age differences in attitudes toward computers. J. Gerontol. B Psychol. Sci. Soc. Sci. **53B**, P329–P340 (1998). https://doi.org/10.1093/geronb/53B.5.P329

32. Eastman, J.K., Iyer, R.: The impact of cognitive age on Internet use of the elderly: an introduction to the public policy implications. Int. J. Consum. Stud. **29**, 125–136 (2005). https://doi.org/10.1111/j.1470-6431.2004.00424.x
33. Ninaus, M., Kiili, K., McMullen, J., Moeller, K.: Assessing fraction knowledge by a digital game. Comput. Hum. Behav. **70**, 197–206 (2017). https://doi.org/10.1016/j.chb.2017.01.004
34. Rheinberg, F., Vollmeyer, R., Engeser, S.: Die erfassung des flow-erlebens (2003)
35. Karrer, K., Glaser, C., Clemens, C., Bruder, C.: Technikaffinität erfassen–der Fragebogen TA-EG. Der Mensch im Mittelpunkt technischer Systeme. **8**, 196–201 (2009)

Learning Geothermal Energy Basics with the Serious Game HotPipe

Liam Mac an Bhaird, Mohammed Al Owayyed, Ronald van Driel, Huinan Jiang, Runar A. Johannessen, Nestor Z. Salamon, J. Timothy Balint, and Rafael Bidarra(✉)

Faculty of Electrical Engineering, Mathematics and Computer Science, Delft University of Technology, Delft, The Netherlands
R.Bidarra@tudelft.nl

Abstract. Burning fossil fuels is a big part of our heat production. Since this process is both non-renewable and polluting, finding other options is important. A clean and underutilized alternative is geothermal energy. However, it is often not considered due to sheer ignorance or misconceptions. HotPipe is a serious game designed to alleviate these problems, particularly among youth populations. Players control a drill to create geothermal wells solving a variety of puzzles, which introduce relevant cases for geothermal heating and show what geothermal wells are made of. The game focuses primarily on conveying the concepts of *water circulation*, *relation between temperature and depth*, and *rock type proprieties*. From our game evaluation, players revealed a solid improvement on their geothermal energy knowledge.

Keywords: Renewable energy · Geothermal heating · Doublet · Drilling · Puzzle · Serious games · Sandstone

1 Introduction

According to figures published by Energie Beheer Nederland [9], heat consumption accounts for nearly 40% of overall primary energy consumption in the Netherlands. This consumption is mainly produced by burning fossil fuels, particularly natural gas. Conventionally, conversion to renewable energy would reduce the established adverse effects of burning fossil fuels [15]. Geothermal energy is regarded as a suitable alternative to fossil fuels [19] as it is eco-friendly, economical in the long term, and efficient. Geothermal systems take advantage of the earth's heat by extracting it from the subsurface. Heat extraction occurs by using pipes to transfer fluids (e.g., water) from subsurface geothermal reservoirs to the surface and vice-versa. Common geothermal reservoirs are *aquifers*, porous ground layers that contain hot fluids. In order to achieve the transfer, a cycle with two wells is needed: one to obtain hot water and the other to inject the water after the heat has been extracted [13]. Such production wells are assumed to last 30 years and require approximately 100 years to regenerate [1].

A. Liapis et al. (Eds.): GALA 2019, LNCS 11899, pp. 312–321, 2019.
https://doi.org/10.1007/978-3-030-34350-7_30

We introduce HotPipe, a serious game that aims at conveying the basic concepts of geothermal heating systems, thus countering ignorance and misconceptions in this domain. Its target audience is the youth, particularly senior high school and undergraduate students. HotPipe is a 2D puzzle game in which the player implements a geothermal system by drilling through a tile-based maze representing the Earth's subsurface, to connect pipes to the underground water reservoirs. A screenshot of one of the early game levels is shown in Fig. 1. Specifically, the game aims at conveying the knowledge of:

- water circulation mechanisms of a geothermal well;
- positive correlation between temperature and depth in the subsurface;
- some rock type properties influence drilling speed; and
- sandstone is the preferable rock type for a water reservoir.

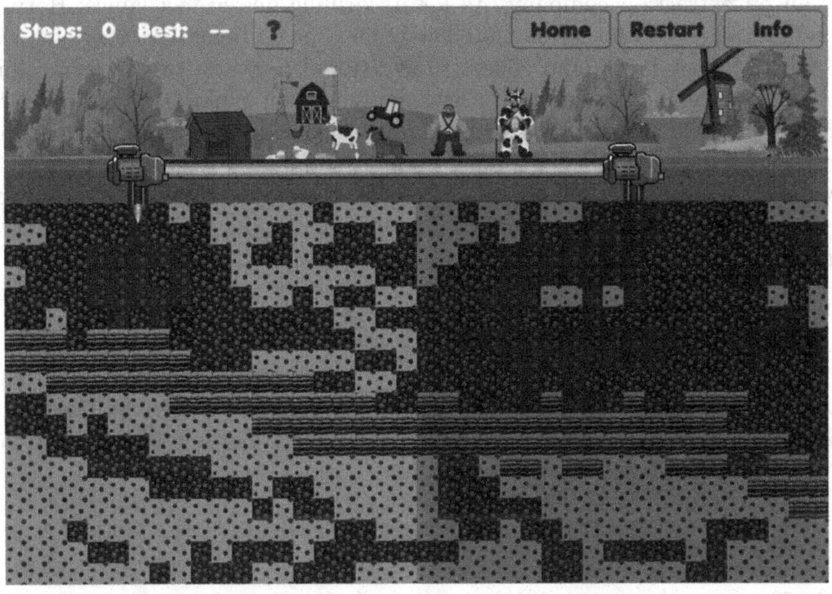

Fig. 1. HotPipe: screen capture of an early game level

2 Related Work

So far, there have been a few proposals to apply gamification techniques to teach geothermal systems to children. Environment for Kids: Geothermal Energy [17] is a post-lesson quiz aiming to measure children's understanding of geothermal energy and the knowledge they gained from lessons. The Groundwater Term

Game [8] takes this concept one step further by providing a more interactive method for answering questions.

To the best of our knowledge, HotPipe is the first serious game about geothermal energy. However, there have been a few other serious games with some remote similarities. Brasil et al. designed a serious 3D game to train operators in oil drilling fields [6]. The game allows operators to exercise their knowledge and practice handling troublesome situations. MAEGUS is a serious game developed to advocate for sustainable energy [16]. Similar to the oil-drilling game, MAEGUS provides players with real-life situations related to a city's energy consumption plans. A player, being a city planner, must adhere to the plans by providing renewable energy to the city (such as geothermal and wind energy).

Several commercially available games have integrated geothermal energy into their gameplay. An example is Turmoil [4], in which the player takes the role of an oil exploration company to gain profit and develop a town. The game simplifies drilling concepts while focusing more on the financial aspects of running an oil extraction company. As for its drilling-puzzle mechanics, Hotpipe can be compared to Motherload [5]. The main concept behind Motherload is to drill through rock layers and collect the scattered rare minerals by controlling a robot-like machine. However, Motherload focuses on exploration and resource management rather than on puzzle solving as in HotPipe. Pipe-based games tend to have the same idea of linking point A to point B (e.g., Line Puzzle [3], Flow Free [2] and Water Pipes [14]). However, these games depend on connecting various pipes on a 2D surface rather than combining them with drilling in different layers.

3 Game Design

In this section we focus on how HotPipe is designed to engage the players, as well as on how its game mechanics guides them towards the essential concepts, including the rock types and the water flow.

3.1 Story Setting

In HotPipe you are a friendly dwarf named Flint who is out to solve other NPCs' (non-playable characters') heating problems using geothermal systems. Each level is split into two puzzles representing the two core elements of a geothermal system: an injection well and a production well, which we refer to as a *level pair*. A water flow animation is played when both wells are complete and the NPC is able to generate a sufficient amount of heat. The setting is designed this way to not only engage with the mechanics of the game but also have an emotional connection to the characters. This gives the player a purpose to complete each level and the reward of seeing more water flow animations.

3.2 Game Mechanics

HotPipe is a tile-based puzzle game. Most people have played puzzle games, so the game is intuitive and does not distract from the educational goals. The player's goal is to create a geothermal well by drilling into the sandstone. The game provides a map with locations for a drilling site just as it would in real life. Next to this, there is also an info page which helps link the game elements to real world applications in the context of geothermal systems. Game elements on the info page contain items such as characters, rock types, geothermal instruments, as well as a tab dedicated to the general workings of a geothermal system. Additionally, the game allows the player to complete level pairs as many times as possible so as to reinforce the educational aspect. The player is further exposed to the general workings of a geothermal system through the level pair complete (water flow) animation.

Controls. The controls in HotPipe are straightforward and intuitive. The arrow controls move the drill in the direction of the key press, and an undo key allows for safe exploration. There is, however, one 'less intuitive' movement, which is key to making HotPipe a unique puzzle experience: the default move (for shale and sandstone) is 2 tiles. This is something that the player must grow familiar with in the early levels. This is also the game mechanics that puts the player in awkward situations. Wonky controls are not only healthy for puzzle games (such as Portal [21] and Snakebird [18]) but, in this case, also represent that in the real world the driller does not have full control over their drill on certain soils.

Rock Tiles. HotPipe features five rock types: shale, granite, limestone, rock salt and sandstone. The behaviour of the different rock types is explained in Table 1. Each level was designed using tiles of these 5 rock types. Aside from these, there are also pipe tiles and a drill head tile. Drilling can be blocked by pipe tiles, granite tiles and limestone tiles.

Progression. Progression in HotPipe is the result of successive puzzle completion. New levels are unlocked progressively as puzzles are completed. Bonus levels are optional, and have increased difficulty, represented with a trickster NPC so the player knows to expect more of a challenge.

Rewards. In-game rewards are based on the amount of steps it takes for the player to complete the level. When players complete a puzzle, they earn either 1, 2 or 3 Golden Dabbing Dwarfs (GDDs), depending on how close to optimal their solution is. This is an addition which represents a cost of inefficiency in the geothermal world. The player receives a reward for completing all non-bonus levels with an end-of-game sequence. Nonetheless, challenging puzzles are very rewarding in themselves to complete. Our careful level design makes the challenge interesting and fair so as to maximize this reward.

Table 1. Rock type tiles and their behavior in HotPipe.

Rock tile	Rock type	Behavior in the game
	Sandstone	Winning condition, players succeed when they drill to the sandstone tiles (in some levels, multiple layers are used, where digging deeper encounters a higher quality sandstone layer).
	Rock salt	Very soft rock and is drilled through very quickly in real life. This is exaggerated in the game and lets the drill move forward until there is no more rock salt.
	Shale	Medium softness rock. The drill moves two steps through these tiles.
	Limestone	Harder than shale. In the game, this is represented by having a tile that must be broken before it can be drilled through. Once limestone has been broken, the properties act as that of shale.
	Granite	Extremely hard and is generally avoided in drilling practices, as it takes a long time to drill through. In the game, this is represented with an impenetrable rock, a well-known tool in level design.

3.3 Visuals

The art style is purposely simple to put focus on the game mechanics and concepts. The tile set is simplified to a single texture for each rock type. This makes different rock types distinguishable albeit less realistic, as our goal is not to teach the player what the rock types look like, but rather to explain their differences in relation to geothermal drilling.

The most important visual element is the animation showing how water flows in a geothermal system, which plays after the player completes a geothermal well (drilling a level pair). This water flow is a core element to the basic workings of geothermal systems. The steam effect animation clearly illustrates that the water being extracted is hotter than the water being pumped down the well (see Fig. 2). This is repeated for each completed well, in an effort to consistently expose players to this essential concept.

4 Level Design

The main reward mechanic of most puzzle games is the actual puzzle. The puzzle must be challenging enough for the player to struggle a little but still end up learning how to complete the puzzle. Unfortunately the amount of challenge that a puzzle provides is very subjective. Therefore, having a target audience makes it easier to design for a specific group in mind. With the target audience of HotPipe, puzzles need to be slightly more challenging than for young children, as this group is assumed to have been exposed to puzzle games before, making the learning process quicker.

The set of tools used for the puzzle design follows the Gamemaker's toolkit principles [10]. In HotPipe, the level design tools align with the following aspects:

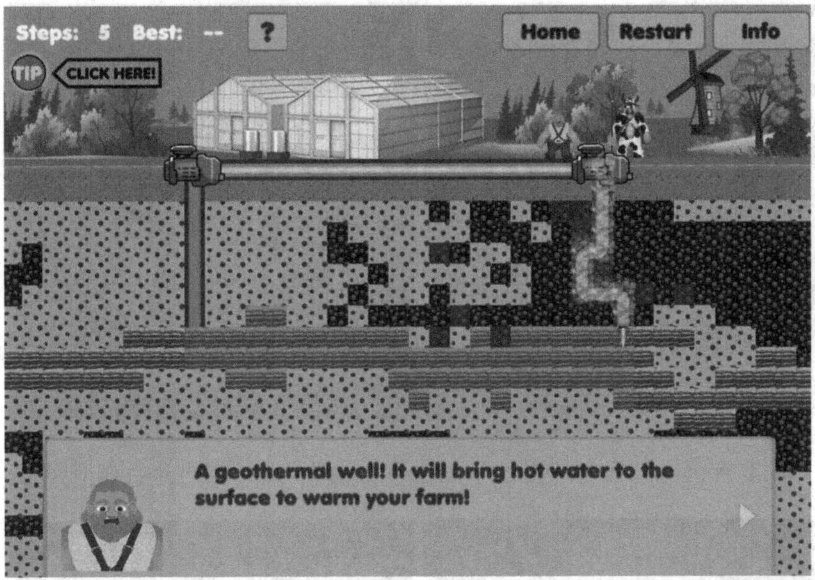

Fig. 2. Water flowing through the system, upon level completion

- **The catch:** a logical contradiction that the player encounters (e.g., turn right to go left).
- **The revelation:** an understanding that the player acquires in order to solve the puzzle (e.g., use an impassable rock to limit further drilling).
- **The assumption:** an assumption can be added to guide a player into the wrong direction, preferably guiding the player into a catch. This assumption must be broken by the player to solve the puzzle (e.g., the player is led to loop around some element).

For the first three levels, the puzzles build upon each other in an introductory fashion, to both retain players and teach them the main workings of the game. Overall, the simplicity of the first levels helps the player focus just on the most relevant game aspects.

Level 1 is an introductory level and is thus kept as simple as possible. Therefore, it only teaches the player the controls and the levels goal.

Level 2 guides the player to the corner of a small corridor. Once the player reaches this corner, they get stuck as there remains no other option but to overshoot the exit, as shown in Fig. 3. Here, they are presented with the catch in that the pipe moves two tiles at a time through this type of rock. This is reinforced if they restart the level and move left. The revelation occurs when they understand that the drill moves two tiles on shale and this is the reason they get trapped leading to the solution shown in Fig. 3.

Level 3 explore the knowledge gained on previous levels. Here the player has already been exposed to the common mechanics of overshooting an exit. Now

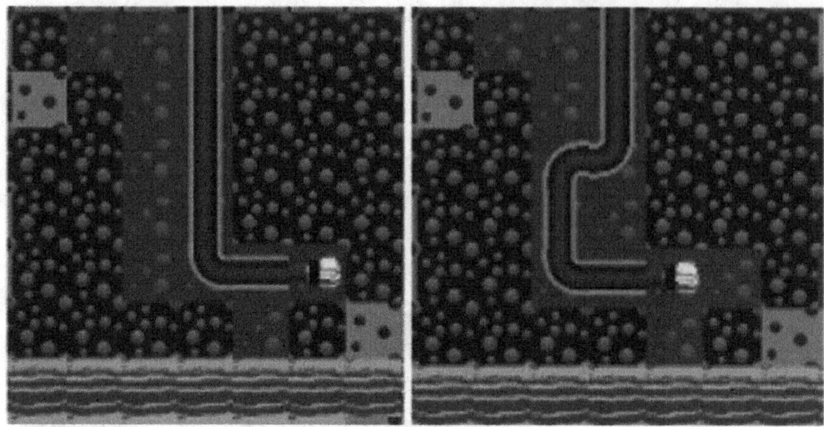

Fig. 3. A player overshooting the exit (left) and the solution learned (right)

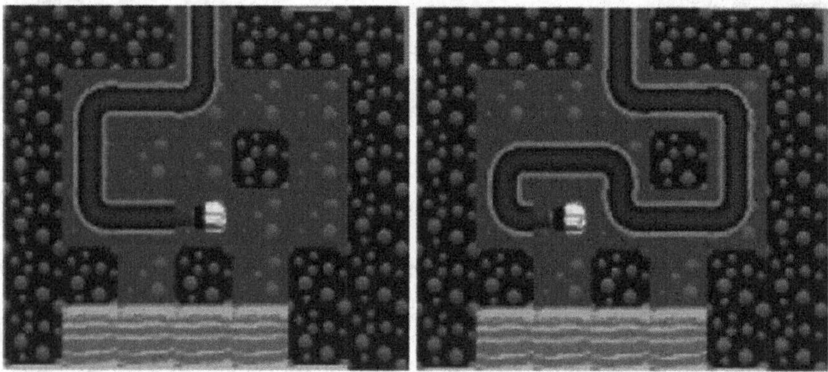

Fig. 4. The player is guided into the revelation that their own pipe can block unwanted drilling progressing.

they only need to be introduced to the not-so-intuitive but common mechanic of using their own pipe to help reach the exit. Again the player is presented with the overshoot problem (Fig. 4). The catch is, this time, they do not have any granite walls that they can use to reach the exit. The player is guided to the solution through: (i) use of minimal possible directions to move at each point, and (ii) the block in the middle of the level, which has no influence on the puzzle's solution other than removing symmetry, but still invites the player to loop around it and further reduces move choice.

After the first three levels, which work as tutorials, the player should be familiar with the controls, the main game mechanics, as well as have experienced two catches. Over the subsequent 17 levels, the player should be able to cope with the increased complexity.

5 Implementation

The game was developed using Unity [20]. Initial level design and testing was done using Puzzlescript [12], an online free-access platform for quickly creating and testing 2D puzzle games.

The game implementation was kept data-oriented, using the same data structure for loading different maps, level backgrounds and character dialogues. For user interface, we implemented window pop-up, fade in, zoom in and scaling effect to enhance players' game feel. The water flow animation in game was done using sprite sequence animation, which simulates the water going through pipes. We also designed particle effects for breaking stones and water steam.

The biggest challenge was the puzzle design. The skill and experience needed to complete each puzzle should not be perceived as too difficult nor too easy. As such it was important that the difficulty started at an accessible level and increased at a good pace to keep the game challenging yet surmountable.

Some technical limitations arose due to the game being 2D and tile-based, the largest one being the simplifications in relation to reality. The tile-based mechanics dictates player movement in that it allows for simple gameplay mechanics and makes puzzle creation easier. On the other hand, it leads the player to drill in an unrealistic fashion by taking sharp turns and not necessarily going straight for the sandstone. While the game is not intended to be a realistic drilling simulator, we did not want to give players a false impression that drilling operations are a simple endeavor. Thus, the info page explains how wells are created in real life and what it requires of planning and calculation to drill correctly.

6 Evaluation

We tested the game with 23 volunteers recruited from TU Delft campus, being 16 volunteers within the audience-targeted range of 15–20 years, and 7 above that range. We designed our evaluation primarily to assess the extent to which the main geothermal concepts and message were captured after playing the game. The participants were asked to play seven levels. On average, they spent two minutes solving introductory levels, and 15 min solving final puzzles.

According to Breuer et al. [7], people tend to learn more if an educational game is engaging. In order to measure the knowledge conveyed by the game, we applied Bloom's taxonomy of educational objectives [11] by defining goals based on the hierarchical levels of the cognitive domain. From the aforementioned domain, the learning goals of HotPipe cover the first three levels: *knowledge* (i.e. remembering learned information), *comprehension* (i.e. understanding the meaning), and the ability to use concepts in a new situation, referred to as *application*. We prepared a brief pre- and post-survey for the participants asking two questions about geothermal systems-related topics (see Fig. 5) to roughly estimate their knowledge before and after playtesting the game. Both surveys had similar questions, but were displayed in randomized order to avoid bias.

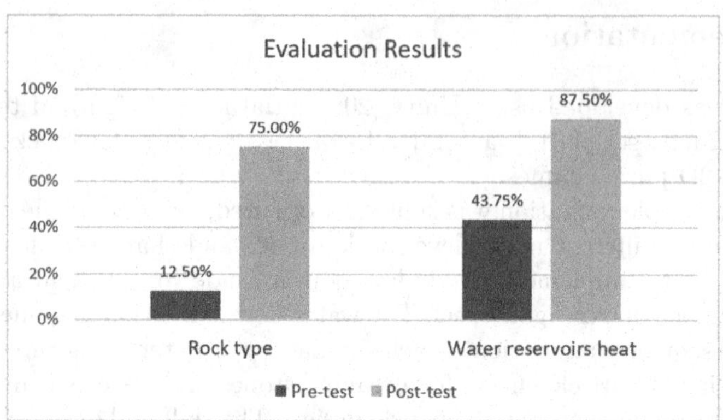

Fig. 5. Percentage of correct answers in pre- and post-surveys.

6.1 Results

The 7 adult participants already had reasonable knowledge about geothermal systems, and thus had little to learn from HotPipe. We therefore focused our analysis on the remaining 16 participants on the target group. Their performance on the surveys increased significantly after playing the game (Fig. 5).

6.2 Discussion

Overall, all participants liked the game and endorsed the controls; most of them described it as easy and intuitive. Almost all the participants figured out the game mechanics by solving the puzzles in order. They did struggle with the last bonus puzzle, but referred to that level as being challenging rather than frustrating, which is a positive indication. We noticed that participants who answered the "rock type" question incorrectly remembered the textures of the rocks. Therefore, we decided to add more elements to the game that display the rock names when hovering over them with a mouse or when a new rock type is introduced in a new level. These elements do not constrict the flow of the puzzles, yet expose the player to rock names more frequently.

7 Conclusions

HotPipe is an intuitive and attractive puzzle game, smoothly integrating education with an enjoyable experience to enhance the appeal of learning. The game focuses on geothermal system fundamentals, including various operations such as drilling and water transfer. As such, HotPipe provides a good introduction to geothermal systems for the target audience. We believe this may be also true for younger groups, due to the atmosphere of friendly competition created.

In the future, we would like to increase the number of levels, as new ideas are still appearing, and some others were put aside for being overly frustrating.

Nonetheless, several other promising geothermal features would deserve further work, including: a store where players can buy drill heads with different properties, a seismic truck for viewing the underground map and ground stimulation techniques.

HotPipe is free to play and is available at: https://hotpipe.itch.io/hotpipe.

Acknowledgement. The authors thank Richard R. Bakker for his helpful suggestions on many geothermal energy-related concepts presented in the game.

References

1. Banwell, C.J.: Life expectancy of geothermal fields. Geother. Energy **2**(7), 12–13 (1974)
2. Big Duck Games LLC: Flow free. http://tiny.cc/ilzocz
3. Bitmango: Line puzzle. http://tiny.cc/vpzocz
4. Bouman, J., Leppen, E.: Turmoil. http://tiny.cc/vrzocz
5. Boyes, S.: Motherload. http://www.xgenstudios.com/play/motherload
6. Brasil, I.S., et al.: An intelligent and persistent browser-based game for oil drilling operators training. In: 2011 IEEE 1st International Conference on Serious Games and Applications for Health (SeGAH), pp. 1–9. IEEE (2011)
7. Breuer, J., Bente, G.: Why so serious? On the relation of serious games and learning. J. Comput. Game Culture **4**, 7–24 (2010)
8. Eirich, M.: The groundwater term game. http://tiny.cc/qxzocz
9. Energie Beheer Nederland B.V. (EBN): Energy in the Netherlands (2016). http://www.energieinnederland.nl/2016
10. Game Maker's Toolkit: What makes a good puzzle? https://youtu.be/zsjC6fa_YBg
11. Krathwohl, D.R., Anderson, L.W.: A Taxonomy for Learning, Teaching, and Assessing: A Revision of Bloom's Taxonomy of Educational Objectives. Longman (2009)
12. Lavelle, S.: Puzzlescript! https://www.puzzlescript.net/
13. Lund, J., Sanner, B., Rybach, L., Curtis, R., Hellstrom, G.: Geothermal (ground-source) heat pumps-a world overview. Geo-Heat Cent. Q. Bull. **25**(3) (2004)
14. Mobiloids: Water pipes. http://tiny.cc/8ozocz
15. Munack, A., Schröder, O., Krahl, J., Bünger, J.: Comparison of relevant exhaust gas emissions from biodiesel and fossil diesel fuel. Agr. Eng. Int.: CIGR J. Sci. Res. Dev. Manuscript EE 01 001 **III** (2001). https://cigrjournal.org/index.php/Ejounral/article/view/195
16. Nataraja, K., Whittinghill, D.: MAEGUS: a sustainable energy simulation to promote energy literacy. In: E-Learn: World Conference on E-Learning in Corporate, Government, Healthcare, and Higher Education (2013)
17. Nelson, K.: Environment for kids: geothermal energy. http://tiny.cc/q2zocz
18. Noumenon Games: Snakebird (2015). http://tiny.cc/kzzocz
19. Omer, A.M.: Ground-source heat pumps systems and applications. Renew. Sustain. Energ. Rev. **12**(2), 344–371 (2008)
20. Unity Technologies: Unity game engine-official site (2019). http://unity.com
21. Valve: Portal. https://store.steampowered.com/app/400/Portal/

Evaluation of Interventions in Blended Learning Using a Communication Skills Serious Game

Raja Lala[1(✉)], Gemma Corbalan[1], and Johan Jeuring[1,2]

[1] Utrecht University, Utrecht, The Netherlands
r.lala@uu.nl

[2] Faculty of Management, Science and Technology, Open University Netherlands, Heerlen, The Netherlands

Abstract. Serious games often employ a scripted dialogue for player interaction with a virtual character. In our serious game Communicate, a domain expert develops a structured, scripted scenario as a sequence of potential interactions in an authoring tool. A player is often a student learning communication skills and a virtual character represents a person that a student talks to. In the original version of Communicate, a player 'converses' with a virtual character by clicking on one of the multiple statement options. Since 2018, we perform blended learning sessions for final year computer science students using Communicate. Our goal is to improve these sessions and in this paper, we apply the action research method over three semesters to iteratively improve these blended learning sessions. In the first semester, our baseline, we conduct sessions where students play a scenario in multiple choice format. In the second semester, we enhance Communicate by enabling a student to enter open text input in an improved scenario. In the third semester, we enhance a session by incorporating peer teaching. Students fill in an evaluation survey after a session and we compare the evaluation of students from the three semesters. Results show that student ratings are significantly higher in sessions incorporating peer teaching compared to the baseline.

1 Introduction

Most professions require communication skills, for example a doctor needs to communicate with a patient [17], while an IT expert discusses system requirements with a client. Generic communication skills such as conflict management, or being assertive are useful for many professionals. Communication skills are best learned through practice, in role play or with a simulated patient [1].

Communicate [4] is a serious game for practising communication skills. A communications expert/teacher scripts a scenario in an authoring tool that provides expressive constructs for variability in a dialogue [6]; see the screenshot at the left hand side in Fig. 1. In the original version of the game, a player

A. Liapis et al. (Eds.): GALA 2019, LNCS 11899, pp. 322–331, 2019.
https://doi.org/10.1007/978-3-030-34350-7_31

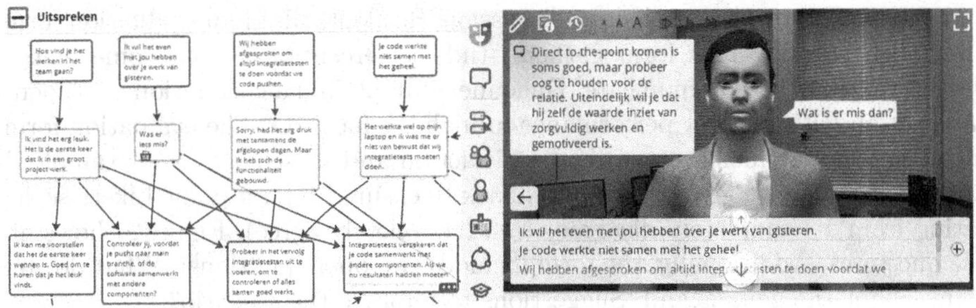

Fig. 1. Communication skills scenario simulation

navigates through a dialogue by selecting a statement option from one of the scripted player statements, see the screenshot at the right hand side in Fig. 1. This is similar to a multiple choice question answer format.

In this paper, we apply the action research method [8] to teach collaboration skills in a blended learning session to final year bachelor computer science students at Utrecht University. We aim to improve these sessions. Lewin [8] describes action research as: 'a spiral of steps, each of which is composed of a circle of planning, action and fact-finding about the result of the action'. In our case, a step is a set of blended learning sessions that we teach per semester. We collect student evaluation in these sessions. At the end of the semester, we critically reflect on the sessions and also analyse the student evaluations to identify potential improvements. We then introduce improvement(s) to the blended learning sessions in the next semester, again collect student evaluations, and compare these to the previous semester.

Final year computer science students at Utrecht University need to work in a project team (of 10 to 12 students each) to develop a software product for a real client. Prior to 2018, we gave a teamwork lecture in a single classroom session to all students. Since the semester spring-summer 2018, we provide a blended learning session: a face-to-face workshop for collaboration skills using Communicate per student project team. We teach a student to handle a collaboration situation where another student in a team (represented as a virtual character in Communicate) does not follow agreed team quality measures (integration tests). In consultation with communication skills experts, we developed a scenario called Collaborate for our students, which uses a protocol consisting of the subject-phases: Approach, Express, Discuss and Agree next steps. We present our study from blended learning sessions with successive batches of final year bachelor computer science students from three semesters: spring-summer 2018, fall-winter 2018 and spring-summer 2019.

We start with sessions where a student plays the Collaborate scenario in a multiple choice manner (in spring-summer 2018). These sessions form our baseline case. In a session an instructor introduces Communicate, students play a scenario, the instructor explains the communication protocol that forms the basis of the scenario, and students play the scenario again. After playing, students and the instructor have a plenary discussion. Students fill in an evaluation form after each session. This form gathers student perceptions about some of the didactic aspects of Communicate. Dhaqane et al. [2] find a correlation of student satisfaction with student performance in higher education. The evaluation form includes five statements on student satisfaction and self-efficacy, for example: I know better how to give relevant feedback, measured on a 5-point Likert scale, rating from 1 (completely disagree) to 5 (completely agree). Figure 2 shows all the questions. Additionally, the form includes two open questions: 'What do you think about the game?' and 'Suggestions to improve the scenario?'

In addition to the evaluation of students, we also look at the application of activity theory to human computer interaction design [5] for potential improvements to our blended learning sessions. Multiple choice versus open text (test)questions are two common forms encountered in learning and education. Choosing from multiple options is similar to a multiple choice test, which often evokes low level cognitive processing, whereas open text response often requires complex thinking [9]. Ozuru et al. [14] conduct a study to compare text comprehension from multiple choice and open text questions. Ozuru et al. find a positive correlation of the performance on open text questions with the quality of an explanation, and a positive correlation of the performance on multiple choice questions with the level of prior knowledge related to the text. In Communicate, a student reads and responds to a text from a virtual character, and gets a score on her performance in a scenario. This is a similar activity as in the study by Ozuru et al. [14], where a student reads a short text while explaining preselected sentences. An open text response should lead a better quality of a response and possibly higher cognitive skills. In fall-winter 2018, we change the activity mechanism for a student to interact with the virtual character by typing open text input.

After fall-winter 2018, we evaluate the blended learning sessions again. A common feedback from students is the wish to play more scenarios. For the activity mechanism we change the interaction between students within a blended learning session to encourage insight in peer behaviour. Goldschmid et al. [3] review peer teaching (when a student teaches another student) in higher education. The authors find that peer teaching among students can enhance active participation, develop skills in cooperation and interaction when used in conjunction with other teaching and learning methods. In spring-summer 2019 we incorporate peer teaching in our blended learning sessions by asking students to play Communicate in pairs and explain their motivation of a statement choice at a step of a scenario to each other. The interaction with a virtual character is reverted to the baseline case of spring-summer 2018, i.e. multiple-choice.

In this paper, we compare student evaluations from the three semesters. Our research question is: 'How does student evaluation vary with different interventions (multiple choice, open text and peer teaching) in blended learning sessions using Communicate?'

This paper is organised as follows. Section 2 discusses related work. Section 3 presents the interventions in the blended learning sessions in more detail and compares the student evaluations from the three semesters, Sect. 4 discusses results and Sect. 5 presents conclusions and future work.

2 Related Work

Provoost et al. [15] perform a scoping review of embodied conversational agents (ECAs) in clinical psychology. The authors find that an ECA has a positive effect on user engagement and effectiveness of the interventions. However, Provoost et al. find only a limited number of evaluation and implementation studies of ECAs, in particular with larger sample sizes and control groups. The authors advocate a 'low tech' (simple) implementation to improve psychological interventions in the field.

Mazza et al. [10] present a learning environment aimed at a student to learn how to interview a patient. A simulation in this environment includes a set of patient videos of interconnected doctor visits. A professional actor plays a virtual patient and simulates moods, attitudes and responses. The authors present a component that matches an open text speech input to a set of available choices. Eight students tested the free speech simulation and were in general positive about this component. However, the students noted problems with input for which no, or an erroneous, match was found. In the former case the software asks a student to rephrase her input, and in the latter case the software matches an input to an incorrect event. To address the problems, the authors propose to extend the set of available choices for a student. This seems to involve hiring the same actor to act responses to the extended set of choices, which might be cumbersome.

Van der Lubbe et al. [18] develop a virtual training environment to teach a player (especially older adults) about situations where a potential swindler tries to gain trust. The author present a prototype consisting of six scenarios. In a scenario, a player interacts with a virtual character by either clicking on an option from multiple choice options or by speaking aloud an option. A speech module detects the level of assertiveness in case of a spoken response. The authors conduct an evaluation with a focus group of five security advisors. The focus group was in general positive about the prototype and expressed desire for more scenarios, being able to go back within a scenario, alter an answer and navigate to the tips/feedback menu.

Ochs et al. [12] develop a virtual reality (VR) based simulation to train a doctor to break bad news. An ECA 'acts' as a virtual patient and follows a scenario. A player's (doctor's) speech input is interpreted real time by a human operator who selects a semantic match to one of the available 136 prototypical sentences. These prototypical sentences are based on a previously transcribed corpus of doctor interactions with trained actors playing a patient. The matched sentence is sent to a dialogue system that generates a verbal and non-verbal response of the ECA. Evaluation of the VR experience shows an positive impact of the environment display on the sense of presence, sense of co-presence, and believability of the virtual patient [13].

The work presented in this paper differs from the research described above: we incorporate multiple interventions (based on feedback from students) using the same learning environment over three semesters with successive student groups. We also compare the evaluation from the students over the three semesters.

3 Method and Results

Action research [8] consists of cycles of taking action, and investigating the effects of the action. A step is a cycle of planning, action and fact finding. Our final year computer science students work in a software project as part of their curriculum towards the end of their bachelor program. Within this course, we provide a workshop session per team to address collaboration skills. Our goal is to improve these sessions and an action step-cycle is described in the Introduction (Sect. 1). Students from each semester fill in the same survey after a session, covering the following questions: five communication learning questions (see Fig. 2) with options on a 5-point Likert scale, and two open evaluation questions *(1. What did you think of the game? 2. Suggestions to improve the scenario?).* We analyse this evaluation and introduce improvements to the blended learning sessions. In this section, we describe the blended learning sessions in each semester in more detail in cycles of action and results.

3.1 Baseline Multiple Choice Sessions of Spring-Summer 2018

In our first version of Communicate **(first intervention)**, a player navigates through a simulation and converses with a virtual character by clicking a statement option from one of the prescripted player statements. This is similar to a multiple choice question answer format; see the right hand side of the screenshot of our learning environment in Fig. 1.

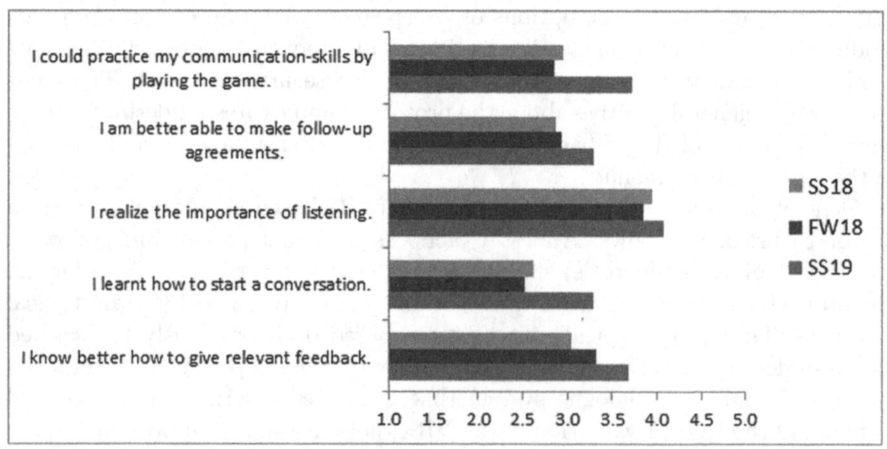

Fig. 2. Chart representation of student rating on the five learning questions

In spring-summer 2018, we organised blended learning sessions where students played the Collaborate scenario. A student interacted with a virtual character by choosing an option from the multiple choice statements at a step of the Collaborate scenario. There were a total of 82 students assigned in eight project teams of 10 to 12 students each. After a project team session, students filled in the evaluation form. A total of 75 students filled in the form. Figure 2 and Table 1 show the student Likert scale ratings on the five learning questions (label SS18 for spring-summer 2018 intervention).

In the feedback to the two open evaluation questions, students expressed the wish to input open text and had reservations about limited statement choices. To address this feedback, we conducted sessions in the same semester to gather open text input from students [16]. Gathering open text input also enabled us to create a dataset to develop and test several NLP methods [16], and to improve the Collaborate scenario. An improved scenario in the game is a teaching material improvement [11]. We applied a clustering algorithm to the list containing students' open text and the predefined statement options for each node in our scenario [7]. Two experts analysed the clustered input and improved the Collaborate scenario in multiple ways. First, if two predefined options at a step of a scenario were contained in the same cluster, then one of them was removed, since they were too similar when compared to the variety of student open text responses. Second, if a number of student open text responses formed a cluster that did not include any predefined scripted statement options, we added a new statement option (similar to the open text responses in the cluster), at that step of the scenario. Third, we modified a response from the virtual character to better frame a context and provide step feedback at some nodes of the scenario. We tested various NLP methods on the dataset created from open text input in spring-summer 2018, but the results were not entirely satisfying [16]. We choose the best matching NLP match method for use in the session of fall-winter 2018.

Another common feedback from the two open evaluation questions was that the VC was seemingly dumb and some students playing the scenario did not want to help/collaborate with the VC. Students also commented about the texture and gestures of the virtual character. We developed a new virtual character with better texture, gestures and animation. We simplified the scenario dialogue to give the VC a 'happy go lucky' character: an engaged and social team member, who works somewhat irregularly.

3.2 Intervention Open Text Input, Fall-Winter 2018

In the blended learning session of fall-winter 2018 (**second intervention** abbreviated to FW18), we incorporate open text in Communicate. A student enters an open text at a step of the scenario Collaborate and the NLP method attempts to match this input to one of the scripted statement choices at that step of Collaborate. Since the NLP match method is not entirely accurate, we scaffold a match result. Communicate highlights the best match when an open text matches to at least one scripted statement and gives a sequence of hints when an open text does not match with any scripted statements at a step. In total 52 students were assigned to five project teams. After playing in open text sessions, 40 students filled in the evaluation form. The evaluation of the students in the five process questions is shown in Fig. 2 and Table 1 (label FW18 for fall-winter 2018 intervention).

The baseline is the evaluation from spring-summer 2018 (abbreviated to SS18) when the students played the Collaborate scenario (Collaborate) in multiple choice format. We compare the (Likert) student ratings on the five learning questions in Table 1 to the student ratings baseline spring-summer 2018. The first column in Table 1 displays the feedback Question that students rated on a 5-point Likert Scale rating from 1 (completely disagree) to 5 (completely agree). The second column denotes the semester and the third column shows the number of students who filled in the evaluation form. The fourth column shows the average rating of the students of the particular question and the fifth column shows the standard deviation to the mean score. In the fifth column, the p-value indicates the likelihood that an increase (or decrease) in rating is due to chance. A *p*-value <0.05 is significant, and a smaller *p*-value indicates a high likelihood that an increase (or decrease) in rating is due to an intervention.

Table 1. Student ratings on the five communication process propositions

Question	Intervention	N	Mean	Std. Dev.	*p*-value
I could practice my communication skills by playing the game	SS18	75	2.95	1.089	
	FW18	40	2.85	1.027	0.639
	SS19	78	3.72	0.952	<0.000
I am better able to make follow up agreements	SS18	75	2.87	1.082	
	FW18	40	2.93	0.971	0.769
	SS19	78	3.29	0.899	0.009
I realize the importance of listening	SS18	75	3.95	1.138	
	FW18	40	3.85	1.075	0.654
	SS19	78	4.08	0.879	0.431
I learnt how to start a conversation	SS18	75	2.61	1.051	
	FW18	40	2.53	0.960	0.651
	SS19	78	3.29	0.955	<0.000
I know better how to give relevant feedback	SS18	75	3.05	0.985	
	FW18	40	3.33	0.917	0.144
	SS19	78	3.68	0.830	<0.000

Despite the extra scaffolding steps there was no significant deterioration (nor improvement) in the five learning questions ratings compared to spring-summer 2018. In the feedback to the two open questions, students were positive about the sessions but had reservations about the matching and expressed a wish to play more scenarios.

3.3 Intervention Students Peer Teach and Play Multiple Scenarios, Spring-Summer 2019

In spring-summer 2019 in our **third intervention** (abbreviated to SS19), we incorporate peer teaching and multiple scenarios in the blended learning sessions. To increase the number of scenarios, we requested communication skills teachers from other faculties to share scenarios and received scenarios on breaking bad news, self reflection, giving feedback etc. In these SS19 sessions, an instructor introduces Communicate, and students play multiple scenarios; at least *Collaborate* and one other scenario (e.g. breaking bad news, giving feedback etc). Students play the scenarios in multiple choice mode. The instructor explains the communication protocol of *Collaborate*: Approach, Express, Discuss and Agree. Thereafter, students play a scenario in pairs of two, where a student explains her statement choice to respond to a virtual character to the other student. We incorporate this action with the goal to provide insight into peer-behaviour, to teach each other and improve interaction in a session [3].

In total 81 students were assigned to eight project teams of which 78 students filled in the evaluation form after the sessions. In SS19 there is a significant improvement in four of the five learning questions ratings compared to the baseline, see Table 1. The fifth question: *'I realize the importance of listening.'* receives high ratings in all three semesters. The scenario seems to elicit the importance of listening in general. In the feedback to the two open questions, some students were 'pleasantly surprised' by the quality of the game and virtual character, some found that the game needed no further improvements, some wished for more feedback in *Collaborate.* We argue that the improved student evaluation is directly related to the third intervention.

4 Discussion

In the student evaluation, student ratings on the Likert scale questions show no significant difference in fall-winter 2018 sessions incorporating open text input versus the baseline of multiple choice input of SS18. In the response to the evaluation form open questions, students made remarks about the quality of an NLP match and that could be a reason that student ratings are not significantly higher. Students also complained about typing multiple times due to the extra scaffolding steps (highlighting and hints) and that could be another reason for no significant rating increase.

Results show that the ratings of the spring-summer 2019 sessions incorporating peer teaching and multiple scenarios are significantly higher for four of the five questions compared to the baseline of spring-summer 2018, see Sect. 3.3. Application of activity theory to human computer interaction design [5] often focusses on interaction. Our results suggest that while interaction (e.g. multiple choice versus open text input) is important, it is crucial to investigate blended learning sessions with respect to pedagogical aspects such as, in our case, peer teaching.

5 Conclusions and Future Work

In this paper we plan, implement and evaluate interventions in our blended learning sessions using Communicate. We start with sessions using multiple choices in Communicate, enhance Communicate by enabling a student to enter open text input in an improved scenario with an improved virtual character and finally incorporate peer teaching and playing multiple scenarios in a session. Results show student ratings of open text input sessions do not significantly differ from multiple choice and that ratings of sessions incorporating peer teaching and multiple scenarios are significantly higher compared to multiple choice sessions.

For future work, we plan to have blended learning sessions again with multiple scenarios and peer teaching. As a difference to spring-summer 2019, we plan to have scenarios in both open text (in Collaborate scenario) and multiple choice (breaking bad news, giving feedback etc.) input modes. In these sessions, for open text input we plan to match with minimal scaffolding, where with matched input a simulation continues as if a virtual character has understood the input (i.e. no extra highlight step) and with unmatched input, we present the available statement options (i.e. no hint step). After playing, a debrief step will be introduced to ask the students in a session to reflect on a recent experience and have a plenary discussion on what went well and what could be improved. After guided sessions with a new batch of students, we can collect student feedback from the sessions.

Acknowledgments. This activity has partially received funding from the European Institute of Innovation and Technology (EIT). This body of the European Union receives support from the European Union's Horizon 2020 research and innovation programme. This research was also partially supported by the 644187 EC H2020 RAGE project.

This work has been developed in collaboration with the Software and Gameproject of the bachelor Computer Science in the faculty of Science, Utrecht University. The authors also acknowledge Majanne Wolters, Marjan van den Akker and Michiel Hulsbergen for their help in teaching and scenario improvement; and to Jordy van Dortmont and Marcell van Geest for implementing the desired changes to Communicate.

References

1. Berkhof, M., van Rijssen, H.J., Schellart, A.J.M., Anema, J.R., van der Beek, A.J.: Effective training strategies for teaching communication skills to physicians: an overview of systematic reviews. Patient Educ. Couns. **84**(2), 152–162 (2011)
2. Dhaqane, M.K., Afrah, N.A.: Satisfaction of students and academic performance in Benadir University. J. Educ. Pract. **7**(24), 59–63 (2016)
3. Goldschmid, B., Goldschmid, M.L.: Peer teaching in higher education: a review. High. Educ. **5**(1), 9–33 (1976)
4. Jeuring, J., et al.: Communicate!—a serious game for communication skills —. In: Conole, G., Klobučar, T., Rensing, C., Konert, J., Lavoué, É. (eds.) EC-TEL 2015. LNCS, vol. 9307, pp. 513–517. Springer, Cham (2015). https://doi.org/10.1007/978-3-319-24258-3_49

5. Kaptelinin, V., Nardi, B.A.: Acting with Technology: Activity Theory and Interaction Design. MIT Press, Cambridge (2006)
6. Lala, R., Jeuring, J., van Dortmont, J., van Geest, M.: Scenarios in virtual learning environments for one-to-one communication skills training. Int. J. Educ. Technol. High. Educ. **14**(1), 17 (2017)
7. Lala, R., et al.: Enhancing free-text interactions in a communication skills learning environment. In: Proceedings of the 13th International Conference on Computer Supported Collaborative Learning, pp. 363–364, June 2019
8. Lewin, K.: Action research and minority problems. J. Soc. Issues **2**(4), 34–46 (1946)
9. Martinez, M.E.: Cognition and the question of test item format. Educ. Psychol. **34**(4), 207–218 (1999)
10. Mazza, R., Ambrosini, L., Catenazzi, N., Vanini, S., Tuggener, D., Tavarnesi, G.: Behavioural simulator for professional training based on natural language interaction. In: EDULEARN18 Proceedings of 10th International Conference on Education and New Learning Technologies, 2–4 July 2018, pp. 3204–3214. IATED (2018)
11. Nieveen, N., Folmer, E.: Formative evaluation in educational design research. Des. Res. **153**, 152–169 (2013)
12. ŠOchs, M., Blache, P. De Montcheuil, G.: What common ground between a human and a virtual agent? The case of task-oriented dialogues for breaking bad news. In: 22nd Workshop on the Semantics and Pragmatics of Dialogue (SemDial 2018) (2018)
13. Ochs, M., et al.: Training doctors' social skills to break bad news: evaluation of the impact of virtual environment displays on the sense of presence. J. Multimodal User Interfaces **13**(1), 41–51 (2019)
14. Ozuru, Y., Briner, S., Kurby, C.A., McNamara, D.S.: Comparing comprehension measured by multiple-choice and open-ended questions. Can. J. Exp. Psychol./Revue canadienne de psychologie expérimentale **67**(3), 215 (2013)
15. Provoost, S., Lau, H.M., Ruwaard, J., Riper, H.: Embodied conversational agents in clinical psychology: a scoping review. J. Med. Internet Res. **19**(5), e151 (2017)
16. Ruseti, S., Lala, R., Gutu-Robu, G., Dascălu, M., Jeuring, J., van Geest, M.: Semantic Matching of Open Texts to Pre-scripted Answers in Dialogue-Based Learning. In: Isotani, S., Millán, E., Ogan, A., Hastings, P., McLaren, B., Luckin, R. (eds.) AIED 2019. LNCS (LNAI), vol. 11626, pp. 242–246. Springer, Cham (2019). https://doi.org/10.1007/978-3-030-23207-8_45
17. Silverman, J., Kurtz, S., Draper, J.: Skills for Communicating with Patients, 3rd edn. Radcliffe Publishing Limited, London (2013)
18. van der Lubbe, L.M., Gerritsen, C., Formolo, D., Otte, M., Bosse, T.: A serious game for training verbal resilience to doorstep scams. In: Gentile, M., Allegra, M., Söbke, H. (eds.) GALA 2018. LNCS, vol. 11385, pp. 110–120. Springer, Cham (2019). https://doi.org/10.1007/978-3-030-11548-7_11

Effects of Game-Based Learning on Academic Performance and Student Interest

Irene Vargianniti[1] and Kostas Karpouzis[2,3(✉)]

[1] Palladio Primary School, Vari, Greece
[2] Intelligent Systems, Content and Interaction Lab, National Technical University of Athens, Athens, Greece
kkarpou@cs.ntua.gr
[3] School of Game Programming, SAE Athens, Moschato, Greece

Abstract. The goal of this paper is to study whether Game-Based Learning (GBL) can be used to improve academic performance and engagement. We present an experiment based on the design and deployment of a Monopoly-like board game, in the context of a primary school Geography curriculum, and look for improvements in students' academic performance and will to learn, interest, and positive motivation. The paper examines if this game had a statistically significant influence on students' performance, as well as how performance and interest are related and how performance differs between boys and girls. Results from the quantitative analysis of the data were positive to all the research queries: students' performance improved substantially after the game, while, the strong correlation between the two variables that resulted made evident the relation between the students' interest and performance.

Keywords: Game-based learning · Geography · Board games · Monopoly · Open data

1 Introduction

Geographical education contributes in formatting citizen's environmental awareness and fostering critical thinking [10]. Utilizing games in the learning process can meet these goals. Games develop skills such as cooperation, communication, critical thinking more than any other learning method. They highly engage players and motivate them. Game-based learning is designed to balance the content of the game and the game itself with the player's ability to apply game's concepts in real world ([6–8]). Prensky reports [5] that education and play have an interrelated relationship. Learning has rich content but little involvement, as opposed to games that lack educational content but engage students very much. Games offer an environment in which learning can thrive. Moreover, games introduce goals and procedures that a student must accomplish in order to evolve. Engagement is associated with learning outcomes [4] and motives are considered games' fundamental elements [1]. Therefore, educational games must be carefully designed in order to engage and motivate students. However, studies haven't found consistent evidence that games would affect academic performance [2]. Educational games can be considered promising learning tools, so if we

A. Liapis et al. (Eds.): GALA 2019, LNCS 11899, pp. 332–341, 2019.
https://doi.org/10.1007/978-3-030-34350-7_32

implement them in classroom, we will combine interest and fun with learning [13]. Today's generation will no longer tolerate being a part of traditional, outdated education, hence, schools and businesses should use games to make learning fun and exciting, but also more effective [9].

Based on existing research, we investigated whether games can find their place in classroom and supplement traditional teaching, by offering an authentic learning environment. The reason behind this study was to find out whether a customized version of the classic board game Monopoly, called "Geopoly", which we implemented in class, affects students' academic performance and interest. More specifically, we sought answers to the following questions:

1. Does Geopoly game help students improve their academic performance in Geography?
2. Are there any differences between boys' and girls' performance?
3. Is there any relevance between interest and academic performance?
4. Which do students find more interesting: game or traditional lesson?

Then, we tested for the following hypotheses:

H1: Students who played the game achieved higher scores than those who attended class.
H2: There isn't any difference between boys' and girls' academic performance.
H3: Students who showed interest about the game achieved higher scores.
H4: Geopoly awakens an interest in Geography more than traditional teaching does.

To evaluate game's impact, we divided 43 6th grader elementary students (N = 43) into two groups: experimental (game replaced traditional lesson) and control (students attended class) and used academic performance and interest as dependent measures and the game as the independent measure.

1.1 Method

Instructional Design. The present intervention aims to introduce students in Game-based learning theory and teach them European Geography alternatively. For this purpose, the classic board game "Monopoly" was adapted, renamed "Geopoly" and embedded in the classroom. Three chapters of school textbook were replaced by the game ("Residents and countries of Europe", "Cultural characteristics of European people" and "Monuments, sights and cultural heritage"). The dashboard was divided into four parts, each of one represented a European region (South, East, Scandinavia, North-Central) as described in the students' school book.

Countries were grouped by color based on their geographical position. At the right, we placed the country with the smallest area (in classic Monopoly, the country with the smallest value is placed at the right of each color group), so students can perceive the concept of relative position. Monopoly's cards were altered to serve our purpose (see Fig. 1).

(a) The adapted game board with a 3D printed player token

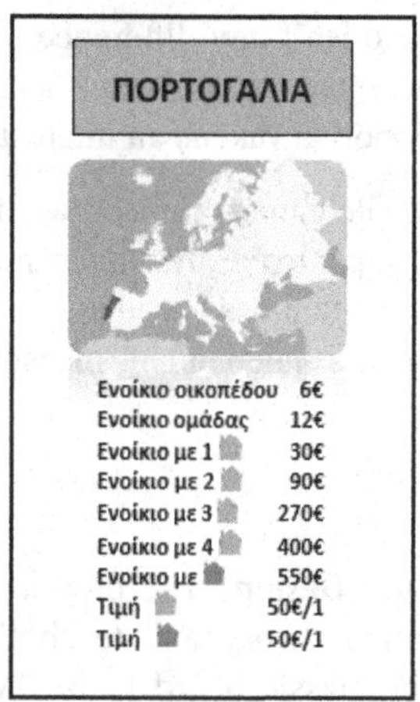

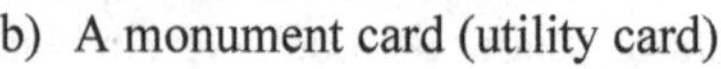

(b) A monument card (utility card) (c) A property card

Fig. 1. The Geopoly game board and cards from the game

Cards. Every game card showed the name of each country and its capital city, while peninsula and island countries were marked with an icon. Utility cards (normally railway stations and energy companies) were replaced with Europe's main sights and monuments. Thus, students linked easily each monument to its country and region.

Upon completion of the educational intervention, students should be able to distinguish the four regions in which Europe is divided, obtain knowledge of a large number of countries and their capitals, distinguish peninsulas and island states, recognize that neighboring countries have common geomorphological and cultural characteristics, compare countries' sizes, and perceive the concept of relative size recognize the main monuments of European culture. 43 6th grade students, participated in this intervention. Students were divided into two groups: experimental group (students played the game instead of attending class) and control group (students attended geography class).

Students in the Experimental group chose the monuments to be modeled and then used the Thingiverse.com website for 3d modeling, assisted by their teacher. All tokens were printed in a 3D printer and depict Europe's iconic landmarks (Colosseum, Big Ben, St Peter's Basilica, Eiffel Tower, Brandenburg's gate, Netherlands' windmills). Then, they took a written test, consisting of 5 exercises aligned with the learning goals of the intervention. Instructions and rules of the game were available on the "Geopoly" website created for this purpose. In the end of each game, teams posted the name of the winner name on the scoreboard (Fig. 2).

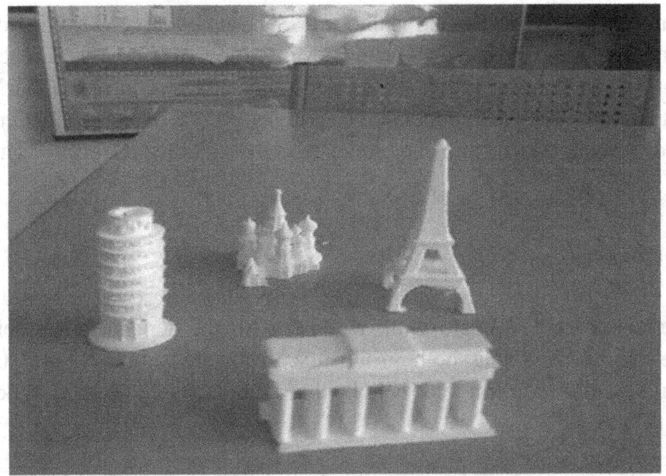

(a) The 3D-printed player tokens

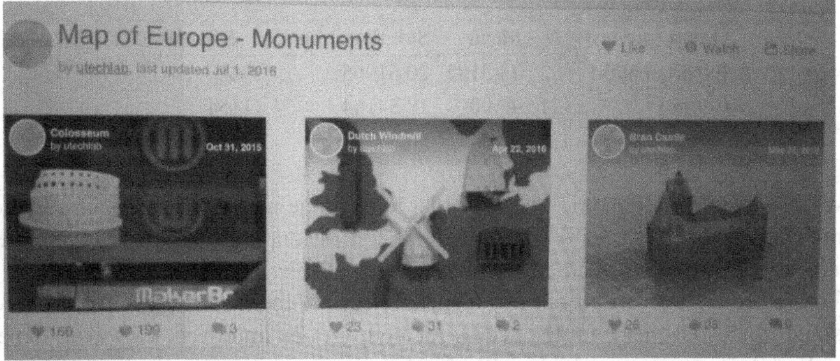

(b) Thingiverse interface to choose and download 3D models

Fig. 2. 3D-printed tokens used in Geopoly

Teams played four consecutive times and each game lasted 40 min. In the end, for five minutes the class reflected on the game and their strategy. Right after the educational intervention, students were tested in a post-test, filled out an Intrinsic Motivation Inventory/IMI (common for the control and test groups), a multidimensional measurement device intended to assess participants subjective experience [14] related to a target activity in laboratory experiments, which it has been used in several experiments related to intrinsic motivation and self-regulation [11]. Finally, students evaluated the game, by answering a questionnaire.

Students in the Control group took a pre-test, were taught three chapters of school textbook and were tested again after. Finally, they filled out an IMI questionnaire and a lesson evaluation questionnaire.

2 Results

Statistical analysis was performed using SPSS. Data were collected from post – questionnaires, pre- and post-tests, Intrinsic Motivation Inventory and teacher observation; statistical processing provided the necessary answers to researcher's assumptions. Relationships between dependent variables (Performance, Gender, Interest, Anxiety, Perceptual Skill) and an independent variable (Geopoly game) were examined.

2.1 Performance

Overall Performance. To begin with, we tested for the dependent variable "performance". Results showed that both groups' scores were similar (~45/100). These below-average scores confirm our beliefs that students a have hard time studying Geography (Table 1).

Table 1. Performance statistics before the intervention

Group (pre-test)	N	Mean	Std. deviation	Std. error mean
Experimental	22	**45.3182**	20.61065	4.39420
Control	21	**45.00**	18.84144	4.11154

We conducted a parametric t-test in order to examine means' equivalence variance. Significance level (p = 0,958) confirmed our first assumption: there isn't statistically significant difference between two groups' scores (Table 2).

Consequently, we carried out a statistical check on the mean scores for each post tests and found out that both the scores for both groups improved. However, experimental group's scores were higher (Table 3).

T-test attested that the game improved students' performance (Table 4).

Table 2. Independent samples test (pre-test)

	Levene's test for equality of variances		t-test for equality of means						
	F	Sig.	t	df	Sig. (2tailed)	Mean difference	Std. error difference	95% confidence interval of the difference	
								Lower	Upper
Equal variances assumed	.294	.591	.053	41	.958	.32	6.03	−11.86	12.49
Equal variances not assumed			.053	40.928	.958	.32	6.01	−11.83	12.47

Table 3. Performance statistics after the intervention

Group (post-test)	N	Mean	Std. deviation	Std. error mean
Experimental	22	78.50	18.44	3.93
Control	21	61.00	15.61	3.41

Table 4. Independent samples test (post-test)

	Levene's test for equality of variances		t-test for equality of means						
Post-test	F	Sig.	t	df	Sig. (2tailed)	Mean difference	Std. error difference	95% confidence interval of the difference	
								Lower	Upper
Equal variances assumed	1.375	.248	3.351	41	.002	17.500	5.223	6.95	28.05
Equal variances not assumed			3.364	40.439	.002	17.500	5.20	6.99	28.01

There is a difference between two groups' means, which is statistically significant (p = 0,02 < 0,05). Statistical control verified our assumption that the game improved students' performance.

Gender Difference. Finally, we tested for a difference between the mean score of boys vs. girls (Table 5).

Table 5. Performance vs. gender

	Gender	Experimental group		Control group	
		N	Mean	N	Mean
Pre-test	Girls	10	40.1	8	44.0
	Boys	12	49.6	13	45.6
Post-test	Girls	10	75.3	8	62.2
	Boys	12	81.1	13	60.2

There are differences in performance of boys - girls in both tests, which are not statistically significant as Levene's test for Equality of Variances showed (Table 6).

Table 6. Performance statistics per gender

	Gender	Experimental group		Control group	
		N	Mean	N	Mean
Def	Girls	10	35.2	8	18.2
	Boys	12	21.5	13	26.3

Due to different scores' starting point, we will proceed to statistical control of students' means (Table 7).

Table 7. Statistical analysis of student performance

Control group	Levene's test for equality of variances				
	F	Sig.	t	df	Sig. (2tailed)
Equal variances assumed	1.632	.217	.352	19	**.728**
Equal variances not assumed			.398	18.992	.695
Experimental group					
Equal variances assumed	.304	.588	.572	20	**.574**
Equal variances not assumed			.556	16.226	.586

Control's group significance level (p = 0,728 > 0,05) verifies our null hypothesis (boys' scores don't vary from girls'), same as experimental group (p = 0,574 > 0,05).

Interest. Moreover, we examined if game had an impact on students' interest about Geography. In order to find answers, we used data from IMI questionnaire which explores students' intrinsic motivation. Then, we correlated academic performance and interest, using Spearman's rank correlation (Fig. 3 and Table 8).

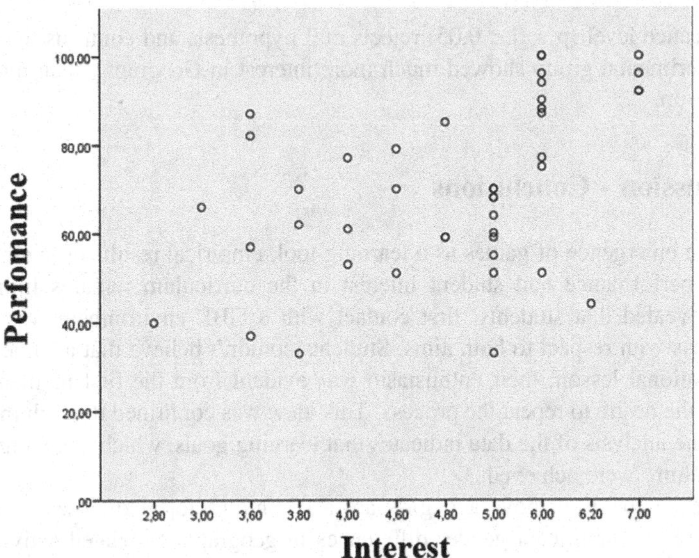

Fig. 3. Correlation between interest and performance

Table 8. Spearman's rank correlation

		Post-test	Interest (IMI)
Post-test	Correlation coefficient	1.000	.844
	N	22	22
Interest (IMI)	Correlation coefficient	.844	1.000
	N	22	22

Spearman's test indicates that there is very strong positive correlation (r = 0,844) between academic performance and interest.

Table 9. Results from the non–parametric Mann Whitney U test

Group	N	Mean rank
Experimental	22	30.30
Control	21	13.31

This scatterplot diagram presents that this high correlation is based on monotony. This correlation signifies that as students' interest increases, their performance increases as well.

Finally, we explored if students who played the game showed as much interest in Geography as students who attended traditional classroom, based on data extracted from IMI questionnaire. Results of the non-parametric Mann Whitney U test (48.500) highlighted that the experimental group has a higher average ranking (30.30) than the control group (13.31), thus mean rank of interest is higher on experimental group (Table 9).

Significance level ($p = 0 < 0,05$) rejects null hypothesis and confirms that students in the experimental group showed much more interest in Geography than those in the control group.

3 Discussion - Conclusions

Despite the emergence of games as a learning tool, empirical results on their effect on academic performance and student interest in the curriculum remains limited. Our analysis revealed that students' first contact with a GBL environment was crowned with success with respect to both aims. Students couldn't believe that a game replaced the conventional lesson; their enthusiasm was evident from the first moment and all expressed the desire to repeat the process. This view was confirmed through the present study, as the analysis of the data indicates that learning goals, which were aligned with the curriculum, were achieved.

Differences between boys and girls are a common subject of research in recent years. There are significant gender differences in geography – related activities [12]. However, this survey's evidence suggested that there was no variation in performance of boys and girls.

A game-based learning environment offers significant potential for increasing motivation and student involvement [4]. Interest, anxiety [15] and perceptual ability, subcategories of internal motivation were measured to provide results on what motivates students. Students found the game interesting, and that caused a positive impact in their academic performance. Students collaborated well, thus we can conclude that playing, cultivated a breeding ground for the development of classroom collaboration. Cooperation, strategy, fun, interest enhanced educational process. Students realized that you can easily learn something and have fun at the same time. Learning and play have been combined to provide the best learning experience. More extensive research is proposed to introduce the GBL in the educational process, so that instructors and learners become more familiar with this learning theory.

At the same time, it would be interesting to adapt the game so that it can be used in other subjects such as Mathematics or Physics, in which performance of boys - girls differs greatly [3].

Finally, implementation of games in the educational environment presupposes their alignment with the curriculum, which is considered obsolete. More space should be provided for teachers to make the most of game's educational value by giving students the opportunity to broaden their knowledge and cultivate 21st century skills.

Acknowledgments. This work has been funded by the iRead project (https://iread-project.eu/) which has received funding from the European Union's Horizon 2020 Research and Innovation program under grant agreement No 731724.

References

1. Schun, D.H.: Motivation—Education.com (2018). https://www.education.com/reference/article/motivation/. Accessed 16 May 2018
2. Ke, F., Abras, T.: Games for engaged learning of middle school children with special learning needs. Br. J. Edu. Technol. **44**(2), 225–242 (2013). https://doi.org/10.1111/j.1467-8535.2012.01326.x
3. Kerkhoven, A.H., Russo, P., Land-Zandstra, A.M., Saxena, A., Rodenburg, F.J.: Gender stereotypes in science education resources: a visual content analysis. PLoS One **11**(11), 1–13 (2016). https://doi.org/10.1371/journal.pone.0165037
4. Deater-Deckard, K., Chang, M., Evans, M.E.: Engagement States and Learning from Educational Games. New Directions for Child and Adolescent Development, (139), 21–30 (2013). https://doi.org/10.1002/cad.20028
5. Pivec, M.: Affective and Emotional Aspects of Human-Computer Interaction: Game-Based and Innovative Learning Approaches Volume 1 Future of Learning. IOS Press, Amsterdam (2006)
6. Karpouzis, K., Yannakakis, G.N. (eds.): Emotion in Games. SC, vol. 4. Springer, Cham (2016). https://doi.org/10.1007/978-3-319-41316-7
7. Yannakakis, G.N., Isbister, K., Paiva, A., Karpouzis, K.: Guest editorial: emotion in games. IEEE Trans. Affect. Comput. **5**(1), 1–2 (2014)
8. Plass, J.L., Homer, B.D., Kinzer, C.K.: Foundations of game-based learning. Educ. Psychol. **50**(4), 258–283 (2015). https://doi.org/10.1080/00461520.2015.1122533
9. Prensky, M.: Digital natives, digital immigrants. Horizon **9**(5), 1–6 (2001). https://doi.org/10.1108/10748120110424816
10. Reinfried, S., Hertig, P.: Geographical Education: How Human- Environment-Society Processes Work, pp. 1–48 (2011)
11. Ryan, R.M., Deci, E.L.: Self-determination theory and the facilitation of intrinsic motivation, social development, and well-being. Am. Psychol. (2000). https://doi.org/10.1037/0003-066X.55.1.68
12. Zernike, K.: Girls a Distant 2nd in Geography Gap Among U.S. Pupils (2000). https://www.nytimes.com. Accessed 29 June 2018
13. Yannakakis, G.N., et al.: Siren: towards adaptive serious games for teaching conflict resolution. In: 2010 European Conference on Game-based learning (ECGBL), pp. 412–418 (2010)
14. Karpouzis, K., Yannakakis, G.N., Shaker, N., Asteriadis, S.: The platformer experience dataset. In: 2015 International Conference on Affective Computing and Intelligent Interaction (ACII), China (2015). https://doi.org/10.1109/acii.2015.7344647
15. Caridakis, G., Karpouzis, K., Wallace, M., Kessous, L., Amir, N.: Multimodal user's affective state analysis in naturalistic interaction. J. Multimodal User Interfaces **3**(1), 49–66 (2010)

'Museum Escape': A Game to Increase Museum Visibility

Angeliki Antoniou(✉), Marios Ilias Dejonai, and George Lepouras

Department of Informatics and Telecommunications, University of Peloponnese, Akadimaikou Vlachou, 22100 Tripolis, Greece
{angelant,tst10071,gl}@uop.gr

Abstract. A peripheral museum with a nevertheless important collection of ancient items, wished to increase its visibility and digital presence in order to become more known and attract new visitors. Among the different solutions designed and implemented, we also designed a series of games of different kinds (i.e. mini vs complex games) for different purposes, like profiling of potential visitors and advertising the venue in social media. Based on lessons learnt from physical games played at museums of the same type in the same region, we designed and implemented a museum escape game. The game is presented here, to provide implementation details regarding the concept, the game mechanics, the interface design, the technical details, as well as the game art. We conclude with primary user testing and future steps that include plans for creating museum escape games with different technologies, like augmented reality and virtual reality.

Keywords: Museum · Games · Escape room

1 The Archaeological Museum of Tripolis

The Archaeological Museum of Tripolis is a medium size, peripheral museum in the Peloponnese Region in Greece. It is housed in a historical building and houses a very important collection of ancient artifacts found in Arcadia, covering a wide historical spectrum (from Neolithic to Mycenaean, Geometric, Classical and Roman times). Regardless of its important collection, the museum remains unknown to the wider public, even to the locals. The visibility of the museum is very low, resulting in very low numbers of visitors.

Trying to understand the reasons for the very low numbers of visitors, we conducted a series of interviews with museum personnel and we also collected data from visitor comments on a popular social site gathering comments from museum visitors (https://www.tripadvisor.com.gr/Attraction_Review-g189490-d6650803-Reviews-Archeological_Museum_of_Tripoli-Tripoli_Arkadia_Region_Peloponnese.html). From our data collection and analysis (extraction and categorization of main issues from the expert and visitor comments), the following reasons emerged as the most important for the low visibility and visitability of the venue:

A. Liapis et al. (Eds.): GALA 2019, LNCS 11899, pp. 342–350, 2019.
https://doi.org/10.1007/978-3-030-34350-7_33

1. Old fashioned museological approach – a sense of storage, rather than exhibition, with items placed one next to the other, often without a obvious connection.
2. Old fashioned and very limited informative material – only a very short label next to same items, providing very basic information, like the location the item was found and the era it belonged.
3. The museum has no digital presence – the museum does not have a website or any presence in social media.

For these reasons, it was decided to build a number of games in order to promote the museum and the collection. The games would be distributed to the public via social media, like Facebook and they would hopefully attract new audiences. There were different games developed, with different characteristics (e.g. mini, complex), and different purposes (e.g. profiling, advertisement, etc.) [1, 2]. Among the games designed and implemented was a museum escape game, based on lessons learnt from a similar physical action, organized by the Ephorate of Antiquities of Arcadia. More specifically, museum escape games were organized for the International Museum Day 2017 in the Archaeological Museum of Tegea (in the same region in Arcadia, as the Tripolis museum) (http://www.tegeamuseum.gr/). The event was very popular and attracted many visitors and press interest. Based on these observations, we proceeded with the design of a digital game for museum escape, which will be presented in the following sections.

2 Escape Rooms

Games have been used in the past to augment the museum experience and address the needs of different visitor groups. For example, games that provide opportunities for shared experiences are effective in increasing visitor engagement [3]. Similarly, collaborative games have been used to enhance the museum learning experience and target specific visitor groups such as children [4].

In addition, in recent years, there has been a growing interest in escape games, as they are used as alternative entertainment practices and attract large audiences. An escape room is a game where players are locked inside a room and play against the clock solving riddles, discover clues and solve puzzles in order to escape in time [5]. In the USA alone, there are more than 2.300 escape rooms and there are reports that the industry is booming [6]. Businesses and corporation are using escape rooms to increase employee bonding, since participants need to collaborate for the common goal [7]. The potential of escape rooms is recognized for a number of purposes like improvement of communication skills, learning specific elements, etc. [8]. This type of games has been used in learning settings, with noticeable success and in different domains, like teaching computer science [9]. In particular, escape games create collaboration opportunities and can function as collaborative learning environments [10]. They also give opportunities to researchers to study group dynamics under the locked conditions of a room and study the behavior of participants. The escape rooms have been used to raise awareness about complex sociotechnical issues, like the use of surveillance technology in cities [11] and they have been also used as testbeds for different learning settings [12].

The mix of the escape room concept with different types of technology is also increasing in popularity. There are studies that try different types of technology to study the changes in human dynamics. For example, it was found that the use of audio in distributed escape rooms can increase social presence and the different variations in using video technology can increase curiosity [13]. Finally, mixed reality in escape rooms can increase group cohesiveness [14].

In regards to museums and cultural heritage, there have been some attempts to employ escape rooms. For example, the Boston Museum of Science has used the escape room concept to enhance human-robot interaction [15]. Therefore, the present work, wishes to incorporate the escape room concept in a museum game, in order to increase the museum's popularity and attract new visitors, while providing opportunities for learning.

3 Game Design

Museum Escape is a game in which the player is called to escape from a museum, based on the Archaeological Museum of Tripolis. It features 2D graphics and runs on a web browser, while it combines elements of puzzle solving and quiz games. The game can be found here: https://pilot3.crosscult.uop.gr/museumEscape/ (last accessed June 2019).

3.1 Main Concept

The Museum Escape is a single player game played with a mouse or touch controls. It consists of a series of puzzles presented in various ways, which will be the means for escaping from one room to another and consequently from the museum. The game targets people of all ages.

The player starts from a room inside the museum and is asked to solve riddles in order to access the key that helps her move to the next room. There is also a countdown of the time available to escape while this time will be reduced if the player makes a mistake and will increase when the player escapes each consecutive room. The riddles include games of discovery and observation (e.g. find the differences in certain images), puzzles, and knowledge-related questions about the exhibits.

We use subdued illumination that simply gives the sense of time but does not lighten the environment excessively. The game graphics are quite simple, though artistic with a cartoon touch, while the music is atmospheric. The walls of the museum's building are imposing, and the building is particularly high-ceilinged and giving the feeling of insecurity and coldness, increasing the need to escape.

3.2 Game Play Mechanics

The player uses a mouse or touch input in order to play the game. She can click or tap on the various exhibits hidden in the game screens. In addition, she has to choose the correct answer to various questions while in some puzzles she should find differences between two pictures or complete a puzzle.

Each level is represented by a room or generally an enclosed space from which the player is called to escape. The room or space has various points of interest that the player can interact with. Each point of interest presents a related riddle to the player. As soon as the player solves it, she can interact with the rest of the items in the room.

There are two types of riddles (Fig. 1):

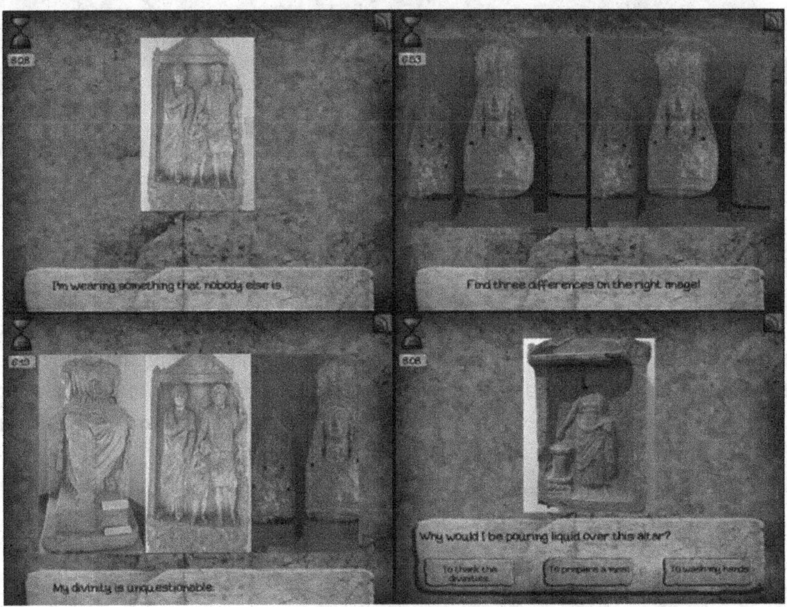

Fig. 1. Examples of riddle screens with real museum objects.

- Quizzes
  - It may fall in one of the following categories:
    - Identify elements on an image such an ornament on a statue.
    - Select an image that matches the description provided.
    - Identify the material from which the object is made.
    - Answer questions related to the image presented.
  - In the event of a mistake, the player will lose one minute of the available time.
  - The quiz questions are designed to educate about different aspects of the exhibits.
- Find the Differences
  - Highlight three points between the original and an altered image of real museum exhibits.
  - If the player makes a mistake, the available time is reduced by 10 s.
  - The "Find the Differences" type of riddles are designed to help put focus on specific parts of the exhibits.

There are 2 difficulty levels that the player can choose from in 2 languages (Greek, English) (Fig. 2). The different levels mean that the initial available time, the extra time given when the player enters a new room and the time lost when a mistake is made, differ.

Fig. 2. Examples of game screens

3.3 Museum Rooms

The museum rooms are all different to each other, in order to provide optical variation to the player. The rooms have a different ambience and feeling and they include different objects in which the different riddle items are hidden. Although, many rooms are added that are not the same as in the physical space, the game map is based on the actual museum map (Fig. 3).

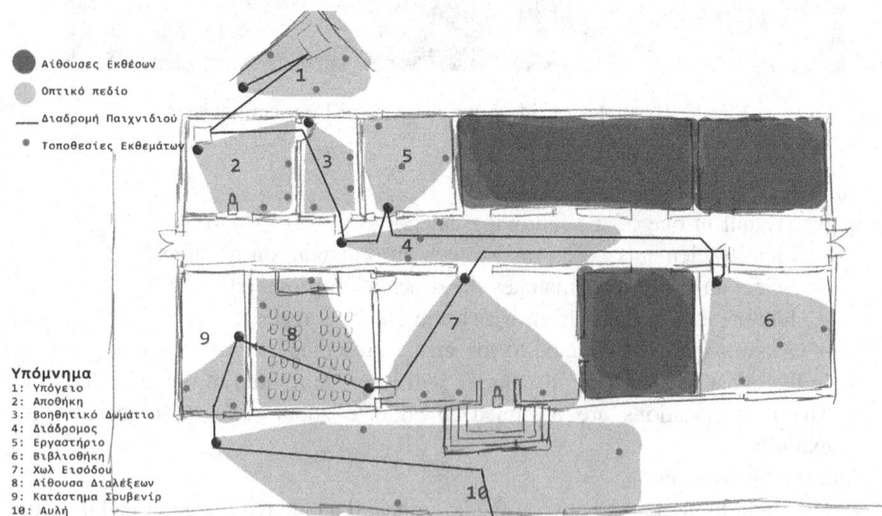

Fig. 3. The game map is based on the actual museum map.

Fig. 4. Examples of museum rooms

The following rooms are implemented (Fig. 4):

Basement - The basement is a dark room with only one light source on the ceiling. The objects in the basement include small wooden boxes, small barrels, some cleaners and an old wooden shelf.

Storage Room - The storage room is used to store findings that are not suitable for exhibition to the public due to excessive wear or findings that have been recently transported and are temporarily stored. It also contains boxes for storing sensitive items. It has a uniform ceiling light as well as two large windows, which are behind the player's field of view. A light from a source on the street is coming in from the windows.

Ancillary Room - This room is used for the storage of cleaning materials as well as for storing personal items of the museum's staff in bulkheads. Objects in this room include brooms, mops, buckets, dustbins, bags and a large shelf.

Hallway - The hallway showcases some exhibits and is the connecting link for the various rooms of the museum. It also has wall light for soft spot lighting and even gentle lighting on the ceiling. In the background and on the sides there are doors and open passages leading to other rooms of the building.

Lab - The lab is used to repair or maintain exhibits. It is a very cold and sterile place with large working benches all over. On the benches there are microscopes, magnifying glasses, papers or maps and various tools such as brushes. It has two large windows with blinds while the ceiling is lit in a uniform way.

Library - The library is a place where visitors and experts can access books and archives. In the library there are bookselves, sofas, armchairs and small lamps on side tables. The lighting mainly comes from the lamps on the tables, which illuminate to allow reading.

Entrance Hall - A very large and bright space. Just opposite the main entrance, which stands out from all the other doors of the building due to both size and color. In addition, there are two large windows, some of which the player can see faint lights from the street outside the museum. In the center of the floor there is a large imposing carpet and on the ceiling a large neoclassical type light. There are some floor lamps in the corners the lighting is soft but warmer than the other parts of the museum.

Conference Room - The conference room is the warmest of the museum. The flooring is made of parquet, the walls have a wooden lining to the middle and soft point lighting at various points, while spot lighting is also on the grid-shaped ceiling.

Souvenir Shop - The souvenir shop is somewhat separated from the rest of the building. There are several souvenirs on display. At the point of the game, the store is closed and only few items are left on the shelves, while lots of rubbish showing a clear image of abandonment.

3.4 Interface Design

In the upper left corner of the game screen is an hourglass and the time available to the player to escape from the museum. Various messages about the riddles are available in clickable text boxes. In the main menu, the player can also access the level button, to indicate whether she prefers an easier level or not. In addition, in the main menu, the player can also find a mute/un-mute button to control the game sound.

The game's graphics are drawn on top of an HTML Canvas element. Various images and text fields are used in the game and every frame is drawn from scratch as the canvas is emptied once per frame. We use many different sounds in the game to enhance the sense of satisfaction in solving the riddles and help create the right atmosphere. Various sound effects are used like:

- A click sound for interaction with the game's buttons.
- A simple countdown sound for when the time left is reduced to a value below 60 s, which becomes more intense as the time goes close to 0.
- A sound for successful moves.
- A sound for mistakes.

Overall, the game has a gentle classical music that enhances the aesthetics of the game and provides a calm background suitable for solving the riddles.

3.5 Technical Details

The game is created in a way that can run in any modern browser that supports HTML5. It is based on two different canvas elements, one for each layer. The back layer contains the room or riddle graphics, while the front is used to display the graphic environment that should appear above the rest of the graphics. There are two xml files which hold all the necessary information for the levels displayed. One relates to the messages displayed to the player while the other relates to the riddle structure and all the information required to run the game. If someone wants to add more levels to the game, all she has to do is add more information to the appropriate spots in the xml files. This makes the game very easy to modify without messing with the game's scripts. The game is developed using Javascript on top of some simple HTML. The messages and level information is stored in two XML files. The game is available in Greek and English. Before the game is loaded, the language is selected and the appropriate XML file is loaded. These are registered using an id with which the appropriate message is selected at a time.

4 Early User Testing

The current version of the game is not yet tested with the public. However, we have proceeded with expert user testing and in particular, we have used a Human Computer Interaction expert and a museum experience expert. The HCI expert found the game highly usable. He mentioned the long duration of the game and the possibility to break the game in smaller parts. The museum experience expert mentioned that the game has a strong educational potential, since it uses real museum exhibits and all riddles are related to the information behind the selected objects. More specifically, she said that it is important that the game provides training in spotting exhibit details, since these are crucial to reveal the exhibits' past. For example, paying attention to what objects the statues might hold, is a way archeologist also use to identify the person represented by the statue (i.e. whether this is a mortal or god, which god this is, the social statues of the mortal, etc.). The game, through the 'find the differences' elements, provides this important aspect of training in observing exhibit details. In addition, the experts also pointed out that the quiz questions make players understand important issues, like status matters in ancient society and elements of the ancient religion. Finally, both experts agreed that even the easy level of the game might be quite difficult for people with no knowledge of history and archaeology. For this reason, they suggested either to make another easier level for people that have no prior knowledge, or leave the game as is, but provide it after the actual museum visit, since the player could acquire some basic information during her visit.

5 Conclusion

The game remains to be tested by the museum visitors and the potential visitors and its different elements need to be assessed. We will proceed with user testing and will check the educational potential of the game, as well as its ability to advertise the venue and the experience and thus, attract new visitors. Our next plans also include the implementation of 2 more museum escape games. The first one is using virtual reality (VR) and the other will use augmented reality (AR). The AR version will be played inside the museum whereas the VR will be played in different locations and it will be portable, allowing people in different locations to play it. Finally, our future plans, also include the incorporation of collaborative interfaces in order to allow more than one player to engage with the game, and support collaboration, as in physical escape rooms.

Acknowledgments. This research received funding from the European Union's Horizon 2020 research and innovation programme under grant agreement No. 693150. We would also like to thank the personnel of the Archaeological Museum of Tripolis and the director of the Ephorate of Antiquities of Arcadia, Dr. Anna Karapanagiotou, for the valuable help and cooperation. Finally, we are grateful to Mr. Yannis Aggelakos for the game graphics.

References

1. Antoniou, A.: Predicting cognitive profiles from a mini quiz: a Facebook game for cultural heritage. In: Gentile, M., Allegra, M., Söbke, H. (eds.) GALA 2018. LNCS, vol. 11385, pp. 422–425. Springer, Cham (2019). https://doi.org/10.1007/978-3-030-11548-7_41
2. Bampatzia, S., Bourlakos, I., Antoniou, A., Vassilakis, C., Lepouras, G., Wallace, M.: Serious games: valuable tools for cultural heritage. In: Bottino, R., Jeuring, J., Veltkamp, R. C. (eds.) GALA 2016. LNCS, vol. 10056, pp. 331–341. Springer, Cham (2016). https://doi.org/10.1007/978-3-319-50182-6_30
3. Dini, R., Paterno, F., Santoro, C.: An environment to support multi-user interaction and cooperation for improving museum visits through games. In: Proceedings of the 9th International Conference on Human Computer Interaction with Mobile Devices and Services, pp. 515–521. ACM (2007)
4. Luyten, K., et al.: Collaborative gaming in the Gallo-Roman museum to increase attractiveness of learning cultural heritage for youngsters. In: Proceedings of the International Conference on Fun and Games, pp. 59–61 (2008)
5. Wiemker, M., Elumir, E., Clare, A.: Game Based Learning – Dialogorientierung & spielerisches Lernen digital und analog. Fachhochschule St. Pölten, St. Pölten (2015)
6. Economist. https://www.economist.com/gulliver/2019/01/11/the-escape-room-games-industry-is-booming
7. Ticktockescaperoom. https://www.ticktockescaperoom.com/the-psychology-behind-the-escape-room/
8. Nicholson, S.: Peeking behind the locked door: a survey of escape room facilities (2015). White Paper http://scottnicholson.com/pubs/erfacwhite.pdf
9. Borrego, C., Fernández, C., Blanes, I., Robles, S.: Room escape at class: escape games activities to facilitate the motivation and learning in computer science. JOTSE **7**(2), 162–171 (2017)
10. Pan, R., Lo, H., Neustaedter, C.: Collaboration, awareness, and communication in real-life escape rooms. In: Proceedings of the 2017 Conference on Designing Interactive Systems, pp. 1353–1364. ACM (2017)
11. Kihara, T., Bendor, R., Lomas, D.: Designing an escape room in the city for public engagement with AI-enhanced surveillance. In: Extended Abstracts of the 2019 CHI Conference on Human Factors in Computing Systems, p. LBW1618. ACM (2019)
12. Menashe, J., Stone, P.: Escape room: a configurable testbed for hierarchical reinforcement learning. In: Proceedings of the 18th International Conference on Autonomous Agents and MultiAgent Systems, pp. 2123–2125. International Foundation for Autonomous Agents and Multiagent Systems (2019)
13. Shakeri, H., Singhal, S., Pan, R., Neustaedter, C., Tang, A.: Escaping together: the design and evaluation of a distributed real-life escape room. In: Proceedings of the Annual Symposium on Computer-Human Interaction in Play, pp. 115–128. ACM (2017)
14. Warmelink, H., et al.: AMELIO: evaluating the team-building potential of a mixed reality escape room game. In: Extended Abstracts Publication of the Annual Symposium on Computer-Human Interaction in Play, pp. 111–123. ACM (2017)
15. Chernova, S., Orkin, J., Breazeal, C.: Crowdsourcing HRI through online multiplayer games. In: 2010 AAAI Fall Symposium Series (2010)

HealthyLunch: A Serious Game for Educating and Promoting the Intake of the Recommended Number of Daily Servings Among Children

Ismael Edrein Espinosa-Curiel[1(✉)], Mitzi Josué Martínez-Rosas[1], Juan Manuel del Hoyo-Ceja[1], Edwin Emeth Delgado-Pérez[2], and Edgar Efrén Pozas-Bogarin[1]

[1] CICESE-UT3, Andador 10 #109, Ciudad del Conocimiento, 63197 Tepic, Nayarit, Mexico
ecuriel@cicese.mx

[2] Centro de Estudios e Investigaciones en Comportamiento, Universidad de Guadalajara (UdG), Francisco de Quevedo 180 Arcos Vallarta, 44130 Guadalajara, Jalisco, Mexico
http://idi.cicese.mx/

Abstract. The intake of bigger portions and the excess in the intake of servings of some foods groups is one of the factors that had been playing major roles in the rising rates of obesity worldwide. To help children to identify the serving size of popular food and the recommended daily number of servings of each food group for them, we developed *HealthyLunch* (HL). It is a serious game where players need to prepare to children lunch boxes that include the food for a day respecting the recommended daily number of servings for children of each food group, and avoiding exceeding the daily recommendations of calories, fat, sugar, and salt. The HL elements are based on nutrition knowledge and constructs from cognitive and behavioral theories. In this paper, we describe the design process of HL and report the results of the usability evaluation study.

Keywords: Childhood obesity · Serious game · Learning · Dietary behavioral change · Serving size · Recommended daily servings · Usability

1 Introduction

During the past two decades, childhood obesity has reached epidemic levels worldwide [16]. Childhood obesity can profoundly affect children's physical health, social, and emotional well-being, and self-esteem [16]. Childhood obesity is a multifactorial problem; however, one of the factors that had been playing

Supported by the Consejo Nacional de Ciencia y Tecnología (CONACyT), Mexico - National Problems Program Ref: PDCPN-2015-824, grant awarded to CICESE.

A. Liapis et al. (Eds.): GALA 2019, LNCS 11899, pp. 351–361, 2019.
https://doi.org/10.1007/978-3-030-34350-7_34

significant roles in the rising rates of obesity worldwide is the energy imbalance caused by the intake of bigger portions and the excess in the consumption of servings of some foods groups [4,16,19]. To ensure children grow appropriately and develop healthy habits, they need guidance on, and support for a healthy diet in early childhood [12] and serious games are an emerging strategy that can fulfill this need [14]. Serious games are innovative and enticing methods for attracting attention, educating, and promoting changes in knowledge, intentions, and human behaviors [2,8]. While there is a growing body of literature on the potential of serious games to influence cognitive development, dietary habits, and physical activity behaviors [2,8,14], Only a reduced number of studies describe the design and evaluation of serious games designed particularly for children [2,8,14]. Baranowski et al. [1], for instance, developed the video games "Escape from Diad" and "Nanoswarm: Invasion from Inner Space". These games were specifically designed to lower risks of type 2 diabetes and obesity by changing youth diet and physical activity behaviors. From an evaluation with children aged 10–12 years old, the authors found that players only increased their intake of fruits and vegetables. Schneider et al. [17] developed "Fitter Critters", an online video game to increase healthy eating and activity knowledge and improve health behaviors. In the game, children need to complete quests to learn how food and physical activity choices influence the behavior and health of a virtual pet called Critter. From an evaluation with students aged 8–12 years old, the authors found that player significantly increased their positive attitudes towards healthy eating and healthy eating self-efficacy, and the game obtain high acceptability by the players. Majumdar et al. [9] developed and evaluated "Creature 101" a game to promote energy balance-related behaviors associated with healthy intake and physical activity. In the game, players need to adopt a creature and help regain health. From an evaluation with students aged between 11 and 13 years old, the authors identified that players only significant decreases in the frequency and amount of consumption of sweetened beverages and processed snacks. Johnson-Glenberg and Hekler [6] developed and evaluated and designed "Alien Health", an embodied video game to teach students about nutrition and several guidelines of the MyPlate guidelines of the U.S. Department of Agriculture. In the game, players learned about nutrition through immediate feedback on how each selected item affected the Alien avatar's alertness/health state. From an evaluation with students aged between 9–10 years old, the authors identified that the players increased their nutrition knowledge and their knowledge regarding MyPlate. Marchetti et al. [10] developed and evaluated "Gustavo in Gnam's planet", a health game to improve knowledge and increase consumption of healthy foods of adolescent (14–18 years old). In the game, players help Gustavo to complete a run taking healthy food and avoiding unhealthy foods. The authors identified that players of this game increased their nutrition knowledge and partially changed dietary behaviors. In addition, they found that while all players found the game easy to use and clear, only 50% found the game interesting.

2 Present Study

Although the studies mentioned above showed positive results, yet, there is still a need to understand the application, limitations, and how to improve this type of game to maximize its effectiveness according to the capacity and interests of children [14]. In particular, we identified the following two opportunities. First, there is sparse evidence of the effectiveness of nutritional education serious games in children aged from 8 to 10 years since most of the current serious video games for nutrition education and behavior change were designed for or tested in children aged 10 years or over. The later latency stage of children development (from 8 to 10 years old) can be relevant to the design of games due to is in this stage when children start to show more independence from parents and have an intense interest in rules and behavioral standards. Besides, the children' self-control is far more reliable, and have an increased ability to remember, pay attention, think, reason, and concentrate. Second, despite the obesity problems related to the intake of bigger portions and the excess in the intake of servings of some foods groups, we did not identify a game explicitly designed to educate and promote the intake of the recommended food portion sizes and the daily food servings among children. Therefore, we developed *HealthyLunch* (HL), a serious game that focuses on help children between 8 to 10 years old to understand and apply three core nutritional concepts: (a) each food have a specific serving size (e.g., while a serving of apple is equal to one piece, a serving of banana is half piece); (b) there is a recommended number of daily servings that children should consume from each food group; and (3) that in addition to complying with the recommendations of servings, children must avoid exceeding the daily recommendations of calories, fat, sugar, and salt for them. The HL elements and mechanics are based on nutrition knowledge and cognitive and behavioral theories. HL is part of IFitKids, a platform that integrates minigames and components related to psychology, nutrition, and physical activity. In this paper, we describe the development process of HL and how constructs from cognitive and behavior theories were operationalized into the game elements to induce changes in the food servings intake of players. We also describe a usability study of HL.

3 Game Design

HL was designed and implemented by a multidisciplinary team composed by software developers, graphical designers, and a human-computer interaction expert, nutritionists and psychologists. We used the following three-step methodology to design and implement HL (see Fig. 1):

- *Step 1.* From a literature review and three multidisciplinary design sessions with two nutritionists and a psychologist, we established the target behaviors, change objectives, the base theories of behavior change, and the behavior change techniques (BCT) that could be integrated into the video game to support the behaviors change objectives.

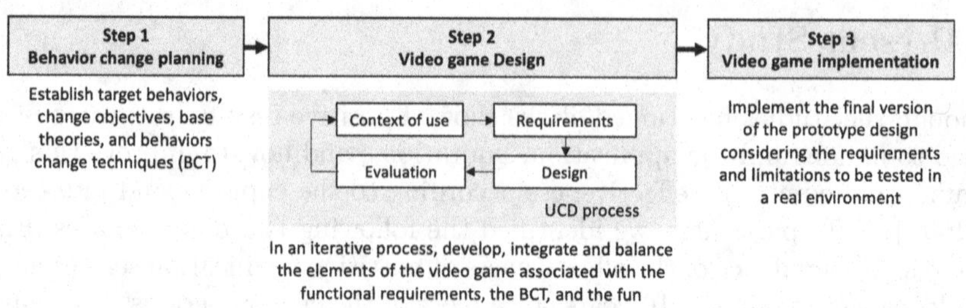

Fig. 1. Overview of activities conducted to design and implement HealthyLunch

- *Step 2.* We used a iterative design process based on the UCD methodology [13] to design HL. We conducted three cycles of UCD until we obtained the final design of HL. In each interaction, we improved the prototype based on the learning obtained from the previous cycle.
  - In the first cycle, we conducted two multidisciplinary design sessions with the participation of two nutritionists, one psychologist, one researcher with expertise in human-computer interaction, and two game designers. The session aimed to propose initial design ideas and requirements, define the nutritional concepts, and to define how to implement the selected BCTs into the gameplay elements. Based on the result of these activities, we designed an initial high-fidelity prototype that we evaluated with five children aged between 8 to 10 years. The children played with the prototype for 10 min and later participated in a focus group were encouraged to talk about their game experience (e.g., instruction, activities, challenges, game flow, human-computer interaction, and fun), and to draw new elements to add the game or new game features. Some suggestions were improve the tutorial, the nutrition explanation, the serving board, and the messages, clarify the mission, and emphasize rewards messages.
  - In the two subsequent cycles, we conducted the following activities. First, a multidisciplinary design session with the participation of the same professional from cycle one. The session aimed to discuss the changes suggested for the game and the new requirements obtained during the evaluation of the first cycle. In addition, to determine how to balance these features with the objectives of change, the BCTs, and fun elements. Based on the results of the session, we redesigned the high-fidelity prototype. Later, we conducted an evaluation session. Six and 15 children aged between 8 to 10 years participated in the second and third cycle evaluation, respectively. The children played with the high-fidelity prototype for 15 min. After that, the children participated in a focus group similar to the one carried out in cycle one. Some suggestions were to add a map to select the affected agent, add difficulty levels and an enemy, make interactive that affects agents, and add more fun elements. Finally, we conducted several multidisciplinary design sessions to discuss and select improvement proposals.

- *Step 3.* Based on the final version of the prototype, we implemented HL in the video game engine Unity. The implemented game also take into account the requirements and limitations to testing the video game in a real environment.

4 HealthyLunch

4.1 Structure

The adventure of HL unfolds in HealthyTown, a city where a group of evil chefs erased the nutrition knowledge of the brain of the health agents and made them eat unhealthily. Therefore, the city mayor assigns to the player the mission of preparing the lunch boxes for the affected agents until they relearn how to eat healthily. HL has three sections. In the *configuration and customization section*, players log-in, play the story of the game, select and buy avatars, and select from a map the next affected agent. In the *educational section*, the players learn about the serving size of popular food, the number of the recommended serving of each food category, and the children recommendations of calories, fat, sugar, and salt. Additionally, learn the game goal, how to play the game, the game options and elements, the indicators, and the results section. In the *training section*, the players prepare the lunch box for their assigned agents. The database of the game included serving size and nutritional information of 300 food popular grouped in eight categories. The lunch box should include the recommended number of daily servings of each food category but without passing the maximum recommended amount of calories, fat, sugar, and salt. For each food, the player has to consider how many servings is the selected portion. In addition, randomly appears questions related to the serving size of a particular food. The player earns coins if answer the questions correctly. We included a curve of increasing difficulty across the 20 levels of the game to encourage players to have fun through the end of the video game. In the first level, only appears the fruits category. While the difficulty increases, the other categories are added. Next, the game includes the calories, fat, sugar, and salt indicators. Finally, the more difficult levels start with a random number of servings assigned to each food categories. Additionally, an evil chef occasionally appears in the game and throws a bomb that changes the serving number of each food category of the lunch box, so the player must make the necessary adjustments in the lunch box to meet the requirements mentioned above. When the players complete the lunch box, start the results and feedback phase. In this phase, the Dr. Yokuro Kokoro review the numbers of servings of each food category added to the lunch box. If a food category has more servings than those recommended, Dr. Kokoro explains player that he/she should not go over the recommended number and does not give him points. Conversely, If it has less than recommended servings, Dr. Kokoro explains player that he/she must comply with the recommended servings and does not give points. Only when the player complies with the recommended servings, earns coins. When the review process is finished, the player sees the results screen that specifies the coins earned, the food categories in which he/she was wrong/right in the number of servings, its performance based on a three-star evaluation, and its position

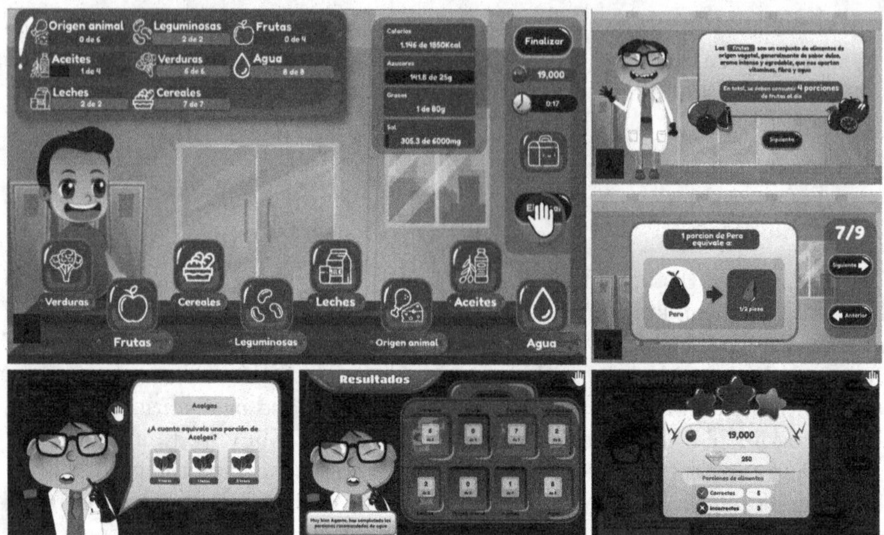

Fig. 2. HL's screens. (1) main screen in the practice phase, (2) explanation of the recommended portion of fruits, (3) explanation of the size of a serving of pear, (4) questions about the size of a serving of chard, (5) evaluation screen, and (6) results screen.

in the global ranking of players. If the player has many errors, he/she will have to repeat that difficulty level until unlocking the next level by obtaining three stars. Figure 2 shows some screens of the three sections.

4.2 Behavioral Change Theories and Techniques

We designed HL as a stimulating and engaging environment in witch key aspect of healthy behaviours and behaviors-specific knowledge are being promoted and strengthened. We used *cognitive behavioral therapy* (CBT) as the base to define the strategies to induce changes in the food serving intake of players. CBT has robust empirical evidence of its efficacy in aiding weight loss in obese patients and other kinds of dietary problems [3], and it is the recommended treatment not only for adults but also for children and adolescents [18]. CBT is based on the combination of the basic principles from behavioral and cognitive models, and group techniques that combine both approaches [7]. The gameplay elements of HL are based on BCTs that relates to the constructs of the cognitive and behavioral theories that are the base of the CBT, and to the social cognitive theory (SCT). Figure 3 explicitly shows the relationship between the gameplay elements, the BCTs, and the base theories. To define and classify the BCTs included in HL, we base our approach on the work of [11]. Related to behavioral theory, we included the constructs *behavioral shaping*, *behavior repetition and substitution*, *stimulus control*, and *learning by consequences*. Related to cognitive theory, we included the *cognitive restructuring* construct. Finally, from the SCT,

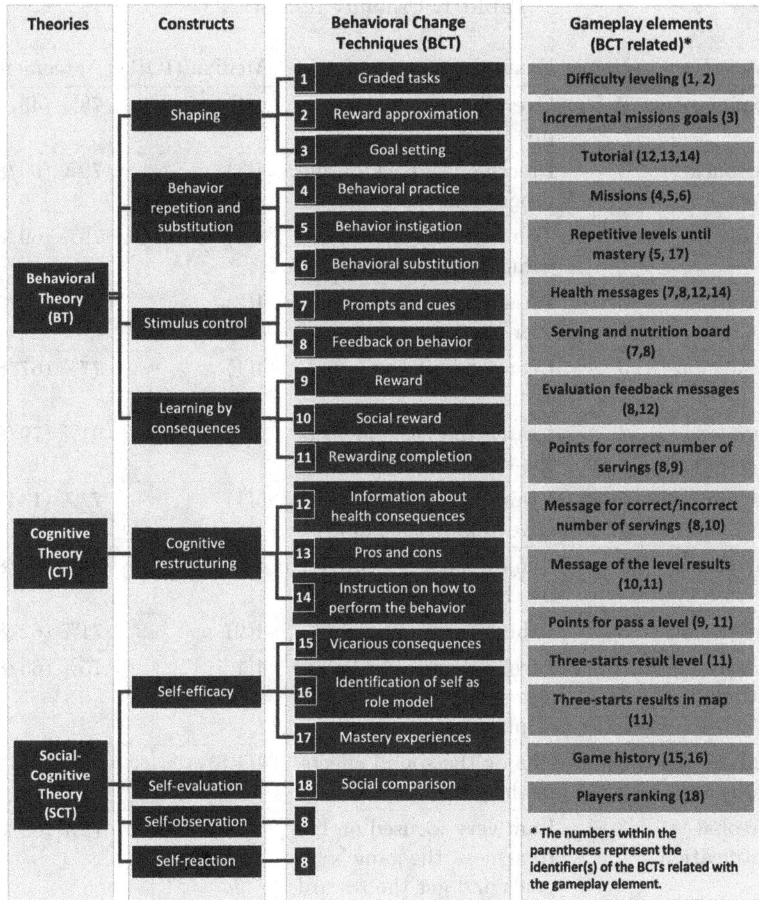

Fig. 3. Theory-based gameplay elements in HL

we included *self-efficacy*, *self-observation* and *self-reaction* constructs. Consult the work of [11] for a broad definition of the BCTs associated with the construct operationalized in HL.

5 Usability Evaluation

We conducted a study to obtain the opinion of children about the characteristics and elements HL. A total of 29 children (n = 15 female, n = 14 male) aged 8–10 (mean age 9.6, SD 0.76 years) of a primary school participated voluntarily in the experiment. Before collecting the data, we obtained written authorization from the school authorities and written consent from parents for the children to take part in the study. Later, the participants conducted seven game sessions of at least ten minutes per session, in 14 days (a session every two days). The total

Table 1. Usability results

#	Category	Items	Example	Median (IQR)	Agreement
1	Goal clarity	2	Overall game goals were presented clearly	4(1)	78% (45/58)
2	Feedback	3	I receive feedback on my progress in the game	4(1)	79% (69/87)
3	Challenge	3	The challenge of the game was adequate to me	4(1)	79% (69/87)
4	Autonomy	2	I feel a sense of control over the game	4(2)	59% (34/58)
5	Immersion	3	I cannot wait to play again	4(1)	77% (67/87)
6	Knowledge improvement	3	I catch the basic ideas of the knowledge taught	4(1)	91% (79/87)
7	Playability	7	I think it is easy to learn how to play the game	5(1)	77% (134/203)
8	Narratives	3	I enjoy the story provided by the game	4(2)	69% (60/87)
9	Enjoyment	3	I think the game is fun	4(2)	71% (62/87)
10	Creative freedom	3	I feel my curiosity is stimulated as the result of playing the game	4(1.5)	75% (65/87)
11	Audio aesthetics	3	I enjoy the sound effects in the game	4(1.5)	75% (65/87)
12	Personal gratification	3	I am very focused on how to achieve the game's goals and get the rewards	4(1)	79% (69/87)
13	Visual aesthetics	3	I enjoy the game's graphics	4(2)	68% (59/87)

Data are expressed as the median (interquartile range) of the participants' scores. The scores are (1) "Strongly disagree"; (2) "agree", (3) "Undecided", (4) "desagree", (5) "Strongly desagree".

average time that the children played was 1.2 h. When the students finished the game sessions, we applied a usability questionnaire. This questionnaire is based on two validated questionnaires [5,15], and had 47 items grouped in 13 categories. For each item, we asked the participants to indicate in a 5-point Liker-Type scale ranging from (1) "Totally disagree" to (5) "Totally agree" the level they believe the game accomplish each one of the questionnaire statements. Table 1, for each category, shows the number of items, an example of the statement, the median and the interquartile range, and the percentage of participants agreed that the game fulfills the statements of the categories. The agreement percentage represents the result of the division of the number of responses with evaluation 4 or 5 by the total number of responses.

6 Discussion

The game received a median score of 4 or above in all dimension which reflects high levels of usability. Most of the participants agreed that HL is fun, easy to use, have clear story, goals, and dialogues, provides useful feedback, and have pleasing sounds and graphics. Another significant result is that the most of the players agreed that the game adapts the difficulty to their capacity and skills, think that the game stimulated its curiosity and allows to be imaginative, helped them to improve their knowledge, and the game constantly motivated them to proceed further to the next stage or level. These characteristics provide them a good level of immersion since the most of the players agreed that forgot about time passing while playing the game, become unaware of the surroundings while playing the game, and cannot wait to play again. Finally, one aspect of improving in the video game is autonomy, because it was the subscale with the lowest rating. It refers to the control that the players feel in the game elements, and the game support provided to players so that they know what the next steps in the game are. The obtained results confirm that serious games for health can obtain good usability results [10,17]. In addition, these results provide evidence that the used development methodology can help to design serious game with good usability. A limitation of this study is that it was conducted in a single school and with few participants. However, given that the objective of this study was not to generalize our findings but to achieve an overall impression of the usability of HL, we consider that our results are valuable for researchers exploring the design space of this type of serious game.

7 Conclusions and Future Work

In this paper, we describe the development process of HL and how constructs from cognitive and behavior theories were operationalized into its elements to induce changes in the food servings intake of players. HL is a serious game to educate and promote the intake of the recommended number of daily servings of food groups among children aged between 8 and 10 years old. We conducted a usability study with 29 children aged between 8 to 9 years to obtain the children opinion about HL. The results showed that the most of the participants perceived HL as fun, easy to use, and immersive. In addition, they perceived that the game stimulates its curiosity and imagination, helped them to improve their knowledge, and provide personal gratification. These results provide insights into the utility of the methodology used to design HL. A future version of HL will include improvements to correct the definitions associated with the scales with the lowest ratings, especially in autonomy. A randomized controlled trial will be conducted to evaluate the effectiveness of HL to support the player learning and to improve the food servings intake of the players.

Acknowledgments. We would like to thank the participating experts and user who helped develop this serious game. We also thank the graphical designer Janeth Aguilar-Partida for participating in the graphical design of HL.

References

1. Baranowski, T., et al.: Video game play, child diet, and physical activity behavior change: a randomized clinical trial. Am. J. Prev. Med. **40**(1), 33–38 (2011). https://doi.org/10.1016/j.amepre.2010.09.029
2. Baranowski, T., et al.: Games for health for children: current status and needed research. Games Health J. **5**(1), 1–12 (2016). https://doi.org/10.1089/g4h.2015.0026
3. Castelnuovo, G., et al.: Cognitive behavioral therapy to aid weight loss in obese patients: current perspectives. Psychol. Res. Behav. Manag. **10**, 165–173 (2017). https://doi.org/10.2147/PRBM.S113278
4. English, L., Lasschuijt, M., Keller, K.L.: Mechanisms of the portion size effect. What is known and where do we go from here? Appetite **88**, 39–49 (2015). https://doi.org/10.1016/j.appet.2014.11.004. Portion Size
5. Fu, F.L., Su, R.C., Yu, S.C.: Egameflow: a scale to measure learners' enjoyment of e-learning games. Comput. Educ. **52**(1), 101–112 (2009). https://doi.org/10.1016/j.compedu.2008.07.004
6. Johnson-Glenberg, M.C., Hekler, E.B.: "Alien health game": an embodied exergame to instruct in nutrition and myplate. Games Health J. **2**(6), 354–361 (2013). https://doi.org/10.1089/g4h.2013.0057
7. Knapp, P., Beck, A.T.: Cognitive therapy: foundations, conceptual models, applications and research. Revista Brasileira de Psiquiatria **30**, s54–s64 (2008)
8. Lu, A.S., Kharrazi, H., Gharghabi, F., Thompson, D.: A systematic review of health video games on childhood obesity prevention and intervention. Games Health J. **2**(3), 131–141 (2013). https://doi.org/10.1089/g4h.2013.0025
9. Majumdar, D., Koch, P.A., Lee, H., Contento, I.R., Islas-Ramos, A.D.L., Fu, D.: "creature-101": a serious game to promote energy balance-related behaviors among middle school adolescents. Games Health J. **2**(5), 280–290 (2013). https://doi.org/10.1089/g4h.2013.0045
10. Marchetti, D., et al.: Preventing adolescents' diabesity: design, development, and first evaluation of "gustavo in gnam's planet". Games Health J. **4**(5), 344–351 (2015). https://doi.org/10.1089/g4h.2014.0107
11. Michie, S., et al.: The behavior change technique taxonomy (v1) of 93 hierarchically clustered techniques: building an international consensus for the reporting of behavior change interventions. Ann. Behav. Med.: Publ. Soc. Behav. Med. **46**(1), 81–95 (2013). https://doi.org/10.1007/s12160-013-9486-6
12. Nishtar, S., Gluckman, P., Armstrong, T.: Ending childhood obesity: a time for action. Lancet **387**(10021), 825–827 (2016). https://doi.org/10.1016/S0140-6736(16)00140-9
13. Norman, D.A., Draper, S.W.: User Centered System Design: New Perspectives on Human-Computer Interaction. L. Erlbaum Associates Inc., Hillsdale (1986)
14. Parisod, H., et al.: Promoting children's health with digital games: a review of reviews. Games Health J. **3**(3), 145–156 (2014). https://doi.org/10.1089/g4h.2013.0086

15. Phan, M.H., Keebler, J.R., Chaparro, B.S.: The development and validation of the game user experience satisfaction scale (guess). Hum. Factors **58**(8), 1217–1247 (2016). https://doi.org/10.1177/0018720816669646. pMID: 27647156
16. Sahoo, K., Sahoo, B., Choudhury, A.K., Sofi, N.Y., Kumar, R., Bhadoria, A.S.: Childhood obesity: causes and consequences. J. Fam. Med. Prim. Care **4**(2), 187–192 (2015). https://doi.org/10.4103/2249-4863.154628
17. Schneider, K.L., et al.: Acceptability of an online health videogame to improve diet and physical activity in elementary school students: "fitter critters". Games Health J. **1**(4), 262–268 (2012)
18. Wilfley, D.E., Kolko, R.P., Kass, A.E.: Cognitive-behavioral therapy for weight management and eating disorders in children and adolescents. Child Adolesc. Psychiatr. Clin. N. Am. **20**(2), 271–285 (2011). https://doi.org/10.1016/j.chc.2011.01.002
19. Young, L.R., Nestle, M.: The contribution of expanding portion sizes to the us obesity epidemic. Am. J. Public Health **92**(2), 246–249 (2002). https://doi.org/10.2105/AJPH.92.2.246. pMID: 11818300

Serious Business Game on Digitalization

Vera Stadler[1] and David Rueckel[2(✉)]

[1] Bissantz & Company GmbH, Nordring 98, 90409 Nuremberg, Germany
[2] Johannes Kepler University Linz, Altenberger Str. 69, 4040 Linz, Austria
david.rueckel@jku.at

Abstract. Through digital transformation programs, companies seek to break new ground to guarantee their long-term stability. Companies try to somehow prepare their employees for novel, technologically-driven trends and highlight the effects of digitalization on their companies. Therefore, serious games seem to be a proper method to train employees' skills in business-related contexts. This paper seeks to prove the need for a serious business game themed around digitalization and digital transformation by applying a qualitative research approach. Eight qualitative interviews with decision-makers in companies, universities and vocational schools were conducted in order to investigate whether such a serious game can achieve a learning effect and whether a digital transformation process can be depicted in a serious game. Data shows evidence for potential of a serious business game on digitalization and digital transformation.

Keywords: Serious business game · Digitalization · Digital transformation · Market potential · Qualitative research

1 Introduction

Employees show understanding for the necessity of digitalization and digital transformation within companies, even though this transformation is associated with fears and uncertainty. Projects dealing with digitalization and digital transformation cannot be successfully implemented in a company if the employees are not prepared for new technologies, processes and structures. Innovations in the company require a learning process among the employees; this includes not only the learning of new technologies, but also a change in the social order. The digital transformation is not only "passively" driven by technology; people must actively drive it. There are several ways to motivate employees to drive transformation, provide training, or offer training. [1, 2] Serious games are commonly used in teaching to impart knowledge in a playful environment. This method aims at the learning effect and the gaining ability of problem solving, whereby real environments are simulated within the structure of a game [3].

The following paper examines whether playing a serious business game centered around digitalization (SBGD) in a business context can increase the understanding of digital transformation. The aim of this game is not only to increase employees' acceptance of digital transformation processes in company settings, but also to provide a teaching method at universities and vocational schools with a focus on business

A. Liapis et al. (Eds.): GALA 2019, LNCS 11899, pp. 362–371, 2019.
https://doi.org/10.1007/978-3-030-34350-7_35

education. The paper is structured as follows: first, we report on the current state of the field on the terms digitalization, digital transformation and serious (business) games. Then, we state our research question and the applied methodology. Finally, we show the results of our study and discuss both the findings and recommendations for future research.

2 State of the Field

In the future, digitalization will increasingly network companies and encourage the formation of alliances. This means that specific knowledge and required capacities can be shared as needed [2]. In the context of digitization, the orientation of many companies has already changed significantly. For example, digital transformation has resulted in new markets, virtual platforms, more efficient processes and targeted customer acquisition [4].

The phrases digitization, digitalization and digital transformation summarize a crosswise related and fuzzy set of semantics, both in research and in practice. While digitization summarizes processes of converting an analog object to a digital one in a technical manner, digitalization describes a wider phenomenon including not only technical entities to be converted or transformed but also sociotechnical phenomena associated with digital technologies [5]. Digital transformation summarizes a long-term process that causes a change through digitalization, enabled by digital technologies and application systems [6]. Digital transformation thereby describes a wide phenomenon that changes companies, markets, people's lives and society lasting. The constant development of information and communication technologies (ICT) demands from companies a targeted implementation of new ideas. At the same time, ICTs must also be strategically embedded in the company [7]. This leads to a steady transformation of a company's structure, business functions, business processes and associated strategies, e.g., (digital) business strategy, IS strategy or digital transformation strategy. According to Matt et al. [8], the digital transformation strategy includes the following elements: use of technologies, change in value creation, change in structure and financing. These four dimensions must be combined; only then can the desired effect of digital change be achieved. Matt et al. [8] furthermore make clear that in order to integrate different transformations on different levels of abstraction into a holistic managerial concept, such transformations need to be categorized and operationalized, defining a strategy for the digital transformation. A strategic approach in the transformation process is crucial for a successful attempt in digital transformation [9–11]. Classical success factors, a common tool in strategic planning, for digital transformation strategies are hard to define, as there is no common consensus of the field in research answering the question of what successful transformation means in practice. It seems unclear whether digital transformation indicates a one-time transformation leading to a definable goal, such as a digital business strategy, or a steady, incremental process with the goal of the establishment of the revolving process.

A framework developed by Muehlburger et al. [12] contains nine enabling factors that have a positive effect on companies' digital transformation programs. These factors are divided into four categories: (1) workforce capabilities, whose enabling factors include individual creativity, innovation capabilities and ICT Literacy; (2) organizational values, which consists of an innovative organizational culture and internal and external collaboration; (3) organizational infrastructure, which contains the factors digital platform infrastructures, IT-agility and institutionalized innovation processes; and (4) management capabilities, which contains the factors strategic embeddedness and digital leadership.

These factors can influence a digital transformation initialization positively and form the basic scaffold for the SBGD. With these factors, the player should be guided through the game and thus experience the digital transformation in all relevant contexts. Serious Games are developed with the aim of solving a real problem or mastering a real situation [13]. This distinguishes them from traditional games, as they are not meant for entertainment but rather as a training method. The aim of these games is to teach and practice learning content in the game environment, while skills are expanded and tasks are trained. Since no uniform definition has existed until today, it can only be described by the characteristics a serious game must have. The game scenario must be designed in such a way that the player can apply learned knowledge in real life. Aspects of entertainment and aspects of education in the game must balance each other out. [14] Greco et al. [15] criticize the term "business game" as often used synonymously with the terms "management simulator". They emphasize that a business game is an intersection of serious games.

Greco et al. [15] characterize business games as serious games in a corporate environment, leading to one or both of the following: players are trained to perform hard and/or soft skills, and the performance of the players is evaluated during the business game – this evaluation can be carried out qualitatively and/or quantitatively [16]. The taxonomy of Greco et al. [15] includes five categories: Environment and Application, User Interface, Target Groups, User Relation and Model. Blažič and Blažič [16] extended the taxonomy of Greco et al. [15] with the category learnability. This taxonomy is considered as state of the art. With a total of 34 subcategories, it is possible to build a coherent application. This parameter-defining characteristics from Greco et al. and Blažič and Blažič must be incorporated in the development of the SBGD. Romero et al. [17] have examined serious games for these abilities and found that these abilities - along with eight others - are trained in serious games, having been found in all the serious games studied: communication, teamwork, ICT skills, social/cultural skills, critical thinking and problem solving. According to Faria et al. [18], business simulation games enable improvements in the areas of experiences, strategy, decision making, learning outcomes and teamwork. De Freitas and Jarvis [19] point out that the use of serious games make it possible to increase social and intercultural competence. There are also advantages to improve the application of methodical competencies and understanding of complex interrelationships. But in comparison to this, the risk of a decreasing educational effect when mapping a company due to the overall complexity is very high [20].

In general, literature does not define a clear target group for business simulation games. A game's degree of complexity must be adapted to the respective target group. As soon as a serious business game is adapted to individual needs, it can be used successfully in any target group. The literature review on the key terms digitization and serious business games concludes that the factors of positive effect on companies' digital transformation programs can be implemented in a serious game taxonomy successfully. To illustrate the relevance of the SBGD, we state the research goal of empirically to reaffirm the statement.

3 Methodology

To achieve the proposed research goal, the following research question was derived:

If a SBGD can strengthen the understanding of digital transformation in the context of corporate development, how must this topic be integrated in the game, and in which areas of the company can it finally be used? As the research is highly exploratory in nature, eight semi-structured expert interviews were conducted over a three-month period of time to answer the research question [21]. The average interview duration was 35 min. The interviews were electronically recorded to be fully transcribed, enabling a code-based qualitative content analysis.

The selection of experts had a central role in this research. The survey of the experts was not aimed exclusively at specific representatives with specialized knowledge in the fields SG and digitalization. Experts from three areas were interviewed; these areas correspond to existing literature and are based on the analysis of well-known providers who also offer their business games in these three areas. The target groups selected were companies, universities and vocational schools. The table (Table 1) below lists the eight interview partners (C for company, U for university, S for school).

Table 1. Interview partners

#	I	Level	Department	Position
1	C	Consulting	Business Process	Senior Manager
2	C	Group (Industry)	Information Technology	Personal Office
3	C	Trade and Service	Human Resources	Personal Management
4	U	University	Information Technology	Head of Department
5	U	University	Information Management	Program Director
6	U	University	Rector's office	Vice Rector Teaching
7	S	Vocational school	Directorship	Principal
8	S	Vocational school	Teacher	Economics

The questionnaire was divided into three subareas. First, the participants were asked about digitalization; second, they were asked about business games; and finally, they were given questions combining both previous topics, which provided information about the acceptance of the SBGD. To establish a common understanding of the topics Serious Games and Digitalization, general questions were asked at the beginning of each topic. Questions about the SBGD always related to the relevant research question. Finally, the interviewee was given time to ask common questions to the interviewer. The results from the individual discussions also leads to new approaches, which can be further discussed. While the relevance of the SBGD was critically appraised by the participants, the answers were sometimes also very critical. However, critical thinking allows for new perspectives on the SBGD.

To answer the research questions, we analyzed the text material using a qualitative content analysis approach. Thirteen deductive categories could be applied, and four inductive categories developed. The following chapter summarizes the results.

4 Results

The results section is structured in two main sections; the first section shows individual results from interviews (i1 … i8) in general, companies, universities and schools, and the second section shows cumulative and quantified results summarizing all interviews.

4.1 Individual Results

As digitalization is part of a steady but yet fastening change process, it must be managed and driven by companies. Since digitalization is a company-wide phenomenon, its management has to be made strategically and company-wide, and it cannot be the task of one department, e.g. IS department (i6). As universities' curricula usually are not only based on theoretical foundations representing the discipline, but also on the demands of business and markets, these institutions are part of the chance process. This is especially true for disciplines like "Business Informatics" or "(Management) Information Systems", which are particularly suitable for contents on digitalization and digital transformation. Even common Computer Science curricula are enriched with topics like automatization ("Industry 4.0") or artificial intelligence. In some instances, even new subjects, such as digital society, are created. Both have to focus on problem solving abilities concerning digitalization (i8). A SBGD thus has to combine all common strategies, business functions and business processes in order to address the complex multi-level nature of the transformation (i7). New ways of thinking must be initiated playing the game, enabling employees to engage creatively and actively participate within the transformation process (i6, i7). The game supports awareness for the necessity of digitalization and insight into the importance of companies' transformation (i7).

Companies' View

All three participants representing companies supported the (high) relevance of the topic and stated that it is a matter of companies' culture to successfully transform. Employees are seen as crucial elements of culture. A successful transformation is highly dependent upon the following factors: ability to change (i1), culture (i1, i2, i3), leadership (i3), flexibility (i2), speed (i2) and competencies (i3). Even though the level of digital transformation varies from company to company, it is crucial to transform strategically on all managerial levels so that all employees are involved (i1). Therefore, employees have to develop further competencies at both the team level and at the individual level (i1, i2, i3). Two companies noted that they already train their employees on topics dealing with digital transformation; one company even has a "roadshow" to show employees the chances gaining from transformation. Even the SME teaches employees about the changes arising from transformation.

Serious business games both support employees in the development of team abilities and communication and strengthens self-consciousness in complex business settings (i1, i2, i3). All companies interviewed currently utilize serious business games, mainly in HR development. Even though companies' strategies and governance must stipulate serious games as method in general, all companies interviewed, independently from industries, support the usefulness of a SBGD for companies. They see their employees as target groups and are willing to pay for such a game. The business game has to be highly customizable depending on the companies' size, its state of transformation and the disruptive ability of digitalization (i1). The target group may also vary, as C-level managers from large companies may already be familiar with the topic (i2). In this case, companies' tactical and operational layers may serve as better target groups, as the combination of business functions and business processes can provide a deeper understanding of potential of transformation (i2). Combining strategic, tactical and operational layers in one game setting may lead to unwanted leadership confusion (i2). Very small companies (e.g. craft business) are not seen as suitable target groups.

The key benefits arising from the application of the SBGD in companies are summarized (i1, i2, i3) in the following: (1) employees get in touch with new ways to gain insights concerning the potential of transformation; (2) employees gain knowledge regarding the complex relations within business functions and processes; and (3) broad application enables knowledge transfer into the companies.

Schools' View

The participants representing schools are aware of the importance of the topic, even though it has not found its way into schools' timetables. Digitalization is part of (multi)-media education and is not taught in the sense of a broader phenomenon.

Serious business games are applied in all schools interrogated. Games dealing with managerial and economical topics were positively adopted by the pupils, even at a rather early age (15–17). The identified benefits are the interactive pupil contact and the chance to interact with companies (e.g., presenting the results outside of school), even though pupils' long-term motivation seems to be a problem.

The question of whether or not the application of the SBGD in schools is useful is a noted controversy. Whereas participants from schools find it rather useful, universities' representatives find it too early to be effective. Schools' representatives find it useful for pupils at the end of high school.

Universities' View

All participants representing universities support the relevance of the topic as they enrich their curricula with topics concerning digitalization and digital transformation. The topic is not only seen as a topic by itself but also as a multidimensional part of different established topics and courses such as process management or human resource management. Therefore, digitalization as a topic has to be integrated in faculties and departments (i6, i7, i8). Universities shall continue teaching core competencies (e.g., communication, social skills, logical thinking), but as these competencies change over time, they must focus on new competencies (e.g., ability to change and digital thinking) as well (i7, i8). Serious business games are common and well established at universities in diverse settings. They are used to display complex relations between different topics, such as production theory and accounting. These complex relations are discussed as students must communicate and therefore set up a theoretical construct. Another benefit arises from the inclusion of students who are typically shy in other settings (i7).

Universities are doubtlessly seen as target groups for the SBGD (i1, i2, i6, i7, i8) and are willing to participate in the development of the game. Students from managerial programs as well as from technical programs are certain target groups, as both programs nowadays are not purely focused on core subjects. In case of technical universities with a stronger focus on (technical) core subjects, a broader introduction into management theory could be necessary. The most relevant programs for the SBGD are interface disciplines, such as (Management) Information Systems or Business Informatics (i6, i7, i8). SBGD could also be used to connect programs, as the game could be applied by mixed teams (e.g., managerial and technical). Independently from the disciplinary background of the program, the SBGD is more suitable for students in master's programs or at the end of their bachelor's programs, as deeper insights can be achieved when findings are combined with theory (i6, i7, i8). All universities interviewed are willing to invest in such a serious game in case of long-term application and further development by its creators (i6, i7, i8).

4.2 Cumulative Results

The participants only spoke positively about the SBGD. Most of them had already taken part in a business plan game themselves (78%) or were already using a business game in their organization (89%). Further training in the field of digitalization has already been implemented at several universities and companies interviewed (44%). All participants (100%) see serious business games as an alternative teaching method for further continuing education in all three target groups. The results from the literature review on serious business games and digitalization were confirmed by the statements of the eight interviews. First, the following table (Table 2) presents the attributes and elements according to the taxonomy of Greco et al. [15] compared to the collected attributes, as noted by the experts.

Second, Fig. 1 presents the recognized positive effects of company simulation on competence development. There is an overlap of seven skills, considered to be future-relevant for employees and expectant employees, in both the literature [17–19] and the experts' interviews: communication, teamwork, ICT skills, social/cultural skills, methodical competencies (problem solving) and decision making (critical thinking).

Finally, the research goal and questions of this paper can be answered. The aim of this research was to investigate the need of a SBGD, used as a teaching tool in various organizations to achieve a comprehensive understanding of the topic of digitalization. The taxonomy of Greco et al. [15] is regarded as a practical approach for the parametrication of serious business games and can be used in the development process of the SBGD. Muehlburger et al. [12] present factors of digital transformation programs must be represented in the SBGD as elements of the storyline of the game and as parametrization of the game. As target groups of the game companies, universities and high schools could be surveyed. In the companies, the target persons are surveyed based on the degree of digitalization's penetration in the company. In the case of

Table 2. Parameters from the literature and the empirical data collection

Category (Greco et al.)	Attribute (Greco et al.)	Element (Greco et al.)	Attribute (Interview)
Environment of application	Use of teacher	Support by coach	Use of a moderator (i3, i7)
Design elements of user interface	Internal time	Self-proceeding	Compressed period of the game (i5)
Target groups, goals & feedback	Debriefing	Collective and individual	Different forms of debriefing depending on the target group (i2, i3)
	Feedback	Immediate and final	Feedback promotes AHA-effects (i2)
	Feedback degree	Complete	Feedback promotes AHA-effects (i2)
User relation/Community	Player composition	Multi-team	Multiple teams in the game (i3, i4, i8)
	Player relation	Static in team	Multiple teams in the game (i3, i4)
	Role playing	Yes	Players take a role in the company (i6)
Model	Domain	Realistic	Realistic illustration (i3)
	Configurability of the model	High	Individualization (i2, i3, i5)
	Fidelity	Medium	Topic of DT should not be too complex (i6)

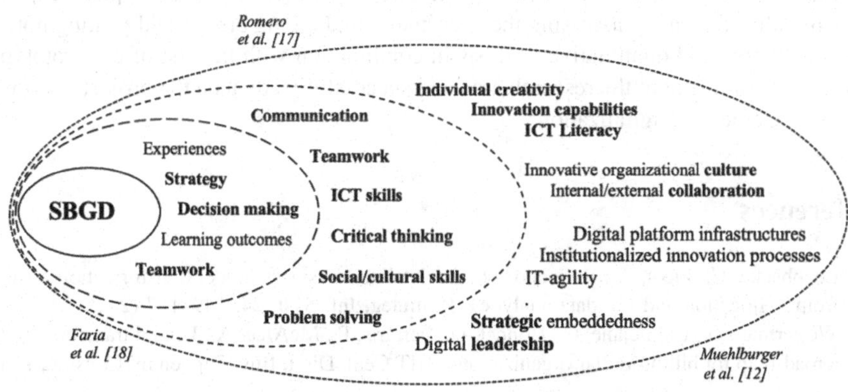

Fig. 1. Focused skills in the SBGD

corporate groups, the operative level was surveyed; in the case of SMEs, a hybrid form (operative and strategic level) is proposed. Finally, the SBGD must fit in companies' strategy and corporate policies. At universities, students of management and technology study path, and in high schools, pupils over the educational level 10, are exemplified.

5 Discussion and Future Work

Technology is not the single driver of digital transformation programs; technology opens up new ways for companies to go. The continuous development of the organization and the development of new business models requires employees who recognize and implement these opportunities. Further training in the fields of digitalization and team building is already being carried out in the companies. Serious business games are used to map many complex topics and relationships; they occur in different forms and areas. The SBGD shows players how the organization as a whole can be viewed with a focus on "digitalization". This teaching method shows digitization from a point of view that not only focuses on individual subareas but recognizes digitization as a whole. As a positive conclusion, it can be summarized that all respondents have reacted positively to the topic of "serious business game". The SBGD can be offered as a teaching method to add value in individual areas. Communication and team building can be strengthened in addition to the general understanding of digitalization and its digital transformation programs. The interpersonal exchange provided can lead to new ideas that can be actively implemented by the employees within the company.

Due to the limited amount of possible interview partners with expertise and the common biases associated with every exploratory, qualitative study, the following procedure is recommended. The first prototype should be implemented with the evaluated parameters (Table 2) and aimed at universities (pilot); students can firstly assume predefined roles and no individual company needs to be mapped – a generic company can be depicted. This method facilitates the implementation, and this procedure is less error-prone. After testing the prototype, students can complete a questionnaire after the game, assessing the user interface, logging errors, and posting notes. This qualitative and quantitative analysis in combination with the test of the prototype can further complement the research area and successfully advance the project "Serious Business Game on Digitalization".

References

1. Loebbecke, C., Picot, A.: Reflections on societal and business model transformation arising from digitization and big data analytics. J. Strateg. Inf. Syst. **24**, 149–157 (2015)
2. Westerman, G., Calméjane, C., Bonnet, D., Ferraris, P., McAfee, A.: Digital transformation: a road-map for billion-dollar organizations. MIT Cent. Digit. Bus. Capgemini Consult., 1–68 (2011)
3. De Lope, R.P., Medina-Medina, N.: A comprehensive taxonomy for serious games. J. Educ. Comput. Res. **55**, 629–672 (2017)
4. von Leipzig, T., et al.: Initialising customer-orientated digital transformation in enterprises. Procedia Manuf. **8**, 517–524 (2017)
5. Legner, C., et al.: Digitalization: opportunity and challenge for the business and information systems engineering community. Bus. Inf. Syst. Eng. **59**, 301–308 (2017)

6. Venkatraman, N.: IT-enabled business transformation: from automation to business scope redefinition. Sloan Manag. Rev. **35**, 73 (1994)
7. Leyh, C., Bley, K.: Digitalisierung: Chance oder Risiko für den deutschen Mittelstand? – Eine Studie ausgewählter Unternehmen. HMD Prax. Wirtsch. **53**, 29–41 (2016)
8. Matt, C., Hess, T., Benlian, A.: Digital transformation strategies. Bus. Inf. Syst. Eng. **57**, 339–343 (2015)
9. Pagani, M.: Digital business strategy and value creation: framing the dynamic cycle of control points. MIS Q. **37**, 617–632 (2013)
10. Bharadwaj, A., El Sawy, O.A., Pavlou, P.A., Venkatraman, N.: Visions and voice on emerging challenges in digital business strategy. MIS Q. **37**, 633–634 (2013)
11. Mithas, S., Tafti, A., Mitchell, W.: How a firm's competitive environment and digital strategic posture influence digital business strategy. MIS Q. **37**, 511–536 (2013)
12. Muehlburger, M., Rueckel, D., Koch, S.: A framework of factors enabling digital transformation. In: Proceedings of the Twenty-fifth AMCIS, Cancun (2019)
13. De Gloria, A., Bellotti, F., Berta, R., Lavagnino, E.: Serious games for education and training. Int. J. Serious Games **1**, 2384–8766 (2014)
14. Abt, C.C.: Serious Games: The Art and Science of Games That Simulate Life. Viking Compass Book, New York (1970)
15. Greco, M., Baldissin, N., Nonino, F.: An exploratory taxonomy of business games. Simul. Gaming **44**, 645–682 (2013)
16. Blažič, A.J., Blažič, B.D.J.: Exploring and upgrading the educational business-game taxonomy. J. Educ. Comput. Res. **52**, 303–340 (2015)
17. Romero, M., Usart, M., Ott, M.: Can serious games contribute to developing and sustaining 21st century skills? Games Cult. **10**, 148–177 (2015)
18. Faria, A.J., Hutchinson, D., Wellington, W.J., Gold, S.: Developments in business gaming: a review of the past 40 years. Bus. Gaming **40**, 1–24 (2008)
19. De Freitas, S., Jarvis, S.: Serious games - engaging training solutions: a research and development project for supporting training needs: colloquium. Br. J. Educ. Technol. **38**, 523–525 (2007)
20. Strzalkowski, T., Symborski, C.: Lessons learned about serious game design and development. Games Cult. **12**, 292–298 (2017)
21. Myers, M.D., Newman, M.: The qualitative interview in IS research: examining the craft. Inf. Organ. **17**, 2–26 (2007)

Understanding Attitudes Towards Emergency Training Modes: Conventional Drills and Serious Games

Hamna Aslam(✉), Irek Almuhametov, and Albert Sakhapov

Artificial Intelligence in Games Development Lab, Innopolis University, 420500 Innopolis, Russian Federation
h.aslam@innopolis.ru

Abstract. Emergency evacuation plans are central to keep people alive and safe in life-threatening situations. However, just making plans is not enough to expect positive outcomes such as no fatalities or injuries. Even a carefully devised evacuation plan becomes worthless if it is not adopted fully. Emergency training and repetitive drills are being carried out to educate people but in most situations, this training is dull. Consequently, the trend is towards other means of delivering emergency education such as games and entertainment. To understand peoples' attitudes towards real drills as well as serious game based training, we developed a game for university students. The game models the university structure and shows fire erupted at certain parts of the university. The player has to evacuate using their knowledge of emergency exits and take other actions like dial an emergency number etc. After gameplay, the participants were interviewed about their preferred means of emergency education. The responses obtained demonstrate how participants feel about the seriousness of emergencies and which means of training (games based or drills) they deem productive for themselves.

Keywords: Serious game · Conventional drills · Emergency training modes · Gamification

1 Introduction

Emergency evacuation plans are not limited to crowded areas and high rise buildings such as shopping centers, educational institutions, residential areas, and workplaces, etc. Evacuation schemes are indispensable for airplanes to ships. However, apart from the challenge of devising evacuation schemes, we also face a challenge of the decent implementation of these schemes [9] and implementation is dependent on training. Invoking the attention of the participant is a big concern in the training sessions where participants perceive themselves rarely facing that emergency in their life. The external obligation by the authorities cannot lead farther than getting attendances from the individuals. The lack of interest of the participants at serious training sessions become evident when they are questioned about the general information provided in these sessions.

A. Liapis et al. (Eds.): GALA 2019, LNCS 11899, pp. 372–382, 2019.
https://doi.org/10.1007/978-3-030-34350-7_36

Serious games have proven to be a productive tool in the sectors of education, training, evaluations, diagnostics, and many more. With the diversity in application areas, Djaouti et al. [3] present a classification of serious games as a G/P/S model. G/P/S stands for *Gameplay, Scope, and Purpose*. This classification system assists in identifying the games according to the needs of the user or domain. Furthermore, [1] provides a relationship between pedagogical elements and game mechanics. This supports alignment between pedagogical goals and game mechanics to achieve the intended results.

In the context of emergency handling and training, Aslam et al. [2] present a serious game that allows players to design relief camps within specified constraints. An Evolutionary Algorithm is implemented, which also finds the best placements according to defined criteria and players can optimize and compare their settings with the evolutionary algorithm's results for best possible designs. Haferkampet al. [4] proposes the DREAD-ED game for training effective communication to transfer personnel at the time of the emergency. Players are the members of the crisis management team and their roles are the same as in a real-life situation. After presenting a disaster, the players must make decisions to deal with the emergency effectively. The disaster damages are measured on scales as causalities, hazard risk, operations, and public relations. The participants involved a team of students and a team of crisis managers. The crisis managers outperformed the students. The results depicted that training is an essential element for dealing with emergencies effectively and serious games enhance the training process by rapid feedback and the possibility of different scenarios to deal with in the game. Furthermore, Ribeiro et al. [5] point out the advantages of virtual video games over physical emergency training. Motivation, higher completion rate, challenging situations and curiosity about outcomes. The game presents a university building and a test was conducted with four types of groups, people with previous knowledge of building and one group video game players and one group, non-players and people with prior knowledge of the building and one group video game players and one group, non-players. The average time to evacuate the building is shortest for the people with the knowledge of the building and who were frequent game players and the longest time was taken by participants with knowledge of the building and no experience of playing games. The evacuation emergency training is as important for ships as for buildings and airplanes. Vanem and Skonj [10] discusses the importance of in time evacuation in case of maritime incidents. Apart from fire, collision and grounding of passenger ships, are the incidents wherein time evacuation is indispensable. For this purpose, International Maritime Organization is undergoing evacuation analysis and the FIRE EXIT project is providing a ship evacuation simulator that considers all possibilities of different types of maritime incidents and carries out evacuation procedure testing for all circumstances. The results obtained from this study highlight areas for improvement to reduce the occurrence of ship incidents and demonstrate risks associated with emergency evacuation in case of fire, collision, and grounding of ships.

To train hospital staff, Silva et al. [7] present a serious game EVA about fire emergency evacuation. The player is presented with a scenario in which a patient on a wheelchair should be carried to the exit at the time of the fire emergency. The time of evacuation, as well as other factors, are recorded for analysis. The results gathered from the game give an insight into different kinds of behaviors that can emerge at the time of chaos and emergency. Each player's behavior and actions are saved in a log data file to analyze their decisions based on their prior knowledge of evacuation rules. Ribeiro et al. [6] also present a serious game for fire evacuation training. The simulator presents a player standing in the Informatics Engineering department. A fire erupts suddenly and the timer starts. A player should run for the nearest emergency exit. The game play statistics have been collected to analyze the behavior of the player in comparison with their prior knowledge about the building. The results showed that sixty-five percent of the players without the previous knowledge of the building missed the emergency exits and left the building through the common exit.

The user study conducted in this research paper presents a serious game to participants to examine their knowledge about emergency guidelines as well as to identify their preferences and attitudes towards conventional emergency drills and serious game based practice. The participants of this study are students at Information Technology University in Russia. The university conducts fire drills regularly to limited engagement. To increase engagement, we have developed an emergency evacuation game that models the structure of the university. The player spawns at a random point in the university and has to escape fire using their knowledge of emergency exits as well as emergency evacuation rules.

The study starts with a survey to analyze participants' behaviour and knowledge about evacuation guidelines. After filling in the survey form, a gameplay session is held. The participants were interviewed after gameplay focusing on their opinion and preferred mode of emergency training. The study design, responses obtained as well as results of the study are elaborated in the following sections.

The remainder of the paper is organized as follows. Section 2 describes the emergency evacuation game modeled on the university's building. Section 3 presents the study design and results of the survey as well as a gameplay session. Section 4 presents the participants' interview feedback. Section 5 presents analysis upon participants' feedback and Sect. 6 draws conclusions.

2 Emergency Evacuation Game

The game has been developed using the Unity 3D Engine. The game setting is the university building where a player emerges randomly in any part of the university. The fire erupts and spreads as shown in Fig. 1 and a player has to exit the university. The game is classified as game-based/training and simulation/teenagers(students), according to G/P/S framework [3].

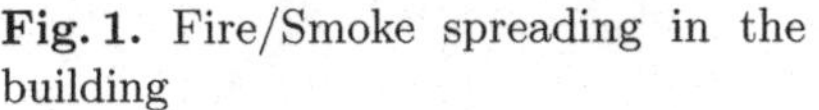

Fig. 1. Fire/Smoke spreading in the building

Fig. 2. Emergency alarm

2.1 Actions Integrated

A player can perform the following actions:

1. Walk freely in the university
2. Use stairs
3. Use elevators
4. Press fire alarm button, as shown in Fig. 2
5. Call an emergency number in the game interface (such as pressing a certain key to input a number)
6. Open doors
7. Jump over the railing of the second, third and fourth floor.

2.2 Game Ending Conditions

The game ends either by the player winning or losing the game. The player wins the game if they exit the university. The game also ends if the player loses under the following conditions:

1. A player jumping over the railing
2. Going into a zone which is on fire.

2.3 Gameplay Information

The action possibilities during gameplay were recorded in the output file. Furthermore, player's start and final exit point is recorded to examine how far they ran from the nearest emergency exit. The output file consists of the following information.

1. Player's starting position
2. Missed nearest exits from the spawn point
3. If the fire alarm is activated by the player or not
4. If the emergency number is dialed or not
5. Distance between player's spawn and final exit point.

3 Survey and Gameplay Results

The study consisted of twenty-nine participants who were the students of the bachelors program in Information Technology. The participants answered a questionnaire followed by a gameplay session. The participants were interviewed by the observer after the gameplay. The interview questions focused on understanding participants' behaviour about emergency training modes. Their feedback and comments were recorded and provide an insight into which training modes are preferred according to individual needs and perceptions.

3.1 Results of Survey

The survey has been filled by twenty-nine participants. The questions included in the survey as well as results obtained are presented as follows:

1. Have you attended a fire drill at the university or before?
   —Twenty-two participants have attended the drill in the university and seven participants have not attended in the university but they have attended several times during school years.
2. How many fire exits you are familiar with in this building?
   —Participants gave an approximate number. Three participants informed that they have no idea and did not guess. Six participants mentioned one exit which is the main exit of the building and rest of the participants were familiar with three emergency exits on average.
3. Have you ever experienced a fire emergency or an earthquake?
   —Eight participants have experienced an emergency in general, either an earthquake or a fire emergency.
4. What are the emergency numbers in case of a fire emergency or any other disaster?
   —Twenty-three participants correctly stated the emergency number. Four participants did not specify the emergency number. Two participants mentioned 911 as the emergency number that is not the emergency number in Russia or in their native countries. Participants informed that this is the first number that came to their mind as they frequently hear it in movies, etc.
5. In case of a sudden emergency such as an earthquake or a fire emergency, what would be your immediate response? Select all that you think you would probably do: (*The number of times each option has been selected is written after the statement*)
   - I will run randomly to exit the building—(*7*)
   - If the emergency alarm is not activated automatically, I will manually pull it to activate—(*18*)
   - If I could find a fire extinguisher, I will attempt to fight the fire (irrespective of the size of the fire)—(*6*)
   - I will try to use an elevator to get to the ground floor as quickly as possible—(*0*)

- I will utilize my knowledge of emergency exits and try to exit from them—(*23*)
- If caught in smoke, I will crawl on my knees to evacuate—(*19*)
- If caught in smoke, I will run as fast possible to exit the building—(*7*)
- I will collect my belongings first and evacuate—(*10*)
- If I have not seen the fire, I would ignore the fire alarm and prefer asking people in student chat groups about the situation—(*18*)
- I would prefer jumping from the window—(*0*)
- I will look at the floor evacuation plan if I do not know where to run—(*22*)
- I will stay calm and keep doing my work—(*3*)
- I will run after other people, hoping that they know where they are going—(*8*)
- In case of an earthquake, I would sit under the table and wait for it to end—(*9*)
- I will try to help other people who cannot escape—(*17*)
- First of all, I will call my family or friends if I suspect an emergency—(*2*)
- I will dial 112, if I suspect an emergency—(*12*).

6. My usual practice is:
   - Familiarizing myself with the emergency exits at my work place or university—(*10 participants selected this option*)
   - I am not interested in getting myself familiarized with emergency plans at my work place or university—(*19 participants selected this option*).

The results identify certain commonalities in participants' behaviour such as if fire is not seen, they would probably ignore the alarm and investigate the situation via student chat groups before taking any action. Upon fire confirmation, some opted for the probability to run randomly or run after other people to find the exit. Majority of the participants also informed that they would try to utilize their knowledge of any emergency exit to evacuate. The survey results are useful for developing further drill sessions. A special concentration on participants' highlighted point during emergency drills can increase the probability of desired behaviours during emergency situations.

3.2 Results of Gameplay

According to game mechanics, a player can win the game by successfully escaping the fire through any emergency exit of the university building. There are seventy spawn points defined in the game and when the game starts, a spawn point is chosen randomly from these seventy points. The output file keeps a record of the player's spawn point and the exits near to this spawn point. Player's exit location and number of nearest exits missed till they evacuated are displayed in the output file. The player does not lose the game by using an elevator or not pressing fire alarm. Output file displays this information after gameplay and also shows if the player has dialed an emergency number or not and if the number was correct or not.

The output file of all participants demonstrates that twenty-five participants won the game (such as successfully exited the university building) and four lost the game. However, winning corresponds to exiting the university and any exit could be used. Twelve participants used the nearest exit from their spawn point to exit the university. Seventeen participants missed seven nearest exits on average. One participant attempted to use the elevator.

The gameplay also provides an opportunity to dial an emergency number. However, the message displayed on the screen was missed by the majority of participants. Participants informed that they would dial an emergency number but they could not understand this option availability as the message was in a small font and was not clearly visible. For further gameplay sessions, this point is noted to improve the game design.

4 Participants' Responses and Feedback

The participants feedback inform that game based training is considered a productive way of learning evacuation rules as well as getting oneself familiarized with the exits of the building. However, participants considered conventional fire drills, a necessity and suggested to incorporate both means in the training process. Responses from some participants are stated as follows:

1. *"I am from a mountainous region and I have witnessed many earthquakes. I remember one incident when I was in school, there was an earthquake and alarms were not working, teachers were running and telling everybody to evacuate. There were multiple training sessions in school and those were helpful. I think, for me, playing a game would be enough but I also need to go through the university and see the exit doors practically. I also believe that alarm system should be accurate in the dormitory as I cannot differentiate if the alarm is ringing because of cooking smoke or real fire emergency."*

2. Another participant stated,

   "I have attended drills in school and I know emergency numbers because I have seen cartoons at the railway station. While waiting for the trains, there was nothing much to do, so I was always watching television on which educational cartoons were shown about emergency responses, therefore, I remember emergency numbers accurately. School training and drills are really important and game based training will work too"

   One participant stated,

3. *I would not prefer game based training. I believe, it is useful to have depiction of real scenario. I have witnessed a fire emergency in my childhood. The training and drills were useful because we knew where to go and what to do. I suggest that the training education should simulate a situation so that people realize the importance of training.*

4. Another response states,

   "Both are useful; fire drills and game based training. Drills are good as you see the real scenario. It is also necessary to be familiar with all the exits of the university. Game is useful to know all emergency exits. It is convenient through the game, as in real-life, I believe nobody would like to walk through the whole university to know all the emergency exits. Game based training is good for children too. I have attended training in school. When the alarm was ringing, we were going to the stadium and teachers were counting all students and were checking the total time it took for everybody to evacuate."

5. One participant suggested to have drills frequently and states,

   "I prefer drills over game based training as I cannot realize the actual emergency situation via a game."

6. Another response,

   "Real drills are useful. But more people will play a game. Game based training is useful for huge places such as shopping malls. People can play before shopping. I would say that, drills should be scheduled during boring lectures that will ensure that many students will attend the drill. Moreover, drills can be in a drama or skit scenario, to make them more interesting"

7. *"Game based training in evacuation situation is useful and convenient. However, real drills are needed as gameplay is something else and experiencing something in reality is something else."*

8. *"It would be more interesting if the game is virtual reality based. Though I did not understand all details through current gameplay, game based training is a nice idea for several sessions of training. I remember, once somebody was making popcorn in oven and smoke alarm started ringing. Initially, I thought, something serious happened. But then I found out that it happened because of popcorn. I believe that there should be a separate alarm system to detect smoke because of cooking and smoke from real serious situations."*

9. *"I like to explore the surroundings. Therefore, I pay attention to maps and emergency plans. Therefore, it can be interesting, if I see the map of the university at the beginning of the game. I would prefer more stress in the game such as some situations creating panic and non-player characters blocking the space."*

The responses from the participants inform that emergency training is considered a necessity and small details affect learning experience such as some would prefer seeing a map before gameplay or drill practice to be aware of all emergency exit locations. Furthermore, as one participant highlighted, the cartoons and safety demonstrations at public places helped them memorize emergency numbers. As mentioned earlier, two participants mentioned 911 as an emergency number as this is the first number that they remembered because of frequently hearing it in the movies. This highlights that in addition to training sessions, emergency guidelines can be emphasized through other means such as digital demonstrations in public places as well as incorporation in the entertainment medium.

5 Participants' Feedback and Attitude Towards Emergency Training Modes

Participants' responses and feedback suggests, ten participants considered the game based training productive for them, four participants preferred being trained through real drills, and fifteen participants considered and suggested both modes of training useful and productive for them.

The participants who mentioned only real drills as an effective mode of training stated the rationale that they prefer to be trained in an environment as close to reality as possible. Another participant informed that they cannot realize the emergency situation via gameplay. Furthermore, one participant informed that drills are a better simulation of an emergency in terms of noise, chaos, and visuals, etc. The drills are definitely worth the cost and effort especially for those who suffer from panic attacks.

The participants who opted for game based training informed that game is useful and convenient to memorize the location of exit doors and emergency rules. Other participants gave similar rationale and stated that real drills are boring and monotonous. Therefore, they would prefer game based training as it would be fun to know if they have won or lost the game.

The responses from participants who preferred incorporation of both modes of training suggested that game is advantageous to get oneself familiarized with the emergency exits and evacuation rules. One participant stated that in case of emergency, it requires more than just knowing evacuation rules and exit locations, in this case, real drills are significant as a person gets the experience of walking through exits in chaos and is more prepared for such situations. Real drills are advantageous to teach corporation in emergencies.

The responses and participants' feedback highlight that game based training is considered an effective mode of training for teaching evacuation rules and exit locations. However, the majority of the participants believe that drills despite their monotonous mechanism should be conducted as they are closer to reality simulation. The suggestions obtained from participants include, the game must include challenging and chaotic situations such as player being stuck among a group of people as well as other hindrances creating panic and stress.

One participant suggested to create an option in a game where player can collect their belongings and they have to decide if they want to use this option or not. The participant mentioned air-crash incident happened on May 5th, 2019. Some of the survivors were seen carrying their belongings that slowed down the evacuation process, hence risking more lives [8]. In this case, adding this option in game can emphasize on such instructions and prevent undesirable behaviours during emergencies.

6 Conclusions

The motivation behind this user study is to identify peoples' perception and attitude towards two prominent modes of emergency training. The participants of the study are a student of bachelors program in Information Technology. Conventional emergency drills are being conducted in the university. The participants were asked to play a game in which the player has to escape the fire in the university. The feedback from participants about their preferred mode of training indicates that the majority of them believe in the conventional form of training as a necessity. They suggested exercising game based training along with real drills. Game based training is deemed useful to get oneself familiarized with emergency exit locations and evacuation rules. The conventional drills are advantageous to be better practiced according to the real scenario.

However, participants suggested improving drills scheme by incorporating themes such as conducting them as a competition to evoke interest. Furthermore, to plan drills as a play in which participants get different roles such as someone panicked, caught in smoke, or a leader who knows all exits and had to guide the crowd, etc.

The research results identified that emergency training is considered advantageous though people prefer a change in the training mechanism to feel immersed as drill mechanism is the same since years. This game based training mechanism was regarded as a productive and effective addition to training programs as game brings those advantages that real drills cannot such as repetitive gameplay till one is familiar with all exit locations as well as self reflection of one's understanding and memory of evacuation rules.

Acknowledgments. Authors would like to thank Dr. Joseph Alexander Brown for his valuable suggestions and feedback on this project.

References

1. Arnab, S., et al.: Mapping learning and game mechanics for serious games analysis. Br. J. Educ. Technol. **46**(2), 391–411 (2015)
2. Aslam, H., Sidorov, A., Bogomazov, N., Berezyuk, F., Brown, J.A.: Relief camp manager: a serious game using the world health organization's relief camp guidelines. In: Squillero, G., Sim, K. (eds.) EvoApplications 2017. LNCS, vol. 10199, pp. 407–417. Springer, Cham (2017). https://doi.org/10.1007/978-3-319-55849-3_27
3. Djaouti, D., Alvarez, J., Jessel, J.P.: Classifying serious games: the G/P/S model. In: Handbook of Research on Improving Learning and Motivation Through Educational Games: Multidisciplinary Approaches, pp. 118–136. IGI Global (2011)
4. Haferkamp, N., Kraemer, N.C., Linehan, C., Schembri, M.: Training disaster communication by means of serious games in virtual environments. Entertain. Comput. **2**(2), 81–88 (2011)
5. Ribeiro, J., Almeida, J.E., Rossetti, R.J., Coelho, A., Coelho, A.L.: Using serious games to train evacuation behaviour. In: 2012 7th Iberian Conference on Information Systems and Technologies (CISTI), pp. 1–6. IEEE (2012)

6. Ribeiro, J., Almeida, J.E., Rossetti, R.J., Coelho, A., Coelho, A.L.: Towards a serious games evacuation simulator. arXiv preprint arXiv:1303.3827 (2013)
7. Silva, J.F., Almeida, J.E., Rossetti, R.J., Coelho, A.L.: A serious game for evacuation training. In: 2013 IEEE 2nd International Conference on Serious Games and Applications for Health (SeGAH), pp. 1–6. IEEE (2013)
8. Thomas, M.: Lessons from the Moscow airport crash: leave your luggage behind, 21 May 2019. https://phys.org/news/2019-05-lessons-moscow-airport-luggage.html. Accessed 27 June 2019
9. Van Manen, S., Avard, G., Martinez-Cruz, M.: Co-ideation of disaster preparedness strategies through a participatory design approach: challenges and opportunities experienced at Turrialba Volcano, Costa Rica. Des. Stud. **40**, 218–245 (2015)
10. Vanem, E., Skjong, R.: Collision and grounding of passenger ships-risk assessment and emergency evacuations. In: Third International Conference on Collision and Grounding of Ships (ICCGS), vol. 195, p. 202 (2004)

Quantum Physics vs. Classical Physics: Introducing the Basics with a Virtual Reality Game

Bob Dorland, Lennard van Hal, Stanley Lageweg, Jurgen Mulder, Rinke Schreuder, Amir Zaidi, Jan Willem David Alderliesten, and Rafael Bidarra(✉)

Faculty of Electrical Engineering, Mathematics and Computer Science, Delft University of Technology, Delft, The Netherlands
R.Bidarra@tudelft.nl

Abstract. Unlike classical physics, quantum physics is harder to explain, as it involves very small scales and phenomena that are not visible to the naked eye. Understanding the differences between classical and quantum physics is difficult, especially for children, who cannot grasp the subtleties conveyed in complicated formulae.

We propose to achieve this in a playful and immersive manner, which is a more familiar and convenient way to introduce children to new concepts. For this we developed *Save Schrödinger's Cat*, a puzzle game in virtual reality featuring a classical physics mode and a quantum physics mode. As virtual objects and phenomena behave differently in each mode, this mechanic encourages players to toggle between modes, in order to explore the differences between quantum and classical physics in an immersive, entertaining and challenging way. A preliminary evaluation showed that players could better identify various distinguishing features of either mode.

Keywords: Classical physics · Quantum physics · Virtual reality · Educational games

1 Introduction

Differences between quantum physics and classical physics can be hard to convey without referring explicitly to in-depth formalisms like formulas [6]. Quantum physics is important for understanding concepts of the universe that are not explicable with classical physics. However, quantum physics is generally considered to be difficult to understand, since this requires knowledge of the underlying theories and classical physics.

How can one convey the differences between quantum physics and classical physics visually, without referring explicitly to in-depth formalisms like formulas? Apart from some videos, there are currently no known accessible mediums that have accomplished this goal successfully for a large audience. Understanding

A. Liapis et al. (Eds.): GALA 2019, LNCS 11899, pp. 383–393, 2019.
https://doi.org/10.1007/978-3-030-34350-7_37

quantum mechanics often involves being familiar with advanced physics concepts, as quantum mechanics go further beyond classical physics.

One possibility is to create an understanding of the basics by using a game. *Save Schrödinger's Cat* is a puzzle game, making use of the differences between classical and quantum physics for the design of puzzles. Players can decide when to enable quantum mechanical effects. All game objects behave differently when these effects are enabled.

1.1 Virtual Reality

The game uses virtual reality technology to immerse the player in an environment in which they can interact with classical and quantum physics directly. It is accessible to anyone with access to an HTC Vive[1] and is designed to introduce the player to differences between classical physics and quantum physics in a playful and visual way.

Empirical experiments involving quantum mechanics are not as easy to conduct as empirical experiments involving classical physics concepts [7]. Computer games allow the creation of a universe with alternate laws of physics, thus it makes sense to show the differences between quantum and macro physics with the use of computer games.

Virtual reality games improve on this by allowing the player to experience a game's universe, almost as if it is reality. By having the effects of quantum mechanics all around the players, they can interact with those effects in an immersive way. Such an environment helps the player learn by empirical experiments, which are shown to be more effective than studying the theory [3,4]. Hence, games in a virtual reality environment are very effective in the field of education.

1.2 Purpose and Idea

Save Schrödinger's Cat is a virtual reality game where the player can experience classical physics and quantum physics. The purpose of the game is to introduce a large audience to the differences between these two different types of physics.

An introduction to the physics types is given in the form of various puzzle rooms. These puzzle rooms utilize the differences between the two physics types by offering the player the ability to switch between two modes with different physics systems. The modes determine the behavior of certain objects, for instance, magnets attract metal boxes in classical mode and bend lasers in quantum mode. Some puzzles can only be solved when being approached in classical mode, others can only be finished in quantum mode or a mix of both. It is up to the player to find out the right way to utilize objects that work differently in each mode for each puzzle.

The most important aspect of this game is the educative part. To support the learning process, the game also has a small story, which is conveyed with the use

[1] https://www.vive.com/eu/product/.

of voice lines. The theory about the quantum mechanics that are displayed in the game is explained through a narrative, where the protagonist, Schrödinger, tries to save his cat from the antagonist by beating all the puzzles described earlier. By letting the player find out how the various objects in the game environment react to quantum physics and classical physics, these mechanics can be experienced.

2 Related Works

Earlier work attempted to find the benefits of gamification in the teaching of quantum physics [2]. The result was that gamification supports education and that educative games are motivating for students. However, the research did not bring conclusive results for all types of games yet.

There are alternative games with similar goals and ambitions to *Save Schrödinger's Cat*. Most have the primary goal of giving the player an enjoyable experience, but some of them focus more on educating the user. Some notable games with the former goal are *Quantum Game with Photons*[2], *Laser Puzzle in VR*[3], and *qCraft*[4]. These games are designed for a wide audience and published on popular platforms to reach this audience. The purely educational games, however, are less known, as they were created as research experiments and abandoned afterwards. Bjaelde and Petersen mention eleven examples of such games during their tests on gamification [2].

Quantum Game with Photons is a game which teaches the player about quantum mechanics. It makes the player solve puzzles with lasers using quantum mechanics. This game is set in a 2D environment instead of in VR, goes a lot more in-depth, and does not show the differences between quantum and classical physics. This game does teach quantum mechanics rather well, but requires prior knowledge about quantum mechanics to properly play. As such, it does not serve as a basic introduction to quantum mechanics.

Laser Puzzle in VR is a VR game in which you have to solve laser puzzles by placing mirrors and other building blocks. It is not very useful for players wanting to learn about quantum mechanics, as it does not cover quantum effects at all.

qCraft is a mod for the game *MineCraft*[5] which adds some new blocks to the game which have quantum properties. This mod focuses on teaching just a couple of different quantum mechanics, but does seem to be doing this rather well. It is very accessible to new users who can quickly learn a couple of things about quantum mechanics by directly interacting with these blocks.

3 Game Design

Before and during development, design decisions were made with regards to the various game mechanics and components. Most of the quantum effects were exaggerated to more clearly communicate them to the player. The story does clearly

[2] http://quantumgame.io/.
[3] https://vr.arvilab.com/products/games/laser-puzzle-in-vr.
[4] https://minecraft.curseforge.com/projects/qcraft.
[5] https://minecraft.net.

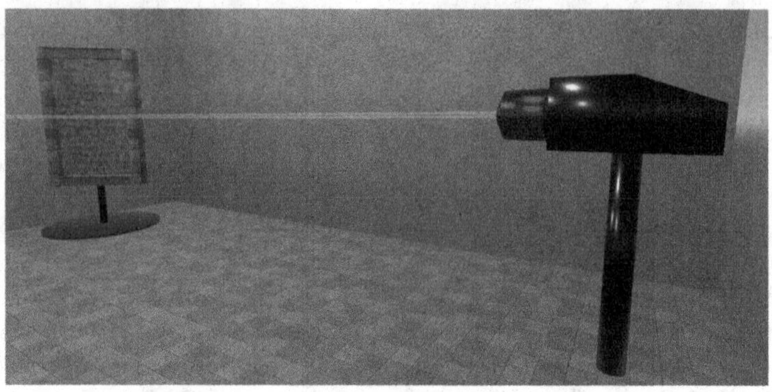

Fig. 1. A laser instead of single photons.

specify that these effects are exaggerated. This way, the player can experience the effects, but still understand that this is not a completely accurate simulation of real life. The goal of the design is to make sure the player can always interact with objects without visual clutter through the scenes. The trailer [6] gives a good idea of the developed game.

Lasers Instead of Single Photons. Most quantum phenomena only work on single photons. The quantum effects were applied to an entire laser, because this would communicate more clearly to the player what is happening. If only single photons would be used, there would have to be a delay between the effects, and the player would have to wait to see what effect a change he has made. The player can now, for example, rotate a mirror and see it affect the laser in real time, allowing for more responsive and clear gameplay (see Fig. 1).

Magnets Bend Lasers. Even though photons have no electric charge, it is possible for magnets to interact with them [1]. However, the effect would be so limited that it would not be visible in the game if it would be implemented realistically. Therefore, the interaction between magnets and photons had to be exaggerated by clearly making entire laser beams bend around a magnet instead of single photons (see Fig. 2).

Metal Box Attraction by Magnets. Magnets will always interact with ferrous objects. However, to allow for more easy to understand features that force the user to keep switching between quantum and classical mode, a decision was made to disregard this fact while the game is in quantum mode. This could have been solved differently by changing the material of the metal objects to something non-ferrous, but that would not be intuitive in this game (see Fig. 3).

[6] https://drive.google.com/file/d/1O27HqhHi5Y2puhz_5sC6iHUy2norCgbx/view?usp=sharing.

Fig. 2. A magnet bending a laser.

Fig. 3. A magnet attracting a metal box.

Enhanced Tunneling Effect. The tunneling effect is usually barely noticeable, even for very thin surfaces. To clearly show this effect to the player, the effect was greatly enhanced by always letting entire lasers tunnel through thin surfaces in quantum mode. This way, the player can see this theoretical effect with their own eyes (see Fig. 4).

Quantum Teleportation. In quantum physics, information can be transferred at extremely high speeds, making it appear as if the information is teleported. The game shows this by letting photons appear instantly in another place. The place is determined by two portals that are linked together in one scene (see Fig. 5).

Hong-Ou-Mandel Effect. The Hong-Ou-Mandel effect is simulated by a beam splitter, which combines two lasers into one stronger laser, or splits one laser into two weaker lasers (see Fig. 6).

Fig. 4. A laser tunneling through a thin wall.

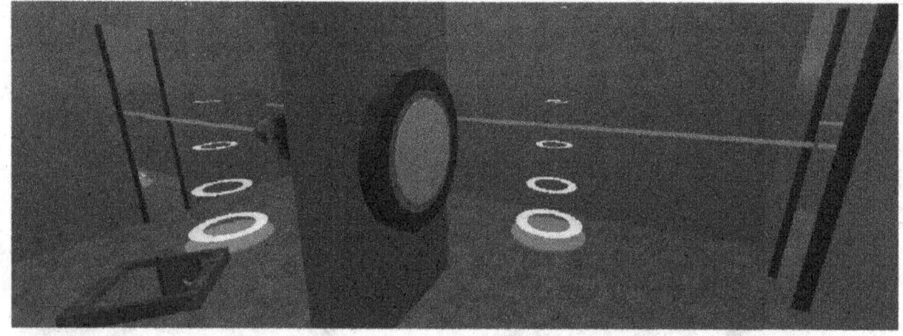

Fig. 5. A portal through which a laser can be teleported.

4 Technology

Save Schrödinger's Cat uses various existing technologies to increase immersion, which consequently improves the educational performance of the game.

4.1 Engine

The game was created on the Unity[7] game engine, utilizing SteamVR[8] for virtual reality support. Unity has a large asset store that provides free assets, which can be used to reduce development time. By using a commercial game engine, *Save Schrödinger's Cat* can promise that there will not be any engine-related problems, except for the limitations that affect all games created in Unity. This is important to ensure that the interaction with objects is stutter-free, as one would expect when physically interacting with objects outside a virtual environment as well.

[7] https://unity.com/.
[8] https://store.steampowered.com/steamvr.

Fig. 6. A beamsplitter, splitting the laser beam into two.

4.2 Hardware Setup

The virtual reality setup that was used includes HTC Vive gear on PC platforms. Other VR hardware was not used due to budget limitations. The hardware components required for playing, besides the headset, are (HTC) controllers and any audio device (see Fig. 7).

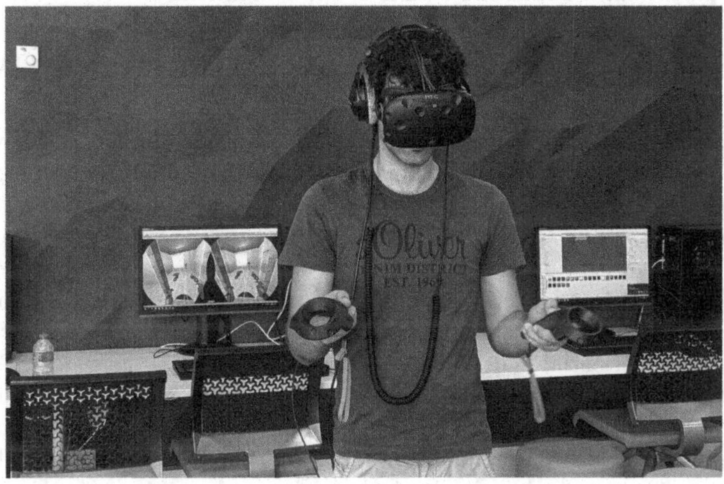

Fig. 7. Player using the virtual reality setup.

The controllers are used as interaction tools to be able to engage with the game's mechanics such as rotating mirrors or picking up boxes. For moving or teleporting the user, the controllers use the touch-pad buttons. For grabbing objects, the trigger buttons on the back of the controllers are used.

Technically, audio is not an essential component for the gameplay. However, the audio does provide some needed clues and explanations about quantum physics and adds another level of immersion that, when missing, may leave users confused or uninterested. Ideally, headphones are used as audio device for an even more immersive experience.

The game does not require a very large play area. The minimum recommended play area has a size of $5\,\mathrm{m}^2$. The ideal play area is a space of at least $8\,\mathrm{m}^2$, as it allows users to walk around freely without bumping into anything.

5 Evaluation

In order to assess whether the game has achieved its educational goal, we invited students to answer questions about differences between quantum physics and classical physics after playing the game, and some others to answer the same questions without playing the game. This way, we could see whether players learned about quantum physics concepts they did not know about before while playing *Save Schrödinger's Cat*. The main question to be answered by the results of these evaluation sessions was: *Does* Save Schrödinger's Cat *manage to teach people with no knowledge of quantum physics some differences between quantum physics and classical physics?* We also asked testers to give their general opinion on *Save Schrödinger's Cat* after playing the game. This would show whether the game provides enough immersion and entertainment, as well as educative elements. Appendix A shows the questionnaire that was used for the evaluation sessions. Appendix B shows the results of the evaluation.

6 Conclusion

Introducing a young audience to concepts of quantum physics and how they compare to classical physics can be done by means of an immersive game for virtual reality. We presented *Save Schrödinger's Cat*, a game developed for young visitors of the Science Centre[9] at Delft University of Technology. Players can directly interact with (virtual) objects or phenomena, in either quantum or classical physics mode, and see the results of the physical laws that apply to them. As a result, it overcomes the need to explain in-depth formalisms (e.g. formulas) with a more experiential and intuitive approach.

The game is aimed at young people with no understanding of quantum physics, as the virtual visualizations help them understand the phenomena. This is an important goal because quantum physics explains phenomena in the universe that are not explicable via classical physics, and quantum physics looks to be an important factor in future technologies and industries [5].

Results from the evaluation show that *Save Schrödinger's Cat* was capable of visually conveying many differences between quantum physics and classical physics. Players were able to identify more quantum physics concepts and differences between quantum physics and classical physics than people who did not play the game. We can, therefore, conclude that this game is a successful addition to the educational exhibit of TU Delft Science Centre.

[9] https://www.tudelft.nl/sciencecentre/.

Appendix A Evaluation Questionnaire

The following two pages were given to play-testers in the TU Delft VR Zone and Science Centre.

Save Schrödinger's Cat - Quiz

Please answer the following questions based on the experiences you gained while playing *Save Schrödinger's Cat.*

Which of the following concepts is possible according to quantum physics but would not be possible in classical physics?
Put a checkmark ✔ in the box next to the applicable concepts.

Concept	**This is made possible by quantum physics**
Tunneling light through thin walls	
Teleportation of light	
Teleportation of a human	
Cloning a cat	
Bending light rays with magnets	
Splitting beams into two weaker beams using a *beam splitter*	
Combining beams into one stronger beam using a *beam splitter*	
Travelling through time	
Evil scientists stealing your cat	
Attracting a metal box with a magnet	
Tunneling light through mirrors	
You cannot know the state of an object before observing it	

	DISAGREE	SOMEWHAT DISAGREE	NEITHER DISAGREE NOR AGREE	SOMEWHAT AGREE	AGREE
1. I understand the **goal of the game** after playing the levels made available for the playtest session.	1	2	3	4	5
2. The **controls are intuitive** and easy to get used to.	1	2	3	4	5
3. The game is **entertaining**.	1	2	3	4	5
4. After playing the game, I feel **I know more about quantum physics** than before playing the game.	1	2	3	4	5
5. Playing the game with **virtual reality hardware has an added value** compared to playing the game on a single screen.	1	2	3	4	5

☐ I participated in this evaluation voluntarily.

☐ I agree to have this data used for further research without any personally identifiable information.

____

Signature

Thank you on behalf of Quantum Studios for taking time to support the development of Save Schrödinger's Cat!

Appendix B Results

Two questions were left out, because of different reasons. The first was "Splitting beams into two with a beam splitter", because the game logic contradicts the real world, so players that have experience in physics will check the box while players that do not will not check the box. The second that was left out was "Evil scientists stealing your cat", because the majority of players considered it a joke and did not seriously answer the question.

Table 1 presents the raw data of filled-in questionnaires, including a computed average for the aggregate of the rows. Each row represents one valid questionnaire. Table 2 presents the results with regard to the questionnaire statements on the game itself.

Table 1. Questionnaire results about differences between quantum physics and classical physics, given to both play-testers and control group members.

	True positive/negative	False positive	False negative
Tester A	100%	0%	0%
Tester B	100%	0%	0%
Tester C	60%	20%	20%
Tester D	30%	40%	30%
Tester E	70%	10%	20%
Tester F	90%	0%	10%
Tester G	80%	0%	20%
Tester H	50%	10%	40%
Tester I	60%	10%	30%
Tester J	80%	0%	20%
Average	**72%**	**9%**	**19%**
Control A	50%	10%	40%
Control B	40%	0%	60%
Control C	70%	0%	30%
Control D	50%	0%	50%
Control E	70%	0%	30%
Control F	60%	10%	30%
Control G	50%	0%	50%
Control H	50%	0%	50%
Control I	50%	20%	30%
Control J	50%	0%	50%
Control K	60%	0%	40%
Control L	50%	0%	50%
Control M	70%	0%	30%
Control N	70%	10%	20%
Control O	60%	10%	30%
Average	**56.7%**	**4%**	**39.3%**

Table 2. Scores for the statements on *Save Schrödinger's Cat*

Question	Average score
I understand the **goal of the game** after playing the levels made available for the playtest session	4.33
The **controls are intuitive** and easy to get used to	3.70
The game is **entertaining**	4.57
After playing the game, I feel **I know more about quantum physics** than before playing the game	3.40
Playing the game with **virtual reality hardware has an added value** compared to playing the game on a single screen	4.47

References

1. Ataman, S.: Vacuum birefringence detection in all-optical scenarios. Phys. Rev. A **97**(6). https://doi.org/10.1103/PhysRevA.97.063811
2. Bjælde, O.E., Pedersen, M.K., Sherson, J.: Gamification of quantum mechanics teaching. In: Bastiaens, T. (ed.) Proceedings of World Conference on E-Learning, pp. 218–222, New Orleans, LA, USA (2014)
3. Deslauriers, L., Wieman, C.: Learning and retention of quantum concepts with different teaching methods. Phys. Rev. Spec. Top. - Phys. Educ. Res. https://doi.org/10.1103/PhysRevSTPER.7.010101
4. Freina, L., Ott, M.: A literature review on immersive virtual reality in education: state of the art and perspectives. In: The International Scientific Conference e-Learning and Software for Education, vol. 1, p. 133. "Carol I" National Defence University, April 2015
5. Quantum technologies to revolutionize 21st century. https://phys.org/news/2016-06-quantum-technologies-revolutionize-21st-century.html. Accessed 12 June 2019
6. Singh, C., Marshman, E.: Review of student difficulties in upper-level quantum mechanics. Phys. Rev. ST Phys. Educ. Res. **11**(2), 020117 (2015). https://doi.org/10.1103/PhysRevSTPER.11.020117
7. Wessel-Berg, T.: Electromagnetic and Quantum Measurements: A Bitemporal Neoclassical Theory, 3rd edn. Springer, Heidelberg (2013). https://doi.org/10.1007/978-1-4615-1603-3

A Serious Game to Inform Young Citizens on Canal Water Maintenance

Yoeri Appel, Yordan Dimitrov, Sjoerd Gnodde, Natasja van Heerden, Pieter Kools, Daniël Swaab, Nestor Z. Salamon, J. Timothy Balint, and Rafael Bidarra(✉)

Faculty of Electrical Engineering, Mathematics and Computer Science, Delft University of Technology, Delft, The Netherlands
R.Bidarra@tudelft.nl

Abstract. In order to support the creation of sustainable and healthy ecosystems, citizens should have knowledge of the necessary maintenance needed. For example, they should be aware of the challenges of maintaining proper urban surface waters, so that they can take on a responsible and proactive role. Ideally, citizens should acquire this knowledge from an early age. We describe the design, implementation, and evaluation of the serious game *Hydro Hero*, aimed at forming and reinforcing this awareness and reasoning. Hydro Hero is an infinite runner game with extended minigames, which show both *what* should not be on the canals as well as *why* they should be removed. We assessed the ability of Hydro Hero to teach young children about canal maintenance by combining a questionnaire with open-ended play-testing sessions at a science museum. On average, players were able to improve their ability to justify why certain items should be removed or left in a canal. It has not been fully confirmed that Hydro Hero conveyed this specific knowledge, due to the absence of quizzing beforehand. However, given the high participants' engagement, we consider the game to have contributed to their awareness about the importance of canal cleaning for a sustainable urban environment.

Keywords: Urban water · Educational games · Behavior change

1 Introduction

Good water management is increasingly important for sustainable ecosystems, in particular for urban environments. Moreover, clean surface water is essential for drinking water, recreation and most plant and animal species. With rapid growing urbanisation, water quality and quantity is under threat. For a sustainable future, water management is especially crucial in the Netherlands, due to its large number of rivers, canals, ditches, levees and lakes. Hence, urban sustainability does not only extends to solar panels and windmills, but also about the mindset and behaviour of citizens. Many people in the Netherlands have limited knowledge about canal cleaning and canal maintenance. The water boards that conduct canal maintenance have tried to make people more aware about the

A. Liapis et al. (Eds.): GALA 2019, LNCS 11899, pp. 394–403, 2019.
https://doi.org/10.1007/978-3-030-34350-7_38

topic, but it has had little effect on public knowledge [10]. This is undesirable, since the general public is also responsible for some of the problems to canal sustainability [5].

Knowledge is important in order to change behaviour: in general, people do not change their mindset and behaviour if they are able to ignore the issue. Therefore, we propose a game to teach children about the importance of water quality on canals. Our research question is:

> "Can children improve their knowledge about canal water maintenance trough playing a serious game?"

Here, knowledge has two aspects: (i) the static knowledge on *what* is favourable and unfavourable to a canal, and (ii) the reason *why* unfavourable items need to be removed.

2 Related Work

Designing educational games for children has been a matter of research for quite some time. Romero and Barma [8] for example, identified many educational possibilities in games for children. Gamification has been often used to enhance learning. This includes digital games, provided certain prerequisites are met [1]. However, the evidence to substantiate this is mainly empirical [3]. A study by Wrzesien and Raya [12] found no significant correlation between children who were taught via games and the control group. They reported, however, more joy, engagement and participation from the children who used serious games. Girard et al. [3] suggest that more empirical research is needed when examining gamification for learning, which is aligned with the topic of this paper.

Various quiz-based games and questionnaires have been deployed as well. For example, with the German game *Prosodiya*, parents and children are tested by answering subjective questions, mainly about the appreciation of the game, while the game assesses a person's presumption about the knowledge that has been gained [4]. Player's motivation has also been analysed. For example, a leader board can work well as a motivator when continuously playing a game [6, p. 34]. When players are only motivated by the reward built into the learning game, they oftentimes do not retain much information [6]. Therefore, it is essential that the player is motivated in the game, by tasks that induce learning. In another paper, Bußwolder and Gebhardt [2] found no significant correlation, between the players' motivation and their performance. Therefore, motivation only affects the attractiveness of longer gameplay sessions.

Furthermore, work has been done in teaching and explanation methods. Wallner et al. [9] empirically concluded that children have the tendency to rush past tutorials. In our game, we took the decision not to implement separate tutorials, but instead make the game self explanatory via minigames.

3 Game Design

Hydro Hero is built around the concept that the player needs to clean and maintain a canal. The player does this by controlling an avatar that has to collect entities that should not be in the water or on the banks. The avatar has a steadily increasing velocity along the direction of the canal. The avatar's lateral movements are limited in range and in speed. Such mechanics makes the game challenging while still being easy to comprehend, in an attempt to lessen the stress of the overall experience.

The canal is an artistic illustration, inspired on a Dutch *boezem* and a *polder* canal. The movement of the entities gives the impression that the avatar is moving along the canal, instead of the water flowing towards the avatar. During the game, the current score is shown in the left top corner, and in the right top corner the three lives, in the form of hearts, are shown. Figure 1 shows a screen capture of the game, illustrating the main visual components.

Fig. 1. Overview of the game. The avatar flies and removes items that are harmful to the canal and banks, while avoiding positive environment entities.

A moderate skill set has to be developed to guide the avatar to collect the objects that do not belong in a canal, called *pickups*, as well as avoid those that do belong there, called *obstacles*. Table 1 lists the in-game *pickups* and *obstacles* and the reasoning for such classification. The player initially does not receive any clues about the nature of the items, either pickup or obstacle. Therefore, the player has to consider what item they have to pick up. The learning goal for the player is to realise that they should remove malicious items from canals, as well as avoid items that belong in or around canals. Later, new pickups are introduced incrementally and explained via minigames.

Table 1. Pickups and obstacles in Hydro Hero

Item	Interaction	Reason
Musk rat	Pickup	Musk rats make holes in levees which weakens them and is a competitor to native species
Garbage bag	Pickup	Perilous to water ecology
Plastic bottle	Pickup	Perilous to water ecology
Duckweed	Pickup	Blocks sunlight and is therefore perilous for water life
Reed	Pickup	Can overgrow large sections of the canal and increases friction of transporting water
Bike	Pickup	Blocks boats
Boat	Obstacle	In general forms no problem to canal
Swan	Obstacle	In general forms no problem to canal
Duck	Obstacle	In general forms no problem to canal
Trees	Obstacle	In general forms no problem to canal and surroundings

During the game, the player loses a "life" for every obstacle it runs into. After losing three lives, the game is finished. By giving players more lives, they will be able to progress through the game more easily, instead of failing at the beginning. Without being able to interact with the subsequent tasks, they would thus fail to meet the learning goals.

Players can enter their name when the game is over, possibly to be featured in the top 10 score list. In addition, the player is also motivated to play the game again via a prominent replay button and attempt to achieve a higher score while learning more about canal maintenance.

3.1 Minigames

For the scope of this project, we focus on the "healthiness" of a canal. After the initial experience relying only the player's previous knowledge and common objects (e.g., ducks and garbage bags), the game starts with teaching children which items do not belong in canals. Also, it is equally important to teach them the reasons why those objects can be harmful to canal health and maintenance. To assist in such explanatory task, we implemented a variety of minigames, showing in an engaging way the positive effects of removing harmful objects from the water.

The minigames are simplistic: the player only has to perform a basic task. Executing this task reveals the reason why the object is harmful for the canal health. Every new pickup item is first introduced with a minigame; only after a minigame is finished can the player continue to the main game. A combination of a minigame and a section of pickups to the next minigame is called a level.

Two minigames are shown in Fig. 2. In minigame Fig. 2a, the aim is to remove duckweed with a net. The explanatory balloon shows why the duckweed is bad for the canal: it blocks the sunlight. While the duckweed is getting removed, the colour of the canal turns brighter. When enough duckweed is removed, the smiley face turns happy and the red circle around the sun is removed. In minigame Fig. 2b the aim is to hit muskrats, while they appear out of their holes. The player sees cracks disappearing, mitigating the danger of levees collapsing.

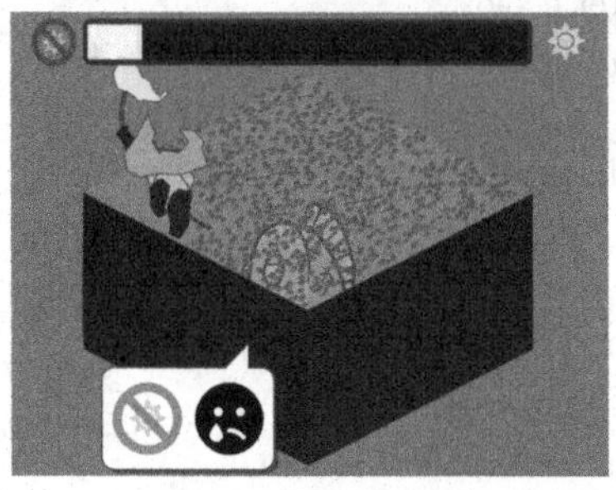

(a) Removing duckweed

(b) Catching muskrats

Fig. 2. Example of two minigames that introduce new pickups. Left: the aim is to remove duckweed, that blocks sunlight into the canal. Right: the goal is to catch muskrats that build holes in levees. (Color figure online)

In our evaluation, we found that the age and prior knowledge of the players had an effect on the players' understanding of why the minigames were included. Furthermore, despite the tempo of the minigames, players were able to understand the concept being conveyed by the game. Finally, after completing a minigame, players has to press a 'Continue' button before proceeding to the topic streak. This consciously reinforces the connection between the main mechanic and the minigame. Figure 3 shows the complete game flow diagram.

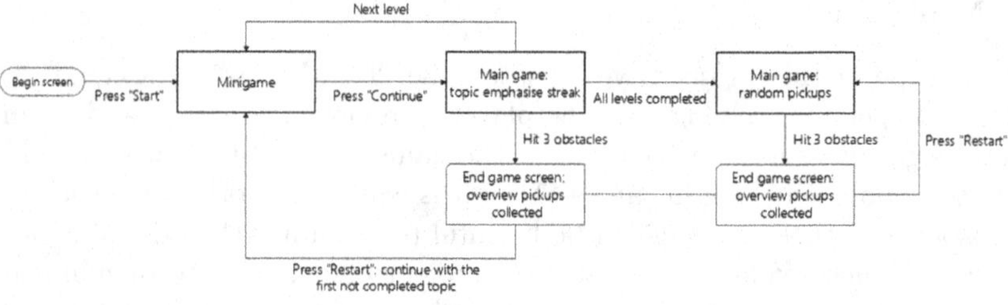

Fig. 3. Game flow: one *minigame* and one *topic emphasise streak* form a level.

3.2 Engagement Mechanism

Many infinite runner games spawn a variety of items from the start, so that players grab entities (either by intuition or by accident) which they believe are possible to be picked up. As a result, without further interaction, players will make no significant progress and, above all, they may fail to capture the rationale behind each item. For Hydro Hero, this would be undesirable and counter-productive. Therefore we opted for deploying after each minigame a *topic emphasise streak level* (see Fig. 3), in which only the specific pickup, together with some obstacles, are presented to the player. This proved to be an useful approach. Many players decided at some point to try out one of these pickups, and realised the nature of the item. Players who persisted in not picking up these items, unavoidably end up hitting one, find it out then. A finish flag is shown after a minimum amount of pickups, and the cycle starts over for a new pickup.

After all the levels have been played and all pickups introduced, the game advances to the final stage: all pickups and obstacles spawn randomly. The player now stays engaged with the game and gets constantly challenged with an increasing navigation and spawn speeds. This goes hand-in-hand with the theory of Wouters et al. [11]: surprises have a positive effect on learning when existing proportional reasoning is included. Players who reached this phase should have a basic understanding of whether an item should be removed. This phase reinforces the ideas through repetition - and competition for high scores.

4 Validation

We implemented Hydro Hero as a browser-based game using Phaser [7]. Relying solely on HTML5 and JavaScript, it prevents players from needing to install additional libraries, which allows the game to reach a wider audience.

In practice, we tested our hypothesis in two ways. Firstly, we tested our approach with non-evaluated playing rounds. This testing delivered solely anecdotal evidence, and was merely used for development of the game. Attention was given to how engaged players were and whether they understood the game. Lately, during the play testing, all the elements of the game were looked at and the engagement, inquisitiveness, amusement, and confusion of players was noted. Components of the game, such as the minigames, were also tested separately to find out its influence on the gameplay and the ability in teaching the player. In this example, the minigames were turned off for certain players and the reaction to new objects was analysed.

Given the nature of the testing place - a public science museum, involvement of the parents/guardians or siblings/friends could not be prevented during the tests. This, however, reflects actually the real world playing, and was therefore not regarded as a problem.

Overall, minigames seemed essential in making clear both what items players had to grab and the reason to do that. The topic emphasise streaks made it even more clear the items that had to be picked up. Without these streaks, players were generally more confused about the function of all items.

The conclusive testing of the prototype was done with a fixed question quiz. The players were quizzed before playing the game first. Five closed questions with the options 'yes', 'no' and 'don't know', were orally asked in order to access the knowledge of the player prior to playing. After the game, the same questions were asked again. However, at this time, if the player gave an answer (right or wrong) that an item did not belong in/near a canal, four plausible options, as well as a 'I don't know'-option were presented to justify the reasoning (Fig. 4).

Prior to the game:
Does a lot of duckweed belong in the canal?

After playing the game:
Does a lot of duckweed belong in the canal?
Why doesn't it?

Fig. 4. Example quiz question. Answer options accepted 'yes', 'no' and 'I don't know', as well as plausible reasoning choices.

5 Results and Discussion

The time played was on average around five stages in six minutes. Overall, players seemed to highly enjoy the game. Next, we applied the quiz described in Sect. 4 to measure the effectiveness of our approach. Results are evaluated on (i) the improvement in static knowledge and (ii) to what extent the players knew about the reason why certain items do not belong in a canal. In total, 20 children participated on the evaluation; the ages are listed in Fig. 5 (right).

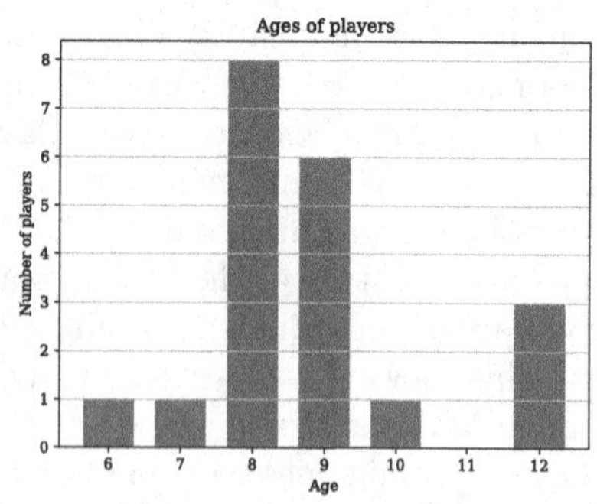

Fig. 5. A child playing the game and the age distribution of the participants.

The improvement of static knowledge (does/does not belong) (i) was tested with the difference in scores of the closed questions prior (X_p) and after (X_a) playing the game, where X_p and X_a depict the sample scores from the user testing. The results are plotted in Fig. 6 (left). The average difference $\mu_{\Delta x}$ was +1.55, and the standard error $\sigma_{\Delta x}$ 1.00 of the test with n = 20. The null hypothesis H_0 was that players did not learn from the game, so $H_0 : \mu_{\Delta X} = 0$. Then $H_1 : \mu_{\Delta X} > 0$. Via a student t-test, a right side p-value was found of 6.452E–07. Therefore, H_0 is rejected and it is likely that H_1 is true.

The reason why certain items are unfavourable for the canal (ii) was measured via the ratio between the correctly selected reasons (R) and the correctly answered closed questions from items that were unfavourable and required a reason ($X_{a,r}$). Here, r and $x_{a,r}$ are the respective sample data. The results are split between players that had no idea, or that gave an answer. In 14% of the cases, the player answered that they had no idea of the reason, which is a significant group. In the case of the other 86%, called r_f, another t-test was done. The total answered reasons are called $x_{a,r,f}$. Being very conservative, it is presumed that two of the four possible answers, were not well-formulated and nobody wanted to select these. The null hypothesis was that the players answered randomly, therefore: $H_0 : \mu_{R_f/X_{a,r,f}} = 0.5$ and $H_1 : \mu_{R_f/X_{a,r,f}} > 0.5$. Of the sample data, $\mu_{R_f/X_{a,r,f}}$ was 0.725, $\sigma_{R_f/X_{a,r,f}} = 0.356$. Therefore, p was 0.005365 and H_0 is rejected, so it is likely that H_1 is true for this 86% group of answers. Thus, players know the reason why some items have to be removed. However, from this data, it cannot be made certain that the knowledge of the reason was acquired by the game, although this is likely because players also significantly improved their (static) knowledge about the subject.

We presumed that quizzing the reasoning before playing the game would have a too big influence on the outcome. Further research with a control group and a higher n, should investigate the influence of the game on R. In that case, and by quizzing beforehand, attention might also be given to different subjects.

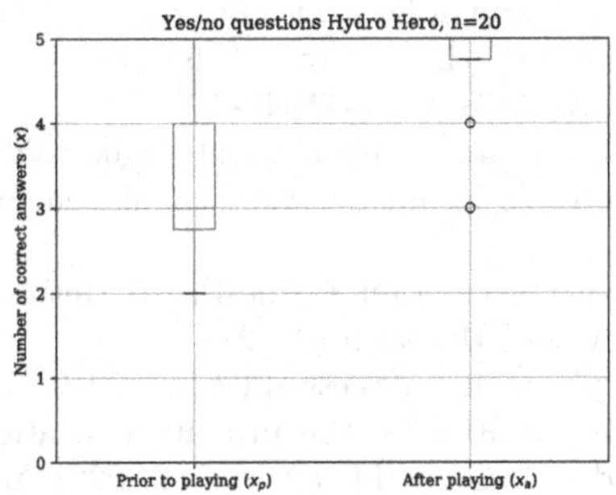

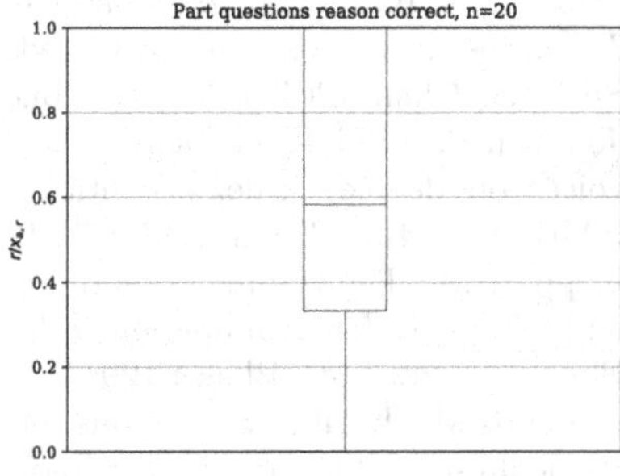

Fig. 6. Results of the quiz. Left: the number of correct answers given by players to the 5 closed questions, before and after playing the game. Right: percentage of correct justification answers (reasoning, only asked after the game).

6 Conclusion

We presented the serious game *Hydro Hero*, designed with the goal of reinforcing children's awareness for the challenges and responsibility of maintaining proper urban surface waters.

The validation data suggest that players of Hydro Hero increase their knowledge about canal cleaning and maintenance, though the exact extent of this increase has not been measured in this research. In addition, data also confirms that a majority of players significantly know why certain items are harmful in the domain of canal cleaning and maintenance; the influence of Hydro Hero in learning such reasons is probable, but has not been confirmed with certainty.

Besides the main research question, the time spent in the game by players proved that the game was moderately engaging, as intended. This helped in teaching the players, as they often mentioned they got the learning goal only after a number of rounds.

Acknowledgements. We owe great thanks to the employees of the Science Centre at the TU Delft, especially Marit Bogert and Jules Dudok, and all visitors of the Science Centre who volunteered to play the game. Furthermore, we thank Sylvia Strijk for the creation of the artwork of the main game.

References

1. All, A., Castellar, E.P.N., Van Looy, J.: Assessing the effectiveness of digital game-based learning: best practices. Comput. Educ. **92**, 90–103 (2016)
2. Bußwolder, P., Gebhardt, A.: Investigating motivation in gamification. In: Dias, J., Santos, P.A., Veltkamp, R.C. (eds.) GALA 2017. LNCS, vol. 10653, pp. 95–104. Springer, Cham (2017). https://doi.org/10.1007/978-3-319-71940-5_9
3. Girard, C., Ecalle, J., Magnan, A.: Serious games as new educational tools: how effective are they? A meta-analysis of recent studies. J. Comput. Assist. Learn. **29**(3), 207–219 (2013)
4. Holz, H., et al.: Prosodiya – a mobile game for German Dyslexic children. In: Dias, J., Santos, P.A., Veltkamp, R.C. (eds.) GALA 2017. LNCS, vol. 10653, pp. 73–82. Springer, Cham (2017). https://doi.org/10.1007/978-3-319-71940-5_7
5. Jonsson, A.: Public participation in water resources management: stakeholder voices on degree, scale, potential, and methods in future water management. AMBIO: J. Hum. Environ. **34**(7), 495–500 (2005)
6. Kapp, K.M.: The Gamification of Learning and Instruction: Game-Based Methods and Strategies for Training and Education. Wiley, Hoboken (2012)
7. Photon Storm Ltd.: Phaser (2019). https://phaser.io/. Accessed 03 Feb 2019
8. Romero, M., Barma, S.: Serious games opportunities for the primary education curriculum in Quebec. In: De Gloria, A. (ed.) GALA 2014. LNCS, vol. 9221, pp. 121–131. Springer, Cham (2015). https://doi.org/10.1007/978-3-319-22960-7_12
9. Wallner, G., Kriglstein, S., Gabriel, S., Loh, C.S., Sheng, Y., Li, I., et al.: Lost my way: an educational geometry game for young children. In: Proceedings of the 13th International Conference on the Foundations of Digital Games. ACM (2018)
10. Waterschap Rijn en IJssel: Uitdagingen voor de planperiode (2018). https://www.wrij.nl/waterbeheerplan/strategie-beleid/uitdagingen/. Accessed 07 Dec 2018

11. Wouters, P., van Oostendorp, H., ter Vrugte, J., vanderCruysse, S., de Jong, T., Elen, J.: The role of surprise in game-based learning for mathematics. In: de De Gloria, A., Veltkamp, R. (eds.) GALA 2015. LNCS, vol. 9599, pp. 401–410. Springer, Cham (2016). https://doi.org/10.1007/978-3-319-40216-1_45
12. Wrzesien, M., Raya, M.A.: Learning in serious virtual worlds: evaluation of learning effectiveness and appeal to students in the E-Junior project. Comput. Educ. **55**(1), 178–187 (2010)

Posters

A Framework for the Development of Serious Games for Assessment

Fatima Hamiye(✉), Bilal Said(✉), and Bader Serhan(✉)

Arts Sciences and Technology University in Lebanon, Beirut, Lebanon
fatimahamiye@gmail.com, bilal.said@gmail.com,
baderserhan@gmail.com

Abstract. The entertaining nature of video games have led to their use for serious purposes, such as in education or assessment, where they become known as serious games (SG). Developing a serious game is a complex task. To reduce this complexity, researchers focus on modeling and code generation tools. Nonetheless, they still fall behind when they try to fit all SG requirements or to cover different game genre within the currently suggested approaches. In our research, we propose a new modeling framework that ease the design and development process of serious game for assessment (SGA). This framework allows the pedagogue to define the game general structure using UML and the game logic using a new DSL language, which is easier and more accessible to non-technical experts. As a proof of concept, we show how two different games can be designed and developed using our framework.

Keywords: Code generation · Xtext · Xtend · DSL · UML · Structure · Logic · Score

1 Introduction

Video games are widespread nowadays; they have positive effects on the player. For instance, they can improve visual, social and spatial skills. They also trigger positive feelings after winning a game [9]. These effects have led to the use of games in serious applications, such as in education [6].

In fact, serious games (SG) are games that are used for a higher purpose than mere entertainment. Hence, they are used as learning tools in military or healthcare sector, or as assessment tools in education or recruitment, where they become known as Serious Games for Assessment (SGA). SG have shown great results in education, since they motivate the students to learn faster and also measure the performance of the players, in a game environment, so that they feel less stressed, which makes the assessment process more credible and realistic [4].

However, developing a serious game is a challenging task, since it requires having clear learning objectives, and must include a challenge to motivate the player to continue playing. Furthermore, a SG must make the right balance between fun and learning so fun does not overcome learning and vice versa, etc. However, this can only be achieved by involving the domain expert, i.e. the pedagogue, in the SG design and

A. Liapis et al. (Eds.): GALA 2019, LNCS 11899, pp. 407–416, 2019.
https://doi.org/10.1007/978-3-030-34350-7_39

testing processes. This would make the development process more complex and sometimes infeasible within fixed budgets or delays.

To overcome this complexity, and facilitate SG development, researchers have often opted to use modeling languages to design models for games and model driven development (MDD) to generate software code from the models. In fact the authors of [2, 5, 7, 8, 13] use Unified Modeling Language (UML) diagrams and a Domain Specific Language (DSL) to model and develop serious games. In addition, in [1, 3, 10, 12] and [11], the authors, model the structure element of SG. Although, these approaches facilitate the development process of SGA, they fail to cover all SG requirements, and none of them takes aspects related to the use of serious games for assessment into consideration. Our aim is to develop a meta-model that allows educators to participate in the development process of SGA, hence to reduce the development complexity, time and effort.

In fact, the work presented in this paper is part of a larger project [1, 4] and [11] called LET'SeGA (Lebanese-Egyptian-Tunisian Serious Game for Assessment) that aims at providing an 34 assessment platform that uses serious games to assess students mastery of certain competencies in order to offer them better orientation and/or assignment to university programs. Although we are currently integrating already existing games in our platform, we are planning to develop our own, or even better, to offer pedagogues the ability to easily define and ideally auto-generate games tailored for our assessment platform.

In the next section, we evaluate existing similar modeling approaches for serious games, and then we present our contribution in Sect. 3, to finally conclude with a primary evaluation of our proposal and a list of our future work.

2 Related Work

In this section, we present various modeling and MDD approaches used for SG development. For instance, the researchers focus on using either visual or textual language to express information in a structured way.

The authors of [13], design an understandable meta-model called GLiSMo, for the structure and the logic of a serious game using UML diagrams. However, it is only used for a specific game genre, which is point and click adventure games. In [5], the authors create a new DSL language called GaML that is used to design a model independent of any platform. Still, it only expresses the reward system and does not capture the game objects and their interactions. In [8], the author uses a graph-based approach to design an understandable DSL meta-model. Yet, it is only used for scenario description and does not offer any means for code generation. In [7], the author takes into consideration all the game aspects such as the structure and logic in his proposed in his SeGMEnt framework. He models these aspects using a custom editor and then generates code from the model using a PHP scripts. However, he did not show the development of a pedagogical assessment scenario using the framework. In addition, the framework could be used only for a specific game genre, which is role-playing. In [2], the author proposes a framework that allows to generate a virtual learning environment, by defining the game aspects using UML Diagrams and combining them with a 3D model game design. This approach was designed for developing a learning environment, but not to create assessment scenarios.

In addition, some researchers only focus on modeling the structure of a game [1, 3, 10, 12] and [11] present all serious game elements using different methodologies. In fact, in [3], the author proposes an ontology, that only facilitate the interdisciplinary communication and collaboration, and does not allow the pedagogue to generate a serious game environment. In addition, the methodology is not evaluated through case studies. In [10], the authors propose a model that represents video games specification. However, they did not focus on serious games for assessment. And in [12], the author creates an ontology diagram that represents serious game elements, however the ontology is only used for documenting SG development and not for code generation. In [1] and [11] the authors capture well all aspects of serious games structures and how they relate to personalization of assessment. Nevertheless, the work does not provide details about the automation of the SGA development process and their code generation.

In conclusion, these approaches aim to facilitate the design and development process of SG largely, however they do not consider all game requirements, and do not cover all game genre. It is also worth noting that none of these approaches is available as a final product, or as an open source repository or any other reproducible research artifact. Therefore, our aim is to develop a framework that fills these gaps in its final version.

3 A Framework for SGA Modeling and Code Generation

In this paper, we aim to create a user friendly SG modeling framework that suits various game genre, covers all the requirements of SGA, and takes into consideration game structure, logic, and scoring system. We aim to make it an open source reproducible research project as well. Hence, Fig. 1 represents the structure of our proposed framework, where we combine the use of visual and textual language to model and design a serious game. We will use a UML diagram to describe the game structure model and a DSL language to describe both the game logic and the scoring rules. Then we generate code from each model using modeling tools and code generators, to finally integrate and combine the generated code with additional extra logic. The following subsections describe the proposed framework much more in detail.

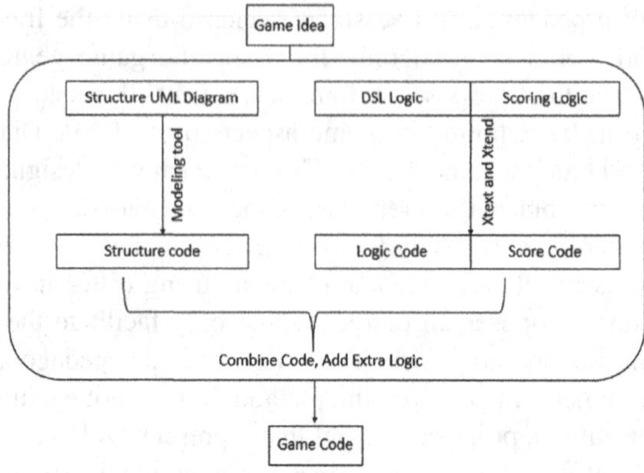

Fig. 1. Proposed framework

3.1 Structure Code Generation

We create a meta-model based on UML diagrams, precisely class diagrams, to describe the game structure. The model is abstract and generic enough to be used in different game genre and correspond 2D/3D games. The pedagogues will use this model to create the main component of a game. They can instantiate and extend this model to add all the features they need. In order to create the meta-model we have to identify the important elements that should be presented in the model to make it compatible with any serious game with any domain, and choose a modeling tool that helps the pedagogues to generate the game structure code from it.

Beyond entertainment, serious games have fixed learning objectives. However, these objectives will be reached by the player when executing specific actions under certain constraints (such as time, game state, etc.). For instance, an objective could be reached when the player successfully moves from one place to another while having an expected score, or when he moves certain game objects from one place to another while destroying other game objects. To capture all these elements in our model, we define the following:

Player, level, actions, objects, scenes, component, non-player character, objective and events.

The meta-model that represent the relationships between all of these elements is represented using UML Class diagram shown in Figs. 2 and 3.

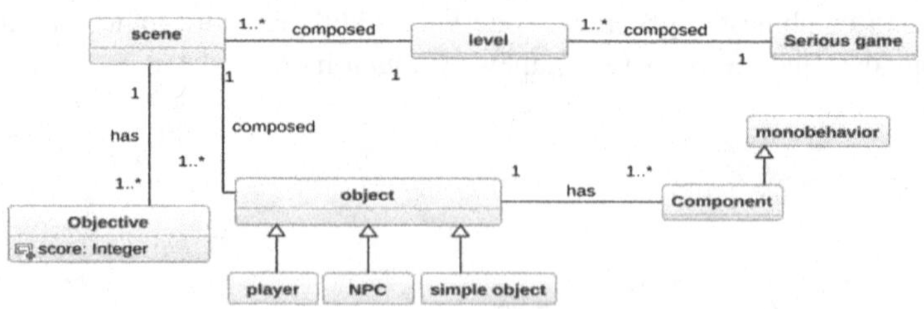

Fig. 2. General structure

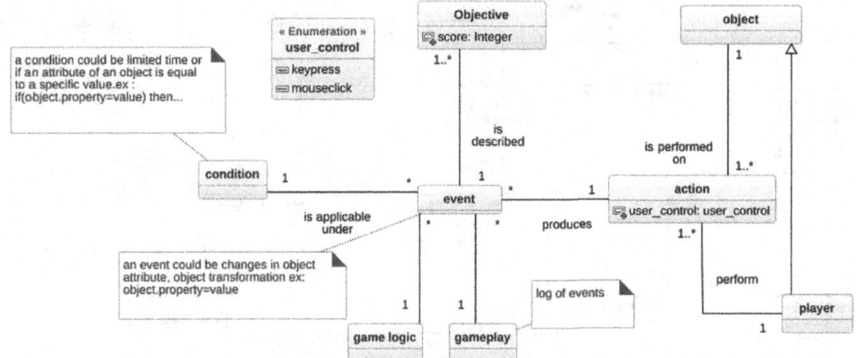

Fig. 3. Player's interaction

Our UML Diagram is composed of two main parts: The first part (Fig. 2) represent the general structure of a serious game where it shows that a SG is composed of levels, each level is composed of scenes, and each scene is composed of objects. The second part (Fig. 3) represent the player interaction within the game play environment and the scoring system. In fact, it shows that, when a player perform a certain action within a specific condition, an event will be triggered, and an objective may be achieved, according to the achieved objective and the triggered event the player will be rewarded.

The pedagogue will use this model to add all the features they need, and then use a suitable modeling tool to help them generate the suitable code that fulfills the semantics of the UML diagrams and shows the class skeleton, getters/setters, and the function's headers for each entity. They can use any tool that has an easy graphical user interface (GUI), allows code generation from a UML diagram and synchronize between the model and the generated code. Examples of such tools are GenMyModel[1], easy UML[2]and Visual Paradigm[3]. Although, we advise them to use GenMyModel because it facilitates collaboration, and it is relatively easy to use online with no software to download.

The UML Object diagram in Fig. 4 gives an example of instantiation of the above model for a specific level in a serious game called "short cuts". This game has been developed and used by Revelian[4], a company specializing in designing serious games for recruitment. The game main aim is to move a blue marble from a start position to end position with minimum number of moves; to measure the fluid reasoning skills of the player.

---

1 https://www.genmymodel.com.

2 http://plugins.netbeans.org/plugin/55435/easyuml.

3 https://www.visual-paradigm.com.

4 www.revelian.com.

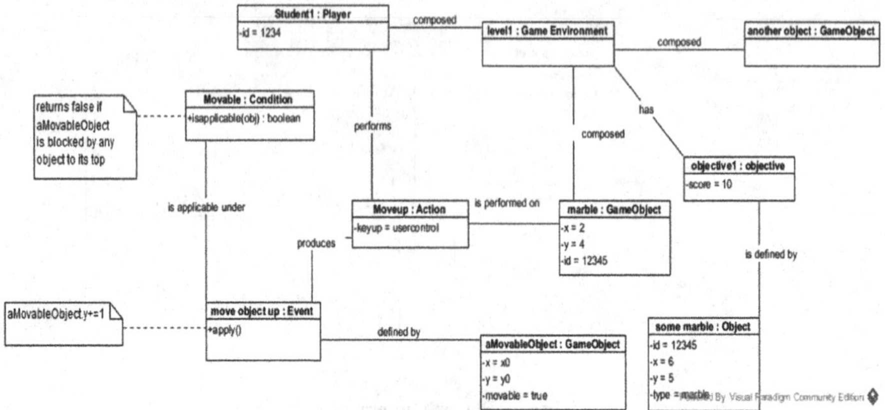

Fig. 4. Object diagram of "Short Cut" mini game

3.2 Logic Code Generation

This section represents the game logic development, where the pedagogue create the logic using a new DSL language, then a code generator will be used to transform the logical modal into software executable code. In fact, the pedagogue define all the possible actions in the game, and for each action, they define its triggered events according to specific conditions. Hence, the following figure shows the representation of an action with its generated code using our DSL. It shows the consequences when a player move up a marble objects (Fig. 5).

```
action:moveup(object)
        event e1: y of object = y of object + 1
        event e2: no changes

begin
        if (no collision) then e1
        if (collision) then e2
end

function moveup(object){
     void OnCollisionExit(Collision col){
                object.position.y= object.position.y+1
     }
}
```

Fig. 5. DSL definition of the "moveup" action of a player on an object

The developing of the DSL language constituted of developing three main elements: DSL Grammar, DSL Validator and DSL generator.

1. DSL Grammar: First, we have to identify the type of instruction that are used in any programing language, and especially in SG development. Such as defining a variable, an array, an expression, if statement, for iteration and son on ….Then we use Xtext, which is an eclipse plugin to represent these instructions in a new rules or format that can be easily understood and used by the pedagogue.
2. Code Validator: A code validator is developed using Xtend to validate the pedagogue's rules before code generation. For example, preventing the user, defining the same variable name twice, or setting a value bigger than x for an attribute y, etc. Therefore, the validator check each instruction to validate it or to show an error to the pedagogues.
3. Code Generator: The code generator will translate the instructions created using our grammar into java code, it checks the type of each instruction, and then depending on the instruction type, it calls the corresponding function that generates its code.

3.3 Scoring System Generation

In this section, we discuss two open source games shown in Fig. 6, where each one measures a specific competency, and we analyze the algorithms used for score calculation in each one, in order to create the rules that allow the pedagogues themselves to define the scoring system of any serious game.

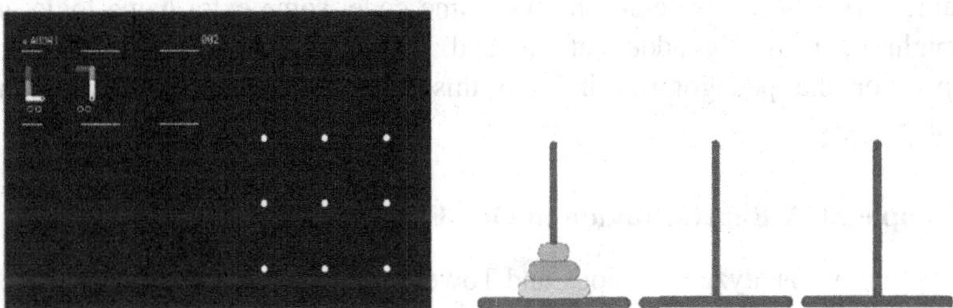

Fig. 6. Screenshots for Breaklock and Tower of Hanoi

Breaklock: This game assesses the "Analysis Techniques" competency of the player, where s/he must unlock an android lock pattern, composed of n dots, by guessing. Each time s/he makes a try s/he *will* know how many dots in the pattern are placed in the correct order and how many dots are in the wrong order. The score of this game depends on the size of the total search space and the length of the winning strategy, which is represented as the number of possible combinations between n dots, and the number of a player's attempts to achieve the goal.

Tower of Hanoi: The objective of this game is that the player moves the disks from one rod to another, while respecting some constraints; namely, that no disk can be put on top of a smaller one. This game assesses the "Knowledge of Programming Algorithms" competency. The pedagogue defines the scores as a mathematical function depending on the number of player's actions to win the game and the number of player's game replay attempts to win, in comparison with the minimum number of steps needed to solve the game.

After analyzing these games we found that the pedagogue rule of score calculation of any game follows a mathematical equation that depends on multiples important elements such as *game final state* that represent whether the objective is achieved, *number of action* to achieve the final state, *number of game replay*, *total number of possible actions*. Our aim is to make an abstraction layer for the pedagogue to help them code their own game scoring rules using a new language and rules that could be used on any serious game. Therefore, our Grammar must allow us to define:

1. Conditions
   - Logical combination of comparisons: Conjunctions (and) OR NOT
   - Comparison: Object.Property, comp_operator Value/ AnotherObject.Property
2. Reward
   - Mathematical Function of Game State.

3.4 Additional Game Logic

The framework will not generate the full game code; some extra game logic or code fixes might be manually added at the end. These additions can be done by the developers or the pedagogues, in case this latter has some basic programming knowledge.

3.5 Sample SGA Representation in Our Framework

In this section, we analyze Breaklock and Tower of Hanoi in detail; we detail the game elements according to our model. For instance, we define an action in each one and map its corresponding event according to specific condition (see Table 1). Hence, the developing of a SG using our framework follows this strategy.

Table 1. Analyze of two games according to the proposed framework

	Breaklock	Tower of Hanoi
Player	Yes	Yes
NPC	No	No
Objects	Dots & the lines that are drawn between the dots to connect them while trying to guess the pattern	Disks and road
Scene	Scene is composed of android lock pattern, i.e. dots and their links	Scene is composed of three rods and three disks that stand on the them (initially they stand on 1 rod while the 2 others are empty, but this changes subsequently)
Objective	Find the correct pattern	Move the disks from one rod to another
Action	Draw pattern	Move disks
Conditions	- **C1**: all dots are placed in the correct order - **C2**: some dots are placed in correct order, others are placed in wrong order, and others does not exist - **C3**: all dots are placed in the wrong order	- **C1**: top disk bigger then the lower - **C2**: lower disk bigger then the top - **C3**: no lower disk - **C4**: last disk
Events	- If **C1** then **e1**: game end, score is shown to the player - If **C2** or **C3** then **e2**: draw a pattern to show the number of correct and incorrect dots to the player	- If **C1**, **e1**: game end and player loose - If **C2** or **C3** then **e2**: increment the number of clicks of player - If **C1** and **C4** then **e3**: player win and the score is calculated

4 Conclusion

In this paper, we propose a framework for modeling and code generation of serious games for assessment, which aims to simplify SGA development. Given the limitations in current approaches (GLiSMo, GaML and Graph-based), we proposed a new UML meta-model to be instantiated in order to define a new game structure, and a DSL to define game logic such as interaction and scoring rules. Nonetheless, some extra coding is needed to glue our code into game engine's APIs to generate a fully functioning game. Finally, we demonstrated how our framework could be used to define two games, as a proof of concept. The implementation of the framework is still a work in progress, which will allow us to make a more thorough evaluation in the future.

In fact, we are currently working on closing the cycle of game definition and generation by integrating with game engines, namely Unity. In parallel, we are planning to offer a visual editor that would ease the task of defining the game structure and its logic, all in one place, and without jumping between UML editors and separate text files for DSL definition. Furthermore, we are working on representing a larger spectrum of game genre, with structures that are more complex or logic to further enrich our model and better study its limitations.

Acknowledgment. We would like to express our gratitude for the Agence Universitaire de la Francophonie (AUF) for funding this research project. We would also like to acknowledge all our colleagues at the LET'SeGA project from Lebanon, Tunisia and Egypt, for their amazing support, team spirit and valuable input.

References

1. Cheniti-Belcadhi, L., El Khayat, G.A., Said, B.: Knowledge engineering for competence assessment on serious games based on semantic web. In: 2019 IEEE Second International Conference on Artificial Intelligence and Knowledge Engineering (AIKE), pp. 163–166. IEEE, Sardinia, Italy (2019)
2. Chevaillier, P., et al.: Semantic modeling of virtual environments using MASCARET. In: 2012 5th Workshop on Software Engineering and Architectures for Realtime Interactive Systems (SEARIS), pp. 1–8. IEEE, Costa Mesa, CA, USA (2012)
3. Elfotouh, A.M.A., Nasr, E.S., Gheith, M.H.: Towards a comprehensive serious educational games' ontology. In: Proceedings of the 3rd Africa and Middle East Conference on Software Engineering - AMECSE 2017, pp. 25–30. ACM Press, Cairo, Egypt (2017)
4. Hamieh, F., Said, B.: Modeling and code generation of serious games for assessment. In: ICT in our Lives, Alexandria, Egypt, p. 8 (2018)
5. Matallaoui, A., Herzig, P., Zarnekow, R.: Model-driven serious game development integration of the gamification modeling language GaML with unity, pp. 643–651. IEEE (2015)
6. Mitchell, A., Savill-Smith, C.: Great Britain, Learning and Skills Development Agency: The Use of Computer and Video Games for Learning: A Review of the Literature. Learning and Skills Development Agency, London (2004)
7. Oon Thean, S.T.: A model-driven framework to support games development: an application to serious games (2013)
8. Prasanna, A.T.: A domain specific modeling language for specifying educational games (2012)
9. Prot, S., Anderson, C.A., Gentile, D.A., Brown, S.C., Swing, E.L.: The positive and negative effects of video game play. In: Media Well - Child Adolescents 109–128 (2014)
10. Reyno, E.M., Cubel, J.Á.C.: A platform-independent model for videogame gameplay specification. In: DiGRA Conference (2009)
11. Said, B., Cheniti-Belcadhi, L., El Khayat, G.: An ontology for personalization in serious games for assessment. In: 2019 IEEE Second International Conference on Artificial Intelligence and Knowledge Engineering (AIKE), pp 148–154. IEEE, Sardinia, Italy (2019)
12. Tang, S., Hanneghan, M.: Game content model: an ontology for documenting serious game design. In: 2011 Developments in E-systems Engineering, pp 431–436. IEEE, Dubai, United Arab Emirates (2011)
13. Thillainathan, N., Leimeister, J.M.: Educators as game developers—model-driven visual programming of serious games. In: Kunifuji, S., Papadopoulos, G.A., Skulimowski, A.M.J., Kacprzyk, J. (eds.) Knowledge, Information and Creativity Support Systems, pp. 335–349. Springer, Cham (2016). https://doi.org/10.1007/978-3-319-27478-2_23

How to Design and Measure a Serious Game Aiming at Emotional Engagement of Social Anxiety

Imre Dániel Báldy, Nikolaj Hansen, and Thomas Bjørner(✉)

Department of Architecture, Design and Media Technology, Aalborg University, Copenhagen, Denmark
tbj@create.aau.dk

Abstract. This experimental study outlines how a serious game can be designed with the aim of simulating an emotional sense of what it is like to have social anxiety disorder. Novel within the study is the use of psychophysiological measures (galvanic skin response and heart rate) as ways to organize specific game events for later interview sessions. Card sorting was used as a projective technique in the interviews as a way to have participants talk about their emotional states. The psychophysiological data, measured by Mionix Naos QG mouse, was used to support self-reported methods consisting of a questionnaire and interviews. The study is based on 28 university students, and tested in a lab environment to minimize external distractions. The game was designed with three different scenarios, and it was concluded that one scenario in particular successfully simulated an emotional sense of what is like to have social anxiety disorder. There is still much future work to do on how to use and interpret psychophysiological measurement within game research. There is also potential for increased validity and reliability using methods other than self-reports, especially with emotional engagement as a research focus.

Keywords: Serious games · Psychophysiological methods · Card sorting · Game design · Social anxiety disorder

1 Introduction

Social anxiety disorder (SAD), otherwise known as social phobia, is a type of anxiety disorder characterized by a strong desire to make a favorable impression on others, along with insecurity about being able to do so [1]. This can lead individuals suffering from SAD to be preoccupied with how others evaluate them, and to notice what went wrong in a social interaction rather than what went right [1]. The tendency of such individuals to construct negative images of themselves and develop anticipatory anxiety about future interactions only further exacerbates the problem. Previous research reports that 10–25% of university students have impaired functioning due to SAD [1–4], with strong correlations with deficits in social skills, relationships, attention difficulties, learning problems, and with increased risk of exam failure and failure to graduate [2]. Seeking professional help can be difficult for students with SAD, since

A. Liapis et al. (Eds.): GALA 2019, LNCS 11899, pp. 417–427, 2019.
https://doi.org/10.1007/978-3-030-34350-7_40

they may find it difficult to express the difficulties they are having due to their social discomfort [1, 2].

The aim of this study is to create a serious game to simulate emotional engagement for university students with SAD and give students information on where they can seek help if they do associate with some of the SAD symptoms. The aim is not to help in the treatment of SAD, but to simulate emotional engagement via a serious game as a way to communicate what suffering from SAD is like. The definition of emotional engagement varies across literature, as it used within many different contexts [2, 8, 10, 15, 18]. However, there is a common understanding that it involves interest, motivation, happiness, fun, anger, empathy, tension, anxiety, and other affective states, any of which factors could affect gamers' involvement or effort to continue playing [15]. For example, empathy as the feeling for and with the characters [18] is accordingly a sub element within emotional engagement [8, 15].

The elements of design and purpose within serious games for mental health are already well covered. However, the evaluation part is understudied [5], including emotional engagement with missing immediate and corresponding content responses. Therefore, advances are needed in the measures of players' emotions in serious games. This study's research question is: How can one design an informative serious game targeting university students with the aim of simulating an emotional sense of what it is like to have social anxiety disorder, and how can emotional engagement be measured by methods other than self-reports?

2 Previous Research

There are already applications designed to provide help with SAD (also targeting university students) in almost all of the six main types of applied serious games for mental health outlined by Fleming et al. [5]. These include, for example, the applications "Journey to the Wild Divine," "Freeze-Framer 2.0," "Pacifia," "Self-Help for Anxiety Management (SAM)," "Challenger" [6], and "SuperBetter [7]." These applications all offer either exercises (e.g. for relaxing or breathing) or community support and feedback. However, there are still missing types of serious games with informative purposes and content associated with SAD.

While there are several existing methods for the measurement of emotional engagement [14–16], an issue still lies in the self-reporting measure used. Most evaluations require that the gameplay either be paused (and thus disrupted) for participants to answer questions, or that questions be completed after the game, which may alter the results as they do not evaluate the here-and-now emotional experience (this method has the problem of recall bias). It is rather difficult for participants to remember specific emotions linked to specific played events. Self-reports (both qualitative and quantitative) also have the limitations of getting participants to register, evaluate, or simply talk about their emotional experiences of the game, as they are not always readily accessible from their consciousness [8, 19]. There is an increase in studies using psychophysiological measures in game research [8, 9, 13, 21], often within a mixed-methods approach to avoid only relying on self-reports. A majority of studies that have examined emotional engagement to game content using psychophysiological measures are based on a combination of arousal and valence, the dimensional model [8]. Arousal is an indication of emotional activation (stimuli producing high arousal are in general remembered better than stimuli producing low arousal), and valence is an indication of how pleasant (positive/negative) an emotion is [8, 19]. Studies often rely on mixed-methods with use of psychophysiological methods to measure arousal [8, 19, 21], and self-reports to measure valence [8, 19]. Affordable and valid methods for measuring arousal through psychophysiological methods include e.g. heart rate (HR), and GSR (galvanic skin response) [11]. GSR, which falls under the umbrella term of electro-dermal activity (EDA), refers to changes in sweat gland activity that are reflective of the intensity of our emotional state, otherwise known as emotional arousal [11]. Both HR and GSR have been shown to have correlation with the intensity of arousal [8, 19, 21].

3 Design

The game is implemented in Unity, and the player experiences a story world with a university context through the eyes of Thomas, a university student who has SAD. There are three different scenarios that all include different social anxiety-provoking events. The scenarios and specific elements of social anxiety are developed based on both literature review [1–7] and collaboration and co-design with a chief psychiatrist with 30 years of expertise in social anxiety. The initial design planning included several interviews with the chief psychiatrist, and the three scenarios were mainly based on his expertise. The three scenarios were classroom, cafeteria, and group exam settings, in that order. The game takes place from a first-person perspective. The first-person perspective was chosen for potentially better identification with Thomas, the main character. Additionally, the first-person perspective makes the feeling of the autonomous physical symptoms of SAD more realistic. In terms of gameplay, the players were dropped into each of the three scenarios one by one and required to navigate through the environment, occasionally being forced into events that would cause the main character's SAD symptoms to occur. Further, there were also simulated autonomous physical symptoms of SAD, including shaking (implemented by camera shake function) and increased heart beat (implemented by changing the volume and the pitch). It was important to put some emphasis on the game's visuals and audio to increase the likelihood of eliciting emotional engagement from the player. We used a low-polygon-count art style because it looked both realistic and stylish at the same time. In addition to this, low-poly graphics are not as computationally demanding as more realistic graphics, which allows the game to run without risk of disengagement from missing frames caused by higher computational requirements. The character models and animations in the game are based on Mixamo [20].

The classroom scenario (Fig. 1, left) begins with the player entering a door and being late for class. After a short conversation with the teacher, the player has to make his or her way to an empty chair in the front row by asking a student sitting in the way to move. Once the player is seated, there is a discussion of who the player should be in a group with, ultimately ending with him being alone and leaving the classroom through the door to work elsewhere. Toward the end of this conversation, the player will begin to hear whispers from fellow students, with dialogue such as "*I don't want to work with him"* and *"It's his fault for being late."* Such whispered dialogue was chosen to illustrate how students with SAD fear being negatively judged. The classroom was purposely designed so the front row seat is the only available seat in the room.

Fig. 1. The classroom and cafeteria scenarios.

The cafeteria scenario (Fig. 1, right) begins with the player entering at the door. The player must then make their way up to the cafeteria cashier, where they ask for a "football" (an unusual request). This request then prompts the character to hear whispers from the cafeteria clerk, and dialogue saying *"What a weird kid"* will appear. As in the classroom scenario, this bit of whispered dialogue was added to reflect how, after making a potentially embarrassing mistake, a person with SAD might be concerned about what others think of him for doing so. After this conversation, the player gets a tray of food and has to find a seat. When the player crosses the threshold of the middle of the room, the player falls over with the tray and food, and the fellow students laugh. The player must then exit the room through the door. The third scenario at which the player arrives is an exam (Fig. 2). This scenario is a common scene for a university student, and was made as a group exam where the player can feel judged by peers.

Fig. 2. Exam scenario.

There is no code or method unique to the exam scenario. It consists entirely of a conversation. At one point the teacher will make an *"mhm..."* sound when Thomas fails to answer a question, which causes the autonomous symptoms effect to intensify. This reflects how people with SAD would dwell on the fact that they performed poorly in a performance context. This event also has a sequence wherein the player character starts hearing whispers. The dialogue displayed at that point includes the lines *"You really should know this," "Come on, we discussed this so many times,"* and *"Just say something."* As with the previous scenarios, this dialogue is meant to reflect the player character's fear of being negatively judged by classmates.

The conversations were made by first creating it visually by a canvas and making a text box with a grey panel acting as a backdrop for the text. The text box contents were altered in code, through a system of Booleans and if-statements (Fig. 3). By progressing step-by-step through conversations, it was ensured that no conversation lines were repeated.

```
else if (CR3) {
    if (Input.GetKeyDown(KeyCode.Alpha1)) {
        talkText.text = "<color=orange><b>Student:</b></color> <i>It's his
        CR4 = true; CR3 = false;
    }
}
```

Fig. 3. Coded example from one part of the classroom conversations

Occasionally we wanted conversations, and other events, to happen after some time had passed. This was implemented using Unity's built-in IEnumerator class and the "WaitForSeconds function", which by set time suspends the execution of the coroutine.

4 Methods

4.1 Research Design and Participants

The psychophysiological methods were used in an explanatory sequential method within a mixed-methods design to ensure measures for both conscious and unconscious experiences, following a study design similar to Heiselberg and Bjørner [19]. A total of 28 university students were recruited for the game test (18 males, 10 females. Age: Mean = 25. Age range: 22–33). All participants were anonymized by ID numbers Students were recruited from the Danish universities Aalborg University CPH and Copenhagen University, and were enrolled in different fields. After a short introduction about the research theme and signing of informed consent (and excluding participants with heart failure and pacemakers [12]), the participants were seated in front of a computer screen and read an introductory script. Then, participants were asked to fill in a form regarding age, gender, field of study, and gaming habits. Participants were informed about the Mionix Naos QG mouse and the GSR and HR measurement. They were also instructed to relax for 30 s before gameplay to establish baseline measurements for GSR and HR. Once participants were finished, they were asked to sit aside and offered refreshments while the researchers analyzed the collected GSR and HR data. The researchers looked for instances where the aforementioned trigger points were accompanied by peaks or lows of GSR and HR, indicating emotional activation.

4.2 Procedure and Measurements

The procedure consisted of three parts: 1. Psychophysiological measurements of GSR and HR throughout the gameplay session. 2. Questionnaire with 5-point Likert items, and 3. Semi-structured interview.

(1) The Mionix Naos QG mouse was used to measure GSR and HR throughout the gameplay sessions. The purpose was to identify game events causing different levels of arousal (low, medium, and high) in response to the three different scenarios. There was established a baseline (measurements while participants were not engaged in any task), as well the test was conducted in an isolated lab environment with minimized external distractions, and even levels of temperature and moisture to avoid unwanted fluctuations [12]. Data corrections (noise filtering) were made, and MATLAB software was used for data processing. The researchers looked for instances where the aforementioned trigger points were accompanied by peaks or lows of GSR and HR, indicating emotional activation.

(2) The questionnaire was handed out after the game-play, and was filled out by the participants meanwhile researchers analyzed the GSR and HR data. One section was dedicated to asking participants about their understanding of SAD after having played the game, while another included questions from the Narrative Engagement Scale [16] and asked participants about their narrative understanding, attentional focus, and emotional engagement.

(3) The semi-structured interview involved questions related directly to the data captured by the psychophysiological methods. Participants were asked about specific events of the gameplay session during which considerably low, high, or medium levels of arousal were detected, similar to the approach of Heiselberg and Bjørner [19]. The first question was "Which event from the game can you immediately recall?" This question was used as a starting point for the interview, with further follow-up questions. Card sorting was used during the interview as a projective technique for asking about emotional engagement in regard to the different in-game events. There were 12 cards with 12 emotions [19]. We used the cards for the measure of valence, while the measure of arousal was provided by the GSR and HR. Both the arousal and valence were compared with the given trigger points. Participants were asked to select three cards (in prioritized order) that best matched their emotional engagement within the three different scenarios. The interviews were recorded and transcribed verbatim. The interviews were analyzed by content analysis [17].

5 Results

5.1 Are the Participants Emotionally Engaged?

The results reveal that almost all participants had an easy time making sense of in-game events. Understanding of the characters was also clear, and participants easily recognized the storyline (Table 1). Questions 1–3 in the questionnaire were related to the participants' narrative understanding, as this is a prerequisite for emotional engagement

[16]. The questions asked were: Question 1: I had an easy time making sense of what was going on in the game. Question 2: My understanding of the characters is clear. Question 3: I had an easy time recognizing the thread of the story.

Table 1. Summary of answers to questions related to narrative understanding (question 1–3) and emotional engagement (question 6–7). Based on questionnaire answers n = 28.

	Disagree	Somewhat disagree	Neutral	Some what agree	Agree
Question 1				10	18
Question 2		1	1	6	20
Question 3			1	5	22
Question 6	3	7	1	11	6
Question 7	3		1	11	13

Participants scored highly regarding narrative understanding (Table 1). The mean value of their answers was 4.67, and the median and mode values were both 5. The data's standard deviation is also low, at 0.58. In terms of the overall game and the story, several participants stated that the experience *"was not confusing"* (ID = 1) or that it was *"pretty straightforward"* (ID = 6). Further, 75% of the participants either agreed or somewhat agreed that they had attentional focus on the game, which was based on the question "I had an easy time paying attention to events in the game."

However, there were some mixed results concerning whether the participants were emotionally engaged if looking only at the questionnaire results based on questions 6 and 7 (Table 1). Question 6 asked "The story affected me emotionally" and question 7 "I felt sorry for some of the characters in the game." Even though the majority of participants either somewhat agreed or agreed with the statement regarding emotional engagement, the results from the questionnaire are a bit mixed. The mean value was 3.72, and both the median and mode were 4. The values are all close to or exactly 4, which suggests that participants were only somewhat emotionally engaged. The standard deviation was 1.32, further supporting that the results from the questionnaire were mixed. Most of the lower ratings were for the statement "*The story affected me emotionally*" (Question 6). One participant (ID = 20) stated in regard to the relatability of the main character Thomas that the lack of context meant "*[he] had no relation to the character, so just jumping into it and having no context to where Thomas is coming from [didn't] help*."

However, both the card sorting within the interviews and the psychophysiological data provide a more nuanced picture in terms of emotional engagement. Through content analysis on an aggregate level (based on 3 cards from 28 participants), it was revealed that participants made their choice of emotion cards for the different events based on one of six categories. Rephrased as statements, the different categories were: *I felt something for Thomas, I felt like I was Thomas, I imagined how I'd feel, I wasn't affected too much, I felt something toward the other characters,* and *I felt something unexpected.* In 55 instances, participants felt something toward Thomas, and 39 times, participants felt as though they were Thomas themselves. This can be considered emotional engagement, as participants were often able to relate to the main character. 33 participants tried to imagine how they themselves would feel in the events.

From the card sorting (Fig. 4), it can be revealed that the predominant emotions were "embarrassed" and "pity." In the classroom scenario in particular, strong tendencies toward "embarrassed" and "pity" were present. Furthermore, "neutral," "angry," and "ashamed" were also often picked.

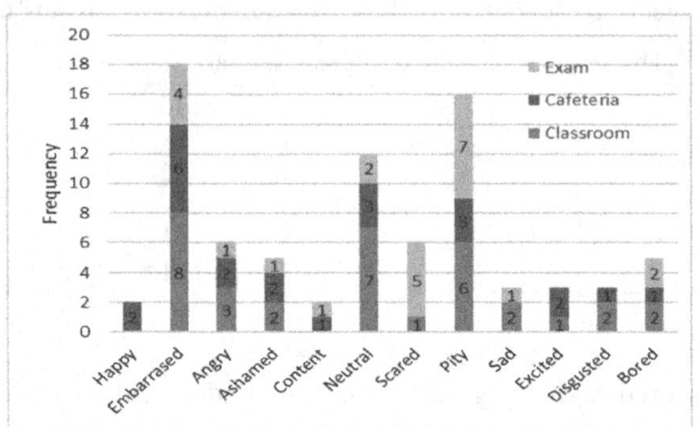

Fig. 4. Card sorting results (first choice) within the three different game scenarios. Based on 12 emotions with 12 cards in qualitative interviewing n = 28.

The data suggests that the exam scenario was more successful in emotionally engaging participants, as many of the emotions they chose—embarrassment, shame, fear, and pity—were directed toward either the character or themselves. An example of the importance of the interview and providing nuanced results can be illustrated by the fact that some participants actually felt anger toward themselves (and by extension, the main character) for being unable to provide an answer in the exam situation: "*[I'd feel] a bit angry, [as] this should be something that I should know*" (ID = 10). However, most participants were angry at the classmates for judging them (ID = 19, 24, 25, 27): "*I felt angry because I was frustrated that others were judging*" (ID = 25). This means that for some participants, the game successfully elicited emotions of feeling judged by others, which was the intention. The final participant failed to clarify what made them angry about the event (ID = 18). 6 participants still chose "neutral," half of whom chose it because they felt emotionally unaffected by the event (IDs = 2, 5, 20). Those who chose "bored" did so because they either felt that nothing interesting was happening in the event (IDs = 2, 26), had no choice or input (IDs = 8, 23, 25), or simply could not relate to the character's feelings (ID = 20).

5.2 Psychophysiological Data

The best-recalled game scenario was the cafeteria, and the best-recalled event was where the main character falls with the tray and gets laughed at by his fellow students. 14 participants recalled this middle scenario most frequently, and 12 (out of 14) participants recalled the tray. This was followed by the first game scenario, with 10 participants recalling the classroom. Only 4 participants recalled the exam scenario the best. Many participants elaborated on the tray event within the interview as being "unexpected and surprising, which made it memorable" (IDs = 2, 10, 11, 13, 14, 15, 27): *"I think it's because it's so sudden compared to the 'building up' nature of the rest of the game"* (ID = 10). *"In this [event], I felt more like I was the one who fell and got embarrassed"* (ID = 13). The self-reported questionnaire and interview results, in which participants reported the highest emotional engagement with the cafeteria scenario, are also supported by the psychophysiological HR data (Fig. 5).

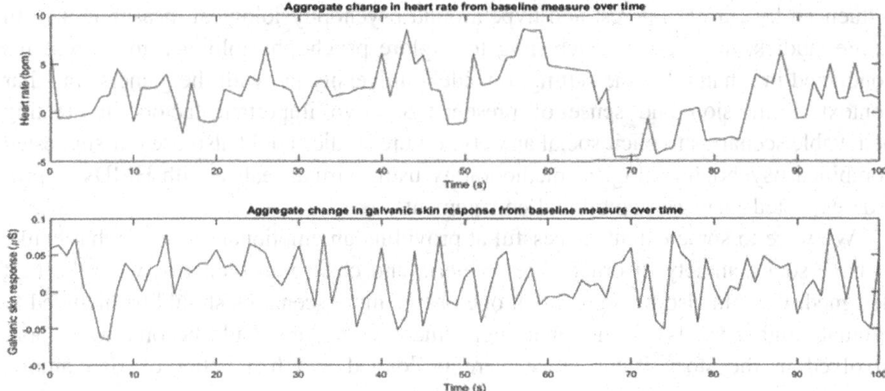

Fig. 5. Aggregated HR and GSR results. Individual datasets made time comparable 0–100 and interpolated (n = 28).

The GSR data appeared to be a bit inconclusive due to equipment failure. In the HR measure, there is a good match of highest arousal within the cafeteria scenario and the tray event (time 50 s–60 s). But another important result is actually the unexpected low recalls and lower arousal within the exam scenario. The triangulated methods can be a good reason to redesign the exam scenario to elicit better social anxiety and emotional engagement. There can be several reasons behind the exam scenario results. First, due to the way the exam setting was designed and implemented, the different anxiety-inducing events (feeling of being judged by the teacher, failing to answer a question, and being judged by groupmates) follow one another back to back, which may cause an overlap among them. Second, if the high-arousal cafeteria scenario was memorable, it can follow that the next scenario would not be, as participants may have been less interested in the game toward the end, while the previous scenarios had already emotionally engaged them.

6 Conclusion and Discussion

Emotional engagement is rather complex to measure. Therefore, there are good validity and reliability reasons to increase the methodological triangulation with psychophysiological measures within serious games for measuring emotional engagement. The psychophysiological measures can be used as a way to organize and categorize later interview sessions, for example, by taking some of the high-, medium-, and low-arousal events into the interview, with the interviews being more detailed and event-specific. The psychophysiological measures can also support and/or provide discussions of results from the self-reported data. However, substantial work is required within the research design to set up useful psychophysiological measures. There is also much further work needed regarding how psychophysiological data could and should be interpreted, then used to design and redesign serious games. At the same time, it is also very important not to allow the psychophysiological data to be too appealing or influenced by current interest and hype around psychophysiological measurements. In future studies, it would be interesting to explore psychophysiological measurements conducted in a natural game setting, outside a university lab with the gamers' familiar context. Immersion and sense of presence are two important factors in creating believable scenarios to elicit social anxiety. Future studies could also use our suggested combined psychophysiological methodology using virtual reality with HMDs to provide expected increased emotional engagement.

We were to some extent successful at providing an emotional sense of what is like to have social anxiety disorder. The cafeteria and classroom scenarios were the best designed. It could also be argued that one or two more scenarios should be included to simulate higher levels of emotional engagement, as players could become even more involved in the story if the story were prolonged and had better overlap among scenarios.

Within this study, card sorting was a good method to get participants to talk about the rather abstract topic of emotional engagement. However, it can be argued that we should have left one card open, on which participants could write down their own emotional engagement labels. "Surprise" could also be included as one of the emotions.

References

1. Purdon, C., Antony, M., Monteiro, S., Swinson, R.P.: Social anxiety in college students. J. Anxiety Disord. **15**(3), 203–215 (2001)
2. Russell, G., Topham, P.: The impact of social anxiety on student learning and well-being in higher education. J. Ment. Health **21**(4), 375–385 (2012)
3. Hakami, R.M., et al.: Social anxiety disorder and its impact in undergraduate students at Jazan Univ. Saudi Arabia. Ment. Illn. **9**(2), 42–47 (2017)
4. Russell, G.C., Shaw, S.: A study to investigate the prevalence of social anxiety in a sample of higher education students in the UK. J. Ment. Health **18**(3), 198–206 (2009)
5. Fleming, T.M., et al.: Serious games and gamification for mental health: current status and promising directions. Front. Psychiatry **7**, 215 (2017)
6. Miloff, A., Marklund, A., Carlbring, P.: The challenger app for social anxiety disorder: new advances in mobile psychological treatment. Internet Interv. **2**(4), 382–391 (2015)
7. Roepke, A., Jaffee, S., Riffle, O., McGonigal, J., Broome, R., Bez, M.: Randomized controlled trial of SuperBetter, a smartphone-based/Internet-based self-help tool to reduce depressive symptoms. Games Health J. **4**(3), 235–246 (2015)
8. Ravaja, N.: Contributions of psychophysiology to media research: review and recommendations. Media Psychol. **6**(2), 193–235 (2004)

9. Parsons, T.D., Reinebold, J.L.: Adaptive virtual environments for neuropsychological assessment in serious games. IEEE Trans. Consum. Electron. **58**(2), 197–204 (2012)
10. Ritterfeld, U., Cody, M., Vorderer, P.: Introduction. In: Ritterfeld, U., Cody, M., Vorderer, P. (eds.) Serious Games: Mechanics and Effects. Routledge, New York (2009). https://link.springer.com/book/10.1007/978-1-4614-1126-0
11. Boucsein, W.: Electrodermal Activity, 2nd edn. Springer, Berlin (2012). https://doi.org/10.1007/978-1-4614-1126-0
12. Figner, B., Murphy, R.O.: Using skin conductance in judgment and decision making research. In: A Handbook of Process Tracing Methods for Decision Research, pp. 163–184 (2011)
13. Jerčić, P., Sundstedt, V.: Practicing emotion-regulation through biofeedback on the decision-making performance in the context of serious games: a systematic review. Entertain. Comput. **29**, 75–86 (2019)
14. Brockmyer, J.H., Fox, C.M., Curtiss, K.A., McBroom, E., Burkhart, K.M., Pidruzny, J.N.: The development of the game engagement questionnaire: a measure of engagement in video gameplaying. J. Exp. Soc. Psychol. **45**(4), 624–634 (2009)
15. Schønau-Fog, H., Bjørner, T.: "Sure, I Would Like to Continue" a method for mapping the experience of engagement in video games. Bull. Sci. Technol. Soc. **32**(5), 405–412 (2012)
16. Busselle, R., Bilandzic, H.: Measuring narrative engagement. Media Psychol. **12**(4), 321–347 (2009)
17. Bjørner, T.: Qualitative Methods for Consumer Research: The Value of the Qualitative Approach in Theory and Practice. Hans Reitzel, Copenhagen (2015)
18. Van Cleemput, K., Vandebosch, H., Poels, K., Bastiaensens, S., DeSmet, A., De Bourdeaudhuij, I.: The development of a serious game on cyberbullying. In: Cyberbullying: from Theory to Intervention, p. 93 (2015)
19. Heiselberg, L., Bjørner, T.: How to evaluate emotional experiences in television drama series: improving viewer evaluations using a combination of psychophysiological measurements and self-reports. Behav. Inf. Technol. **37**(9), 884–893 (2018)
20. Adobe Inc. Mixamo. https://www.mixamo.com/#/. Accessed 1 July 2019
21. Kivikangas, J.M., et al.: A review of the use of psychophysiological methods in game research. J. Gaming Virtual Worlds **3**(3), 181–199 (2011)

On the Design of Gamification Elements in Moodle Courses

Ioannis Petroulis[1(✉)], Maria Tzelepi[2], and Kyparissia Papanikolaou[3]

[1] Department of Informatics and Telecommunications, National and Kapodistrian University of Athens, Athens, Greece
johnyend@di.uoa.gr

[2] Department of Psychology, National and Kapodistrian University of Athens, Athens, Greece
tzelepimaria@yahoo.com

[3] School of Pedagogical and Technological Education, Athens, Greece
kpapanikolaou@aspete.gr

Abstract. This study proposes a rewarding system for blended learning courses delivered through the Moodle platform. The proposed rewarding system consists of two types of rewards, those that are automatically provided by Moodle and those that are provided manually by the tutor. The specific rewarding system follows the principles of the Gamified e-Learning Model, focusing on the way students should be rewarded in order to become engaged in the course and form a Community of Inquiry. An empirical study in which the proposed rewarding system was implemented in a blended learning course on educational technology, is described. The rewards provided by the teacher are based on analysis of the Moodle log files and data collected for each student using a learning analytics tool. The results of the study provide evidence about students' appreciation of the various types of rewards rewarding individual and collaborative effort.

Keywords: Gamification · Communities of Inquiry · Moodle · Forum

1 Introduction

Gamification can be defined as the use of game design elements and game like mechanisms, aesthetics and thinking in non-game contexts or processes (such as education) in order to engage system users, motivate them, promote learning and even, solve problems [1, 2]. According to Lee and Hammer [3], games are motivating, because of the impact they have on the cognitive, emotional and social perspective of a user/player. The most popular gamification elements that can engage users/learners, enhance their intrinsic motivation and push them to achieve better results are points, levels, leaderboards and badges [4].

According to Pavlus [5], gamification, as a concept to raise user's motivation and engagement towards a system, can be embedded in an e-learning environment. Moreover, Ehlers [6] has stated that the learning process should be developed through collaboration and communication towards the creation of a learning community.

A. Liapis et al. (Eds.): GALA 2019, LNCS 11899, pp. 428–437, 2019.
https://doi.org/10.1007/978-3-030-34350-7_41

So gamification in this context could contribute to the creation of a collaborative and communicative environment. A well-known model in the area of virtual learning communities, is the Community of Inquiry model (CoI) [7] where educational experience between learners and educators is considered to occur through interaction among social, cognitive and teaching presence inside the community. Especially, the cognitive presence evolves through four phases [7]: (a) triggering event, (b) exploration, (c) integration and (d) resolution. Social presence is described as the ability of learners to display their personal characteristics while communicating with their peers and expressing themselves in the classroom [8]. Finally, regarding the teaching presence, it concerns the planning design and management of the learning process [9].

In this paper the approach followed for enhancing a blended course with gamification elements towards the development of a Community of Inquiry is presented. An empirical study in which the proposed approach was implemented in a blended learning course on educational technology in order to explore the potential of gamification for promoting learners' engagement, is described.

2 Design Principles of a Rewarding System Based on Badges

The rewarding system proposed in this paper is based on the Gamified e-Learning Model [10], a learning model which uses rewards to promote CoI [8] within online courses. Below the main theoretical axes behind the proposed system are briefly presented:

1. According to Utomo and his colleagues [10], learners who participate in Online Learning Systems, learn not only through studying the material provided by the tutor and answering to questions, but also through a productive discussion with their peers (peer learning) and the tutor. During the learning process, through discussion and communication, the teaching presence appears not only on the part of the educator, but also on the part of the learners. In this context, gamification elements, such as badges, that the educator or the course designer provides to learners should encourage open communication [11]. So, it is suggested that the facilitators (the educator and the researchers) of the discussion should provide messages that will be gradually shifting from direct guidance to simple facilitation, helping learners to become more autonomous during the discussion. Moreover, relevant badges promoting student's undertaking the role of facilitator should be provided.
2. The Gamified e-Learning Model also, indicates that after discussing on the new knowledge, learners should work on several tasks (such as quizzes, assignments and final test) organized by the educator. Gamification mechanisms that highlight the learners' progress are, also, suitable for this phase. Following the specific guideline proposed by the Gamified e-Learning Model, the learners, after participating in a discussion, they have to submit a quiz relevant to the topic of the discussion and the issues analyzed through the discussion. Additionally, learners should be informed on the results of the quiz. To this end, learners are provided with relevant badges and personalized feedback.

3. Levels and leaderboards, where the learners' progress can be put in a ranking way, are considered as motivating them to engage through the learning process [2]. So, following the specific guideline (a) the provision of badges rewarding individual contribution is suggested through the "Level up!" Moodle plugin in combination with (b) the provision of a group reward to the community, based on the learners' teamwork and interaction throughout the discussions that took place through the course.

3 Design Rational of a Blended Learning Course Enriched with Gamification Elements

In this section, the design of an educational technology course for pre-service teachers enhanced with the rewarding system presented in Sect. 2 is presented. The course was organized as a series of eight (8) workshops enhanced with discussions. Through the workshops, students work on activities (individually and in groups) in order to familiarize themselves with WebQuests, explore digital tools, participate in discussions using the Moodle forum and they answer to quizzes of ten (10) questions relevant to the previous discussion. In the course discussions the teacher, two researchers (authors of this paper) and twenty-six (26) students separated into two laboratory sessions, participate. The teacher is the one who raises the topic for each discussion, and then, in consultation with the researchers, they coordinate the discussion. The teacher's and researchers' presence in the first and second discussion is quite instructive, in contrast to the next two (2) discussions, where their teaching presence is fading aiming to promote students to undertake teaching presence action. Finally, the main assignment of the course is the collaborative design and development of a WebQuest on a particular platform such as Weebly, Googlesites, Winx. Table 1 presents the structure of the course in terms of the main topics included, the discussions that took place, the quizzes that students had to answer and the rewards they received.

Table 1. Curriculum of the technology enhanced learning course organized in face to face (F2F) workshops and online discussions.

Topic	Discussions	Quizzes	Rewards
F2F Workshop 1: Introduction to WebQuests and principal design guidelines by evaluating real paradigms of WebQuests **Discussion 1:** "The best WebQuest"	Discussion on best practices in designing WebQuests based on specific criteria	✘	✘
F2F Workshop 2: Group work: Students select subject for their WebQuests,	✘	Quiz 1 based on	LevelUp!

(*continued*)

Table 1. *(continued)*

Topic	Discussions	Quizzes	Rewards
exploring the text books and appropriate resources. Introduction to defining learning outcomes		Discussion 1	
F2F Workshop 3 **Discussion 2**: "Designing the Introduction of a WebQuest"	Exploring the scope and the design of the Introduction field of several WebQuests as well as the role of the Web 2.0 objects integrated	✖	Cognitive Excellence and Sociability
F2F Workshop 4: Presentation of the Product Design Cycle as an instructional approach as well as of several educational scenarios based on the particular approach. Proposed digital tools: Simulations, Googlearth, SketchUp, FreeCAD	✖	Quiz 2 based on the Discussion 2	Quiz & Level Up!
F2F Workshop 5 **Discussion 3:** "Design the Task/Process field of a WebQuest"	Design the Task/Process field of a WebQuest on a specific subject	✖	Cognitive Excellence & Sociability & Quiz & LevelUp!
F2F Workshop 6 on (a) site development on Weebly, Wordpress, Wix, Googlesite (b) WebQuest design on Learning Designer	✖	Quiz 3 based on the Discussion 3	LevelUp!
F2F Workshop 7 **Discussion 4:** "Design the Process/Evaluation field of a WebQuest"	Design the Process/Evaluation field of the WebQuest of Workshop 5	✖	Quiz & Participation & Cognitive Excellence & LevelUp!
F2F Workshop 7 Students work in groups on the development of a WebQuest	✖	Quiz 4 based on the Discussion 4	Presentation of all the rewards

During the learning process, students were achieving rewards coming from: (a) the system automatically during the interaction, and (b) the facilitators in the form of badges (provided at each lesson and explained by the teacher). Specifically, the system rewarded automatically the students through "Level up!" gamification plugin [12]. "Level up!" classifies students in leaderboard depending on various actions they take inside the Moodle platform, such as, their forum posts, the comments they make to their peers' posts, the quizzes submission and the assignments submission. In general, "Level up!" attributes points to students for their actions, when they create, edit or read course contents. For example, they would receive 45 points, when creating a new forum discussion and receive 9 points, when reading course resources. These are the default rules whilst educators can add more ones. All these events usually relate to a user's learning experience for example, posting to a forum or submitting an assignment, and even updating a calendar or viewing a message [13].

Two types of badges were also provided to students as rewards: individual badges and group badges. The *individual badges* reward activities that require independent work and group badges reward activities that require interaction with peers. The individual badges provided are (see Table 2): (a) the *Participation* badge which reflects activities such as number of messages posted, period of navigation in the Moodle platform, times of access, etc., and (b) the *Quiz* badge. The group badges are (c) the badge of *Cognitive Excellence* which reflects the messages contributed by the student in the discussion based on the four faces of cognitive presence of CoI, and (d) the *Sociability* badge which reflects the interaction among students. These rewards were provided to the learners in a text form organized in tables. At the beginning of each course, the teacher was explaining the rewards of the students in relation to the CoI model. The individual rewards were shared among the students.

The value of each reward was manually calculated using (a) the SNA learning analytics tool that is a Moodle plug-in and (b) the Moodle log files as follows (see Table 2):

(a) The Participation badge reflected the sum of each student's activities as they were recorded in the Moodle log files.
(b) The Quiz badge reflected the percentage of the right answers on the quizzes. These data were provided by the Moodle Quiz activity file.
(c) The Cognitive Excellence badge reflected the student's level on the Cognitive presence of the CoI model. The data used were provided by the Moodle log files and the content of the discussions and they were analyzed according to the Cognitive phases descriptors [8]. This badge represents the multitude of the cognitive presence messages that the students contribute to each discussion, i.e. the cognitive phase (triggering event, exploration, integration, resolution) in which the messages belong.
(d) The Sociability badge reflected the Density and the Centrality measurement of social network analysis. These measurements were provided by the SNA learning analytics tool.

4 Empirical Study

The study performed in the context of an undergraduate course on educational technology at the Department of Civil Engineering Educators of the School of Pedagogical and Technological Education (ASPETE) in Athens, Greece. The participants of the

Table 2. The proposed rewarding system: types of rewards with their values

Types of reward	Values for each reward
A. Participation badge	**Gold:** The student who navigated to the platform, viewed educational content, downloaded content and submitted assignments with a frequency higher than the 60% of his peers **Silver:** The student who visited, navigated to the platform, viewed the sources, downloaded material and submitted assignments with a frequency lower than the 30% and higher than the 60% of his peers **Bronze:** The student who visited, navigated to the platform, viewed the sources, downloaded material and submitted assignments with a frequency lower than the 30% of their peers
B. Quiz badge	**Player:** The student who has responded correctly to a number of questions less than the Average of the correct answers of all the students of the specific group **Scorer!:** The student who has responded correctly to a number of questions equal to or greater than the average of the correct answers of all the students of the specific group
C. Cognitive Excellence badge	**Abstract:** The student who has contributed under the 25% of the average number of messages posted by each participant of the discussion. Also, s/he has not approached the solution of the problem discussed **Explorer:** The student who has contributed under the 50% of the average number of messages posted from each participant to the discussion. Also, he/she has not approached the solution of the problem **Builder:** The learner who has contributed over the 50% of the average number of messages posted from each participant but he/she has not approached the solution of the problem, or the learner has contributed below the 50% of the average number of messages posted from each participant to the discussion but he/she has conquered the solution of the problem **Conqueror:** The one who has contributed over the 50% of the average number of messages posted from each participant to the discussion, with high cognitive quality and has conquered the solution of the problem
D. Sociability badge	**Sun, Planet, Satellite, Comet**: The classification is based on the measurements of the centrality of each student in the community

study were 26 undergraduate students enrolled in the course and organised in two laboratory groups. The students participated in four asynchronous discussions according to the proposed course design presented in Sect. 3.

The research focus of the study is on the students' perceptions about the proposed rewarding system. The research question of the study is "How did the students evaluate the types of rewards they receive during the course?"

4.1 Data Collection and Analysis

In order to address the research question, two types of data were gathered: (1) the students' discussion messages and (2) the students' answers to the Badge Questionnaire which the students submitted at the end of the course.

The Badge Questionnaire was created by the authors, based on the "Internal Gamification Questionnaire (IGQ)" [14]. IGQ reflects the behaviour of the system users during the interaction with their colleagues and the system. Moreover, it evaluates the binding of the users with the system and the experience that the users had through their interaction with the gamified system. Appropriate questions that match the educational sector have been selected as the IGQ has been designed for business contexts.

The Badge Questionnaire (see Table 3) consists of twelve (12) closed ended questions of five-point Likert scale type and two open questions. The closed ended questions pertain to every form of reward given to the students during the course. The options given to these questions are scored from 1 to 5, where 1 is the lowest value (meaning "strongly disagree") and 5 is the highest value (meaning "strongly agree").

The data analysis process took place through the course and after the course. The aim was to combine data from various sources such as questionnaires and more objective data such as the rewards that students got, in order to shed light on the characteristics of students that appreciate more or less the rewards provided. The data analysis process included (a) statistical analysis of the twenty-six (26) badge questionnaires collected, as well as (b) content analysis of the four (4) discussions that included 1094 student messages.

In particular, the mean and standard deviation for each question of the Badge Questionnaire and for each type of reward given, were calculated.

Through the course, after each discussion activity, the content of the students' messages were analyzed by two independent researchers based on the four phases' indicators defined in the CoI model [7]. The unit of analysis was each single message. Inter-rater reliability was calculated using Holsti's coefficient of reliability and Cohen's Kappa, which was 93.6% and .92 respectively. This provided an estimate of reliability between the coders, before the adoption and advantage of a negotiated coding approach. Through this content analysis the students' cognitive contribution to each discussion was calculated supporting the reward provision process.

Aiming to provide more precise data on students' perceptions about the various types of rewards given, we divided the students into two groups, in order to determine whether students whose cognitive presence showed progress in each subsequent discussion, evaluated differently the provided rewards than the underperformed students. The students in Group 1 increased their cognitive contribution in each subsequent discussion while the students in Group 2 did not.

4.2 Results

We quantitatively analyzed the learner's answers to the Badges Questionnaire, reflecting students' perceptions for each type of badge they received. The Cronbach's Alpha for the twelve (12) items of the questionnaire was 0.97.

Table 3 shows a breakdown of the statistics calculated for each of the 12 questions of the Badge Questionnaire, each one examining all the five types of rewards provided to learners i.e. Cognitive Excellence, Sociability, Quiz, Course Participation and the "Level up!" reward, – this is reflected by the star (*) accompanying the particular questions. The mean of all the questions was high enough to show the students' positive perception for the rewards given during the course. Specifically, it shows the tendency of the learners to agree that the rewards given were understandable (question 9), in an appropriate form of presentation (question 6) and motivated them to participate in the discussions (question 1).

Table 3. Descriptive statistics of the Badge Questionnaire reflecting students' perceptions for all the rewards provided through the course.

Questions	Mean	s.d.
1. After participating in the discussion, I was looking forward to seeing the reward*	4.2	.7
2. I was trying harder to achieve my goals while waiting for the reward*	4.1	.7
3. I was dedicating time to the lesson due to the reward*	3.8	1.0
4. I was finishing my lesson duties more successfully because of the reward*	4.0	.8
5. I was finishing my lesson duties more quickly because of the reward*	3.9	.8
6. I can characterize as appropriate the form of the reward*	4.2	.7
7. I was staying focused on the discussion because of the reward*	3.9	.8
8. The discussion time of the lesson was very pleasant because of the reward*	3.9	.8
9. I could easily understand the meaning of the reward*	4.2	.6
10. The reward* helped to observe my learning progress	4.1	.7
11. I consider it helpful my group to stay informed for my reward*	4.0	.9
12. I consider it helpful, being informed about my peers' reward*	3.7	1.1
Open Questions		
1. Add a comment or suggestion for those rewards that their meaning was difficult for you to understand		
2. Suggest new rewards that you consider useful		

Regarding the open questions, most students were satisfied from the type and form of the rewards. Only two students encountered difficulty with rewards: the first one found difficult to understand the reward of Sociability, and the second one stated that he did not feel comfortable communicating his reward to the rest of the community. In the second open question, one student suggests rewarding to be also provided from one student to another. This feature can be enabled by the Moodle add-on which is called "Stamp collection".

Additionally, independent samples t-tests were performed on the means and revealed similarities and significant differences between Group 1 and Group 2 of students for each type of reward provided (see Table 4). Specifically, although the students of Group 1, whose cognitive presence showed progress through the discussions, were slightly more positive to all the rewards than those of Group 2, however, no significant differences were observed in the perception of both groups for the Cognitive Excellence, Participation, Sociability and Quiz reward (t(24) = 1.084, p > 0.05, t(24) = 1.309, p > 0.05, t(24) = .743, p > 0.05 and t(24) = 1.370, p > 0.05 respectively). On the other hand students of Group 1 show significantly higher perception for the "Level up!" reward than those of Group2 (t(24) = 1.904, p < 0.05). These results suggest that the students' progress i.e. their performance in cognitive presence, has a significant effect on their perception for the "LevelUp!" reward.

Table 4. Descriptive and t-test statistics for the two groups of learners for the various types of rewards provided

Types of reward	Groups	N	Mean	s.d.	t
A. The Cognitive Excellence reward (Abstract, Explorer, Builder, Conqueror)	1	11	4.0	.5	p > .05
	2	15	3.7	.8	
B. The Sociability reward (Meteorite, Planet, Satellite, Sun)	1	11	4.0	.6	p > .05
	2	15	3.8	.8	
C. The Quiz reward (Player, Scorer!)	1	11	4.1	.4	p < .05
	2	15	3.8	.8	
D. The Course Participation reward (Bronze, Silver, Gold)	1	11	4.2	.5	p < .05
	2	15	3.9	.8	
E. The "Level up!" reward (Level 1 to 10)	1	11	4.4	.5	p < .05
	2	15	3.9	.8	

5 Conclusions

In this research, rewards were considered as the key design factor of a blended learning course, promoting students to engage and evolve throughout the course.

Particularly important is the fact that most students were satisfied from the type and form of the rewards provided. So, the positive evaluation by the students, lead us to retain the existing rewards and enrich them according to the students' suggestions.

The results of this preliminary research also provide evidence about the impact of the students' progress on their perception for the given rewards. Especially, the students' progress in their cognitive presence seems to have an actual impact on their perception for the "Level up!" reward. However, what remains to be further investigated is how the particular rewards affect students' progress.

The students, also, rated slightly more positively the rewards that reflect their individual performance (Participation and "LevelUp") than the rewards that reflect their performance in the discussions and within the community (Sociability, Quiz, Cognitive Excellence). This evidence also should be further investigated, how the students perceive individual contribution to the community and how they value the community evolution.

Concluding, the proposed course design enhanced with the rewarding system, looks promising for promoting Communities of Inquiry. The work presented in this paper will be continued since the limited number of students of this study prevents generalization of the findings. Also, based on the current evidence we intent to redesign the study in order to investigate whether there are effects of the given rewards to the students' performance on CoI and to explore the qualitative characteristics of these effects.

References

1. Deterding, S., Dixon, D., Khaled, R., Nacke, L.: From game design elements to gamefulness: defining gamification. In: The 15th International Academic MindTrek Conference: Envisioning Future Media Environments Proceedings, pp. 9–15. ACM (2011)
2. Dominguez, A., Navarrete, J.S., Marcos, L., Sanz, L.F., Pages, C., Herraiz, J.J.M.: Gamifying learning experiences: practical implications and outcomes. J. Comput. Educ. **63**, 380–392 (2013)
3. Lee, J., Hammer, J.: Gamification in education: what, how, why bother? Definitions and uses. Exch. Organ. Behav. Teach. J. **15**(2), 1–5 (2011)
4. Mekler, E.D., Brühlmann, F., Touch, A.N., Opwis, K.: Towards understanding the effects of individual gamification elements on intrinsic motivation and performance. Comput. Hum. Behav. **71**, 525–534 (2017). https://doi.org/10.1016/j.chb.2015.08.048
5. Pavlus, J.: The game of life. Sci. Am. **303**, 43–44 (2010)
6. Ehlers, U.D.: Web 2.0 e-learning 2.0 quality 2.0? Quality for new learning cultures. Qual. Assur. Educ. **17**, 296–314 (2009)
7. Garrison, D.R., Anderson, T., Archer, W.: Critical thinking, cognitive presence, and computer conferencing in distance education. Am. J. Dist. Educ. **15**(1), 7–23 (2001)
8. Garrison, D.R., Anderson, T., Archer, W.: Critical inquiry in a text-based environment: computer conferencing in higher education. Internet High. Educ. **2**, 87–105 (1999)
9. Anderson, T., Rourke, L., Garrison, D.R., Archer, W.: Assessing teaching presence in a computer conferencing context. J. Asynchronous Learn. Netw. **5**(2), 1–17 (2001)
10. Utomo, A.Y., Amriani, A., Aji, A.F., Wahidah, F.R.N., Junus, K.M.: Gamified e-learning model based on community of inquiry. In: 2014 International Conference on Advanced Computer Science and Information Systems (ICACSIS) Proceedings, pp. 474–480. IEEE, Jakarta (2014)
11. Hakulinen, L., Auvinen, T., Korhonen, A.: Empirical study on the effect of achievement badges in TRAKLA2 online learning environment. In: The 1st Learning and Teaching in Computing and Engineering (LaTiCE) Proceedings, Macau, pp. 47–54 (2013)
12. Level up! Docs. https://levelup.branchup.tech/docs/article/how-are-experience-points-calculated. Accessed 11 Sept 2019
13. Moodle. https://docs.moodle.org/37/en/Events_list_report. Accessed 11 Sept 2019
14. Interactive Systems: Internal Gamification Questionnaire (IGQ). http://gdp.interactivesystems.info/gameful-design-process/resources/InternalGamificationQuestionnaire.pdf. Accessed 02 July 2019

A Serious Game Design and Evaluation Approach to Enhance Cultural Heritage Understanding

Christina Tsita(✉) and Maya Satratzemi

Department of Applied Informatics, University of Macedonia, Thessaloniki, Greece
{c.tsita,maya}@uom.edu.gr

Abstract. One of the most promising means regarding the potential of supporting both, entertainment and learning, in cultural heritage sector are the Serious Games (SGs). During last decades, Cultural Heritage Serious Games (CHSGs) are being developed with the use of different technologies, in order to facilitate learning of cultural heritage via an entertaining manner. Although, there are evidences about CHSGs effects, there is the need of extracting more reliable results about their effectiveness, meaning the extent to which the initial intentions achieved their purpose. Regarding CHSGs, this purpose is twofold, which means the measurements are as much about entertainment as learning. Moreover, there is the need of increasing evidences on CHSGs' effectiveness regarding higher-cognitive processes in learning. The aim of the present paper is to describe a CHSG design and evaluation approach, which is oriented to the enhancement CHSGs effectiveness in terms of entertaining and learning, as well as the extraction of more reliable results. Regarding learning aspects, the proposed approach focuses on extracting results about cultural heritage understanding. The suggested approach will be applied in a CHSG for the understanding of the Roman Forum of Thessaloniki, Greece.

Keywords: Serious Games · Cultural Heritage · Game design

1 Introduction

In recent years, serious games are being used as means to communicate cultural heritage, through the use of various technologies such as AR, VR, projection-based applications, desktop and web applications [1–5]. CHSGs that take place in 3D virtual worlds offer the opportunity to the user not only to view the representations of the past, but also to interact with them. In addition, game mechanics allow the user to execute quests and earn rewards for completing activities that promote learning and thinking on the related cultural content. Such games promote the explorative behaviour, while the user is triggered by game mechanics to explore the virtual world [6]. During the exploration the user receives visual stimuli, which enhances the understanding of the past. The users also have higher motive to think about the past in order to make decisions to progress in the game. The other hand Although, CHSGs can be highly effective in communicating cultural heritage content, there is the need of more reliable

A. Liapis et al. (Eds.): GALA 2019, LNCS 11899, pp. 438–446, 2019.
https://doi.org/10.1007/978-3-030-34350-7_42

evidence on their effectiveness [1, 9]. Moreover, the results on their effectiveness regarding higher cognitive processes, are limited [1, 2, 4]. Thus, it is important to highlight the positive effects that serious games can have on cultural heritage cognition in a systematic and reliable way in order to create more high-level games and spread their use. Additionally, the integration of personalized experiences in CHSGs, can increase their effectiveness in terms of entertainment and learning, and reach wider audience [4].

This paper aims to present the early design phase of a CHSG approach that targets to enhance the understanding of cultural heritage. More specifically, the proposed approach aims to meet these objectives: (a) increase serious games effectiveness by design [1, 10], (b) contribute to the collection of more rigorous CHSGs research results [1, 2, 4, 9], (c) examine the CHSG's effectiveness on higher cognitive processes [1, 2, 4], (d) analyse log data and use artificial intelligence to increase SG effectiveness in terms of user experience and learning [1, 4, 11].

The rest of the paper is structured as follows. Next section, which consists of four sub-sections, presents the objectives of the CHSG research study. In the third section, the suggested design approach is presented, while in the fourth section, the progress and the upcoming work are being described. Finally, the last section presents the conclusions.

2 The Proposed CHSG Objectives

The proposed CHSG approach aims to meet the following four objectives defined on a literature review of the field:

2.1 Increase Serious Game Effectiveness by Design

One of the objectives of this work is to contribute to the serious game design methodology to enhance their effectiveness, through the definition of the targeted effectiveness goals, in early stages of SG design. Serious games are widely used in various fields, while there are evidences that they facilitate learning through an attractive and entertaining manner. Serious games aim by definition in entertaining and learning [13], while their effectiveness should be defined in terms of whether they achieved the initial goals in relation to these two parameters. In recent years, discussions on serious games focus on ways to increase the evidences in order to spread their use. In the last few decades, many design frameworks have been introduced as tools within the research community to ensure some level of effectiveness [10]. Although, evaluation frameworks have been also introduced, it is not common to take into account the evaluation process, during the design phase [10]. A different approach comes from the education field, where every educational process, in design phase has built-in mechanisms that will allow the measurement of the results according to the objectives set. Thus, to enhance effectiveness, is suggested to define from the very beginning in a specific verbal manner the expected outcomes of the gameplay (What will be measured?), as well as the way that these outcomes will be measured (How they will be measured?). Thereby, during final evaluation, it will be clear if the initial goals of the game achieved and to what extent (see Fig. 1). The initial measurable goals and their evaluation should concern parameters related to (a) the users' experience, including entertainment and (b) learning. These parameters could be evaluated using a framework for a systematic evaluation of educational games, such as MEEGA+ model [14]. This framework provides quality factors that can be used to evaluate a SG in terms of user experience (focused attention, fun, challenge, social interaction, relevance, satisfaction, usability) and learning (knowledge, skills, attitude).

2.2 Extract Rigorous Results About CHSGs, Through the Use of Log Data

This work also aims to contribute to the CHSGs research with more rigorous results about their effectiveness, through the use of log data. The effectiveness of the CHSGs is related not only with the results themselves, but also with the reliability of the measurement process to extract the results. According to [1], most of the recent studies on CHSGs, conducted non-experimental methods with one intervention group and lack of comparison group, making difficult to draw conclusions about what would happen without the game session. Moreover, most of the non-experimental studies did not use a pre-test in order to compare the intervention group before and after the session. In addition, only few studies utilized the ability to observe user's behaviour through log data. Taking into account the additional small size of the participants in most of the studies, it is evident that more rigorous results need to be extracted to promote CHSGs potentials. The parameters that will be defined as effectiveness factors should be measured during gameplay, by integrating the collection of log data in the game architecture. These data, in combination with the results from other evaluation tools (questionnaires, pre-test, post-tests), is expected to enhance the reliability of the results (see Fig. 1).

2.3 Examine the Effectiveness of CHSG on Facilitating Higher Cognitive Processes

Another goal of this work is to examine the effectiveness of CHSGs on facilitating higher-level cognitive processes. The entertainment factor is included in user's experience parameters and can be evaluated among other factors that contribute to a pleasant experience [14]. On the other hand, learning may concern cognitive (knowledge), affective (emotions - attitude) and psychomotor (actions - skills) domains [7, 8, 14]. Cognitive domain refers to different levels. The understanding level of cognition targets higher learning objectives than the first remember level, which usually is being examined. The remember level concerns the information retention and recalling, while the next levels concern the understanding, applying, analysing, evaluating and creating [7, 8]. Although, the goal of the serious games is twofold: entertainment and learning, recent studies focus more in the users' experience and examine less or not at all the learning outcomes of the games. Furthermore, most of the evidence are limited to the cognitive level of remembering, while there is a little effort on enhancing higher level cognitive processes, and by extension there are few relevant results [1]. This work will examine the three first levels of Bloom's taxonomy (remember, understand, apply) focusing on understanding level of cognition. According to needs, and measurement tools available it is possible to include parameters regarding higher levels (analysing, evaluating, creating). It is expected to contribute to the evidence that exists on whether a digital CHSG is able to enhance the understanding of cultural heritage.

2.4 Increase CHSG's Effectiveness Through the Use of Data Analysis and Artificial Intelligence

Last but not least, current study aims to improve the effectiveness of CHSG regarding user's experience and learning by using data analysis and artificial intelligence (AI). The data collection during gameplay, can inform us about the users' behaviour inside the virtual world [11]. Some of the collected data can be exploited not only for the final evaluation, but also for the formative evaluation, during game session (see Fig. 1). Those data can be analysed and part of them can be used as input to the artificial intelligence module, which will configure part of the game. In this way, the CHSG can offer a more personalised experience, that is more satisfying in terms of entertainment and learning. Thus, the data that will be collected will be defined, as well as the types of analyses, the input parameters for the AI and the output parameterized content of the game. Moreover, the data analysis can provide more reliable results in final evaluation in combination with the rest of the log data. Finally, through data analysis is possible to extract results not only for users' experience but also for the learning process.

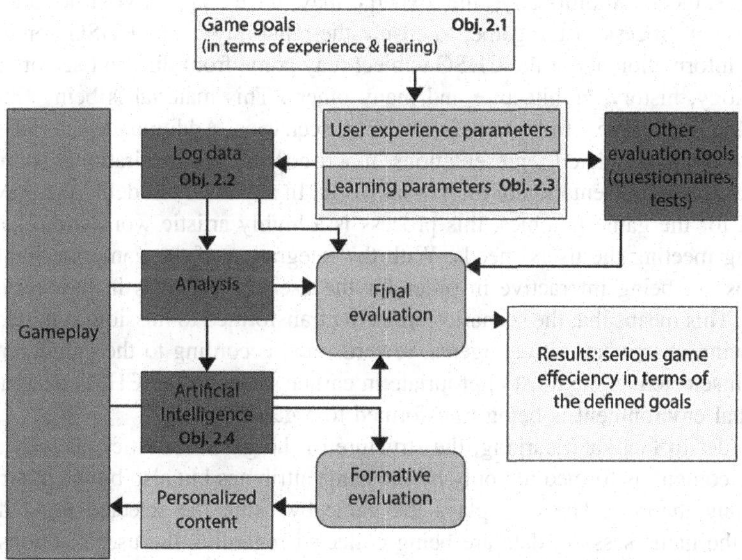

Fig. 1. Visual representation of the proposed CHSG evaluation process

3 CHSG Design Approach to Enhance Understanding of Cultural Heritage

The visual representation of the CHSG design is presented in Fig. 2. The main subject of the CHSG emerges from tangible or intangible cultural heritage that is intended to be disseminated to the public. The main subject may vary from an emblematic museum exhibit, to a monument or an archaeological site. Interesting to communicate with a 3D CHSG is a historical theme or a whole era, due to the fact that a whole virtual world can be created in the game, as well as myths and traditions, where imaginary creatures can get alive and heroes can revive. An interesting aspect is to create CHSGs for monuments, or cultural heritage objects, that are difficult or even impossible to reach the wide public. Often monuments are accessible only for researchers (e.g. tombs), or it is impossible for the public to reach them, due the restrictions of the physical space (e.g. underwater). Additionally, important cultural heritage objects that cannot be exhibited because of their fragile materials can reach the wide public through CHSGs delivered via web.

Fortunately, for cultural heritage sites, objects or monuments, there is at least one institution or utility that is responsible for its protection and communication. The same goes for the intangible cultural heritage, which is widely being digitized in recent years. Regarding historical themes and myths there are also the responsible organizations or specialists (universities, research teams etc.). The collaboration with the experts, facilitates the identification of the scientific knowledge that exists for the cultural heritage subject. Additionally, the experts may have supportive role during the development process of the game, to ensure the reliability of the CHSG content.

The information about the CHSG subject may come from different sectors such as archaeology, history, architecture and many others. This material is being filter with storytelling techniques, to be transformed into scenarios. Additional, material such as similar projects or related representations, mood boards, and inspirational sources can feed the visual representation of the virtual world. In any level of fidelity that have been selected for the game graphics, this process is a highly artistic work with challenges regarding meeting the users' needs. With the integration of the game mechanics, the scenarios are being interactive in order for the users to progress in the story, while playing. This means that the scenarios are being transformed to missions, quests, levels, non-playing characters, virtual agents, rewards etc., according to the game genre that has been selected as the most appropriate in earlier stages of the CHSG design. Thus, the virtual environment is being transformed to a game.

In order to facilitate learning, the structure of the game activities, as well as their learning content, is formed not only by the game attributes but also by the contribution of learning theories. The user plays the game by using the selected input devices. During the game session, data are being collected regarding the user's actions inside the virtual world. These data are being analysed and, through the use of artificial intelligence, part of the experience is being personalized to the behaviour of the user. At the same time these data, are used to evaluate the game, enhancing the reliability of the evidences CHSGs' effectiveness in terms of entertainment and learning.

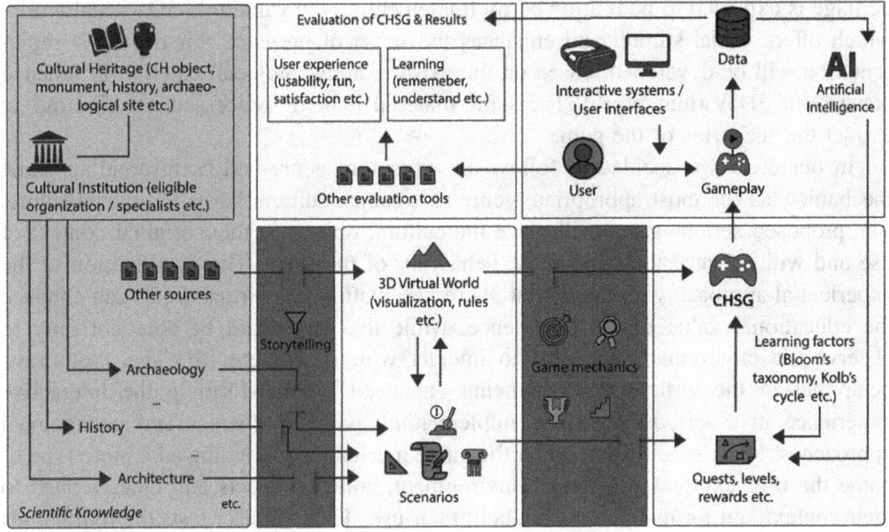

Fig. 2. Visual representation of the proposed CHSG design

4 Current and Future Work

The aforementioned approach is intended to be applied for the creation of a CHSG for the Roman Forum of Thessaloniki[1], Greece. The monument was the administrative centre of the ancient city. Its construction began at the end of the second century A.D. on the site of an older forum dating from early Imperial times. The complex of the forum was arranged around a rectangular paved square. There were stoas on the three sides, each of which consisted of a double row of columns and provided access to a surrounding zone of public buildings. The southern stoa stood on a vaulted substructure (cryptoporticus) – an impressive double arcade which was partly underground, making use of the natural slope of the land. To the south, along the cryptoporticus, there was a row of shops fronting the ancient shopping street. There is also a building for public performances that must have functioned as an odeon. The Roman Forum Museum (Ancient Agora)[2] is underground and is located inside the archaeological site. The exhibition of the museum includes mainly informative material and emphasis is given to the clarity of the information and the comprehensive way of presentation, with the goal to make the content easy to understand for everyone.

The organization that research and protects the archaeological site is the Ephorate of Antiquities of Thessaloniki City (EATC), which under the Hellenic Ministry of Culture and Sports. In collaboration with the EATC, we decided to develop a serious game to enhance the understanding of the Roman Forum. The understanding of cultural

[1] In Thessaloniki page, http://inthessaloniki.com/item/roman-forum-museum-ancient-agora/, last accessed 2019/6/15.

[2] In Odysseus page, http://odysseus.culture.gr/h/3/eh351.jsp?obj_id=2457, last accessed 2019/6/15.

heritage is expected to be reinforced by implementing the game in a 3D virtual world, which offers visual stimuli and enhances the sense of presence. Firstly, a 3D representation will be developed, based on the existing archaeological material, in order to consist our 3D Virtual World. The same material is being processed, at this time, to extract the scenarios of the game.

In our case, we decided to follow the adventure genre and corresponding game mechanics, as the most appropriate genre to enhance cultural heritage understanding. The proposed serious game will place the cultural objects in their original context of use and will enhance the explorative behaviour of the users. The combination of the experiential approach with the digital 3D representation in a virtual world can enhance the educational value of the experience, while the user could be able not only to observe the environment but also to interact with its content [6]. The explorative behaviour in the virtual world is being enhanced by transforming the interactive experience in a serious game, by implementing game mechanics and pedagogical approaches. More specifically, when the game mechanics follow the adventure type of game the user explores the virtual environment, collects objects and clues related to their context and forms hypotheses about their use. Then the user tests the hypotheses by using the objects in the environment, in order to solve game's puzzles and executes the missions to progress in the game. This approach leads itself to the use of Kolb's theory and application of the experiential cycle of learning, where the user thinks about how to solve a task and experiments to the point that the approach tested leads to the solution of the riddle [12]. Additional to the experimentation activities, Vygotsky's scaffolding [15] (hints, help on demand, etc.) will be used, among other facilitating learning factors [10].

During gameplay log data will be collected in order to export more rigorous results on users' experience. Moreover, by analysing those data it will be possible to offer a more personalized experience to the users, while part of them will be used as input to the Artificial Intelligence (AI) module, which will adjust part of the game, based on the users' behaviour. The interaction will be offered in lower (desktop) and higher (virtual reality system) level of immersion. The log data will be used for formative evaluation (during gameplay) and the final evaluation, combined with other tools (pre-tests, post-test, questionnaires). This CHSG will be evaluated in terms of the cognitive level, and more specifically in understanding and higher-level processes. In terms of user experience fun, satisfaction, usability and other factors will be measured.

The collection of the related scientific material has been completed, meaning the archaeological research that have been published by the EATC. The scenarios are work in progress, as well as the design of the virtual world rules and environment. In parallel, decisions are being made in more detail regarding game user experience and learning intentions, as well as other factors, based on our previous work [10]. According to the intentions, the metrics will be defined, as well as the corresponding parameters for the log data, the type of analysis and the input/output of the artificial intelligence module, aligned with the game activities.

5 Conclusions

The results of this study are expected to contribute to the creation of experiences with high educational and entertaining value in the CH field. It is evident that SGs are able to offer such experiences, while existing studies have highlighted their potential for enhancing learning and entertainment. However, the results of CHSGs that have been extracted with systematic ways are limited. Many of the studies, evaluate the user's experience, which includes the entertainment factor, and do not evaluate the learning aspects of the game, while most of them evaluate the first cognitive level (remember) [7, 8]. The evidence regarding the effectiveness of the CHSGs in terms of higher cognitive levels are limited [1]. This study proposes that the CHSGs effectiveness can be enhanced by defining the game goals in terms of user experience and learning, along with the tools that will be used to measure the results, from the early stages of the design process. Thus, it is possible to integrate evaluation mechanisms in the architecture of the game, in order to collect data regarding the behaviour of the users, during gameplay. Additionally, those data will be analysed to extract more rigorous results. Moreover, part of the data will be used as input to the artificial intelligence module in order to adapt a part of the game content to the user's behaviour and offer a more personalized experience. The goal is to extract evidence of CHSGs effectiveness with more systematic ways, and provide rigorous results regarding their potential to offer a pleasant experience (entertainment) and to support cultural awareness and understanding of cultural heritage (learning), in order to spread their use. The use of 3D environment and immersive technologies will support the communication of cultural heritage, and is expected to trigger the participants' interest on the cultural heritage content of the game.

Main aspects of the proposed CHSG approach are (a) the use of log data and the data analytics to increase the reliability of the evaluation and the extraction of more reliable results, (b) the use of artificial intelligence to adapt content of the game based on user's behaviour, (c) the use of 3D virtual world to facilitate cultural heritage understanding, (d) the indication of the adventure games as suitable game genre for the understanding of cultural heritage, and for the support of higher-level cognitive processes.

References

1. Tsita, C., Satratzemi, M.: How serious games in cultural heritage are being evaluated. In: Proceedings of the 11th Pan-Hellenic & International Conference, ICT in Education (HCICTE), Thessaloniki (2018)
2. Malegiannaki, I., Daradoumis, T.: Analyzing the educational design, use and effect of spatial games for cultural heritage: a literature review. Comput. Educ. **108**, 1–10 (2017)
3. Paliokas, I., Sylaiou, S.: The use of serious games in museum visits and exhibitions: a systematic mapping study. In: 8th International Conference on Games and Virtual Worlds for Serious Applications (VS-Games), pp. 1–8. IEEE (2016)
4. Mortara, M., Catalano, C.E., Bellotti, F., Fiucci, G., Houry-Panchetti, M., Petridis, P.: Learning cultural heritage by serious games. J. Cult. Heritage **15**(3), 318–325 (2014)

5. Anderson, F.E., McLoughlin, L., Liarokapis, F., Peters, C., Petridis, P., de Freitas, S.: Developing serious games for cultural heritage: a state-of-the-art review. Virtual Reality **14** (4), 255–275 (2010)
6. Bellotti, F., Berta, R., De Gloria, A., D'ursi, A., Fiore, V.: A serious game model for cultural heritage. J. Comput. Cult. Heritage (JOCCH) **5**(4), 1–27 (2012). https://doi.org/10.1145/2399180.2399185
7. Bloom, B.S.: Taxonomy of Educational Objectives, Vol. 1: Cognitive Domain. McKay, New York (1956)
8. Krathwohl, D.R.: A revision of Bloom's taxonomy: an overview. Theory Pract. **41**(4), 212–218 (2002)
9. Catalano, C.E., Luccini, A.M., Mortara, M.: Guidelines for an effective design of serious games. Int. J. Serious Games 1(1) (2014)
10. Tsita, C., Satratzemi, M.: Conceptual factors for the design of serious games. In: Gentile, M., Allegra, M., Söbke, H. (eds.) GALA 2018. LNCS, vol. 11385, pp. 232–241. Springer, Cham (2019). https://doi.org/10.1007/978-3-030-11548-7_22
11. Yannakakis, G.N., Togelius, J.: Artificial Intelligence and Games. Springer, New York (2018). https://doi.org/10.1007/978-3-319-63519-4
12. Kolb, D.A.: Experiential learning: experience as the source of learning and development. FT press, London (2014)
13. Susi, T., Johannesson, M., Backlund, P.: Serious games: an overview (2007)
14. Petri, G., von Wangenheim, C.G., Borgatto, A.F.: MEEGA+: an evolution of a model for the evaluation of educational games. INCoD/GQS, 3 (2016)
15. Vygotsky, L.: Interaction between learning and development. Read. Dev. Child. **23**(3), 34–41 (1978)

A Focused Conversational Model for Game Design and Play-Tests

Joseph Alexander Brown(✉)

Artificial Intelligence in Games Development Lab, Innopolis University, Innopolis, Republic of Tatarstan, Russia
j.brown@innopolis.ru

Abstract. Ludic examinations are close in scope to appreciations in other fields such as art criticism, which has utilized methods, such as focused conversations in order to derive the truth from several viewpoints. Best practices of lesson planning, such as that based off of the Context-Activity-Reflection-Documentation (CARD) model, requires a reflective stage of development. The Focused Conversation Model or ORID question model are both examined with the application to a playtesting case study in order to encourage the application of lesson planning to the field of games appreciation and design.

Keywords: Educational game · Focused conversation model · ORID model · CARD model · Playtesting

1 Introduction

The focused conversation model was first developed by United States Army Chaplain and Art Professor, Joseph Mathews, as a method of art appreciation and reflection [8]. The conversational approach eschews the idea of a single expert in the teaching model and instead relies on the assumption that there is no universal truth to the appreciative process. The only method to come to meaning is to have a series of viewpoints. A truth is based on observing several subjective opinions, and not a result due to the existence of a truth objectively. Upon examining the world of games—avoiding the common folly of stating analog or digital games are completely unrelated design tasks—we realize the need for the development of such shared truths in the rules sets. That being a set of rules by which the players will abide by setting out the expectations for play and those actions which are out of bounds.

Suits defines a game as "the voluntary attempt to overcome unnecessary obstacles" and states further that "to play a game is to attempt to achieve a specific state of affairs [prelusory goal], using only means permitted by rules [lusory means], where the rules prohibit use of more efficient in favour of less efficient means [constitutive rules], and where the rules are accepted just because they make possible such activity [lusory attitude]" [9]. This definition is an operationalization of games as rules sets. However, the play does not always have explicit rules.

A. Liapis et al. (Eds.): GALA 2019, LNCS 11899, pp. 447–456, 2019.
https://doi.org/10.1007/978-3-030-34350-7_43

Children at play also reveal these implicit structures [2,4]. They will start to form the basis of the space about them and the objects available to them. They quickly define a basis for the collective play, toss aside previous methods, and declare other actions outside of a norm as 'cheating' or 'unfair' in order to maintain a collective law. The children in their attitudes set forward a lusory means as a matter of play and develop manners to ensure constructive rules are not unduly influencing the play session to another player's advantage.

Such methods have also been used implicitly by game designers and developers. Such behaviours as those engaged in the Blackmoor campaign [7] would serve as the foundation for Arneson and Gygax in the codified rules of D&D. When the campaign was ongoing, Arneson was asked to provide the rules for the campaign only to hear the response of "Rules? What rules!?"[1]. Of course, there were rules; they were implicitly known by the players, defined over a multitude of play sessions, drafted, agreed upon, ratified, and revised. When an event occurred which was beyond of the agreed-upon limits of the game, the community would dispute and a new rule would be developed. Arneson would even eventually go back on the statement and present a set of rules to Gygax, and other elements such as the use of the 7-die polyhedral set instituted by Dave Wesley would also be adopted from Blackmoor [10]. However, the Blackmoor system was not "constructed with any consideration to instructing someone who had not already experienced it", and thus Gygax would mould Arneson's "20 or so pages of handwritten rules" through a process of "adopting, expanding and repurposing them" [7]. This was not a new creation from the request, but a codification of a collective oral history of a community's laws.

In the development of a game, there is a balance. Rules create enjoyable games where players have choices of actions. Thus, there is fairness to the players, and players find a clear direction to make a reliable strategy. However, a game with too many rules limits interactions, as it becomes too hard to understand what a legal interaction is, and the rule set becomes self-contradictory and internally consistent. Further, games have narrative and themes outside of the mechanical actions of the rule. Rules should reflect these narrative choices and themes of the game. Participatory Design has been claimed to provide a manner of games production [1,5]; however, it lacks rigor in the process. The focused conversational model presented provides a methodology.

The focused conversational model allows for an examination and reflective process, and it works effectively when combined with an activity-based learning model. The CARD model is an activity-based reflective process of lesson planning. It has been used as part of the set of training processed which is used in the Instructional Skills Workshop (ISW). The ISW is internationally recognized/utilized as a best practice for faculty development for instructional skills and lesson planning [3,6,11]. Section 2 reviews the lesson planning model of CARD with an examination of its applicability to playtesting. Section 3 overviews the focused conversation model or ORID. A case study of a game rule process is examined in Sect. 4 with a sample set of facilitator questions. Section 5

[1] Attributed to Different Worlds issue 3 in July of 1979 by Peterson's account.

examines the findings of the case study. Finally, Sect. 6 gives conclusions and a future direction for games educational methods.

2 The CARD Model

The Context-Activity-Reflection-Documentation (CARD) model of planning focuses on providing an experiential and outcomes-based learning environment. The goal of the model is to reflect a shared activity. Which is modelled for an experiential learning process, especially for those with an outcome-based learning model. In terms of game design and design of rules, there is no clear, measurable objective, yet there is an expected outcome of finding flaws in the design or understanding of players using features of the game's mechanics.

2.1 Context

The contextual phase readies the space for learning and sets the plan for the activity to come. It sets some expectations as to the method but does not intend to limit the scope of the participants to provide feedback. The context should make the activity clear for all participants in terms of their roles, the method of which they will use to engage with the artifacts of the game objects, and what rules will be introduced.

2.2 Activity

The participants engage in the outlined activity. The facilitator is monitoring and making observations of the behaviours in order to have an objective record of the event. The activity may also be filmed or otherwise recorded: keystroke logs, actions made in the game, etc.

2.3 Reflection

The participants are asked to reflect upon the previous activity. This phase is primarily where the discovery or learning event occurs. The role of the facilitator is to elicit ideas from the participants. This can be done in several manners. The facilitator can use a survey-based approach giving a series of closed questions (with generally quantitative results) and open questions (to give qualitative results). This may also adopt the format for a larger group as a conversational model, such as the ORID Model.

2.4 Documentation

The end phase is a collection of the documentation for both the facilitators and the participants. In a learning environment, this is valuable to students as an artifact of the process to be reviewed for tests and projects or as an example for their future processes.

As a design tool, the documentation is for the designer to have a record which allows for both analysis for the developer for improvements. Moreover, it allows the participants an appreciation.

2.5 Play-Tests

To contextualize this model into the application in playtesting a new game, we need to see the game objects itself as the target for a learning process. The expected outcome of our play-testers is an understanding of the game objects, rules, interactions, and strategies. For those who are just seeing the game from the first time, we are interested in the learning process of a novice in understanding possible conceptual models of gameplay. For those who have interacted with previous editions of the game, the designer is interested in seeing the evolution of thinking about more complex conceptual models and moving from short term tactics of playing into more long term strategies.

3 The Focused Conversation Model - ORID

The focused conversation model or the Objective - Relational - Interpretive - Decisional (ORID) model is applied in the following manner. It first examines the data—Objective. Then makes a call for personal feelings and reactions—Relational. It encourages the group to delve deeper—Interpretive. Only then does it require the group to make either a collective or personal statement as to what the situation or object has taught them or what actions should be made next—Decisional. Given is a more detailed look at the model and some example/sample questions used in our examination.

3.1 Objective

Objective based questions are those which explore the situation or object based upon the objective facts without recourse to emotions, beliefs, interpretations. The goal of this stage is to have a collective and clear agreement as to the question of "what happened?" It is often the case in this stage that facilitators need to keep participants clearly on task by limiting the comments at this stage. It is a natural want of the participants to want to skip over this step in their responses and move on to their beliefs and interpretations of their actions. This is folly. Allowing this will lead to confusion for other participants and will lead to statements about actions without everyone understanding what happened from the various perspectives and will not allow an objective view of the situation or object to emerge.

3.2 Relational

Relational questions examine the feelings and base level thoughts of the participants. The role of this level of questioning is to have the immediate and quite often personal reaction to the data. This is often the emotional response suppressed in the objectives level of the questioning. This level examined the surface relations between the facts.

3.3 Interpretive

The *interpretive* level of questioning examines the meaning of connections. These questions examine the values of the participants and the implication of the thoughts about the situation or object. This stage of questioning has been built into by the previous questioning stages allowing for a firm foundation for insights to emerge.

3.4 Decisional

The *decisional* level examines, based on the interpretations, what actions should now be undertaken. The questions of this phase create resolutions and close the conversation while laying out the next steps. This stage also naturally lends itself to the documentation of an action plan.

4 Case Study

4.1 Context

The players are told to join in on the development of a game. The room is cleared of any obstructions and facilitator(s) lead the group(s) of 5 to 10 players arranged into circles, see Fig. 1. They hand several game objects to the players. The players are then informed that they will be constructing a game rule by rule, each player in the circle receiving a chance to add a rule. If at any time the

Fig. 1. Instructor Gives the *Context* of the Process. Photo by Lesia Poliakova, used with permission.

group believes that the rules have become too complex, the game is ended, and the number of rules is recorded. The game is then reset to having no rules.

4.2 Activity

During the activity stage, the groups are arranged, and the facilitator provides a set of game objects, such as balls, mats, etc. During the gameplay, the facilitator is observing the process and making mental and perhaps physical notes on the actions made in the game. Their note taking aim is to allow for better questioning rounds during the reflective conversation. In addition, the facilitator is there to ensure participant safety and to be able to answer any questions about the process from participants. They also act as a time keeper for the rounds of the playtesting between rules changes and for the activity overall (Fig. 2).

Fig. 2. Students Engage with the Development of a Rule Set Adding One Rule at a Time During the *Activity*. Photo by Lesia Poliakova, used with permission.

4.3 Reflection

The reflection method has two parts. The first is at the end of every round of the game, see Fig. 3, in which the players declare the number of rounds to be over as the game has become to complex. The facilitator will check with the group in order to note anything they would like to have a remembrance upon and examines the comfort of the group before the next round.

In the grand reflection phase, the ORID model is used with each participant keeping their own record and the facilitator writing a group finding on a white-board. Each individual is asked the following questions as a minimal set—with deeper probes by the facilitator.

Fig. 3. The Group Meets again to *Reflect* on the Rules Sets Created. Photo by Lesia Poliakova, used with permission.

Objective Questions

- What instructions were given by the facilitator?
- What objects did you use?
- How many rules did you make?
- What were the rules you produced?
- What rule caused you to end the game?

Relational Questions

- How did you feel when engaging in the activity?
- Why did you choose these objects?
- As the number of rules increased, what did you notice?
- What were your feelings about the rules you produced?
- How did you feel as the game went on towards the end?

Interpretive Questions

- What rules were better for the game?
- What rules were contradictory and how did you solve this problem?
- Why did that rule cause to end the game?

Decisional Questions

- What rules would you want to keep in future games?
- What rules would you want to avoid in future games?
- What did you learn about rule systems?

4.4 Documentation

Each participant has their notes and record of the playtest questions, and the grand collection is sent as a picture of the whiteboard to the class.

5 Findings

5.1 Later Rounds Could Go Longer

In the multiple times this process has been run the initial rounds of the game creation lead quickly to games where the participants wish them to stop. Later examples of games will have more rules added before called to end.

The speculated reasoning is that as players learn the actions which lead to a reduction of the fun, fairness or are contradictory. It was noted by several participants that with a few rules the game was not fun due to the lack of challenge and too many rules leads to frustration. For example, there are physical limitations of being to stand on one foot, while dropping the ball, shouting the name of who passed the ball, and then passing the ball to someone who had not yet passed the ball. There is also the problem of the cognitive load of knowing when and in what order to pass the ball.

5.2 Development of Anti-rules

In multiple instances, players would engage in the creation of rules which would counter what they perceived as unfairness or cheating in the game. Having a short period of play between the addition of rules allowed for a clear understanding of the effect of playing the current ruleset.

In one illustrative instance, a rule was instituted which eliminated players tossing the ball if the ball was not caught. This leads quickly to players to which is ball was being thrown intentionally dropping, or refusing the catch the ball, wanting other players to then. After a few such eliminations, a player with the ball just held it, much to the dismay of those assembled who realized that he was attempting to avoid elimination by refusing to play.

This was then countered in the next rulemaking round by a rule which required a player to pass the ball under a five-second shot clock. That, while fixing the issue of the player just holding onto the ball, reverted the game to the previous state of having an elimination on each pass of the ball, still considered to be unfair. The next rule added was to counter this deficiency by eliminating both the passing player and the receiving player when the ball was dropped. This process of creating rules and exceptions left behind the shot timer which would persist in the rules for the remainder of the game.

The vestigial nature of this rule would later emerge during the focused conversation. During the relational phase, it emerged to this group via the question that this stage of the game rules was very frustrating, hard, and trying. The interpretive phase of questions examined these statements further, and it was decided that the shot clock was added to remove the immediate issue of the lack of action in the game, however, the longer term fix of eliminating both the passer and receiver was what lead back to the fun/challenge in the game.

5.3 Facilitator as an Appeal

As a facilitator, there may be questions when these perceived offences occur—that is the facilitator as a court of appeal or a rule meta-maker. The practice was adopted is to remind the participants that (1) they can collectively reset the rules any time to nothing with a consensus of the players, and (2) at the end of the play round if an exploitation in the rules is perceived, then the rule can be changed by the next rule maker unilaterally.

However, it is best if the facilitator engaged when rules declared are sexist, racist, exclusionary, or directed at individual players and not behaviours in the game. Thankfully, in the author's experience this has only occurred once in the formation of an anti-rule to prevent perceived cheating actions by a specific player, and a reminder of "well what would happen if someone else made the same action?" from a facilitator was enough to focus the team and revise the proposed new rule with no offense taken.

6 Conclusions

The process of the focused conversational model allows for a lesson which can examine a topic without a clear objective based outcomes. The model is inherently experience based, allowing for active learning. It also a reflective process which has been demonstrated to improve learning outcomes. The model also allows for a method, when used in conjunction with the CARD framework to be used in lesson planning, making the process of active examination of grams following a clear pedagogical process and allows for the replication in course syllabi, which games education is sadly missing.

The future development of education in games development is not in retesting the theoretical basis of the pedagogical models. There are existing good methods such as focused conversation and CARD which are well framed, used in several practices in the related field of artistic appreciation, and trained in accepted international pedagogical best practices used in many countries.

The future work should surround: (1) Putting into practice clear and existing leading pedagogical models. Firstly, via the development of laboratory, industry, and research leaders trained in better distribution of their works to students. This interfacing with the training of upcoming graduate students and teaching assistant roles who have more contact hours with students in smaller group lab and tutorial settings were such techniques as the CARD and focused conversational models applied in their most useful context. (2) The development of exemplary classes using the models to fit with a games development curriculum. The need for a curriculum is perhaps the great challenge, a clear games development curriculum, as there is currently no generally accepted elements which separate a games design or development degree as a type of specialization. This conversation should be undertaken by practitioners and stakeholders to create a standard for the specialization and will need to emerge to move game design and development from what is now an early academic field into maturity.

References

1. Benton, L., Varotsis, G., Vasaloua, A.: Leading by example: exploring the influence of design examples on children's creative ideation. Int. J. Hum. Comput. Stud. **122**, 174–183 (2019)
2. Castle, K.: Children's rule knowledge in invented games. J. Res. Child. Educ. **12**(2), 197–209 (1998)
3. Dawson, D., Borin, P., Meadows, K., Britnell, J., Olsen, K., McIntryre, G.: The impact of the instructional skills workshop on faculty approaches to teaching. Technical report, Higher Education Quality Council of Ontario (2014)
4. Golomb, C., Kuersten, R.: On the transition from pretence play to reality: what are the rules of the game? Br. J. Dev. Psychol. **14**, 203–217 (1996)
5. Khaled, R., Vasalou, A.: Bridging serious games and participatory design. Int. J. Child-Comput. Interact. **2**(2), 93–100 (2014)
6. Macpherson, A.: The instructional Skills Workshop as a transformative learning process. Ph.D. thesis, Simon Fraser University, Burnaby, BC (2012)
7. Peterson, J.: Playing at the World. Unreason Press, San Diego (2012)
8. Stanfield, R.B.: The Art of Focused Conversation: 100 Ways to Access Group Wisdom in the Workplace. New Society Publishers, Gabriola (2000)
9. Suits, B.: The Grasshopper: Games, Life and Utopia. University of Toronto Press, Toronto (1978)
10. Tresca, M.J.: The Evolution of Fantasy Role-Playing Games. McFarland & Company Publishers Inc., Jefferson (2011)
11. Zhirosh, O., Brown, J.A., Tickner, D.: Democratizing faculty development - establishing a training program at a new computer science university in Russia. In: ASEE Annual Conference and Exposition, Conference Proceedings, p. Paper ID #25473, Tampa, Florida (2019)

Alternative Teaching of History Subject in Primary School: The Case of the 3D HIT Playful Activity

Dimitrios Rammos and Tharrenos Bratitsis(✉)

University of Western Macedonia, 3rd km National Road Florinas-Nikis, 53100 Florina, Greece
dimrammos@yahoo.gr, bratitsis@uowm.gr

Abstract. History as a school subject is difficult for young pupils, especially when teaching is based on bulky texts and lacks audio-visual auxiliary material. This paper presents a differentiated teaching proposal based on the use of the playful activity '3D Heroes Introduce Themselves' (3D HIT). It is based on the projection of 3d models on mobile devices as augmented spreads on images included in a worksheet. Together with the manipulation of 3d models, students are invited to create digital stories with relevant information. Thus, a final video is created in which heroes and mythical figures from the History subject introduce themselves with the voice of the pupils. The contribution of the activity to the students' performance and the level of engagement and participation was examined in this study. Also, whether the production of digital narratives in combination with the manipulation of 3d models reinforced the expressiveness of pupils was examined. Observation-based data indicated interesting positive results.

Keywords: Serious games · Digital Storytelling · Augmented reality · History

1 Introduction

Teaching History in Primary School has many difficulties since pupils are not used to process bulk tests and to critically work with the information in them. On the other hand, historical knowledge is valuable both in terms of knowledge acquisition and skills development. The choice of teaching methodology is an important criterion that influences and shapes the general attitude of students towards the course of history. A differentiated teaching scenario for the chapter of Greek mythology in presented in this paper. Greek Mythology is taught in the small classes of elementary school in Greece.

The scenario includes a playful/gamified educational activity with the use of ICT through which pupils themselves innovatively are required to present history characters from their school books that have been taught in previous sessions. This activity falls within the context of serious games utilization in education so it will be referred to as '3D Heroes Introduce Themselves' (3D HIT) game or gamified activity, hereinafter.

A. Liapis et al. (Eds.): GALA 2019, LNCS 11899, pp. 457–467, 2019.
https://doi.org/10.1007/978-3-030-34350-7_44

This paper initially presents the theoretical background of the study. The contents of the gamified educational activity are then described. Finally, the results of a short research study conducted to evaluate the contribution of the use of 3D HIT game in gaining knowledge and developing skills are discussed.

2 Background of the Study

2.1 History Teaching in Primary School

Teaching History aims to transmit knowledge that connects the past with the present and provides students with useful information about the place in which they live [1]. At the same time, the study of the historical evolution brings out the relations between people and the impact of their actions over a wide range of time [2]. Students have the opportunity to compare facts and compose information that lead, in combination, to logical results [3].

Thus, they can understand historical elements as reasonable implications of human behaviour. Analytical and compositional thinking is one of the most important and useful skills for modern pupils since they come into contact with a vast amount of information at school or through the internet [4]. The development of analytical and synthetic thinking presupposes the study of many historical resources and the search for historical truth through detailed check and intersection of these sources [1]. Students should be encouraged to look for authoritative resources and filter the content of their findings [3]. This filtering is implemented individually or at group level as part of a team activity. This effort is greatly enhanced by easy access to digital material and collections with audio-visual historical content.

The extraction of conclusions follows the search and analysis of historical information. The oral or written wording of these conclusions completes the cognitive processes of the pupils by reinforcing the communication with others and the ability to transmit knowledge through the reasoning of the meanings [5]. The narrative of historical events with a synthetic and critical sense is a particularly difficult learning objective [2]. Learning style and characteristics of pupils must, therefore, be taken into account in every step of the learning process.

ICT changes the way History is employed and studied. The visualization of historical facts and the ability to easily access and manage/manipulate historical material impose new teaching forms [3]. Exploring the capabilities of digital tools and the extent to which they affect the way history is studied, is the main question for planning teaching activities using ICT. The contribution of learning theories developed in recent years have significantly influenced the design of ICT learning environments for the study of history [1]. Most of them are mainly based on the theories of Behaviourism, Cognitive Constructivism and Social Constructivism [6]. In addition, some basic principles of the modern learning activities in History field [3] demonstrate that:

- Learning focuses on pupils' interests and abilities.
- Knowledge is discovered and acquired by students driven to it by different pathways and through varied sources of information.

- Teachers facilitate the linking of knowledge with reality by presenting information in authentic activities.
- The learning process is based on social interaction and cooperation.

New technologies contribute to these guidelines, mainly to the ability to visualise historical elements and create interactive social environments [3]. Digital applications and serious games with educational context create opportunities for dialogue and knowledge building through activities in authentic environments that require students' research and active participation [5]. In this case, the support of the learning process is achieved through new cognitive tools that support narration and reasoning skills [6].

2.2 Serious Games and Playful Activities for Teaching

A 'serious' game is one that is applied in the context of a teaching scenario and emphasizes the cognitive content and benefits that students gain after playing [7]. Such games maintain their pleasant and relaxed character on the one hand, but on the other they serve clear educational purposes [8]. Thus, they hold a constant educational value. Serious games are played on electronic devices using digital media and applications. The use of ICT is nowadays very widespread in educational context, mainly because digital applications are used by educators to differentiate teaching methodology and activate pupils [5]. Playful activities and games in their devices inside the school context is supposed to activate pupils since they match their desires and suit their characteristics [3].

The focus of using ICT and specifically serious games is to integrate them into teaching in a scientific and pedagogical way [9]. Digital media should be suitable for the age of the children and tailored to the educational needs of all pupils. Also, the selection of applications must be targeted and linked to the learning objectives [5]. Knowledge gain should always be the core axis when designing or choosing a game for teaching purposes. This way, the risk for pupils being distracted by the use of the game is reduced. Still, it is important to allocate the time that children will use the game. Playing the game can be done individually or in groups. In both cases it is important to give all children the opportunity to equally participate in the process. In addition to the knowledge that children can acquire, it is also important that they develop digital skills [4]. Thus, the teacher must guide the realization of teaching activities in a way that promotes interaction between pupils [10].

Finally, it is important for children themselves to know the educational purpose for playing the game as part of their lesson. At any age, from very early, children are capable of understanding the link between each activity and the content of their textbooks. This is a skill that is cultivated with their experience. Educators can strengthen this characteristic by providing clear instructions and references before starting the gamified activity [10]. Students, in this way, feel more confident since they understand that educators want to involve them actively instead of only treating them as listeners.

2.3 Digital Storytelling and Augmented Reality in Playful Activities

One of the main objectives of primary education is to enable pupils to express themselves with structure and clarity [4]. They should also be able to present their perspectives to others in a clear and comprehensible manner [3]. When achieving such goals, the confidence of students is significantly enhanced and teamwork within the classroom is facilitated [6]. The skill of communication is considered, after all, to be among the most important ones for the pupils of the 21st century [10].

It has become increasingly clear nowadays that the ways pupils are communicating and expressing themselves evolve and become more digital [11]. These changes are consistent with the evolution of technology and society itself [6]. In the school context, the ability of pupils to record their stories digitally should additionally ensure greater productivity since this practice keeps up with their daily out of school habits [3].

In terms of content, storytelling is characterised by freedom and flexibility, thus ensuring the disconnection with the traditional oral storytelling and the rigorous structure of an evaluation [12]. Digital Storytelling (DS) is one of the educational methods using technological devices allowing computer users to become creative storytellers by developing their own interesting stories [13]. It constitutes a creative process used to capture personal stories in a 3–5 min digital clip [14]. Lately it has been utilized as a teaching approach in many disciplinary areas and education level [15–18].

The 3D HIT playful activity is based on cutting-edge technology and features that confront the characteristics of the commercial digital games that children play. Augmented reality technology follows the above judgement. Integrating digital elements into the real world introduces impressive possibilities to modern electronic devices [11, 19]. In education, the use of augmented reality can add interactivity to educational materials by converting, for example, a 2d image into a 3d animated model. This practice can then be utilized for the design of serious games in educational context. The use of augmented reality can transfuse the sense of surprise and subversion to serious gamification activities [3]. Thus, mystery and exploration among pupils are increased.

The 3D HIT playful activity, is a combination of augmented reality with DS. This combination enhances educational quality as it ensures the ability to use and configure the three-dimensional models with the digital recording of students' descriptions. Moreover, the aim was to diversify History teaching in order to allow the pupils to perceive it as a digital, serious game. The activity is described in the next section.

3 Methodology

Within this study a playful, game-like activity was designed, following the principles of serious games. It cannot be characterized as a game, as no application was implemented by using a software development tool (e.g. a programming language or an authoring tool). Also, it cannot be characterized as a gamified activity exactly, as it didn't involve fundamental gamification elements, such as score tracking, etc. Rather, it was a differentiated, playful activity for teaching History, focusing on divine and mythical creatures, as explained in the next subsection.

3.1 Gods, Demigods and Mythical Creatures

One of the chapters included in the History subject, in primary school is Greek mythology. The study of Greek mythology is of great interest to students because it includes the action of Gods, Demigods and various forms of mythical creatures, as shown in Fig. 1. The main focus are the 12 Olympian Gods who are presented as regulators of people's lives. At the same time, there are the Demigods, such as Hercules, who have half human and divine qualities. Finally, very often many supernatural creatures emerge that complicate human actions and reveal the intentions of the Gods. People, Gods and mythical creatures take part in adventures with unexpected evolution and great twists.

Through these adventures the relationship of people with the divine element is presented together with the consequences of human acts that contradict the will of the Gods. They also capture the feelings of people and their efforts to meet the rules of the ethical order, in times when life was not developed in organized societies [2].

All the above transfuse attractiveness to the study of Greek mythology. Historical events are presented in the form of myths and understanding of historical meanings becomes easier for young learners. This is crucially important since it reinforces the positive attitude to the study of History subject in general [1, 3].

Fig. 1. Captions of 3d models used in 3D HIT. Trojan Horse, Neptune, Athena, Apollo, Hercules, Minotaur, Labyrinth of Knossos and Prometheus were some of the historical characters and constructions pupils described in their digital stories.

3.2 The Implemented Teaching Approach

The teaching scenario includes the production of digital stories through the 3D HIT playful activity. It is about creating digital narratives related to mythical figures of the Greek mythology in the context of the 4th Grade History Subject (Fig. 1). These narratives should describe these characters and provide information about their lives. Stories are created and recorded at the same time that students manipulate 3d models of these characters. At the end of each activity, each child has created a video with the recording of the 3d characters' movements along with the story narrated by him/her. The 3d models are displayed through portable electronic devices, with Augmented Reality software. Using their devices, pupils choose and scan images in an enriched worksheet prepared by the teacher. The enrichment of the images involves their connection with the 3d models which is realized with Augment, open Augmented Reality tool. Thus, from each image, the 3d form of a character is displayed in real context.

The selection of images for the design of the worksheet and the 3d models follow the historical knowledge that has already been taught in previous lessons, during the same school year. Therefore, the use of the game aimed to assess the acquired knowledge and to create an incentive for pupils to express themselves freely and creatively [20]. Pupils are informed from the beginning that their stories will be recorded and presented in the classroom. Therefore, the criterion of quality and reliability of the content is automatically determined. Methodologically, the innovative element lies in the ability to narrate stories *in tandem with the manipulation of 3d digital mode* while moving 3d History models in pupils' mobile devices. Moreover, digital stories together with the recorded videos (through screen capturing software) were compiled into a digital repository that can be further utilized at any time.

The search for the 3d digital material and the preparation of the worksheet was carried out by the teacher. The sources were mainly existing collections of 3d models and personal web pages of 3d digital content designers. The age of children who played 3D HIT in this teaching intervention was 10–11 years. Their age only allowed an experimental use of the game designed by the teacher.

There were three stages in the implementation of the activity (Fig. 2). The first, the design stage which was carried out by the teacher. It included research for material, the creation of the activities' worksheet and the synthesis of the gamified activity 3D HIT.

Then, the stage of implementation followed, in which children chose images from the worksheet, they displayed and manipulated the 3d character that corresponded to the image and finally composed their final video. This final video was in the form of presentation of each character. That's because it looks like he/she is introducing him/herself while moving and spinning around.

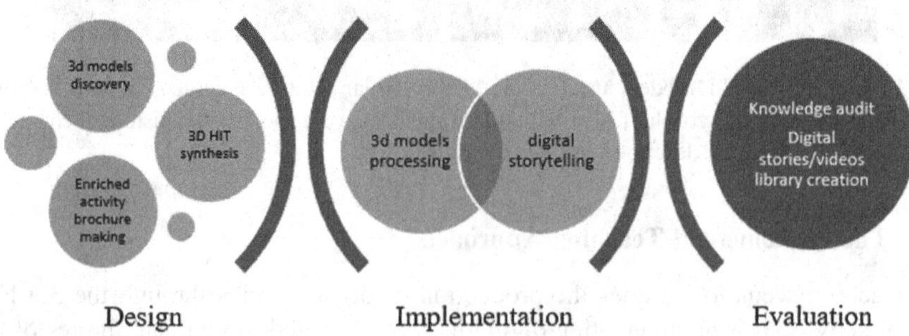

Fig. 2. Stages of the activity.

Finally, there was the evaluation stage in which the videos were played with the integrated digital narratives of all children and discussed within the classroom, in a plenary session. During this process the teacher had the opportunity to assess children's knowledge and attempted to further facilitate knowledge acquisition through dialogue.

The final stage also included the creation of a digital library with all the pupils' digital material created through playing the 3D HIT game. This library was finally posted on the school's website in an open and easily accessible way for students and educators, using personalized codes.

3.3 Research Design

In order to evaluate the effectiveness of teaching history concepts through 3D HIT, a small-scale, qualitative ethnographical study was designed. The main objectives were to examine the level of students' previous knowledge on an already taught Greek Mythology chapter. Also, the aim was to investigate the contribution of the activity to the engagement and participation of pupils in the teaching process so as to cultivate better communication among them [15]. Therefore, three research questions were formulated as follows: (a) did pupils perform better than their usual mark rates indicate after playing 3D HIT, (b) was their engagement and participation level higher than in similar activities in the History subject, and (c) did pupils improve their ability to express themselves fluently and with clarity during the digital storytelling process of the activity?

Systematic observation was selected as a data collection tool. This choice was made because the researcher was also the teacher of the specific class for a long time and many different disciplinary areas (which is very common in Primary Education). Therefore, it was easier to record and understand the changes that occurred in the behaviour of the pupils during the game's performance.

Moreover, since it is not easy to quantify or accurately evaluate the gained historical knowledge in small age groups, it is equally important for educators to elaborate the skills development after each teaching activity [3]. This process is dynamic and constantly evolving. Therefore, the systematic observation and recording of pupils' behaviour is considered to be more accurate [21]. The teacher could be described as a 'participant observer'. At the same time, he facilitates the activity in technical needs.

The sample population of this study consisted of 24 students aged 9–10 years old. The duration of the study was 2 weeks, including five 45-minutes sessions in total.

4 Results

A positive contribution of the activity to knowledge and skills building was indicated by the results of the systematic observation.

As far as the level of knowledge of pupils is concerned, it was recorded that the majority (15/24) showed a performance improvement, compared to their usual average grades (Fig. 3). What was actually measured was the ability of pupils to use historical knowledge during the narration of their digital stories. That was compared with traditional evaluation processes in which they were also asked to orally narrate historical facts previously taught by the teacher. The mail difference lies to the fact that during the playful activity 3D HIT, historical Knowledge is processed and produced by pupils themselves. Eight out of twenty-four pupils performed equally to their usual grades and only one student performed worse than usually. A greatest improvement was recorded

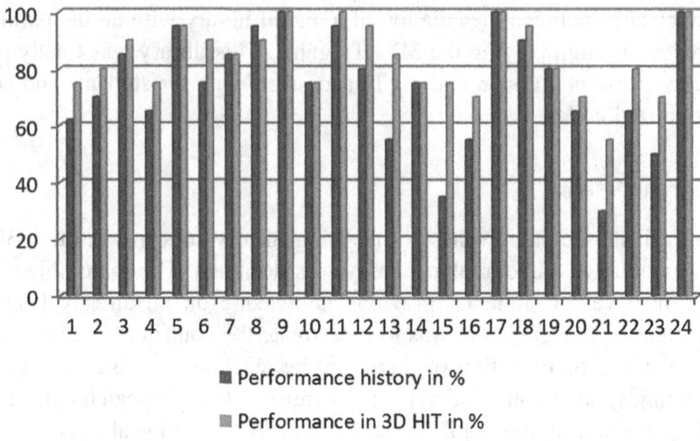

Fig. 3. Pupils' performance comparison after playing 3D HIT game.

for average students while those who had a very high performance, retained their scores after playing the 3D HIT game. Although grading in primary education follows the scale of 10, the percentage presentation is used for the needs of this study.

Moreover, according to the data, in all the five session that the game was utilized, the improvement of the pupils' participation level was equally increased (Fig. 4). A scoring rubric was used in which pupils' attitude and reactions during the whole activity were recorded in detail. This involved the objective evaluation of the teacher for these variables, based on the overview of the class status that he had developed over time. A 10-grade scale was used, following the normal grading approach of Primary School. It is important to say that any teacher is obliged to follow similar grading approaches through the year in order to report pupils' overall performance to parents and the School. There were no signs of leakage in stage of the game implementation while the pupils' interest and participation showed an upward trend as the sessions progressed. This is particularly important for the History subject since research shows high rates of difficulty and leakage, especially in younger ages [2]. Large and obscure texts discourage young learners while the supervisory material is often limited to two-dimensional images and historical maps [1]. The findings of this small-scale study indicate that the utilization of a differentiated teaching practice such as the 3D HIT gamified activity had boosted pupils' interest and desire to participate.

Also, a corresponding improvement was recorded in the expression capacity of the children. This improvement gradually evolved from the first session to the completion of the digital stories and the final videos (Fig. 4). Although a two-week period is considered to be short for such an important research sector, in the case of text production for their digital narratives, a remarkable evolution was observed in pupils' stories. For data collection, a scoring rubric was used to keep track of pupils' oral expressions whether used in their digital stories or not.

The whole activity inspired them to express themselves more, since they found it particularly appealing that historical figures and heroes introduced themselves to the public using their own voice. In a sense, pupils' digital stories and the movement of the

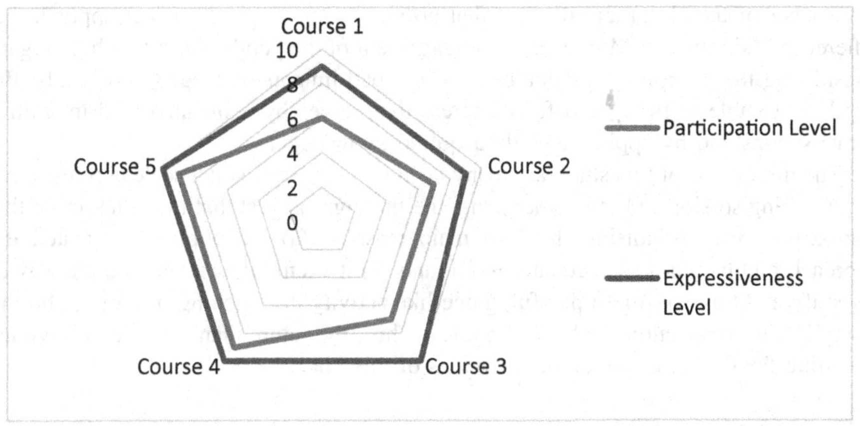

Fig. 4. Records of pupils' engagement and participation level during playing 3D HIT game.

three-dimensional model brought to life the characters of their own school books. This led them to continually enrich their texts with expressive elements. It also urged them to check the validity of the information used.

The lack of time pressure and the lack of evaluation by the teacher also contributed to the increase of expressiveness. Pupils were only given instructions for the game and the task to produce their videos. During their work there were no interventions or corrective remarks. Thus, the playful form of the teaching activity was maintained in every stage of it. All of the above contributed to reducing stress. This is particularly important since stress is very evident in cases where young pupils are asked to create stories and orally share them with classmates. Observation findings together with the comments of pupils themselves, showed that the fact that only their voice was used in the final videos and not their face also reduced stress and anxiety. On the contrary, the use of screen recording software made them feel comfortable and concentrated in their work. Finally, as the majority of pupils commented, the simultaneous exploitation of 3d models in their devices inspired them in the production of their digital stories, offering them visualisation of the historical content.

5 Conclusions

Within this study a playful, game-like activity was designed, following the principles of serious games, for teaching History in a diversified manner. The main objectives were to examine the level of students' previous knowledge on an already taught Greek Mythology chapter and to investigate the contribution of the playful activity to the engagement and participation of pupils in the teaching process so as to cultivate better communication among them [15].

The data indicate that the pupils performed better within this activity when graded in an ordinary manner (Fig. 3). Although at first the difference may not seem big enough, considering the disciplinary area, the perspective of the researcher (being also the teacher of the class) and the fact that no significant preparation was applied, this difference is significant. Moreover, the engagement of the pupils was rather high (again considering the discipline), gradually reaching total immersion (Fig. 4). Similarly, the pupils were able to freely and fully express themselves by being involved in fruitful conversations and by applied already acquired knowledge.

The limitations of this study are many, as it was of a very small scale and restricted to 5 teaching sessions. On the other hand, the findings suggest that the potential of this approach is very promising, for two main reasons: (a) the pupils appreciated the approach highly and it seemed successful, and (b) it exemplifies a very simple way to diversify and transform into playful, game-like activity the teaching of a rather boring discipline, utilizing cutting edge technology. Thus, the future plans are rather obvious, including the design of additional activities of this kind.

References

1. Bourdillon, H.: Teaching History. Routledge, Abingdon (2013)
2. Arthur, J.: Issues in history teaching. Routledge, Abingdon (2012)
3. Rammos, D., Bratitsis, T.: Inclusive strategies for the History Subject in 6th Grade of Greek Primary School: gamifying the curriculum with digital storytelling and augmented reality. In: Proceedings of the 8th International Conference on Software Development and Technologies for Enhancing Accessibility and Fighting Info-exclusion. ACM (2018)
4. Boyaci, S.D.B., Atalay, N.: A scale development for 21st century skills of primary school students: a validity and reliability study. Int. J. Instr. **9**(1), 133–148 (2016)
5. Chalkiadaki, A.: A systematic literature review of 21st century skills and competencies in primary education. Int. J. Instr. **11**(3), 1–16 (2018)
6. Cantu, D.A., Warren, W.J.: Teaching History in the Digital Classroom. Routledge, Abingdon (2016)
7. Protopsaltis, A.; Pannese, L.; Pappa, D., Hetzner, S.: Serious games and formal and informal learning. E-Learning Papers, 1887–1542 (2011)
8. Nistor, G.C., Iacob, A.: The advantages of gamification and game-based learning and their benefits in the development of education. In: International Scientific Conference eLearning and Software for Education, Vol. 1. "Carol I" National Defence University (2018)
9. Maragos, K., Grigoriadou, M.: Towards the design of intelligent educational gaming systems. In: Proceedings of AIED05 WORKSHOP5: Educational Games as Intelligent Learning Environments, pp. 35–38 (2005)
10. De Freitas, S.: Are games effective learning tools? A review of educational games. J. Educ. Technol. Soc. **21**(2), 74–84 (2018)
11. Liestøl, G.: Story and storage–narrative theory as a tool for creativity in augmented reality storytelling. Virtual Creativity **8**(1), 75–89 (2018)
12. Rieber, L.P., Smith, L., Noah, D.: The value of serious play. Educ. Technol. **38**(6), 29–37 (1998)
13. Robin, B.R.: The power of digital storytelling to support teaching and learning. Digit. Educ. Rev. **30**, 17–29 (2016)
14. Lambert, J.: Digital Storytelling: Capturing Lives, Creating Community, 4th edn. Routledge, New York (2013)

15. Bratitsis, T., Kotopoulos, T., Mandila, K.: Kindergarten children as story makers: the effect of the digital medium. In: Xhafa, F., Barolli, L., Köppen, M. (eds.) Proceedings of the IEEE 3rd International Conference on Intelligent Networking and Collaborative Systems, INCoS 2011, Fukuoka, Japan, pp. 84–91, 30 November–2 December (2011)
16. Bratitsis, T.: Experiences from digital storytelling training seminars for educators. The case of Greece. In: 9th Panhellenic Conference "ICTs in Education", 3–5 October 2014, University of Crete, Rethymno (2014)
17. Melliou, K., Moutafidou, A., Bratitsis, T.: Children's rights: using digital storytelling and visible thinking approaches to create a narrative video in early childhood classroom. Int. J. Electron. Governance **7**(4), 333–348 (2015)
18. Bratitsis, T., Ziannas, P.: From early childhood to special education: Interactive digital storytelling as a coaching approach for fostering social empathy. Procedia Comput. Sci. **67**, 231–240 (2015)
19. Darzentas, D., Flintham, M., Benford, S.: Object-focused mixed reality storytelling: technology-driven content creation and dissemination for engaging user experiences. In: Proceedings of the 22nd Pan-Hellenic Conference on Informatics. ACM (2018)
20. Wang, M., Nunes, M.B.: Matching serious games with museum's educational roles: smart education in practice. Interact. Technol. Smart Educ. **16**, 319–342 (2019)
21. Claire, H.: Values in the primary history curriculum. In: Values in History Teacher Education and Research, pp. 54–70. History Teacher Education Network in Association with St Martin's College, Lancaster (2002)

A Serious Logistical Game of Paediatric Emergency Medicine: Proposed Scoring Mechanism and Pilot Test

Cevin Zhang[1(✉)], Jannicke Baalsrud Hauge[2,4], Karin Pukk Härenstam[3], and Sebastiaan Meijer[1]

[1] Department of Biomedical Engineering and Health Systems, Kungliga Tekniska Högskolan, 14157 Huddinge, Sweden
chenzh@kth.se

[2] Department of Sustainable Production Development, Kungliga Tekniska Högskolan, 15136 Södertalje, Sweden

[3] Pediatric Emergency Department, Karolinska University Hospital, 14157 Huddinge, Sweden

[4] Bremer Institut fuer Produktion und Logistik, 28359 Bremen, Germany

Abstract. Outcomes of care for various diseases and urgent conditions in an emergency department are dependent on balancing the patient's need and available resources through management and coordination under often rapidly changing preconditions. However, although it is central to resilient operations, decision-making in dynamic resource management is rarely visible to managers. Sometimes the identification of successful strategies is apparent only through adverse event reports. A simulation game could be helpful for the acquisition of non-technical skills in addressing operational conundrums that could threaten the defence ability of a paediatric emergency department under care production pressures. This contribution presents a Sandtable serious logistical game of the care production system and, in particular, proposes its scoring mechanism, which was tested in a set of logistical experiments. The results show that through gamification, participants were challenged in terms of their intrinsic self-interest when it came to approaching the work. More importantly, the proposed extrinsic reward system allows all parallel functional roles to be equally rewarded as the game evolves. Anticipatory human resource management is identified as a successful strategy for achieving a sustainable working environment if the organizational resilience is confronted with patient inflow surges during the busiest hours of the busiest day.

Keywords: Game design · Game mechanics · Scoring system · Emergency department · Performance outcomes · Resource management · Decision making · Training

1 Introduction

Emergency departments (ED) are responders in the immediate aftermath of incidents and catastrophic situations, as well as the only part of the entire healthcare system that delivers the greatest health benefits to acutely ill patients. At the same time, it is one

A. Liapis et al. (Eds.): GALA 2019, LNCS 11899, pp. 468–478, 2019.
https://doi.org/10.1007/978-3-030-34350-7_45

type of organization that faces challenges with regard to creating a sustainable working environment [1]. Overall resiliency in low-resource settings requires dynamic resource management to encourage proactive safety measures, which has attracted more attention, particularly with regard to facilitating sustainable practices to realize a resilient work system.

The ability to manage resources, especially when human resources are deeply involved in health organizations, is a non-technical skill (NTS) that requires decision-making, coordination, and leadership. According to definitions in this field, non- NTS are defined as cognitive, social, and personal skills related to organizational robustness and resilience in management [2]. Coordination, decision-making, and situational awareness are considered core NTS in several industries requiring maximum levels of safety and quality under conditions of stress and disruption.

Practices such as staffing strategies and controlling, rostering and capacity building in human resource management (HRM) have received attention from process and system engineers [3]; for these practices, simulations and gaming can be used to train individuals and teams until they are technically proficient in the skills needed for a collective, reliable high-performance working system [4].

Technology-enhanced learning can be used to teach NTS related to resource management. The benefits of using technology relies on modelling of real systems, experiential learning, debriefing, evaluation of play, and systematic analysis [5]. Progress in the field necessitates that the evaluation of play and outcomes of the game be systematically performed with self-assessment tools, meaningful scoring and gamification, and direct measurements of performance. Most studies up to now have only considered indirect measurements, and further studies on direct measurements are needed [6]. The work by Rusnock et al. is one of the few healthcare simulation studies that have examined mental workload changes in situations such as increases in patient inflow and human resource strategies [7]. In addition, there is a lack of studies on how scoring systems should be constructed for HRM-related games and simulations that contribute to learning NTS, especially when dynamic scheduling and staffing of health human resources are strongly connected to organizational performance and workload reduction.

2 The Need of Gaming in Non-technical Skills Training: Review

In the ED, resource management is central to operations and affects the length of stay, quality of care, waiting time, task distribution and workload reduction for employees. Operations depend on highly functioning, interconnected teams. Crew Resource Management (CRM) was developed in aviation in 1980 as a response to a series of accidents in which the lack of teamwork and communication, a hierarchical culture, and suppressive leadership led to disasters [8]. The goal of CRM is to create a highly reliable organization through a focus on training NTS. In everyday work, CRM aims to train teams to use all available resources in terms of information, equipment, and people to support resilient operations [9]. E-learning and serious games have been used successfully to train NTS [10] or have shown potential as an efficient technique to test management, leadership, and organizational models [11].

The knowledge and acquisition of skills are achieved as long as the simulation game is not separate but rather connects to experimental learning, with the game design framework applying and organizing game development, participation, debriefing, evaluation, and analysis. The Kriz framework could be an exemplar, bringing together all apparatuses [12]. Alternative templates are Olszewski and Wolbrink's work that frames simulator development in medical education [13]; the Experience, Experiment and Evaluate framework dedicated to the assessment of serious games [14]; and the Metrics Feedback Cycle for improving gamification features and user engagement [15]. Based on these observations, the research question asked in this study is: How should a game scoring mechanism be designed to generate a fair and meaningful playing field on which individuals and team can learn the skills needed to coordinate resources in an ED? The driving force behind the research question is that there are no such alternative scoring systems in recently published gaming articles on care production systems, nor are there solutions or innovations pertaining to gamifying the delivery of care inside a paediatric ED [3].

This study was designed to explore the usefulness of a proposed scoring mechanism as an extrinsic reward system in a training game. The theme of the game was practising NTS in the dynamic resource management of a paediatric ED that faces challenges from case mix and low acuity inflows.

3 Methodology and Research Design

3.1 Main Game Elements

The gaming structure was presented in a previous work [16], and it requires participation from six players. The players represent inspectorates of the care production system. In this work, the structure is materialized into an analogue game. The managers are represented by players in the game. The players are managing the triage station and five normal modules as parallel functioning production units of an ED (see Table 1). They expect a fast throughput and timely emergency medicine delivery. Players collaborate and compete with each other to develop a resilient paediatric ED from available human resources and stretchers. Each session is populated with mixed low-acuity and high-acuity incoming patients distributed in sixteen rounds. The first six rounds are to simulate daily operations from the middle of the day, known as the busiest hours. To avoid preventable access blocks, the intended learning goal of the game is that players are expected to use NTS to communicate, coordinate and collaborate with other players who are under production pressures. The only Key Performance Indicator (KPI) for winning is the amount of tokens, which is awarded based on the flow performance, service delay, failure of accountabilities and errors leading to misplaced human resources.

Table 1. Roles, functions, decision making and motivations for the serious logistical game

Game roles	Functions	Decisions to make	Motivations
Triage manager	Control inflows	Priority assignment to patients and referral control based on narratives	Balanced inflow through the ED
Red module manager	Resuscitate critically ill patients	Resource management to accomplish tasks of patients in the activity log; fill in the time for first doctor diagnose; discharge planning	Revive patients; provide timely emergency medicine
Orange module manager	Take care of patients with mixed acuity levels		Provide timely emergency medicine; fast discharging
Yellow module manager			
Green module manager			
Blue module manager			

3.2 Gaming Process

The ED receives a predefined number of incoming patients into triage each round based on actual patient flow data from a large paediatric ED. Decisions need to be made by the triage nurse regarding whether the patient is referred or stays in the ED.

The patients are represented using cards, as illustrated in Fig. 1. There are ninety such cards. They are prioritized before being diagnosed or treated by doctors and nurses who work at the modules. Each patient has a unique profile with regard to priority and activities that require an individual resource plan from the responsible person at the appropriate module. The use of stretchers and the priority levels of patients are decided on by negotiation between modules and the triage station. Urgent patients, the only level indicated on the cards, must be sent to the red module. The game encourages the organizational dynamic between individual key performance indicators and a high-performance working system at the organizational level with a better patient flow and shorter lead time. Part of the coordination process is to be situationally aware of the ongoing workload of the different modules and to manage flows while simultaneously meeting the demands of patients.

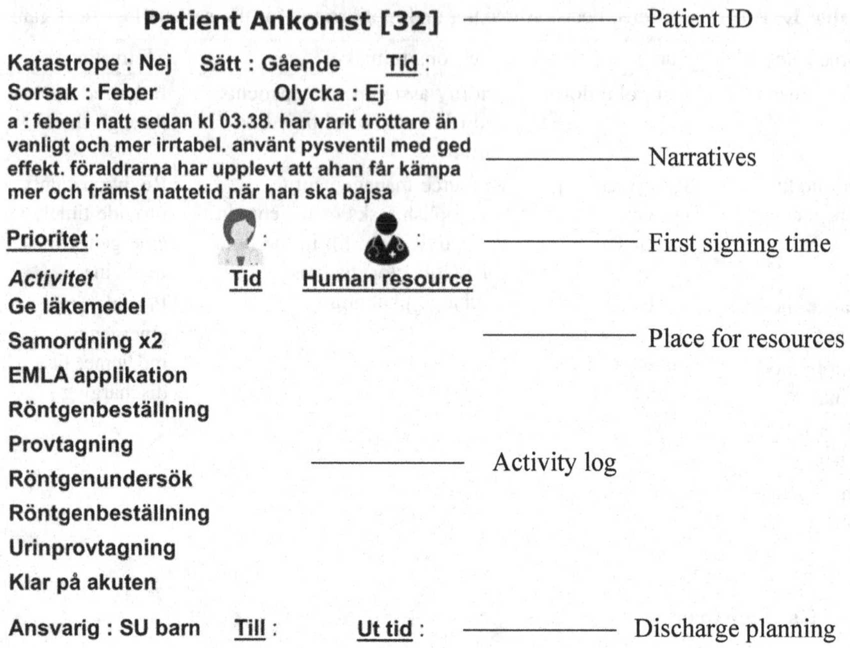

Patient Ankomst [32] —— Patient ID

Katastrope : Nej Sätt : Gående Tid :
Sorsak : Feber Olycka : Ej
a : feber i natt sedan kl 03.38. har varit tröttare än vanligt och mer irrtabel. använt pysventil med ged effekt. föraldrarna har upplevt att ahan får kämpa mer och främst nattetid när han ska bajsa —— Narratives

Prioritet : : : —— First signing time

Activitet **Tid Human resource**
Ge läkemedel
Samordning x2 —— Place for resources
EMLA applikation
Röntgenbeställning
Provtagning
Röntgenundersök —— Activity log
Röntgenbeställning
Urinprovtagning
Klar på akuten

Ansvarig : SU barn Till : Ut tid : —— Discharge planning

Fig. 1. Patient representation

3.3 Research Design

The main objective of this study was two-fold. First, it was designed to develop a scoring mechanism that does not currently exist in the literature regarding operational sciences pertaining to paediatric emergency medicine to support NTS acquisition in a fair and meaningful playing field; second, it was designed to determine, through in-game decision-making consequences, whether participants achieve the intended learning goal. A set of experiments was carried out.

To address the research questions (evaluating learning and the design of the scoring mechanism), a framework that part of the research team has used on several occasions to evaluate learning in different settings was selected [12]. This framework allows the organization of the game-based experiment with understanding the complexity of a work system as a keyword. The justification is as follows: (1) Because we are handling complex resource management problems, the game must be designed as an artefact (form) to simulate (function) system processes that activate proactive participation, aiming for the adoption of strategic management; (2) as mentioned before and in addition to a wide variety of applications, the Kriz gaming framework is a validated design guideline that can efficiently organize all apparatuses; (3) because the goal is for the participants to take away valuable knowledge from technology-enhanced learning, a continuum arises in *design-in-the-small* (focusing on gamification) and *design-in-the-large* (focusing on the interpretation of outputs and the translational knowledge) in the game design process; and (4) debriefing is delivered.

Participants in the pilot study and those evaluating the gaming effect were recruited from student groups participating in a relevant course. They differ from the main target group of the game, which is medical personnel working in ED. The reason is that to investigate how scoring mechanisms are working, a relatively large sample size is required, and it is necessary to be able to repeat the experiment with similar attendees after changing the game. That is not possible with ED personnel with limited time. The participants received a briefing about the roles, resources, and rules of the game. Progress through the game was photographed to record how gaming evolved. To evaluate gameplay, the mental workload was scored based on visual, auditory, cognitive, and psychomotor workload methodology framework to calculate such values as patient tasks that are unique to each profile [7]. Additionally, data on resource utilization and lead times were collected. The game does not end with a winning or losing person because the aim is not completion but collaborative decision making (Fig. 2).

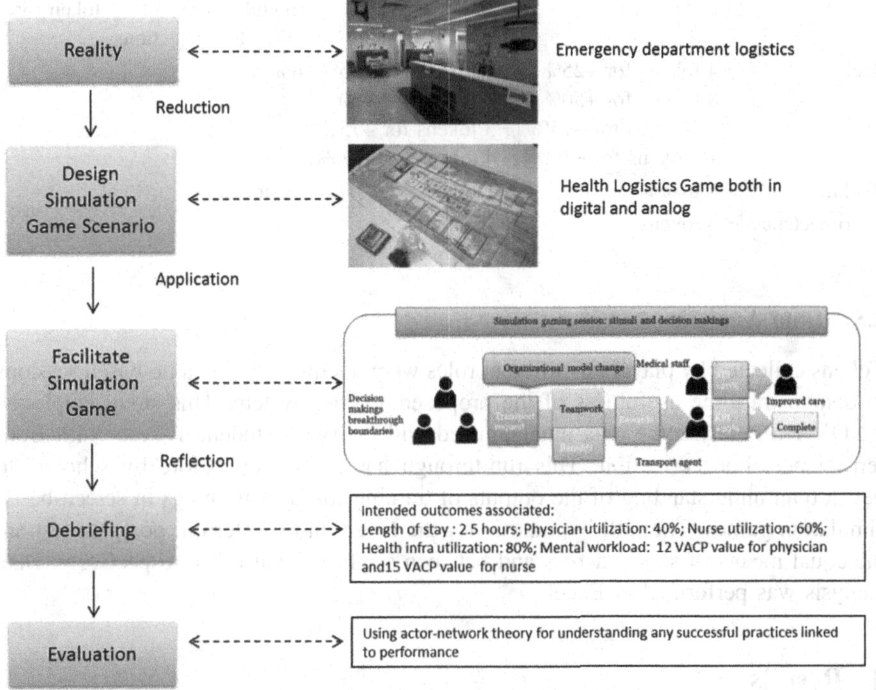

Fig. 2. Flowchart of the game

3.4 A Scoring System for Meaningful Gamification of Emergency Care Production

To evaluate the learning outcome, a scoring system, as shown in Table 2, is built into the game. A scoring system needs to be meaningful so that players are given the same opportunity to grow. The flow criterion is for all the roles to accrue tokens after successfully discharging each patient. Penalties are issued once delay, failure, and incompetency criteria are met. With reference to the criteria, a pairwise comparison of an individual resource plan in game play and the real parameters of resource planning is performed for each simulated patient. The length of stay in the game is compared to the real length of stay. It is considered a failure when a task is not implemented by the appropriate personnel. An incompetency penalty is issued when a particular task that should have taken care of by a doctor is implemented by a nurse due to a lack of resources. A total score is available by summing the tokens collected and lost.

Table 2. Overview of the Health Logistics Game scoring system (+25% stands for a 25% increase in the standard value)

Criterion	Red module responsible	Normal modules responsible	Triage place
Flow	+16 tokens	+4 tokens	¼ of the tokens the receiving module earns but −1 token for every two rejections
Delay	−4 tokens for +25% −8 tokens for +50% −12 tokens for +75% −16 tokens for +100%	−1 tokens for +25% −2 tokens for +50% −3 tokens for +75% −4 tokens for +100%	n/a
Failure	−4 tokens	−1 token	−1 token
Incompetency	−4 tokens	−1 token	n/a

3.5 Data Analysis

Tokens collected by players in different roles were documented in game-based sessions to demonstrate the usefulness of the proposed scoring system. This study employed ANOVA to analyse the data amalgamated with pairwise student T-Tests with Bonferroni post hoc correction. This run-through has been used before by scholars to develop an understanding of the outputs of training for NTS trainings in screen-based simulation games. The null hypothesis for the F-test and Bonferroni post hoc test are the equal means of scores across and between six functional roles, respectively. Data analysis was performed in Excel.

4 Results

In total, twelve workshops with 81 participants were held. The participants were all students at KTH and participated on a voluntary basis. The scoring mechanism was fair, although the scoring plays different roles. The scores on modules that work with healthier patients tended to be higher than the score for modules working with less healthy patients. The null hypothesis for the F-test was investigated under a probability of rejecting the proposed scoring system at the $\alpha = 0.05$ level. Fifteen pairwise comparisons needed to be performed based on a Bonferroni correction value of 0.003. The data show no significant score disparities among the roles.

By investigating in-game data, it can be observed that the participants made more collaborative decisions in later rounds of the game. This reflects that the better outcomes in later rounds might be the result of the increased complexity and visibility of the effects of decisions as the number of patients in the ED grows. In early rounds, participants were cautious about delaying the patients and attempted to organize flows in the most efficient way possible. As more patients came into the ED, the key performance indicators generally became worse compared to the estimated average values from the ED. Nevertheless, it was evident from the outputs that the management of the ED improved even though incoming patients continued to pile up (Fig. 3, Table 3).

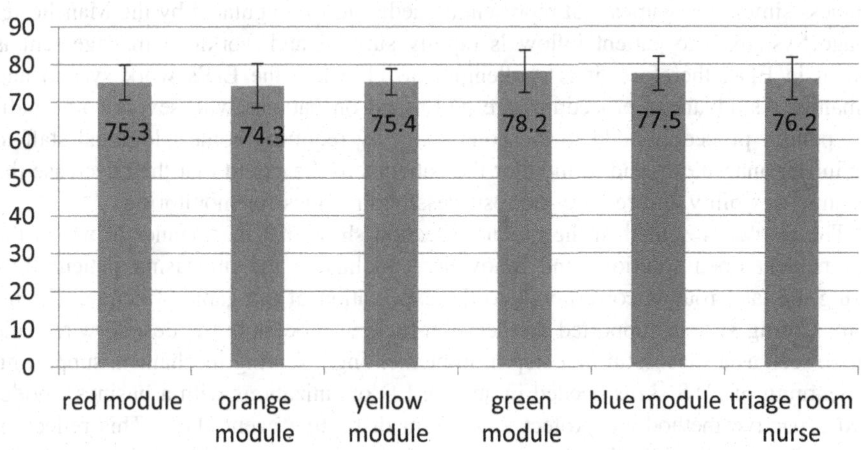

Fig. 3. Score results between roles

Table 3. Changes of key performance indicator in the simulated busiest hours of the day

KPI (entity)	Round 1	Round 2	Round 3	Round 4	Round 5	Round 6
Length of stay (patients)	−10.2%	−8.3%	−2.5%	+5,2%	+4.6%	+1.4%
Utilization (doctor)	−5.3%	−6.2%	+5.6%	+8.2%	+5.5%	+4.2%
Utilization (nurse)	−2.3%	+2.0%	−3.2%	+4.2%	+3.5%	+3.3%
Utilization (observation room)	−5.1%	+2.8%	+7.3%	+15.6%	+12.5%	+8.9%
Mental workload (doctor)	−8.4%	−6.2%	+5.2%	+12.1%	+6.3%	+3.2%
Mental workload (nurse)	−3.5%	−5.7%	+8.5%	+13.3%	+8.9%	+6.3%

Reactions from the debriefing were positive. Participants stated that the development and implementation of planned changes could be visualized. Meanwhile, decisions made by the leading physician and nurse with regard to managing employees were based on leadership or monitoring performances. Another lesson from the trials is that proposed HRM for a sustainable working environment is a successful strategy after evaluating the outcomes of play. Proactive safety operations can be facilitated by negotiation and participation (i.e., sharing risks through management leaders). This is evident from the dynamics of the organizational performance in gaming. In approximately round 4, all human resources became interchangeable in the modules. In addition, workload, occupation, and length of stay markedly decreased even as the projected increasing logistical flows from round 3 to round 4 were challenging the availability of resources. Players successfully handled the demand-capacity gap even though the simulated ED was more congested in the last two rounds of the game.

5 Discussion and Conclusion

Overall, game designers could apply the proposed scoring structure to newly developed business simulation games that represent a paediatric ED regulated by the Manchester Triage System. The patient inflow is rapidly surging and workload management is critical in EDs; therefore, it is challenging to elucidate the ED's work system and demands. As advanced procedures are performed on patients with severe comorbidities, painful procedures add to the complexity by requiring some additional staff to administer anaesthesia and to monitor the patients, to the extent that they decrease the systemic flexibility and require more successful strategies for monitoring.

The results presented in the previous section show that the manner in which the players developed solutions and innovations to handle the increasing patient flow during the later rounds corresponds to the expectation of the game principle. The in-game scoring system supported the decision-making process in the desired way. This can be seen as a successful first step in implementing a scoring mechanism supporting the learning of NTS skills needed in an ED. ED organizations with a business model need proactive methods to protect them from disruptive events [17]. This reflection from participation shows that the game can capture and render visible the core logistics challenge of managing an ED. The managers reasoned that without a combined decision-making ability and proper management of employees, there was no point in trying a planned change. The managers' central role in the implementation work, as they described, was not only monitoring but also engaging, facilitating work-as-done, and encouraging self-reflection and determination. A simulation-based game mirroring a real work process, as presented in this study, can be used to teach HRM in an ED setting. Competition is not recommended as part of the team atmosphere, which was a contribution from emergency medicine shareholders during the game co-design process. The proposed scoring system is not aimed to overemphasize the winning situation but to provide information to players on how gaming evolves through organizational performance in simulated scenarios.

However, as noted earlier, in this first evaluation of the scoring mechanism, all eighty-one participants were students, and not all game interactions were genuinely realistic. Therefore, in the next step, the presented result will be used to refine the built-in scoring system and to make the tasks more in line with the current situation in an ED. This will then be tested both with students in next year's class from the same course and ED staff. A more structured and systemic evaluation methodology is proposed and validated by Carvalho et al.'s work [18]. This is a suitable framework given that a favourable view of game-based training for healthcare logistics has yet to be shown. This framework will be used to measure the learning curve and the gap between gaming outcomes and observed performance outcomes to further support debriefing and evaluation.

References

1. Bragard, I., Dupuis, G., Fleet, R.: Quality of work life, burnout, and stress in emergency department physicians: a qualitative review. Eur. J. Emerg. Med. **22**(4), 227–234 (2015)
2. Crichton, M., O'Connor, P., Flin, R.: Safety at the Sharp End: A Guide to Non-technical Skills. Ashgate Publishing Ltd., Farnham (2013)
3. Zhang, C., Grandits, T., Härenstam, K.P., Hauge, J.B., Meijer, S.: A systematic literature review of simulation models for non-technical skill training in healthcare logistics. Adv. Simul. **3**(1), 15 (2018)
4. Baker, D.P., Day, R., Salas, E.: Teamwork as an essential component of high-reliability organizations. Health Serv. Res. **41**(4), 1576–1598 (2006)
5. Kriz, W.C.: Types of gaming simulation applications. Simul. Gaming **48**(1), 3–7 (2017)
6. Barré, J., et al.: Does repeated exposure to critical situations in a screen-based simulation improve the self-assessment of non-technical skills in postpartum hemorrhage management? Simul. Gaming **50**(2), 102–123 (2019)
7. Rusnock, C.F., Maxheimer, E.W., Oyama, K.F., Valencia, V.V.: Simulation-based evaluation of the effects of patient load on mental workload of healthcare staff. Simul. Healthc.: J. Soc. Simul. Healthc. **12**(4), 260–267 (2017)
8. Flin, R., O'Connor, P., Mearns, K.: Crew resource management: improving team work in high reliability industries. Team Perform. Manag. **8**(3/4), 68–78 (2002)
9. Chassin, M.R.: The urgent need to improve health care quality: institute of medicine national roundtable on health care quality. JAMA **280**(11), 1000 (1998)
10. Creutzfeldt, J., Hedman, L., Felländer-Tsai, L.: Effects of pre-training using serious game technology on CPR performance – an exploratory quasi-experimental transfer study. Scand. J. Trauma Resusc. Emerg. Med. **20**(1), 79 (2012)
11. Ligtenberg, A., van Lammeren, R.J.A., Bregt, A.K., Beulens, A.J.M.: Validation of an agent-based model for spatial planning: a role-playing approach. Comput. Environ. Urban Syst. **34**(5), 424–434 (2010)
12. Kriz, W.C., Manahl, W.: Gaming simulation as a science of design approach. In: Naweed, A., Wardaszko, M., Leigh, E., Meijer, S. (eds.) ISAGA/SimTecT 2016. LNCS, vol. 10711, pp. 380–393. Springer, Cham (2018). https://doi.org/10.1007/978-3-319-78795-4_27
13. Olszewski, A.E., Wolbrink, T.A.: Serious gaming in medical education: a proposed structured framework for game development. Simul. Healthc.: J. Soc. Simul. Healthc. **12**(4), 240–253 (2017)
14. Lytle, N., Floryan, M., Amin, D.: Experience, experiment, evaluate: a framework for assessing experiential games, vol. 4, no. 1, March 2017
15. Atkins, A., Wanick, V., Wills, G.: Metrics feedback cycle: measuring and improving user engagement in gamified eLearning systems. Int. J. Serious Games **4**(4), 3–19 (2017)
16. Zhang, C., Meijer, S.: A simulation game of patient transportation. In: Hamada, R., et al. (eds.) Neo-Simulation and Gaming Toward Active Learning, vol. 18, pp. 53–66. Springer, Singapore (2019). https://doi.org/10.1007/978-981-13-8039-6_5

17. Sahebjamnia, N., Torabi, S.A., Mansouri, S.A.: Integrated business continuity and disaster recovery planning: Towards organizational resilience. Eur. J. Oper. Res. **242**(1), 261–273 (2015)
18. de Carvalho, C.V., Cano, P., Roa, J.M., Wanka, A., Kolland, F.: Technology enhanced learning for senior citizens. In: Hancke, G., Spaniol, M., Osathanunkul, K., Unankard, S., Klamma, R. (eds.) ICWL 2018. LNCS, vol. 11007, pp. 37–46. Springer, Cham (2018). https://doi.org/10.1007/978-3-319-96565-9_4

Economic Evaluation of Business Models in Video Gaming Industry from Publisher Perspective

Erik Massarczyk(✉), Peter Winzer, and Sina Bender

Hochschule RheinMain, Unter den Eichen 5, 65195 Wiesbaden, Germany
{erik.massarczyk, peter.winzer}@hs-rm.de

Abstract. Against the background of rising development costs for video games, it is becoming increasingly important for game developers and publishers to assess, which business model (a) best fits the newly developed video game and (b) promises the highest financial returns. In this respect, the advantages and disadvantages of the various business models of video games must also be examined and evaluated within the framework of game development. Here, the business models (a) free to play, (b) pay to play, and (c) buy to play are explained and compared from the publisher perspective. The comparison was made on the basis of a self-developed evaluation system. In this system, free to play business model achieves the best ranking value, although this model does not guarantee fixed financial returns for the game developers. In this respect, it should be examined whether and to what extent this business model can assert itself on the video game market.

Keywords: Business models · Free to play · Buy to play · Pay to play · Video game

1 Introduction

This paper considers specifically the video game industry as a part of the software entertainment industry. Although the gaming segment is often assigned as a niche market in the past, nowadays the worldwide video game market represents a business volume of 137.9 billion USD and 2.3 billion active video gamers [14, 24]. Like the entire entertainment industry, the games industry aims to reach as many Internet users as possible [9, 11]. In recent years, sharply rising development costs for video games are observed. Average development costs are now around USD 15 to 30 million per game. In individual cases, even high double-digit to three-digit million development budgets are achieved [26, 27]. Against the background of these high development costs, it is of crucial economic importance for the future to choose or develop business models that enable them to refinance their investment budgets.

Despite the increased development budgets for video games, the increasing abundance and complexity of content, and the competition with its increasing supply of games by game developers and a rising demand by video gamers, the prices paid for video games decrease or stay relatively stable [2, 19, 26]. Thus, most video games

A. Liapis et al. (Eds.): GALA 2019, LNCS 11899, pp. 479–489, 2019.
https://doi.org/10.1007/978-3-030-34350-7_46

struggle in reaching the break-even by declining revenues [2, 19, 26, 27]. This means that in a game industry with increasing user and sales figures [11], the primary challenge for game developers and publishers is to find the business models that are best suited to generating adequate sales despite a fundamental reluctance on the part of consumers to pay.

This paper has the following structure. After the introduction in the first section, the term video game and the different types of business models will be explained in section two. In the subsequent third section, the underlying methodology is presented. In section four the business models will be evaluated based on the introduced criteria. The paper is finalized by the conclusions in section five.

2 Business Models

2.1 Video Games

The first video games were developed in the 1950s and were normally the computerized form of games or sports which exist in real world [1, 13, 26]. In general, to play a video game, the three following components are necessary: (a) hardware, (b) software, and (c) a playing human. The hardware is the device through which the players can use or operate the game, while the software represents the virtualized content of the video game [26]. That is, each video game has a technical device, a computer program with a specific design and virtualized images [5, 20, 22]. The aim of the publishers is to bind the users to themselves for as long as possible with the help of the attractive design of the aforementioned features of a video game. To achieve the user interest, the video game needs (a) specific game mechanics, (b) rules, (c) an interface, (d) sound, (e) game environment, and (f) content [5].

2.2 Gaming Types

The definition of game types depends on several factors as e.g. (a) the device for which the game will be originally developed, (b) the design of the game, (c) the gamers' willingness to pay, (d) the played and consumed video game genre, and (e) the division into single-player and multi-player gamers [2, 18, 26]. This distinction is essential, since e.g. the development of video games for smartphones, handhelds and consoles depend on different kinds of platforms resulting in development costs, which differ, distinctively from the costs for video games produced for computers [26]. In addition, the preferred video game genre of the players influences their demand concerning content and design. Lastly, the business models are driven by the willingness to pay of the video gamers, since more than half of the video gamers are not willing to invest money for gaming [24], which means that they are prone to use video games for free.

Considering the diversity of video gamers, the focus in this research will be on those gamers who primarily play on the computer or consoles, regardless of any single-player or multi-player preferences. Furthermore, the further evaluation of business models for video games is based on video games with average expenses between at least USD 15 to USD 30 million of production costs [26, 27].

2.3 Buy to Play (B2P)

The business model *buy to play* counts as the traditional model to market video games to the customers. The idea is that the customers do a one-off payment and get the full-developed video game [6, 23, 26]. The different gaming types (single-player or multi-player) and the distribution over retailers or digital platforms can lead to price variations but do not change the basic pricing model [17]. In the B2P model, every video game sold is usually provided individually to the user, e.g. on a medium (such as a CD) or by individual download. From the perspective of the customers, the buy to play business model is very simply, since the customers pay and get the full-developed product.

Although the one-off payment usually allows the financial return to be planned well, game developers and publishers must firstly bear the entire development and marketing risks (average development costs between USD 15 and 30 million per game [26, 27]. In addition, the one-off payment video games can be often found in the highest video game price segments [11]. Developers and publishers try to keep the customers in the loop and skim off any additional willingness to pay. Therefore, publishers often enable micro-transactions within video games. In so-called in game shops, users can buy additional content, game benefits or cosmetic adjustments [2, 23]. In view of the fact that customers have already spent an average of 30 to 40 Euros on the purchase of the game, such micro-transactions are generally little accepted by users [26, 27]. Rather, they often feel that they cannot fully experience the video game without additional payments, which seems unacceptable to them.

2.4 Pay to Play (P2P)

The *pay to play* business model requires users to subscribe to the video game [4, 6, 26]. Typically, this business model is used to market online multiplayer video games. Since such multiplayer video games usually also have high development costs, it is often the case that players first pay a "starting price" which at least partially covers the development costs. The current income from subscription payments primarily covers the costs for the provision of servers, the development of further content, support and the necessary reinvestment in the system [11]. The regular subscription payments provide game developers and publishers with a secure planning basis.

However, subscriptions are increasingly losing acceptance as fewer and fewer players are willing to pay usage-independent prices. Therefore, more game developers decide to transform the business model from a pay to play to a free to play model with in game shop and micro-transactions.

2.5 Free to Play (F2P)

With the *free to play* business model, players can use a (basic) video game without payment. In this regard, any market entry barrier by the price for the willing users do not exist [16]. It is only necessary to create a user account and provide some personal data, whereby it is to be assumed that a possible marketing of this data for game developers and publishers promises at best relatively low revenues and would not cover costs if necessary. In this respect, the free to play business model appears at first glance to be economically unreasonable, since regularly revenues and payments are not guaranteed [2, 11]. However, the free introduction of the game hinders competitors to create a price competition and the pressure to setting low prices [2].

The idea behind this business model is that users can firstly get to know the basic game free of charge, which means that a relatively large (registered) customer base can then be targeted with regard to the purchase of additional offers [6, 10, 23, 26]. This means that the revenue is generated solely from the sales of these additional offers (additional features, enhanced design, additional game levels, etc.), which should help to keep the video gamers' attention on the game [14, 15]. In contrast to the B2P and P2P models, in which users can easily overlook the fixed one-off or monthly payments, F2P video games make it easier for players to lose track of the amounts actually paid, so that they often spend more money than they would spend on video games in the other business models. The core problem from the perspective of game developers and publishers is that the proportion (=the conversion rate) of players who become paying users through these additional offers is usually very low at 1% to 5% [7, 11, 12, 15]. In order to cover the costs (especially the development costs) despite such a low conversion rate, it is economically necessary to reach initially a very large number of video players as registered users. Nonetheless, game developers often decide to publish a video game on the base of a F2P business model, as long as the game development costs are relatively low and the financial loss in the case of non-acceptance of the game by the customers is limited. Therefore, it is no surprise that especially mobile games are released with a F2P business model combined with optional in game sales [10, 21]. However, in case of video game development with high investment costs, the F2P with an unsecured backflow of financial resources does not seem to be the right choice for compensating the taken financial efforts [2]. Nonetheless, developers and publishers often fear that the costs cannot be compensated.

3 Methodology

In the following, this paper evaluates which business models are most advantageous for game developers and publishers as a whole and under which conditions. For this purpose, a comprehensive catalogue of criteria is used, which not only concentrates on the costs and revenues of video games, but also uses other criteria and characteristics to compare the business models. Finally, the results for each of the business models are summarized in a combined index. The target of the own created self-developed evaluation system is to firstly estimate the advantages and disadvantages of the general business models and distinguish from a publisher point of view, why one of the business models is more preferred than the other ones.

The rating of the single criterion follows the binary coding system (1 = criterion positively, 0 = criterion negatively). If a unique valuation is not possible, the value 0.5 is used. If a criterion is defined by different sub-criteria, each sub-criterion will be coded in the binary coding system as well. At the end, all the sub-criteria will be summarized by calculating the simple mean. A corresponding method is used for the combined index, which summarizes all the criteria.

4 List and Evaluation of Criteria

4.1 Obtainment of Payments

The three business models differ about the regularity and security of sales and incoming payments [2]. From the publisher and developer perspective, it must be assumed that regular revenues are to be preferred to one-off payments, as these guarantee stable long-term earnings and therefore, a high degree of planning security and calculability. Most critically for developers and publishers would be if they were not able to estimate the gain of financial backflows at all, which are described in the F2P model.

In the B2P model, only one-off revenues are generated, there is no possibility of current income (valuation = 0). Although the payment covers the costs, before the revenues can be achieved, the developers bear high financial risks with the production costs [19]. The P2P model, on the other hand, can generate relatively secure regular revenues, which are able to cover the occurring costs over time (e.g. for servers, updates etc.) (valuation = 1) [23]. With the F2P model, neither one-off nor current revenues are guaranteed. However, the F2P model attracts a relatively large number of customers, of whom a certain proportion (depending on the conversation rate between 1% and 5% [7, 12]) also generates follow-up sales. In this respect, regular revenues can be assumed, albeit at a lower level and with less certainty than with the P2P model. Therefore, the F2P model is rated at 0.5.

4.2 Customer Data

In general, in case video gamers consume a video game, they create an amount of user information. For this reason, the evaluation of the considered criterion includes the valuation if the created user information are linked to a personal account for the video game and the necessity to create such a user account.

A player account is required for online video games. Similarly, a customer account will usually be required when purchasing a video game online, whereby a distinction must be made here between whether the customer (a) buys the game directly from the publisher or via (b) an (intermediary) dealer, in the latter case the publisher should not have access to the customer account data [8]. After all, when buying from a stationary retailer (in conjunction with the B2P model), no customer account or individual data is usually required. From the point of view of game developers and publishers, a player account has the following advantages. Firstly, the customer provides personal information such as email address, name, date of birth, and payment information.

Secondly, publishers can track the purchases and, in some cases, the gaming activities of their registered customers. This means that publishers usually have extensive information about their (registered) customers and can use this data for cross-selling activities. Finally, it is also possible to use the customer data for advertising purposes by selling it to third parties.

When selling B2P video games, there is usually no need to register or set up a user account. In this respect, publishers do not have any customer data (apart from buying via publishers' own digital distribution platforms), so the B2P model is valued at 0. However, in case the full price video game titles are sold through a digital platform, a user account and the distribution of personal information would be necessary. Although the customers could choose, which purchasing platform they use, more and more developers and publishers implement the requirement to activate the purchased game via a digital platform. For this reason, the prevention to use a personal account cannot be completely achieved. Nonetheless, the B2P model with purchases of full price titles enables a greater liberty than the two other considered business models.

In contrast, the purchase or use of video games based on the P2P or F2P model generally requires the registration and creation of a customer account. This results in extensive cross-selling options. In this respect, P2P and F2P models will be valued at 1.

4.3 Compulsory Permanent Internet Connection

The compulsory permanent internet connection criterion is closely related to the previously discussed customer data criterion. From the publishers' point of view, it is generally desirable that a game can only be used with a permanent login and a permanent online connection. The reasons for this are, (a) that software piracy can be better prevented in this way (with software keys), (b) that more easily additional content can be automatically provided, and in particular (c) that individual gaming behavior can be recorded, and user profiles created. On this base, customers can be offered highly personalized additional offers.

With the paid subscription (P2P), video players must be permanently registered in the video game system in order to be able to use the respective video game. In this respect, the P2P model is rated 1. Likewise, a permanent login is usually a prerequisite for the use of the game with F2P, so that this is also rated as 1. This conclusion can be naturally drawn, due to P2P and F2P business models are most likely implemented in online multiplayer games. In contrast, most video games purchased based on the B2P model do not necessarily require a permanent Internet connection. In this respect, this model is rated 0.

4.4 In-game Shop

It has already been discussed that publishers can use in-game shops for the distribution of additional functional content and/or optical game elements, which can be purchased using so-called micro-transactions, and (depending on the selected business model) represent the main source of revenues (F2P), or should generate additional revenues (B2P/P2P) [2]. The main motivation for the purchase of such additional functions/elements is (from the user's point of view) to increase the gaming experience or to improve one's own gaming result.

Although most video players generally refuse to reach the goal of the game faster through "buyable" game advantages ("Pay to Win"), in fact many users still spend money to achieve exactly such advantages. Nonetheless, users also spend financial resources to gain access to further cosmetic designs as well as further game mechanics. Since the revenues, which can be generated in this way, are to be valued higher from the publishers' point of view than the principled rejection by most players [3]. In addition, the costs for setting up and operating such an in-game shop are usually much lower than the expected sales. For F2P video games, an in-game shop is obligatory, as this is the only way to handle the (micro-)transactions that are economically necessary. In this respect, the F2P model is valued at 1. The B2P and P2P business models are generally financed by one-off payments or subscriptions and therefore do not necessarily require an in-game shop. However, even in these business models, additional features are increasingly being offered via in-game shops, especially when multiplayer games are involved. These two models are therefore rated 0.5 each.

4.5 Ongoing Costs

The economic life of a video game depends primarily on how long it makes economic sense for game developers and publishers to maintain the operation and (further) development of the game in question. This means how long the expected revenues will exceed the corresponding costs. In a single-player video game, there is no "real" economic lifespan, as such a game could usually be played on almost "indefinitely". Here, the lack of updates and improvements and the lack of adaptation to new operating systems will lead to a "creeping" decline in game usage.

The evaluation of long-term orientation is based on three sub-criteria: (a) provision of servers for continuous gaming, (b) provision of patches, and (c) provision of further content, which all cause corresponding costs. Nonetheless, the keeping of connectivity and the provision of content and patches mainly induce that video gamers stay longer on the game [15]. With the P2P business model, customers pay monthly for game usage. This means that these games have to be provided by the server constantly and trouble-free, and possible problems or errors have to be solved in the shortest possible time. However, customers expect the games to remain attractive over a longer period through further continuous development of the game content. In this respect, the P2P model incurs relatively high costs for all three sub-criteria, which leads to a rating of 0 for all sub-criteria.

Table 1. Evaluation of the long-term orientation criterion

Criteria	B2P	P2P	F2P
Server availability	1	0	0
Provision of patches	0.5	0	0.5
Provision of content	0.5	0	0.5
Sum	2	0	1
Mean	0.67	0	0.33

Also with the F2P model, the constant availability of the games (on the servers) is the prerequisite for the game to be able to be used and, in particular, for the customers to be able to buy additional elements in the in game shop, which is the economic basis for this business model. In this respect, there are relatively high costs for the permanent server availability, so that this sub-criterion must be evaluated with the value 0. Since the users of the F2P model (in contrast to the P2P model) do not pay fixed (monthly) prices, the customer expectations and the resulting expenses for the operators with regard to the two sub-criteria provision of patches and provision of further content are significantly lower (than in the P2P model) and therefore have to be valued at 0.5. In the B2P model, the game can usually be played independently of a (permanent) server connection. In this respect, this sub-criterion is rated 1. However, it makes sense for customer satisfaction that errors are corrected by patches and that the content is regularly further developed, resulting in a certain amount of effort. Therefore, these two sub-criteria are evaluated with the value 0.5. The results are presented in Table 1.

4.6 Advertisement

In principle, it is also possible to generate additional revenues with advertising in video games and thus improve the profitability of such games [25]. The advantages of such additional revenues must be weighed against possible disadvantages, such as acceptance problems on the part of users. There is a risk that such advertising may disrupt the game flow and intensity in the perception of players. This means that ads should be used and placed very carefully. In other words, the central question is which business models such advertising (which is fundamentally economically desirable from the provider's point of view) is most likely to be accepted by customers and thus does not lead to negative effects in terms of game usage.

In the F2P model, it is known that users do not pay one-off or regular user charges. This means that in this model the customers will probably have a relatively high acceptance for advertising and in this model the providers are also most dependent on advertising revenues. In this respect, this model is rated 1. In contrast, users in the other models (B2P & P2P) pay one-off or current prices. This means that customer acceptance of advertising is likely to be significantly lower (than with the F2P model). Moreover, with these models' publishers are less dependent on advertising revenues, which such additional revenues are of course desirable. These two models are therefore rated 0.5 each.

5 Conclusion

Regarding Table 2, the rating for all the three business models is presented. The F2P business model achieves the highest-ranking value from publisher point of view. Although this model does not guarantee fixed financial returns, the possibilities outweigh (a) to generate additional revenues in in-game shops, (b) to place successfully advertising due to relatively high advertising acceptance, (c) to reach quickly high customer numbers due to low customer access barriers, and (d) to obtain relatively comprehensive customer information. The fact that this business model seems to be the most advantageous is also underlined by the fact that more and more multiplayer video games are changing their business model towards F2P. In contrast, traditional business models achieve lower valuations. The B2P model appears to be the most unattractive overall, which is not surprising, as B2P video games have high development costs without (with a high probability) recurring revenues. The main problem with P2P video games is the relatively high running costs and limited revenue potential. The F2P business model is therefore the most recent of the business models considered. Because more and more players are willing to shop on in-game marketplaces, it is to be expected that more and more video games will be offered based on the F2P model (with an in-game shop). Furthermore, it needs to be determined that the F2P model guarantees that publishers avoid a possible price competition with other enterprises in the market, and customers can use a game without spending money.

Table 2. Evaluation of the criteria

Criteria	B2P	P2P	F2P
Obtainment of payments	0	1	0.5
Customer data	0	1	1
Compulsory permanent internet connection	0	1	1
In-game shop	0.5	0.5	1
Ongoing costs	0.67	0	0.33
Advertisement	0.5	0.5	1
Sum	1.67	4	4.83
Mean value	0.28	0.67	0.81

Although the model is unreasonable from an economical perspective at first glance, more and more publishers choose to combine the traditional business models B2P (one purchase) and P2P (subscription purchase) with an in game market place and micro transactions to skim the willingness to pay of the video game users. On this base, it can be underlined that video games with a F2P model are able to survive in the market. To exploit the willingness to pay and to yield further revenues by low implementation costs of an in game shop, publishers and developers are shifting to hybrid business models. The current analysis supports the raison d'être of the F2P business model and displays the benefits of an implementation in combination with other business models.

References

1. Bit-Museum: Level 1: Bits aus der Anfangsphase (2010). http://www.8bit-museum.de. Accessed 09 Nov 2019
2. Anderie, L.: Games Industry Management. Springer, Heidelberg (2016). https://doi.org/10.1007/978-3-662-49425-7
3. BIU – Bundesverband Interaktive Unterhaltungssoftware e.V.: Jahresreport der Computer- und Videospielbranche in Deutschland (2017). https://www.vau.net/system/files/documents/biu_jahresreport_2017_interaktiv.pdf. Accessed 09 Nov 2019
4. Castendyk, O., Müller-Lietzkow, J.: Studie zur Computer- und Videospielindustrie in Deutschland. Daten und Fakten zum deutschen Entwicklungs- und Vertriebsmarkt für digitale Spiele (2017). https://projektzukunft.berlin.de/fileadmin/user_upload/pdf/studien/Bundesweite_Studie_Computer-_und_Videospieleindustrie_HMS.pdf. Accessed 09 Nov 2019
5. Clais, J-B., Dubois, P.: Game story. Une histoire de jeu vidéo, Paris (2011)

6. Feijoo, C., Gómez-Barroso, J.-L., Aguado, J.-M., Ramos, S.: Mobile gaming: industry challenges and policy implications. Telecommun. Policy **36**(3), 212–221 (2012)
7. Flunger, R., Mladenow, A., Strauss, C.: The free-to-play business model. In: Indrawan-Santiago, M. (Ed.) Proceedings of the 19th International Conference on Information Integration and Web-based Applications & Services, pp. 373–379 (2017)
8. Game – Verband der deutschen Games-Branche e.V.: Vier von zehn Games werden als Download gekauft (2018). https://www.game.de/blog/2018/04/16/vier-von-zehn-games-werden-als-download-gekauft/. Accessed 09 Nov 2019
9. González-Piñero, M.: Redefining the value chain of the video game industry. Knowledge Works National Centre for cultural industries, pp. 6–60 (2017). https://kunnskapsverket.org/sites/default/files/Redefining%20the%20Value%20Chain%20of%20Video%20Games%20Industry%202017_final.pdf. Accessed 09 Nov 2019
10. Hodge, V.J., et al.: How the Business Model of Customisable Card Games Influences Player Engagement. IEEE Xplore Digital Library (2018)
11. Kelly, C., Mishra, B., Jequinto, J.: The Pulse of Gaming – Gaming Disruption. Accenture, pp 1–18 (2018). https://www.accenture.com/us-en/~/media/Accenture/Conversion-Assets/LandingPage/Documents/3/Accenture-3-LT-10-Pulse-Gaming-Disruption.pdf. Accessed 09 Nov 2019
12. Koch, O.F., Benlian, A.: The effect of free sampling strategies on freemium conversion rates. Electron. Mark. **27**(1), 67–76 (2017)
13. Lago Moneo, J. A.: El Mercado de Videojuegos 2014. EAE Business School. https://de.slideshare.net/daoletrang/eae-business-school-el-mercado-de-videojuegos-2014-45069001. Accessed 09 Nov 2019
14. Leimeister, J.M.: Einführung in die Wirtschaftsinformatik. Springer, Heidelberg (2015). https://doi.org/10.1007/978-3-540-77847-9
15. Linnemeijer, I., van Goor, E.: Gaming in the Netherlands – virtual goods in video games: a business model with prospects. PricewaterhouseCoopers, pp. 2–15 (2013). https://www.kidsenjongeren.nl/wp-content/uploads/2012/09/pwc-gaming-in-the-netherlands.pdf. Accessed 09 Nov 2019
16. MacInnes, I., Moneta, J., Caraballo, J., Sarni, D.: Business models for mobile content: the case of m-games. Electron. Mark. **12**(4), 218–227 (2002)
17. Newzoo: 2017 Free Global games Market Report. http://progamedev.net/wp-content/uploads/2017/06/Newzoo_Global_Games_Market_Report_2017_Light.pdf. Accessed 09 Nov 2019
18. Olbrich, R., Battenfeld, D.: Preispolitik. S. Springer, Heidelberg (2014). https://doi.org/10.1007/978-3-642-37947-5
19. Polygon: The State of Games: State of AAA. In part one of a five-part series, Polygon evaluates the state of the blockbuster "AAA" game development industry (2012). https://www.polygon.com/2012/10/1/3439738/the-state-of-games-state-of-aaa. Accessed 09 Nov 2019
20. Rodríguez, E.: Jóvenes y videojuegos. Espacio, significación y conflictos. FAD –Injuve, Madrid (2002)
21. Soh, J., Tan, B.: Mobile gaming. Commun. ACM **51**(3), 35–39 (2008)
22. Tejeiro, R., Pelegrino, M.: Los videojuegos. Qué son y cómo nos afectan, Barcelona (2003)
23. Vanhatupa, J.-M.: Business Model of Long-Term Browser-Based Games – Income Without Game Packages. IEEE Xplore Digital Library (2011)
24. Wijman, T.: Newzoo's 2018 Report: Insights Into the $137.9 Billion Global Games Market. https://newzoo.com/insights/articles/newzoos-2018-report-insights-into-the-137-9-billion-global-games-market/. Accessed 09 Nov 2019

25. Williamson Smith, M.: Game advertising. A conceptual framework and exploration of advertising prevalence. Comput. Games J. **3**(1), 95–124 (2014)
26. Wirtz, B.W.: Medien-und Internetmanagement, 9th edn. Springer, Wiesbaden (2016)
27. Wolters, O.: Elektronische Spiele: Wachstumsmarkt mit großer Wertschöpfung. In: Picot, A., Zahedani, S., Ziemer, A. (eds.) Spielend die Zukunft gewinnen. Springer, Berlin (2008). https://doi.org/10.1007/978-3-540-78717-4_3

Cultural Heritage, Serious Games and User Personas Based on Gardner's Theory of Multiple Intelligences: "The Stolen Painting" Game

Markos Konstantakis[1,2](✉), Eirini Kalatha[1,2], and George Caridakis[1,2]

[1] Department of Cultural Technology and Communication, University of the Aegean, Mytilene, Greece
{mkonstadakis, ekalatha, gcari}@aegean.gr
[2] Intelligent Interaction Research Group, Mytilene, Greece

Abstract. The main feature of a Serious Game (SG) is its objective of supporting the player to achieve learning targets through a fun experience. The paper focuses on the creation of a digital cultural SG, named "The stolen painting". The main goal of this game is to initiate users into art painting, through game activities that encourage the users to learn about some of the most famous paintings in the world and their creators. The theory of Gardner's Multiple Intelligences (MI) is used for game profile identification through social media data mining techniques, or alternatively, through Multiple Intelligences Profiling Questionnaire (MIPQ) in order to reveal and quantify the different types of intellectual strengths (intelligences) that each user exhibits. Game's progress is based on the three strongest intelligences of the player and the main objective of the player is to reveal the stolen painting's identity.

Keywords: Multiple Intelligences · Serious games · User personas · Cultural heritage

1 Introduction

Over the last few years, SGs have been widely adopted in the CH field [17] as a new and promising tool to promote cultural education in an engaging way [16]. The fact that SGs combine aspects of learning with the playfulness of video games [2] and maximize user's motivation, increase their popularity, even in public that may not be familiar with the arts and culture [5].

One of the main advantages of SGs is that motivates the user to activate and extend his/her knowledge, by transforming him/her from a passive data receiver to an actor [10] who plays, explores, makes mistakes and, also, his/her own choices [3].

Personalized SGs can promote motivated usage, increased user acceptance, and user identification [21]. Personalized learning games could offer all players-learners the possibility to learn in a motivating manner, due to the fact that these games take into account that each person prefers different learning styles.

A. Liapis et al. (Eds.): GALA 2019, LNCS 11899, pp. 490–500, 2019.
https://doi.org/10.1007/978-3-030-34350-7_47

Although personalization in cultural heritage is useful, creating correct visitor profiles is a rather demanding task basically due to the short duration of most visits and the fact that most visitors might only visit a specific institution only once. Within these time restrictions, visitor profiles need to be created quickly and effectively in terms of their appropriateness for the different visitors. The problem is that although visitors enjoy the benefits of personalization in cultural heritage, they are at the same time reluctant at dealing with form-filling activities and researchers have to become more creative in applying indirect approaches for the collection of the needed information for the creation of user profiles. The question of how to start creating these profiles and where to find the necessary information is studied on our current analysis thus, we assume that User personas is one of the most complete user analysis methodology. User Personas is one of the most established methods of personalization and profiling of users. It allows for an initial categorization of the user to a certain Persona, which has specific needs and expectations from the Game (and consequently from the platform) [12].

Sajjadi [19, 20] explored individual differences among players from a more pedagogical perspective, including learning styles and intelligence, based on his work on the theory of "Multiple Intelligences (MI)" [7]. Sajjadi argued that exploiting the potential relation between multiple intelligences and game constructs could prove to be important in personalized or player-centered game design.

Therefore, Gardner's theory of MI, that is considered as one of the key discoveries of educational psychology of the late 20th century, could be exploited in the concept of game personalization in order to help the user to learn easily. Specifically, the theory of MI draws a framework for defining individual differences between people in terms of their intelligences.

According to Gardner, intelligence is "*the ability to solve problems, or to create products, that are valued within one or more cultural settings*". The profiles of intelligence and their basic description defined by the MI Gardner's theory are:

- ***Verbal/linguistic*** – represents the primary means of communication amongst humans. It is reflected in symbolic thinking, language, reading, writing. An individual with strong verbal/linguistic intelligence learns better by speaking, listening and seeing the words, writing, reading;
- ***Logical/mathematical*** – is used for data processing, pattern recognition, working with numbers, geometric shapes. Persons with strong logical/mathematical intelligence learn better by playing with numbers, collecting and sorting objects, engaging in the function of things and in role-play activities, exploiting the conditional statement "if-then";
- ***Visual/spatial*** – navigation, map making, visual arts, architecture, perspective. Colors, images, maps, and graphs are useful learning tools. More specific, by observing, dream stilling, designing, photographing, assembling, individuals who are in strong visual/spatial intelligence learn better;
- ***Bodily/kinesthetic*** – reflects the precise self-body motion control, non-verbal emotion expression, dance, fine hand-eye coordination. Individuals with strong bodily/kinesthetic intelligence learn better when they can move around and engage their small and large muscle groups, by touching and interacting in a place;

- ***Musical/rhythmic*** – recognition and use of rhythmic and tonal patterns, recognition of sound, speech and musical instruments. It is used to interpret and create music. By exploiting all these "tools", people with strong musical/rhythmic intelligence manage to learn easily;
- ***Natural*** – recognizing patterns in nature, classification of objects and types of wildlife;
- ***Interpersonal*** – the possibility of cooperation in small groups, communication with other people, a person's ability to recognize other people's intentions, moods, motivation, non-verbal signs;
- ***Intrapersonal*** – recognizing one's own abilities, capacities, feelings and emotional reactions, self-reflection, and intuition. Through teamwork, games or by comparing and correlating, facilitated learning for individuals with strong intrapersonal intelligence.

As stated by [15], everyone possesses every intelligence but to different degrees. All dimensions work together in an orchestrated way.

2 Related Work

Research on MI and SG in CH is rather scarce. The studies focused on MI and SG in CH can be divided into two groups: the first group, are studies and projects that discussed possible connections between SG and CH, while the second group contains studies that focus on multiple intelligences by playing SG [19].

In the first group, the "Gossip at palace" is a location-based mobile game with a storytelling approach and offers contextual information to the visitors in order to help them discover characters, traditions, and events that characterized the palace in the 18th century [18]. This approach can be particularly intuitive and helps users easily connect the cultural contents with the physical context of the museum.

In the ViaAppia SG application, users are able to explore the notion of narrative movement and travel across space and time due to the fact that, in the context of the game, 1 km of the Via Appia Antica was reconstructed in three time periods (320 CE, 71 BCE, and 49 BCE) [13].

Furthermore, in ARCO project, an AR cultural heritage game, that was based on a historical and archaeological context, was developed and evaluated [22]. The main goal of the game was to test the user's ability to discover information about Fishbourne Roman Palace, UK, and its archaeological artifacts by answering related questions.

The second group of studies consists of works that have focused on the development of players' intelligences through SG. For instance, [9] provide an overview of several educational games that can aid the development of a player's logical-mathematical intelligence. Similarly, [4] have claimed that games can be used as a tool to enhance players' intelligence dimensions and learning outcomes, specifically in relation to visual-spatial, logical-mathematical, bodily-kinesthetic, linguistic and interpersonal intelligences. Also, [16] provides an extensive portrait of the current proposition of SG in the cultural sector, highlighting the educational objectives of games in this domain and analysing the complex relations between genre, context of use, technological solutions and learning effectiveness. Finally, [6] is the online serious game ThIATRO that immerses the player into an exhibition and helps students learn about art history. Its playful approach not only increases motivation to learn but also raises interest in art history and cultural heritage in general.

3 SG Scenario and Architecture

"The stolen painting" is designed for everyone who wants to combine fun with learning. The user can play the game in a mobile device (smartphone, tablet) and after his/her login, he/she is able to choose the personalization method that he/she prefers. The user can choose which of the two modes will use to start playing the game. It is true that by answering the questionnaire, he/she would devote enough time, as the number of questions is relatively large (31 questions) and the process is relatively time consuming. The system, however, store the data of the questionnaire and the related result, so the user can immediately start the game every next time. The alternative of social media data is definitely less time consuming that leads to the conclusion that maybe consist a better option in cases that the user will use the system only one time or has limited time [23, 24]. Further system's evaluation by a larger sample of users is required, in order to substantiate whether both alternatives give the same result or the degree of divergence they may have. This consists one of our future goals we have set.

Personalized user experience acquires profiled data which can be found from various repositories (mobile device, social media). Due to the complexity and diversity of the multiple data sources, data mining techniques and natural language recognition are required to retrieve the profiled data of a user for a game that supports MI, data that will need to be modelled and reasoned. The abundance of social media user input and the subsequent opinion mining on it will allow a better user classification and overall the fusion of heterogeneous data streams will associate the user with a personalized way, allowing a better understanding of the user's needs and goals. Sentiment analysis will be performed on the profiled and behavioral data, extracting usable information about the user profile.

The Questionnaire will ask the player to rate 31 statements on a scale of 1 to 5 to measure the eight MI dimensions. Each dimension will be measured using four questions, except for the naturalist intelligence dimension that will be measured by three questions. After the system quantify the different types of intellectual strengths (intelligences) that each user exhibits, the game is adapted based on the three strongest intelligences of the player. For instance, if the three strongest intelligences of a user are linguistic, visual/spatial and musical intelligence, mini games based on the above intelligences will be played by the user in order to find the missing pieces of the stolen painting.

Therefore, the "Stolen Painting" is a proposed SG platform that intends to combine established and emerging technologies into an ecosystem with elements of cultural heritage through multiple intelligences. The architecture of the "Stolen Painting" platform is depicted in Fig. 1. There are 4 modules that are connected to the Code module of the platform, each one involving a couple of components.

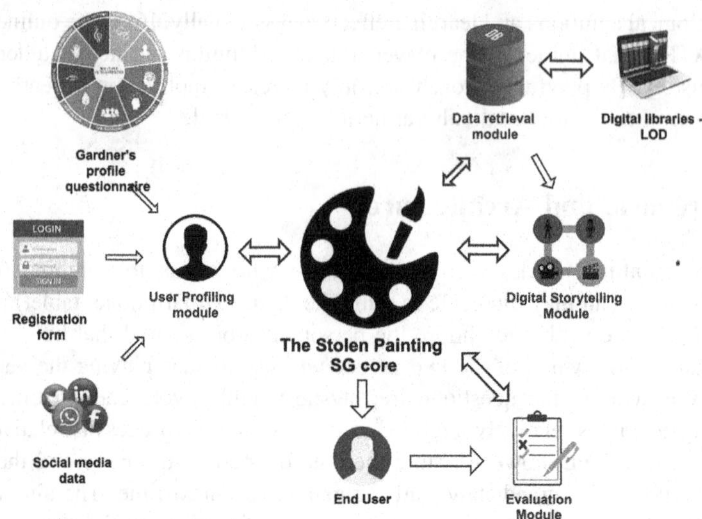

Fig. 1. The Stolen Painting SG core architecture

User Profiling Module: The first module involves the necessary steps to initialize the platform, consisting of the main components of the User Persona Identification through Gardner's MI Questionnaire, the Registration Component and the Social media data component. Both receive data from the users, to accordingly adapt the initial personalization of the SG. At first, the personalization procedure is refined with the use of registration data from the user, which is processed and analyzed into higher level of information concerning the user. The first section of the module contains six questions that inquire about the demographic information of the participants (gender, age range, and level of education), as well as their game-related background information (frequency of gaming, experience with different game platforms or devices, preferred game genres). This information would enable us to determine the heterogeneity of the sample, as well as investigating the effect of personal and contextual factors such as age, education and prior experiences. The next step includes the data acquisition from profiled data derived from mobile devices and social media that allow a refinement of the associated user persona. An alternative solution for the user's clustering procedure (when the participants anticipate privacy risks for the data generated in game playing) is the use of the MIPQ Questionnaire in order to reveal and quantify the different types of intellectual strengths (intelligences) that each user exhibits.

Overall, the user profiling module provides a setup for the platform to know where to start from, eliminating the cold-start issue, which characterizes situations when the system lacks any information about the user and thus cannot offer any personalization but relies on default settings [12].

Data Retrieval Module**:** After user profiling, the platform has to select the game data that will accompany the game types that are appropriate for the persona of the user. Most of the data will be stored in the game Database, while the rich resources of the Linked Open Data Cloud (LOD) will be exploited as well. Linking to such data repositories (e.g. Europeana) will allow for further enrichment of the multimedia content of the game, also addressing the issue of dynamic update of game content from external sources.

Digital Storytelling Module: Closely related to the previous module, the third one continues the process of game data presentation. Game data may include textual, visual (images, videos) and audio materials of actors, objects or events related to CH field. Digital storytelling represents an evolution of traditional storytelling, for the technical means used for the creation and the delivery of the story, the introduction of new narrative models and the enhancement of the relations between user, narration and context [14].

Evaluation Module: The final module is responsible to evaluate the user experience of the SG platform. Users will be prompted to express their opinion about the game, its mechanics, the content and whether the platform has helped towards a better engagement with cultural heritage elements. The evaluation metrics will be stored and analyzed in order to improve the platform's behavior. The evaluation methods will include a mobile questionnaire, focus groups techniques, combined with other CH evaluation methodologies.

3.1 Technologies

New ways of cultural expression are being developed through modern technology, while new tools for creating cultural products are emerging. At the same time, new, more effective methods of protecting cultural heritage are emerging and innovative practices are created to promote its global visibility.

Linked Open Data: Linked Open Data (LOD) Cloud uses the infrastructure of the World Wide Web to publish and link datasets that can then be examined and processed by applications accessing them, while also these datasets are continuously updated and linked with new assets. Linked Data is one of the most practical parts of the Semantic Web, as it is a model for representing and accessing data that are flexible enough to allow adding or changing sources of data, to link with other databases and data and to process the information according to its meaning.

In the context of "The Lost Painting", LOD aim to enrich the content of the game and improve user experience. The conceptualization of user personas and game data can organize and correlate the information included in different game types of the platform. Moreover, the initial game datasets can be matched with external resources which are similarly related. By expanding the game possibilities with the use of cultural LOD, the user will be able to explore and learn historic, artistic, geographical etc. Information in a playful way. Eventually, cultural multimedia and textual content displayed on "The Lost Painting" will be dynamically updated, since the connected resources perpetually store and provide new data [1].

Digital Storytelling: Handler Miller [14] defines digital storytelling as the use of digital media platforms and interactivity for narrative purposes, either for fictional or for non-fiction stories. Storytelling or the use of narrative elements can be found in many games [8]. On a theoretical level, it incorporates a pre-designed story, but also includes integration of the player and enables freedom of interaction during the action. Interactive stories may create a connection to the storyline for the user by making their own decisions and completing quests and can make them curious about further progress for more than one session.

User Experience Evaluation: The evaluation of the SGs visitors' experience is a crucial part, since it will determine the outcome of this research and validate the research objectives. There are various evaluation methods available for cultural heritage SG, such as formative evaluation, summative evaluation, and front-end evaluation. The choice of methodology to be used in the current SG is based on the scope and aspects of the research itself. In addition, the choice of methodology used must also be in accordance with the components that will be evaluated [11, 12].

4 SG Prototype and Use Case Scenario

We created a prototype that incorporates the basic concepts of our framework, helping us in the constant evaluation of its development. The use case scenario that was tested, is described in the screenshots below (Figs. 2 and 3):

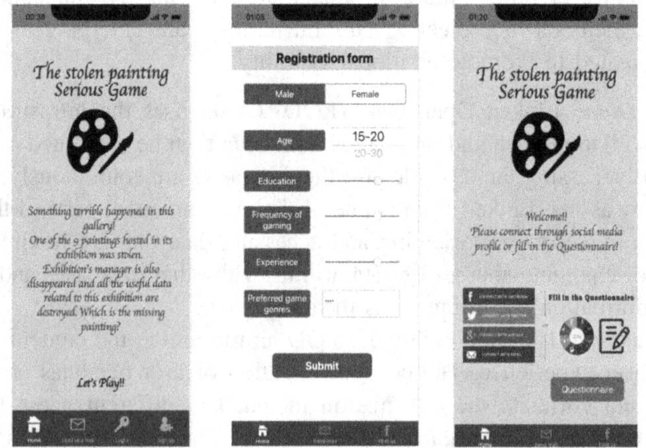

Fig. 2. The Stolen Painting SG login screenshots

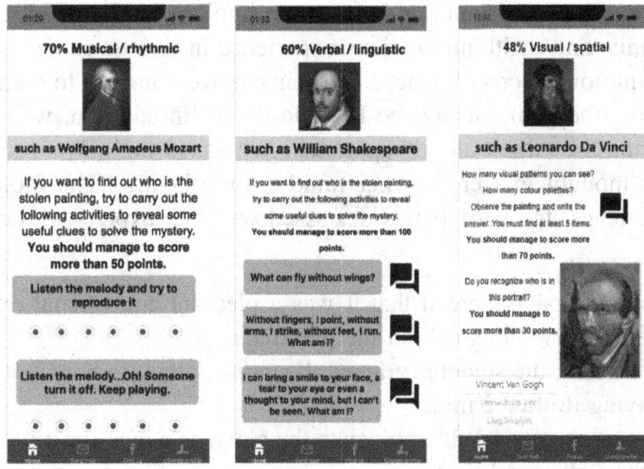

Fig. 3. The Stolen Painting SG MI tasks screenshots

This prototype is a mobile application that implements examples of the mini games and evaluates the validity and the efficiency of the technologies, by using the Proto.io[1] development tool (Fig. 4).

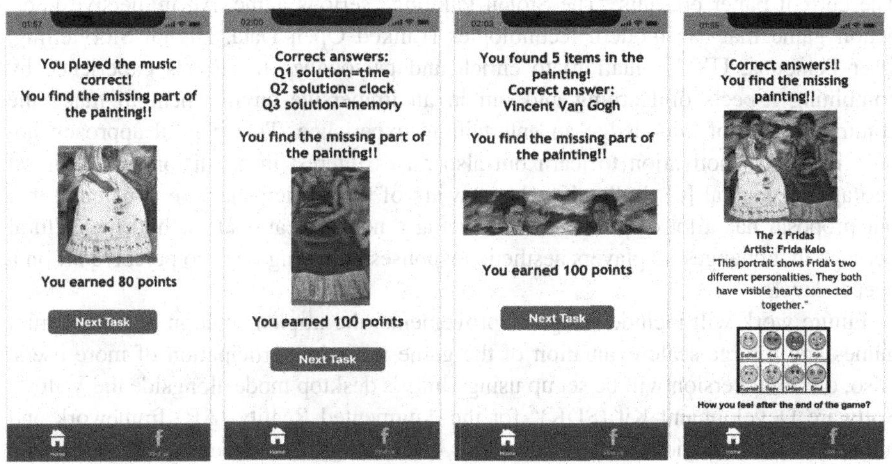

Fig. 4. The Stolen Painting SG MI tasks solutions screenshots

Evaluation

In this section, we present the results from the test of the usability and effectiveness of our prototype and evaluate the feedback received from the testing users based on the

[1] https://proto.io/.

answers to our questionnaire and the focus group implementation. 20 users were from outside of the university, with no previous experience in serious games but all of them were familiar with touch screen devices. Participants were invited to complete a series of tasks regarding the game, using the Proto.io demo. In addition, we organized test sessions following the "think-aloud" approach. We asked the players to immediately verbalize every thought that crosses her mind while playing "The Stolen Painting". After their experience, the participants discussed with our experts who concluded the following:

- Most of the participants agreed that it was a pleasant educational experience and that they learned new things about the paintings,
- On a scale of 1 to 5, the students granted the game with 4 on how it attracts them to continue playing it after 2 min.
- Most of the participants would appreciate the game as a massive multiplayer online experience through social data login.
- Some of the players found the tasks very easy and suggested to have a longer version, adding tasks not strictly related to educational content and including rewards.
- Users also argue about the importance of the guidelines provided during the experiment to perform the tasks needed.

Conclusion

The current paper presents "The Stolen Painting" serious game. An immersive interaction game that use modern technologies (Linked Open Data, Digital Storytelling, User Personas, UX Evaluation) to enrich and personalize the user's experience by combining aspects of learning and fun in an immersive environment to make the communication of knowledge an entertaining experience. This playful approach not only increases motivation to learn but also raises interest in art history and cultural heritage in general [6]. Following the answers of the participants, we concluded that our proposal has a lot of potential introducing a new educational method for cultural heritage that changes its players aesthetic responses, allowing them to perceive art on a deeper level.

Future work will include design improvements, the implementation of further mini games and a large-scale evaluation of the game with the participation of more users. Also, our final version will be set up using Unity's desktop mode alongside the Vuforia Software Development Kit (SDK)[2] for the Augmented Reality (AR) framework and immersive technologies, such as Bluetooth Low Energy (BLE) beacons (interior) and GPS (exterior) based context-aware architecture, AR UI with head-mounted display (for example a Google Cardboard) and narrative based serious game using digital storytelling techniques through social data mining procedures.

Acknowledgments. The research and writing of this paper were financially supported by the General Secretariat for Research and Technology (GSRT).

[2] https://developer.vuforia.com/downloads/sdk.

References

1. Aliprantis, J., Kalatha, E., Konstantakis, M., Michalakis, K., Caridakis, G.: Linked open data as universal markers for mobile augmented reality applications in cultural heritage. In: Ioannides, M. (ed.) Digital Cultural Heritage. LNCS, vol. 10605, pp. 79–90. Springer, Cham (2018). https://doi.org/10.1007/978-3-319-75826-8_7
2. Alvarez, J., Rampnoux, O., Jessel, J.P., Methel, G.: Serious game: just a question of posture. Artif. Ambient Intell. AISB **7**, 420–423 (2007)
3. Anolli, L., Mantovani, F., Confalonieri, L., Ascolese, A., Peveri, L.: Emotions in serious games: from experience to assessment. Int. J. Emerg. Technol. Learn. (iJET) **5** (2010)
4. Chuang, T., Sheng-Hsiung, S.: Using mobile console games for multiple intelligences and education. Int. J. Mob. Learn. Organ. **6**(3–4), 204–217 (2012)
5. Foni, A.E., Papagiannakis, G., Magnenat-Thalmann, N.: A taxonomy of visualization strategies for cultural heritage applications. J. Comput. Cult. Herit. (JOCCH) **3**(1), 1 (2010)
6. Froschauer, J., Arends, M., Goldfarb, D., Merkl, D.: A serious heritage game for art history: design and evaluation of ThIATRO. In: 2012 18th International Conference on Virtual Systems and Multimedia (2012)
7. Gardner, H.E.: Multiple Intelligences: The Theory in Practice. Basic Books, New York (1993)
8. Jenkins, H.: Game design as narrative architecture. In: First Person: New Media as Story, Performance, and Game, pp. 118–130. MIT Press, Cambridge (2004)
9. Li, J., Ma, S., Ma, L.: The study on the effect of educational games for the development of students' logic-mathematics of multiple intelligence. Phys. Proc. **33**, 1749–1752 (2012)
10. Kalatha, E., Aliprantis, J., Konstantakis, M., Michalakis, K., Moraitou, T., Caridakis, G.: Cultural heritage engagement via serious games: the ARCADE augmented reality, context-aware, linked open data personalized ecosystem. In: 1st International Conference On Cultural Informatics, Communication and Media Studies (CICMS 2018), 3–4 May, Kuşadası, Turkey (2018)
11. Konstantakis, M., Michalakis, K., Aliprantis, J., Kalatha, E., Caridakis, G..: Formalizing and evaluating cultural user experience. In: SMAP Special Session Personalized Delivery of Cultural Heritage Content (2017)
12. Konstantakis, M., Aliprantis, J., Michalakis, K., Caridakis, G..: Recommending user experiences based on extracted cultural personas for mobile applications-REPEAT methodology. In: Mobile HCI (2018)
13. Liestøl, G.: Along the appian way. Storytelling and memory across time and space in mobile augmented reality. In: Ioannides, M., Magnenat-Thalmann, N., Fink, E., Žarnić, R., Yen, A.-Y., Quak, E. (eds.) EuroMed 2014. LNCS, vol. 8740, pp. 248–257. Springer, Cham (2014). https://doi.org/10.1007/978-3-319-13695-0_24
14. Miller, C.: Digital Storytelling: A Creator's Guide to Interactive Entertainment. Focal Press, Waltham (2004)
15. Moran, S., Kornhaber, M., Gardner, H.: Orchestrating multiple intelligences. Educ. Leadersh. **64**(1), 22–27 (2006)
16. Mortara, M., Catalano, C.E., Bellotti, F., Fiucci, G., Houry-Panchetti, M., Petridis, P.: Learning cultural heritage by serious games. J. Cult. Herit. **15**(3), 318–325 (2014)
17. Paliokas, I., Sylaiou, S.: The use of serious games in museum visits and exhibitions: a systematic mapping study. In: 2016 8th International Conference on Games and Virtual Worlds for Serious Applications (VS-Games), pp. 1–8. IEEE (2016)

18. Rubino, I., Barberis, C., Xhembulla, J., Malnati, G.: Integrating a location-based mobile game in the museum visit: evaluating visitors' behavior and learning. J. Comput. Cult. Herit. (JOCCH) **8**(3), 15 (2015)
19. Sajjadi, P., Vlieghe, J. De Troyer, O.: Evidence-based mapping between the theory of multiple intelligences and game mechanics for the purpose of player-centered serious game design. In: VS-Games, 8th International Conference on Games and Virtual Worlds for Serious Applications, p. 18. IEEE (2016)
20. Sajjadi, P., Vlieghe, J., De Troyer, O.: Exploring the relation between the theory of multiple intelligences and games for the purpose of player-centred game design. Electron. J. e-Learn. **15**(4), 320–334 (2017)
21. Streicher, A., Smeddinck, J.D.: Personalized and adaptive serious games. In: Dörner, R., Göbel, S., K-R, M., Masuch, M., Zweig, K. (eds.) Entertainment Computing and Serious Games. LNCS, vol. 9970, pp. 332–377. Springer, Cham (2016). https://doi.org/10.1007/978-3-319-46152-6_14
22. Sylaiou, S., et al.: Evaluation of a cultural heritage augmented reality game. Cartographies of Mind, Soul and Knowledge. Special Issue for Prof. em. Myron Myridis, School of Rural and Surveying Engineers. AUTH (2015)
23. Tirri, K., Nokelainen, P.: Identification of multiple intelligences with the multiple intelligence profiling questionnaire III. Psychol. Sci. **50**(2), 206 (2008)
24. Tirri, K., Nokelainen, P.: Multiple Intelligences profiling questionnaire. In: Measuring Multiple Intelligences and Moral Sensitivities in Education, pp. 1–13. Sense Publishers (2011)

Effect of Whole-Body Movement on Performance and Efficiency: A Comparison of Three Controlling Methods for a Math Game

Antero Lindstedt[1](✉) and Kristian Kiili[2]

[1] Information Technology and Communication, Tampere University, Pori, Finland
antero.lindstedt@tuni.fi

[2] Faculty of Education and Culture, Tampere University, Tampere, Finland
kristian.kiili@tuni.fi

Abstract. During the last decade, the number of studies investigating learning effectiveness and motivational aspects of game-based learning has increased. Nevertheless, research that considers the meaning of the User Interface (UI) in game-based learning has been sparse. This paper reports a within-subject study in which we investigated how the implementation of the UI affects students' performance (accuracy), training efficiency (task completion duration), and user experience in a number line based math game. Ninety-three fifth graders played the same math game with three different UIs in a counter balanced order. The results revealed that the implementation of the UI influenced significantly on performance and training efficiency. Students' estimation performance with the chair-based exertion UI (whole-body movement) was significantly worse than with the tilting UI (controlled with hands) and virtual directional pad UI (controlled with fingers). Nevertheless, the players felt that the controlling of the game was equally easy with the gaming chair than with the other two controlling methods. Actually, the majority of the students named the chair as the most preferable controlling method. The results suggest that a whole-body movement can be an engaging and viable controlling method for learning games, but its effects on performance and efficiency should be considered, especially in game-based assessment context.

Keywords: User interface · Human-computer interaction · Whole-body movement · Game-based learning · User experience · Number line estimation

1 Introduction

The introduction of digital games in the field of mathematics education has presented new ways to improve mathematical skills. The games can contain simple drills, similar to pen-and-paper tasks, but also more inventive learning content. For example, Devlin [1] has argued that video games can provide an alternative presentation to the traditional, symbol-based expressions that is easier and more natural to use. According to

A. Liapis et al. (Eds.): GALA 2019, LNCS 11899, pp. 501–511, 2019.
https://doi.org/10.1007/978-3-030-34350-7_48

Moeller and colleagues [2], the latest technological developments have created new possibilities to train mathematical competencies with, for example, digital game-based learning solutions that provide interactive math training or allow the player to solve mathematical tasks in an embodied fashion. Digital games can also offer immediate feedback to the student without the need for the teacher to check the answers. For the teacher, the game could offer data about the students' progress. In fact, digital game-based learning have the potential to support learning assessment (e.g. [3–5]).

1.1 Movement-Based User Interfaces in Games

During the past decade we have witnessed more attempts at using body movement in digital games [6] and exertion interfaces have been utilized also in game-based learning field (e.g. [7]). So-called exergames use player's own physical movement for game controlling. According to Staiano and Calfert [8], this can lead to physical and cognitive development, but also have other benefits by providing opportunities for social interaction. For an educational game, the physical component could help to alleviate cognitive load (embedded cognition) and promote learning by drawing on previous sensorimotor experiences (embodied cognition) [9]. There has also been evidence that exergame interventions in schools can reduce negative classroom behaviors and absenteeism while improving academic performance [10]. Exergames have been implemented using special devices, such as Kinect™ [11] or dance mats [12], but as mobile devices like phones and tablets have become better and more common, their accelerometers have been used to implement embodied number line trainings [3, 13].

It is important to implement controls based on physical movement properly, or otherwise it can distract the players from the actual gameplay [7]. A well-designed UI allows the player to master the game controls and lets the player focus on the game content. This might not be satisfying in itself, but the mastery of controls is necessary for meeting the player's psychological needs [14]. In fact, previous research has argued that the increase of physical movement in games increases positive emotional and social responses [15, 16].

Although the gamification of learning and exertion interfaces have the potential to increase engagement, we should also consider their consequences to other learning dimensions such as learning effectiveness and learning analytics. Game elements that increase enjoyment may in turn make performance less certain. This may be irrelevant in the training context if the learning is not impeded, but could become more problematic if the results are used for assessment (grading) purposes [17]. Kiili and Ketamo [3] considered game-based math test to be a valid and fair assessment approach regarding gender and students' previous gaming experience even though they also found that the performance was significantly worse with a game-based math test than with a paper-and-pencil based test. Game-based assessment in education is relatively new and only a little evidence exists on maximizing the validity and effect of it without losing engagement [18]. Thus, it is important to study how the user interfaces influence on students' performance in game-based learning solutions.

1.2 Present Study and Hypotheses

Despite the increasing interest in utilizing movement in digital games, very little is known how exertion interfaces influence on students' performance and attitudes in game-based learning. The aim of the current study is to shed light on this open question. In order to study the meaning of the user interface, we developed a number line based math game and three different controlling user interfaces: Chair UI (whole body), Tilt UI (hands), and virtual D-pad (directional pad) UI (fingers). In this within-subject study, we compared these user interfaces with respect to the number line estimation accuracy (performance), answering duration (efficiency), and students' opinions about the user interfaces (user experience).

Based on previous research we formed two hypotheses. As large whole body movements are not as precise as smaller hand and finger gestures, we hypothesize that answering accuracy is worse and task completion duration is longer with the Chair UI than with the Tilt and the D-pad UI (Hypothesis 1). Because previous research has shown that when the controller requires increased body movement, the player's engagement level improves [15], we hypothesize that the students will select the chair as the best user interface (Hypothesis 2).

2 Methods

2.1 Participants

A total of 93 fourth graders (age 11–12) from three Finnish schools participated in this study. 50 were male and 43 were female.

2.2 Game-Based Learning Solutions

A mathematics learning game, created using a number line based game engine developed by the researchers, was used in this study (a screenshot in Fig. 1). Using the game engine, three versions of a rational number learning game were built. The games were played on an iPad device and they utilized the device's accelerometer and touch input. The contents of the game were exactly the same with each version, but three different controlling user interfaces were developed:

- *D-pad UI.* The game character was controlled with fingers using an onscreen virtual Directional pad and answering was done with an onscreen button.
- *Tilting UI.* To make the game character move, the tablet had to be tilted by hand movement towards left or right, which made the character walk in that direction. Tapping the screen made the character jump. An onscreen button was used for answering.
- *Chair UI.* This version required a special chair to play (Fig. 1). The player sat on the chair with the tablet device fixed to the chair in front. The player had to lean his/her body towards one of the four directions. Tilting the chair to either side made the character walk towards that direction. Tilting the chair backwards resulted in a jump and tilting forwards was interpreted as an answer. These controls required

upper-body movement, but the exertion applied to legs, arms, and midriff too, even if these parts remained quite stationary.

The game content was divided into levels, each containing 10 tasks. The first task of each level was a tutorial task that provided a soft start for the student, and explained if there was some new game mechanic introduced in the level. The first level had trivial to solve whole number tasks with the correct answer visible. This was used as an onboarding level to measure how fast the player could get acquainted with the controlling method without mathematical competency affecting the results. The game characters' walking distance to the correct answer was the same in each of these tasks. The second level contained basic fraction number tasks. The third level introduced traps, which required additional estimating. The fourth level had enemies that had to be evaded or destroyed by jumping on them. The fifth level and all the levels afterwards mixed the same elements, but increased gradually in difficulty.

Fig. 1. On the left: a screenshot of the game. In this task, the player had to estimate a fraction 1/5 while having to avoid a trap at 3/5. On the right: Students playing with the gaming chair.

2.3 Measures and Analyses

Data was collected using online questionnaires and in-game data storing. All the data was anonymized. The answer accuracy and duration for each task were stored in a database. The player had a maximum of two attempts per task. If the first attempt did not reach 90% or better accuracy, a second attempt was allowed. Some tasks showed additional hints on the second attempt. Therefore, only the accuracy of the first answer was stored. Additionally, the playing sessions were observed by the supervisor.

Statistical analysis was performed in IBM SPSS Statistics, version 25. A one way repeated measures ANOVA was conducted to determine whether there were differences in the accuracy and duration on per level basis. All the analyzed data were tested using Mauchly's sphericity, and in case the sphericity assumption was violated, the resulted F-test values were adjusted using Greenhouse-Geisser correction. In pairwise comparisons, a Post hoc analysis with Bonferroni adjustment was used.

2.4 Procedure

For the gaming sessions, a separate space was arranged where the gaming chairs were set up. Five students took part in each session, while the rest of the students continued in their own class normally. Each session lasted about 1.5 h. This consisted of starting instructions, playing of each of the three game versions and filling out the required questionnaires. The students had 15 min to play each game version. The rest of the actions lasted until everybody was finished.

During a session, the students played the same game version at a time and then filled in a questionnaire about that game design. Then the same procedure was repeated for the other two designs. In the end, there was still one questionnaire to be filled. The order in which the game designs were played within each group was distributed so that each version was equally often the first, the second and the last one to be played. Since the behavior of students may differ at different times of a school day, the order of the game designs was similarly distributed evenly to morning, midday and afternoon.

3 Results

There was a significant effect of user interface (UI) on the number of completed tasks, $F(2, 184) = 40.195$, $p < .001$, $\eta_p^2 = .304$. Most tasks were completed with the D-pad UI (47.55 tasks, SD = 9.60), followed by the Tilt UI (44.31, SD = 10.68), and least tasks were completed with the Chair UI (38.18, SD = 8.98). Pairwise comparisons showed that students completed 9.37 (95% CI, 6.68 to 12.05) tasks fewer with the Chair UI than with the Tilt UI, $p < .001$, and 6.13 (95% CI, 3.46 to 8.80) tasks fewer than with the D-pad UI, $p < .001$. With the Tilt UI students completed 3.24 (95% CI, 0.84 to 5.63) tasks fewer than with the D-pad UI, $p < .001$.

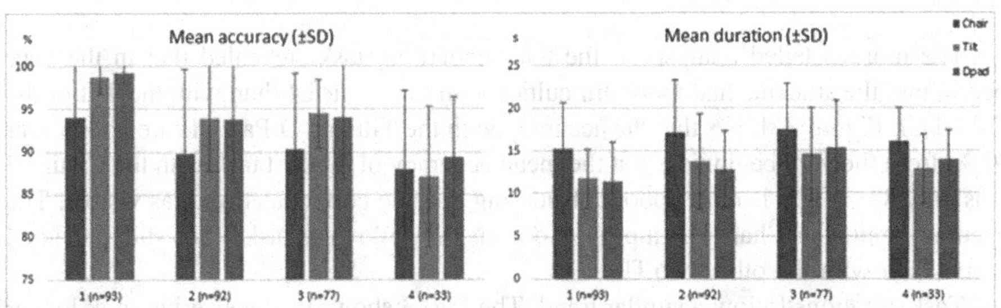

Fig. 2. The mean accuracy (left) and duration (right) for each of the game's four first levels. The horizontal axis shows the level number and participant count who completed it

As the students completed a differing amount of levels and the levels varied in design, in the following sections, students' performance is handled level by level (Fig. 2). This means that only those students that completed the level with each of the three user interfaces were included in the level-based analyses.

3.1 Analyses of the Onboarding Level

Every student completed the first level (onboarding) successfully (N = 93). There was a significant effect of the user interface both on accuracy, $F(1.11, 101.90) = 28.34$, $p < .001$, $\eta_p^2 = .235$ and on answering duration, $F(1.70, 156.46) = 24.21$, $p < .001$, $\eta_p^2 = .208$. Pairwise comparisons indicated that the mean accuracy with the Chair UI was 4.78 (95% CI, 2.47 to 7.09) percentage points lower than with the Tilt UI, $p < .001$, and 5.34 (95% CI, 3.07 to 7.61) percentage points lower than with the D-pad UI, $p < .001$. In line with this, the mean answering duration with the Chair UI took 3.47 (95% CI, 1.96 to 4.98) seconds longer than with the Tilt UI, $p < .001$, and 3.80 (95% CI, 2.10 to 5.45) seconds longer than with the D-pad UI, $p < .001$. On the other hand, there was no statistically significant difference in mean accuracy ($p = .084$) or in mean duration ($p = 1.000$) between the Tilt and D-pad UIs. The rest of the levels showed no difference either. Thus, pairwise comparison results between Tilt and D-pad UIs are not reported in analyses of the rest of the levels.

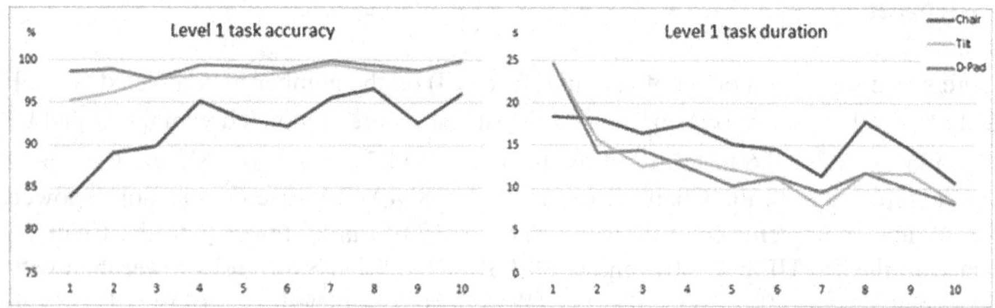

Fig. 3. The answer accuracy (left) and duration (right) for each task on the first level. Task number on horizontal axis

The more detailed analysis of the ten onboarding tasks revealed that in the very beginning, the students had more difficulties with the Chair UI than with the Tilt or the D-Pad UI. Figure 3 shows that the accuracy with the Tilt and D-Pad UIs are good (over 95%) from the very beginning, but the mean accuracy of the first task with the Chair UI was only 84%. This is rather poor considering that the correct answer was visible. The accuracy with the Chair UI improved during the following tasks, but still remained worse than with the other two UIs.

Task durations follow a similar trend. The Fig. 3 shows that answering took longer with the Chair UI than with other UIs. An exception to this is the first task, in which the duration was smaller with the Chair condition. This is likely due to accidental answering that some of the players faced in the beginning. The same was not experienced to the same extent with the Tilt or D-pad UI. These accidental answers lowered the mean accuracy and explain much of the poor accuracy on the first task with the Chair UI. After the first task, the unintended answers diminished with the Chair UI too.

3.2 Analyses of the Basic Levels

The second level contained basic fraction estimation tasks without any obstacles. One student had already dropped from the analyses at this point (n = 92). There was a significant difference in accuracy between the user interfaces, $F(1.68, 152.64) = 10.99$, $p < .001$, $\eta_p^2 = .108$. Pairwise comparisons indicated that the mean accuracy with the Chair UI was 4.14 (95% CI, 1.84 to 6.45) percentage points lower than with the Tilt UI, $p < .001$, and 3.99 (95% CI, 1.08 to 6.91) percentage points lower than with the D-pad UI, $p < .004$. There was a significant difference also in answering duration between the user interfaces, $F(2, 182) = 23.27$, $p < .001$, $\eta_p^2 = .204$. Answering with the Chair UI took 3.33 (95% CI, 1.65 to 5.02) seconds longer than with the Tilt UI, $p < .001$, and 4.29 (95% CI, 2.56 to 6.02) seconds longer than with the D-pad UI, $p < .001$.

In the third level, in addition to the basic task, the students had to estimate the locations of traps and jump over them. Level 3 was completed by 77 students. Again there was a significant difference in accuracy between the user interfaces $F(1.78, 135.44) = 12.34$, $p < .001$, $\eta_p^2 = .140$. The mean accuracy with the Chair UI was 4.15 (95% CI, 1.63 to 6.68) percentage points lower than with the tilt UI, $p < .001$, and 3.67 (95% CI, 1.37 to 6.00) percentage points lower than with the D-pad UI, $p < .001$. Like in level 2, there was a significant difference also in answering duration between the user interfaces, $F(2, 152) = 8.74$, $p < .001$, $\eta_p^2 = .103$. Answering with the Chair UI was 2.91 (95% CI, 1.12 to 4.71) seconds slower than with the Tilt UI, $p < .001$, and 2.13 (95% CI, .33 to 3.94) seconds slower than with the D-pad UI, $p = .015$.

In the fourth level, the students also faced enemies that had to be avoided or destroyed by jumping on them. Only a third of the students (n = 31) were able to finish this level. This time, accuracy did not reveal any statistically significant differences between the user interfaces, $F(2, 60) = 1.92$, $p = .16$, $\eta_p^2 = .060$. Nevertheless, like in the previous levels, there was a significant difference in answering duration between the user interfaces $F(2, 60) = 8.73$, $p < .001$, $\eta_p^2 = .225$. With the Chair UI, answering was 3.24 (95% CI, 1.36 to 5.12) seconds slower than with the Tilt UI, $p < .001$, and 2.14 (95% CI, .08 to 4.19) seconds slower than with the D-pad UI, $p = .015$.

Only four students completed level 5 with all the user interfaces. It is not meaningful to analyze such a small sample.

3.3 User Experiences

While the analysis showed that the Chair UI was less accurate and took more time to use, the question of preference was much more positive for the Chair UI. When the students had to name the best and the worst UI, the one receiving the most "best" votes was the Chair UI (77.6%). The D-pad UI (12.2%) and the Tilt UI (10.2%) followed at quite a distance. The "worst" votes followed a similar trend as the Tilt UI (44.9%) and the D-pad UI (43.9%) received votes roughly evenly and the Chair UI (11.2%) got much less.

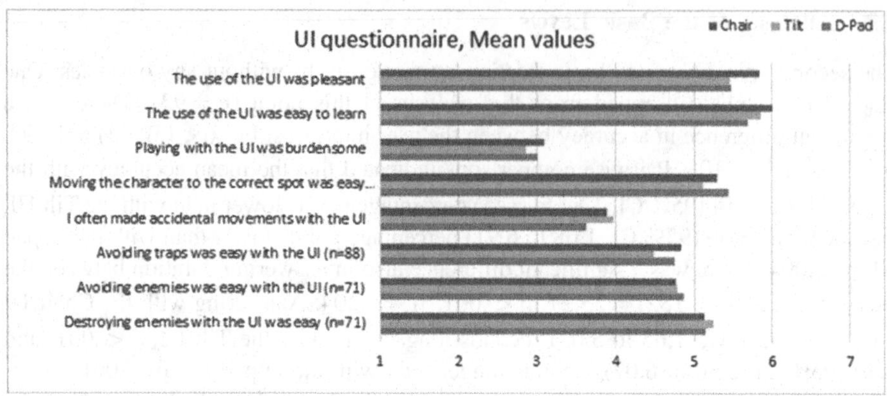

Fig. 4. Questions asked after each UI version. Answers on a 7-point Likert scale (1 = totally disagree, 7 = totally agree).

Based on the questionnaires about each UI (Fig. 4), there was very little difference between the three UIs, and none of the question showed any statistical significance. Sample size was a bit smaller on the three last questions as answers for those were omitted if the player had not actually faced traps and/or enemies.

4 Discussion and Conclusions

In the current study, we aimed at evaluating how the user interface implementation influences on playing performance, efficiency, and user experience of a mathematical game-based learning solution. Particularly, we explored how whole-body game controller influenced on these metrics. In the following, we will first discuss the results concerning the player performance and efficiency before we will elaborate results about students' user experiences and adoption of the different user interface implementations.

4.1 Player Performance and Efficiency

One objective of the current study was to evaluate the usefulness of the whole-body user interface in a math game founded on the number line estimation task. The results revealed that the implementation of the user interface influenced significantly on answering accuracy and task completion duration as the effect sizes varied from medium to large. The students' answering accuracy with the Chair UI (whole-body movement) was significantly worse than with the other user interfaces that did not involve whole-body movement as a controlling method. In line with this, the Chair UI was also significantly slower to use than the other user interfaces. These results are consistent with our first hypothesis. One exception was the fourth level, where the accuracy no longer showed statistical significance. An explanation could be that the players who managed to complete the level 4 (n = 31) were generally more competent with the UI and therefore its effect to the accuracy was diminished. The smaller sample size could also have an effect. The Tilt (hand movement) and the D-Pad (finger movement) UIs produced very similar results throughout the whole study. The only statistically significant difference was the completed tasks count, where the D-Pad condition fared slightly better.

The lowered performance and efficiency has clear implications to educational practices. Educators should be aware of how user interface solutions affect students' performance so that they can utilize the learning analytics or in-game metrics that the games may provide in a reasonable manner. We argue that game controlling methods that may influence negatively on performance (educational competences) suit best for training or for formative assessment context. That is, if the game is used in summative assessment, the user interface should be optimized with respect to controlling accuracy and fairness. The results also showed that the whole-body user interface was inefficient compared to other studied user interfaces as the students managed to complete fewer tasks with the Chair UI. With that respect, when selecting games, educators should consider whether the amount of training of the learning subject is more important than the physical training and other beneficial effects gained at the same time through the game controls.

4.2 User Experiences and User Interface Adoption

Although exact answering was harder and it took more time with the whole-body user interface than with the other user interfaces, the students appreciated it more. As we expected in our second hypothesis, the students were enthusiastic to play with the gaming chair and it was the most popular controlling method by far despite its limitations, with 77.6% of the students naming it the best UI. The user experience questions did not show any significant difference on the perceived easiness of use between the UIs.

The onboarding tasks showed that the two first tasks produced many unintended answers for the Chair UI, some for the Tilt UI and none for the D-pad UI. The rest of the onboarding tasks had only a few unintended answers meaning the players got the hang of the controls quickly. This highlights the usefulness of a soft start to playing, like having a couple of tutorial tasks first where the players are free to experience the controls of the game. This means that the results from the tutorial tasks should be omitted if the game is used for assessment purposes. The soft start is especially important for controlling methods using whole-body movement, as the player has to familiarize her/himself with not only the execution of the commands but also the required intensity of the exertion.

4.3 Limitations and Further Research

One limitation of the study is that much of the Chair UI's appeal could be attributed to the novelty effect of getting to play with the gaming chair. On the other hand, it is a good sign if the players feel like they are playing with a toy when they are controlling an educational game. While this case required special equipment, it still shows that physical movement based educational games can be engaging. Secondly, the treatment duration of 15 min per UI might not be enough to reveal all the aspects of the UIs. To further investigate the subject, a between-subject study in which students play the game for a longer period could be conducted. This could negate the effect of having to play the same content for multiple times and the longer playing period could decrease the novelty effect. Moreover, longer playing sessions could reveal how physical demands of the chair (exhaustion) influence on students' user interface preferences and answering accuracy. By having the player focus on only one UI, the player could proceed further in the game content, which would open up possibilities to study learning gains.

References

1. Devlin, K.: The music of math games. Am. Sci. **101**(2), 87–91 (2013)
2. Moeller, K., Fischer, U., Nuerk, H.C., Cress, U.: Computers in mathematics education – training the mental number line. Comput. Hum. Behav. **48**, 597–607 (2015)
3. Kiili, K., Ketamo, H.: Evaluating cognitive and affective outcomes of a digital game-based math test. IEEE Trans. Learn. Technol. **11**(2), 255–263 (2018)
4. Shute, V.J., Wang, L., Greiff, S., Zhao, W., Moore, G.: Measuring problem solving skills via stealth assessment in an engaging video game. Comput. Hum. Behav. **63**, 106–117 (2016)
5. Serrano-Laguna, A., Torrente, J., Moreno-Ger, P., Fernandez-Manjon, B.: Application of learning analytics in educational video-games. Entertain. Comput. **5**(4), 313–322 (2014)
6. Márquez Segura, E., Waern, A., Moen, J., Johansson, C.: The design space of body games: technological, physical, and social design. In: Proceedings of the SIGCHI Conference on Human Factors in Computing Systems, pp. 3365–3374. ACM (2013)
7. Lindstedt, A., Kiili, K., Tuomi, P., Perttula, A.: A user experience case study: two embodied cognition user interface solutions for a math learning game. Seminar.net – Int. J. Media technol. Lifelong learn. **2**(12) (2016)
8. Staiano, A., Calvert, S.: Exergames for physical education courses: physical, social, and cognitive benefits. Child. Dev. Perspect. **5**(2), 93–98 (2011)
9. Pouw, W.T., Van Gog, T., Paas, F.: An embedded and embodied cognition review of instructional manipulatives. Educ. Psychol. Rev. **26**(1), 51–72 (2014)
10. Lieberman, D., Chamberlin, B., Medina, E., Franklin, B., Sanner, B., Vafiadis, D.: The power of play: innovations in getting active summit 2011: a science panel proceedings report from the american heart association. Circulation **123**, 2507–2516 (2011)
11. Link, T., Moeller, K., Huber, S., Fischer, U., Nuerk, H.C.: Walk the number line – an embodied training of numerical concepts. Trends Neurosci. Educ. **2**, 74–84 (2013)
12. Moeller, K., Fischer, U., Nuerk, H.C., Cress, U.: Computers in mathematics education – training the mental number line. Comput. Human Behavior **48**, 597–607 (2015)
13. Riconscente, M.M.: Results from a controlled study of the iPad fractions game Motion Math. Games Cult. **8**(4), 186–214 (2013)
14. Przybylski, A.K., Rigby, C.S., Ryan, R.M.: A motivational model of video game engagement. Rev. Gener. Psychol. **14**(2), 154 (2010)
15. Bianchi-Berthouze, N., Kim, W.W., Patel, D.: Does body movement engage you more in digital game play? and Why? In: Paiva, A.C.R., Prada, R., Picard, R.W. (eds.) ACII 2007. LNCS, vol. 4738, pp. 102–113. Springer, Heidelberg (2007). https://doi.org/10.1007/978-3-540-74889-2_10
16. Lindley, S.E., Le Couteur, J., Berthouze, N.L.: Stirring up experience through movement in game play: effects on engagement and social behaviour. In: Proceedings of CHI 2008, pp. 511–514. ACM press (2008)

17. Greipl, S., Ninaus, M., Bauer, D., Kiili, K., Moeller, K.: A fun-accuracy trade-off in game-based learning. In: Gentile, M., Allegra, M., Söbke, H. (eds.) GALA 2018. LNCS, vol. 11385, pp. 167–177. Springer, Cham (2019). https://doi.org/10.1007/978-3-030-11548-7_16
18. Kim, Y.J., Shute, V.J.: The interplay of game elements with psychometric qualities, learning, and enjoyment in game-based assessment. Comput. Educ. **87**, 340–356 (2015)

Reinforcing Stealth Assessment in Serious Games

Konstantinos Georgiadis[1](✉), Giel van Lankveld[2], Kiavash Bahreini[1], and Wim Westera[1]

[1] Open University of the Netherlands, 6419 AT Heerlen, The Netherlands
{konstantinos.georgiadis,wim.westera}@ou.nl, kiavashbahreini@gmail.com

[2] Fontys Applied University of Eindhoven, 5612 AR Eindhoven, The Netherlands
gielvanlankveld@protonmail.com

Abstract. Stealth assessment is a principled assessment methodology proposed for serious games that uses statistical models and machine learning technology to infer players' mastery levels from logged gameplay data. Although stealth assessment has been proven to be valid and reliable, its application is complex, laborious, and time-consuming. A generic stealth assessment tool (GSAT), proven for its robustness with simulation data, has been proposed to resolve these issues. In this study, GSAT's robustness is further investigated by using real-world data collected from a serious game on personality traits and validated with an associated personality questionnaire (NEO PI-R). To achieve this, (a) a stepwise regression approach was followed for generating statistical models from logged data for the big five personality traits (OCEAN model), (b) the statistical models are then used with GSAT to produce inferences regarding learners' mastery level on these personality traits, and (c) the validity of GSAT's outcomes are examined through a correlation analysis using the results of the NEO PI-R questionnaire. Despite the small dataset GSAT was capable of making inferences on players' personality traits. This study has demonstrated the practicable feasibility of the SA methodology with GSAT and provides a showcase for its wider application in serious games.

Keywords: Stealth assessment · Serious games · Generic tool · Statistical model · Machine learning · Stepwise regression · Personality traits

1 Introduction

During the last couple of decades the educational community has been putting an increased effort on gradually transcending from traditional classrooms to digital educational environments. These digital learning environments require and can promote specific skills, e.g. critical 21st century skills and abilities, and thus prepare learners for future challenges in workplace and generally in life [1]. Among the most promising forms of digital education are serious games, due to their potential for enabling active learning in rich simulation environments. In these highly dynamic and interactive

A. Liapis et al. (Eds.): GALA 2019, LNCS 11899, pp. 512–521, 2019.
https://doi.org/10.1007/978-3-030-34350-7_49

learning environments it is of vital importance to accurately diagnose the progressing competence level of learners for properly tailoring the learning process.

One of the most promising assessment methodologies proposed for usage in serious games is stealth assessment (SA) [2]. SA combines a principled assessment design framework, namely the Evidence-Centered Design (ECD) [3], with machine learning (ML) technology in order to produce inferences about the learner's competences. The ECD serves as a framework for designing conceptual models for relating competencies (i.e. knowledge, skills, abilities, traits, etc.) and in-game tasks, whilst it also allows for developing computational models that express the relationship of these constructs with evidence (i.e. data) collected during gameplay. These computational models can be processed by ML algorithms and hence produce classifications of the learner's competence levels.

Although it has already been proven in several cases [4–6] that SA can produce valid and reliable assessments, its practical application is troublesome since it is a complex, laborious, and time-consuming process [7]. SA is inherently complex due to the diversity of expertise that is required in several domains beyond the learning content such as game development and design, machine learning, learning materials, statistics, etc. SA is laborious insofar it has only been applied in a hardcoded manner as an integral part of the games' source code. Such solutions limit the transferability of SA, while it requires each time software development and validation from scratch. As a result, applying SA in a game becomes a time-consuming process that is vulnerable to mistakes.

To overcome the practical drawbacks of SA and accommodate its wider application, a generic solution has been proposed [8, 9]. That is a stand-alone software tool, the Generic Stealth Assessment Tool (GSAT), which (1) allows the use of numerical datasets from any serious game, (2) automates the ML processes, and (3) allows the easy arrangement of different ECD models. GSAT has already been proven for its robustness against simulation datasets [10]. The aim of this study is to examine the use of GSAT with real-world data from a serious game, while concurrently allowing the detailing of the methodology that needs to be followed for this purpose.

To achieve this, data collected in another study [11] from a serious game called *THE POISONED LAKE* is used. This game is intended to allow for capturing behavioural responses that relate to personality traits. These personality traits are described by a five factor model called the OCEAN model [12]. In specific, the personality traits are: (1) Openness to new experiences, (2) Conscientiousness, (3) Extraversion, (4) Agreeableness, and (5) Neuroticism. These traits are also referred to as the "big five personality traits". Apart from collected game data, the study included the data collected from of a valid external measurement for these traits: the NEO PI-R [13] questionnaire. Based on the aforementioned datasets, the authors of the study managed to generate computational models (i.e. statistical models) to relate in-game behaviours with the personality traits, following a stepwise regression analysis method.

In this study, the produced computational models from *THE POISONED LAKE* game are being used with GSAT to directly determine the competence level of the learners on the big five personality traits from the logged player data. The outcomes of GSAT are then compared to the normed scores of the participants from the NEO PI-R questionnaire.

The structure of this paper is as follows. Background information about SA is provided in Sect. 2. Information on GSAT is presented in Sect. 3. Background information on the big five personality traits can be found in Sect. 4. Details regarding the game, the collected data, and the produced computational models are presented in Sect. 5. The methodology that was used for the purposes of the study is described in Sect. 6. Section 7 presents the results of this study, while a discussion over the results and our final conclusions are in Sect. 8.

2 Stealth Assessment Background

As previously mentioned, SA combines the use of the ECD framework with ML technology. These two ingredients are briefly presented in this section.

2.1 Evidence-Centered Design

To arrange assessments in serious games, SA uses a principled assessment design framework called ECD. The ECD consists of several generic conceptual models. In particular, these models are: (1) the competency model, (2) the task model, and (3) the evidence model. The competency model describes the assessed competency as a construct that includes its underlying factors (i.e. facets, sub-skills, etc.). The task model describes a set of in-game tasks that can elicit evidence for the assessed competency. The evidence model allows for describing the relationships of the observed in-game behaviour (i.e. observables or game variables) to both the in-game tasks and the competency construct. Therefore, the evidence model consists of two sub-models, that is (1) the evidence rules and (2) the statistical model (i.e. computational model). The evidence rules describe the relationship between the observed performances and the in-game tasks, while the statistical model describes the relationship between the observed performances and the competency construct.

Within the scope of this study, the only relevant models are the competency model and the statistical model, since only these two models are essential for the evaluation of the learners' performance from logged data. The task model and the evidence rules become important only when the SA is to be integrated within the game source code itself, which requires close attuning of the game's design to these models. GSAT, however, does not concern about these aspects as it exclusively deals with the diagnostic aspect of SA and its generic application even in games that have not been developed with respect to ECD.

2.2 Machine Learning Technology

Serious games are frequently portrayed as one of the most promising digital vehicles for capturing rich learner data, far beyond of what is usually possible in traditional education settings. This rich data can be used to fathom the behaviour of the learners and evaluate their competence level even for imponderables such as soft skills (i.e. communication, collaboration, team-work, etc.) and even personality traits. Machine learning is a field artificial intelligence that uses data to build models for pattern recognition and inferences. For SA, ML is the most suitable technology for making predictions about competence levels from logged data. Originally, Bayesian Networks were examined as an ML methodology for SA [2]; however other ML algorithms such as Decision Trees, Neural Networks, Logistic Regression, Support Vector Machines, and Deep Learning have been explored for SA [14, 15].

3 GSAT

The main motivation for developing GSAT was to lift the barriers of SA and allow its wider application in serious games. While SA served its purpose well in several case-specific empirical studies, the concept of directly integrating it within the gaming environment has hindered its full potential. Hence, the idea of detaching SA from hardcoded solutions led to developing GSAT as a practicable stand-alone software tool. Fundamentally that was possible due to the generic nature of the main ingredients that constitute SA (i.e. ECD and ML). As a result, GSAT not only allows the wider adoption of SA by the serious game community, but also offers research opportunities for examining SA when exposed to various boundary conditions.

GSAT was developed as a client-side console application in the C# programming language using the.NET framework. Currently an early version has been developed which fulfils all its core functional requirements [9], be it without a user interface, help widgets, and additional support functions (future work will address these issues to enhance the usability of the tool). GSAT's workflow design, as well as the external libraries that were used to realize it, has been extensively presented in a previous study [10], which used a simulation-based approach to examine the robustness of GSAT for numerical datasets of different sample sizes and normality significance levels, for different competency constructs and statistical models, and when using different ML algorithms. The results have shown that GSAT is a highly robust tool that ranked high in all the used performance measures for all the tested conditions.

4 Big Five Personality Traits

Since early 20th century, efforts were made concerning the development of a descriptive model for personality. These efforts led to a five factor model [16], referring to the following factors: (1) Openness to new experiences, (2) Conscientiousness, (3) Extraversion, (4) Agreeableness, and (5) Neuroticism (abbreviated to OCEAN). Accordingly, a valid and reliable test instrument for the OCEAN personality traits is available: the NEO PI-R questionnaire. The NEO PI-R divides every trait into six facets (see Table 1) and consists of 240 items measuring the five domains and their facets. In the reference study [11] that provided us with the *THE POISONED LAKE* datasets, data was also collected using the NEO PI-R questionnaire. The final scores of the learners that participated in this study were normed according to a respective valid norm table that takes into account the distributions on large sample groups.

Table 1. The five personality traits followed by their general description and respective facets.

Personality traits	Description	Facets
Openness	The interest in novel stimuli. A high score is typically accompanied by curiosity and willingness to deviate from social conventions	Fantasy Aesthetics Feelings Actions Ideas Values
Conscientiousness	The propensity to adhere to rules, both social and personal. This trait is also tied to the ability to restrain oneself and the ability to stick to a plan during periods of stress and difficulty	Competence Order Dutifulness Achievement Striving Self-Discipline Deliberation
Extraversion	High scorers seek excitement and positive stimuli. This often leads to individuals seeking the company of others and seeking exhilarating situations like high speed driving, roller coasters, and other high adrenaline activities	Warmth Gregariousness Assertiveness Activity Excitement Seeking Positive Emotion
Agreeableness	Explained as compliance, willingness to cooperate, and friendliness. Low scorers tend to follow their own needs over those of others. High scorers are seen as empathic	Trust Straightforwardness Altruism Compliance Modesty Tendermindedness
Neuroticism	This trait is connected to fluctuating and negative emotions such as anger and fear. High scorers are more likely to check situations for safety. There is also a relationship to shyness and social anxiety	Anxiety Hostility Depression Self-consciousness Impulsiveness Vulnerability to Stress

5 The Poisoned Lake

THE POISONED LAKE game (see Fig. 1) was developed as a mod of the popular leisure game called *NEVERWINTER'S NIGHT*. Information regarding the gameplay, the data that was logged during gameplay, and the statistical models that were finally produced from this data as reported in [11] are presented below.

5.1 Gameplay

The gameplay of *THE POISONED LAKE* involves a storyline that is divided into three parts: (1) a training part so that the learners become familiar with the game controls,

(2) the main part at which the learners have to execute a mission of solving the mystery of the poisoned lake and finding a way to stop the poisoning, (3) a couple of optional side stories were the learners can investigate how to save various non-playing characters (NPCs). The main actions that learners can perform during gameplay are to venture in the map and converse with NPCs in order to find a way to solve the mystery. The maximum amount of gameplay time for the learners was set to 60 min.

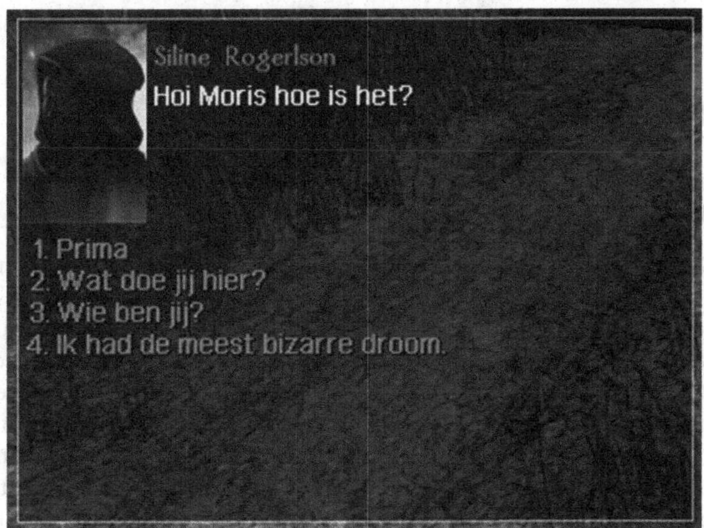

Fig. 1. A screenshot from *THE POISONED LAKE* game were a learner talks to an NPC [11].

5.2 Game Logs

Discrete numerical data was logged during gameplay for 80 learners (same for the NEO PI-R questionnaire). The logged data referred to three distinct types of variables: (1) data related to conversations with NPCs, (2) data related to the movement of the learners in the map logged at certain trigger points, and (3) general data relating the total time spend in game as well as aggregated (i.e. pooled) data regarding both conversation and movement data. A total of 260 game variables were logged [11].

5.3 Statistical Models

A linear stepwise regression analysis was performed in order to generate statistical models for each personality based on the collected game data. To achieve this, the final normed scores of the learners for each of the big five personality were set as dependent variables, while all the logged game variables were set as independent variables. Hence, five statistical models were generated each one explaining a certain amount of the variance by the models according to the size effect statistic R^2. Table 2 depicts the results of the stepwise regression analysis including validity and reliability relevant statistics (R^2 and Cronbach's α) [11].

Table 2. Overview of the statistical models produces from the linear stepwise regression analysis based on the logged for the big five personality traits [11].

Personality traits	R^2	α	No. of variables in model
Openness	.768	.54	17
Conscientiousness	.559	.31	10
Extraversion	.351	.07	6
Agreeableness	.724	.07	15
Neuroticism	.568	.55	9

6 Methodology

6.1 Using Statistical Models for the Big Five Personality Traits with GSAT

We configured GSAT to run the statistical models that were provided by the reference study in order to produce inferences about the personality traits of the learners. A Gaussian Naïve Bayesian Network (GNBN) was used for each personality trait. A percentage split rule was used to decide the number of samples included for the training (65%) and testing (35%) purposes of the classifiers. The GNBNs were set to produce inferences for three classes (Low, Medium, and High performance). Several performance measures [17] were used in this study to evaluate the performance of GSAT, such as the classification accuracy (CA), the kappa statistic (KS), the mean absolute error (MAE), the root mean squared error (RMSE), the relative absolute error (RAE), and the root relative squared error (RRSE).

6.2 Validation of the Results

A bivariate correlation analysis approach is used in this study in an attempt to validate the outcomes of GSAT regarding the big five personality traits of the learners. That is, we examined the Spearman's *rho* correlation coefficients between the normed results from the NEO PI-R questionnaire and the classifications produced by GSAT.

7 Results

This section includes results relating to both the performance of GSAT and the validity of the used statistical models.

7.1 GSAT Performance

The results for each GNBN classifier used per personality trait can be found in Table 3.

Table 3. Results regarding the performance of GSAT on the big five personality traits.

Personality traits	CA	KS	MAE	RMSE	RAE (%)	RRSE (%)
Openness	0.96	0.94	0.04	0.19	6.1	26.7
Conscientiousness	0.74	0.51	0.26	0.51	56.3	85.3
Extraversion	1	1	0	0	0	0
Agreeableness	1	1	0	0	0	0
Neuroticism	0.78	0.64	0.22	0.47	35.16	64.0

7.2 Correlation Analysis Results

A bivariate correlation analysis between the outcomes of GSAT and NEO PI-R was performed for each of the big five personality trait of the OCEAN model in order to validate the GSAT's outcomes with respect to the used statistical models. The results of this analysis are depicted in Table 4.

Table 4. Results from the bivariate correlation between the outcomes from NEO PI-R and GSAT with respect to Spearman's rho coefficient. The ** sign suggests significant correlation at the 0.01 level (2-tailed)

Personality traits	Spearman's rho
Openness	−.104
Conscientiousness	−.099
Extraversion	−.270
Agreeableness	.504**
Neuroticism	.357

8 Discussion and Conclusion

This study examined GSAT's performance with real-world data collected from a serious game. When examining the performance of GSAT by using standard classification performance measures it was found that the GNBN classifiers were able to perform at a high level despite the small sample size. Most notably, high classification accuracies (100%) were found for extraversion and agreeableness, while the lowest classification accuracy was found for conscientiousness (74%). These results confirm the robustness of GSAT with real-world data.

The bivariate correlation analysis of the GSAT outcomes with the respective outcomes from the NEO PI-R shows a strong and significant correlation only for agreeableness. This is reassuring as such, be it only a partial success. The reason for not being able to validate all the statistical models may lie on possible overfitting issues in the original model. Another possible explanation is that the original statistical models were not fully explaining the variance dependent variables in the first place. Indeed, an additional analysis of the data has revealed some flaws. In specific, we examined regression assumptions such as linearity, collinearity, normality, outliers, etc. Not to mention that the sample size was probably too small [18–20] for the number of descriptors included in the regression.

Nevertheless, this study was an excellent opportunity to test GSAT with real-world data. Even with a small dataset (only 80 users) GSAT was capable of training the SA model, and making inferences on the users' personality traits, be it only partially. This provides a favourable starting point for follow-up studies with larger sample sizes and more reliable statistical models. Moreover, by testing GSAT this study as demonstrated the practicable feasibility of the SA methodology. It also has shown that the generation of valid and reliable statistical models is essential for full and reliable coverage of assessments in serious games. Overall, this study contributes to improving the visibility, feasibility, and practicability of a principled assessment methodology for serious games such as SA.

References

1. Larson, L.C., Miller, T.N.: 21st century skills: prepare students for the future. Kappa Delta Pi Rec. **47**(3), 121–123 (2011)
2. Shute, V.J.: Stealth assessment in computer-based games to support learning. Comput. Games Instr. **55**(2), 503–524 (2011)
3. Mislevy, R.J.: Evidence-centered design for simulation-based assessment. CRESST Report 800. National Center for Research on Evaluation, Standards, and Student Testing (CRESST) (2011)
4. Shute, V.J., Ventura, M., Kim, Y.J.: Assessment and learning of qualitative physics in newton's playground. J. Educ. Res. **106**(6), 423–430 (2013)
5. Ventura, M., Shute, V., Small, M.: Assessing persistence in educational games. Design Recomm. Adapt. Intell. Tutor. Syst.: Learn. Model. **2**, 93–101 (2014)
6. Shute, V.J., Wang, L., Greiff, S., Zhao, W., Moore, G.: Measuring problem solving skills via stealth assessment in an engaging video game. Comput. Hum. Behav. **63**, 106–117 (2016)
7. Moore, G.R., Shute, V.J.: Improving learning through stealth assessment of conscientiousness. In: Marcus-Quinn, A., Hourigan, T. (eds.) Handbook on Digital Learning for K-12 Schools, pp. 355–368. Springer, Cham (2017). https://doi.org/10.1007/978-3-319-33808-8_21
8. Georgiadis, K., Van Lankveld, G., Bahreini, K., Westera, W.: Accommodating stealth assessment in serious games: towards developing a generic tool. In 2018 10th International Conference on Virtual Worlds and Games for Serious Applications (VS-Games), pp. 1–4. IEEE (2018)
9. Georgiadis, K., Van Lankveld, G., Bahreini, K., Westera, W.: Learning analytics should analyse the learning: proposing a generic stealth assessment tool. Accepted at the IEEE Conference on Games (CoG) (2019)
10. Georgiadis, K., Van Lankveld, G., Bahreini, K., Westera, W.: On the robustness of steath assessment. IEEE Trans. Games (2019, submitted)
11. Van Lankveld, G., Spronck, P., Van den Herik, J., Arntz, A.: Games as personality profiling tools. In: 2011 IEEE Conference on Computational Intelligence and Games (CIG 2011), pp. 197–202. IEEE (2011)
12. McCrae, R.R., Costa Jr., P.T.: Personality trait structure as a human universal. Am. Psychol. **52**(5), 509 (1997)
13. Costa, P.T., McCrae, R.R.: The revised neo personality inventory (neo-pi-r). SAGE Handb. Pers. Theory Assess. **2**(2), 179–198 (2008)

14. Sabourin, J.L.: Stealth assessment of self-regulated learning in game-based learning environments (2013)
15. Min, W., et al.: DeepStealth: leveraging deep learning models for stealth assessment in game-based learning environments. In: Conati, C., Heffernan, N., Mitrovic, A., Verdejo, M. F. (eds.) AIED 2015. LNCS (LNAI), vol. 9112, pp. 277–286. Springer, Cham (2015). https://doi.org/10.1007/978-3-319-19773-9_28
16. Wiggins, J.S. (ed.): The Five-Factor Model of Personality: Theoretical Perspectives. Guilford Press, New York (1996)
17. Domingos, P.M.: A few useful things to know about machine learning. Commun. ACM **55** (10), 78–87 (2012)
18. Field, A.: Discovering Statistics Using SPSS. Sage Publications, London (2009)
19. Green, S.B.: How many subjects does it take to do a regression analysis. Multivar. Behav. Res. **26**(3), 499–510 (1991)
20. Maxwell, S.E.: Sample size and multiple regression analysis. Psychol. Methods **5**(4), 434 (2000)

Exploring a Mixed Method Approach: Simulation Games and Q Methodology

Anique Kuijpers(✉), Heide Lukosch, and Alexander Verbraeck

Faculty of Technology, Policy and Management,
Delft University of Technology, Jaffalaan 5, 2628 BX Delft, The Netherlands
a.g.j.kuijpers@tudelft.nl

Abstract. In this paper we explore the possibilities to combine two research methods we regard as being very useful when interacting with stakeholders in complex systems. We discuss a mixed research methods approach, based on the Q methodology and a simulation game. In a game design process, translating the real or reference system into the game design is an intricate process and rather challenging due to the complexity of today's societal systems. As shown by various studies, different data techniques are proposed in order to translate reality aspects. One of the proposed data gathering techniques in combination with simulation games is Q methodology. Q methodology is a suitable method to retrieve social perspectives of stakeholders on a particular topic. Yet it is still elusive how the results of a Q methodology can be used in a game design process. In this paper, we explore the possibilities how to combine the two methods and how to translate the results of the Q analysis into a game design concept. In the context of a case within the domain of transport and logistics, we discuss how such mixed research methods approach could look like. We conclude with a future outlook on our research.

Keywords: Simulation games · Q methodology · Mixed method approach · Game mechanics

1 Introduction

Simulation gaming is an appropriate method to analyze, understand, represent and design complex systems [1–4]. Analysis and translation of reality aspects into a game environment is important since it is a starting point for the game design process [2, 5]. While this translation is important, it is also difficult because current societal systems, such as the domain of transport and logistics, are rather complex. They consist of social subsystems (e.g. individuals, organizations) and technical systems (e.g. innovations) that interact with each other [6], while having interdependent processes. Illustrating this in the transport and logistics system, it comes obvious that global and local organizations interact with each other by means of technical and social innovations. Additionally, each organization has its own needs, interest and processes. When developing an instrument to be used in such system, for example to support decision-making, or to foster communication, one has to develop a proper understanding of this reference system, including its subsystems and dynamic relationships. In complex systems,

A. Liapis et al. (Eds.): GALA 2019, LNCS 11899, pp. 522–529, 2019.
https://doi.org/10.1007/978-3-030-34350-7_50

phenomena occur that are difficult to capture and fully understand, for example situational awareness and trust. Actors in the system may have different viewpoints on such phenomena. These different viewpoints, however, provide a better understanding of the communication around a topic within a complex system that is interesting to take into account when designing a simulation game.

To create a good understanding of the processes, communication streams and phenomena that emerge in the system, simulation games can be used in conjunction with additional methods. According to [7] and [4], simulation games are an appropriate method to combine with other instruments. One of the methodologies that can be used to complement the game design process is the Q methodology [7]. A Q study allows researchers to study and explore patterns and social perspectives of stakeholders on a specific topic [8]. It is a systematic way to explore and cluster various, subjective perspectives of stakeholders on a topic. As aforementioned, a complex system consists of a multitude of actors each with their own perspectives on a topic or issue that exists in the system. In our opinion, Q methodology is a suitable tool to analyze expressions and communication of actors on a particular phenomenon in a complex system. This method provides insights into different aspects of the topic and moreover the subjectivity of opinions is analyzed systematically. This paper aims to explore the possibilities to use a Q study in the design process of simulation gaming.

Although this approach is discussed as a suitable research methodology in relation to simulation games, it did not receive a lot of attention in the field of simulation games yet. Therefore, in this paper, we explore the possibilities to combine the Q-methodology and simulation games. First, we discuss how these two methods can complement each other. Subsequently, the essential steps of a Q methodology are described in Sect. 2. Followed by a description of a case study where we want to apply Q methodology in combination with simulation games. We conclude with a future outlook.

2 Combining the Q-Methodology and Simulation Games

Simulation games are used as research instruments, training tools or instruments to raise awareness, transmit knowledge or to enable a learning process. When designing a simulation game, one of the important aspects is the translation of the reference system towards the gaming system [2]. A multitude of game design approaches propose how to translate the reality aspect into a simulation game, for example, [2] or [9]. Both of these approaches discuss the importance of translating the reality aspect into a simulation game. By including subject-matter experts [2] or the target group [9] with the design process, information is shared that help to clarify and identify important aspects of a complex system. The Q methodology can be used to support this game design step.

Based on related game design approaches, literature studies, interviews and workshops with experts and practitioners are suitable tools to understand the system in-depth and moreover to clarify the problem [10]. The data retrieved from the above-mentioned tools serve as a basis to map the system in a systematic way [11]. Besides these tools, in our opinion other research methodologies, such as Q methodology, are suitable in conjunction with simulation games to gather data, for example different viewpoints of stakeholders. During the design process, it is challenging to include all viewpoints of the different actors in the system on a particular topic. Yet, for the analysis of the system it is interesting to collect similar and dissimilar viewpoints to create a thorough analysis of the complex system.

Combining simulation games with other research methodologies is discussed in a few papers. [7] showed that games create a suitable environment for a mixed method research approach. As shown in this paper, a Q study is considered as an appropriate methodology to collect data. With a Q study, data is gathered that gives insights into the opinions or motivations of stakeholders on a certain topic [12]. Another study that elaborates on the combination of different research tools is the study by [4]. This study discusses different types of simulation games by game design and evaluation. From the various case studies it is learned that transferring reality aspects during the game design process is an intricate process and interviews with experts and workshops help to support this translation.

In our opinion, one methodology that is useful in relation to game design is the Q methodology. A Q study consists of both qualitative and quantitative elements [8, 13, 14]. This methodology is used to analyze social perspectives of a variety of stakeholders [14] as well as to extract patterns of these perspectives [15].

2.1 Q Methodology

A Q study is suitable to study a social phenomenon which is subjected to different understandings and which is debated quite a lot [8]. A Q study will provide insights and feedback on a topic as well as knowledge of the reference system. According to [8, 12, 14], conducting a Q study consists of 5 subsequent steps. The first step of a Q study is the demarcation of concourse. In this first step, expressions and information flows on a topic are identified that reflect the diversity of perspectives from actors in a system [12, 14]. Based on the concourse, statements are defined that reflect the diversity of the perspective. This second research step is called the selection of statements. After the selection of the statements, the respondents are selected who will perform the Q sort. These respondents are selected based on their different perspectives on a topic [14]. The fourth step is the Q sort. In this step the respondent are asked to rank the statements according to a research question. Respondents sort the statements on a grid which is shaped as a normal distribution. Grounded on the different Q sorts by respondents, a data analysis is conducted as the fifth research step. The final step is the analysis and interpretation of the different Q sorts by means of a quantitative statistical analysis that provides to a set of factors [13, 14]. These set of factors give an overview of the shared perspectives of actors on a topic. A Q study is a systematic analysis to study a topic in a complex system. By analyzing and retrieving feedback from experts and practitioners a better understanding of the real system is created and moreover game designers are able to transfer the reality aspects into a game environment [3, 4]. In doing so, the Q methodology helps to carry out this design step in a structured way.

3 Case Study: A Game of Trust

Combining the Q methodology and simulation games did not receive a great deal of attention yet. How to combine these two methodologies is explored in the Trans-SONIC project. Within the Trans-SONIC project, the impact of trust on collaboration in light of the innovation process is studied by means of simulation games. The context of the study is the transport and logistics system, and in more detail the port-hinterland system. This system can be characterized as a complex system [6], where actors have interdependent processes and interact with each other by means of novel technologies in order to transport goods from A to B. With the introduction of novel technologies, procedures and processes of actors may change. Additionally, actors need to decide if they want to compete or collaborate with competitors. Trust in this case is key as it enhances collaboration [16]. Consider, for instance, the implementation of truck platooning in the transport and logistics system. Truck platooning is a concept where a number of trucks, from different truck companies, drive together with a fixed vehicle distance by means of communication technologies. This innovation provides advantages for truck companies, for example fuel reduction. Yet, it also causes some challenges. In order to establish a platoon, truck companies need to share information, such as departure times or truck driver schedules, with other truck companies. In order to exploit the advantages of truck platooning, collaboration and moreover trust is vital.

In the Trans-SONIC project, we develop a trust game according to the Triadic Game Design (TGD) Philosophy proposed by [2]. According to the TGD philosophy, a game design approach should be balanced along three aspects, i.e. reality (i.e. translation of the reference system), meaning (i.e. the purpose/learning goal of the game) and play (i.e. game elements/mechanics). We develop a round-based game where players experience the influence of a low trusted environment or a high trusted environment. In the game we are interested how trust influences initial collaborative relationships in the port-hinterland system, thus in an inter-organizational environment.

The port-hinterland system is rather complex and to understand the system in-depth, a system analysis is conducted to gain insight into the actors, their relations and interests. Subsequently, we visualized the information and communication stream of the actors by means of a business modelling approach. For example, the actors and their processes are visualized by the use of a swimming lanes model. With the system analysis we are able to represent the main roles in the game as well as the communication streams.

As aforementioned, the main concept in the game is trust. In order to translate this social phenomenon in a game, first a literature review is conducted. The results of this literature review show that the concept of trust is multidimensional. It evolves over time and emerges in different stages [17], for instance on a personal level as well as on an institutional level. Deriving from the literature review, trust is defined as an expectancy that emerges in a technological environment or a social environment [18]. Since the purpose of the game is to study the influence of inter-organizational trust (i.e. low and high trust) on initial collaborative relationships, our concept of trust is based on the definition proposed by [19]. According to this study, trust is an organizations expectancy that another actor will fulfil its obligations, behaves in a predictable manner and is not opportunistically [19]. The role descriptions are based on the trust characteristics of this definition. For instance, one player in the game will behave opportunistically compared to another player who will behave predictable.

We are aware that trust embedded in a system and is influenced by various factors, for example power and risk. Grounded on literature from a broad range of disciplines (e.g. sociology, management) we could derive that information is a construct that influences the process of trusting another actor [20]. In other words, the choice whether or not to collaborate is moderated by the received information and this varies per stakeholder.

3.1 Q Methodology: Input for Game Mechanics

To translate the relation between information, trust and collaboration we first need to create a better understanding what the role of information is in the transport and logistics system. We do this by means of a Q study. For example, the construct information consists of different types such as fixed information (e.g. container code) or future events (e.g. turnaround times terminal) [21]. A Q study allows researchers to identify underlying patterns of the stakeholders on a social perspective [21], in our case information in relation to trust. Our hypothesis is that the Q methodology allows us to ensure that critical elements of the relation information and trust are translated to the game environment.

As explained in Sect. 2, conducting a Q study consists of 5 subsequent steps [8]. To set up the concourse, we will analyze journal articles and grey literature (expert reports and news articles) in depth. This will provide us with a better insight of the relation between information and trust, as well as the communication about this topic in the port hinterland system. Following from the concourse, Q statements will be defined that cover all the relevant aspects of the topic. For example, information in relation to trusted third parties or what type of information (e.g. feedback ratings, operational information) is trusted by the stakeholders. After formulating the Q statements we select port-hinterland stakeholders who have different viewpoints. The stakeholders then need to sort the statements on a grid-shaped normal distribution from strongly disagree to agree which are afterwards analyzed by a factor analysis [13]. Resulting from the factor analysis is a set of shared perspectives from a multitude of port-hinterland stakeholders on the topic information in relation to trust.

Our hypothesis is that the outcomes of a Q study will reveal the most important elements of the topic information in relation to trust, since it will provide us with the viewpoints of the port-hinterland stakeholders. Based on this data, game mechanics will be designed (Fig. 1).

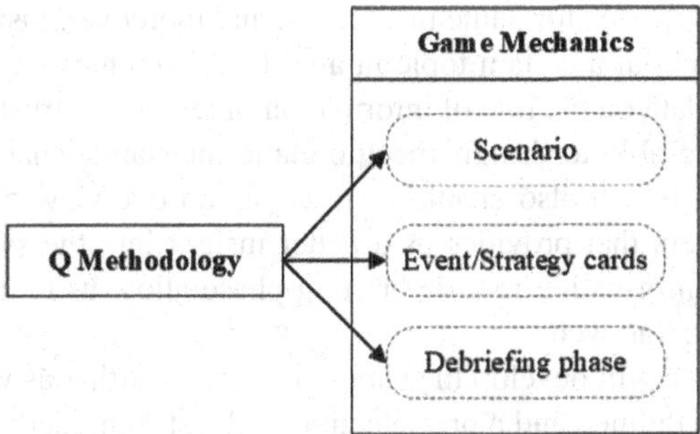

Fig. 1. Q methodology translated to game mechanics

Since the game is a round based game, one of the social perspective deriving from the Q study can serve as a scenario in one of the rounds. The output of a Q study is the shared perspectives, positive or negative, of different stakeholders on a topic. For example, possible shared perspectives of stakeholders in the transport and logistics system could be: sharing of different types of information should be regulated or the role of trust and security in relation to information is necessary. A Q study reveals in more detail the concerns and issues of stakeholders. To illustrate, take for example the shared perspective of trust and security. Stakeholders may be concerned that trusting others may be difficult and they have a positive attitude towards implementing regulations in order to increase their trust level. Grounded on this shared perspective, scenarios could be designed that provides a linkage towards reality and used to influence the game play of players. For instance, a scenario can be introduced where new rules and regulations are mentioned that affect the trust level of players. Another alternative is to use the different perspectives as input for the strategy cards where players are able to influence the environment (e.g. low trusted environment or high trusted environment). Strategy cards are a suitable game mechanic to differentiate between a high trusted environment and a low trusted environment. For example, certain information can be left out during specific game rounds. When playing one of the strategy cards certain information what is important in relation to trust is not shared by a player. Additionally, while conducting a Q study, more information and insights will be retrieved from the stakeholders. After sorting the statements, it is possible to ask more in-depth questions relating to the Q sorting. This information can also be used in a debriefing phase, where the role of information in relation to trust will be made explicit.

4 Conclusion and Future Outlook

In this paper, we explored Q methodology in conjunction with simulation games. In the literature, Q methodology is discussed as one of the possibilities to gather data. While a couple of studies discussed the opportunities of combining different research methodologies, the combination of the Q methodology and simulation games did not receive a great deal of attention. In our opinion, a Q study is beneficial for the game design, i.e. serves as a basis for game mechanics, and moreover, insights are created on the communication about a certain topic in a system. We envision that a Q study will allow us to retrieve data on the role of information in relation to trust. By gathering data on this topic, we are able to design specific game mechanics that influence the trust level of the players. It will also enable us to create an overview of the opinions of a variety of stakeholders that provides us a better insight into the system itself. Subsequently, using this information in a de-briefing phase allow us to expand the learning process of the players as well.

In future work, we will develop the simulation game further as well as the Q study. Q statements will be defined and a pre-selection of the stakeholder will be asked to sort these statements according to a scale from strongly disagree to agree. Subsequently, the results will be analyzed which provides us perspective that can serve as input for the game design. In parallel the game of trust will be further developed. Game mechanics are designed will be designed that partially comply with the results retrieved from the Q study. Additionally, experiments will be designed to study the role of trust on collaboration in the port-hinterland system.

The overall aim of the Trans-SONIC approach is to create a better understanding of the role of trust in a socio-technical system when novel technologies are introduced.

References

1. Duke, R.D.: Gaming: The Future's Language, 2nd edn. Sage Publications, Beverly Hills (1974)
2. Harteveld, C.: Triadic Game Design: Balancing Reality, Meaning and Play, 1st edn. Springer, London (2011). https://doi.org/10.1007/978-1-84996-157-8
3. Kriz, W.C.: Creating effective learning environments and learning organizations through gaming simulation design. Simul. Gaming **34**(4), 495–511 (2003)
4. Lukosch, H.K., Bekebrede, G., Kurapti, S., Lukosch, S.G.: A scientific foundation of simulation games for the analysis and design of complex systems. Simul. Gaming **49**(3), 279–314 (2018)
5. Peters, V., Vissers, G., Heijne, G.: The validity of games. Simul. Gaming **29**(2), 20–30 (1998)
6. De Bruijn, H., Herder, P.M.: System and actors perspectives on sociotechnical systems. IEEE Trans. Syst. Man Cybern. Part A: Syst. Hum. **39**(5), 981–992 (2009)
7. Mayer, I.S.: The research and evaluation of serious games: toward a comprehensive methodology. Br. J. Educ. Technol. **45**(3), 502–527 (2014)
8. Cuppen, E., Bosch-Rekveldt, M.G.C., Pikaar, E., Mehos, D.C.: Stakeholder engagement in large-scale energy infrastructure projects: revealing perspectives using Q methodology. Int. J. Project Manage. **34**(7), 1347–1359 (2016)
9. Duke, R.D.: The game design process. In: Greenblat, C.S., Duke, R.D. (eds.) Gaming and Simulation: Rationale Design and Applications, pp. 99–168. Wiley, New York (1981)
10. Geurts, J.L.A., Duke, R.D., Vermeulen, P.A.M.: Policy gaming for strategy and change. Long Range Plan. **40**(6), 535–558 (2007)
11. Peters, V., Van de Westelaken, M.: Spelsimulaties – een Beknopte Inleiding in het Ontwerpproces (Simulation Games – A Brief Introduction tot he Design Process), Nijmegen, The Netherlands (2011)

12. Webler, T., Danielson, S., Tuler, S.: Using Q method to reveal social perspectives in environmental research, Greenfield, MA (2009)
13. Brown, S.R.: Q methodology and qualitative research. Qual. Health Res. **6**(4), 561–567 (1996)
14. Ligtvoet, A., et al.: New future perspectives through constructive conflict: exploring the future of gas in the Netherlands. Futures **78–79**, 19–33 (2016)
15. Barry, J., Proops, J.: Seeking sustainability discourses with Q methodology. Ecol. Econ. **28** (3), 337–345 (1999)
16. Nooteboom, B.: Collaboration, trust and the structure of relationships. In: Nooteboom, B., Stam, E. (eds.) Micro-Foundations for Innovation Policy, pp. 199–218. Amsterdam University Press, Amsterdam (2008)
17. Lewis, J.D., Weigert, A.: Trust as a social reality. Soc. Forces **63**(4), 967–985 (1985)
18. Mcknight, D.H., Carter, M., Thatcher, J.B., Clay, P.F.: Trust in a specific technology: An investigation of its components and measures. ACM Trans. Manage. Inform. Syst. **2**(2), 1–25 (2011)
19. Zaheer, A., McEvily, B., Perrone, V.: Does trust matter? Exploring the effects of interorganizational and interpersonal trust on performance. Organ. Sci. **9**(2), 141–159 (1998)
20. Lewicki, R.J., Bunker, B.B.: Trust in Relationships: A Model of Development and Decline, 1st edn. Jossey-Bass, San Francisco (1995)
21. Wiegmans, B., Menger, I., Behdani, B., van Arem, B.: Communication between deep sea container terminals and hinterland stakeholders: information needs and the relevance of information exchange. Marit. Econ. Logist. **20**, 531–548 (2017)

Creating Serious Games with the Game Design Matrix

Aaron Pendleton(✉) and James Okolica

Air Force Institute of Technology, Dayton, OH 45433, USA
aaron.pendleton@afit.edu

Abstract. Serious Games can be a powerful tool for educators to boost the level of student engagement in academic environments, but the level of game expertise and knowledge required in order to design a game with playable mechanics and well integrated learning objectives can be overwhelming. This high barrier to entry for inexperienced designers attempting to employ serious games has not been addressed in a commonly available or recognized step-by-step game design framework. This paper creates a framework which uses the Mechanics, Dynamics, and Aesthetics (MDA) design process as the cornerstone of a step-by-step design matrix targeted at new game designers. It empowers someone with a minimal background in game design to have a much greater level of effectiveness. This is accomplished by using learning objectives and environmental constraints to map ideal game dynamics and game mechanics. A static analysis of existing games is used to assess the effectiveness of the game dynamic and game mechanics mapping matrix. A dynamic analysis of the framework is conducted by creating a cyber education focused serious game using the learning objectives and environmental constraints from an active classroom.

Keywords: Serious games · Game design · Design process

1 Introduction

Serious Games as first introduced by Clark Abt can be defined as games which are not played primarily for amusement, but for a carefully thought out education purpose [1]. They can be a powerful tool to boost the level of engagement in many academic environments [18], but the level of game knowledge required in order to design a game with playable mechanics and well integrated learning objectives can be overwhelming to an educator.

This paper creates a model which uses the Mechanics, Dynamics, and Aesthetics (MDA) design framework developed by Hunicke [9] paired with the Krathwohl revision of Bloom's Taxonomy [11] as the cornerstones of a serious game design process. It empowers someone with minimal background in game design to have a much greater level of effectiveness. This is accomplished by

A. Liapis et al. (Eds.): GALA 2019, LNCS 11899, pp. 530–539, 2019.
https://doi.org/10.1007/978-3-030-34350-7_51

employing pre-defined learning objectives and environmental constraints to map requirements to specific game dynamics, mechanics, and learning outcomes.

2 Related Work

2.1 Game Design Elements

Serious Game design draws from traditional game design in many applications. An overview of traditional game design yields many frameworks for designing games that engage players but notably miss incorporating learning objectives at the earliest stages of planning and development.

MDA Framework. The Mechanics, Dynamics, and Aesthetics (MDA) approach to game research is one of the cornerstones of current game design [19]. It develops a simple and effective framework which defines the three distinct components of games. The elements of MDA build upon each other to form the complete player experience. The basic framework is shown in Fig. 1. MDA can be used as the cornerstone of the game design process, but it does not provide a step-by-step process [19]. MDA is an ideal framework to be extended for outlining a more direct process to design serious games. MDA places emphasis on the designer's selection of mechanics to drive the dynamics and aesthetics that are created. This is shown in Fig. 1 as the framework develops from left to right.

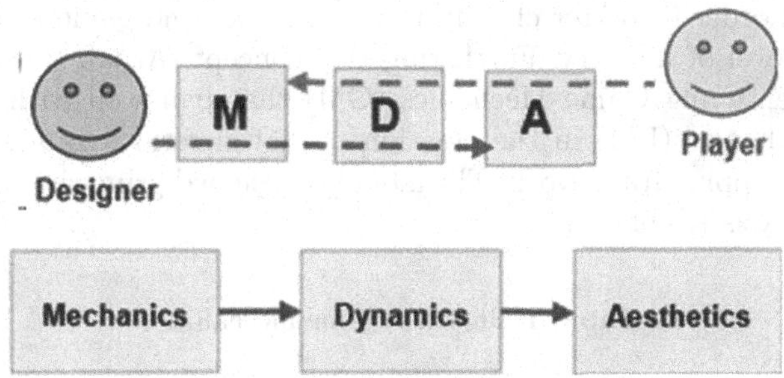

Fig. 1. Mechanics, dynamics, and aesthetics framework [9]

Extensions to MDA. Walk [19]approaches several perceived weaknesses in the MDA framework through the Design, Dynamics, and Experience (DDE) framework. Multiple arguments are posed against the MDA framework, but they are concisely summarized as situational. MDA neglects to give designers direct influence over Dynamics and Aesthetics, instead claiming they are reliant on the players and mechanics. DDE remedies the perceived weaknesses in the MDA framework with a complex and scrupulously detailed framework which can now account for interactions in nearly any game at the cost of simplicity and brevity [19]. For the purposes of this paper, the recognized shortcomings of MDA are not prohibitive and will not be directly addressed.

2.2 Learning Assessment Methods

Bloom's Taxonomy. Bloom's taxonomy was originally intended to be used as a measurement tool to aid curriculum developers and educators by creating a common language with which to define the specific targeted levels of education measured by a course or assessment [11]. It has since been applied to the development of learning objectives as well. Krathwohl [11] proposes a revision to the original framework to better provide specification when creating requirements based on each of the six categories. This provides a meaningful improvement over the original, as both the matrices of keywords used to relate each category and evolution of the applications for the original taxonomy are beyond the scope of the original intentions [11].

2.3 Categorizing Learning Objectives

Starr [17] advocates for the concept of using Bloom's taxonomy to aide in the development of learning objectives in the same manner it can be used to create learning assessments. As originally intended, Bloom's was a tool to gauge levels of mastery in a subject matter. Starr creates a meta-level analysis with which to apply Bloom's Taxonomy within the scope of a lesson objective.

2.4 Applying Bloom's Taxonomy to Serious Games

Buchanan [6] breaks down the levels of Bloom's taxonomy as applicable to Serious Games in order to better classify types of games and game mechanics with a particular level of mastery. Furthering this concept, Arnab [2] addresses the process of identifying Game Mechanics (GM) that pair well with a particular Learning Mechanics (LM) in the creation of digital serious games by creating the LM-GM mapping framework. The model is designed primarily to aid in game design or analysis (Table 1).

Table 1. Järvinen game mechanics

Accelerating/decelerating	Bidding	Allocating	Arranging
Attacking/Defending	Conquering	Browsing	Building
Buying/Selling	Catching	Choosing	Composing
Aiming & Shooting	Contracting	Controlling	Conversing
Discarding	Enclosing	Expressing	Herding
Information-seeking	Jumping	Manoeuvring	Motion
Moving	Operating	Performing	Placing
Point-to-point Movement	Powering	Sequencing	Voting
Sprinting/Slowing	Storytelling	Submitting	Substituting
Upgrading/Downgrading	Taking	Trading	Transforming

2.5 Defining Game Mechanics

Järvinen [10] defines a list of mechanics shown in Table 2 which is designed to encompass any form of game. Game mechanics are considered specific actions and defined as primarily verbs. This definition allows different player options to be classified as either a mechanic or a higher level system interaction (Game Dynamic) [10].

2.6 Establishing Game Dynamics

Game dynamics are defined by Järvinen as the system-behavior of a game, but a comprehensive list is not created. A suitably complete list of serious game or traditional game dynamics has not been found. Table 2 introduces an inclusive list of game dynamics developed for the Game Design Matrix.

Table 2. List of game dynamics

Modular game board	Fog of war	Deck/hand building
Bluffing	Chance	Cooperation
Competition	Conflict	Collaborating
Level of communication	Information Control	Time Scarcity
Multiple Strategies	Multiple endings	Infinite Gameplay
Player substitution	Player Autonomy	Team Modeling
Real Time Play	Hidden Objectives	Limited Actions
Feedback	Realism	Negotiation
Diplomacy	Player Ethics	Asymmetric abilities
Resource Scarcity	Adversary Tracking	Teams

3 Basic GDM Structure

The principle idea behind the GDM concept is that all games at their most basic level can be generally categorized as a combination of the interactions of Mechanics and Dynamics, and therefore there will be mechanics and dynamics best suited for any game created to achieve a certain objective. This takes the building blocks of MDA and reorients them for serious game creation to first select the dynamics of a game in order to allow for the focus to be placed on the primary driver of the learning outcome.

Environmental constraints and learning objectives are used to identify, isolate, and map an optimized set of game mechanics and game dynamics for a given design. The game components and aesthetics are developed based on the mechanics and dynamics selected using GDM. Figure 1 shows the steps of GDM in order of interaction a dependency (Fig. 2).

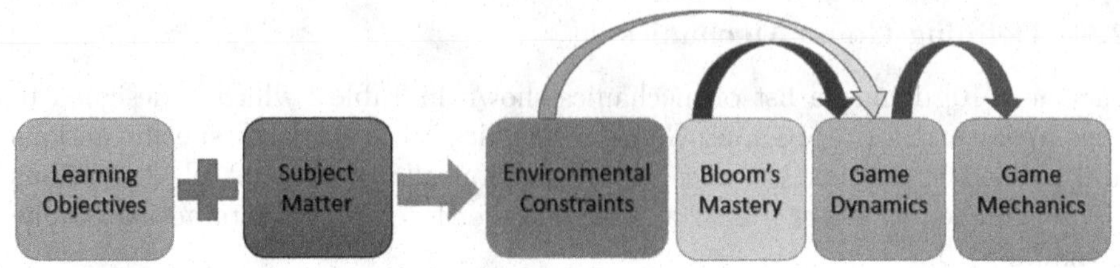

Fig. 2. Game design and assembly matrix structure

3.1 Step One: Identify Learning Objectives and Subject Matter

The designer must first determine the subject matter or topic of the game, and then the desired learning objectives and learning outcomes for the players. The learning objectives will be used to isolate the level of Bloom's taxonomy (revised) that the game is targeting by employing Starr's association methodology.

3.2 Step Two: Identify Environmental Constraints

Environmental constraints must be identified and anticipated by the game designer in order to narrow the scope of selected dynamics and mechanics. Accurate identification of environmental constraints is one of the primary cornerstones of GDM, and enables more effective game designs. An example of commonly identified environmental constraints are shown in Table 3, but the designer may need to define additional unique constraints in order to optimize performance.

All environmental constraints must be addressed prior to selecting dynamics. If new constraints are realized during the game dynamics or game mechanics selection, then the designer must return to the environmental constraints identification step. The environmental constraints should also be used to eliminate game dynamics that are not compatible with the desired classroom application.

Table 3. Environmental constraints

Class size	Introduction time
Seating/Table Space	Playtime
Student Knowledge Level	Camaraderie
Budget	Technology

Refining the list of game dynamics at this stage allows for a more targeted output. Nearly every classroom situation can be adapted to GDM because this mechanism allows for an abstract implementation, but a game may not be realistic in situations where environmental constraints eliminate all game dynamics.

3.3 Step Three: Isolate Game Dynamics

The user should select dynamics which have familiarity, extensibility, and pair well with each other. This is accomplished using two strategies: elimination of dynamics precluded by the environmental constraints, and identification of dynamics which best support the level of Bloom's taxonomy targeted in the learning objectives.

Table 4. Bloom's mastery levels to game dynamics

Level of mastery	Mapped dynamic
IV. Creating	Not directly targeted
V. Evaluating	Targeted through a combination of level 4 dynamics
VI. Analyzing	Multiple Strategies, Modular Game Board Resource Scarcity, Adversary Tracking Hidden Objectives, Fog of War, Feedback Bluffing, Player Ethics, Limited Actions Diplomacy Team Modeling, Information Control Multiple Endings, Deck/Hand Building Asymmetric Abilities
III. Applying	Chance, Cooperation, Collaboration Conflict, Negotiation,
II. Understanding	Teams, Realism, Real-Time Play Time Scarcity, Player Autonomy
I. Remembering	Infinite Game Play, Competition Player Substitution, Turn Based

Table 4 maps game dynamics to a level of Bloom's Taxonomy that it is likely to reach when properly implemented. Using this as a baseline to choose a primary game dynamic, secondary and tertiary dynamics can also be chosen to increase the complexity and depth of the game.

In situations where a broad array of game dynamics is available after the environmental constraints and learning objective isolation step, it is recommended to create several individual game profiles and select the course of action which best adheres to design and learning outcome requirements.

3.4 Step Four: Select Game Mechanics

The core of the GDM process is the selection of game mechanics that can enable the intended game dynamics. It is often only necessary to employ one or two mechanics to create a dynamic, and it is similarly important to group like dynamics by using the same mechanics to achieve them in order to keep game complexity approachable. Table 5 is a suggested mapping of game mechanics to game dynamics that can be used to optimize selections based on an analysis of existing games and their mechanic - dynamic interactions.

Table 5. Game dynamics to game mechanics

Game dynamics	Mapped game mechanics
Modular Game Board	Building, Allocating, Choosing Controlling, Discarding Enclosing, Placing, Substituting Taking, Transforming Upgrading/Downgrading
Fog of war	Moving, Point-to-Point Movement Controlling Enclosing, Herding Information-seeking
Asymmetric abilities	Allocating, Browsing, Choosing Substituting, Taking Upgrading/Downgrading
Hidden Objectives	Buying/Selling, Contracting Controlling, Enclosing Herding, Information-seeking
Teams	Contracting, Conversing
Adversary Tracking	Controlling, Herding Point-to-point Movement
Resource Scarcity	Allocating, Choosing, Controlling Enclosing, Herding, Placing Taking, Trading, Transforming Upgrading/Downgrading
Player Ethics	Buying/Selling, Enclosing, Placing, Substituting, Taking
Diplomacy	Conquering, Contracting, Controlling Conversing, Enclosing, Storytelling Information-seeking, Voting, Trading
Deck/Hand Building	Arranging, Building, Controlling Discarding, Taking, Trading Upgrading/Downgrading
Bluffing	Conversing, Expressing, Storytelling
Chance	Operating
Cooperation	Conquering, Contracting, Conversing Substituting, Attacking/Defending
Competition	Conquering, Enclosing, Choosing
Conflict	Buying/Selling, Conquering, Controlling, Enclosing, Taking Trading, Attacking/Defending
Collaborating	Contracting, Conversing, Substituting Voting, Attacking/Defending
Level of communication	Controlling, Conversing, Expressing Information-seeking, Storytelling
Information Control	Controlling, Conversing, Enclosing, Taking, Expressing Choosing, Information-seeking, Storytelling, Trading
Time Scarcity	Operating
Feedback	Conversing, Expressing, Information-seeking, Submitting, Voting
Limited Actions	No Mechanic Required
Infinite Game Play	No Mechanic Required
Real Time Play	Accelerating/Decelerating, Expressing, Catching, Conversing Aiming & Shooting, Manoeuvring, Motion Moving, Powering Sprinting/Slowing, Jumping
Team Modeling	Choosing, Contracting, Conversing
Multiple Strategies	Buying/Selling, Choosing, Conquering, Enclosing Taking, Transforming, Upgrading/Downgrading
Multiple endings	Choosing, Controlling, Storytelling
Player substitution	Choosing, Conversing, Substituting
Player autonomy	Taking, Placing, Point-to-point Movement, Submitting Choosing, Transforming, Upgrading/Downgrading
Realism	Operating, Sequencing, Voting
Negotiation	Bidding, Buying/Selling, Contracting, Conversing Controlling, Enclosing, Storytelling

4 Introducing "Enterprise": A Game Designed Using GDM

Enterprise is designed using GDM to select the mechanics and dynamics based on teaching students to apply principles of mission assurance and cybersecurity risk management in enterprise network operations. These learning objectives and subject matter were selected from a cybersecurity continuing education course, and the game was built to replace an exercise designed to accompany a lecture. This desired learning outcome drove the selection of dynamics based on level three and level four of Bloom's taxonomy. The environmental constraints required support for larger class sizes (more than fifty students), quick playtime (fifteen minutes or less), and to model the real life teamwork of a workplace. Three primary dynamics were selected based on these requirements to target in the game design: Chance, Collaboration, and Asymmetric Abilities. These dynamics can all be supported by the mechanics Upgrading/Downgrading, and Choosing. This enabled a targeted development focused on creating the components and aesthetics within established constraints, using the selected mechanics and dynamics. This resulted in a playable draft within 15 h of game conception, and a developed classroom ready iteration with only 25 h of total design, testing, and production time. Shown in Fig. 3 is the basic board and player positions. It allows 4–5 players to take on different roles within the network operations, information assurance, network maintenance, and cybersecurity functions of a large network. The player is to keep the network operational for 10 rounds while addressing cyber attacks, hardware failures, user errors, and equipment upgrades. Players must collaborate to make purchases/network upgrades, mitigate attacks, fix failures, and ultimately restore services if they are out. The game is designed to be played in 10–15 min and requires a 5–10 min introduction time. It is intended to be played by students that already understand basic enterprise operations concepts as taught by the preceding lecture, and does not explain roles or equipment used during play. This allows for significant time savings, and students are expected to immediately begin applying their knowledge to "emergencies" created in the game.

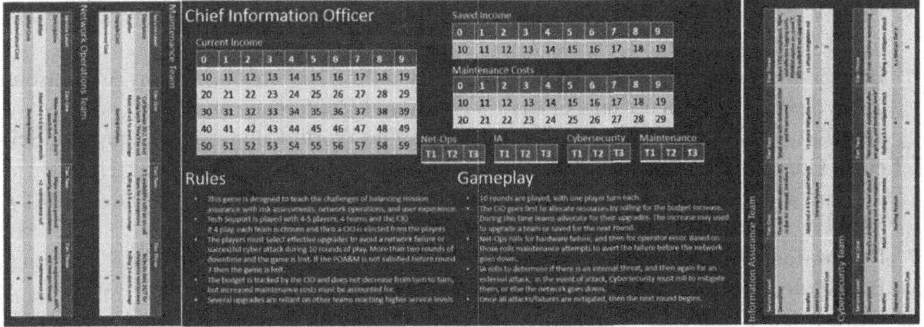

Fig. 3. Player cards and board of enterprise

5 Conclusion and Future Work

GDM is a game design process intended to give educators a step by step method to create serious games. The core of the design process is selecting game dynamics that are targeted at the level of mastery the learning objectives prescribe, and optimizing them for the specific classroom environment. This emphasis on dynamics requires selecting mechanics suitable to their environmental constraints and learning objectives. The result of employing GDM is a game framework that begins with user defined learning objectives and subject matter, and outputs dynamics and mechanics yielding potential increases in game effectiveness and decreased development time.

The next stage of testing is developing additional games using designs outputted by the model. Enterprise is designed using the first iteration of the GDM framework, and based off the short development time this aspect of the process is effective. Classroom testing of Enterprise is planned for future work alongside the second phase of game design which will include Agile Software Development and Secure Software Design learning objectives. This long term study will examine the result of games created by multiple educators with learning objectives targeted at different levels of mastery in order to assess the entirety of the framework rather than the single example used in this paper. Testing more games in a variety of environments will demonstrate the robust and extensible design of the model, including the ability to design board games, live action games, and digital games.

References

1. Abt, C.C.: Serious Games. University Press of America, Lanham (1987)
2. Arnab, S., et al.: Mapping learning and game mechanics for serious games analysis. Br. J. Educ. Technol. **46**, 391–411 (2015)
3. Bishop, J.L., Verleger, M.A.: The flipped classroom: a survey of the research. In: ASEE National Conference Proceedings, Atlanta, GA, vol. 30, no. 9, pp. 1–18 (2013)
4. Bloom, B.S.: Taxonomy of Educational Objectives. Vol. 1: Cognitive Domain. McKay, New York (1956)
5. Breuer, J., Bente, G.: Why so serious? On the relation of serious games and learning. J. Comput. Game Cult. **4**, 7–24 (2010)
6. Buchanan, L., Wolanczyk, F., Zinghini, F.: Blending Bloom's taxonomy and serious game design. In: Proceedings of the International Conference on Security and Management (SAM). The Steering Committee of The World Congress in Computer Science, Computer Engineering and Applied Computing (WorldComp) (2011). Learning and game mechanics for serious games analysis. Br. J. Educ. Technol. **46**(2), 391–411 (2015)
7. De Freitas, S.: Learning in immersive worlds: a review of game-based learning. Bristol Joint Information Systems Committee
8. Girard, C., Ecalle, J., Magnan, A.: Serious games as new educational tools: how effective are they? A meta-analysis of recent studies. J. Comput. Assist. Learn. **29**(3), 207–219 (2013)

9. Hunicke, R., LeBlanc, M., Zubek, R.: MDA: A formal approach to game design and game research. In: Proceedings of the AAAI Workshop on Challenges in Game AI, vol. 4, no. 1, p. 1722 (2004)
10. Järvinen, A.: Games Without Frontiers: Theories and Methods for Game Studies and Design. Tampere University Press, Tampere (2008)
11. Krathwohl, D.R.: A revision of Bloom's taxonomy: an overview. Theory Pract. **41**(4), 212–218 (2002)
12. Lameras, P., Arnab, S., Dunwell, I., Stewart, C., Clarke, S., Petridis, P.: Essential features of serious games design in higher education: linking learning attributes to game mechanics. Br. J. Educ. Technol. **48**(4), 972–994 (2017)
13. Michael, D.R., Chen, S.L.: Serious Games: Games that Educate, Train, and Inform. Muska & Lipman/Premier-Trade (2005)
14. Overbaugh, R., Schultz, L.: Bloom's Taxonomy. Old Dominion University, Norfolk (2008)
15. Serrano-Laguna, Á., Martínez-Ortiz, I., Haag, J., Regan, D., Johnson, A., Fernández-Manjón, B.: Applying standards to systematize learning analytics in serious games. Comput. Stand. Interfaces **50**, 116–123 (2017)
16. Sicart, M.: Defining game mechanics. Game Stud. **8**(2) (2008)
17. Starr, C.W., Manaris, B., Stalvey, R.H.: Bloom's taxonomy revisited: specifying assessable learning objectives in computer science. In: ACM SIGCSE Bulletin, vol. 40, no. 1, pp. 261–265. ACM (2008)
18. Susi, T., Johannesson, M., Backlund, P.: Serious games: an overview (2007)
19. Walk, W., Görlich, D., Barrett, M.: Design, dynamics, experience (DDE): an advancement of the MDA framework for game design. In: Korn, O., Lee, N. (eds.) Game Dynamics, pp. 27–45. Springer, Cham (2017). https://doi.org/10.1007/978-3-319-53088-8_3

Digital Games in Non-formal and Informal Learning Practices for Science Learning: A Case Study

Iro Voulgari(✉) and Georgios N. Yannakakis

Institute of Digital Games, University of Malta, Msida 2080, Malta
{iro.voulgari,georgios.yannakakis}@um.edu.mt

Abstract. This paper examines non-formal and informal learning practices for science learning. Through a case study and an exploratory, qualitative approach we identify aspects involved such as the content, the goals, the pedagogical approaches, the settings, the role of fun and playfulness, challenges, and the role of the practitioner. Data was collected through interviews and a survey. Despite the diversity in the format, settings, structure, and target group of the practices examined in this study, there seems to be a convergence in certain themes such as the objectives of the practices, the pedagogical approaches involved, and the importance of fun. These aspects are linked with the design and implementation of digital games in the context of informal and non-formal science learning. Further issues emerged from the analysis such as gender representation, resources required for efficient implementation of practices, and the role of the parents. Strengthening the links between formal and informal or non-formal science learning practices could benefit not only formal education but access of students to and effectiveness of non-formal and informal practices as well.

Keywords: Science learning · Informal learning · Non-formal learning · Digital games · Game based learning

1 Introduction

In this study we focus on non-formal and informal practices and activities for science learning within which digital games may be integrated, and explore aspects which could be addressed during the organization and design of such practices in order to increase their learning effectiveness. Research has linked digital games to scientific learning and science education not only as media through which players can explore and understand the learning content but also as artifacts that can trigger the interest for science and technology [1–4]. The context within which the gaming practices are situated are also of interest either as a framework supporting the gaming and learning practices or as emerging communities of practice spontaneously formed by the players [5]. As digital games offer players worlds to inhabit and explore, embed problem-solving situations, and support scientific inquiry, we can only assume that they can also promote scientific thinking. On that basis, games have been described as "*well suited for informal learning environments*" [9].

A. Liapis et al. (Eds.): GALA 2019, LNCS 11899, pp. 540–549, 2019.
https://doi.org/10.1007/978-3-030-34350-7_52

Although in the literature the notions of *informal* and *non-formal learning* are often used interchangeably, in this study we adopt the definition of [10] describing **informal learning** as *emerging spontaneously with no authority figure or mediator* (e.g. at home, or with friends), while **non-formal learning** *occurs in a planned manner beyond the formal or informal education settings*.

Although informal learning practices involving digital games have been studied to a degree, there is still limited research focusing on non-formal practices. Mapping the field of informal science learning through games [6] has identified four main contexts: everyday peer cultures, intentional gaming groups and communities, family and home life, and commercial and public media culture. Moreover, Fowler [7] and Arya [8], discussed Game Jams as "an informal STEM learning environment" with an educational potential involving interdisciplinarity and the acquisition of knowledge and skills. In [9] attributes of informal education settings are presented in comparison to formal (e.g. schools). Such settings include the flexible time structure, the voluntary participation, the emergent educational goals, and the flexible disciplinary boundaries. Practices such as Game Jams or after-school programs do not share some of these attributes since, for instance, they have a fixed time structure and a set of objectives.

In this study we focus on *non-formal science learning* practices and our main goal is to explore and describe aspects such as the *content*, the *objectives*, the *challenges*, and the *role of the practitioner*, and their *implications* on the design of such practices and relevant digital games. Our main research questions were: *What is the context and content of the informal and non-formal learning activities? What is the role of fun and engagement? What is their relation to learning and formal education? What are the challenges involved in planning and running such activities?*

This study was conducted within the framework of the EU funded project *COMnPLAY Science*[1] aiming to explore non-formal and informal science learning through coding, making, and play activities. In this study we focus on the case Malta as one of the partner countries.

2 Research Methodology

In the case study reported in this paper we combine quantitative (survey) and qualitative (semi-structured interviews) data for our analysis. In this section we describe the data collection process we followed, outline our data analysis methods and present the participants of the study.

2.1 Instruments and Data Collection

The survey and interviews were conducted concurrently in October and November 2018. The survey we used for this study was developed by the COMnPLAY Science project consortium [11] and was addressed to practitioners and facilitators of non-formal and informal activities relevant to science learning. In particular, the survey

[1] https://comnplayscience.eu/.

includes 38 closed (multiple-choice, Likert-scale) and open-ended questions focusing on dimensions such as the content, the goals, and the context of the participants' activities. The survey was distributed through an online link securing free anonymous access via social media and direct emails to institutions organizing such activities such as universities, museums, and science fairs hosts; for more details on the instrument and process followed for its design the reader is referred to [11].

The interviews, designed also by the project consortium, involved 5 main dimensions: the *content* of the activity, possible *challenges*, the *relation of the activity to formal education*, the background and the *role of the practitioner*, and *fun and playfulness*. These dimensions would allow us to gain a better insight of the context and nature of the activities. Interviews were mainly conducted via online teleconferencing platforms and their duration was approximately 45 min.

2.2 Data Analysis

The interviews were recorded, transcribed, and coded in two cycles: (a) structural coding based on the 5 dimensions described earlier and *in-vivo* coding for identifying emerging and potentially interesting phenomena and (b) pattern coding for summarising the issues identified into meaningful categories [15, p. 66, 74, 152]. Open-ended survey questions were similarly coded and analyzed. Quotes from the interviews and open-ended questions are referenced in the text so as to validate results and give a better insight of the issue addressed. Each quote is followed by the reference number of the interview (e.g. "int01"). For the closed survey questions, although the frequencies of the responses are described, no statistical analysis was conducted due to the small sample examined.

2.3 Case Study Participants

The total number of survey responses (N) from several European countries is 128, at the moment of writing. In this paper, however, we only focus on respondents from Malta (N = 7) as our initial analysis of the underlying practices of informal learning on that country. The interviewees were 3 experts from Malta that were purposefully sampled. They were, therefore, specifically invited for their potentially interesting and information-rich cases [16, p. 230]. All participants were volunteers and practitioners or facilitators of informal or non-formal science learning activities. They had different backgrounds, such as law, biology, and education. They were all affiliated with different institutions such as universities, museums, and governmental organisations. Three of the survey respondents were male and four female. All three of the interviewees were male and their practices involved digital games.

3 Results

In this section we describe the results obtained from our analysis in relation to our research questions.

3.1 Description of Activities

The activities described vary regarding their context, settings, subject, duration, age range, and gender representation of the participants. Respondents in our survey and interviews described contexts such as invited workshops at schools, coding and robotics workshops, guided experiments, science theatre, playing digital games, summer camps, after-school programmes, science events, career orientation days, game exhibitions, demonstrations, and game development contests (e.g. Game Jams).

Sciences such as Technology, Biology, Chemistry, Mathematics, and Computer Science were the fields most activities were situated in. In particular cases though (1 case in the survey and 3 cases in the interviews) the activities were also oriented towards Arts, Philosophy, and social issues.

The activities take place either in classroom settings (invited by the teacher), or in fairs, museums, science centres, outreach centres, depending on who is organising or hosting the activity. The duration of the activities described varied from a few minutes, to 6 h, or 5 consecutive days, usually as a single-occasion activity, as reported in the interviews and in 6 out of 7 survey cases, with groups usually participating in the activity only once (see Fig. 1).

Fig. 1. Indicative non-formal learning practices with digital games

The ages of the participants also ranged from 4 to 18 years old, or even families and the general public, in most cases separated in age-groups. Regarding the gender of the participants, although girls and boys seemed to have equal representation in the activities in most cases–approximately 50%, as reported in the survey–one of the respondents reported a near 0% of girls for robotics and coding activities. This was consistent with another response indicating a 4% of girls also for activities in robotics and coding. Similar findings were also described in [11]. The same respondent further observed that "*If booked by school, [the percentage of girls/females is] 50%. If booked by parents, 10% to 70% depending on the topic and name [...]*".

3.2 Engagement, Playfulness and Fun

Fun, playfulness, and engagement were reported as the strong points of their activities by the survey respondents in 5 of the 7 cases, for instance: "*Children like to play games during these events, they are engaged and like to spend time.*", "*it is fun and the participants are very engaged and excited*". Engagement, playfulness, and fun are actually primary goals when designing such activities e.g. "[fun and playfulness for achieving the goal are] *very important. That if the children in particular don't feel that they are having fun and you are trying especially to do extra work or work about the school work, you are just going to drive them more away. There is such a thing as bad science communication where you get negative outcomes. It doesn't mean because you are doing an intervention it's going to make them better*" (int02).

Fun and engagement, though, is one of the most challenging goals to achieve mainly due to the heterogeneity and diversity of the participants and the quick turnaround. An indicative quote: *"One of the challenges is that there is no universal definition of fun. So when you are making an experience fun you have to tailor it very specifically to the audience. Like I was saying, some kids love to draw and explore and see while other kids just want to shoot things in a video game. It's more challenging to make a game that appeals to both, or to everybody's sense of fun"* (int01).

But what motivates children and young people to participate in such activities in the first place? As reported by the practitioners in this study, the novelty and distinction from the school environment were strong motivations. Commenting on the aspects of the activity they thought young people appreciated the most, the majority of the participants selected the option "Doing something that is not 'school-like' (in 6 of the 7 cases), followed by "Making something by themselves" (5 out of 7), and "Doing something new" (4 out of 7). The contrast between the school setting and informal or non-formal activities as a motivation was also reported by 1 of the interviewees: *"[...] it's really different from when I used to teach. You know, when the bell for the break rings they are already out of the room. But in these workshops, they want to stay there [...]"* (int03).

Specifically, for practices involving digital games, the use of digital games was reported to be an *a-priori* motivator: *"[...] immediately, when you are talking about games students are already enjoying. They haven't even started playing the game and they are already looking forward and enjoying the session [...]"* (int03). For sustaining, though, this engagement, the appeal of the games used during the activity in relation to commercial games is critical, as reported by one of the interviewees *"The problem is that often there is better games on their mobile. So at this age, 16, the game on their mobile is more appealing than a lot of this stuff that we show them"* (int01).

It seems that parents and educators also play an important role in the selection of the activity. In a 5 point Likert-scale question on the frequency young people, parents, and educators decide participation of the children in the activity, in 5 cases it was the parents that "often" made that decision, in 4 cases it was the educators, and in 3 cases it was the young people. The highest label ("always") was not selected in any of the cases. As one interviewee similarly commented on what makes children join their informal activity: *"Their parents. Basically they are public events. The parents take them and they walk around the city"* (int01).

The concepts of fun and playfulness were further elaborated by the participants in our interviews recognising that even though these terms seem to overlap, playfulness tends to involve action and interaction. Two indicative quotes: *"I think playfulness is maybe more interactive. You can have fun watching, but it's not playful."* (int01), *"Fun is something enjoyable, laughter, whatever. Playful is something maybe related more to doing, and activities, and games* (int02).

3.3 The Learning Aspect

Learning Goals. It seems that informal and non-formal activities are not necessarily designed to achieve specific learning goals but rather raise the awareness and interest on a topic; as one survey respondent commented *"they are not focused on conveying the content of a scientific concept."* More specifically, "Engagement or interest in a particular scientific topic, concept, phenomenon, theory or career" was selected by the majority of the survey participants (5 out of 7) as the main aim of their activity. When asked specifically about the objectives, 4 of the 7 respondents agreed that their activities had explicit learning goals and elaborated providing examples such as "coding", "collaborative work", and "acquiring a few key facts". Similarly, when discussing the strong points and success indicators of their activities, survey respondents described objectives such as "improving people's confidence towards science." and "raise awareness". One interviewee elaborated on similar learning outcomes: *"the content, the scientific content, the technological content, whatever we want that to be. So we would want them to learn that. But if, for example, they do something collaboratively, we would want them to learn how to work in a team and so on. We have other learning outcomes such as motivation towards science or science careers, or confidence in science. Those are the underlying goals in many of the things that we do: building their own self esteem, empowerment, and ability in that field"* (int02).

Two interview participants that reported using digital games for their activities also agreed that an additional goal for their use was the awareness that digital games, beyond entertainment, can be tools for learning, for expression, or career opportunities. Indicatively: *"they can see that they can do more philosophical more meaningful game development and more meaningful coding in the sense that they can make something that makes people think."* (int01) and *"Through these workshops, the parents start to realise that the games aren't just a waste of time. So they start to realise that there is some potential of learning in using games. [...] mainly we want to let children know that there are also games that can be used for learning purposes"* (int03).

The short-term involvement and short duration of the activities though seem to make it difficult to assess or follow-up the learning outcomes. An indicative quote: *"The response and learning results are difficult to say because they are there for like 5 min and then they go out again"* (int01).

Relation to Formal Education. There was a slight shift regarding the learning goals when these non-formal learning activities were transferred into formal education settings, e.g. when schools invited the practitioners to organise the activities in their classrooms. In many cases, both in the surveys and the interviews, the participants commented that in such settings the activity would have to align to "specific syllabi" and curricula: *"We are more concerned with engagement, but teachers want to see explicit learning objectives to justify booking with us, especially in Secondary where it's harder to organise/justify outings as they're so disruptive to the school day."* (survey response, open question) and *"If we are going to schools then we have to align to the curriculum. Because you don't want the teacher to feel like she or he is wasting their time. You want to make it that you are helping them. So you are covering content for them."* (int02). Three out of seven survey respondents agreed that the goals and objectives of their activity were explicitly connected to school curricula; three respondents disagreed, and the remaining respondent did not answer this question.

An interesting finding is that the fun and playful aspect of the activities is linked to the learning outcomes and is also an element distinguishing them from formal education. As one of the interviewees commented: *"I think the main difference between these informal and non-formal activities and the formal, traditional school setting is that students are actually learning through fun."* (int03).

Learning Strategies Involved. Constructivist and social constructivist approaches to learning emerged as the main learning approaches involved. The active role of the participants was further highlighted as a strong point of the activity and an indication of success for 3 of our survey respondents: "[people] *show interest by doing the hands on activities, many ask questions.", "Often they also interject and collaborate with other players", "interactive and not passive"*. In the survey question on what describes best what happens during the activity, 5 reported discovery-learning, 4 reported problem-based learning, and 3 reported collaborative-learning. Similar approaches were also commented in the interviews: "[during the Game Jams] *the fact that you are in a team, that really helps because you get guidance from other people. [...] you are still learning things because you're explaining them"* (int01), and *"I try to make the students work in [groups of] two. Because I think it's important for them to have this collaborative aspect between two."* (int03).

3.4 Challenges

Respondents and interviewees identified specific challenges with respect to the resources and support required for running such activities. Survey respondents described the (lack of) institutional support, the resources, the (limited) number of activities and volunteers, and the appropriate marketing for communicating and disseminating the activities to the public, as weak points that needed improvement.

Similar issues were described in the interviews. Indicatively: *"recruiting volunteers, [...] monitoring that, training them [...] having the money to run these sort of things. And the people, the institutional stuff to run this. [...] Logistical staff [...]."* (int02). In one case the cost of making games for learning that could compete with commercial games and appeal to children and young people was mentioned as a challenge requiring more resources and funding: *"[...] a lot of the educational games that we have are graphically far inferior. So the challenge is to find the budget and investment for people to make the graphics. You have to make a game that attracts [the children's] attention at least in the beginning* [...]*"* (int01).

The crowded areas and the distractions particularly in public events and science fairs, and the short duration were further reported in the interviews and in 4 instances in the survey as some of the challenges of such activities that need improvement. Our study participants reported that such challenges make it difficult to employ more personalised learning approaches and increase the risk that children may disengage the activity. Indicative quote: *"We only get 1 h with the kids, so no opportunity for larger or long-term projects. 1 or at most 2 presenters/facilitators with 25 kids, so very little one-on-one".*

3.5 Discussion and Conclusions

Despite the diversity in the context and content (i.e. format, settings, structure, and target group) of the non-formal learning practices examined in this study, there seems to be a convergence in certain themes such as the objectives, the pedagogical approaches involved, the importance of fun and the challenges for achieving it. The participants of this initial study within the Maltese context, emphasized awareness and interest for a topic as a core objective, similarly to findings in [12] and [17], and favoured learner-centered approaches. Links (curriculum subjects) and differences (playfulness) to formal education settings were identified. Also, challenges such as the resources required, the time constraints and their implications, were described. Some additional interesting issues, though, also emerged from the data, such as the mediating role of the parents and gender representation.

The mediating role of the parents in the participation of minors to such activities may be an issue to further consider, particularly in the cases where digital games are involved. Parents, as reported in the interviews, are likely to be biased against digital games ("a waste of time"). Such stereotypes and attitudes towards games could potentially affect their decision of the activities their children–particularly younger children- will attend or not attend. The role of the parents may also be an issue for further study regarding the gender representation in such activities. As reported by a facilitator in robotics and coding workshops when children were registered by their parents the percentage of girls is nearly 0%; this percentage however increase substantially when children are invited by educators at schools. This seems to be a case where integration of such activities to formal education settings could support access by a wider range of children regardless of their gender.

The implications of these issues on the design of digital games to be implemented in informal and non-formal science learning practices involve the diversity, the goals, the settings, and the time constraints of the practices. Their diversity could give game designers the freedom and opportunity to create a variety of games, as also noted in [9], but also be a challenge to adapt a game to the different learning practices. The development of games for science learning seems to be presented with the additional challenge of competing with the budget and marketing of commercial games as also noted in [13]. Additionally, although games can support the development of expertise and the formation of a scientific identity [14] the short-term engagement in activities and practices that last one hour or even a few minutes as described here could rather

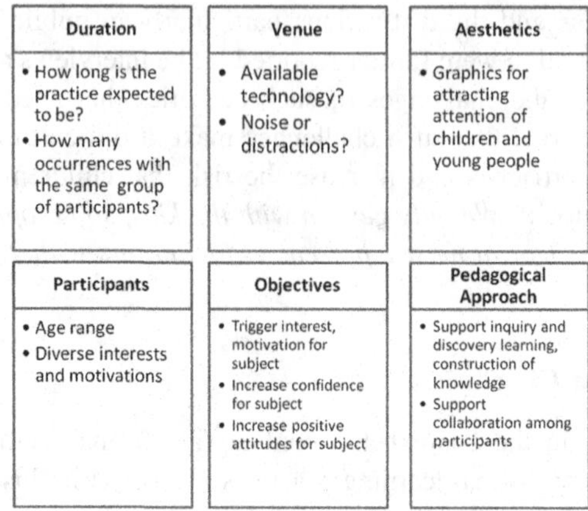

Duration
• How long is the practice expected to be?
• How many occurrences with the same group of participants?
Venue
• Available technology?
• Noise or distractions?
Aesthetics
• Graphics for attracting attention of children and young people
Participants
• Age range
• Diverse interests and motivations
Objectives
• Trigger interest, motivation for subject
• Increase confidence for subject
• Increase positive attitudes for subject
Pedagogical Approach
• Support inquiry and discovery learning, construction of knowledge
• Support collaboration among participants

Fig. 2. Game design considerations for non-formal and informal learning practices for science learning.

raise interest for a specific topic [13]. In Fig. 2, we summarise the considerations–as emerged from our data–to be considered for the design of digital games directed to non-formal and informal learning practices.

The implementation of digital games in informal or no-formal learning practices has to further consider and address factors such as the marketing of commercial games and parents' stereotypes that shape the selection and use of games in informal settings such as for recreation at home [6]. By doing so, more structured or guided practices with the appropriate learning context could expand the use of games for science learning to a wider audience of children and young people and support the understanding and learning of science concepts and positive attitudes towards science.

Science education and science literacy may benefit from research in public engagement with science and links to everyday life as described by Feinstein in [18]. Since this papers offers an initial study of a specific case with a relatively small number of participants, our findings are limited to the local context and cannot be general enough. The in-depth accounts of the practitioners and the themes that emerged, however, can provide some first insights for the study of informal and the design of non-formal practices for science learning, as well as the design of digital games that can support such practices.

Acknowledgments. The authors wish to thank the participants in the survey and interviews, the COMnPLAY project partners, and our colleagues Jasper Schellekens and Anonios Liapis who collaborated with us for conducting this study and with comments on this manuscript. This work was supported by the EU funded Horizon 2020 project COMnPLAY Science.

References

1. Biles, M.: Leveraging insights from mainstream gameplay to inform STEM game design: great idea, but what comes next? Cult. Stud. Sci. Educ. **7**(4), 903–908 (2012)
2. Bricker, L.A., Bell, P.: "GodMode is his video game name": situating learning and identity in structures of social practice. Cult. Stud. Sci. Educ. **7**(4), 883–902 (2012)
3. Jeremiassen, K.S.: Differences in students' stem identity, game play motivations, and game preferences. Doctoral Dissertation, University of Houston-Clear Lake (2018)
4. Mayo, M.J.: Video games: a route to large-scale stem education? Science **323**(5910), 79–82 (2009)
5. Williamson, B., Facer, K.: More than "just a game": the implications for schools of children's computer games communities. Educ. Commun. Inform. **4**, 255–270 (2004)
6. Ito, M.: Sociocultural contexts of game-based learning. The National Academies of Sciences, Engineering, Medicine. Paper presented at the workshop for the National Academy of Science's Committee on Learning Science: Computer Games, Simulations, and Education (2009)
7. Fowler, A.: Informal STEM learning in game jams, hackathons and game creation events. In: Proceedings of the International Conference on Game Jams, Hackathons, and Game Creation Events, New York, NY, USA, pp. 38–41 (2016)
8. Arya, A., Chastine, J., Preston, J., Fowler, A.: An international study on learning and process choices in the global game jam. IJGBL **3**(4), 27–46 (2013)
9. Squire, K., Patterson, N.: Games and simulations in informal science education. The National Academies of Sciences, Engineering, Medicine, Washington, DC, Paper commissioned for the National Research Council Workshop on Gaming and Simulations, October 2009
10. Eshach, H.: Bridging in-school and out-of-school learning: formal, non-formal, and informal education. J. Sci. Educ. Technol. **16**(2), 171–190 (2007)
11. Tisza, G., et al.: The role of age and gender on implementing informal and non-formal science learning activities for children. In: Proceedings of the FabLearn Europe 2019 Conference, New York, NY, USA, pp. 10:1–10:9 (2019)
12. Falk, J.H., Hall, W.: Understanding the informal science education landscape: an exploratory study. Public Underst. Sci. **21**(7), 865–874 (2012)
13. Honey, M., Hilton, M.L.: Learning Science Through Computer Games and Simulations. National Academies Press, Washington (2011)
14. Shaffer, D.W.: Epistemic frames for epistemic games. Comput. Educ. **46**(3), 223–234 (2006)
15. Saldaña, J.: The Coding Manual for Qualitative Researchers. Sage Publications Ltd., London (2009)
16. Patton, M.Q.: Qualitative Research and Evaluation Methods, 3rd edn. Sage Publications, Thousand Oaks (2002)
17. Allen, S., Peterman, K.: Evaluating informal STEM education: issues and challenges in context. New Direct. Eval. **2019**(161), 17–33 (2019)
18. Feinstein, N.: Salvaging science literacy. Sci. Educ. **95**(1), 168–185 (2011)

Oppidum - A Serious-AR-Game About Celtic Life and History

David A. Plecher(✉), Christian Eichhorn, Annette Köhler, and Gudrun Klinker

Chair for Computer Aided Medical Procedures and Augmented Reality, The Technical University of Munich, Munich, Germany
{plecher,koehlean,klinker}@in.tum.de, christian.eichhorn@tum.de

Abstract. Augmented Reality (AR) and (Serious) Games have been used to support cultural heritage experiences for a widespread audience. Combining both methods, we present a multiplayer Serious-AR-Game for Celtic Life and History. As a game the player experiences fun and competition which leads to intrinsic motivation. In contrast to existing games with a Celtic theme, our approach has been focused on historical accuracy to ensure a learning-centered foundation. The goal is to build a Celtic village with a functioning economic cycle. Especially by interacting in AR, the game becomes more perceptible, intriguing and vivid. Based on tangibles (markers tracked by a camera), playful, interactable replications of historically accurate Celtic buildings can be explored. The player can see their interior and also get information about the Celts by interacting with various objects or tools of their daily life. The collected knowledge is necessary to succeed in the 'quiz-war' against an opponent. This project was evaluated (N = 20) based on a questionnaire (GEQ) [10] to measure the game experience as well as the transferred knowledge and to get directed feedback for further development.

Keywords: Serious games · Augmented reality games · Flow · Interactive learning environments

1 Introduction

Even though the Celts didn't produce many written artifacts themselves [21], descriptions of Celtic legends can be found throughout human history. Today's interest in this past civilization is vast and visible in video games, comics and movies. In the process, historical facts are overlooked and the complex living structure based around a self-sustaining village is often missed. The Celtic lifestyle and their struggle for survival can be an interesting topic for a game with serious content.

In this paper, we propose a concept of a **Serious Game** combined with **Augmented Reality (AR)**, that is also used for educational purposes [3], as curiosity sparking visualization tool for knowledge transfer This design, filled

A. Liapis et al. (Eds.): GALA 2019, LNCS 11899, pp. 550–559, 2019.
https://doi.org/10.1007/978-3-030-34350-7_53

with rich and playful **interactions**, is embedded in an economic simulation of the processes occurring in the daily life of a more accurate Celtic village of that time, thereby conveying **Celtic knowledge**. Furthermore, we introduce spontaneous, active **competition** by letting two players play against each other. This should result in a more challenging game experience. Our concept combines two readily available technologies: By using Elements of classic **board games** in combination with **mobile** devices with wireless communication, tethering is avoided, the game can be played anywhere. By using AR-technology on today's smartphones, the players explore the Celtic life and history through augmented markers directly, showing 3D models of buildings and objects of daily life, accompanied by corresponding descriptions. With such a setting, we go back to the traditional table game with classic elements, such as markers and cards which are now extended with a new, virtual dimension. The outcome of the game depends on the knowledge gained in the AR views, combined with strategic decisions. We have evaluated our approach, using the Game Experience Questionnaire (GEQ) [10] to measure variables such as the immersion, flow and social presence of the player. We have also measured the learning outcome, using score comparison.

2 Serious-AR-Games

A Serious Game is defined as "a digital game created with the intention to entertain and to achieve at least one additional goal (e.g., learning or health)" [7] or also as "the use of complete games for non-entertainment purposes" [6]. Mortara et al. [15] introduced following taxonomie in respect of Serious Games for cultural heritage: *cultural awareness, historical reconstruction* and *heritage awareness*. Our game matches cultural awareness by introducing the Celtic writing system (runes) and also traditions respectively religions (druids) to the player. Regarding the historical reconstruction we are focusing on the life in a Celtic village and show a simple ecological system like producing weapons or tools with wood (woodchopper) and coal and ore from the mines. The requirements for heritage awareness for archaeological and architectural heritage are full filled by the historical accurate modelled houses. Mixed Reality (AR&VR) is often used for Cultural Heritage. A well known example is the ARCHEOGUIDE Project [24] which augmented the excavation of Olympia with 3D modells of the ancient temples on top of the ruins. It is also used inside museums to augment for example ancient statues with colors [19] or missing body parts and attributes [18]. A Game about the Battle of Thermopylae shows already an very immersive way of teaching ancient history [4] using the combination of a Serious Game and Virtual Reality (VR).

Our goal is to motivate the player to get in touch with Celtic life and history while playing and to learn subconsciously. Therefore, we have laid great importance on historical correctness. Corresponding to the "added-value"-approach [14] we used AR to enhance the player's motivation by showing virtual and historically accurate 3D-models from the player's individual perspective. There are already some games about the Celts, using either AR or other (serious) Games. A project in the area of conveying historically accurate knowledge about the Celtic lifestyle is "The Celts - Living History" for the Museum zu Allerheiligen in Schaffhausen (Switzerland) [12]. In the augmented book basic knowledge about the Celtic history, art, living conditions and warfare is visualized in an innovative and playful manner by carefully integrating AR. A similar concept applies to the somewhat popular rune game genre like Rune Writer 2 [16], where the idea of teaching interesting Celtic topics is brought to life. This strategy utilizes the technology in a way to spark interest for the topic, but leaves out the potential of actually using the learned content in a strategic way (e.g. through competition), hence represents a form of gamification [6]. A similar project can be found in the Museum of Celtic Heritage in Salzburg and is called "The Speaking Celt" [22]. Avatars are trying to transfer knowledge for children.

We followed previous research that suggested the combination of *presence* and *realism* for active game-based learning [2]. On top of that, Weibel [25] determined that *presence* and flow are two separate constructs, but connected through the experience of immersion. Thereby *presence* is defined as "the sensation of being there in the mediated world" and flow as "the sensation of being involved in the gaming action" [25, p. 1]. Game-based learning thereby has multiple advantages through engagement and *presence* (triggering flow&immersion), such as reflection of situations, practical learning, improved memory recall, contribution to a better world (moral building) [8].

3 Game Design

Our Oppidum game is designed for two players using a tablet or smartphone connected via internet and printed markers. The challenge is setting up and managing a Celtic village (archaeological terminus: "Oppidum"). Additionally the players have to explore the virtual buildings to find runestones and to gain information for the quiz-war against the opponent (competition).

Fig. 1. Historically accurate model of a Celtic building (Museum für Archäologie und Frühgeschichte Gutenstetten, Germany) [9]

3.1 Historical Model Design

As the game tries to simulate a Celtic village as historically accurately as possible, we need to model individual buildings with high precision and authencity.

In Fig. 1 the left picture shows an example of visualizations and images provided by historical sources [13,21]. On the right picture our corresponding model in the game is shown. Such models include both the interior and the exterior of buildings with realistic tools and other furniture inside.

Furthermore, we have created a playful environment by including details such as changing the appearance of the crop field for different seasons. The Celtic period has undergone changes between 800-250 B.C., with a few significant topics emerging: Trading, migrations and war. The game integrates these topics in the form of an economical model (story-telling). The player has to decide how to invest resources in the need to re-position buildings throughout the game phases to improve their production. Last but not least, war is represented as competition (quiz war) between the two players and the growth of their villages.

Fig. 2. Marker design (left) and quest cards with VuMark in the upper left corner

3.2 AR Markers

For the augmentation Vuforia Image Targets have been used with custom designs which allow robust tracking of multiple building markers at once. The markers have been printed on beer mats (see Fig. 2). The used icons (e.g. axe) on the marker referring to the houses (e.g. woodchopper) that could be build and shown on.

3.3 Quiz War

The game is turn-based and after deciding how to distribute the resources the players have the option to battle each other in a quiz. The questions are focused on the Celtic history [21]. Players implicitly learn about it when exploring the village and reading the information boxes. Both players have to answer the same set of questions. The player who correctly answers more questions receives a victory point. We provide instant feedback by showing the correct answer when a question is answered incorrectly. Multiple quiz wars are offered throughout the course of the game. To improve the learning outcome, questions which have been answered incorrectly, reappear in a later duel.

3.4 Rune System

Shining runestones are distributed throughout the village. They can be collected by clicking on the virtual stones and be stored in a rune book. Afterwards they can be combined to cast powerful spells with the help of a druid. Exploring and collecting are major game elements that are frequently used in gaming concepts with the intention to motivate players. These spells can be activated in the endgame to either boost the performance of the own village or hinder the development of the other player.

3.5 Quest Cards

Quest cards (see Fig. 2) have been added to help the player focus on a task. They are similar to event and chance cards, adding to the board game character. They provide additional suspense throughout the game due to the involved chance and opportunities Additionally, quest cards fit the concept of an AR board game. Every term, a card is drawn by each player. It has to be scanned by the camera for its activation. To achieve consistency for the design of the cards, Vuforia VuMarks are used. This allows to take one single marker template and generate various marker patterns which have consistent background, indistinguishable for the human eye. There are various types of quests, including beneficial ones which add production performance. Other quests inflict damage on the village, if not being solved before an expiration date. Each such card presents a short story with Celtic background.

3.6 Game Interface

The game basically consists of two combined systems: On the one hand players are to explore the village and the objects using an AR mode. Secondly, players need overview and control information concerning turn taking and the simulated economic model. The interface has to tailor to both needs (see Fig. 3). A top bar contains all necessary information about resources and gives access to main views like the rune book. On the right side, status updates about quests and building progress are shown. Furthermore, by tapping on virtual buildings, such as the woodchopper house, a specific resource management system can be accessed. On top of that, a technology tree gives the player more options to expand the buildings with functionality, modeled after real world Celtic processes. When starting the game, a Celtic chieftain from a neighboring village introduces the player to the game mechanics and provides hints in the upcoming game rounds.

4 AR Interactions

The simulation phase of the game focuses on the element of exploration to gain knowledge about the Celtic life and technology which is tested during the quiz phase [5]. The three-dimensional virtual view of the buildings allows a realistic

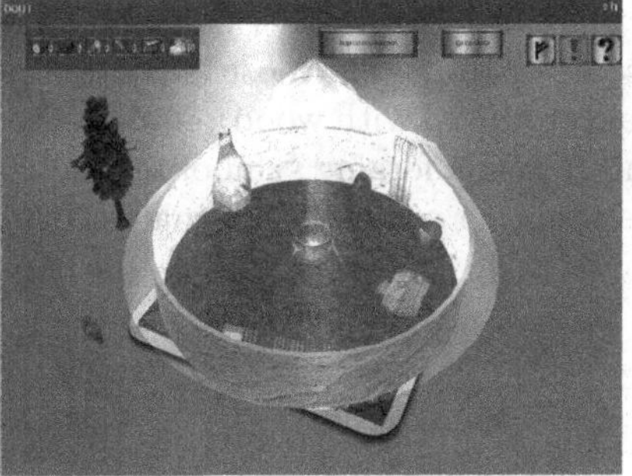

Fig. 3. Positioning the markers (left) and exploring the interior of a building (right)

perception of the living condition in a Celtic village. All exploration is performed by AR interactions with the augmented virtual buildings and objects.

Changing the Device Distance to the Buildings or Markers: When moving closer to a virtual building, the roof becomes transparent (see Fig. 4) and the player can explore the interior, representing our understanding of playful learning environment. This technique has already been used in the *AR Towering Defense Game* [23]. The player gets the opportunity to interact with various objects and tools necessary in the daily life of the Celts. Each house represents a task of the people in the village and hence contains different tools to perform them. By touching an object, text boxes appear with important information. This helps the player later in the quizzes.

Tapping on a Building: A building can also be selected via touchscreen when the marker is detected. At the beginning, a hammer is visible which indicates the option to build the house if enough resources are available. Later on, tapping on the building allows to open a menu for enhancements. Upgrades expand the production capabilities, while extensions via the individual building dependent technology tree allow the production of new types of resources. Furthermore, the view contains information about the production rate.

Varying the Position of the Buildings to Each Other: The player can rearrange the markers to increase efficiency of the production, as the path to needed resources is reduced (see Fig. 4).

5 Economic Model

The game is based on an economic simulation. Hence, the players' understanding of the production chain will determine the progress of buildings and technology in the village. Therefore, choices by the player will result in personalised learning through the discovery of their consequences, hence the combination of *presence* and *realism* [11]. There are three types of natural resources and four processed goods. Out of those, food (all processes and tasks in the village consume it to function) and wood (mainly used for buildings) are considered the starting resources. Iron is the most important long-term resource, as in combination with coal (produced with wood), it allows the production of iron objects and weapons. This focus on forging symbolizes the importance of iron in the Celtic history and the resulting resources are mandatory for succeeding in the endgame.

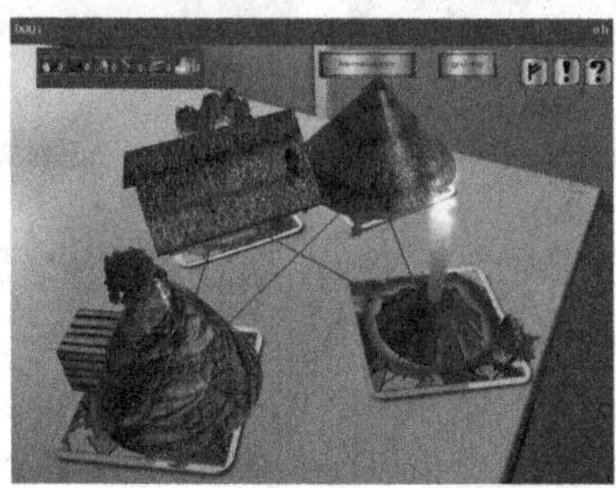

Fig. 4. Distances between the markers have an influence on the production rate

6 Evaluation

20 students (17 male and 3 female) took part in our study. All of them were in the age group 19–29 and were experienced gamers. 6 participants hadn't used AR before. We also tested the players' previous knowledge about the Celts. 16 players stated that they encountered the Celts in school, movies, books or museums before. We used the Game-Experience-Questionnaire (GEQ) [10] and also asked open questions about the usage of AR and the interaction techniques in the game. The GEQ defines categories. For each category, we have calculated the average across all participants according to the scoring guidelines (0 very low - 4 very high), see Table 1.

Table 1. Scores of GEQ core module & in-game version (left) and the scores of GEQ social presence module (rigtht)

GEQ Core Module & In-Game version	
Competence	2,116071429
Immersion	2,46875
Flow	2,348214286
Tension/Annoyance	0,4
Challenge	1,285714286
Positive affect	2,475961538
Negative affect	0,578125

GEQ Social Presence Module	
Empathy	2,135416667
Negative Feeling	1,525
Behavioural Involvement	1,322916667

As described flow and immersion play an important role for knowledge transfer. According to the evaluation of the GEQ, the players rated these and the positive affect with above-average values, just as competence. Tension/annoyance and negative affects recieved very low score. Challenge reached a score of 1,28. This should be improved in the future. According to Reichart and Brügge [20], many Serious Games are lacking social interaction like a multiplayer mode. For Bachen et al. [2] the idea of socially-oriented tasks and their impact on the learning outcome is a particularly interesting concept. Furthermore, in the study by Admiraal et al. [1] flow could already be associated with team performance, hinting the connection to rich competition. The Social Presence Module of the GEQ showed an above-average score for empathy. Thus, the participants could empathize with their opponent, e.g. in case of winning the quiz-war. Vice versa, negative feelings arose in case of loosing. Previous studies showed a correlation between experienced feelings such as empathy and the interest in learning [2]. In a future iteration of the game, it could be helpful to expand the concept of empathy by directly connecting the player to the fate of the people living in the village. We received a number of comments to the open questions about AR and the gameplay itself:

- Players commented favorably on the fact that buildings were presented with a high level of detail, stressing historical correctness.
- Players also liked the usage of AR. The ability to look at the Celtic buildings both from outside and inside was much appreciated.
- The multiplayer feature, sparking rich competition, was perceived as very motivating.
- The test persons explicitly commented that the difficult issue of combining a fun game experience with serious learning was addressed very well.
- One participant noted that he was surprised how much knowledge he had gained while playing an immersive game.

In the quiz-wars on Celtic knowledge, all players demonstrated a positive learning outcome. On average, two thirds of the questions were answered correctly.

7 Future Work

- **3D printed, trackable figures:** Toady's AR tracking capabilities are not limited to 2D markers, but it is also possible to track objects. This would introduce another typical board game element and a more haptic, perceptible element to the game.
- **Expanding the influence of seasons on the village:** This could greatly improve the playful nature by also adding more realism to the game. An example is already implemented in the form of the crops field which changes with season. Besides the visual diversity, a season simulation could teach the player a better understanding of the lifestyle and challenges faced during the different seasons, e.g. in winter the food income is low or the annual celebrations.

– **AR writing of the runes and Celtic symbols:** The rune system can be expanded to include a deeper focus on learning by having to draw the rune combinations (bind runes) for casting. This will improve memorizing the strokes and their meaning, hence enhances the Serious Game aspect. For the realization of this feature, two approaches would be possible. Either finger drawing and gesture recognition in the AR view or with a simpler solution by just writing on the screen [17].

8 Conclusion

In conclusion, we did reach the goal of implementing a game that teaches players information about Celtic life and history subconsciously. Combining elements of traditional board games (real, touchable) such as cards with historically correct 3D virtual objects was successful. Furthermore, the users liked the AR content very much and were fascinated by interacting with the virtual objects. Thus, we designed a multiplayer Serious-AR-Game about the Celts, that reached very good scores for flow, immersion and (social) presence, followed by an high documented knowledge transfer. Yet, our user tests also uncovered a number of challenges for future work, opening interesting research opportunities towards combining tangible, physical objects and settings with virtual content.

References

1. Admiraal, W., Huizenga, J., Akkerman, S., Ten Dam, G.: The concept of flow in collaborative game-based learning. Comput. Hum. Behav. **27**(3), 1185–1194 (2011)
2. Bachen, C.M., Hernández-Ramos, P., Raphael, C., Waldron, A.: How do presence, flow, and character identification affect players' empathy and interest in learning from a serious computer game? Comput. Hum. Behav. **64**, 77–87 (2016)
3. Cheng, K.H., Tsai, C.C.: Affordances of augmented reality in science learning: suggestions for future research. J. Sci. Educ. Technol. **22**(4), 449–462 (2013)
4. Christopoulos, D., Mavridis, P., Andreadis, A., Karigiannis, J.N.: Using virtual environments to tell the story: the battle of thermopylae. In: 2011 Third International Conference on Games and Virtual Worlds for Serious Applications, pp. 84–91. IEEE (2011)
5. Csikszentmihalyi, M., Abuhamdeh, S., Nakamura, J.: Flow. In: Flow and the foundations of positive psychology, pp. 227–238. Springer (2014)
6. Deterding, S., Dixon, D., Khaled, R., Nacke, L.: From game design elements to gamefulness: defining gamification. In: Proceedings of the 15th International Academic MindTrek Conference: Envisioning Future Media Environments, pp. 9–15. ACM (2011)
7. Dörner, R., Göbel, S., Effelsberg, W., Wiemeyer, J.: Serious Games: Foundations, Concepts and Practice. Springer, Heidelberg (2016). https://doi.org/10.1007/978-3-319-40612-1
8. Gamelearn: Game-based Learning und Serious Games (2017). https://bit.ly/2Z3qF2S. Accessed 30 Mar 2019
9. Gutenstetten: Museum für Archäologie und Frühgeschichte Gutenstetten, Germany (2008). http://www.acm.org/class/how_to_use.html. Accessed 26 Nov 2018

10. IJsselsteijn, W., et al.: Measuring the experience of digital game enjoyment. In: Proceedings of Measuring Behavior, pp. 88–89. Noldus Information Technology Wageningen, Netherlands (2008)
11. Konijn, E.A., Bijvank, M.N.: Doors to another me: identity construction through digital game play. In: Serious Games, pp. 201–225. Routledge (2009)
12. Kovacovsky, M.: The Celts - Living History (2013). http://martinkovacovsky.ch/die-kelten/
13. Maier, B.: Geschichte und Kultur der Kelten, vol. 3. CH Beck (2012)
14. Mayer, R.E.: Computer Games for Learning: An Evidence-Based Approach. MIT Press, Cambridge (2014)
15. Mortara, M., Catalano, C.E., Bellotti, F., Fiucci, G., Houry-Panchetti, M., Petridis, P.: Learning cultural heritage by serious games. J. Cult. Herit. **15**(3), 318–325 (2014)
16. PB Softworks: Rune writer 2. App. PB Softworks, Karlsruhe, Germany (2015)
17. Plecher, D.A., Eichhorn, C., Kindl, J., Kreisig, S., Wintergerst, M., Klinker, G.: Dragon tale-a serious game for learning Japanese Kanji. In: Proceedings of the 2018 Annual Symposium on Computer-Human Interaction in Play Companion Extended Abstracts, pp. 577–583. ACM (2018)
18. Plecher, D.A., Wandinger, M., Klinker, G.: Mixed reality for cultural heritage. In: 2019 IEEE Conference on Virtual Reality and 3D User Interfaces (VR), pp. 1618–1622. IEEE (2019)
19. Pujol, L., Roussou, M., Poulou, S., Balet, O., Vayanou, M., Ioannidis, Y.: Personalizing interactive digital storytelling in archaeological museums: the chess project. In: 40th Annual Conference of Computer Applications and Quantitative Methods in Archaeology. Amsterdam University Press (2012)
20. Reichart, B., Bruegge, B.: Social interaction patterns for learning in serious games. In: Proceedings of the 19th European Conference on Pattern Languages of Programs, p. 22. ACM (2014)
21. Rieckhoff, S., Biel, J., Abels, B.U.: Die Kelten in Deutschland. Stuttgart (2001)
22. Schneeweis. Technology: The Speaking Celt (2016). https://www.wikitude.com/showcase/speaking-celt-museum-experience/
23. Tolstoi, P., Dippon, A.: Towering defense: an augmented reality multi-device game. In: Proceedings of the 33rd Annual ACM Conference Extended Abstracts on Human Factors in Computing Systems, pp. 89–92. ACM (2015)
24. Vlahakis, V., et al.: Archeoguide: an augmented reality guide for archaeological sites. IEEE Comput. Graph. Appl. **22**(5), 52–60 (2002)
25. Weibel, D., Wissmath, B.: Immersion in computer games: the role of spatial presence and flow. Int. J. Comput. Games Technol. **2011**, 6 (2011)

A Quantitative Approach for Developing Serious Games for Aptitude and Trait Assessment

Brenton M. Wiernik(✉) and Michael D. Coovert

University of South Florida, Tampa, FL, USA
brenton@wiernik.org

Abstract. We describe a development process for serious games to create psychometrically rigorous measures of individual aptitudes (abilities, skills) and traits (habits, tendencies, behaviors). We begin with a discussion of serious games and how they can instantiate appropriate cognitive states for relevant aptitudes and traits to manifest. This can have numerous advantages over traditional assessment modalities. We then describe the iterative approach to aptitude and trait measurement that emphasizes (1) careful definition and specification of the traits and aptitudes to be measured, (2) rigorous assessment of reliability and validity, and (3) revision of gameplay elements and metrics to improve measurement properties.

Keywords: Assessment · Validity · Factor analysis · Personality · Cognitive ability

1 Overview

Selecting employees with necessary competencies to perform their jobs is critical to ensure workforces are productive and able to meet organizational goals, especially for cognitively demanding careers, such as software development, data science, and cybersecurity. Identifying the most capable employees requires precise, valid assessment of job-relevant aptitudes and traits that contribute to employees' performance. In this proposal, we lay the groundwork for a philosophy of measurement for assessing aptitudes and traits using serious games. We begin with a discussion of serious games and their potential advantages and disadvantages compared with traditional assessment modalities. We emphasize the potential power of serious games to create an experience for the player with high psychological fidelity to the future work environment [1]. This allows players' in-game behavior to reflect their standing on job-relevant traits and aptitudes and to predict future on-the-job performance. Next, we describe a development sequence to ensure that serious game-based measures are psychometrically sound before applying them in operations. This sequence involves careful definition and specification of the traits and aptitudes to be measured, assessment of measures' reliability and validity following traditional psychometric standards [2], and iterative revision and refinement of gameplay-related metrics to improve psychometric properties.

A. Liapis et al. (Eds.): GALA 2019, LNCS 11899, pp. 560–571, 2019.
https://doi.org/10.1007/978-3-030-34350-7_54

1.1 Serious Games

Serious games are an evolving tool in organizations. Most current applications focus on education and training [3, 4]. An emerging area of interest seeks to also apply games as part of a technologically enhanced *employee selection process*. Here, the goal is to use information collected during gameplay to assess a player's standing on job-relevant aptitudes and traits to determine their suitability for specific work roles. Below, we review existing types of serious games, consider common features of serious games that may prove useful for personnel assessment, and consider advantages and disadvantages of serious games relative to traditional assessment modalities.

1.2 Existing Classifications of Serious Games

We can consider the potential scope of serious game-based assessment by examining existing serious game taxonomies. A widely-used taxonomy describes six major categories of competencies (aptitudes and traits) that serious games have been designed to develop or assess [5, 6]:

1. Cognitive and perceptual competencies (e.g., problem-solving, planning)
2. Sensory-motor competencies (e.g., reaction time, eye-hand coordination)
3. Emotional and volitional competencies (e.g., stress control, endurance)
4. Personal and attitudinal competencies (e.g., self-efficacy, interest)
5. Social competencies (e.g., cooperation, communication)
6. Domain-specific competencies (e.g., media knowledge, job knowledge)

These categories of competencies (aptitudes and traits) are similar to major categories of competencies identified in job analysis and competency modeling practice in industrial psychology [7]. Ludoscience [8] has developed another serious game classification system that provides a directory of available games with summaries and searchable keywords. One may also examine the Serious Games Association directory [9].

1.3 Psychological Fidelity as a Strength of Game-Based Assessment

The key potential strength of serious games as a modality for employee assessment is their ability to create an immersive experience with high psychological fidelity to the on-the-job work environment [9, 10]. That is, the game can place the player into cognitive and emotional states that resemble those experienced on the job [11]. All the elements of game design can be leveraged to evoke key work-relevant competencies, permitting each player's relative standings on key aptitudes and traits to manifest themselves through gameplay. These elements include (1) mechanics—procedures and rules of the game; (2) theme and story—the context and sequence of events that unfold in the game; (3) aesthetics—how the game looks, sounds, and feels; and (4) the technological media through which players interact with the game (e.g., displays, keyboards, physical apparatuses, or augmented reality devices [12] (p. 41). For example, strong themes and well-designed aesthetics can evoke specific emotional states. Using time limits, a fast pace, low lighting, or emotional or startling imagery or sounds can induce feelings of stress, urgency, or confusion. Assessing players' responses to such situations can be useful for many occupations, such as public safety and medicine. Similarly, game mechanics might be designed so that a team of players must cooperate to achieve shared goals; such a design could be used to assess individuals' cooperativeness or to assess a teams' communication skills or shared mental models. The sequence of game experiences over time can also be used as part of assessment. For example, games can be designed so that gameplay becomes progressively harder, permitting assessment of players' ability to acquire new skills or adapt to changing circumstances.

1.4 Advantages and Disadvantages of Assessment via Serious Games

Traditional aptitude assessments typically take the form of text-based questions and response options presented to applicants on paper or a computer screen. Questions may assess general capabilities (e.g., reasoning ability) or domain-specific knowledge. Their target aptitudes are obvious to applicants, and their presentation is not contextualized for a specific goal other than assessment. Traditional trait assessments typically involve self-report responses to questions about typical behaviors in various settings. Trait assessment relies on applicants' descriptions of their own behavior, rather than observable performance. Alternative assessment modalities, such as work samples, simulations, and situational judgment tests, aim to provide higher fidelity assessment of job-relevant competencies [11]. Serious games can be understood as a new approach in this tradition of high-fidelity, performance-based assessment.

Compared to traditional assessment modalities, serious games may have several advantages for assessing cognitive workers. First, serious games may elicit more favorable reactions from assessed applicants. Although traditional aptitude measures (e.g., general cognitive ability or reasoning measures) are widely applied in employment contexts, advanced employees may feel that such measures are inappropriate or insulting for employees of their level [13, 14]. Similarly, high-level applicants may respond negatively to traditional self-report trait measures, for example, believing that such measures are too easily "faked" or otherwise are unable to accurately predict future performance [15]. Although such beliefs are likely inaccurate [16], applicants may respond better to serious game assessments due to their greater job fidelity and higher production values. Second, related to the first point, serious games may be more engaging for applicants and produce greater test-taker motivation [17]. Traditional cognitive assessments may be perceived as boring or uninteresting; even if applicants are extrinsically motivated to perform well in order to be selected for a position, uninteresting tasks may reduce intrinsic motivation, preventing applicants from performing at maximal levels and potentially contaminating assessments with extraneous capabilities (e.g., attentional control). By providing an assessment experience that is intrinsically motivating, serious games may help to elicit maximal performance during applicant assessment. Third, compared to traditional self-report trait measures, serious game assessments may be less prone to impression management [18] (but cf. [16]). Applicants may be less able to discern the targeted traits in a serious game compared to traditional assessments, so they are less able to modify their responses to inflate their expected scores. Fourth, serious games may be able to assess multiple aptitudes and traits at one time by using a variety of gameplay metrics recorded concurrently. This can potentially reduce assessment time compared to traditional multi-scale assessment batteries.

Despite these potential advantages, serious games also have several potential disadvantages that must be overcome to ensure reliable and valid assessment. First, it may be difficult to develop gameplay metrics that can function as indicators of targeted aptitudes and traits without contamination by undesired characteristics (e.g., video game familiarity, psychomotor skills). Second, if multiple traits or aptitudes are assessed using performance on the same gameplay tasks, these scores may show a lack of discriminant validity (unique variance for each assessment), even if they are scored using distinct gameplay metrics. For example, many performance-based metrics (e.g., achievement of game objectives, resource management, gameplay speed) are likely to be influenced by general cognitive ability and overall game skill, leading to substantial correlations among these measures. Third, some traits or aptitudes may be difficult to assess within the context of a game and may be better assessed through traditional methods. For example, Conscientiousness-related traits (responsibility, dependability, achievement striving) refer primarily to behaviors exhibited over the long term. Valid measures of these characteristics may be difficult to obtain during a short gameplay period; more accurate assessment could likely be realized using self-report, other-report, or other methods than can refer to long-term typical behavioral patterns. Fourth, relatedly, some traits may take longer to assess reliably using a serious game than using a traditional method. In designing serious games for personnel assessment, developers must take caution to avoid these disadvantages and ensure that the serious game provides real benefits over traditional alternative assessment modalities.

2 Development Sequence for Game-Based Assessments

2.1 Serious Games as a Means to an End

When designing a serious game for personnel assessment, it is *critical* to remember that the purpose of the game is to obtain reliable, predictive assessments of applicant traits and aptitudes—the game is only a means to this end. It does not matter how clean, slick, expensive, or useful the game *appears*; if it cannot reliably assess the targeted competencies, the game will be unable to provide useful information to aid organizations' decision making. This purpose must guide all game design, development, validation, and deployment decisions. This purpose of personnel assessment games—to accurately measure job-relevant traits, not merely entertain—is the game's "characterizing goal" [9] (p. 3). Achieving this goal requires not only quality game design, but clear specification of the assessment purposes and rigorous evidence of psychometric validity.

2.2 Assessment Purpose: Construct Definition and Specification

Development of serious game assessments must follow rigorous procedures to ensure reliability, validity, utility, and fairness [2]. The first step of this process is to clearly define the traits and aptitudes ("constructs") that the game will measure and to specify how these characteristics are linked with on-the-job performance (e.g., what level of an ability is relevant for the job? under what circumstances must employees demonstrate a trait?). These decisions should be informed by job analysis, a process through which key work tasks are described and the necessary aptitudes and traits to perform them are delineated [19]. The constructs to be assessed must be carefully chosen so they are (1) necessary for effective job performance, (2) amenable to assessment using gameplay performance, and (3) not already well-assessed using existing measures and methods.

2.3 Selecting Game Assessment Metrics

After specifying the aptitudes and skills to be measured, the next step is to select the specific metrics that will be used to quantify these competences. Assessment in a serious game typically occurs via three primary methods—(1) direct assessment by the game engine during gameplay, (2) ratings by trained observers, or (3) player responses to questions during or after play [10, 20]. Some constructs, such as decision-making ability, may be amenable to direct assessment by the game engine (e.g., by achievement of game objectives), whereas others (e.g., team cohesion, emotional states) may be better-assessed using observer ratings or player responses to post-game reflection questions.

When selecting performance metrics to monitor as assessments of target constructs, it is important to align assessment granularity with the level needed to inform decisions. Human performance occurs at multiple levels of specificity—for example, neurological, biomechanical, cognitive, and social. The same phenomenon can be described simultaneously at multiple levels. For example, in a resource management game, performance could be assessed at the biomechanical level using a stream of individual clicks and movements. It could also be assessed more abstractly at the cognitive level by capturing the aggregate number of errors and efficiency of the player's allocation decisions. In many cases, focusing assessment at the more abstract cognitive and social levels will produce more actionable performance information than minute neurological or biomechanical information [21]. For a summary, see [22] (pp. 275–277).

In designing serious game assessments, developers must conceive of observable performance behaviors and outcomes as *indicators* of the underlying latent traits and aptitudes they wish to assess [10]. Game performance itself is not of interest; performance metrics are only valuable to the degree that they can be used to infer players' standing on targeted job-relevant traits and aptitudes. Directly observable behaviors and responses may be driven by multiple traits and aptitudes; game designers must carefully consider the myriad of factors that may contribute to performance behaviors and select metrics (or apply analytic models) to isolate relevant trait and aptitude information. Gameplay must also be designed to avoid evoking unintended responses.

For example, game difficulty should be increased at an appropriate rate to engage and challenge players without inducing frustration or anxiety.

Performance evolves over the course of gameplay, and changes over time may impact the validity of assessments. Considering the stage of gameplay is critical for serious game assessment. For example, early in gameplay, players may need time to become familiar with the game controls and objectives. Early performance may thus more reflect factors such as prior gaming experience (i.e., "game wise-ness"), rather than the constructs of interest. To counter such effects, developers might consider providing a warmup period for the player to practice and become comfortable with play before beginning scored assessment. The constructs driving successful game performance may also change over the course of play. For example, in a team simulation, early team-level performance might capture team trust—willingness to work with and rely on other people. Later in play, when players are more comfortable with each other, successful performance may be more driven by effective communication and teamwork skills.

Assessment metrics might also consider players' dynamic performance over time. Does performance improve over time? Is it consistent or highly variable? How does performance vary across different situations, task types, stimuli, or difficulty levels? These qualities are often difficult to assess in the staffing process; thus, a game's ability to capture performance dynamics is a potential advantage over traditional modalities.

2.4 Measurement and Modeling

This section considers the issue of measurement—how observable game performance metrics are used to infer underlying trait and aptitude levels. After identifying candidate metrics to assess each construct, formal models must be built and evaluated to convert raw performance metrics into scores for targeted constructs. A variety of psychometric and statistical models are available to model latent traits and aptitudes. We review three common models that may be particularly useful for serious game-based assessment.

Common Factor Model

A common factor model specifies that each observed indicator comprises two parts—(1) variance shared with other indicators due to a common factor, taken to represent the construct of interest and (2) variance unique to each indicator, usually taken to represent measurement error. For example, several game objectives may be designed to capture decision-making ability. Success/failure for each objective can be modeled as indicators (a la test items) of a latent Decision-Making factor. We show such a model in Fig. 1 with standard RAM notation from structural equation modeling. Ellipses are latent constructs, boxes are observed/measured variables, single-headed arrows are factor loadings/regression paths, and double-headed arrows are variances or residual/error variances. Here, G is a common factor purported to underlie performance on the six observed indicators $M1$–$M6$. The λ values are factor loadings—regression coefficients predicting each observed variable using the latent factor.

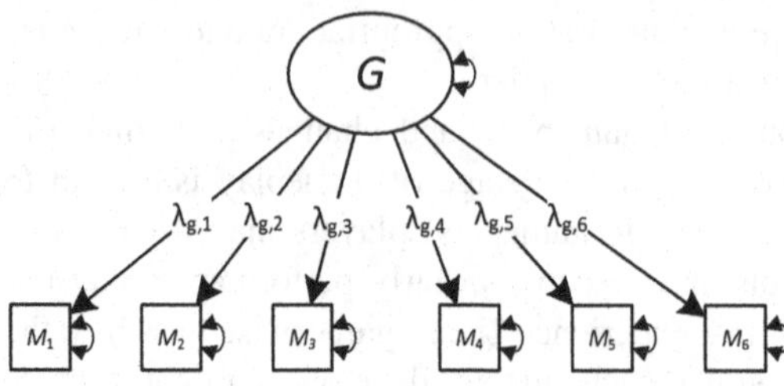

Fig. 1. A common factor model with six indicators. Each indicator loads onto the general factor (G).

A common factor model is appropriate when a weighted composite of indicators can well-represent the construct. For an overall score to be interpretable, the measure should be unidimensional or at least possess a strong general factor that captures most of the variance in observed indicators [23, 24]. For guidelines on common factor models, see [25, 26].

Bifactor Model

A bifactor model (Fig. 2) specifies that each observed indicator comprises three parts—(1) variance shared with *all* other indicators due to a common general factor, G, (2) variance shared with a *subset* of other indicators due to "group factors", S, and (3) variance unique to each indicator (again interpreted as measurement error) [27].

Bifactor models are useful when indicators violate the unidimensional common factor model's strict conditional independence assumption—that indicators are independent after accounting for a single common factor [27]. The general and group factors in a bifactor model could all be substantively meaningful (e.g., a broad trait and subtraits), or one or the other could be interpreted as a measurement artefact. For example, a bifactor model may be useful in serious game assessment to increase discriminant validity (reduce collinearity) between scores for different constructs. Performance-based metrics based on the same gameplay sequence are likely to be highly correlated. These correlations may be substantive (e.g., overall skill or aptitude), but they may also reflect shared method artefacts. Removing this common variance using a bifactor model can help to produce more distinct scores for specific aptitudes, permitting differential assessment and comparison of players across multiple constructs. Caution is warranted, however; if the general factor is strong, group factor scores after removing it may be very unreliable (imprecisely estimated) [24, 28]. For guidance on bifactor models, see [27, 29].

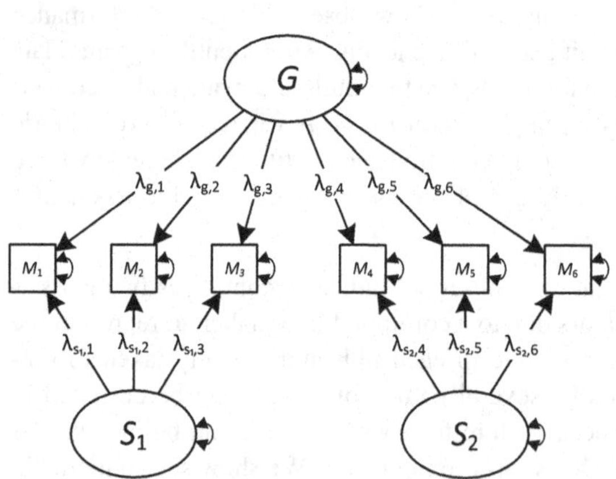

Fig. 2. A bifactor model with six indicators. Each indicator loads onto the general factor (G) and onto one group factor (S_1 or S_2).

Growth Curve and Latent Change Score Models

A third useful model is a growth curve model (Fig. 3), as well as the related latent change score model [30]. In a latent growth curve model, a construct is assessed repeatedly over time, and changes in the scores are used to model growth trajectories for each person. Each person's growth is modeled using an intercept factor, with all loadings fixed to 1, and one or more slope factors, with loadings fixed to values based on the amount of time elapsed or number of measurements taken. Different types of growth trajectories can be modeled (e.g., linear, quadratic). Growth curve models are useful for assessing development or change. For example, they could be used to quantify how quickly players learn a skill. Coovert et al. [31] used growth curve models to assess teammate trust development. For guidance on growth curve models, see [32].

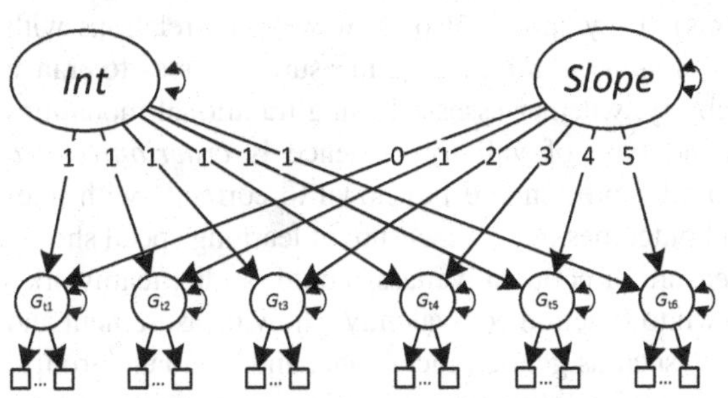

Fig. 3. A latent growth curve model with six time points (G_{t1}–G_{t2}), an intercept (*Int*), and a linear growth term (*Slope*). Each timepoint is a common factor model with observed indicators (□; full measurement models not shown).

Typically, the number of candidate metrics will be relatively small, as they will be specifically designed to assess specific constructs. If a large number of metrics are being considered, other modeling approaches, such as regularized regression or genetic algorithms, may also be useful [33].

Reliability and Measurement Precision

Trait and aptitude scores derived from serious game-based assessments must be estimated with sufficient precision (1) to discern applicants' specific competency levels and (2) to discriminate between applicants with different competency levels. This means that standard errors for individual scores must be small. This is the concept of measure reliability [2]. If the estimated models yield scores with large standard errors, assessments should be revised until standard errors are small enough to meet decision-making needs. This can include revising metrics to be higher quality or more reliable or adding additional metrics to the scoring model. To predict future job performance, scores must also have high test–retest reliability (stability over time) [2].

2.5 Validation

After designing a serious game, choosing performance metrics, and modeling these metrics to estimate reliable scores, further analyses are needed to evaluate the *validity* of the scores—whether they can be accurately interpreted as reflecting individuals' standing on the intended traits or aptitudes, as well as whether they accurately predict on-the-job performance [2]. Several types of validity evidence of must be gathered before operational use of a serious game-based assessment can be justified. The first is *construct validity* evidence. The serious game-based scores should be shown to correlate with scores on other measures of the same or similar constructs (*convergent validity*; e.g., problem-solving game scores should correlate with traditional deductive and inductive reasoning assessments). They should also show weak correlations with measures of other constructs (*discriminant validity*; e.g., a measure of stress tolerance should be unrelated to reasoning ability, whether assessed using traditional modalities or game-based metrics). The second type of validity evidence is *criterion-related validity* evidence. Serious game-based scores should be shown to correlate with relevant job performance behaviors and outcomes (e.g., a measure of learning speed should predict training performance; a measure of cooperativeness should predict teamwork). Finally, assessments should be shown to function equivalently (show measurement and predictive invariance) across groups, such as gender, racial, age, and language groups.

Collecting data to show these types of validity evidence helps to ensure that scores can be accurately interpreted as reflecting the intended competencies and to rule out alternative interpretations (e.g., that scores merely reflect game-playing skill, gender bias, or noise). The role of sound psychometric analysis in this work cannot be overstated; without accurate and rigorous psychometric evidence supporting proposed interpretations of calculated scores, it is impossible know whether assessment results can usefully inform decision making practice. Unless robust reliability and validity evidence is presented, there is no way to know whether a serious game is useful or merely a pleasant diversion.

2.6 Iteration and Refinement

Developing a serious game that can reliably and validly assess job-relevant aptitudes and traits is a challenging process. In most cases, many rounds of revision and refinement will be needed before an assessment meets psychometric standards for operational use. Game performance metrics that were initially expected to reliably indicate a specific construct may prove unreliable or unrelated to existing measures of these constructs. Even reliable and valid metrics may show insufficient variance to discriminate individuals with different construct levels (e.g., if game tasks are too easy or challenging for the job applicant population). Serious game-based measures, just like traditional psychometric assessments, require extensive testing and revision before measures can be validly applied in practice. Even the game design itself (separate from design of game-based assessments—controls, audiovisual assets, difficulty, etc.) requires extensive playtesting and revision to ensure the game is playable and engaging for players.

Given the need for extensive testing and revision, serious game developers should adopt an iterative or spiral development model [12] (p. 83), beginning with an initial prototype followed by testing, revision, further testing, further revision, and so forth. This process continues until acceptable levels of playability and assessment reliability and validity are achieved.

3 Summary

Developing psychometrically reliable and valid measures of aptitudes and traits is critical to inform selection of employees, especially for cognitively demanding jobs. Serious games present an exciting new technology that may address important limitations of traditional assessment modalities. Attention to the psychometric properties of assessments during serious game development is paramount. Designing a serious game that creates a terrific play experience is of no benefit if it fails to deliver an accurate assessment the targeted aptitudes and traits. In this paper, we described a framework for developing and iteratively evaluating and refining game-based assessments to ensure the resulting assessment products can meaningfully inform personnel decision-making.

References

1. Kozlowski, S.W.J., DeShon, R.P.: A psychological fidelity approach to simulation-based training: theory, research and principles. In: Schiflett, S.G., Elliott, L.R., Salas, E., Coovert, M.D. (eds.) Scaled Worlds: Development, Validation and Applications. Routledge, London (2017). https://doi.org/10.4324/9781315243771
2. Society for Industrial and Organizational Psychology, American Psychological Association: Principles for the validation and use of personnel selection procedures (Fifth edition) (2018). https://www.apa.org/ed/accreditation/about/policies/personnel-selection-procedures.pdf
3. Ford, J.K., Meyer, T.: Advances in training technology: meeting the workplace challenges of talent development, deep specialization, and collaborative learning. In: Coovert, M.D., Thompson, L.F. (eds.) The Psychology of Workplace Technology. Routledge, New York (2013). https://doi.org/10.4324/9780203735565
4. Long, D.T., Mulch, C.M.: Interactive wargaming cyberwar: 2025 (2017). https://apps.dtic.mil/docs/citations/AD1053350
5. Wiemeyer, J., Hardy, S.: Serious games and motor learning: concepts, evidence, technology. In: Bredl, B., Bösche, W. (eds.) Serious Games and Virtual Worlds in Education, Professional Development, and Healthcare, pp. 197–220. IGI Global, Hershey (2013). https://doi.org/10.4018/978-1-4666-3673-6.ch013
6. Wiemeyer, J., Kliem, A.: Serious games in prevention and rehabilitation—a new panacea for elderly people? Eur. Rev. Aging Phys. Act. **9**, 41–50 (2012). https://doi.org/10.1007/s11556-011-0093-x
7. The O*NET® Content Model. https://www.onetcenter.org/content.html
8. Ludoscience: A collaborative classification of serious games. http://serious.gameclassification.com/
9. Dörner, R., Göbel, S., Effelsberg, W., Wiemeyer, J. (eds.): Serious Games: Foundations, Concepts and Practice. Springer, Cham (2016). https://doi.org/10.1007/978-3-319-40612-1
10. Coovert, M.D., Winner, J., Bennett, W.: Construct development and validation in game-based research. Simul. Gaming. **48**, 236–248 (2017). https://doi.org/10.1177/1046878116682661
11. Lievens, F., Patterson, F.: The validity and incremental validity of knowledge tests, low-fidelity simulations, and high-fidelity simulations for predicting job performance in advanced-level high-stakes selection. J. Appl. Psychol. **96**, 927–940 (2011). https://doi.org/10.1037/a0023496

12. Schell, J.: The Art of Game Design: A Book of Lenses CRC Press, Boca Raton (2008). https://doi.org/10.1201/9780080919171
13. Anderson, N., Salgado, J.F., Hülsheger, U.R.: Applicant reactions in selection: comprehensive meta-analysis into reaction generalization versus situational specificity. Int. J. Sel. Assess. **18**, 291–304 (2010). https://doi.org/10.1111/j.1468-2389.2010.00512.x
14. Anderson, N.: Applicant and recruiter reactions to new technology in selection: a critical review and agenda for future research. Int. J. Sel. Assess. **11**, 121–136 (2003). https://doi.org/10.1111/1468-2389.00235
15. Gilliland, S.W.: Fairness from the applicant's perspective: reactions to employee selection procedures. Int. J. Sel. Assess. 3, 11–18 (1995). https://doi.org/10.1111/j.1468-2389.1995.tb00002.x
16. Ones, D.S., Viswesvaran, C., Reiss, A.D.: Role of social desirability in personality testing for personnel selection: the red herring. J. Appl. Psychol. **81**, 660–679 (1996). https://doi.org/10.1037/0021-9010.81.6.660
17. Eklöf, H.: Skill and will: test taking motivation and assessment quality. Assess. Educ. Princ. Policy Pract. **17**, 345–356 (2010). https://doi.org/10.1080/0969594X.2010.516569
18. McFarland, L.A., Yun, G.J., Harold, C.M., Viera, L., Moore, L.G.: An examination of impression management use and effectiveness across assessment center exercises: the role of competency demands. Pers. Psychol. **58**, 949–980 (2005). https://doi.org/10.1111/j.1744-6570.2005.00374.x
19. Wilson, M.A. (ed.): The Handbook of Work Analysis: Methods, Systems, Applications and Science of Work Measurement in Organizations. Routledge, New York (2013). https://doi.org/10.4324/9780203136324
20. Coovert, M.D., Winner, J., Bennett, Jr., W., Howard, D.J.: Serious games are a serious tool for team research. Int. J. Serious Games. **4** (2017). https://doi.org/10.17083/ijsg.v4i1.141
21. Campbell, J.P., Wiernik, B.M.: The modeling and assessment of work performance. Annu. Rev. Organ. Psychol. Organ. Behav. **2** 47–74 (2015). https://doi.org/10.1146/annurev-orgpsych-032414-111427
22. Wiemeyer, J., Kickmeier-Rust, M., Steiner, Christina M.: Performance assessment in serious games. In: Dörner, R., Göbel, S., Effelsberg, W., Wiemeyer, J. (eds.) Serious Games, pp. 273–302. Springer, Cham (2016). https://doi.org/10.1007/978-3-319-40612-1_10
23. Nandakumar, R.: Assessing essential unidimensionality of real data. Appl. Psychol. Meas. **17**, 29–38 (1993). https://doi.org/10.1177/014662169301700108
24. Gignac, G.E., Watkins, M.W.: Bifactor modeling and the estimation of model-based reliability in the WAIS-IV. Multivar. Behav. Res. **48**, 639–662 (2013). https://doi.org/10.1080/00273171.2013.804398
25. Coovert, M.D., McNelis, K.: Determining the number of common factors in factor analysis: a review and program. Educ. Psychol. Meas. **48**, 687–692 (1988). https://doi.org/10.1177/0013164488483012
26. Comrey, A.L.: A First Course in Factor Analysis, 2 edn. Psychology Press, New York (2013). https://doi.org/10.4324/9781315827506
27. Reise, S.P.: The rediscovery of bifactor measurement models. Multivar. Behav. Res. **47**, 667–696 (2012). https://doi.org/10.1080/00273171.2012.715555
28. Wiernik, B.M., Wilmot, M.P., Kostal, J.W.: How data analysis can dominate interpretations of dominant general factors. Ind. Organ. Psychol. **8**, 438–445 (2015). https://doi.org/10.1017/iop.2015.60
29. Giordano, C.A., Waller, N.G.: Recovering bifactor models: a comparison of seven methods. Psychol. Methods (2019). https://doi.org/10.1037/met0000227

30. McArdle, J.J.: Latent variable modeling of differences and changes with longitudinal data. Annu. Rev. Psychol. **60**, 577–605 (2009). https://doi.org/10.1146/annurev.psych.60.110707.163612
31. Coovert, M., Miller, E., Bennett, Jr., W.: Assessing trust and effectiveness in virtual teams: latent growth curve and latent change score models. Soc. Sci. **6**, 87 (2017). https://doi.org/10.3390/socsci6030087
32. Bollen, K.A., Curran, P.J.: Latent Curve Models: A Structural Equation Perspective. Wiley, Hoboken (2005). https://doi.org/10.1002/0471746096
33. Kuhn, M., Johnson, K.: Applied Predictive Modeling. Springer, New York (2013). https://doi.org/10.1007/978-1-4614-6849-3

Designing a Serious Game to Motivate Energy Savings in a Museum: Opportunities & Challenges

Dimosthenis Kotsopoulos[1(✉)], Cleopatra Bardaki[2], Thanasis G. Papaioannou[3], Stavros Lounis[1], George D. Stamoulis[3], and Katerina Pramatari[1]

[1] ELTRUN e-Business Research Center, Athens University of Economics and Business, 47A Evelpidon Street & 33 Lefkados Street, 11362 Athens, Greece
{dkotsopoulos, slounis, k.pramatari}@aueb.gr

[2] Department of Informatics and Telematics, Harokopio University, 9 Omirou Street, 17778 Tavros-Athens, Greece
cleobar@hua.gr

[3] Network Economics and Services (NES) Group, Athens University of Economics and Business, 76 Patission Street, 10434 Athens, Greece
{pathan, gstamoul}@aueb.gr

Abstract. The ongoing global environmental crisis has led to the identification of energy-saving as a worldwide necessity. Public buildings hold great unexploited opportunities towards that end. Moreover, the occupants' behavior is an impactful factor that can potentially lead to significant energy-savings therein. Recognizing the engaging power of games towards that end, our research aim is to motivate human-driven energy conservation in an especially challenging organizational context: an art museum. Through a survey of our context, we recognized the energy-saving opportunities for employees and visitors therein. Consequently we designed and present an effective serious game that fits the special characteristics of a museum's exhibition area, as well as the users' requirements, thus providing a mutually engaging experience for personnel and visitors alike. We also present and discuss the results from the participation of museum visitors in the game, as well as the actual energy savings achieved. Furthermore, we discuss our collected insights while designing and applying the serious game, so that future game designers can get a head start in their own projects, by keeping the challenges that may lay ahead in mind.

Keywords: Serious game · Engagement · Energy conservation · Museum

1 Introduction

Worldwide energy conservation has been widely recognized as the most important measure towards reducing CO_2 emissions and protecting the environment (International Energy Agency 2016; UNFCCC 2016). However, electricity demand features an

A. Liapis et al. (Eds.): GALA 2019, LNCS 11899, pp. 572–584, 2019.
https://doi.org/10.1007/978-3-030-34350-7_55

average yearly growth of 1.6% in the commercial sector (Conti et al. 2016). Therefore, it is important to increase our efforts in reducing energy consumption in public buildings. At the same time, human behavior can add – or save – one-third to a building's designed energy performance (Nguyen and Aiello 2013). Moreover, the application of games to reduce energy consumption has led to savings in the range of 3–6% – with more than 10% achievable (Grossberg *et al.* 2015). Through our research, we aim to utilize serious games, towards increasing the occupants' motivation for energy conservation in a museum exhibition area. In this paper, we present the design characteristics, as well as implementation challenges we faced, in order to provide an engaging game experience for museum employees and visitors alike, which would lead to energy behavior change. Furthermore, we provide evidence that, by participating in the proposed energy-saving game museum visitors achieved actual energy savings, and there is great energy saving potential provided that visitor participation increases. Moreover, this study provides guidelines for future practitioners and researchers that aspire to design effective energy-saving games for challenging inflexible environments with strict security regulations, such as museums.

2 Background

2.1 Energy-Saving Behavior at Work

Energy in commercial buildings is mostly consumed through heating and cooling systems, lights, computers, and other equipment (Conti et al. 2016). Energy conservation through technological improvements should be accompanied by efforts towards improving occupants' behavior, since it also significantly affects the successfulness of technology-based efficiency improvements (Delmas *et al.* 2013; Lutzenhiser 1993). Although studies in energy conservation through behavior change emerged with the oil shocks of the 1970s (Stephenson et al. 2010), the role of the human factor has been largely overlooked in energy consumption analysis, especially in work environments (Lo et al. 2012; Lutzenhiser 1993). Motivations and incentive structures towards energy conservation are different for users in organizational settings and private households, as no personal monetary gains are normally expected, and more altruistic motives – like supporting the organization in energy and monetary savings, contributing to environmental protection, or complying with peer expectations – can be leveraged to engage in energy saving at work (Matthies *et al.* 2011). More importantly, an average 7.4% energy savings have been reported in the literature as a result of behavioral interventions (Darby 2006; Delmas et al. 2013). Therefore, significant energy savings can be achieved by carefully designing behavioral interventions aimed at conserving energy in organizational environments.

2.2 Games for Energy-Saving

Games have a history of being utilized at the workplace as human resources tools and as entertainment interfaces for repetitive tasks (Nikkila *et al.* 2011). Moreover, the engagement mechanisms used in games can also be leveraged to promote real-world energy saving behaviors (Fijnheer *et al.* 2016; Reeves *et al.* 2012). Feedback, tips, challenges, ranking and rewards have been included in "EnergyLife" and the "Energy Battle" apps (Gamberini et al. 2012; Geelen *et al.* 2012). More importantly, energy efficiency games, such as "Cool Choices", "WeSpire", "Ecoinomy" and "Carbon4Square", or "Energic" have been used in workplace environments, with very positive results (Cool Choices 2019; Energic 2019; Grossberg *et al.* 2015; WeSpire 2019). The empirically measured effects of a number of serious games in changing knowledge, behavior and attitude towards energy-saving have overall been positive (Fijnheer and Van Oostendorp 2016), with reported energy savings in the range of 3–6% on average and >10% achievable on a number of studies (Grossberg *et al.* 2015). Interestingly, various approaches, including gamification have also been designed to motivate the usage of stairs instead of the elevator in various real-world settings, such as "ClimbTheWorld" (Aiolli *et al.* 2014), or "The Piano Stairs" (Matsumura *et al.* 2015). However, there is room for improving existing energy game designs, especially towards meeting their goals for behavior change (Fijnheer and Van Oostendorp 2016). Bearing in mind the intricacies of a workplace environment, especially involving internal (employees) and external (visitors) customers, we aim to leverage the motivating power of games to effect energy conservation behavior at a museum.

3 The Museum Game Design – Approach and Characteristics

In order to design a game that would motivate employees, as well as visitors, of a museum to conserve energy, we followed a structured process, visited three workplaces across the EU, including an art museum in Luxembourg, and conducted a users' survey with regards to energy consumption therein. Based on the results of this survey, and our observations of the daily energy consumption actions – that are analyzed and can be reviewed in more detail in (Kotsopoulos *et al.* 2017; Lounis *et al.* 2017) – we designed an energy-saving game for use in work environments accordingly. The characteristics of the game, along with corresponding screenshots of the interface, can be reviewed in (Kotsopoulos *et al.* 2018). Additionally, the enablement of the game operation was made possible through the utilization of a specially designed hardware infrastructure that was installed throughout the pilot areas and includes IoT-enabled devices, such as real-time energy-consumption monitoring equipment in a per-area, per-person, as well as per-device level of detail, as well as low cost NFC stickers. More detailed information on the characteristics of this infrastructure that enables the operation of the game can be found in (Papaioannou et al. 2018; Papaioannou et al. 2017). We involved the users in all steps of the game design process to ensure that the designed game would fit their preferences and needs, and indeed, encouraging usability and user experience results were attained during preliminary usability tests performed with employees (Kotsopoulos *et al.* 2018).

In short, the game revolves around a common concept, across all game scenarios: a living tree. The more energy-saving is performed by the participants, the more the tree grows on screen. Moreover, players can view information regarding their progress in the game (e.g. light switching actions they have performed, stairs they have climbed instead of using the elevator) in the lower part of the screen. Screenshots of the game's interface can be found in (Kotsopoulos *et al.* 2018). For the special use-case of the museum, two different game interfaces were materialized: One designed around employees – the "museum lights challenge" – and one around visitors – the "museum visitor's game" – that involves using the stairs instead of the elevator. Their main difference lies in the fact that the employees' "museum lights challenge" is designed to last a longer period of time, whereas visitors are bound to just play the game during a daily visit. The visitors can only review information regarding their progress in climbing stairs, which in turn leads to their tree growing from a branch to a fully grown flourishing organism. In contrast, the museum lights challenge is designed to include, apart from the tree growth feature (according to the energy saved by optimal light operation): (i) a leaderboard feature where the participants can review and compare their personal and teams' progress in the game with other participants, as well as the points they have accrued, and (ii) badges represented by animated birds that reside on their personal/team tree, whenever challenges are won in the game. In order to make sure that the game design would befit the museum employees' characteristics and motivations to play the game, we relied on the results from a survey we conducted accordingly. The results from this survey can be reviewed in more detail in (Kotsopoulos *et al.* 2018). We explored Employee Motivations to Participate in Gamification at work (EMPG) and identified the needs for (i) Self-Actualisation, (ii) Self-Regulation, (iii) Rewards & Recognition and (iv) Affiliation as most prominent. Moreover, we mapped their connections with preferences in game elements, as well as specific energy-saving actions at work. As we found no correlation between the action of "switching off lights in a room" and any of the players' underlying motivations to play, we designed the game to tend to the most preferred game elements across all user profiles instead. Therefore, the elements of progression (growth in the tree), and rewards (points) were chosen to be included in the museum guards game.

The game was designed to be simpler for the visitors, due to the very limited time scope in playing it (only once by each player and in the duration of a museum visit), and was played solo – not as part of a team. Consequently, as there was no time or opportunity for the visitors to accumulate a high score during their visit, and no opportunity for direct comparison of their score with other visitors, or contribution towards team score, we decided that including the game element of points would not be fitting to this particular game scenario, and focused on the element of progression in the game via the virtual tree growth instead. Moreover, this visual reference to the progression in the game was more easily followed by the participants, who viewed the game on screens that were mounted on the wall, instead of their own mobile devices. A more detailed account of the characteristics of the two game scenarios (the museum lights challenge and the visitor game) is provided in the following sub-sections.

3.1 The Museum Lights Challenge

Overview

A multitude of technical solutions currently exist in the modern workplace that can automate the lights operation. However, the introduction of lights automation may require costly alterations to the building and electrical infrastructure. Furthermore, when it comes to energy consumption at work, employees are by no means passive, no matter how little agency they may in some cases be allocated by extant automated systems, and adopt various measures – such as placing post-it notes on light sensors to disable them – in order to resolve practical problems they may face at work (Pettersen *et al.* 2017). Moreover, in public buildings and especially museum exhibition areas, the automated operation of lights can potentially cause problems, as in some cases lights may need to remain on in unoccupied areas for various reasons (mainly regarding security), and operation of the lights by the museum personnel remains the solution of choice. Therefore, in order to ensure that lights are optimally used in the museum (lights at the museum's exhibition areas are kept always-on by default during operating hours) a corresponding challenge was designed. The challenge is played based on good cooperation and communication between the museums' guards and control room employees. To conserve energy, guards are encouraged by the game to inform the control room personnel to turn OFF the lights in vacant areas, where at the same time no visitors are approaching. As soon as a guard notices visitors approaching an area where the lights have been switched off, they notify the control room employees to turn the lights back ON. These messages are transferred to the control room by scanning NFC on/off tags in each museum room. By sending appropriate on/off signals, the guards thus ensure that lights are kept on when visitors are present in the museum areas, and off when the rooms are completely empty. Overall, the control room employees close the action loop that leads to optimal energy consumption by ensuring that the guards' on/off signals are turned into actual lights on/off actions. Moreover, on/off signals are transferred by the museum guards to the control room by swiping on specially positioned NFC tags in each museum area. At the end of the day the actions of all participants in the challenge are corroborated and points are assigned according to the total lights on/off events sent by the guards, as well as the actual time these actions were materialized by control room employees.

The game has been designed as a team-based competition, with guards and control room personnel belonging to competing teams, in a "Guards vs Control room" scenario. Two different viewpoints coexist in this game scenario, as analyzed below.

The Museum Guard Viewpoint is reviewed in Fig. 1 and summarized as follows:

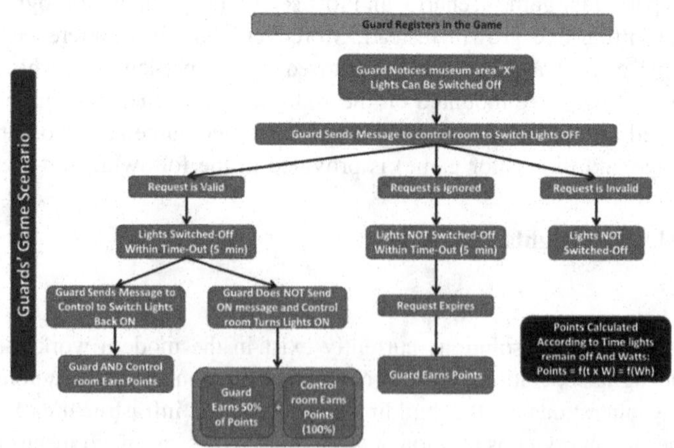

Fig. 1. The game scenario, according to the museum Guards' viewpoint

- Every time a room is empty and no visitors are approaching, the guard sends an "OK to turn OFF lights in area XX" signal to the control room. As soon as a visitor is approaching after that, the guard sends a new signal to "Turn ON lights in area XX".
- Both signals are cross-checked and flagged by the control room (flags = ascertains if the suggested action is valid or invalid) and valid signals are executed by the control room personnel, as requested by the guard. Points are provided according to Δ(delta)-time between the two (valid) messages and the Δ-power of turning off lights (the impact of the action in Watt-Hours - Wh).
- A Time-out (originally set to 5') exists. If the control room ignores a guards' message for 5 min, it expires, the guard earns the corresponding points, and can re-send the same message (because the control room did not respond promptly). Even though this specific action was not enacted by the control room and the lights were not switched off to save energy, the guard did their part and they are rewarded.
- If, after a Guard has sent a message to turn off lights (and while the control room personnel have not proceeded to already turn off the lights), it must be cancelled (e.g. a visitor is approaching), then the Guard can send a CANCEL – "Visitor approaching" signal to the control room, so that the lights are not switched off after all.
- Switch-on lights messages are accompanied by a characteristic sound in the game interface (that the control room won't "miss") and can be repeated (sent more than once by the guards if necessary) until the lights are turned on by the control room.

The Control Room Personnel Viewpoint is reviewed in Fig. 2 and can be summarized as follows:

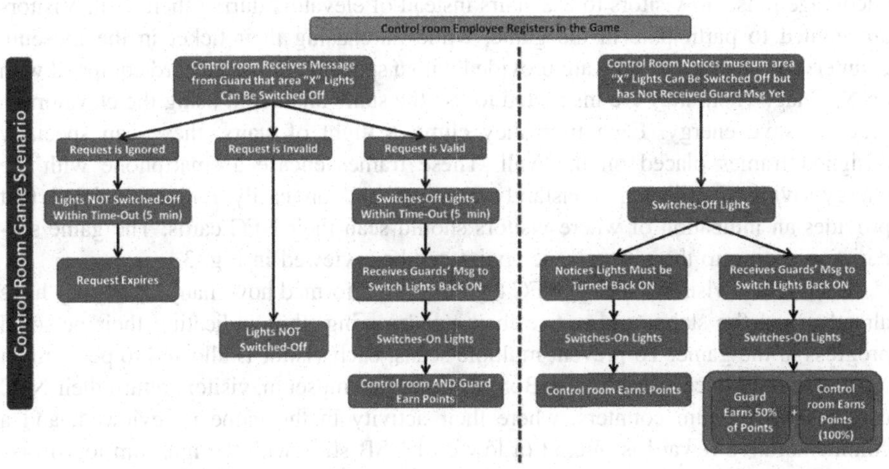

Fig. 2. The game scenario, according to the control room employees' viewpoint

- As soon as a "turn ON" or "turn OFF" lights message is received, the control room personnel follow a three-step process:

  - *Step A – validity check:* Are there any visitors present in the area?
  - *Step B – message flagging*: If not, then message is marked "checked and valid".
  - *Step C – action:* The action is performed – lights are turned off/on as suggested.
- If the lights are turned ON/OFF as requested by the guards, both employees are awarded the same amount of points (according to the energy saved).
- If the control room employee flags the message as "invalid" then neither them, nor the guard that sent the request, receive any points.
- In the meantime, if the control room employee discovers an area that is vacant from visitors, and lights can be turned off, but has not received a relative message by a guard yet, they can initiate the turn-off the lights process independently and earn the corresponding points on their own.

Combining Viewpoints: In some of the actual life scenarios, the two viewpoints described above intertwine. Such cases include the points' allocation, for whenever the messages to switch ON/OFF lights are sent by players belonging to different teams. In these cases Guards get 50%, and Control room 100% of the points earnable:

- A guard sent the lights-off signal but a control room employee noticed that the lights needed to be turned back on without receiving a message from a guard first.
- A control room employee turned the lights off without receiving a message by the guards, but the guards noticed that the lights needed to be turned on again and sent the message before the control room noticed it.

3.2 The Museum Visitor Game

The museum visitor game was designed to be simple and straightforward to follow, and encourage museum visitors to use stairs instead of elevators during their visit. Visitors are invited to participate in the game, while purchasing their ticket in the museum counters. If they accept, they are provided with a specially designed card equipped with an NFC tag. Then, they are instructed to use the stairs and avoid using the elevators in order to save energy. Each time they climb a flight of stairs, they scan specially designed frames placed on the wall. These frames encase a smartphone with the energy-saving mobile app constantly running, and an easily noticeable label that provides an indication of where visitors should scan their NFC cards. The game scenario according to the visitors' viewpoint can be reviewed in Fig. 3.

Each time a visitor scans an NFC tag, they are informed how many times they have already used the stairs, and notice their tree growing, thus indicating their personal progress in the game. To prevent multiple scans, each visitor is allowed to perform an NFC scan only once every 5 min. Before exiting the museum, visitors return their NFC card to the museum counters, where their activity in the game is reviewed, and a commemorative reward is offered (a low cost USB stick with the museum logo).

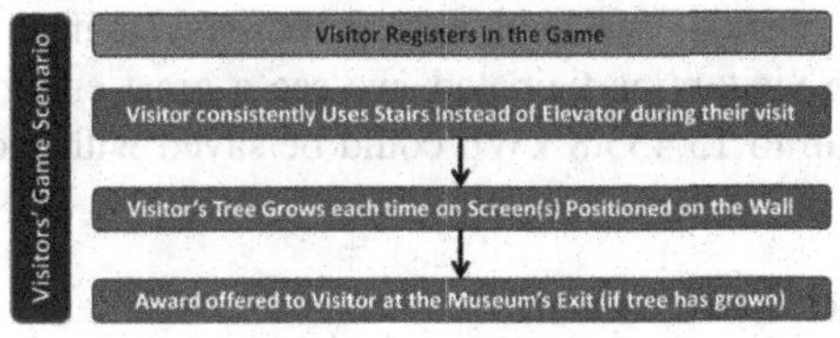

Fig. 3. The game scenario, according to the visitors' viewpoint

4 Preliminary Results from the Museum Visitor Game

The visitor's stairs challenge was played in the MNHA museum between March 1, 2019 and April 29, 2019 (2 months). All the museum visitors that were eligible for the pilot test were invited to participate by the personnel at the entrance of the museum, after being provided with an introduction to the game. The prospective participants were clearly told that the aim of participating in the game was to conserve energy by using the stairs instead of the elevators during their visit. Non-eligible visitors included those that visited the museum as part of a group (pre-booked group visit tickets), and elderly/disabled, that were not available to use the stairs instead of the elevator due to logistic issues. Therefore, the pool of prospective participants was smaller than the total number of the museum's visitors in the two months that the game was active.

When interpreting the game statistics, as well as recorded energy readings from the energy-measurement infrastructure installed in the museum (briefly outlined in Sect. 3 of this paper), we adopted the assumption that those who opted to use the stairs instead of elevators during the pilot period, did so because of playing the game. Therefore, the savings recorded were attributed exclusively to not using the museum's lifts. The statistics regarding the museum visitors' game are summarized in Table 1.

Table 1. Museum visitors' game statistics, 01/03/2019–29/04/2019 (2 months)

Key performance indicator (KPI)	Value
# of visitors in the museum	13,489
# of visitors belonging to a group	5,100
# of unique visitors available to participate in the game	8,389
# of actual participants in the game – stairs challenge	271 (3.23%)
Total # of staircases climbed	1,633
Avg. # of staircases climbed per museum visitor	6.03
Energy savings recorded	498.72 kWh (4.79%)
Staircases that would have been climbed if all visitors played the game	81,339
Maximum energy savings achievable if all visitors played the game	15,435.8 kWh

Reviewing the table above, we see that 3.23% of the museum visitors participated in the game during the test period. A total of 1,633 staircases were used instead of the museum lifts, or, 6.03 staircases per person on average. The energy savings recorded during the pilot period were 4.79%, with each participant saving 1.84 kWh on average. As only 3.23% of the visitors participated, we see a great energy-saving potential in this challenge since, up to 15,435.8 kWh could be saved with increased participation.

5 Discussion and Conclusion

Through this research, we provide both specific design characteristics that a game focused on energy-savings in a museum by employees and visitors should include, as well as insight on the actual implementation process. Furthermore, we provide evidence of the actual energy savings achievable by involving museum visitors in an energy-saving game promoting using stairs instead of elevators. Moreover, by following a structured user-centered procedure while designing the game, good usability and user acceptance results have been recorded by a sample of employees (Kotsopoulos et al. 2018). In essence, our work also constitutes a step towards designing effective energy-game design and, to the best of our knowledge, the first attempt to design a game for energy-savings in a museum, involving both visitors and employees.

Based on our experience from designing a game for energy-saving by both employees and visitors in a museum, we collected various insights. With regards to the design challenges faced, we found that designing one game that would fit all the participants' requirements was impractical. Visitors have significantly different opportunities to conserve energy than employees, as well as different timeframes to their interaction with the building. While employees interact with the building on a daily basis as part of their work routine, visitors only interact with the building during their short visit in just one day. Therefore, when designing a game, the characteristics need to evolve for a longer time period when it comes to employees, and a more varied collection of game elements can be utilized accordingly. In contrast, the game play in the visitors' case must be quickly progressing and simple in its nature, as the timeframe of their visit, combined with the fact that the interface they interact with is embedded in the building, do not allow for more complex game designs.

In addition to the above, by surveying the premises, we found that the energy saving opportunities in an art museum were limited. Coordinating the optimal operation of lights was the only possible point of intervention for employees in the exhibition area, while opting to use the stairs instead of the elevator was the only energy-saving action available for museum visitors. The opportunity to save energy in a museum is further limited, due to strict operating procedures in such an environment, where ambient conditions and security issues come above and beyond any energy-saving plan.

Bearing in mind this significant difference in time scope, the visitors' game was specifically designed to be used once in the duration of a visit to the museum and, as a limited time usage scenario, no meaning was found in using other game elements than progression in the tree growth. Furthermore, as the visitors had limited time to visit the museum, and no long-term engagement with the building, they preferred to devote it on visiting the exhibition. Thus the gameplay had to be simpler and less time consuming to engage them. Moreover, there was no profile, history of their past behavior, or "daily routine" available, as they were visiting the museum for the first time.

Having designed a plausible game scenario befitting to the occupants of the museum, we set forth to implementing it. We found that, with regards museum exhibition area personnel scenario, a number of operating procedures must be altered before applying it in practice as, for instance, turning off lights during operating hours is normally prohibited during the museum operating hours. Therefore, the implementation of our designed game scenario for energy savings via optimal operation of the museum lights was delayed, in view of a need for altering internal security rules which needed central approval. This leads us to suggest that future practitioners in this field of application should take this need for an extended preparation period into account when scheduling the initiation of the behavioral intervention period.

In the case of the museum visitor scenario, we found that scheduling the implementation was easier, since utilizing stairs instead of the elevator was readily allowed by the museum. However, engaging one-off visitors of a museum in energy-saving was not such an easy task, as proven by the relatively low percentage of actual participants in the game (3.23%). One must also take into account that only single visitors were notified by the museum personnel to participate in the game (group visits were shown in without passing through the same ticket rims). A future game scenario must also provide alternate means of providing the NFC-card to visitors belonging to a group (e.g. a pick-up location before entering the museum) to increase participation. However, although a relatively low percentage of visitors opted to participate in the energy-saving game, the energy-savings achieved in the elevator circuit were significant (498.72 kWh = 4.79%). Moreover, an extrapolation of these figures leads us to the conclusion that large savings are available by extending the scenario to engage more users, as total participation by all the museum's visitors in the game could lead to energy savings of up to 15,435.8 kWh in the museum for a two-month period.

As all research, our study does not come without its limitations. With regards to the stairs challenge, we unfortunately did not have any available past data regarding the usage of stairs/elevators in the museum before the study was conducted, and therefore resorted to following an approximation approach that included energy baseline calculations to extrapolate behavior change instead. Additionally, as no control group was available in our studies, further research would be needed in order to exclude the possibility that the measured behavioral effect from the intervention includes a Hawthorne effect (i.e. that the alteration of the participants' behavior was in part due to their awareness of being observed). Moreover, future research should focus on delineating the personal attributes of the participants (and non-participants) in the visitor challenge, in order to more effectively approach prospective future participants towards participating in the game. The significant amounts of energy savings achievable by a higher rate of participation in the museum visitor game would thus become more reachable in future interventions with the aim of conserving energy in museums by involving visitors. Utilizing a control group, as well as a longer testing period would also provide for more accurate and dependable results. An improved participant elicitation process and a game scenario for the groups of visitors could also improve the rates of participation in the museum visitor game. Another avenue of research could examine ways in which energy-saving challenges can be designed to allow visitors to affect the operation of lighting in the building, or ways in which automated lights operation could be mixed with the manual decision process currently in effect at the museum. However, these latter scenarios would require that the buildings' operating rules be revised accordingly.

Acknowledgments. This research study is partially funded by the project ChArGED (CleAn-web Gamified Energy Disaggregation), that receives funding from the EU Horizon 2020 research and innovation program, under grant agreement No 696170.

The research of Dr. Kotsopoulos and Dr. Papaioannou is partially financed by the Research Centre of Athens University of Economics and Business, in the context of the project entitled "Original Scientific Publications".

The graphic design of the user interfaces of the game app discussed in this paper, and its software implementation, have been performed by Evi Ioannidou and Kostas Vasilakis & Themis Apostologlou respectively, for European Dynamics S.A. (http://www.eurodyn.com) – the coordinator of project ChArGED.

References

Aiolli, F., Ciman, M., Donini, M., Ombretta, G.: Serious game to persuade people to use stairs. In: Persuasive 2014 Posters, pp. 11–13 (2014)

Conti, J., Holtberg, P., Diefenderfer, J., LaRose, A., Turnure, J.T., Westfall, L.: International Energy Outlook 2016, With Projections to 2040 (May 2016). U.S. Energy Information Administration (EIA), Washington, D.C. (2016)

Cool Choices. Employee Engagement Sustainability Game (2019). https://coolchoices.com/. Accessed 14 Feb 2019

Darby, S.: The effectiveness of feedback on energy consumption: a review for Defra of the literature on metering, billing and direct displays. Environ. Chang. Inst. Univ. Oxf. **22**(April), 1–21 (2006). https://doi.org/10.4236/ojee.2013.21002

Delmas, M.A., Fischlein, M., Asensio, O.I.: Information strategies and energy conservation behavior: a meta-analysis of experimental studies from 1975 to 2012. Energy Policy **61**, 729–739 (2013). https://doi.org/10.1016/j.enpol.2013.05.109

Energic. Energic - Smart Energy Challenge (2019). http://www.energic.io/. Accessed 6 Apr 2019

Fijnheer, J.D., Van Oostendorp, H., Veltkamp, R.C.: Gamification in a prototype household energy game. In: Proceedings of the 10th European Conference on Games Based Learning, pp. 192–201 (2016)

Fijnheer, J.D., Van Oostendorp, H.: Steps to design a household energy game. Int. J. Serious Games **3**(3), 12–22 (2016). https://doi.org/10.17083/ijsg.v3i3.131

Gamberini, L., et al.: Tailoring feedback to users' actions in a persuasive game for household electricity conservation. In: Bang, M., Ragnemalm, E.L. (eds.) PERSUASIVE 2012. LNCS, vol. 7284, pp. 100–111. Springer, Heidelberg (2012). https://doi.org/10.1007/978-3-642-31037-9_9

Geelen, D., Keyson, D., Stella, B., Brezet, H.: Exploring the use of a game to stimulate energy saving in households. J. Des. Res. **10**, 102–120 (2012). https://doi.org/10.1504/JDR.2012.046096

Grossberg, F., Wolfson, M., Mazur-Stommen, S., Farley, K., Nadel, S.: Gamified Energy Efficiency Programs. Washington, D.C. (2015). http://www.climateaccess.org/sites/default/files/aceee.pdf

International Energy Agency. World Energy Outlook, Paris, France (2016)

Kotsopoulos, D., Bardaki, C., Lounis, S., Papaioannou, T., Pramatari, K.: Designing an IoT-enabled gamification application for energy conservation at the workplace: exploring personal and contextual characteristics. In: 30th Bled e-Conference: Digital Transformation – From Connecting Things to Transforming Our Lives, pp. 369–383. University of Maribor Press (2017). https://doi.org/10.18690/978-961-286-043-1.26

Kotsopoulos, D., Bardaki, C., Papaioannou, T.G., Lounis, S., Pramatari, K.: Agile user-centered design of an IoT-enabled gamified intervention for energy conservation. IADIS Int. J. WWW/Internet **16**(1), 1–25 (2018). http://www.iadisportal.org/ijwi/papers/2018161101.pdf

Kotsopoulos, D., Bardaki, C., Papaioannou, T.G., Lounis, S., Pramatari, K.: Gamification at work: employee motivations to participate and preferences for energy conservation. In: Mediterranean Conference on Information Systems (MCIS) 2018 Proceedings, pp. 1–17 (2018b). https://aisel.aisnet.org/mcis2018/19

Lo, S.H., Peters, G.J.Y., Kok, G.: Energy-related behaviors in office buildings: a qualitative study on individual and organisational determinants. Appl. Psychol. **61**(2), 227–249 (2012). https://doi.org/10.1111/j.1464-0597.2011.00464.x

Lounis, S., Kotsopoulos, D., Bardaki, C., Papaioannou, T.G., Pramatari, K.: Waste no more: gamification for energy efficient behaviour at the workplace. In: CEUR Workshop Proceedings, vol. 1857 (2017)

Lutzenhiser, L.: Social and behavioral aspects of energy use. Annu. Rev. Energy Environ. **18**, 247–289 (1993)

Matsumura, N., Fruchter, R., Leifer, L.: Shikakeology: designing triggers for behavior change. AI Soc. **30**(4), 419–429 (2015). https://doi.org/10.1007/s00146-014-0556-5

Matthies, E., Kastner, I., Klesse, A., Wagner, H.-J.: High reduction potentials for energy user behavior in public buildings: how much can psychology-based interventions achieve? J. Environ. Stud. Sci. **1**(3), 241–255 (2011). https://doi.org/10.1007/s13412-011-0024-1

Nguyen, T.A., Aiello, M.: Energy intelligent buildings based on user activity: a survey. Energy Build. **56**, 244–257 (2013). https://doi.org/10.1016/j.enbuild.2012.09.005

Nikkila, S., Linn, S., Sundaram, H., Kelliher, A.: Playing in Taskville: designing a social game for the workplace. In: CHI 2011 Workshop on Gamification: Using Game Design Elements in Non-Game Contexts, pp. 1–4 (2011)

Papaioannou, T., et al.: An IoT-based gamified approach for reducing occupants' energy wastage in public buildings. Sensors **18**(2), 537 (2018). https://doi.org/10.3390/s18020537

Papaioannou, T.G., et al.: IoT-enabled gamification for energy conservation in public buildings. In: GIoTS 2017 - Global Internet of Things Summit, Proceedings (2017). https://doi.org/10.1109/GIOTS.2017.8016269

Pettersen, I.N., Verhulst, E., Valle Kinloch, R., Junghans, A., Berker, T.: Ambitions at work: professional practices and the energy performance of non-residential buildings in Norway. Energy Res. Soc. Sci. **32**, 112–120 (2017). https://doi.org/10.1016/j.erss.2017.02.013

Reeves, B., Cummings, J.J., Scarborough, J.K., Flora, J., Anderson, D.: Leveraging the engagement of games to change energy behavior. In: Proceedings of the 2012 International Conference on Collaboration Technologies and Systems, CTS 2012, pp. 354–358 (2012). https://doi.org/10.1109/CTS.2012.6261074

Stephenson, J., Barton, B., Carrington, G., Gnoth, D., Lawson, R., Thorsnes, P.: Energy cultures: a framework for understanding energy behaviours. Energy Policy **38**(10), 6120–6129 (2010). https://doi.org/10.1016/j.enpol.2010.05.069

UNFCCC. United Nations Framework Convention on Climate Change: Paris Agreement - Status of Ratification (2016). http://unfccc.int/2860.php. Accessed 30 Nov 2016

WeSpire. WeSpire - Employee Engagement Platform Powered by Behavioral Science (2019). https://www.wespire.com/. Accessed 14 Feb 2019

Interactive Spatial Storytelling for Location-Based Games: A Case Study

Chrysanthi Nika(✉), Ioannis Varelas, Nikos Bubaris, and Vlasios Kasapakis

Department of Cultural Technology and Communication, University of the Aegean, Mitilini, Greece
ch.nika@hotmail.com, johnnybmailbox@yahoo.gr, nbubaris@ct.aegean.gr, v.kasapakis@aegean.gr

Abstract. In this paper we discuss the distinctive role of interactive stories in the design of location-based games. Interactive spatial storytelling becomes a powerful tool for creating experiences of mixed reality where the story is related to specific facts that occurred in the same location in which the player is physically present. Moreover, player's immersion in mixed reality is increased when she follows or enacts as a real character of a historically documented story, infused with imaginative elements in accordance to the objectives of the game. Following this line of thought, we introduce the location-based mobile game "Inside Old Town of Athens", and its accompanying website, in which we creatively combine elements and principles of interactive storytelling with the distinctive attributes of location-based games that generate site-specific experiences. We also, discuss our design choices that concern the integration of the story scenario and game structure with the route in the area of Plaka, in Athens, as well as the graphic and interaction design of the mobile application that stimulate and enable the player to act in both digital and physical space.

Keywords: Interactive storytelling · Location-based game · Mixed reality

1 Introduction

In location-based games (LBG), the spatial position of the player is key to the development of gameplay and of the gaming experience. LBG combine features, technologies and principles from pervasive and mobile games with physical activities of the player performed in the real world. Through this combination, LBG generate hybrid spaces [1, 2]. Under this scope, the use of stories related to places becomes a creative tool for designing meaningful interactions that enhance the engaging experience of mixed reality, as LBG pursues. In particular, LBG combine spatial stories with interactive storytelling, creating a transmedia mode of storytelling that could be termed as "interactive spatial storytelling".

Resonating the persevering debate "ludology vs. narratology", many game designers argue that the more game-like an experience is, the less impact the emerging

A. Liapis et al. (Eds.): GALA 2019, LNCS 11899, pp. 585–594, 2019.
https://doi.org/10.1007/978-3-030-34350-7_56

narrative will have, and the more the narrative is designed for impact, the less options to influence it will be allowed. On the other hand, interactive storytelling has been recognized for a long time as a distinctive sub-field of game design [3] and it is a "medium where the narrative, and its evolution, can be influenced in real-time by a user" [4]. Therefore, one big challenge in interactive storytelling applications lies in blending the opposing design features of narratives and games [10].

The purpose of this paper is to stimulate and contribute to the discussion of the role and techniques of interactive spatial storytelling in LBG. In general, we consider that interactive spatial storytelling integrates selectively, existing principles and techniques of interactive storytelling in games, with the specific features that LBG places as site-specific media experiences. In this direction we will introduce the location-based game "Inside Old Town of Athens" in which we sought to creatively combine the playful character of the game with interactive storytelling. The rest of this paper will refer to our design choices in relation to the story scenario, game structure, graphic design, and finally the evaluation results placing emphasis on the learning objectives of the game.

2 Towards Interactive Spatial Storytelling

Interactive spatial storytelling becomes a powerful tool of creating experiences of mixed reality where the story is related to facts that occurred in the same location in which the player is physically present. In particular, the combination of historical data with imaginative events is considered a case of what Avouris & Yiannoutsoy call "Mobile Fiction" [4]. In mobile fiction, players move from place to place following and activating the spatial events of a game's story. Mobile fiction blends the ludic tradition with the pedagogical tradition of LBG [7], developing a gamified method of knowledge about the multiple and often hidden stories of a place.

Riot! is an apt case in point [12]. Riot! is a location sensitive interactive play which is based on a real riot that had taken place in Queen's Square one hundred and seventy-three years earlier [13]. The game utilizes hand-held computing technology and the Global Positioning System (GPS) to deliver audio files triggered in relation to public space. Another interesting example of interactive spatial storytelling is GEMS [11]. In GEMS players are allowed to create their own stories and bind them to specific physical locations thus creating records. Those locations can then be visited by other players who collect those records. GEIST is a 3D based narrative educational system in which players walk on a sightseeing tour at the castle of Heidelberg. With the use of GPS localization and interactive rendering [14], they encounter ghosts that tell them stories that happened in the site during the Thirty-Year War [15]. In Barbarossa [16, 17], players trace, locate and open a chest, locked and hidden by pirates in the city of Mytilene (Lesvos, Greece). The scenario of Barbarossa has largely been inspired by the medieval story of the pirate brothers Barbarossa, set in the Aegean Sea. Players must cooperate in teams of three, and complete individual and complementary game scenarios with the use of various technologies like AR, QR codes, GPS and Interactive 3D Maps.

Reviewing the examples presented above, we can firstly conclude that the sense of being part of a mixed reality experience becomes even more intense when the player embodies, follows or enacts, a real character of a historically documented story, which may however be infused with imaginative elements in accordance to the objectives of the game. With regard to the games presented above, we note that the various techniques of interactive spatial storytelling (e.g. using real places bound with historical information, creating fictional characters who recite historical information), converge to the mixture of historical and fictional elements with the use of various location-aware technologies in order to provide immersive gaming experiences to the players.

In the following text we will present the location-based learning game "Inside Old Town of Athens" (IOTA), which was created by adapting existing interacting spatial storytelling techniques and experimenting with new ones, emphasizing at fiction blending with non-fictional, digital with physical space, present with past, location-aware technologies with representational mobile media.

3 Inside Old Town of Athens

At the "Inside Old Town of Athens" (IOTA), the player can select and play stories that take place in the center of old Athens, mainly during the 19th century. The player walks through the streets and visits the buildings that existed at the time of the story and are still retaining their functionality today. An important feature of the game is interactive narrative, composed of text, image, sound, and video. During the game, the player can make decisions that affect the route that she follows. The game is played individually by each player on her mobile phone and is a typical location-aware game, as GPS has a decisive impact on gameplay. It also possesses adventure game features, as there is narration, riddles to solve and inventory for clues collected by the player.

IOTA combines the gamification of an educational application, with exploring and interacting in the real space of a location-based game. The application's goal is to activate the player (physically and mentally) throughout the game and assist her into acquiring knowledge through real space interaction and also through the application's complementary website.

3.1 Game Scenario

Scenario-based design [18] is a method that allows designers and users to describe existing activities, or to envision new activities that can be generated through interactions. The story has a beginning, middle and end, and follows the activity of the central character - player. It is crucial that the player's course of action is based upon an action-reaction pattern, which in turn affects the player in such a way that eventually leads to the creation of a new action [19]. As Alan Armer [20] says, "every story, every plot, is a Character with a Problem".

According to scenario-based design, the protagonist of the story holds the dominant role in the creation of the script and in the evolution of the plot. The primary concern for the choice of the protagonist in our game was the existence of factual data about her, an adventure, a fact or a purpose associated with her, so that the script could be more easily developed. In this direction, exceptional emphasis was put on the research to find, collect and process historical data using various techniques and methods such as research in historical texts, maps and images, historical interviews, spot observation, etc. Through this process we identified George Cochrane (male) as the protagonist [21]. Regarding the historical period of action, we set the game in 1835 as it is documented that Cochrane was in Athens during that year.

In summary, the structure of the scenario is as follows: Cochrane arrives at the port of Piraeus on 24/6/1835. He feels worried about the course his proposition to the Greek government has taken, as he was planning to be the first to establish a shipping route on East Mediterranean. Originally, he is heading to the only Athens hotel (the player is looking for its location and name at this point). The next day, Cochrane leaves the hotel to meet Mr. Finley (his uncle's old friend). Accidentally he encounters General Church, who invites him to his home. Here the player can choose one of the two routes, either to follow General Church or visit Mr. Finley's house. In any case, in the end, Cochrane arrives at the Hill School where he meets Miss Kondaxaki, who reveals the futility of his venture. Although Cochrane has paid enough money in the form of a guarantee, he realizes he has no hope of getting it back. The story ends with his own words, as he will write a book about his experiences in Greece.

3.2 Flow Chart in Hybrid Space

The flow chart of IOTA forms the cartography of the hybrid space rather than an abstract visual representation of the digital-only space of the application. Arrow lines are correlated to the physical movement in the streets and nodes are associated with specific locations in which the player gets information and makes decisions for his subsequent route. In this sense, the selection of the route in real space is equally important and intertwined with the design of the mobile application.

Game's starting point and routes were designed in the area of Plaka, which is a quiet area in the historical center of Athens, with narrow alleys to walk between buildings that refer to the game story's era. Players move indoors (buildings) and outdoors (streets). Figure 1, presents the main nodes in which the game progresses according to the interaction options. Specifically, the nodes are divided into road clues (which give the player guidance for the route), exterior stations (which give the player information on the plot and the opportunity to collect objects - clues for the inventory) and the interior of the two buildings (in which most of the story evolves).

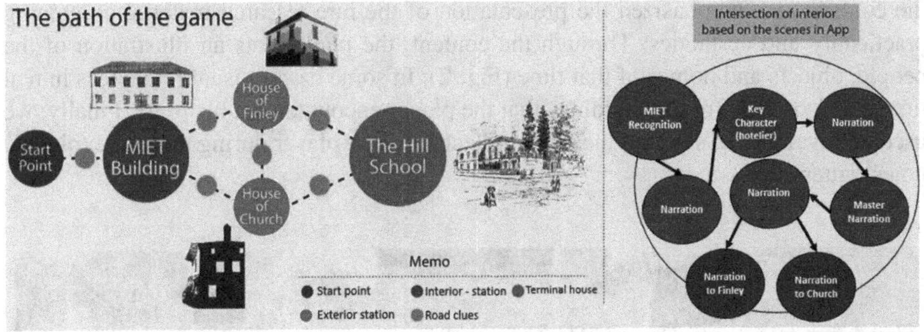

Fig. 1. IOTA story flow

In location-based games, physical space does not act merely as a backdrop for the story of the game but plays an active role in its evolution [22]. The interior spaces of the two buildings form a key role in IOTA. The criteria for selecting the buildings were the existence of evidence for their operation at that time, 1835, their accessibility and the close distance between them. Also, these buildings are relatively unknown to the general public, which, along with their interior design, adds a sense of mystery to the game experience. Where MIET stands today, in 1835 was located the first hotel operating in Athens, under the name 'EUROPE', which indeed hosted all of the city's visitors. During the game, the player enters the patio and the inner veranda of the first floor. The second major building of the game is the Hill School, the first school that operated in Athens after the establishment of the New Hellenic Nation. This building is where the final action of the game takes place. Here, the player enters the professor's office on the first floor and interacts with the offices, the library and all of Mr. Hill's personal belongings that survive from 1835 to this day.

3.3 Interactions and Graphic Design

Concerning the design of the interface and interactions, both in the application as well as the hybrid space, the main goal was to place the players in the centre of the plot, urging them to act on their own. During the game, the player takes advantage of specific locations – spots of the route, meets the story characters, collects clues, certifies his position via GPS, hears sounds, talks, implements AR, etc. The user's interaction, sometimes in the real space and sometimes in the digital space, sometimes with imagination and sometimes through physical presence gives life to the story.

The user's information and interactions through the application are visual, acoustic, vibrating, and sometimes combined. The players' encounter with the characters of the story is of central importance and a more realistic rendering of the provided information was achieved by voice recording, in the form of dialogue with the player, often in a mysterious or comic sense.

The application interface has been designed to provide a user-friendly gaming environment. We deliberately avoided using Google maps, as this would give the player a navigation styled interaction, removing the sense gaming and wandering. On the contrary, we emphasized the presentation of the rare research material combining practicality and aesthetics. Through the content, the player gets an illustration of the people, objects and homes of that time (Fig. 2). In some cases, visual references in real time are also made for the buildings that the player encounters on his route. Finally, we used an inventory to store all the clues collected by the player during the game (photos, notes, letters, etc.).

Fig. 2. Scenes from mobile application

An important part of the game is also the interactions in the hybrid world. The player is required to walk, observe, enter a room, climb a ladder, look out of a window, read and sit in the places where the characters of the story really lived. Furthermore, the recognition of some spaces is realised by viewing the image of the building front and exterior so that the player understands that she is in the right place. To provide clues we also used AR where the game action takes place simultaneously in the digital and real space. Using AR, the player must point her phone camera to a specific real space in order to see an overlaid to it digital animation and acquire a clue.

However, the use of AR proved to be problematic in some cases due to limitations imposed by unstable lighting in the real world, preventing some users to properly see the game content. To solve this issue, we have incorporated photos of the real space the user would have to point her phone camera to in order to enable AR content into a booklet and made them part of the game scenario. Therefore, if a user had issues when using AR in the real space, she could use the booklet to acquire the information instead. The booklet was handed out to players at the beginning of the game. Its design was similar to the application and had multiple functions such as instructions for playing the game, historical information, riddles, etc. The booklet enhances the interaction with the real space and acts as a link to the digital one, as the player takes it with her and consults it throughout the game.

3.4 Website

Along with the mobile application, the website www.insideoldathens.com was created to complement the learning objectives of the project. The purpose of the website is to provide the user with scientifically substantiated information about the historical period, the characters and the locations of the game. The website design aims to motivate the player to read all the story information (Fig. 3). Only after finishing the game, does the player acquire a password that allows her to enter the appropriate door on the website, which corresponds to the door of the last building on the route of the game. Once she entered, the player hears soundmarks and sees landmarks of old Athens while reading short and easily readable texts. In conjunction with the multi-modal presentation of information, the content design of the website focuses on the fact that all the places that the player visits and plays in, are preserved almost unchanged until now, 200 years later. These spaces are a living monument of the history of the New Hellenic Nation and continue their silent journey in time.

Fig. 3. Scenes from the website

4 Evaluation

The evaluation of "Inside Old Town of Athens" was carried out using questionnaires and interviews, which are common methods in pervasive games evaluation [23]. In the evaluation there were 2 groups of 15 participants, while consistency was ensured concerning age and educational level. The evaluation lasted a total of 2 weeks (Fig. 4). After the first week, we selectively integrated the key feedback from respondents, in order to test it on the next week's participants. Almost all users were playing for the first time a location-based game like IOTA. The game flow as experienced by real users during the evaluation period can be found at https://youtu.be/efWpqs96d40.

(a) (b)

Fig. 4. (a) User searching for a specific real book; (b) User acquiring clues with the use of AR

The evaluation focused on the user experience of the hybrid space, emphasising on the choice of area, route and buildings along with usability issues of the mobile application and the website as a learning tool.

All respondents found the choice of the area and route selection to be an important aspect of the game experience. 80% of the participants would like more indoor interactions (e.g. use of AR), using mixed reality technologies revealing the potential of those technologies in interactive spatial storytelling. Another interesting result was that 75% of the users found that the deliberate absence of the map increased the mystery and the atmosphere of the game, showing that allowing users to wander while playing such a game can serve as a useful tool while designing LBG which incorporate interactive spatial storytelling. Finally, all users found the recorded dialogues pleasant and important for the evolution of story.

Regarding the mobile application issues, 40% of the first group experienced some mainly because of the fragmentary reading of the texts in the application, the difficulty of recognizing the exterior of the buildings and the problematic use of AR which could be however solved using the booklet. Those issues were looked at and improvements were made prior to the second evaluation group, were the percentage of users facing them dropped to 25%. Correspondingly, in the booklet, we incorporated the comments of the first group, adding a riddle about the Hill school. The riddle was designed to prompt visitors to interact in the physical space and search for a specific book in the school's large wooden library. As a result, the entire second group found the booklet very helpful in conducting the game, but also in creating atmosphere and mystery.

All the respondents agreed that the real elements of the story had a decisive effect on the stimulation of interest and involvement in the game.

Finally, the use of the website by the players revealed interesting issues about the learning procedure that the game incites. The evaluation was carried out by two different player groups in order to find out the usefulness and effectiveness of a website containing information about the game story. 60% of the first group of players, who did not know about the website, said that would search information about the story and characters after playing the game. 88% of the second group of players, who knew about the website, actually visited it after playing the game and was informed of the real historical events, characters and locations of the game. These findings reveal the potential of such LBG as IOTA to increase players' interest to deepen their knowledge of the real aspects of the gameworld. Moreover, they showcase the importance of a complementary tool, such as the website, for easing players' access to additional information after the end of the game.

5 Conclusion and Future Developments

IOTA is a location-based game that blends physical with digital space, historical events with fiction and today's reality. The main goal of this blending is the creative combination of live experience with the acquisition of knowledge. To this end, interactive spatial storytelling plays a key role in motivating players to engage cognitively and kinaesthetically in playing the game.

The evaluation of IOTA revealed several interesting results towards interactive spatial storytelling in LGB. At first, the evaluation results revealed the importance of choosing a story that can be seamlessly assigned to real locations as this aspect greatly increased players' interest and immersion. Moreover, rich interaction is a key element for interactive spatial storytelling in LGB as most of the IOTA players wished for more in-game elements to interact with. In particular, interaction with solely real objects during gameplay should be considered to increase players' interest and immersion in such games, as revealed by the use of the booklet and the riddle about the Hill school. Moreover, navigation assistance such as the use of interactive maps, commonly used in LGB like the ones presented in Sect. 2, should not be considered as mandatory as its absence can increase players' interest and immersion. In IOTA, players were implicitly or explicitly guided in space through the location-specific activation of the events and the digital characters of the story.

All the design choices in IOTA aim at stimulating the players' interest in the historical capital of the area in which the game takes place. In particular, interactive spatial story facilitates the mixture of ludic and pedagogic elements [4] through which players encounter historical characters, search and document old buildings, participate and partly determine the sequence of the events. Finally, the use of other media platforms (e.g. the website in IOTA) can greatly assist into achieving the learning goal of such mobile games, stimulating players to be further educated towards the game concept. In other words, reading the website after playing the game, is not only an act of learning about the historical importance of the game's locations but it is also a process of self-reflecting on game experience in its historical context.

To further develop IOTA we plan to redesign the first story, and add two new stories, enhancing the experience of mixed reality by offering more choices of routes and physical spaces. This will allow us to cross evaluate the scenarios in order to verify the evaluation results of IOTA. Furthermore, by incorporating other technologies such as internet of things in indoors, social media connectivity to motivate participation, and also more sophisticated visualization and improved audio quality of compelling textual information in the mobile application, the game enables to efficiently capture the player's attention to the digital as well as the physical space. We believe that this type of application that combines features of diffuse play and also has an educational implementation in correlation to the physical space is particularly important because they can appeal to a vast audience of different characteristics and background who do not need to have any particular familiarity or previous experience in order to benefit from the full potential of the game.

References

1. Montola, M., Stenros, J., Waern, A.: Pervasive Games: Theory and Design. Morgan Kaufmann Game Design Books. CRC Press, Boca Raton (2009)
2. De Souza e Silva, A.: From cyber to hybrid: mobile technologies as interfaces of hybrid spaces. SAGE J. **9**(3), 261–278 (2006). Sims, K.: Paul Ricoeur. Routledge, London (2003)
3. Crawford, C.: Chris Crawford on Interactive Storytelling, 2nd edn. New Riders (2012)

4. Avouris, N., Yiannoutsou, N.: A review of mobile location-based games for learning across physical and virtual spaces. J. Univers. Comput. Sci. **18**, 2120–2142 (2012)
5. Paul, R., Charles, D., McNeill, M., McSherry, D.: Adaptive storytelling and story repair in a dynamic environment. In: Si, M., Thue, D., André, E., Lester, James C., Tanenbaum, J., Zammitto, V. (eds.) ICIDS 2011. LNCS, vol. 7069, pp. 128–139. Springer, Heidelberg (2011). https://doi.org/10.1007/978-3-642-25289-1_14
6. Klimmt, C., Hartmann, T., Frey, A.: Effectance and control as determinants of video game enjoyment. Cyberpsychol. Behav. **10**(6), 845–847 (2007)
7. Procyk, J., Neustaedter, C.: GEMS: a location-based game for supporting family storytelling. In: CHI 2013 Extended Abstracts on Human Factors in Computing Systems, pp. 1083–1088. ACM (2013)
8. Blythe, M., Reid, J., Wright, P., Geelhoed, E.: Interdisciplinary criticism: analysing the experience of riot! A location-sensitive digital narrative. Behav. Inf. Technol. **25**(2), 127–139 (2006)
9. Foot, P.: Shoy Hoys reform: the fight for the 1832 reform act. Edward Pearce London Review of Books **26**(9), 29 (2004)
10. Rauterberg, M. (ed.): ICEC 2004. LNCS, vol. 3166. Springer, Heidelberg (2004). https://doi.org/10.1007/b99837
11. Malaka, R., Schneider, K., Kretschmer, U.: Stage-based augmented edutainment. In: Butz, A., Krüger, A., Olivier, P. (eds.) SG 2004. LNCS, vol. 3031, pp. 54–65. Springer, Heidelberg (2004). https://doi.org/10.1007/978-3-540-24678-7_6
12. Kasapakis, V., Gavalas, D., Bubaris, N.: Pervasive games field trials: recruitment of eligible participants through preliminary game phases. Pers. Ubiquitous Comput. **19**, 523–536 (2015)
13. Kasapakis, V., Gavalas, D., Bubaris, N.: Addressing openness and portability in outdoor pervasive roleplaying games. In: Proceedings of the 2013 3rd International Conference on Communications and Information Technology (ICCIT 2013), pp. 93–97 (2013)
14. Carroll, J.M.: Scenario-Based Design. Wiley, New York (1995)
15. Brady, B., Lee, L.: The Understructure of Writing for Film and Television, 1st edn. University of Texas Press, Austin (1988)
16. Miller, W.: Screenwriting for Film and Television. Ohio University, Athens (1998)
17. Cochrane, G.: ESQ. Wanderings in Greece I & II. Henry Colburn, London (1837)
18. Davenport, G.: When place becomes character: a critical framing of place for mobile and situated narratives. In: Reiser, M. (ed.) The Mobile Audience: Art and New Technologies of the screen. FBI, London (2005)
19. Saarenpää, H.: Data gathering methods for evaluating playability of pervasive mobile games. Master thesis. University of Tampere (2008)

Investigating the Effect of Personality Traits on Performance Under Frustration

Zeinab El Nashar[1], Alia El Bolock[1,2], Jailan Salah[1], Cornelia Herbert[2], and Slim Abdennadher[1(✉)]

[1] German University in Cairo, Cairo, Egypt
slim.abdennadher@guc.edu.eg
[2] University Ulm, Ulm, Germany

Abstract. Life is full of frustration, and the ability to withstand it differs from one person to another. Accordingly, their behavior and reaction vary. This paper is an initial attempt to determine the relationship between the big five personality traits and performance under frustration. We present the design of an educational game that induces frustration within a certain level, to compare the performance under different conditions. A self-assessment test was given to the participants, and bio-sensors were used to detect the effect of frustration on both heart rate and skin conductivity. The results indicated that participants with high extraversion performed better under frustration, while those with high conscientiousness or high neuroticism had a decrease in performance.

Keywords: Frustration · Frustration mode · Performance · Big five traits · Affective computing

1 Introduction

Frustration occurs in situations where a person is blocked from achieving the desired goal [5]. When frequently frustrated, people can face problems in their jobs or relationships. Frustration has various modes; aggression, resignation, fixation and regression [4]. Frustration tolerance differs from one person to another, and accordingly, their performance under frustration will vary [5]. This study examines the effect of frustration on the quality of performance and its diversity, relative to the big five personality traits. It was achieved by implementing an educational computer game that induces frustration across two identical challenging levels and comparing the performance in which frustration is, or is not induced since computers are becoming increasingly context-aware.

Computers are beginning to acquire the ability to express and recognize affect [1]. They can use anything to detect and interpret human emotions, starting from facial expressions, to the temperature changes of the hand [2]. Affective computing is not a new field but one that is becoming more relevant today, especially if you combine them with big data, robotics, and machine learning [1]. This study aims to examine the performance under frustration concerning the big five personality traits so the results can be used then as data for affective computing applications.

A. Liapis et al. (Eds.): GALA 2019, LNCS 11899, pp. 595–604, 2019.
https://doi.org/10.1007/978-3-030-34350-7_57

Frustration causes a blockage that is captured by all negative vibrations of emotion [3]. Any individual experiencing a situation opposite to the desired or obligated to respond to something that he wants to avoid can encounter frustration [3].

Frustration has a specific system. It has four modes of reactions to a situation [4]. Aggression, where frustration leads to forms of attack and may be expressed in terms of irritation, quarreling, and fighting [4]. Resignation, is escapism from reality, with the elimination of needs and lack of interest in surroundings [4]. Regression, where there is a backward step in development, and the amount of regression is related to the strength of frustration [4]. Finally, fixation where the person is being stereotyped and is usually attached to interests and emotional attitudes belonging to an early stage of development [4]. At times frustration seems to lead to better performance, while at other times it seems to produce disorganization and decrease in performance [5].

Personality is the way people learn and adapt, and its different characteristics can be detected by the big five traits and these five categories are usually described as follows: High levels in neuroticism are characterized by frequent worries as well as emotional instability including more frequent and more intense negative affect [6]. High levels in extraversion are characterized by seeking and enjoying social interactions frequently, while high levels in openness are characterized by enjoying intellectual activities and new experiences in different domains. High levels of agreeableness are characterized by being cooperative and avoiding conflicts [6], while high levels of conscientiousness are characterized by pursuing a tenacious goal and great task orientation [6].

The relationship between personality and job performance has been frequently studied in the past century [7]. High extraversion and conscientiousness and low neuroticism predicted successful performance during and after stressful conditions [15], but in this study, we specify the performance under frustration. We expect our results to define the quality of performance according to the personality traits.

2 Related Work

The effect of frustration on the quality of performance was previously studied in the experimental study [5], it proved that the frustration effect would vary according to a person's general habits of response to frustration, at times frustration can lead to more effective performance, at other times it can produce disorganization and less effective performance [5]. In our study, we related this proof to the big five personality traits, as this variance in quality of performance under frustration depends on the type and characteristics of personality for each individual.

Moreover, the induction of frustration has been studied in interactive games. For example, in [8], they brought subjects to participate in a computer game.

Subjects received ten dollars for their participation, but the game was also a competition. However, the experimenters had designed the mouse to fail at irregular intervals, to frustrate the participants [8]. The mouse failure and the competition game idea used in the study [8] were references in designing our experiment, as they were added to the sources used in arousing frustration. We added in our study the measurement of the users' performance, and we correlated the performance under frustration to the big five personality traits.

Affective Pacman, a game that also induced frustration to study the effects of frustration on the brain-computer interface used in games [9]. A self-assessment was integrated into the game to track changes in the users' conditions. Preliminary results indicated a significant effect of frustration induction on the brain signals [9]. This study is similar to ours in the part of inducing frustration and using the SAM test to track the users' state. However, our study focused on detecting the performance when the participants got frustrated and when in neutral condition and correlated the difference in performance to the big five personality traits.

The relationship between the Big Five personality traits and job performance was carried out in [11]. Results showed that to make a difference in job performance is a behavioral trait for conscientiousness and extraversion. Neuroticism is recognized to be the second most important big five. Agreeableness and openness do not seem to make a significant difference in job performance [11]. Our study specified the performance under frustration, and also correlated the big five personality traits to whether they had a decrease or an increase in the quality of performance when frustrated.

In [15], they investigated if the big five personality traits are linked to stress sensitivity and baseline physiology. The results indicated that high extraversion and conscientiousness and low neuroticism predict successful performance during and after stressful conditions [15]. This study has many similarities with ours, but we induced stress in a broader range that blocked the user from reaching his goal to arouse frustration. Neuroticism and extraversion had the same results under stress and frustration, but the conscientiousness could not successfully perform under frustration as they did under stress.

3 Approach

In our study, we are comparing the participants' performance when in neutral condition and when subjected to frustration caused by different means. We used a self-assessment test (SAM) after each state, which is a non-verbal pictorial assessment technique that directly measures the pleasure, arousal, and dominance, associated with a person's affective reaction to a wide variety of stimuli [16], to regulate the participants' emotions. The heart rate and the galvanic skin response (GSR) were also detected to measure the participants' conditions in different situations. GSR is an autonomic physiological signal that is extracted from the level of sweat in the skin and describes the changes in the skins' ability to conduct electricity [13]. GSR increases when the subjects secrete more sweat, where their skin can conduct electricity [13]. These measurements were detected in both conditions using a wrist band called Empatica E4 [17], which is equipped with sensors designed to gather high-quality data. Each participant took a big five personality traits test. Through data analysis, the correlation between big five personality traits and performance under frustration was perceived.

3.1 Game Design

With a randomly chosen sample, we made each person undergo an educational game; it is a piano game with three levels. Each level consisted of a theoretical information lesson followed by multiple-choice questions shown in Fig. 1, the first level was added as a preface to make the user acclimate to the game objective to avoid score diversity between the second and third levels due to unfamiliarity with the game and to ensure he gets equal opportunities at both levels. In the multiple-choice questions, the game keeps track of the current score and displays it to stimulate the user in addition to a timer. The user also has the option to skip a question and a help option where he can review the information lesson but would lose ten points when choosing to use one of these options, as shown in Fig. 1. A challenging color game in Fig. 2 interrupts the user just before starting the last multiple-choice in level three to frustrate him to be able to compare his performance in neutral condition in level two and when frustrated in level three. The self-assessment test (SAM) was added twice, first at the beginning of the game to measure the participants' emotions before starting the game while in the neutral state, and the second time at the end of the experiment asking about their emotions when subjected to frustration.

3.2 Experimental Design

The color challenge game was intended to frustrate the user to a great extent, so we used several sources to reach the frustration level. Firstly, the selective attention theory [18]. This process involves differential processing of different stimuli, where there is a limit for the information that one can process at a given time, and selective attention allows us to filter irrelevant stimuli and focus on the important ones [18]. Consequently, we added names of colors to texts in multiple colored boxes as in Fig. 2, while each box is colored in a different color than that was mentioned in its text. Giving the user a smaller colored box, he was asked to click on the box having a text matching the color name of the small box, as shown in Fig. 2. Thus in Fig. 2 example, the user has to click on the red box having the word yellow. This task lasts for 2 min; each level lasted two and a half seconds (featured in milliseconds) to make it unwinnable to be a blockage source for frustration. It gets more difficult as levels increase, where at some levels the small box can move vertically or horizontally quickly before the user can even detect the exact color.

Moreover, the boxes having the texts can get changed in colors several times quickly, which arouses frustration as it makes it difficult for the user to reach his goal. Also, as the level increases the number of boxes with texts increases, with little changes in the small box. For example, it can have more than one color, and the user has to search for a text with more than one word, for example, "yellow and green" text.

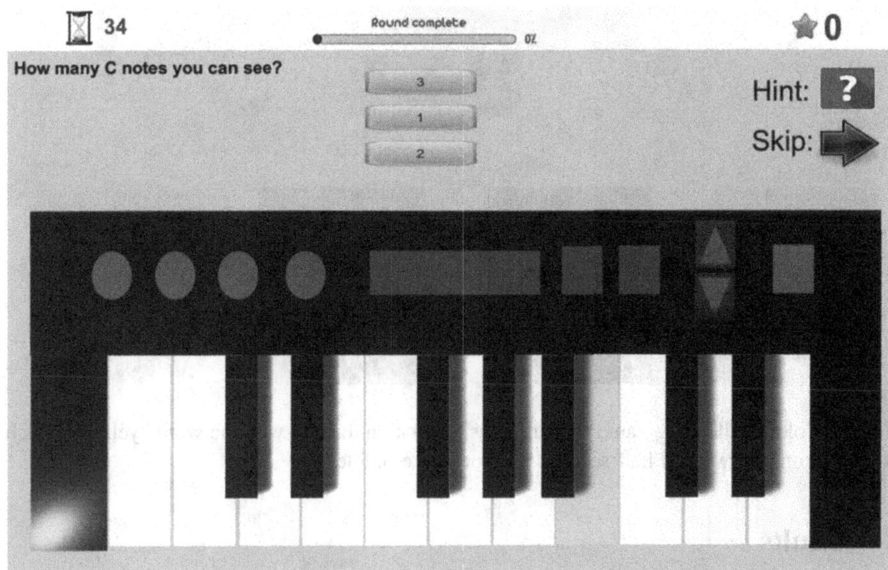

Fig. 1. A question level in the piano educational game.

The second source of frustration was the mouse being designed to fail at irregular intervals during the color game. That was done previously in the frustration experiment [8]. Limiting the timing as done in [12] aroused frustration, as to reach frustration level we had to minimize the timer to a great extent to block the participants and to make it almost impossible for them to resolve it. To avoid any suspicious thoughts or doubts from the participants, and to make it more challenging we convinced them that it is a challenge and previewed the top users and that was also done in the frustration experiment [8]. The sound was also added, where a frustrating timer sound accompanied the decrease in timing, right answer and wrong answer sounds were also added to be played when the user clicks on one of the available boxes. Finally, to arouse frustration, we also used colors that affected arousal and stress, like yellow and red [14]. The Big Five is a way of classifying personality differences and is the most widely used. Research experts have used the recent measure of personality traits to predict entrepreneurial intention. These personality dimensions include extraversion, neuroticism, conscientiousness, agreeableness, and openness to experience [10]. Participants were given this test after finishing the experiment, to avoid any knowledge about the experiment and that it is related to a personality test. The results were used to find the correlation with the performance under frustration using the T-tests.

Fig. 2. Color challenging game. The user has to click on the box with the word "yellow" which is the red one in two and half seconds. (Color figure online)

4 Results

Our sample involved thirty-five subjects, twelve male and twenty-three female, with average age twenty-nine. Two participants were excluded, as it was challenging to find openness trait in our sample, also the agreeableness trait was found in only two participants. Consequently, we concentrated on extraversion, neuroticism, and conscientiousness traits. The participants were subjected to the experiment in our lab, where it was certain that there was not any source of external distraction, and they have been asked not to come unless they were in a relaxed condition.

We classified all collected data for all participants in the following manner: The score of Level two, where the user is in a neutral condition. The score of Level three, where the user was subjected to the frustrating color game just before answering the questions. The Keyboard strokes for both levels. Minimum, Maximum, and average heart rate under both the neutral and frustration conditions, which was collected from the Empatica E4 wristband results. Minimum, Maximum, and average GSR when subjected to the two different conditions. The two SAM tests results for pleasure and arousal, scaled from one to nine.

The percentage of each personality trait for every participant measured by the big five personality test. Data analysis was done through the Paired Sample Ttest. First, we observed that all participants who had a decrease in their score, had the highest percentage in either neuroticism or conscientiousness traits, so the worrying overwhelmed any other personality trait and was the highest even if they had a high percentage in another trait like extraversion. Moreover, those with high extraversion but not with high neuroticism or conscientiousness had a medium or low percentage in all other traits. Accordingly, participants' data were classified relative to the highest personality trait, into three groups (extraversion, neuroticism, and conscientiousness) to test if there is a significant difference, ten participants for extraversion, ten for conscientiousness, and thirteen for the neuroticism. Then all collected data in the neutral condition was compared with that under frustration.

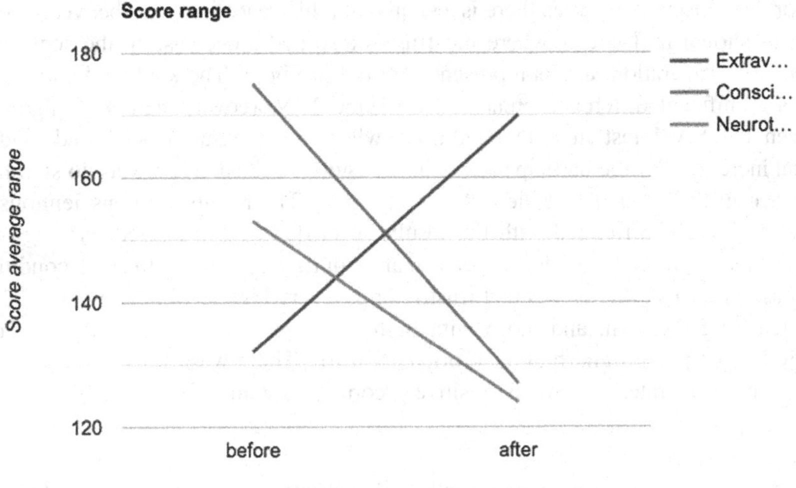

Fig. 3. The average score range before and after frustration (Color figure online)

The results revealed that for the neuroticism trait, there is a significant difference in scores between the two levels, as shown in Table 1, where most users' scores decreased when subjected to frustration, represented in yellow in Fig. 3. There was also a significant difference between the SAM tests in both conditions as the pleasure decreased, and the arousal and frustration intensity increased for the participants, shown in Table 1. Finally, there was a significant difference between the Minimum, Maximum and average heart rate in both conditions where most of the participants' heart rates increased when subjected to the challenging game, notably that they all reported being frustrated and some refused to proceed with the challenging color game. These results for the neuroticism trait were expected as all participants who had neuroticism trait with the highest percentage, reported that they need a calm atmosphere to perform better and that the frustration game affected the quality of their performance negatively in the third level. There was no significant difference between the other data collected as ($p > 0.05$). The results for neuroticism trait are positively correlated with the results of [15], which computed the quality of performance under stress relative to the big five personality traits.

Table 1. Paired samples test for neuroticism trait. (Paired difference between frustration and neutral condition)

	Mean	Standard deviation	t(9)	Sig, (2-tailed)
Pair1 Score	28.750	3.268	2.925	0.005
Pair2 SAM test (Pleasure)	3.250	1.570	8.277	0.000
Pair3 SAM test (Arousal)	−4.062	2.462	−6.600	0.000
Pair4 Minimum heart rate	−9.095	11.798	−3.083	0.008
Pair5 Average heart rate	−7.265	11.495	−2.528	0.023
Pair6 Maximum heart rate	−6.219	10.038	−2.478	0.026

For the conscientiousness, there is a significant difference in scores between the two levels as shown in Table 2, where most users also had a decrease in the score when subjected to frustration, and is represented in red in Fig. 3. The keyboard strokes also have a significant difference erence as in Table 2. Moreover, there is a significant between the SAM test in both conditions where the pleasured decreased, and the arousal increased for the participants when they got frustrated. There was no significant difference in the other data collected as ($p > 0.05$). The results for conscientiousness trait is negatively correlated with the results of [15], where it proved that high conscientiousness predicts successful performance during and after stressful conditions. The reason for this difference is that frustration is a very high level of stress, that blocks from reaching the goal, and those with high conscientiousness are characterized by tenacious goal pursuit and high task orientation [6]. There wasn't a significant difference in the heart rate, and that is positively correlated with [15].

Table 2. Paired samples test for conscientiousness trait. (Paired difference between frustration and neutral condition)

	Mean	Standard deviation	t(9)	Sig, (2-tailed)
Pair1 Score	44.444	45.582	2.925	0.019
Pair2 Key stroke	4.666	4.031	3.473	0.008
Pair3 SAM test (Pleasure)	1.777	1.481	3.600	0.007
Pair4 SAM test (Arousal)	−3.444	2.128	−4.856	0.001

As for the extraversion trait analysis, there is a significant difference in scores between the two levels, shown in Table 3 where most users' scores increased when subjected to frustration, and is represented in blue in Fig. 3. Maximum GSR has a significant difference, where most participants had an increase in the GSR under frustration. Finally, there was a significant difference in the minimum heart rate in both conditions, as in Table 3. The results were expected as those with high extraversion are characterized by frequently seeking and enjoying social interactions and can change situations [6]. That is positively correlated with the results in [15], where participants with high extraversion predicted successful performance during and after stressful conditions.

Table 3. Paired samples test for extraversion trait. (Paired difference between frustration and neutral condition)

	Mean	Standard deviation	t(9)	Sig, (2-tailed)
Pair1 Score	−36.000	16.733	−4.811	.009
Pair2 Maximum GSR	−0.055	0.036	−3.421	0.027
Pair3 Minimum heart rate	−6.718	1.661	−9.041	0.001

5 Discussion

By analyzing the results, it indicated that the participants reacted differently under frustration. The neuroticism participants were worried, and that is due to being characterized by constant worries [6]. All participants had a decrease in their performance when they got frustrated and had difficulty in concentration. Most of them reported that they need a calm atmosphere to perform well. That is similar to when they are stressed as in [15]. The conscientiousness participants were very angry, and some of them refused to pursue the frustrating level, as this personality trait needs to reach the goal precisely [6] and the challenging color game was blocking them, so they didn't perform well which is opposite to [15], and they all reported that the frustration level was annoying. Finally, most of the extraversion participants were not provoked by frustration, and most of them reacted by laughing at the situation, where they were not able to accomplish the task during the frustrating color game. They were very challenged to do better and concentrate more compared to when in neutral condition as they can change situations [6]. Their performance increased under frustration, and they reported that they perform at their best when they are challenged. These results are positively correlated to the results in [15].

6 Conclusion and Future Work

The ability to manage frustration is required in order to remain positive with all the difficulties we face. People perform differently under frustration; some would quit with a reduction in performance while others would be challenged and motivated to do their best with an increase in performance level [5]. This difference is correlated to the big five personality traits that each person has. In our work, we investigated the effect of the big five personality traits on performance under frustration, by comparing the performance in neutral condition and when subjected to frustration caused by a blockage from reaching the goal. The objective of this study is to help in understanding the appropriate conditions needed for every person to perform at their best, according to their personality traits. The users reported that the challenging part was very frustrating and some refused to proceed in the game, but we asked them not to stop. The results indicated that high extraversion performed better under frustration, while high conscientiousness and high neuroticism had a decrease in performance under frustration. Future applications can adapt to the users behavior under frustration, depending on his personality to improve his performance.

References

1. Picard, R.W.: Affective computing M.I.T media laboratory perceptual computing section. Technical report No. 321
2. Nakasone, A., Prendinger, H., Ishizuka, M.: Emotion recognition from electromyography and skin conductance. In: Proceedings of the 5th International Workshop on Biosignal Interpretation, pp. 219–222 (2005)

3. Andalib, T.W., Darun, M.R., Azizan, A.: Frustration of employees: reasons, dimensions and resolving techniques. WCIK E J. Integr. Knowl. 1–11 (2013)
4. Kaur, B.: Mode of frustration. Int. Multidiscip. E-J. **IV**(VI), 239 (2015)
5. Waterhouse, I.K., Child, I.L.: Frustration and the Quality of Performance: III. An Experimental Study. Journal of personality, 21(3), 298–311 (1953). https://doi.org/10.1111/j.1467-6494.1953.tb01773.x
6. Wrzus, C., Wagner, G.G., Riediger, M.: Personality-situation transactions from adolescence to old age
7. Rothmann, S., Coetzer, E.: The big five personality dimensions and job performance. SA J. Ind. Psychol. **29**(1), 68–74 (2003)
8. Scheirer, J., Fernandez, R., Klein, J., Picard, R.W.: Frustrating the user on purpose: a step toward building an affective computer. Interact. Comput. **14**(2), 93–118 (2001)
9. Reuderink, B., Nijholt, A., Poel, M.: Affective pacman: a frustrating game for brain-computer interface experiments. In: Nijholt, A., Reidsma, D., Hondorp, H. (eds.) Intelligent Technologies for Interactive Entertainment INTETAIN 2009, vol. 9, pp. 221–227. Springer, Heidelberg (2009). https://doi.org/10.1007/978-3-642-02315-6_23
10. Murugesan, R., Jayavelu, R.: The influence of big five personality traits and self-efficacy on entrepreneurial intention: the role of gender. J. Entrep. Innov. Emerg. Econ. **3**(1), 41–61 (2017)
11. Ceschi, A., Costantini, A., Scalco, A., Charkhabi, M., Sartori, R.: The relationship between the big five personality traits and job performance in business workers and employees perception. Int. J. Bus. Res **16**, 63–76 (2016)
12. Ho, C.J.: The effects of frustration on intellectual performance. Sci. Educ. **50**(5), 457–460 (1966)
13. Civitello, D., Finn, D., Flood, M., Salievski, E., Schwarz, M., Storck, Z.: How do physiological responses such as respiratory frequency, heart rate, and galvanic skin response (GSR) change under emotional stress. J. Adv. Stud. Sci **1**, 1–20 (2014)
14. Valdez, P., Mehrabian, A.: Effects of color on emotions. J. Exp. Psychol. Gen. **123**(4), 394 (1994)
15. Brouwer, A.M., Van Schaik, M.G., Korteling, J.H., van Erp, J.B., Toet, A.: Neuroticism, extraversion, conscientiousness and stress: physiological correlates. IEEE Trans. Affect. Comput. **6**(2), 109–117 (2014)
16. Bradley, M.M., Lang, P.J.: Measuring emotion: the self-assessment manikin and the semantic differential. J. Behav. Ther. Exp. Psychiatry **25**(1), 4959 (1994)
17. E4 wristband user manual
18. Dayan, P., Kakade, S., Montague, P.R.: Learning and selective attention. Nat. Neurosci. **3**(11s), 1218 (2000)

Author Index

Printed in the United States
By Bookmasters